The Organizational Behaviour Discussion students in the transition from textbook learning to real-world application.

Integrative Running Case

Organizational Behaviour

Organizational Behaviour

MANAGING PEOPLE AND ORGANIZATIONS

Second Canadian Edition

P. Gregory Irving
Wilfrid Laurier University

Daniel F. Coleman
University of New Brunswick

Ricky W. Griffin
Texas A&M University

Gregory Moorhead
Arizona State University

Houghton Mifflin Harcourt Publishing Company
Boston   New York

For my partner, Shelley Miller, and my parents, Ray and Lorain. —G.I.
For my family: Michele, Nick, J., and Sam. —DFC

V.P., Executive Publisher: *George Hoffman*
Executive Editor: *Lisé Johnson*
Development Editor: *Glen Herbert*
Senior Project Editor: *Fred Burns*
Senior Marketing Manager: *David Tonen*
Art and Design Manager: *Jill Haber*
Cover Design Director: *Tony Saizon*
Senior Composition Buyer: *Chuck Dutton*
New Title Project Manager: *James Lonergan*

Cover image credit: Le-Dung Ly/Getty Images

Photo Credits:
Chapter 1: Page 2: CP/Jonathan Hayward; page 5: Honda of America/AP/Wide World; page 13: Richard Vogel/AP Wide World; page 17: CP/Kevin Frayer. **Chapter 2:** Page 40: © Ed Quinn/Corbis; page 41: CP/Richard Lam; page 44: Greg Girard/Contact Press Images; page 48: © Tim Shaffer/Corbis; page 54: AP/Wide World; page 62: AP/Wide World. **Chapter 3:** Page 70: AP/Douglas Rea; page 75: Lockheed Martin; page 82: AP/Wide World; page 88: AP/Paul Sakuma. **Chapter 4:** Page 97: AP/Wide World; page 117: CP/Jonathan Hayward; page 122: AP/Wide World. **Chapter 5:** Page 137: AP/Wide World; page 144: JPL NASA; page 146: Christina Caturano/Boston Globe; page 148: CP/Kevin Frayer. **Chapter 6:** Page 163: copyright Dorothy Low/People Weekly/Time; page 167: Justin Lane/NY Times; page 176: AP/Wide World; page 183: AP/Wide World. **Chapter 7:** Page 190: AP/Wide World; page 196: Larry Dale Gordon/The Image Bank/Getty Images; page 198: AP/Wide World; page 202: CP/Larry MacDougal. **Chapter 8:** Page 224: AP/Wide World; page 228: © Jim Craigmyle/Corbis; page 230: Barbel Schmidt; page 242: AP/Wide World. **Chapter 9:** Page 261: Tim Pelling/First Light; page 267: CP/Richard Lam; page 274: AP/Wide World; page 276: Toronto Star/Rick Madonik. **Chapter 10:** Page 293: CP/Richard Lam; page 301: CP/Jonathan Hayward; Page 302: CP/Ryan Remiorz. **Chapter 11:** Page 324: © Kim Kulish/Corbis; page 325: CP/Tom Hanson; page 331: copyright Koester Axel/Corbis Sygma; page 336: copyright Margaret Salmon and Dean Wiand; page 340: AP/Wide World; page 342: AP/Wide World; page 350: AP/Wide World. **Chapter 12:** Page 355: Guy Stubbs, Photographer; page 358: AP/Wide World; page 368: CP/Adrian Wyld. **Chapter 13:** Page 385: AP/Wide World; page 391: AP/Wide World. **Chapter 14:** Page 413: Toronto Star/Stuart Nimmo; page 426: AP/Wide World; page 428: Greg Miller. **Chapter 15:** Page 441: Mark Ralston/SCMP; page 445: AP/Wide World; page 449: The Indianapolis Star/AP/Wide World; page 451: AP/Wide World; page 466: AP/Wide World.

Printed in the U.S.A.

Library of Congress Control Number: 2008921466

ISBN 13: 978-0-618-88865-8
ISBN 10: 0-618-88865-9

1 2 3 4 5 6 7 8 9—CRK—12 11 10 09 08

Brief Contents

Contents

Preface

Change continues to be the watchword for managers everywhere. Now more than ever, managers need a complete and sophisticated understanding of the assets, tools, and resources they can draw upon to compete most effectively. Understanding the people who live and work in organizations—operating employees, managers, engineers, support people, sales representatives, decision makers, professionals, maintenance workers, and administrative employees—is critical for any manager who aspires to understand change and how his or her organization needs to respond to that change.

As we prepared this edition of *Organizational Behaviour: Managing People and Organizations*, we again relied on a fundamental assumption: We must equip today's students (and tomorrow's managers) with a perspective on managing people that allows them to create, interpret, judge, imagine, and build behaviours and relationships. This perspective requires students to gain a firm grasp of the fundamentals of human behaviour in organizations—the basic foundations of behaviour—so that they can develop new answers to the new problems they encounter. As new challenges are thrust upon us from around the world by global competition, new technologies, newer and faster information processes, new worldwide uncertainties, and customers who demand the best in quality and service, the next generation of managers will need to go back to basics—the fundamentals—and then combine those basics with valid new experiences in a complex world, and ultimately develop creative new solutions, processes, products, or services to gain competitive advantage.

The Text That Meets the Challenge

This edition of *Organizational Behaviour: Managing People and Organizations* takes on that charge by providing the basics in each area, bolstered by the latest research in the field. This is further emphasized by the inclusion of recent Canadian research in each chapter. The content is reinforced with examples of what companies are doing in each area. To help meet our goals, we have made several structural changes in the book, which are detailed below. In terms of the chapters themselves, we open each one with a textual introduction that weaves in a new opening incident and provides an immediate example of how the topic of the chapter is relevant in Canadian organizations. Chapter outlines and learning objectives are also presented at the beginning of each chapter. We continue to build and reinforce learning techniques at the end of each chapter in order to provide more opportunities to work with the chapter content. In addition to the end-of-chapter case, experiential exercise, and self-assessment exercise, we have added an opportunity for students to build their own managerial skills with the building managerial skills exercise. We have also kept the in-depth running case that is presented at the end of each part of the book. The running case for this edition follows the stunning success of Starbucks.

Organizational Behaviour: Managing People and Organizations, Second Canadian Edition, prepares and energizes managers of the future for the complex and challenging tasks of the new century while it preserves the past contributions of the classics. It is comprehensive in its presentation of practical perspectives, backed up by the research and learning of the experts. We expect each reader to be inspired by the most exciting task of the new century: managing people in organizations.

Content and Organization

The Second Canadian edition of *Organizational Behaviour: Managing People and Organizations* retains the same basic overall organization that has worked so well in previous U.S. and Canadian editions. But within that framework, we are also introducing several exciting and innovative changes that will further enhance the book's usefulness.

Part 1 discusses the managerial context of organizational behaviour. In Chapter 1 we introduce the basic concepts of the field, discuss the importance of the study of organizational behaviour, and relate organizational behaviour to the broader field of management. Chapter 2 focuses on the changing environment of organizations. The key topics addressed in this chapter are globalization, diversity, technology, ethics and corporate governance, and new employment relationships.

Part 2 includes four chapters that focus on the fundamental individual processes in organizations: individual behaviour, motivation, and managing stress and the work-life balance. Chapter 3 presents the foundations for understanding individual behaviour in organizations by discussing the psychological nature of people, elements of personality, individual attitudes, perceptual processes, and workplace behaviour. Chapter 4 focuses on the historical perspectives on motivation, and then turns to consider current theories of motivation. Chapter 5, meanwhile, moves away from theory per se and describes some of the more important methods and techniques used by organizations to actually implement the theories of motivation, Work stress, another important element of individual behaviour in organizations, is covered in Chapter 6.

In Part 3 we move from the individual aspects of organizational behaviour to the more interpersonal aspects of the field, including communication, groups and teams, leadership and influence processes, power and politics, and conflict and negotiations. Chapter 7 describes the behavioural aspects of communication in organizations. Chapter 8 begins with a presentation of the basics of understanding the dynamics of small group behaviour, then discusses the more applied material on teams. In this manner readers get to understand the more basic processes first before attacking the more complex issues in developing teams in organizations. Decision making—a process that is increasingly group-oriented in modern organizations—is covered in Chapter 9. Closely related to decision making are the concepts of power, politics, and workplace justice which are explained in Chapter 10. Part 3 closes with Chapter 11, devoted to the vital consideration of leadership in organizations. We believe users will especially enjoy the latter portion of Chapter 11, with its new coverage of strategic, ethical, and virtual leadership, as well as gender and cross-cultural impacts on leadership.

In Part 4 we address more macro and system-wide aspects of organizational behaviour. Chapter 12, the first of a two-chapter sequence on organization structure and design, describes the basic building blocks of organizations—division of labour, specialization, centralization, formalization, responsibility, and authority—and then presents the classical view of organizations. Chapter 13 describes more about the factors and the process through which the structure of an organization is matched to fit the demands of change, new technology, and expanding competition, including global issues. Chapter 14 moves on to the more elusive concept of organizational culture. The final chapter, Chapter 15, could really be the cornerstone of every chapter, because it presents the classical and contemporary views of organizational change. Due to the demands on organizations today, as stated earlier and by every management writer alive, change is the order of the day, the year, the decade, and the new century. Finally, two appendixes provide additional coverage of research in organizational behaviour and the historical foundations of the field.

Features of the Book

This edition of *Organizational Behaviour: Managing People and Organizations* is guided by our continuing devotion to the preparation of the next generation of managers. This is reflected in four key elements of the book which we believe stem from this guiding principle: a strong student orientation; contemporary content; a real-world, applied approach; and effective pedagogy.

Student Orientation

We believe that students, instructors, and other readers will agree with our students' reactions to the book as being easy and even enjoyable to read with its direct and active style. We have tried to retain the comprehensive nature of the book while writing in a style that is active, lively, and geared to the student reader. We want your students to enjoy reading the book while they learn from it. The cartoons and their content-rich captions tie the humorous intent of the cartoons to the concepts in the text. All of the figures include meaningful captions, again to tie the figure directly to the concepts. The end-of-chapter features retain the popular experiential exercises and the diagnostic questionnaire, or self-assessments, and the real-world cases that show how the chapter material relates to actual practice.

Contemporary Content Coverage

This edition continues our tradition of presenting the most modern management approaches as expressed in the popular press and in academic research. The basic structure of the book remains the same, but you will find new coverage that represents the most recent research in many areas of the book.

Real World, Applied Approach

The organizations cited in the opening incidents, examples, cases, and boxed features throughout this edition represent a blend of large, well-known and smaller, less well-known organizations so that students will see the applicability of the material in a variety of organizational settings. Each chapter opens and closes with concrete Canadian examples of relevant topics from the chapter. The running end-of-part case on Starbucks provides a more in-depth case for class discussion. Boxed features appear in each of the chapters, and are identified with icons to distinguish their focus. Also included are ". . . and Research" boxes that summarize research either complete or underway that relates to specific discussion topics. Our experience has shown that this feature helps illustrate concepts from each chapter and demonstrates to students that world-class, relevant research is being done close to home.

 Each ". . . and Technology" box describes how a company uses advances in computer and information technology to improve its business.

 Each ". . . and Change" box shows an organization rethinking its methods of operation to respond to changes in the business climate.

 Each ". . . and Globalization" box describes an organization meeting the needs of its increasingly complex global environment.

Each ". . . and Diversity" box shows an organization dealing with its increasingly diverse work force.

 Each ". . . and Ethics" box shows an organization's ethical perspective when making decisions or dealing with complicated situations.

 Each ". . . and Research" box presents recent and relevant research done by Canadian scholars to highlight concepts presented in each chapter.

Effective Pedagogy

Guiding intent continues to be to put together a package that enhances student learning. The package includes several features of the book, many of which have already been mentioned.

- Each chapter begins with a chapter outline and objectives and ends with a synopsis.
- Discussion questions at the end of each chapter stimulate interaction among students and provide a guide to complete studying of the chapter concepts.
- An "Experiencing Organizational Behaviour" exercise at the end of each chapter helps students make the transition from textbook learning to real-world applications. The end-of-chapter case, "Organizational Behaviour Case for Discussion," also assists in this transition.
- A "Self Assessment" activity at the end of each chapter gives students the opportunity to apply a concept from the chapter to a brief self-assessment or diagnostic activity.
- The "Building Managerial Skills" activity provides an opportunity for students to "get their hands dirty" and really use something discussed in the chapter.
- The opening and closing cases, and accompanying boxed inserts, illustrate chapter concepts with real-life applications.
- The Integrative Running Case on Starbucks at the end of each part provides an opportunity for students to discuss an actual ongoing management situation with significant organizational behaviour facets.
- A self-test is found at the end of each chapter, serving as a handy review and study tool. Each self-test offers questions with answers appearing at the end of the text so students can evaluate their own progress.
- Figures, tables, photographs, and cartoons offer visual and humorous support for the text content. Explanatory captions to figures, photographs, and cartoons enhance their pedagogical value.
- A running marginal glossary and a complete glossary on the textbook website provide additional support for identifying and learning key concepts.

The new design for this second Canadian edition reflects this edition's content, style, and pedagogical program. The colours remain bold to reflect the dynamic nature of the behavioural and managerial challenges facing managers today, and all interior photographs are new to this edition and have been specially selected to highlight the dynamic world of organizational behaviour.

A Complete Teaching and Learning Package

A complete package of teaching and learning support materials accompanies the second Canadian edition.

For Students

Canadian *Student Website (www.hmco.ca/ob)* provides chapter synopses and objectives, ACE practice tests, links to companies highlighted in the text, Flashcards, a visual glossary, career snapshots, OB Online, Experiencing Organizational Behaviour and Self-Assessment exercises from the end-of-chapter sections, a resource centre with links to OB-related sites, and additional cases and experiential exercises.

OB in Action, Eighth Edition, written by Steven B. Wolff, provides additional cases and hands-on experiential exercises to help students bridge the gap between theory and practice. Working individually or with teams, students tackle problems and find solutions, using organizational theories as their foundation.

For Instructors

Online OB in Action **Instructor's Resource Manual** correlates with *OB in Action* exercises. It includes a topic area grid, a section with icebreaker materials, and teaching notes for all cases and exercises in the *OB in Action* text.

Online Canadian Instructor's Resource Manual, includes a chapter overview, chapter learning objectives, lecture outline, text discussion questions with suggested answers, notes on the experiential exercises (Building Managerial Skills, Experiencing Organizational Behaviour, Self-Assessment), Organizational Behaviour case questions with suggested answers, a mini-lecture, and additional experiential exercise ideas. Also included are a table of contents, a transition guide, sample syllabi, suggested course outlines, and a section on learning and teaching ideologies. Printed copies are available upon request from your local Houghton Mifflin Harcourt Canadian sales representative.

Canadian Digital Test Bank contains true/false, multiple-choice, matching, completion, and essay questions for each chapter. A text page reference and a learning-level indicator accompany each question. It allows instructors to select, edit, and add questions, or to generate randomly selected questions to produce a test master for easy duplication. The digital test bank and testing software are available to adopters for download and printed copies are available upon request. Please contact your local Canadian Houghton Mifflin Harcourt sales representative for access to these items.

Canadian Instructor Website (www.hmco.ca/ob) includes downloadable files for the IRM, PowerPoint slides, Video Guide, and Transparencies, as well as a resource centre that includes sample syllabi, a table of contents, learning and teaching ideologies, a visual glossary, chapter overviews, mini-lectures, notes on the experiential exercises (Building Managerial Skills, Experiencing Organizational Behaviour, OB Online, Self-Assessments), text discussion questions with suggested answers, *OB in Action* Instructor Notes and notes on additional cases, Organizational Behaviour case questions with suggested answers, and additional cases and notes.

PowerPoint Slides are available in both basic and premium versions. Basic PowerPoint Slides follow the text's structure, including headings and figures. The Premium Slides offer all of the content found in the Basic Slides, along with video and photos.

Online Transparencies contain all of the figures from the main text. Printed copies are available upon request to your Canadian Houghton Mifflin Harcourt sales representative.

HMClassPrep™ CD-ROM includes the complete Instructor's Resource Manual in electronic format (Word and PDF formats), PowerPoint Slides for classroom presentation, the Online Transparencies, sample syllabi, transition guide, chapter overviews, mini-lectures, lecture outlines, a visual glossary, video guide and select video case segments, learning and teaching ideologies, notes on the experiential exercises (Building Managerial Skills, Experiencing Organizational Behaviour, OB Online, Self-Assessments), text discussion questions with suggested answers, Organizational Behaviour case questions with suggested answers, additional experiential exercises and cases with notes, and end-of-chapter exercises.

Video features video case segments highlighting management and organizational behaviour scenarios. A correlated Video Guide is available.

Blackboard ® /*WebCT* ® includes ACE practice tests plus additional self-test questions, additional cases and experiential exercises, text discussion questions with suggested answers, end-of-chapter experiential exercises with instructor notes (Building Managerial Skills, Experiencing Organizational Behaviour, OB Online, Self-Assessments), *OB in Action* Instructor Notes and notes on additional cases, Power-Point slides, HMTesting, Online Transparencies, sample syllabi, transition guide, learning and teaching ideologies, Career Snapshot and Visual Glossary video segments, a video guide, chapter overviews and objectives, mini-lectures, lecture outlines, Flashcards, Organizational Behaviour cases with questions and suggested answers, and links to the instructor and student websites, and to companies highlighted in the text.

Acknowledgments

Although this book bears our names, numerous people have contributed to it. Through the years we have had the good fortune to work with many fine professionals who helped us to sharpen our thinking about this complex field and to develop new and more effective ways of discussing it. Their contributions were essential to the development of this edition. Any and all errors of omission, interpretation, and emphasis remain the responsibility of the authors.

Several reviewers made essential contributions to the development of this and previous editions. We would like to express a special thanks to them for taking the time to provide us with their valuable assistance:

Jane Haddad	Seneca College
Jules Carrière	University of Ottawa
Jean Helms Mills	St. Mary's University
Jamie Gruman	University of Guelph
Catherine Connelly	McMaster University
Glenn Brophy	Nipissing University
Joan Finegan	University of Western Ontario
Ian Gellatly	University of Alberta
Susan Quinn	Mt Royal College
Kim Richter	Kwantlen College
Choon Hian Chan	Kwantlen College

We thank the production team at Houghton Mifflin Harcourt, especially Glen Herbert, development editor, and Debbie Underhill, National Sales Manager.

We would like to thank the administrations at the Wilfrid Laurier University and the University of New Brunswick for their direct and indirect support to us while we prepared this second edition.

Greg Irving would particularly like to thank his colleagues at the School of Business and Economics for their interest and support. Thanks also to the many O.B. students over the years who have helped to shape my ideas about how an O.B. text can enhance their learning experience. My parents, Ray and Lorain Irving, provided me with the inspiration and dedication to higher education as well as supporting all my endeavours. My daughter, Bridget, challenges me intellectually every day as she embarks on her own journey through her university education. Finally, thanks to Shelley Miller for her constant love, support, humour, and sound advice on all matters.

At UNB, Dan Coleman, who is currently the Dean of the Faculty of Business Administration, would like to acknowledge Drs. Angelo Belcastro and Jane Fritz, Vice-Presidents (Academic) who tolerated his frequent but brief "disappearances" to work on the book. Thanks also to my administrative assistant, Anna Ward, who covered for my absences. Special thanks to Isabelle Gingras who provided invaluable research assistance. Overdue thanks to my mother, Loretta Coleman, who long ago instilled in me a love of reading and learning, and demonstrated true everyday leadership while raising nine children. Finally, thanks to my family, wife Michele, and children Nick, Julia, and Sam for providing a supportive environment to complete this work over many nights and weekends.

Organizational Behaviour

An Overview of Organizational Behaviour

CHAPTER 1

After studying this chapter, you should be able to:

▶ Describe the field of organizational behaviour and explain its importance.

▶ Trace the historical roots of the field of organizational behaviour.

▶ Discuss the emergence of contemporary organizational behaviour, including its precursors, the Hawthorne studies, and the human relations perspective.

▶ Explain the characteristics and concepts of contemporary organizational behaviour.

▶ Identify and discuss contextual perspectives on organizational behaviour.

▶ Explain the importance of theory and research to the field of organizational behaviour.

1

People Matter in the High Technology Sector

Research in Motion (RIM) is a world leader in the development, design, and manufacture of wireless communication technology. The Waterloo, Ontario, based company is probably best known for its Blackberry wireless handheld device that incorporates phone, email, and Internet browser capability in a pocket-sized package. Since the company was founded in 1984, the company has grown to hold assets of nearly $2.5 billion. In addition to the spectacular financial success that RIM has enjoyed since the launch of the Blackberry in 1999, the company is a highly sought after employer. And for good reason! The company values innovation and hires hundreds of cooperative-education students, interns, and new graduates each year. RIM offers its employees many perks, including a free Blackberry device, training, and numerous social activities. To celebrate its twentieth anniversary, the company staged a private rock concert for its employees featuring Aerosmith. In addition, the company is concerned with employee well-being as evidenced by its Healthy@RIM program, which includes on-site massage, subsidized gym memberships, blood pressure/cholesterol clinics, and on-site weight management and smoking cessation programs, among other things.

All of these benefits reflect the views of RIM co-CEOs Mike Lazaridis and Jim Balsillie that success comes from attracting the best people and keeping them happy, productive, and proud of their company. And RIM is certainly a successful company! In 2006, the company had annual revenues exceeding

Organizational behaviour is the study of organizations and the people who work in them. An understanding of the many aspects of OB can play a vital role in managerial work, contributing to the overall success of an organization as well as to the efficiency and morale of individual employees. Jim Balsillie, pictured here, of Research in Motion, is a good example of someone who leads through an intimate understanding of the organization and the people within it. As a result, RIM is one of the most successful companies in Canada.

$2 billion and the number of Blackberry users worldwide surpassed 6 million. And in an era when high profile scandals have meant that corporate ethics and social responsibility have become a major concern, RIM strives to be a good corporate citizen by operating a corporate philanthropy program. The co-CEOs have led by example. Lazaridis donated $100 million to establish the Waterloo-based Perimeter Institute for Theoretical Physics as well as another $50 million to the University of Waterloo to establish the Institute for Quantum Computing. For his part, Balsillie provided major gifts to establish the Centre for International Governance Innovation, also in Waterloo, and to the cancer care unit at the Grand River Hospital.

The success of RIM is based on a number of factors, including the skills of Lazaridis and Balsillie as managers and their understanding of the importance of people. They clearly recognize the value of control and operational systems in a successful organization. But perhaps even more important, they see the value of people and innovation as a key determinant of success. Indeed, no manager can succeed without the assistance of others. Any manager—whether responsible for large organizations such as McCain's, the Toronto Blue Jays baseball team, or the Royal Bank, or small organizations such as a local Pizza Hut restaurant—must strive to understand the people who work in the organization.

This book is about those people. It is also about organizations and the managers who operate them. The study of organizations and of the people who work in them together constitute the field of organizational behaviour. In this introductory chapter, we begin with a comprehensive definition of organizational behaviour and discuss a framework for its study. Then we trace the field's historical roots and its emergence as an independent field. Next, we discuss contemporary organizational behaviour and present an overview of the rest of this book. We also examine several contextual perspectives that provide a general framework for a more comprehensive examination of human behaviour at work. Finally, because theories and research are critical to the development of knowledge in the field of organizational behaviour, we examine how theories and research findings about organizational behaviour are developed.

What Is Organizational Behaviour?

What exactly is meant by the term "organizational behaviour"? And why should it be studied? Our starting point is to answer these two fundamental questions.

The Meaning of Organizational Behaviour

Organizational behaviour (OB) is the study of human behaviour in organizational settings, of the interface between human behaviour and the organization, and of the organization itself.[1] Although we can focus on any one of these three areas, we must remember that all three are ultimately necessary for a comprehensive understanding of organizational behaviour. For example, we can study individual behaviour (such as the behaviour of Jim Balsillie or of one of his Research in Motion employees) without explicitly considering the organization. But because the organization influences and is

> **Organizational behaviour** is the study of human behaviour in organizational settings, the interface between human behaviour and the organization, and the organization itself.

3

FIGURE 1.1

The Nature of Organizational Behaviour

The field of organizational behaviour attempts to understand human behaviour in organizational settings, the organization itself, and the individual–organization interface. As illustrated here, these areas are highly interrelated. Thus, although it is possible to focus on only one of these areas at a time, a complete understanding of organizational behaviour requires knowledge of all three areas.

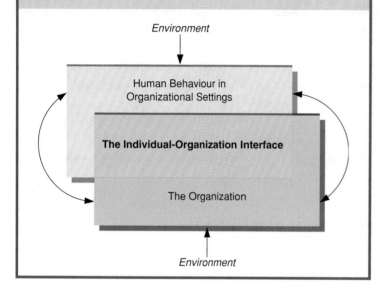

influenced by the individual, we cannot fully understand the individual's behaviour without learning something about the organization. Similarly, we can study organizations (such as Research in Motion itself) without focusing explicitly on the people within them. Again, we are looking at only a portion of the puzzle. Eventually we must consider the other pieces, as well as the whole.

Figure 1.1 illustrates this view of organizational behaviour. It shows the linkages among human behaviour in organizational settings, the individual–organization interface, the organization, and the environment surrounding the organization. Each individual brings to an organization a unique personal background and set of characteristics and experiences from other organizations.

In considering the people who work in organizations, therefore, a manager must look at the unique perspective each individual brings to the work setting. For example, suppose Canadian Tire hires a consultant to investigate employee turnover. As a starting point, the consultant might analyze the types of people the company usually hires. The goal would be to learn as much as possible about the nature of the company's workforce as individuals—their expectations, their personal goals, and so forth.

But individuals do not work in isolation. They come in contact with other people and with the organization in a variety of ways. Points of contact include managers, coworkers, the formal policies and procedures of the organization, and various changes implemented by the organization. Over time, the individual also changes as a function both of personal experiences and maturity and of work experiences and the organization. The organization, in turn, is affected by the presence and eventual absence of the individual. Clearly, then, managers must also consider how the individual and the organization interact. Thus, the consultant studying turnover at Canadian Tire might next look at the orientation procedures for newcomers to the organization. The goal of this phase of the study would be to understand some of the dynamics of how incoming individuals interact with the broader organizational context.

An organization, of course, exists before a particular person joins it and continues to exist after he or she leaves. Thus, the organization itself represents a crucial third perspective from which to view organizational behaviour. For instance, the consultant studying turnover would also need to study the structure and culture of Canadian Tire. An understanding of factors such as the performance evaluation and reward systems, the decision-making and communication patterns, and the design of the firm itself can provide added insight into why some people choose to leave a company and others elect to stay.

Thus, the field of organizational behaviour is both exciting and complex. Myriad variables and concepts accompany the interactions just described, and together these factors greatly complicate the manager's ability to understand, appreciate, and manage others in the organization. They also provide unique and important opportunities to enhance personal and organizational effectiveness.

The Importance of Organizational Behaviour

The importance of organizational behaviour may now be clear, but we should take a few moments to make it even more explicit. Most people are born and educated in organizations, acquire most of their material possessions from organizations, and die as members of organizations. Many of our activities are regulated by the various organizations that make up our governments. Most adults spend the better part of their lives working in organizations. Because organizations influence our lives so powerfully, we have every reason to be concerned about how and why those organizations function.[2]

In our relationships with organizations, we can adopt any one of several roles or identities. For example, we can be consumers, employees, or investors. Because most readers of this book are either present or future managers, we will adopt a managerial perspective throughout our discussion. The study of organizational behaviour can greatly clarify the factors affecting how managers manage. It is the field's job to describe the complex human context in which managers work and to define the problems associated with that realm. The value of organizational behaviour is that it isolates important aspects of the manager's job and offers specific perspectives on the human side of management: people as organizations, people as resources, and people as people. Indeed, managers today continually search for ways to better integrate organizations and the people who constitute them, especially in the face of constant change. As the Change box illustrates, it is critical to engage the organization's employees in order to create a culture that will lead to success.

Clearly, then, an understanding of organizational behaviour can play a vital role in managerial work. To most effectively use the knowledge provided by this field, however, managers must thoroughly understand its various concepts, assumptions, and premises. To provide the groundwork for this understanding, we start by looking at the field's historical roots.

People represent the essence of an organization, regardless of the size of the organization or the technology it uses. Honda, for instance, relies on automated robotic assembly systems to create automobiles. But people design, install, operate, and repair those systems. These Honda employees are celebrating the launch of a new product line coming off the assembly line.

The Historical Roots of Organizational Behaviour

Many disciplines, such as physics and chemistry, are literally thousands of years old. **Management** has also been around in one form or another for centuries. For example, the writings of Aristotle and Plato abound with references to and examples of management concepts and practices. But because serious interest in the study of

Management is a relatively new field of study, having emerged only within the past 100 years.

Organizational Culture and . . .   **CHANGE**

Developing a Strong Organizational Culture

A study conducted by Toronto-based Waterstone Human Capital revealed that 82 percent of executives believe that corporate culture affects an organization's ability to attract and retain the best employees as well as its long-term financial performance. The study classified weak cultures as those that are bureaucratic, top-down, over-regulated, and have an underlying fear of making a mistake. How does this happen? In some cases, it could be the result of upheaval from a merger or acquisition. In others, it could result from leadership changes or restructuring due to failed strategies.

Not all organizations fall prey to having their culture slide as a result of these occurrences. But it can take visionary leadership and communication with employees to ensure it doesn't happen. When the Trillium Health Centre was formed from the forced merger of Mississauga Hospital and Queensway General Hospital over a decade ago, CEO Ken White abandoned the hierarchical approach to organizing typical of health care organizations in favour of distributed leadership. This approach, which Trillium dubbed "1001 Leaders," involves encouraging all 4,200 employees to seize leadership opportunities, irrespective of their position within the organization. Using a decentralized organizational structure, Trillium steers individuals into leading specific projects designed to improve organizational effectiveness and patient care. In addition, responsibility for setting the vision, goals, and objectives of each of Trillium's divisions are delegated rather than handed down from top management.

Explicitly valuing employees can take other forms. Several years ago, Winnipeg-based Ceridian Canada surveyed its 1,400 employees about what values were important to them and the extent to which they perceived the values of the organization as being aligned with them. At eBay Canada's head office in Toronto, employees vote on the Hat Trick Award, given each quarter to an individual employee who demonstrates a great performance as it relates to integrity, excellence, and innovation. The focus is less on the outcome than it is on the manner in which the employee conducts him- or herself. These examples demonstrate the importance of communicating with employees about the values that are central to the organization and of rewarding behaviours that reflect those values.

Sources: Andrew Wahl, "Stop the Rot," *Canadian Business*, October 2005, www.canadianbusiness.com (Accessed on February 21, 2007); Suzanne Bowness, "Healthy Leadership: Trillium Motivates from the Ground Up," *Canadian Business*, 8 January 2007, www.canadianbusiness.com, on February 21, 2007).

management did not emerge until around the turn of the twentieth century, the study of organizational behaviour is only a few decades old.[3]

One reason for the relatively late development of management as a scientific field is that few large business organizations existed until the nineteenth century. Although management is just as important to a small organization as to a large one, large firms were needed to provide both a stimulus and a laboratory for management research. A second reason is that many of the first people who took an interest in studying organizations were economists who initially assumed that management practices at the organizational level are by nature efficient and effective; therefore, they concentrated on higher levels of analyses such as national economic policy and industrial structures.

Interestingly, many contemporary managers have come to appreciate the value of history. For example, managers glean insights from Homer's *Iliad*, Machiavelli's *The Prince*, Sun Tsu's *The Art of* War, Musashi's *The Book of Five Rings*, and Chaucer's *The Canterbury Tales*. Some organizations, such as Polaroid, even have corporate historians. Others, such as Manufacturers Life Insurance and Bata, openly proclaim their heritage as part of their employee-orientation programs.

Scientific Management

One of the first approaches to the study of management, popularized during the early 1900s, was **scientific management**. Several individuals helped develop and promote scientific management, including Frank and Lillian Gilbreth (whose lives were portrayed in a book and a subsequent movie, *Cheaper by the Dozen*), Henry Gantt, and Harrington Emerson. But Frederick W. Taylor is most closely identified with this approach.[4] Early in his life, Taylor developed an interest in efficiency and productivity. He identified a phenomenon he called *soldiering*—employees working at a pace much slower than their capabilities. Because most managers had never systematically studied jobs in the plant—and, in fact, had little idea how to gauge worker productivity—they were completely unaware of this practice.

To counteract the effects of soldiering, Taylor developed several innovative techniques. For example, he developed a standardized method for performing each job. He also installed a piece-rate pay system in which each worker was paid for the amount of work that individual completed during the workday rather than for the time spent on the job. (Taylor believed that money was the only important motivational factor in the workplace.) These innovations boosted productivity markedly and are the foundation of scientific management.

In addition to piece-rate pay systems, Taylor developed several efficiency techniques, redesigned jobs, and introduced rest breaks to combat fatigue. He claimed his ideas and methods greatly improved worker output. Taylor's book *Principles of Scientific Management*, published in 1911, was greeted with enthusiasm by practising managers and quickly became a standard reference.

Scientific management quickly became a mainstay of business practice. Among other things, it facilitated job specialization and mass production, profoundly influencing the manner in which businesses operated. It also demonstrated to managers the importance of enhancing performance and productivity and confirmed their influence on these matters. Even today, some firms use some of the basic concepts of scientific management in their efforts to become more efficient. However, it should be noted that technological advances throughout the twentieth century reduced the role of manual labour as such work was taken over by computers and robots.

Taylor did have his critics, however. Labour opposed scientific management because its explicit goal was to get more output from workers. Critics have argued that Taylor's incentive system would dehumanize the workplace and reduce workers to little more than drones. Later theorists recognized that Taylor's views of employee motivation were inadequate and narrow. Nevertheless, scientific management represents a key milestone in the development of management thought.

Classical Organization Theory

During the same era, another perspective on management theory and practice was also emerging. Generally referred to as **classical organization theory**, this perspective was concerned with structuring organizations effectively. Whereas scientific management studied how individual workers could be made more efficient, classical organization theory focused on how a large number of workers and managers could be organized most effectively into an overall structure.

Henri Fayol and Max Weber were major contributors to classical organization theory. Weber proposed a "bureaucratic" structure that he believed would work for all organizations.[5] Although today the term "bureaucracy" conjures up images of paperwork, red tape, and inflexibility, in Weber's model **bureaucracy** embraced logic,

Scientific management, popular during the early twentieth century, was one of the first approaches to management. It focused on the efficiency of individual workers.

Taylor identified a phenomenon he called "soldiering"—the practice of working considerably slower than one can.

Classical organization theory focused on how organizations can be structured most effectively to meet their goals.

The bureaucracy model, as described by Weber, was an early universal approach to organization structure. In ideal form, a bureaucracy is logical, rational, and efficient.

Google and . . . **DIVERSITY**

The Diversity of Googlers

Sergey Brin and Larry Page founded Google as computer science graduate students at Stanford University. From the beginning, the firm sought diversity as a way to increase innovation. Google employees are a diverse group, with a diverse mix of prior work experiences. According to the Google website, Googlers (as employees are called) "range from former neurosurgeons, CEOs, and U.S. puzzle champions to alligator wrestlers and Marines." The result is a variety of perspectives, skills, and values that lead to enhanced creativity.

Google employees speak dozens of languages and represent many nationalities, which supports the company's international users and customers. The majority of Googlers are young and male, as in many high-tech firms, but there are a number of older workers and women in key roles throughout the company.

When employees are diverse, multiple viewpoints help the company to identify many opportunities for improvement. For example, Google search depends on properly spelled search words. One engineer responded to the problem of typing errors by creating a clever spell checker.

Diversity is imbedded in Google in an even more fundamental way—through its users. The search technique used by Google relies on feedback from users. In effect, users are "voting" on the best search results. Those 82 million users per month come from hundreds of countries, access Google through one of 97 languages, and represent a tremendous pool of diverse needs and ideas.

> *"Googlers range from former neurosurgeons and CEOs to alligator wrestlers."*
>
> GOOGLE WEBSITE

Arthur Schopenhauer, a nineteenth-century philosopher, famously said, "Talent hits a target no one else can hit. Genius hits a target no one else can see." Diversity is an important factor in helping Google repeatedly find those targets that no other competitor can see. The chapter closing case highlights more factors that contribute to Google's success.

Sources: "Corporate Information," Google website, www.google.com on January 12, 2005 (quotation); Ben Elgin, "Google: Whiz Kids or Naughty Boys?" *BusinessWeek*, August 19, 2004, www.businessweek.com on February 12, 2005; Paul S. Piper, "Google Spawn: The Culture Surrounding Google," *Information Today*, June 2004, www.infotoday.com on February 7, 2005.

rationality, and efficiency. Weber assumed that the bureaucratic structure would always be the most efficient approach. (Such a blanket prescription represents what is now called a universal approach.) Table 1.1 summarizes the elements of Weber's ideal bureaucracy.

In contrast to Weber's views, contemporary organization theorists recognize that different organization structures may be appropriate in different situations. However, like scientific management, this perspective played a key role in the development of management thought, and Weber's ideas and the concepts associated with his bureaucratic structure are still interesting and relevant today. (Chapters 13 and 14 discuss contemporary organization theory.)

Clearly, then, an understanding of organizational behaviour can play a vital role in managerial work. To most effectively use the knowledge provided by this field, however, managers must thoroughly understand its concepts, assumptions, and premises. To provide a groundwork for this understanding, we look further at the field's historical roots.

Key contributors to classical organization theory included Henri Fayol, Lyndall Urwick, and Max Weber.

Elements	Comments
1. Rules and Procedures	A consistent set of abstract rules and procedures should exist to ensure uniform performance.
2. Distinct Division of Labour	Each position should be filled by an expert.
3. Hierarchy of Authority	The chain of command should be clearly established.
4. Technical Competence	Employment and advancement should be based on merit.
5. Segregation of Ownership	Professional managers, rather than owners, should run the organization.
6. Rights and Properties of the Position	These should be associated with the organization, not the person who holds the office.
7. Documentation	A record of actions should be kept regarding administrative decisions, rules, and procedures.

TABLE **1.1**

Elements of Weber's
Ideal Bureaucracy

The Emergence of Organizational Behaviour

Rationality, efficiency, and standardization were the central themes of both scientific management and classical organization theory. The roles of individuals and groups in organizations were either ignored altogether or given only minimal attention. This, however, changed with the Hawthorne studies.

The Hawthorne Studies

The **Hawthorne studies** were conducted between 1927 and 1932 at Western Electric's Hawthorne plant near Chicago.[6] The first major experiment at Hawthorne investigated the effects of different levels of lighting on productivity. The researchers systematically manipulated the lighting of the area in which a group of women worked. The group's productivity was measured and compared with that of another group (the control group), whose lighting was left unchanged. As lighting was increased for the experimental group, productivity went up—but, surprisingly, so did the productivity of the control group. Even when lighting was subsequently reduced, the productivity of both groups continued to increase. Not until the lighting had become almost as dim as moonlight did productivity start to decline. This led the researchers to conclude that lighting had no relationship to productivity.

The Hawthorne studies, conducted between 1927 and 1932, led to some of the first discoveries of the importance of human behaviour in organizations.

In another major experiment, a piecework incentive system was established for a nine-member group that assembled terminal banks for telephone exchanges. Scientific management would have predicted that each person would work as hard as possible to maximize his or her personal income. But the Hawthorne researchers instead found that the group as a whole established an acceptable level of output for its members. Individuals who failed to meet this level were dubbed "chisellers," and those who exceeded it by too much were branded "rate busters." A worker who wanted to be accepted by the group could not produce at too high or too low a level. Thus, as a worker approached the accepted level each day, that worker slowed down to avoid overproducing.

After a follow-up interview program with several thousand workers, the Hawthorne researchers concluded that the human element in the workplace was considerably more important than previously believed. The lighting experiment, for example, suggested that productivity might increase simply because workers were singled out for special treatment and thus perhaps felt more valued.

The earliest approaches to management, such as scientific management and classical organization theory, gave little regard to the value and importance of human behaviour to organizational effectiveness. Thus, people were viewed from a "machine" perspective as robots who did as they were told and were interchangeable with others. While the changeable Hawthorne studies undermined this mentality and illustrated the importance of human behaviour, some managers today, still fail to acknowledge the role and importance of human behaviour. For example, they may ignore the individual needs of their employees and assume that work always takes precedence over other things.

Despite the conclusions drawn from the Hawthorne studies, managers may still sometimes forget the importance of people and focus too heavily on the mechanistic side of business. Like scientific management, the Hawthorne studies played a major role in the advancement of the field and are still among its most frequently cited works.[7]

The Human Relations Movement

Human relationists believed that employee satisfaction is a key determinant of performance.

The Hawthorne studies created quite a stir among managers, providing the foundation for an entirely new approach to management known as the human relations movement. Following the Hawthorne studies, the human relations movement emerged. **Human relationists** believed that employee satisfaction is a key determinant of performance. The basic premises underlying the human relations movement were that people respond primarily to their social environment, that motivation depends more on social needs than on economic needs, and that satisfied employees work harder than unsatisfied employees. This perspective represented a fundamental shift away from the philosophy and values of scientific management and classical organization theory.

Abraham Maslow, another pioneer in the human relations movement, developed the well-known hierarchy of human needs.

The works of Douglas McGregor and Abraham Maslow perhaps best exemplified the values of the human relations approach to management.[8] McGregor is best known for his classic book, *The Human Side of Enterprise*, in which he identified two opposing perspectives that he believed typified managerial views of employees. Some managers, McGregor said, subscribed to what he labelled **Theory X**, whose characteristics are summarized in Table 1.2.

Theory X takes a pessimistic view of human nature and employee behaviour. In many ways, it is consistent with the premises of scientific management. A much more optimistic and positive view of employees is found in **Theory Y**, also summarized in Table 1.2. Theory Y, which is generally representative of the human relations perspective, was the approach McGregor himself advocated.

A prominent human relations writer, Douglas McGregor developed the concepts of **Theory X** and **Theory Y**. Theory X takes a negative and pessimistic view of workers, Theory Y a more positive and optimistic perspective. McGregor advocated the adoption of Theory Y.

In 1943, Abraham Maslow published a pioneering theory of employee motivation that became well known and widely accepted among managers. Maslow's theory assumes that motivation arises from a hierarchical series of needs. As the needs at each level are satisfied, the individual progresses to the next higher level.

The Hawthorne studies and the human relations movement played major roles in developing the foundations for the field of organizational behaviour. Some of the early theorists' basic premises and assumptions were incorrect, however. For example, most human relationists believed that employee attitudes, such as job satisfaction, are the major causes of employee behaviours, such as job performance. As we explain in Chapter 3, however, this is not always the case. Also, many of the human relationists' views were unnecessarily limited and situation specific. Thus, there was still plenty of room for refinement and development in the emerging field of human behaviour in organizations.

Toward Organizational Behaviour: The Value of People

Organizational behaviour began to emerge as a mature field of study in the late 1950s and early 1960s.[9] That period saw the field's evolution from the simple assumptions

Theory X Assumptions	Theory Y Assumptions	TABLE 1.2
1. People do not like work and try to avoid it. 2. People do not like work, so managers have to control, direct, coerce, and threaten employees to get them to work toward organizational goals. 3. People prefer to be directed, to avoid responsibility, to want security; they have little ambition.	1. People do not naturally dislike work; work is a natural part of their lives. 2. People are internally motivated to reach objectives to which they are committed. 3. People are committed to goals to the degree that they receive personal rewards when they reach their objectives. 4. People will seek and accept responsibility under favourable conditions. 5. People have the capacity to be innovative in solving organizational problems. 6. People are bright, but under most organizational conditions their potentials are underutilized.	**Theory X and Theory Y**

Source: Douglas McGregor, *The Human Side of Enterprise* (New York: McGraw-Hill, 1960), pp. 33, 47–48. Reprint by permission of The McGraw-Hill Companies.

and behavioural models of the human relationists to the concepts and methodologies of a true scientific discipline. Since that time, organizational behaviour as a scientific field of inquiry has made considerable strides, although there have been occasional steps backward as well. Overall, however, managers increasingly recognize the value of human resources and strive to better understand people and their role in complex organizations and competitive business situations. Many of the ideas discussed in this book have emerged over the past two decades. We turn now to contemporary organizational behaviour.[10]

> Organizational behaviour began to emerge as a mature field of study in the late 1950s and early 1960s.

Contemporary Organizational Behaviour

Two fundamental characteristics of contemporary organizational behaviour warrant special discussion. Furthermore, a particular set of concepts is generally accepted as defining the field's domain.

Characteristics of the Field

Researchers and managers who use concepts and ideas from organizational behaviour must recognize that it has an interdisciplinary focus and a descriptive nature; that is, it draws from a variety of other fields, and it attempts to describe behaviour (rather than to prescribe how behaviour can be changed in consistent and predictable ways).

An Interdisciplinary Focus   In many ways, organizational behaviour synthesizes several other fields of study. Perhaps the greatest contribution is from psychology, especially organizational psychology. Psychologists study human behaviour, whereas organizational psychologists deal specifically with the behaviour of people in organizational settings. Many of the concepts that interest psychologists, such as individual differences and motivation, are also central to students of organizational behaviour. These concepts are covered in Chapters 3 to 5.

Sociology, too, has had a major impact on the field of organizational behaviour. Sociologists study social systems such as families, occupational classes, and organizations.

> Contemporary organizational behaviour has an interdisciplinary focus, drawing from fields such as psychology, sociology, and other related areas.

Stress has emerged as an important individual-level outcome in many organizations. Organizational factors can both cause and be affected by stress among the firm's workers. While few employees may actually exhibit the stress levels shown here, many firms do actively seek ways to help people better cope with stress.

Because a major concern of organizational behaviour is the study of organization structures, the field clearly overlaps with areas of sociology that focus on the organization as a social system. Chapters 12 to 15 reflect the influence of sociology on the field of organizational behaviour.

Anthropology is concerned with the interactions between people and their environments, especially their cultural environment. Culture is a major influence on the structure of organizations and on the behaviour of people in organizations. Culture is discussed in Chapter 14.

Political science also interests organizational behaviourists. We usually think of political science as the study of political systems such as governments. But themes of interest to political scientists include how and why people acquire power and such topics as political behaviour, decision making, conflict, the behaviour of interest groups, and coalition formation. These are also major areas of interest in organizational behaviour, as is reflected in Chapters 9 and 10.

Economists study the production, distribution, and consumption of goods and services. Students of organizational behaviour share the economists' interest in areas such as labour market dynamics, productivity, human resource planning and forecasting, and cost–benefit analysis. Chapters 2 and 5 most strongly illustrate these issues.

Engineering has also influenced the field of organizational behaviour. Industrial engineering in particular has long been concerned with work measurement, productivity measurement, workflow analysis and design, job design, and labour relations. Obviously these areas are also relevant to organizational behaviour and are discussed in Chapters 2, 5, and 10.

Most recently, medicine has come into play in connection with the study of human behaviour at work, specifically in the area of stress. Increasingly, research is showing that controlling the causes and consequences of stress in and out of organizational settings is important for the well-being of both the individual and the organization. Chapter 6 is devoted to stress.

A Descriptive Nature   A primary goal of studying organizational behaviour is to describe relationships among two or more behavioural variables. The theories and concepts of the field, for example, cannot predict with certainty that changing a specific set of workplace variables will improve an individual employee's performance by a certain amount. At best, the field can suggest that certain general concepts or variables tend to be related to one another in particular settings. For instance, research might indicate that in one organization, employee satisfaction and individual perceptions of working conditions are positively related. However, we may not know if better working conditions lead to more satisfaction, if more-satisfied people see their jobs differently than dissatisfied people, or if both satisfaction and perceptions of working conditions are actually related through other variables. Also,

Contemporary organizational behaviour reinforces the need for a strong interdisciplinary focus. For example, consider these Vietnamese employees working in a Nike contract factory in their homeland. Managers cannot simply take their understanding of workers based in North America and blindly apply it in a setting such as this. Instead, managers need to have an understanding of how psychological, sociological, anthropological, political, and economic forces vary across cultures in general and how they apply to Vietnam in particular if they are to work effectively in that country.

the relationship between satisfaction and perceptions of working conditions observed in one setting may be considerably stronger, or weaker, or even nonexistent in other settings.

Organizational behaviour is descriptive for several reasons: the immaturity of the field; the complexities inherent in studying human behaviour; and the lack of valid, reliable, and accepted definitions and measures. Whether the field will ever be able to make definitive predictions and prescriptions is still an open question. Nonetheless, the value of studying organizational behaviour is firmly established. Because behavioural processes pervade most managerial functions and roles, and because the work of organizations is done primarily by people, the knowledge and understanding gained from the field can significantly help managers in many ways.[11]

> Organizational behaviour attempts to describe relationships between two or more behavioural variables.

Basic Concepts of the Field

The central concepts of organizational behaviour can be grouped into three basic categories: (1) individual processes, (2) interpersonal processes, and (3) organizational processes and characteristics. As Figure 1.2 shows, these categories provide the basic framework for this book.

Chapter 2 develops a managerial perspective on organizational behaviour and links the core concepts of organizational behaviour with actual management for organizational effectiveness. Together, the two chapters in Part 1 provide a fundamental introduction to organizational behaviour.

The four chapters of Part 2 cover individual processes in organizations. Chapter 3 explores key individual differences in such characteristics as personality and attitudes. Chapters 4 and 5 provide in-depth coverage of an especially important topic, employee motivation in organizations, as well as various methods and strategies that managers

> The central concepts of organizational behaviour can be divided into three basic categories: individual processes, interpersonal processes, and organizational processes and characteristics.

FIGURE 1.2

The Framework for Understanding Organizational Behaviour

Organizational behaviour is an exciting and complex field of study. The specific concepts and topics that constitute the field can be grouped into three categories: individual, interpersonal, and organizational processes and characteristics. Here these concepts and classifications are used to provide an overall framework for the organization of this book.

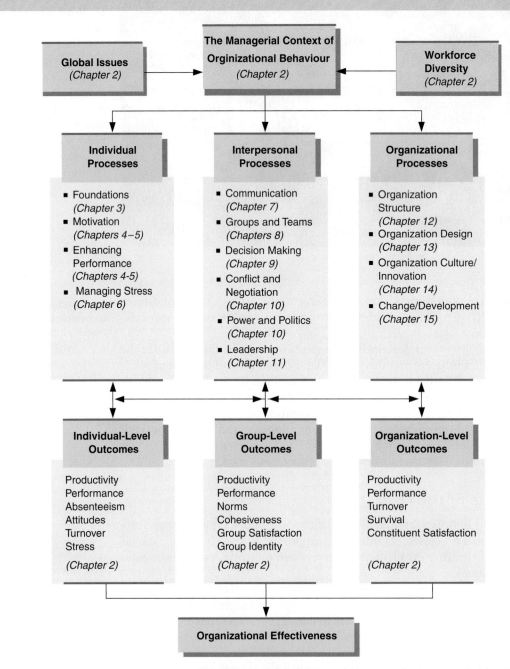

can use to enhance employee motivation and performance. Chapter 6 covers the causes and consequences of stress in the workplace.

Part 3 is devoted to interpersonal processes in organizations. Chapter 7 covers interpersonal communication, and Chapter 8 is devoted to group dynamics and how managers are using teams in organizations today. Chapter 9 explores various aspects of decision making, and Chapter 10 covers conflict, negotiation, power, and politics. Chapter 11 discusses leadership models and concepts.

Part 4 is devoted to organizational processes and characteristics. Chapter 12 describes organization structure; Chapter 13 is an in-depth treatment of organization design. Organization culture and innovation are discussed in Chapter 14, and organization change and development are covered in Chapter 15.

Contextual Perspectives on Organizational Behaviour

Several contextual perspectives have increasingly influenced organizational behaviour: the systems and contingency perspectives, the interactional view, and contemporary applied perspectives. Many of the concepts and theories discussed in the chapters that follow reflect these perspectives; they represent basic points of view that influence much of our contemporary thinking about behaviour in organizations.

Systems and Contingency Perspectives

The systems and contingency perspectives share related viewpoints on organizations and how they function. Each is concerned with interrelationships among organizational elements and between organizational and environmental elements.

The Systems Perspective   The systems perspective, or the theory of systems, was first developed in the physical sciences, but it has been extended to other areas, such as management.[12] A **system** is an interrelated set of elements that function as a whole. Figure 1.3 shows a general framework for viewing organizations as systems.

> A **system** is a set of interrelated elements functioning as a whole.

According to this perspective, an organizational system receives four kinds of inputs from its environment: material, human, financial, and information. The organization then combines and transforms the inputs and returns them to the environment in the form of products or services, employee behaviours, profits or losses, and additional information. Then the system receives feedback from the environment regarding these outputs.

As an example, we can apply systems theory to Petro-Canada. Material inputs include pipelines, crude oil, and the machinery used to refine petroleum. Human inputs are oil field workers, refinery workers, office staff, and other people employed by the company. Financial inputs take the form of money received from oil and gas sales, shareholder investment, and so forth. Finally, the company receives information inputs from forecasts about future oil supplies, geological surveys on potential drilling sites, sales projections, and similar analyses.

Through complex refining and other processes, these inputs are combined and transformed to create products such as gasoline and motor oil. As outputs, these products are sold to the consuming public. Profits from operations are fed back into the environment through taxes, investments, and dividends; losses, when they occur, hit the environment by reducing shareholders' incomes. In addition to having on-the-job contacts with customers and suppliers, employees live in the community and participate in

---

FIGURE 1.3

The Systems Approach to Organizations

The systems approach to organizations provides a useful framework for understanding how the elements of an organization interact among themselves and with their environment. Various inputs are transformed into different outputs, with important feedback from the environment. If managers do not understand these interrelations, they may tend to ignore their environment or to overlook important interrelationships within their organization.

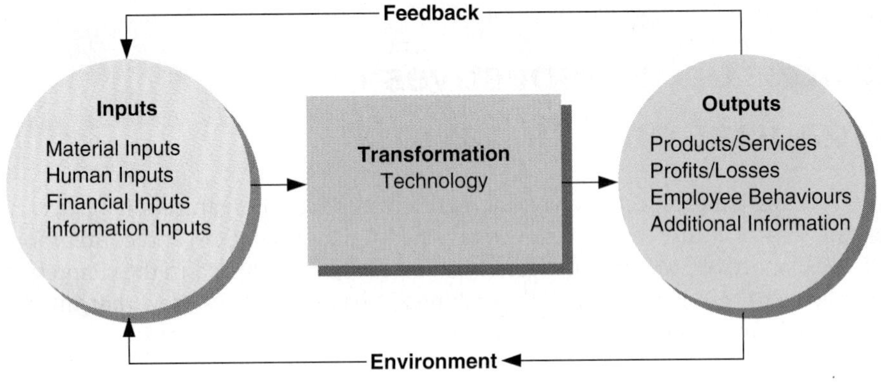

---

activities away from the workplace, and their behaviour is influenced in part by their experiences as Petro-Canada workers. Finally, information about the company and its operations is also released into the environment. The environment, in turn, responds to these outputs and influences future inputs. For example, consumers may buy more or less gasoline depending on the quality and price of Petro-Canada's product, and banks may be more or less willing to lend Petro-Canada money based on financial information released about the company.

The systems perspective is valuable to managers for a variety of reasons. First, it underscores the importance of an organization's environment. Failing to acquire the appropriate resources and to heed feedback from the environment, for instance, can be disastrous. The systems perspective also helps managers conceptualize the flow and interaction of various elements of the organization as they enter the system, are transformed by it, and then re-enter the environment. Many of the basic management concepts introduced in Chapter 2 rely heavily on the systems perspective.

The Contingency Perspective   Another useful viewpoint for understanding behaviour in organizations comes from the **contingency perspective**. In the earlier days of management studies, managers searched for universal answers to organizational questions. They sought prescriptions, the one best way that could be used in any organization under any conditions, searching, for example, for forms of leadership behaviour that would always lead employees to be more satisfied and to work harder. Eventually, however, researchers realized that the complexities of human behaviour and organizational settings make universal conclusions virtually impossible. They discovered that, in organizations, most situations and outcomes are contingent; that is, the relationship between any two variables is likely to be contingent on, or to depend on, other variables.[13]

The **contingency perspective** suggests that in most organizations situations and outcomes are contingent on, or influenced by, other variables.

Figure 1.4 distinguishes the universal and contingency perspectives. The universal model, shown at the top of the figure, presumes a direct cause-and-effect linkage between variables. For example, it suggests that whenever a manager encounters a certain problem or situation (such as motivating employees to work harder), a universal approach exists (such as raising pay or increasing autonomy) that will lead to the desired outcome. The contingency perspective, on the other hand, acknowledges that several other variables alter the direct relationship. In other words, the appropriate managerial action or behaviour in any given situation depends on elements of that situation.

The field of organizational behaviour gradually has shifted from a universal approach in the 1950s and early 1960s to a contingency perspective. The contingency perspective is especially strong in the areas of motivation and job design (Chapters 4 and 5), leadership (Chapter 11), and organization design (Chapter 13), but it is becoming increasingly important throughout the field.

Interactionalism: People and Situations

Interactionalism is a relatively new approach to understanding behaviour in organizational settings. First presented in terms of interactional psychology, this view assumes that individual behaviour results from a continual

The contingency perspective notes that various factors can alter the way an organization responds to a situation. In the wake of the 9/11 attacks on the World Trade Center and the Pentagon, airport security methods changed to prevent future occurrences. With each new terrorist threat, security methods have changed accordingly. Recently, following a failed plot to blow up airplanes, passengers were banned from carrying liquids on planes. The rules are constantly being adjusted to ensure maximum passenger safety and minimum inconvenience.

FIGURE 1.4

Universal Versus Contingency Approaches

Managers once believed that they could identify the one best way of solving problems or reacting to situations. Here we illustrate a more realistic view, the contingency approach. The contingency approach suggests that approaches to problems and situations are contingent on elements of the situation.

Universal Approach

| Organizational problems or situations determine . . . | → | the one best way of responding. |

Contingency Approach

| Organizational problems or situations must be evaluated in terms of . . . | → | elements of the situation, which then suggest . . . | → | contingent ways of responding. |

FIGURE 1.5

The Interactionist Perspective on Behaviour in Organizations

When people enter an organization, their own behaviours and actions shape that organization in various ways. Similarly, the organization itself shapes the behaviours and actions of each individual who becomes a part of it. This interactionist perspective can be useful in explaining organizational behaviour.

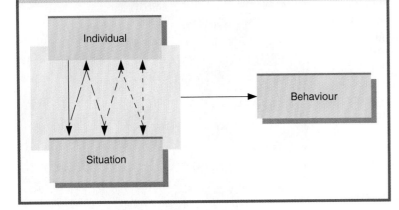

Interactionalism suggests that individuals and situations interact continually to determine individuals' behaviour.

and multidirectional interaction among characteristics of the person and characteristics of the situation. More specifically, **interactionalism** attempts to explain how people select, interpret, and change various situations.[14] Figure 1.5 illustrates this perspective. Note that the individual and the situation are presumed to interact continually. This interaction is what determines the individual's behaviour.

The interactional view implies that simple cause-and-effect descriptions of organizational phenomena are not enough. For example, one set of research studies may suggest that job changes lead to improved employee attitudes.

Another set of studies may propose that attitudes influence how people perceive their jobs in the first place. Both positions probably are incomplete: Employee attitudes may influence job perceptions, but these perceptions may in turn influence future attitudes. Because interactionalism is a fairly recent contribution to the field, it is less prominent in the chapters that follow than the systems and contingency theories. Nonetheless, the interactional view appears to offer many promising ideas for future development.

Research Methods in Organizational Behaviour

We will be referring to theories and research findings as a basis for our discussion throughout this book. In many chapters, we will also highlight important Canadian organizational behaviour research. In this section, we further examine how theories and research findings about organizational behaviour are developed. First, we highlight the role of theory and research. Then we identify the purposes of research and describe the steps in the research process, the types of research designs, and the methods of gathering data. We conclude with a brief discussion of some related issues.

The Role of Theory and Research

Some managers—and many students—fail to see the need for research. They seem confused by what appears to be an endless litany of theories and by sets of contradictory research findings. They often ask, "Why bother?" Indeed, few absolute truths have emerged from studies of organizational behaviour. Management in general and organizational behaviour in particular, however, are in many ways fields of study still in their infancy. Thus, it stands to reason that researchers in these fields have few theories that always work. In addition, their research cannot always be generalized to settings other than those in which it was originally conducted.

Still, theory and research play valuable roles.[15] Theories help investigators organize what they do know. They provide a framework that managers can use to diagnose problems and implement changes. They also serve as road signs that help managers solve many problems involving people. Research also plays an important role. Each study conducted and published adds a little more to the storehouse of knowledge available to practising managers. Questions are posed and answers developed. Over time, researchers can become increasingly confident of findings as they are applied across different settings.[16]

Purposes of Research

As much as possible, researchers try to approach problems and questions of organizational behaviour scientifically. **Scientific research** is the systematic investigation of hypothesized propositions about the relationships among natural phenomena. The aims of science are to describe, explain, and predict phenomena.[17] Research can be classified as basic or applied. **Basic research** is concerned with discovering new knowledge rather than solving particular problems. The knowledge made available through basic research may not have much direct application to organizations, at least when it is first discovered.[18] Research scientists and university professors are the people who most often conduct basic research in organizational behaviour.

Applied research, on the other hand, is conducted to solve particular problems or answer specific questions. The findings of applied research are, by definition, immediately applicable to managers. Consultants, university professors, and managers themselves conduct much of the applied research performed in organizations.

The Scientific Research Process

To result in valid findings, research should be conducted according to the scientific process shown in Figure 1.6. The starting point is a question or problem.[19] For example, a manager wants to design a new reward system to enhance employee motivation, but is unsure about what types of rewards to offer or how to tie them to performance. This manager's questions, therefore, are "What kinds of rewards will motivate my employees?" and "How should those rewards be tied to performance?"

The next step is to review existing literature to determine what is already known about the phenomenon. Something has been written about most problems or questions today's managers face. Thus, the goal of the literature review is to avoid "reinventing the wheel" by finding out what others have already learned. Basic research generally is available in journals such as the *Academy of Management Journal*, *Academy of Management Review*, *Administrative Science Quarterly*, *Journal of Applied Psychology*, *Organizational Behaviuor and Human Decision Processes*, *Journal of Management*, and *Organization Science*. Applied research findings are more likely to be found in sources such as the *Harvard Business Review*, *Academy of Management Perspectives*, *Organizational Dynamics*, *HRMagazine*, and *Personnel Psychology*.

Based on the original question and the review of the literature, researchers formulate hypotheses—predictions of what they expect to find. The hypothesis is an important guide for the researcher's design of the study because it provides a very clear and precise statement of what the researcher wants to test. That means a study can be specifically designed to test the hypothesis.

The research design is the plan for doing the research. (We discuss the more common research designs later.) As part of the research design, the researcher must determine how variables will be measured. Thus, if satisfaction is one factor being considered, the researcher must decide how to measure it.

Scientific research is the systematic investigation of hypothesized propositions about the relationships among natural phenomena.

Basic research involves discovering new knowledge rather than solving specific problems.

Applied research is conducted to solve particular problems or answer specific questions.

FIGURE 1.6

The Research Process

The scientific research process follows a logical and rational sequence of activities. Using this process enables researchers to place greater confidence in their findings. Of course, in some instances, compromises may be necessary to study some phenomena in certain settings. For example, studying potentially controversial subjects like power, politics, or ethics may be difficult if the process is followed rigidly.

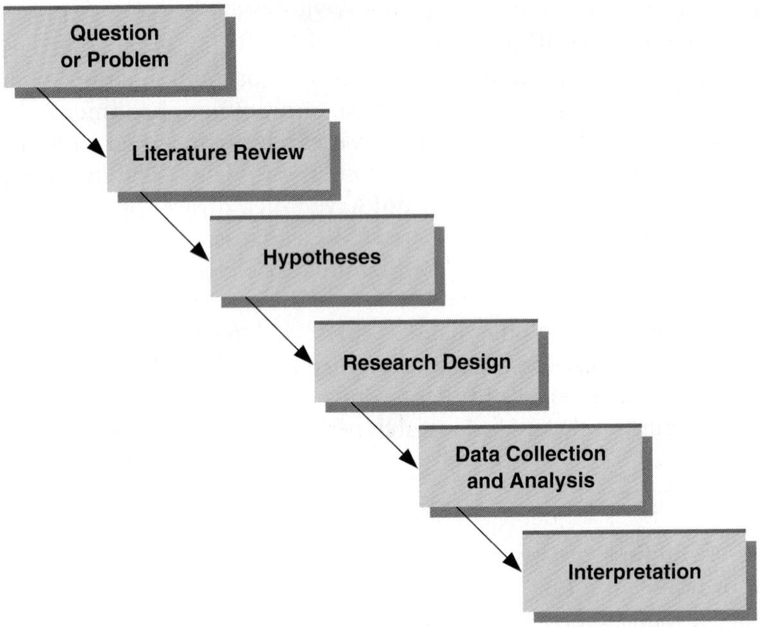

```
┌─────────────────┐
│    Question     │
│   or Problem    │
└─────────────────┘
       ↓
   ┌─────────────────┐
   │ Literature Review│
   └─────────────────┘
          ↓
      ┌─────────────┐
      │ Hypotheses  │
      └─────────────┘
             ↓
         ┌─────────────────┐
         │ Research Design │
         └─────────────────┘
                ↓
            ┌─────────────────┐
            │ Data Collection │
            │  and Analysis   │
            └─────────────────┘
                   ↓
               ┌─────────────────┐
               │ Interpretation  │
               └─────────────────┘
```

After data have been collected, they must be analyzed. (We also discuss common methods for gathering data later.) Depending on the study design and hypotheses, data analysis may be relatively simple and straightforward or require elaborate statistical procedures. Methods for analyzing data are beyond the scope of this discussion.

Finally, the results of the study are interpreted; that is, the researcher figures out what they mean. They may provide support for the hypothesis, fail to support the hypothesis, or suggest a relationship other than that proposed in the hypothesis. An important part of the interpretation process is recognizing the limitations imposed on the findings by weaknesses in the research design.

Many researchers go a step further and try to publish their findings. Several potential sources for publication are the journals mentioned in the discussion of literature review. Publication is important because it helps educate other researchers and managers and also provides additional information for future literature reviews.[20]

Types of Research Designs

A **research design** is the set of procedures used to test the predicted relationships among natural phenomena. The design addresses issues such as how the relevant variables are to be defined, measured, and related to one another. Managers and researchers

A **research design** is the set of procedures used to test the predicted relationships among natural phenomena.

Type	Dominant Characteristic
Case Study	Useful for thorough exploration of unknown phenomena
Field Survey	Provides easily quantifiable data
Laboratory Experiment	Allows researcher high control of variables
Field Experiment	Takes place in realistic setting

TABLE 1.3

Types of Research Designs

can draw on a variety of research designs, each with its own strengths and weaknesses. Four general types of research designs often are used in the study of organizational behaviour (Table 1.3); each type has several variations.[21]

Case Study A **case study** is an in-depth analysis of a single setting. This design frequently is used when little is known about the phenomena being studied and the researcher wants to look at relevant concepts intensively and thoroughly. A variety of methods are used to gather information, including interviews, questionnaires, and personal observation.[22]

A **case study** is an in-depth analysis of one setting.

The case study research design offers several advantages. First, it allows the researcher to probe one situation in detail, yielding a wealth of descriptive and explanatory information. The case study also facilitates the discovery of unexpected relationships. Because the researcher observes virtually everything that happens in a given situation, she or he may learn about issues beyond those originally chosen for study.

The case study design also has several disadvantages. The data it provides cannot be readily generalized to other situations because the information is so closely tied to the situation studied. In addition, case study information may be biased by the researcher's closeness to the situation. Case study research also tends to be very time consuming.

Nevertheless, the case study can be an effective and useful research design as long as the researcher understands its limitations and takes them into account when formulating conclusions.

Field Survey A **field survey** usually relies on a questionnaire distributed to a sample of people chosen from a larger population.

A **field survey** typically relies on a questionnaire distributed to a sample of people selected from a larger population.

If a manager is conducting the study, the sample often is drawn from a group or department within her or his organization. If a researcher is conducting the study, the sample typically is negotiated with a host organization interested in the questions being addressed. The questionnaire generally is mailed or delivered by hand to participants at home or at work and may be returned by mail or picked up by the researcher. The respondents answer the questions and return the questionnaire as directed. The researcher analyzes the responses and tries to make inferences about the larger population from the representative sample.[23] Field surveys can focus on a variety of topics relevant to organizational behaviour, including employees' attitudes toward other people (such as leaders and coworkers), attitudes toward their jobs (such as satisfaction with the job and commitment to the organization), and perceptions of organizational characteristics (such as the challenge inherent in the job and the degree of decentralization in the organization).[24]

Field surveys provide information about a much larger segment of the population than do case studies. They also provide an abundance of data in easily quantifiable form, which facilitates statistical analysis and the compilation of normative data for comparative purposes.

Field surveys also have several disadvantages. First, survey information may reveal only superficial feelings and reactions to situations rather than deeply held feelings, attitudes, or emotions. Second, the design and development of field surveys require a great deal of expertise and can be very time consuming. Furthermore, relationships among variables tend to be accentuated in responses to questionnaires because of what is called common method variance. This means that people may tend to answer all the questions in the same way, creating a misleading impression. A final, very important point is that field surveys give the researcher little or no control. The researcher may lack control over who completes the questionnaire, when it is filled out, the mental or physical state of the respondent, and many other important conditions. Thus, the typical field survey has many inherent sources of potential error.[25]

Nonetheless, surveys can be a very useful means of gathering large quantities of data and assessing general patterns of relationships among variables.

Laboratory Experiment   The **laboratory experiment** gives the researcher the most control. By creating an artificial setting similar to a real work situation, the researcher can control almost every possible factor in that setting. He or she can then manipulate the variables in the study and examine their effects on other variables.[26]

As an example of how laboratory experiments work, consider the relationship between how goals are developed for subordinates and the subordinates' subsequent level of satisfaction. To explore this relationship, the researcher structures a situation in which some subjects (usually students, but occasionally people hired or recruited from the community) are assigned goals while others determine their own goals. Both groups then work on a hypothetical task relevant to the goals, and afterward all subjects fill out a questionnaire designed to measure satisfaction. Differences in satisfaction between the two groups could be attributed to the method used for goal setting.

Laboratory experiments prevent some of the problems of other types of research. Advantages include a high degree of control over variables and precise measurement of variables. A major disadvantage is the lack of realism; rarely does the laboratory setting exactly duplicate the real-life situation. A related problem is the difficulty in generalizing the findings to organizational settings. Finally, some organizational situations, such as plant closings or employee firings, cannot be realistically simulated in a laboratory.

Field Experiment   A **field experiment** is similar to a laboratory experiment except that it is conducted in a real organization. In a field experiment, the researcher attempts to control certain variables and manipulate others to assess the effects of the manipulated variables on outcome variables. For example, a manager interested in the effects of flexible working hours on absenteeism and turnover might design a field experiment in which one plant adopts a flexible work schedule program and another plant, as similar as possible to the first, serves as a control site. Attendance and turnover are monitored at both plants. If attendance increases and turnover decreases in the experimental plant and there are no changes at the control site, the manager probably will conclude that the flexible work schedule program was successful.

The field experiment has certain advantages over the laboratory experiment. The organizational setting provides greater realism, making generalization to other organizational situations more valid. Disadvantages include the lack of control over other events that might occur in the organizational setting (such as additional changes the firm introduces), contamination of the results if the various groups discover their respective roles in the experiment and behave differently because of that knowledge, greater expense, and the risk that the experimental manipulations will contribute to problems within the company.

A **laboratory experiment** involves creating an artificial setting similar to a real work situation to allow control over almost every possible factor in that setting.

A **field experiment** is similar to a laboratory experiment, but is conducted in a real organization.

Methods of Gathering Data

The method of gathering data is a critical concern of the research design. Data-gathering methods may be grouped into four categories: questionnaires, interviews, observation, and nonreactive measures.[27]

Data-gathering methods may be grouped into four categories: questionnaires, interviews, observation, and nonreactive measures.

Questionnaires

A *questionnaire* is a collection of written questions about the respondents' attitudes, opinions, perceptions, demographic characteristics, or some combination of these factors. Usually the respondent fills out the questionnaire and returns it to the researcher. To facilitate scoring, the researcher typically uses questions with a variety of answers, each of which has an associated score. Some questionnaires have a few open-ended questions that allow respondents to elaborate on their answers. Designing a questionnaire that will provide the information the researcher desires is a very complex task and one that has received considerable attention. Some researchers have recently begun using computer networks to distribute questionnaires and collect responses.

Interviews

An *interview* resembles a questionnaire, but the questions are presented to the respondent orally by an interviewer. The respondent usually is allowed to answer questions spontaneously rather than asked to choose among alternatives defined by the researcher. Interviews generally take much more time to administer than questionnaires, and they are more difficult to score. The benefit of interviews is the opportunity for the respondent to speak at length on a topic, thereby providing a richness and depth of information not normally yielded by questionnaires.

Observation

Observation, in its simplest form, is watching events and recording what is observed. Researchers use several types of observation. In structured observation, the observer is trained to look for and record certain activities or types of events. In participant observation, the trained observer actually participates in the organizational events as a member of the work team and records impressions and observations in a diary or daily log. In hidden observation, the trained observer is not visible to the subjects. A hidden camera or a specially designed observation room may be used.

Nonreactive Measures

When a situation is changed because of data gathering, we say the activity has caused a reaction in the situation. *Nonreactive measures*, also called "unobtrusive measures," have been developed for gathering data without disturbing the situation being studied. When questionnaires, interviews, and obtrusive observations may cause problems in the research situation, the use of nonreactive measures may be an appropriate substitute. Nonreactive measures include examination of physical traces, use of archives, and simple observation. At some universities, for example, sidewalks are not laid down around a new building until it has been in use for some time. Rather than ask students and faculty about their traffic patterns or try to anticipate them, the designers observe the building in use, see where the grass is most heavily worn, and put sidewalks there.

Related Issues in Research

Three other issues are of particular interest to researchers: causality, reliability and validity, and ethical concerns.[28]

Causality

Scientific research attempts to describe, explain, and predict phenomena. In many cases, the purpose of the research is to reveal causality; that is, researchers attempt to describe, explain, and predict the cause of a certain event. In everyday life, people commonly observe a series of events and infer causality about the relationship among them. For example, you might observe that a good friend is skipping one of her classes regularly. You also know that she is failing that class. You might infer that she is failing the class because of her poor attendance. But the causal relationship may be just the reverse: your friend may have had a good attendance record until her poor performance on the first test destroyed her motivation and led her to stop attending class. Given the complexities associated with human behaviour in organizational settings, the issues of causality, causal inference, and causal relations are of considerable interest to managers and researchers alike.

In the behavioural sciences, causality is difficult to determine because of the interrelationships among variables in a social system. Causality cannot always be empirically proven, but it may be possible to infer causality in certain circumstances. Generally, two conditions must be met for causality to be attributed to an observed relationship among variables. The first is temporal order: if x causes y, then x must occur before y. Many studies, especially field surveys, describe the degree of association among variables with highly sophisticated mathematical techniques, but inferring a causal relationship is difficult because the variables are measured at the same point in time. On the basis of such evidence, we cannot say whether one variable or event caused the other, whether they were both caused by another variable, or whether they are totally independent of each other.

The second condition is the elimination of spuriousness. If we want to infer that x caused y, we must eliminate all other possible causes of y. Often a seemingly causal relationship between two variables is due to their joint association with a third variable, z. To be able to say the relationship between x and y is causal, we must rule out z as a possible cause of y. In the behavioural sciences, so many variables may influence one another that tracing causal relationships is like walking in an endless maze. Despite the difficulties of the task, we must continue trying to describe, explain, and predict social phenomena in organizational settings if we are to advance our understanding of organizational behaviour.[29]

Reliability and Validity

The **reliability** of a measure is the extent to which it is consistent over time. Suppose that a researcher measures a group's job satisfaction today with a questionnaire and then measures the same thing in two months. Assuming that nothing has changed, individual responses should be very similar. If they are, the measure can be assessed as having a high level of reliability. Likewise, if question 2 and question 10 ask about the same thing, responses to these questions should be consistent. If measures lack reliability, little confidence can be placed in the results they provide.

Validity describes the extent to which research measures what it was intended to measure. Suppose that a researcher is interested in employees' satisfaction with their jobs. To determine this, the employees are asked a series of questions about their pay, supervisors, and working conditions. The researcher then averages their answers and uses the average to represent job satisfaction. We might argue that this is not a valid measure. Pay, supervision, and working conditions, for example, may be unrelated to the job itself. Thus, the researcher has obtained data that do not mean what he or she thinks they mean—they are not valid. The researcher, then, must use measures that are valid as well as reliable.[30]

Ethical Concerns

Last, but certainly not least, the researcher must contend with ethical concerns. Two concerns are particularly important.[31] First, the researcher must provide adequate protection for participants in the study and not violate their privacy without their permission. For example, suppose that a researcher is studying the behaviour of a group of operating employees. A good way to increase people's willingness to participate is to promise that their identities will not be revealed. Having made such a guarantee, the researcher is obligated to keep it.

Likewise, participation should be voluntary. All prospective subjects should have the right not to participate or to withdraw their participation after the study has begun. The researchers should explain all procedures to participants in advance and should not subject them to any experimental conditions that could harm them either physically or psychologically. Many government agencies, universities, and professional associations have developed guidelines for researchers to use to guarantee the protection of human subjects.

The other issue involves how the researcher reports the results. In particular, it is important that research procedures and methods be reported faithfully and candidly. This enables readers to assess for themselves the validity of the results reported. It also allows others to do a better job of replicating (repeating) the study, perhaps with a different sample, to learn more about how its findings generalize.

Summary of Key Points

■ Organizational behaviour is the study of human behaviour in organizational settings, the interface between human behaviour and the organization, and the organization itself. The study of organizational behaviour is important because organizations have a powerful influence over our lives.

■ Serious interest in the study of management first developed around the beginning of this century. Two of the earliest approaches were scientific management (best represented by the work of Taylor) and classical organization theory (exemplified by the work of Weber).

■ Organizational behaviour began to emerge as a scientific discipline as a result of the Hawthorne studies. McGregor and Maslow led the human relations movement that grew from those studies.

■ Contemporary organizational behaviour attempts to describe, rather than prescribe, behavioural forces in organizations. Ties to psychology, sociology, anthropology, political science, economics, engineering, and medicine make organizational behaviour an interdisciplinary field.

■ The basic concepts of the field are divided into three categories: individual processes, interpersonal processes, and organizational processes and characteristics. Those categories form the framework for the organization of this book.

■ Important contextual perspectives on the field of organizational behaviour are the systems and contingency perspectives, interactionism, and contemporary applied perspectives.

■ Much of what we know about organizational behaviour is the result of research. This research can take many forms, such as experimental and field research. Concerns when conducting research include causality, reliability and validity, and ethics.

Discussion Questions

1. Some people have suggested that understanding human behaviour at work is the single most important requirement for managerial success. Do you agree or disagree with this statement? Why?

2. In what ways is organizational behaviour comparable to functional areas such as finance, marketing, and production? In what ways is it different from these areas? Is it similar to statistics in any way?

3. Identify some managerial jobs that are highly affected by human behaviour and others that are less so. Which would you prefer? Why?

4. Besides those cited in the text, what reasons can you think of for the importance of organizational behaviour?

5. Suppose you have to hire a new manager. One candidate has outstanding technical skills, but poor interpersonal skills. The other has exactly the opposite mix of skills. Which candidate would you hire? Why?

6. Some people believe that individuals working in an organization have a basic human right to satisfaction with their work and to the opportunity to grow and develop. How would you defend this position? How would you argue against it?

7. Many universities offer a course in industrial/organizational psychology. The content of those courses is quite similar to the content of this one. Do you think that behavioural material is best taught in a business or psychology program, or is it best to teach it in both?

8. Do you believe the field of organizational behaviour has the potential to become prescriptive as opposed to descriptive? Why or why not?

9. Are the notions of systems, contingency, and interactionism mutually exclusive? If not, describe ways in which they are related.

10. Get a recent issue of a popular business magazine such as *The Globe and Mail Report on Business* or *Canadian Business* and scan its major articles. Do any of them reflect organizational behaviour concepts? Describe.

11. Do you read *Dilbert*? Do you think it accurately describes organization life? Are there other comic strips that reflect life and work in contemporary organizations?

Purpose: This exercise will help you appreciate the importance and pervasiveness of organizational behaviour concepts and processes in both contemporary organizational settings and popular culture.

Format: Your instructor will divide the class into groups of three to five members. Each group will be assigned a specific television program to watch before the next class meeting.

Procedure: Arrange to watch the program as a group. Each person should have a pad of paper and a pencil handy. As you watch the show, jot down examples of individual behaviour, interpersonal dynamics, organizational characteristics, and other concepts and processes relevant to organizational behaviour. After the show, spend a few minutes comparing notes. Compile one list for the entire group. (It is advisable to turn off the television set during this discussion!)

During the next class meeting, have someone in the group summarize the plot of the show and list the concepts it illustrated. The following television shows are especially good for illustrating behavioural concepts in organizational settings:

Network Shows	Syndicated Shows
Survivor	DaVinci's Inquest
Corner Gas	Seinfeld
The Sopranos	Home Improvement
The Office	Made in Canada
C.S.I.	Cheers
Grey's Anatomy	Star Trek

Follow-up Questions

1. What does this exercise illustrate about the pervasiveness of organizations in our contemporary society?

2. What recent or classic movies might provide similar kinds of examples?

3. Do you think television programs from countries other than Canada or the United States would provide more or fewer examples set in organizations?

Assessing Your Own Management Skills

The questions below are intended to provide insights into your confidence about your capabilities regarding the management skills discussed in this chapter. Answer each question by circling the scale value that best reflects your feelings.

1. I generally do well in quantitative courses like math, statistics, accounting, and finance.

5	4	3	2	1
Strongly Agree	Agree	Neither Agree Nor Disagree	Disagree	Strongly Disagree

2. I get along well with most people.

5	4	3	2	1
Strongly Agree	Agree	Neither Agree Nor Disagree	Disagree	Strongly Disagree

3. It is usually easy for me to see how material in one of my classes relates to material in other classes.

5	4	3	2	1
Strongly Agree	Agree	Neither Agree Nor Disagree	Disagree	Strongly Disagree

4. I can usually figure out why a problem occurred.

5	4	3	2	1
Strongly Agree	Agree	Neither Agree Nor Disagree	Disagree	Strongly Disagree

5. When I am asked to perform a task or to do some work, I usually know how to do it or else can figure it out pretty quickly.

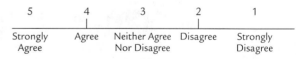

5	4	3	2	1
Strongly Agree	Agree	Neither Agree Nor Disagree	Disagree	Strongly Disagree

6. I can usually understand why people behave as they do.

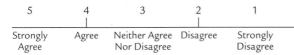

7. I enjoy classes that deal with theories and concepts.

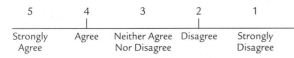

8. I usually understand why things happen as they do.

9. I like classes that require me to "do things"—write papers, solve problems, research new areas, and so forth.

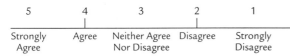

10. Whenever I work in a group, I can usually get others to accept my opinions and ideas.

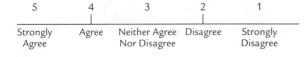

11. I am much more interested in understanding the "big picture" than in dealing with narrow, focused issues.

12. When I know what I am supposed to do, I can usually figure out how to do it.

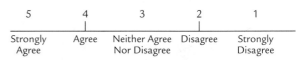

Instructions: Add up your point values for questions 1, 5, and 9; this total reflects your assessment of your technical skills. The point total for questions 2, 6, and 10 reflects interpersonal skills; the point total for questions 3, 7, and 11 reflects conceptual skills; the point total for questions 4, 8, and 12 reflects diagnostic skills. Higher scores indicate stronger confidence in that realm of management. [*Note:* This brief instrument has not been scientifically validated and is to be used for classroom discussion only.]

Management Skillbuilder

Exercise Overview: Conceptual skills refer to a manager's ability to think in the abstract, while diagnostic skills focus on responses to situations. These skills must frequently be used together to better understand the behaviour of others in the organization, as illustrated by this exercise.

Exercise Background: Human behaviour is a complex phenomenon in any setting, but especially so in organizations. Understanding how and why people choose particular behaviours can be difficult, frustrating, but quite important. Consider, for example, the following scenario.

Sandra Buckley has worked in your department for several years. Until recently, she has been a "model" employee. She was always on time, or early, for work, and stayed late whenever necessary to get her work done. She was upbeat, cheerful, and worked very hard. She frequently said that the company was the best place she had ever worked, and that you were the perfect boss.

About six months ago, however, you began to see changes in Sandra's behaviour. She began to occasionally come in late, and you cannot remember the last time she agreed to work past 5:00. She also complains a lot. Other workers have started to avoid her, because she is so negative all the time. You also suspect that she may be looking for a new job.

Exercise Task: Using the scenario described above as background, do the following:

1. Assume that you have done some background work to find out what has happened. Write a brief case with more information that explains why Sandra's behaviour has changed (i.e., your case might include the fact that you recently promoted someone else when Sandra might have expected to get the job). Make the case as descriptive as possible.

2. Relate elements of your case to the various behavioural concepts discussed in this chapter.

3. Decide whether or not you might be about to resolve things with Sandra in order to overcome whatever issues have arisen.

4. Which behavioural process or concept discussed in this chapter is easiest to change? Which is the most difficult to change?

**Organizational Behaviour
Case for Discussion**

Employees to the 100th Power

Google, a provider of Internet search capability, was named after "googol," the number 10 raised to the 100th power (the numeral 1 followed by 100 zeros), to reflect the company's ability to organize the immense amount of information available on the World Wide Web.

Every month, 82 million individuals, half of them from outside the United States, access the Google website, one of the five most popular Internet sites in the world. There they find more than eight billion web pages presented in an easy-to-use format. The company charges firms to sponsor links to corporate websites so the service is free to customers and avoids irritating pop-up ads.

How does Google continue to develop innovative technology and techniques, staying ahead of such tough competitors as Yahoo! and Microsoft? The key ingredient in Google's success is people.

Google began as a project of two Stanford graduate students, Larry Page and Sergey Brin, and an informal, collegial spirit still guides the firm. Googlers are encouraged to work on projects of their own choosing for one day each week. The time to freely experiment has led to innovations such as the ability to translate pages into various languages. Innovation is so important to the firm that its website states, "We don't talk much about what lies ahead, because . . . one of our chief competitive advantages is surprise. Surprise and innovation."

Collaboration is another key value for Google workers. Google facilities contain on-site sports fields and shared office spaces. Employees from new hires to the CEO eat lunch together, play on the same hockey team, and mingle in the office lounges. Google's website claims, "Google . . . favors ability over experience." Position within the corporate hierarchy plays a relatively minor role.

In an environment where pressure can be intense, Googlers must know how to relax. Employees play billiards or ping pong and bring their dogs to work. Even recruiting is fun. When Google sought new programmers, the company didn't use traditional techniques. Instead, it conducted an online programming skills contest, giving cash prizes and job offers to top-performing competitors.

In spite of their emphasis on fun, Googlers are serious about productivity, quality, and cost cutting. To stay focused on customer needs, a large world map is prominently displayed at headquarters. Points of light represent current searches while colour coding shows the language used by the searcher. Current searches are displayed around the office too, so staff remain constantly aware of their far-flung customers.

Google's commitment to excellence is characterized on the company's website: "[We] continue to look for those who share an obsessive commitment to creating search perfection." Although Google uses diversity to drive innovation, the firm concentrates on just one aspect of Internet service: search. One of the company's key values, stated on the website, is "It's best to do one thing really, really well." "Never settle for the best," the Google corporate philosophy, sums up the company's relentless drive to perfection.

Of course, Google isn't perfect. While top leaders are technology wizards, their business expertise is not as strong. Managers made serious missteps during the company's initial public offering of stock in 2004. The mistakes were serious enough to spark a Securities and Exchange Commission inquiry, which found errors but no intent to defraud. Observers credit those mistakes to arrogance. One investment banker characterizes Brin and Page as "challenging and difficult" and speculates that the stock market will "crush" that arrogance.

Looking to the future, stock analysts and investors have expressed concerns about the ability of Google managers to handle an organization that is rapidly growing. A more complex corporate structure, with facilities located on three continents, also adds to the management challenges.

Google's greatest challenge at this time, however, seems to be increased competition. While Internet searching has thus far escaped the attention of larger competitors, that is about to change. Microsoft, for example, has recently introduced a test version of a new search engine. Google's search procedures yield better-quality results, yet it's only a matter of time before a well-funded and smart competitor will duplicate their methods. To ensure continued success, Google must keep its expert workforce loyal, motivated, and productive.

❝ Never settle for the best. ❞
GOOGLE CORPORATE PHILOSOPHY

Only then will Google innovate and stay ahead of its competition.

Case Questions

1. In your opinion, what types of management skills are most important at Google? Explain your answer.

2. How do individual processes at Google reflect the company's focus on customer needs, innovation, and teamwork? How do team processes and organizational processes reflect the company's priorities? Use Figure 1.2, "The Framework for Understanding Organizational Behaviour," to help you answer these questions.

3. Consider Google as a system. Give an example of each type of input available to Google. Give examples of transformation processes and outputs at Google. What impact does the environment have on Google and what impact does Google have on the environment?

Sources: "Corporate Information," "Google Job Opportunities," Google website, www.google.com on February 12, 2005 (quotation); Sergey Brin and Lawrence Page, "The Anatomy of a Large-Scale Hypertextual Web Search Engine," *Computer Networks and ISDN Syste*ms, 1998, www.db .stanford.edu on February 7, 2005; Fernando Ribeiro Correa, "Interview with Google's Sergey Brin," *Linux Gaze*tte, November 2000, www .linuxgazette.com on February 7, 2005; Ben Elgin, "Google: Whiz Kid or Naughty Boys?" *Business*Week, August 19, 2004, www.businessweek.com on February 12, 2005; Stephanie Olsen, "Google Seeking a Few Good Code Jockeys," C/Net News.com, September 17, 2003, news.com.com on February 7, 2005; Paul S. Piper, "Google Spawn: The Culture Surrounding Google," *Information To*day, June 2004, www.infotoday.com on February 7, 2005.

SELF TEST

You have read the chapter and studied the key terms. Think you're ready to ace the exam? Take this sample test to gauge your comprehension of chapter material and check your answers at the back of the book. Want more test questions? Take the ACE quizzes found on the student website: www.hmco.ca/ob.

T F   1. Organizational behaviour (OB) is the study of how companies expand their market shares, deal with competitors, and successfully satisfy customer expectations.

T F   2. Many students who take an organizational behaviour course go on to become Organizational Behaviour Managers in their future careers.

T F   3. The scientific management approach focused on worker attitudes.

T F   4. A laboratory experiment involves creating an artificial setting similar to a real work situation to allow control over almost every possible factor in that setting.

T F   5. An understanding of organizational behaviour allows managers to make specific, accurate predictions about their employees.

T F   6. The systems perspective says organizations receive inputs from the environment, combine and transform them, and then return them to the environment.

T F   7. A person's behaviour is likely influenced by his or her personal characteristics as well as characteristics of the situation the person is in.

8. This is probably your first course in organizational behaviour. You will learn about all of the following by reading this text, except
a. human behaviour in organizational settings.
b. the unique perspectives employees bring to work settings.
c. the interface between human behaviour and the organization.
d. competition and how it affects the stock prices of publicly held firms.
e. organizations themselves.

9. Adherents of this approach to studying organizational behaviour believed that employee satisfaction was a key determinant of productivity.
a. Scientific management
b. Theory X
c. Human relations
d. Classical organization theory
e. Bureaucracy

10. The extent to which a measure is consistent over time refers to the measure's
a. Reliability
b. Validity
c. Utility
d. Causality
e. Ethicality

11. TD Canada Trust sends out a questionnaire to its employees asking them about their satisfaction with their jobs. What type of research design is TD using?
a. Laboratory experiment
b. Field experiment
c. Case study
d. Field survey
e. Observation

12. The field of organizational behaviour is best described as
a. scientific and individual in nature.
b. behavioural and organizational in nature.
c. innovative and traditional in nature.
d. interdisciplinary and descriptive in nature.
e. cross-functional and predictive in nature.

13. Organizational behaviour examines outcomes at which three levels?
a. Organization, industry, division
b. Organization, division, department
c. Department, individual, group
d. Individual, group, organization
e. Group, organization, industry

14. A collection of written questions about the respondents' attitudes, opinions, perceptions, demographic characteristics, or some combination of these factors is:
a. an interview
b. a questionnaire
c. an experiment
d. a case study
e. an observation

CHAPTER 2

Managing People, Organizations, and Diversity

▶ **Explain managerial perspectives on organizational behaviour.**

▶ **Describe the manager's job in terms of managerial functions, roles, and skills. Identify major organizational challenges and relate them to organizational behaviour.**

▶ **Identify major environmental challenges and relate them to organizational behaviour.**

▶ **Discuss how to use a knowledge of organizational behaviour to manage for effectiveness.**

Chapter Outline

Managerial Perspectives on Organizational Behaviour

Basic Management Functions, Roles, and Skills

Fundamental Managerial Functions
Basic Managerial Roles
Critical Managerial Skills

Diversity and Other Organizational Challenges

Downsizing
Workforce Diversity
The New Workforce
Organization Change
Information Technology
New Ways of Organizing

Environmental Challenges

Competitive Strategy
Globalization

Ethics and Corporate Governance

Contemporary Ethical Issues
Ethical Issues in Corporate Governance
Ethical Issues in Information Technology

New Employment Relationships

The Management of Knowledge Workers
Outsourcing
Quality and Productivity
Manufacturing and Service Technology

Managing for Effectiveness

Individual-Level Outcomes
Group- and Team-Level Outcomes
Organization-Level Outcomes

Effective Management Means Success

Effective management is the key to organizational success. Of course, figuring out how to manage effectively is sometimes akin to searching for the proverbial alchemist's stone. There is no one best way to manage effectively and organizations use a variety of approaches to achieve success. Each year, the *Financial Post* publishes a list of the 50 Best Managed companies in Canada. A common thread among many of these highly successful firms is the importance they place on human resources in achieving that success.

For example, Dessau-Soprin, based in Laval, Quebec, is the second largest engineering and construction management company in that province. The company conducts projects in Asia, Africa, and North and South America and its annual revenues recently surpassed $300 million. Although not a household name among Canadian companies, it has been involved in some very well known projects such as the electric transmission system that delivers electricity from James Bay to Montreal, the Bell Centre (home of the National Hockey League's Montreal Canadiens), and the Canadian Space Agency's building in St. Hubert. Dessau-Soprin achieves all of this success by placing strong emphasis on employee satisfaction. A recent internal poll demonstrated an overall 94 percent satisfaction rating among its employees. CEO Jean-Paul Sauriol suggests that the level of satisfaction is the result of the company maintaining a flat management structure, by training and motivating employees, maintaining open communication channels, providing clear goals, and involving employees in decision making.

Employee involvement is a key component of the success of two Alberta companies deemed to be among Canada's best-managed. CCI Thermal Technologies is based in Edmonton and has operations in Ontario and the United States with demanding, high profile customers such as NASA and Atomic Energy of Canada. CCI products include gas recovery systems for nuclear reactors and explosion-proof heaters for oil and gas facilities. Not surprisingly, then, quality is essential to the success of the company. CCI president Bernie Moore believes that employees must be kept in the loop if quality is to be maintained and he achieves this by holding regular round-table meetings with staff during which he collects their suggestions in a notebook that he carries with him. CCI also maintains a bulletin board at each plant so that employees can see the impact they are having on key process indicators.

Blue Falls Manufacturing makes the Arctic Spas line of hot tubs in tiny Thorsby, Alberta. In addition to its Thorsby plant, Blue Falls operates two other facilities in small Alberta towns, employing 400 people. Like CCI, Blue Falls maintains a corporate culture that emphasizes the importance of employees to the success of the firm. Management is always open to new ideas from employees, minimizes red tape, and rewards employees who go the extra mile for the company.[1]

Organizational behaviour is not a designated organization function or area; rather, an understanding of organizational behaviour provides a perspective that all managers can use to perform their jobs more effectively.

I n today's competitive environment, driven by such forces as globalization, rapidly changing technology, and downsizing, it is more important than ever for managers to hone their craft. Managers are constantly seeking new ways to perform their tasks more effectively. The nature of managerial work varies from company to company and continues to evolve, but one factor permeates virtually all managerial activity: interacting with other people. Indeed, the typical day for most managers is devoted almost entirely to interacting with others. Thus, the management process and the behaviour of people in organizations are undeniably intertwined.

This chapter relates the general field of management to the more specific field of organizational behaviour. We start by developing a managerial perspective on organizational behaviour. Then we characterize the manager's job in terms of its functions, roles, and requisite skills. Next, we identify and discuss a variety of organizational and environmental challenges in a context of organizational behaviour. Finally, we discuss how an understanding of organizational behaviour can enhance the manager's ability to manage effectively.

Managerial Perspectives on Organizational Behaviour

Virtually all organizations have managers with titles such as marketing manager, director of public relations, vice president of human resources, and plant manager. But probably no organization has a position titled organizational behaviour manager. The reason is simple: organizational behaviour is not a designated function or area. It is, rather, an understanding of organizational behaviour as a perspective or set of tools that all managers can use to carry out their jobs more effectively.[2]

A knowledge of organizational behaviour helps managers better understand the behaviour of those around them.[3] For example, most managers in an organization are directly responsible for the work-related behaviours of a group of other people—their immediate subordinates. Typical managerial activities in this realm include motivating employees to work harder, ensuring that employees' jobs are properly designed, resolving conflicts, evaluating performance, and helping workers set goals to achieve rewards. The field of organizational behaviour abounds with theory and research on each of these functions.[4]

Unless they happen to be chief executive officers (CEOs), managers also report to others in the organization (and even the CEO reports to the board of directors). In dealing with these individuals, an understanding of basic issues associated with leadership, power and political behaviour, decision making, organization structure and design, and organization culture can be quite beneficial. Again, the field of organizational behaviour provides numerous valuable insights into these processes.

Managers can use their knowledge of organizational behaviour to better understand their own needs, motives, behaviours, and feelings that will help them improve their decision-making capabilities, control stress, communicate better, and comprehend how career dynamics unfold. The study of organizational behaviour provides insights into all of these concepts and processes.

Managers can use their knowledge of organizational behaviour to better understand themselves, their subordinates, their peers and colleagues, and their superiors.

Managers interact with a variety of colleagues, peers, and coworkers inside the organization. An understanding of attitudinal processes, individual differences, group dynamics, intergroup dynamics, organization culture, and power and political behaviour can help managers handle such interactions more effectively. Organizational behaviour provides a variety of practical insights into these processes. Virtually all of the behavioural processes already mentioned are also valuable in interactions with people outside the organization—suppliers, customers, competitors, government officials, representatives of citizens' groups, union officials, and potential joint-venture partners. In addition, an understanding of the environment, technology, and global issues is valuable. Again, organizational behaviour offers managers many insights into how and why things happen as they do.

Finally, these patterns of interactions hold true regardless of the type of organization. Whether a business is large or small, domestic or international, growing or stagnating, its managers perform their work within a social context. The same can be said of managers in health care, education, government, student organizations such as fraternities and sororities, and professional clubs.

We see, then, that it is essentially impossible to understand and practise management without considering the numerous areas of organizational behaviour. We now turn to the nature of the manager's job in more detail.

Basic Management Functions, Roles, and Skills

There are many different ways to conceptualize the job of a contemporary manager.[5] The most widely accepted approaches, however, are from the perspectives of basic managerial functions, common managerial roles, and fundamental managerial skills.

Fundamental Managerial Functions

Managers in all organizations engage in four basic functions. These functions are generally referred to as planning, organizing, leading, and controlling. All organizations also use four kinds of resources: human, financial, physical, and information. As illustrated in Figure 2.1, managers combine these resources through the four basic functions. That is, the figure shows how managers apply the basic functions across resources to advance the organization toward its goals.

> The manager's job involves four basic functions: planning, organizing, leading, and controlling.

Planning   **Planning**, the first managerial function, is the process of determining the organization's desired future position and deciding how best to get there. The planning process at The Bay, for example, includes studying and analyzing the environment, deciding on appropriate goals, outlining strategies for achieving those goals, and developing tactics to help execute the strategies. Behavioural processes and characteristics pervade each of these activities. Perception, for instance, plays a major role in environmental scanning, and creativity and motivation influence how managers set goals, strategies, and tactics. Larger organizations usually rely on top management to handle planning activities. In smaller firms, the owner usually takes care of planning.

> **Planning** is the process of determining an organization's desired future position and the best means of getting there.

Organizing   The second managerial function is **organizing**—the process of designing jobs, grouping jobs into manageable units, and establishing patterns of authority among jobs and groups of jobs. This process produces the basic structure, or framework, of the organization. For large organizations such as The Bay, that structure can be extensive and complicated. Smaller firms can often function with a relatively simple and straightforward form of organization. As noted earlier, the processes and characteristics of the organization itself are a major theme of organizational behaviour.

> **Organizing** is the process of designing jobs, grouping jobs, into units and establishing patterns of authority between jobs and units.

Leading   **Leading**, the third managerial function, is the process of motivating members of the organization to work together toward the organization's goals. A manager at the Body Shop, for example, must hire people, train them, and motivate them. Major

> **Leading** is the process of getting the organization's members to work together toward the organization's goals.

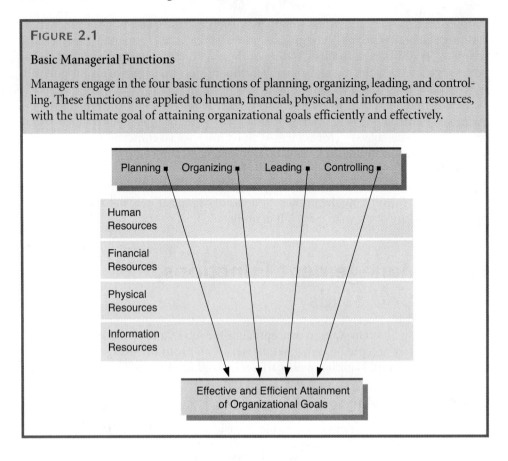

> **FIGURE 2.1**
>
> **Basic Managerial Functions**
>
> Managers engage in the four basic functions of planning, organizing, leading, and controlling. These functions are applied to human, financial, physical, and information resources, with the ultimate goal of attaining organizational goals efficiently and effectively.

components of leading include motivating employees, managing group dynamics, and actually leading. These are all closely related to major areas of organizational behaviour. All managers, whether they work in a huge multinational corporation or a small neighbourhood business, must understand the importance of leading.

Controlling is the process of monitoring and correcting the actions of the organization and its members to keep them directed toward their goals.

Controlling   The fourth managerial function, **controlling**, is the process of monitoring and correcting the actions of the organization and its people to keep them headed toward their goals. A Bay manager has to control costs, inventory, and so on. Again, behavioural processes and characteristics are key parts of this function. Performance evaluation, reward systems, and motivation, for example, all apply to control. Control is of vital importance to all businesses, but it may be especially critical to smaller ones. General Motors, for example, can withstand a loss of several thousand dollars due to poor control, but a similar loss can be devastating to a small firm.

Managers play ten basic roles in their jobs.

Basic Managerial Roles

In an organization, as in a play or a movie, a role is the part a person plays in a given situation. Managers often play a number of different roles. Much of our knowledge about managerial roles comes from the work of Henry Mintzberg.[6] Mintzberg identified ten basic managerial roles clustered into three general categories; see Table 2.1.

Three important **interpersonal roles** are the figurehead, the leader, and the liaison.

Interpersonal Roles   Mintzberg's **interpersonal roles** are primarily social in nature; that is, they are roles in which the manager's main task is to relate to other people

Management Myths and . . . **RESEARCH**

Mastering Myth

Management and organizational behaviour textbooks discuss the activities of managers in terms of the four basic functions: planning, organizing, leading, and controlling. Such discussions may give the impression that the daily life of managers can easily be compartmentalized. In a classic article published in 1975 that is still widely cited, however, McGill University management professor Henry Mintzberg suggested that the daily worklife of managers is much more chaotic than we would be led to believe.

In his article, Mintzberg took direct aim at four myths concerning the job of manager. First, rather than engaging in reflective, systematic planning, Mintzberg reported that managers are very action oriented and their activities are typically very brief and quite various in nature. In his own observation of top managers, Mintzberg found that about half of the activities engaged in by managers lasted less than nine minutes!

A second myth dispelled by Mintzberg's study concerned the extent to which managers engaged in regular duties. Rather than simply planning and delegating, managers perform a significant number of routine activities, such as meeting with customers and presiding at company events. Third, whereas popular myth holds that managers rely on formal management information systems, reality suggests that managers spend a considerable amount of time obtaining information via verbal communication. Finally, rather than a science or profession, Mintzberg found that the practice of management relies heavily on judgment and intuition. By addressing these myths, Mintzberg has highlighted the fact that the job of manager is far more complex than can be captured by the fundamental managerial functions.

Source: Henry Mintzberg, "The Manager's Job: Folklore and Fact," *Harvard Business Review*, 1975, vol. 53, pp. 49–61.

in certain ways. The manager may serve as a figurehead for the organization. Taking visitors to dinner and attending ribbon-cutting ceremonies are part of the figurehead role. In the role of leader, the manager works to hire, train, and motivate employees. Finally, they have a liaison role that consists of relating to others outside the group or organization. For example, a manager at Intel might be responsible for handling all price negotiations with a key supplier of electronic circuit boards. Obviously, each of these interpersonal roles involves behavioural processes.

Informational Roles   Mintzberg's three **informational roles** involve some aspect of information processing. The monitor actively seeks information that might be of value to the organization in general or to specific managers. The manager who

Three key **informational roles** are the monitor, the disseminator, and the spokesperson.

Category	Role	Example
Interpersonal	Figurehead	attend employee retirement ceremony
	Leader	encourage workers to increase productivity
	Liaison	coordinate activities of two committees
Informational	Monitor	scan *National Post* for information about competition
	Disseminator	send out memos outlining new policies
	Spokesperson	hold press conference to announce new plant
Decision making	Entrepreneur	develop idea for new product and convince others of its merits
	Disturbance handler	resolve dispute
	Resource allocator	allocate budget requests
	Negotiator	settle new labour contract

TABLE 2.1

Important Managerial Roles

transmits this information to others is carrying out the role of disseminator. The spokesperson speaks for the organization to outsiders. A manager chosen by Corel to appear at a press conference announcing a new product launch or a major deal would be serving in this role. Again, behavioural processes are part of each of these roles, because information is almost always exchanged between people.

Decision-Making Roles   Finally, Mintzberg identified four **decision-making roles.** The entrepreneur voluntarily initiates change, such as innovations or new strategies, in the organization. The disturbance handler helps settle disputes between various parties, such as other managers and their subordinates. The resource allocator decides who will get what—how resources will be distributed among individuals and groups. The negotiator represents the organization in reaching agreements with other organizations, such as in contracts between management and labour unions. Again, behavioural processes clearly are crucial in each of these decisional roles.

> Four basic **decision-making roles** are the entrepreneur, the disturbance handler, the resource allocator, and the negotiator.

Critical Managerial Skills

Another important element of managerial work is the skills necessary to carry out basic functions and fill fundamental roles. Generally, most successful managers have a strong combination of technical, interpersonal, conceptual, and diagnostic skills.[7]

> Most successful managers have effective technical, interpersonal, conceptual, and diagnostic skills.

Technical Skills   **Technical skills** are skills necessary to accomplish specific tasks within the organization. Designing a board game for Irwin Toys, developing a new formula for a frozen food additive for McCain, and writing a press release for TransCanada Pipelines require technical skills. Hence, these skills are generally associated with the operations employed by the organization in its production processes. For example, in 2001, when the telecom industry was in the process of collapsing, Cisco Systems shut down PixStream, a Waterloo, Ontario-based video-networking company it had acquired for $554 million just four months earlier. Dave Caputo, one of the engineers who founded PixStream decided that, rather than lose the collective engineering talent within the company, he and his team would found Sandvine, which today is a fast-growing company that develops and markets network equipment for DSL, cable and wireless residential broadband service providers. Certainly, in addition to his entrepreneurial drive, Caputo's technical skills are an important part of his success. Another example of a manager with strong technical skills is Richard Waugh, CEO of Scotiabank, who started his career as an employee at one of the company's Winnipeg branches.

> **Technical skills** are the skills necessary to accomplish specific tasks within the organization.

Interpersonal Skills   The manager uses **interpersonal skills** to communicate with, understand, and motivate individuals and groups. As we noted, managers spend a large portion of their time interacting with others, so it is clearly important that they get along with other people. Paul Godfrey, CEO of the Toronto Blue Jays baseball club, frequently has both athletes and non-athletes in the organization approach him regarding personal issues. Godfrey has an open-door policy to employees from all levels of the organization and goes to great lengths to ensure that employees are recognized for good performance.[8]

> The manager uses **interpersonal skills** to communicate with, understand, and motivate individuals and groups.

Conceptual Skills   **Conceptual skills** are the manager's ability to think in the abstract. A manager with strong conceptual skills is able to see the "big picture." That is, she or he can see opportunity where others see roadblocks or problems. For example, Michael Budman and Don Green had a lifestyle ideal that they transformed into an international manufacturing and retailing chain of high-quality casual clothing. In 1973, they began with a single store and a single product (the "earth" shoe). Thus was born Roots Canada.

> The manager uses **conceptual skills** to think in the abstract.

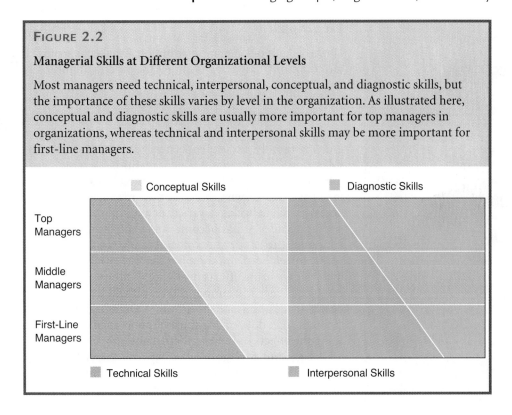

FIGURE 2.2

Managerial Skills at Different Organizational Levels

Most managers need technical, interpersonal, conceptual, and diagnostic skills, but the importance of these skills varies by level in the organization. As illustrated here, conceptual and diagnostic skills are usually more important for top managers in organizations, whereas technical and interpersonal skills may be more important for first-line managers.

Conceptual Skills   Diagnostic Skills

Top Managers

Middle Managers

First-Line Managers

Technical Skills   Interpersonal Skills

Diagnostic Skills   Most successful managers also bring **diagnostic skills** to the organization. Diagnostic skills allow managers to better understand cause-and-effect relationships and to recognize the optimal solutions to problems. For example, in response to high prices and stiff competition at home, managers at Cadillac Fairview, a large Canadian real estate firm, decided to diversify its holdings outside of Canada in order to take advantage of opportunities in developing markets such as South America and South Africa.[9]

Of course, not every manager has an equal measure of these four basic types of skills. Nor are equal measures critical. As shown in Figure 2.2, for example, the optimal skills mix varies with the manager's level in the organization. First-line managers generally need to depend more on their technical and interpersonal skills and less on their conceptual and diagnostic skills. Top managers tend to exhibit the reverse combination—more emphasis on conceptual and diagnostic skills and less dependence on technical and interpersonal skills. Middle managers require a more even distribution of skills.

> The manager uses **diagnostic skills** to understand cause-and-effect relationships and to recognize the optimal solutions to problems.

Diversity and Other Organizational Challenges

Organizational behaviour has several implications for various organizational and environmental challenges. From the organizational perspective, particularly important challenges are downsizing and cutbacks, workforce diversity, the new workforce, organization change, information technology, and new ways of organizing.

Downsizing

Downsizing is one major organizational challenge that is all too common today. **Downsizing** is the process of purposely becoming smaller by reducing the size of the workforce or by shedding entire divisions or businesses. During the 1960s and 1970s, many Canadian firms dramatically increased new operations and positions at all levels. Their sales were growing rapidly, and expenses needed relatively little consideration. As international competition became more intense in the early 1980s, however, these firms found that their costs had grown faster than their revenues. It was then necessary to cut back in a variety of areas, including payroll.

For decades, it has become commonplace for firms to announce the elimination of thousands of jobs. In recent years Nortel, Ford, and Bombardier have each undergone major downsizing efforts involving thousands of employees. Nortel recently announced that it will be eliminating nearly three thousand positions.[10] Organizations going through such downsizing must be concerned about managing the effects of these cutbacks, not only for those who are let go, but for those who stay—albeit with reduced security. Research has demonstrated on numerous occasions that "survivors" of downsizing efforts suffer negative effects. For example, research by Marjorie Armstrong-Stassen and her colleagues at the University of Windsor suggest that employees who remain after downsizing, even those employees in management-level positions, often experience elevated levels of stress.[11]

We should note that downsizing sometimes has surprisingly positive results. The firm that cuts staff presumably lowers its costs. But the people who leave may find that they are happier as well. Many start their own businesses, and some find employment with companies that better meet their needs and goals. Unfortunately, others suffer the indignities of unemployment and financial insecurity.

Diversity training is a common method used in businesses today to better enable their employees to accept and value differences. These workers, for instance, are participating in a role-playing exercise as part of a diversity training program. Various individuals wear labels branding themselves as "complainer," "rookie-new hire," "opposed to change," "overweight," and so forth. As they interact with one another, they begin to see how labels affect their interactions with others at work.

Downsizing is the process of purposely becoming smaller by reducing the size of the workforce or shedding divisions or businesses.

Workforce demographic variables such as age, gender, and ethnic composition are all changing.

Workforce Diversity

A second important challenge today is the management of diversity.[12] The term *diversity* refers to differences among people. Royal Bank of Canada and Loblaws are excellent examples of firms that use diversity to their competitive advantage. Diversity may be reflected along numerous dimensions, but most managers focus on age, gender, ethnicity, and physical abilities and disabilities.

For example, the average age of workers in Canada is gradually increasing. This is partly because of declining birthrates and partly because people are living and working longer. Many organizations have found that retirees are excellent part-time and temporary employees. McDonald's has hired hundreds of older workers over the years. Apple Computer has used many retired workers for temporary assignments and projects. By hiring retirees, the organizations get the expertise of skilled workers and the individuals get extra income and an opportunity to continue to use their skills. Most provincial governments have rescinded mandatory retirement laws, the most recent of which was Ontario in 2006.

An increasing number of women have also entered the Canadian workforce. In the 1950s, fewer than a third of Canadian women worked outside their homes; today almost two-thirds are employed outside the home. Many occupations traditionally dominated by women—nursing, teaching, being a secretary—continue to be popular with females. But women have also moved increasingly into occupations previously dominated by males, becoming lawyers, physicians, and executives. Further, many blue-collar jobs are being increasingly sought by women. Also, more and more men are entering occupations previously dominated by women. For example, there are more male secretaries and nurses today than ever before. The percentage of new and smaller businesses started by women is also increasing rapidly.

The ethnic composition of the workplace is also changing. One obvious change has been the increasing number of visible minorities entering the workplace. Further, many of these individuals now hold executive positions. In addition, there has been a dramatic influx of immigrant workers in the last few years. British Columbia in particular has experienced tremendous growth in its Asian population in recent years and it is estimated that over 40 percent of the population of Toronto is made up of visible minorities who are projected to form the majority of Toronto's population within the next decade.

Cultural displays, such as this New Year parade in Vancouver in 2007, are for many the most obvious sign of the diversity Canadians enjoy. While often less obvious, our diversity includes that of tradition, lifestyle, heritage, and opinion, all of which are important for organizations to be mindful of, and to embrace within their workforce.

In addition to the changing ethnic character of the country's workforce, Canada has two official languages, English and French, and nearly a quarter of the population are francophones. Many Canadian managers must be able to function in both languages, as well as understand the cultures that exist throughout the regions of Canada.

The passage of human rights codes and employment equity legislation at both the federal and provincial levels has brought to the forefront the importance of providing equal employment opportunities for people with disabilities. As a result, organizations are attracting qualified employees from groups that they may perhaps once have ignored. Clearly, then, along just about any dimension imaginable, the workforce is becoming more diverse. Workforce diversity enhances the effectiveness of most organizations, but it also provides special challenges for managers.

Not paying attention to diversity can be very costly to an organization. In addition to blocking minority involvement in communication and decision making, there can also be tension among workers, lower productivity, increased costs due to increased absenteeism, turnover, equal employment opportunity and harassment suits, and lower morale among workers. On the contrary, organizations that embrace diversity can thrive. Saskatchewan telephone company SaskTel is widely viewed as an employer of choice in the province. Approximately 8 percent of its workforce is drawn from the First Nations and Métis population. In order to service the significant aboriginal customer base, the organization maintains a call centre that offers service in three First Nations languages.[13]

Fast Company; February–March 1999; p. 66.
Richard Cline.

Fitting into the corporate model is not exactly what it used to be with all of the Internet start-ups these days. In this situation, the "boss" expects the older gentleman in the suit and tie to conform to the more informal "dress code." But fitting in is not necessarily the best in every situation. Doing the right job in the right way is more important than wearing the right clothes and fitting in. The lessons of valuing diversity should have shown us that.

The New Workforce

Aside from its demographic composition, the workforce today is changing in other ways. During the 1980s, many people entering the workforce were what came to be called *yuppies*, slang for young urban professionals. These individuals were highly motivated by career prospects, sought employment with big corporations, and were often willing to make work their highest priority. Thus, they put in long hours and could be expected to remain loyal to the company, regardless of what happened.

Younger people entering the workforce today, however, are frequently different from their predecessors. Sometimes called "Generation Y," these workers are less devoted to long-term career prospects and less willing to adapt to a corporate mindset that stresses conformity and uniformity. Instead, they may seek work in smaller, more entrepreneurial firms that allow flexibility and individuality. They also put a premium on lifestyle considerations, often putting location high on their list of priorities when selecting an employer. They are the first generation to have lived their entire lives with information technology.

Thus, managers are increasingly faced with the challenge of first creating an environment that will be attractive to today's worker. Then, managers must address the challenge of providing new and different incentives to keep people motivated and interested in their work. Finally, they must build enough flexibility in the organization to accommodate an ever-changing set of lifestyles and preferences.

Organization Change

Managers must be prepared to address organization change. This has always been a concern, but the rapid, constant environmental changes faced by businesses today have made change management even more critical. Simply put, an organization that fails to monitor its environment and to change to keep pace with that environment is doomed to failure. But more and more managers are seeing change as an opportunity, not a cause for alarm. Indeed, some managers think that if things get too calm in an organization and people start to become complacent, managers should shake things up to get everyone energized.[14] We discuss the management of organizational change in more detail in Chapter 15.

Information Technology

New technology, especially as it relates to information, also poses an increasingly important challenge for managers. Most people are very familiar with advances in information technology. Cellular telephones, PDAs, the iPod, and digital cameras are just a few of the many recent technological innovations that have changed how people live and work. Breakthroughs in information technology have resulted in leaner organizations, more flexible operations, increased collaboration among employees, more flexible work sites, and improved management processes and systems. On the other hand, they have also resulted in less personal communication, less "down time" for managers and employees, and an increased sense of urgency vis-à-vis decision making and communication—changes that have not necessarily always been beneficial. These innovations have increased the work pace for managers, cut into their time for thoughtful contemplation of decisions, and increased the amount of information they must process.[15]

Although these tools make it easier to acquire, process, and disseminate information, they also increase the risk that the manager will get distracted by superfluous information or become so wrapped up in communication as to give too little time to other important management functions. A related issue is the increased capabilities this technology provides for people to work at places other than their office. Chapter 7 examines some of these issues in more depth.

New Ways of Organizing

A final organizational challenge today is the complex array of new ways of organizing that managers can consider.[16] Recall from Chapter 1 that early organization theorists such as Max Weber advocated "one best way" of organizing. These organizational prototypes generally resembled pyramids—tall structures with power controlled at the top and rigid policies and procedures governing most activities. Now, however, many organizations seek greater flexibility and the ability to respond more quickly to their environment by adopting flatter structures. These flat structures are characterized by few levels of management; broad, wide spans of management; and fewer rules and regulations. The increased use of work teams also goes hand in hand with this new approach to organizing. We will examine ways of organizing in Chapters 8 and 13.

Environmental Challenges

Managers also face numerous environmental challenges. The environmental issues most relevant to the domain of organizational behaviour are competitive strategy, globalization, ethics and corporate governance, new employment relationships, quality and productivity, and manufacturing and service technology.

Competitive Strategy

A firm's **competitive strategy** explains how it intends to compete with other firms in the same industry. Most firms generally adopt one of three business strategies.[17] A firm using a *differentiation strategy* attempts to make its products or services at least appear to be different from others in the marketplace. For example, Rolex has created the image that its watches are of higher quality and prestige than those offered by its competitors, so it can charge a higher price. Other firms that have successfully used this model are BMW, Calvin Klein, and Nikon.

A firm that adopts a *cost leadership strategy*, on the other hand, works aggressively to push its costs as low as possible. This allows the firm to charge a lower price for its products or services and thus gain more market share. Bic, the French firm, uses cost leadership to sell its inexpensive disposable ballpoint pens. WalMart successfully entered the Canadian retail market by pursuing a low cost leadership strategy.

Finally, a *focus strategy* involves establishing a niche by concentrating on a particular market segment using either a differentiation or cost leadership strategy. Irving Oil, based in Saint John, New Brunswick, focuses its efforts primarily in the Maritimes, where it is the dominant producer and distributor of petroleum products.

A firm's managers must know its business strategy when hiring employees. For example, if the business strategy calls for differentiation, the firm will need employees who can produce higher-quality products or services and project a differentiated image. On the other hand, a cost leadership strategy dictates the need for people who can keep focused on cost cutting and who respond well to tight cost controls. Finally, a focus strategy requires people who clearly understand the target population being courted.[18]

Important environmental challenges for managers include competitive strategy, global competition, ethics and social responsibility, quality and productivity, and the management of technology.

A **competitive strategy** is an outline of how a business intends to compete with other firms in the same industry.

These four workers in Alcatel's switch-making plant in Shanghai, China, exemplify the rapid changes in manufacturing in that country. Once known for cheap and low-skilled labour that made cheap trinkets, toys, textiles, and knock-offs of higher-quality goods, China has become a haven for high-tech manufacturing. China's emergence is creating rapid shifts in investment around the world, as manufacturers move to take advantage of the cheaper labour, high-quality workmanship, sophisticated engineering expertise, and proximity to the huge Chinese marketplace. Investment that used to go to Japan and other countries in Southeast Asia is now going to China.

The same manager behaves differently in different cultures.

Globalization

It is no secret that the world economy is becoming increasingly global. But often people do not realize the true magnitude of this globalization trend or the complexities it creates for managers. Consider, for example, the impact of international businesses on our daily lives. We wake to the sound of Panasonic alarm clocks made in Japan. For breakfast we might drink milk from Beatrice—a subsidiary of Parmalat, an Italian firm—with coffee ground from Colombian beans. We dress in clothes sewn in Taiwan and drive in a Japanese automobile. Of course, Canadians are not alone in experiencing the effects of globalization. Indeed, people in many countries of the world eat at McDonald's restaurants and snack on Mars candy bars and drink Coca-Cola soft drinks. They drive Fords, use IBM computers, and wear Levi's jeans. They use Canon cameras and fly on Bombardier airplanes.

The globalization trend started right after World War II. The Canadian economy emerged from the war strong and intact. Canadian businesses became successful exporters in a variety of industries. But war-torn Europe and the Far East rebuilt. Businesses there were forced to build new plants and other facilities, and their citizens turned to their work as a source of economic security. As a result, these economies strengthened and each developed competitive advantages. Today those advantages are being exploited to their fullest.

Managing in a global economy poses many different challenges and opportunities. For example, at a macro level, property ownership arrangements vary widely. So does the availability of natural resources and components of the infrastructure, as well as the role of government in business. For our purposes, a very important consideration is how behavioural processes vary widely across cultural and national boundaries. Values, symbols, and beliefs differ sharply among cultures. Different work norms and the role work plays in a person's life influence patterns of both work-related behaviour and attitudes toward work. They also affect the nature of supervisory relationships, decision-making styles and processes, and organizational configurations. Group and intergroup processes, responses to stress, and the nature of political behaviours also differ from culture to culture.

Geert Hofstede, a Dutch researcher, studied workers and managers in 60 countries and found that attitudes and behaviours differed significantly due to the values and beliefs in the various countries.[19] Table 2.2 shows how Hofstede's categories help us summarize differences for several countries.

Diversity Works! and . . . 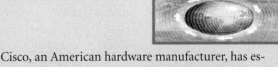 GLOBALIZATION

How Do You Say "G'Day" in Chinese?

Australia is a diverse country, including indigenous people, Europeans, and others, with Asians as the largest minority group. The Australian government uses a program called Diversity Works! to educate and encourage companies about the beneficial aspects of diversity. Several of the projects recently undertaken at Diversity Works! focus on China, because Chinese-Australians make up the largest group of non-English speakers in the country. Almost half a million Australians speak Mandarin or Cantonese as their primary language and know little or no English.

Sovereign Hill, a historical park, teaches visitors about Australia's gold rush, which included 9,000 Chinese immigrant miners. Multilingual tour guides aid foreign guests and Chinese-Australian staff from Diversity Works! train all of Sovereign Hill's staff in cultural awareness. A Chinese-speaking marketer visits China to establish relationships with tour operators. "What has been most powerful is the increased understanding of the context for language and behaviour," says Tim Sullivan, Deputy CEO. "This includes knowing something about the places the visitors come from, what their lives are like, and how they like to work and play."

Cisco, an American hardware manufacturer, has established a technical support centre in Australia to support its Asian clients. Half of the workforce speaks a language other than English, ranging from Hindi to Thai to Mandarin. Diversity Works! sponsors multicultural and language education. "It is not just language skills that are important. Cultural skills are also very important, even when English is being spoken," claims senior director Karen McFadzen. Cisco and Diversity Works! support non-English-speaking personnel with cross-cultural training and events.

China is clearly important to Australian businesses. Seventeen percent of exports go to Chinese-speaking countries, including the People's Republic of China, Singapore, Hong Kong, and Taiwan. With help from Diversity Works! Australian organizations can increase their understanding of this important international market. (How *do* you say "G'day" in Chinese? "Wu an.")

For more about Australia's approach to encouraging diversity initiatives in business, see the chapter's closing case, "Diversity, Aussie Style."

Country	Individualism/ Collectivism	Power Distance	Uncertainty Avoidance	Masculinity	Long-term Orientation
Canada	H	M	M	M	L
Germany	M	M	M	M	M
Italy	H	M	M	H	(no data)
Israel	M	L	M	M	(no data)
Japan	M	M	H	H	H
Mexico	H	H	H	M	(no data)
Pakistan	L	M	M	M	L
Sweden	H	M	L	L	M
United States	H	M	M	M	L
Venezuela	L	H	M	H	(no data)

TABLE 2.2

Work-Related Differences in Ten Countries

Note: H = high; M = moderate; L = low. These are only ten of the more than sixty countries that Hofstede and others have studied. Titles of the categories have been adapted from Hofstede's original titles to make them more easily understood.

Sources: Adapted from Geert Hofstede, "Motivation, Leadership, and Organization: Do American Theories Apply Abroad?" *Organizational Dynamics*, Summer 1980, pp. 42–63; Geert Hofstede and Michael Harris Bond, "The Confucius Connection: From Cultural Roots to Economic Growth," *Organizational Dynamics*, Spring 1988, pp. 5–21.

Individualism is the extent to which people place primary value on themselves.

Collectivism is the extent to which people emphasize the good of the group or society.

Power distance is the extent to which less powerful persons accept the unequal distribution of power.

Uncertainty avoidance is the extent to which people prefer to be in clear and unambiguous situations.

Masculinity is the extent to which the dominant values in a society emphasize aggressiveness and the acquisition of money and material goods, rather than concern for people, relationships among people, and the overall quality of life.

People with a **short-term orientation** focus on the past or present; people with a **long-term orientation** focus on the future.

The two primary dimensions that Hofstede found are the individualism–collectivism continuum and power distance. **Individualism** exists to the extent that people in a culture define themselves by referring to themselves as singular persons rather than as part of one or more groups or organizations. At work, people from more individualistic cultures tend to be more concerned about themselves rather than their work group, individual tasks are more important than relationships, and hiring and promotion are based on skills and rules. **Collectivism** is characterized by tight social frameworks in which people tend to base their identities on the group or organization to which they belong. At work, this means that employee–employer links are more like family relationships, relationships are more important than individuals or tasks, and hiring and promotion are based on group membership. In Canada, a very individualistic culture, it is important to perform better than others and try to stand out from the crowd. In Japan, a more collectivist culture, an individual tries to fit in with the group, strives for harmony, and prefers stability.

Power distance, which can also be called orientation to authority, is the extent to which less powerful people accept the unequal distribution of power. In countries such as Mexico and Venezuela, for example, people prefer to be in a situation where the authority is clearly understood and lines of authority are never bypassed. In countries such as Israel and Denmark, authority is not as highly respected and employees are quite comfortable circumventing lines of authority to accomplish something. People in Canada tend to be mixed, accepting authority in some situations but not others.

Uncertainty avoidance, which can also be called **preference for stability**, is the extent to which people feel threatened by unknown situations and prefer to be in clear and unambiguous situations. People in Japan and Mexico prefer stability over uncertainty, whereas uncertainty is normal and accepted in Sweden, Hong Kong, and the United Kingdom. **Masculinity**, which is also called **assertiveness** or **materialism**, is the extent to which the dominant values in a society emphasize aggressiveness and the acquisition of money and things, as opposed to concern for people, relationships among people, and the overall quality of life. People in Canada are moderate on both the uncertainty avoidance and masculinity scales. Japan and Italy score high on the masculinity scale, while Sweden scores low.

Hofstede's framework was later expanded to include **long-term** versus **short-term orientation**. Long-term values include focusing on the future, working on projects that have a distant payoff, persistence, and thrift. Short-term values are more oriented toward the past and the present and include respect for traditions and social obligations. Japan, Hong Kong, and China are highly long-term oriented. The Netherlands and Germany are moderately long-term oriented. Canada, the United States, Indonesia, West Africa, and Russia are more short-term oriented.

Hofstede's research is only one of several ways to categorize differences across many different countries and cultures. His system is, however, widely accepted and used by many companies. The important point is that people from diverse cultures value things differently from each other. All employees need to take these differences into account as they work.

Ethics and Corporate Governance

While ethics have long been of relevance to businesses, what seems like an epidemic of ethical breaches in recent years has placed ethics in the mainstream of managerial thought today. One special aspect of business ethics, corporate governance, has also taken on increased importance. Ethics also increasingly relate to information technology.

Contemporary Ethical Issues

A central issue revolves around the fact that rapid changes in business relationships, organizational structures, and financial systems pose unsurpassed difficulties in keeping accurate track of a company's financial position. The public—current and potential investors—often get blurred pictures of a firm's competitive health. Stakeholders, however—employees, stockholders, consumers, unions, creditors, and government—are entitled to a fair accounting so they can make enlightened personal and business decisions. Even the American Institute for Certified Public Accountants (AICPA) admits that keeping up with today's increasingly fast-paced business activities is putting a strain on the accounting profession's traditional methods for auditing, financial reporting, and time-honoured standards of professional ethics.

The Enron scandal, for example, involved extended enterprises using fast-moving financial transactions among layers of subsidiary firms, some domestic and many off-shore, with large-scale borrowing from some of the world's largest financial institutions. Electronic transactions flooded through a vast network of quickly formed and rapidly dissolved partnerships among energy brokers and buyers. This network was so complex that Enron's accounting reports failed completely to reflect the firm's disastrous financial and managerial condition. In a blatant display of unethical conduct, Enron's public reports concealed many of its partnerships with (and obligations to) other companies, thus hiding its true operating condition.

Furthermore, why did Arthur Andersen, the accounting firm that audited Enron's finances, not catch its client's distorted reports? Auditors are supposed to provide an objective and independent assessment of the accuracy of financial information reported by corporations to key stakeholders, such as investors and governmental agencies. Indeed, publicly traded corporations are legally required to use an external auditor for just this purpose.

The answer to this question reveals a further illustration of the hazards faced by today's extended firm. Andersen, like other major accounting firms, had expanded from auditing into more lucrative non-accounting areas such as management consulting. Reports suggest that Andersen's desire for future high-revenue consulting services with Enron may have motivated the CPA's auditors to turn a blind eye on questionable practices that eventually turned up during audits of Enron's finances.

Beyond these large-scale issues, other contemporary ethical concerns involve such areas as executive compensation, environmental protection, working conditions in foreign factories, pricing policies, and the pressures to balance profits against costs as businesses continue to globalize. We discuss ethical issues in several places later in this book, including Chapter 9 (decision making) and Chapter 11 (contemporary views of leadership).

Ethical Issues in Corporate Governance

A related area of emerging concern relates to ethical issues in **corporate governance**—the oversight of a public corporation by its board of directors. The board of a public corporation is expected to ensure that the business is being properly managed and that the decisions made by its senior management are in the best interests of shareholders and other stakeholders. But in far too many cases the spate of ethical scandals of the late 1990s and early 2000s alluded to above have actually started with a breakdown in the corporate governance structure. For instance, WorldCom's board approved a $366 million personal loan to the firm's CEO, Bernard Ebbers, when there was little evidence that he could repay it. Likewise, former Hollinger International CEO Conrad Black was accused of receiving millions of dollars in unauthorized payments from company coffers as well as using company funds for private use.

> **Corporate governance** refers to the oversight of a public corporation by its board of directors.

Corporate governance has become a major issue in recent years. One of the more visible examples has been the long-running feud between two former Walt Disney Company directors, Roy Disney and Stanley Gold, and the current board. Disney and Gold claim that the current board lacks independence, has been too slow in forcing longtime CEO Michael Eisner to leave the company's top spot, and too slow in developing an executive succession plan. Recent events have placated Disney and Gold, but they nevertheless are keeping a careful eye on the Disney board's activities.

But boards of directors are also increasingly criticized even when they are not directly implicated in wrongdoing. The biggest complaint here often relates to board independence. Disney, for instance, has faced this problem. Several key members of the firm's board of directors are from companies that do business with Disney, and others are longtime friends of former Disney CEO Michael Eisner. The concern, then, is that Eisner may have been given more autonomy than might otherwise be warranted because of his various relationships with board members. While board members need to have some familiarity with both the firm and its industry in order to function effectively, they also need to have sufficient independence as might be necessary to carry out their oversight function.[20]

Ethical Issues in Information Technology

Another set of issues that have emerged in recent times involves information technology. Among the specific questions in this area are individual rights to privacy and the potential abuse of information technology by individuals. Indeed, online privacy has become a hot issue as companies sort out the ethical and management issues. DoubleClick, an online advertising network, is one of the firms at the centre of the privacy debate. The company has collected data on the habits of millions of Web surfers, recording which sites they visit and on which ads they click. DoubleClick insists the profiles are anonymous and are used to better match surfers with appropriate ads. However, after the company announced a plan to add names and addresses to its database, it was forced to back down because of public concerns over invasion of online privacy.

DoubleClick isn't the only firm gathering personal data about people's Internet activities. People who register at Yahoo!.com are asked to list their date of birth, among other details. Amazon, eBay, and other sites also ask for personal information. As Internet usage increases, however, surveys show that people are troubled by the amount of information being collected and who gets to see it.

One way many companies have addressed these concerns is by posting a privacy policy on their websites. The policy usually explains what data the company collects and who gets to see it, which gives people a choice about having their information shared with others, and provides an option to bypass data collection altogether. Disney, IBM, and other companies support this position by refusing to advertise on websites that have no posted privacy policies.

In addition, companies can offer Web surfers the opportunity to review and correct information that has been collected, especially medical and financial data. In the offline

Corporate Citizenship and . . .  **ETHICS**

Good Corporate Citizenship Is Good for Business

Although it seems that ethical scandals in business have become almost commonplace, the organizations that emphasize social responsibility are also reaping the benefits on their bottom line. A well-known example of such an organization is The Body Shop, a major cosmetics chain that commits itself to not test its products on animals and contributes to a number of social causes such as Greenpeace and Amnesty International.

Other large organizations are following suit, sometimes by partnering with nonprofit social agencies or by sponsoring events. For example, Pratt and Whitney Canada and McDonald's both partner with the Missing Children's Network Canada. Kellogg Canada partnered with the Vancouver International Children's Festival as a means of marketing the Vancouver launch of its Rice Krispie cereal bars. By linking business objectives and corporate social responsibility, organizations are able to leverage corporate donations by combining them with marketing opportunities. Companies have good reason to believe that this strategy will be successful. The Cone/Roper Cause-Related Marketing Trends Report, a national survey of consumer attitudes, reported that 76 percent of consumers would switch to brands associated with a good cause, all else being equal. The likelihood of switching is even greater with younger customers. The 2006 Cone Millennial Cause Study of individuals born between 1979 and 2001 revealed that 89 percent of respondents would likely or very likely switch brands (assuming price and quality were equal).

Other organizations have approached social responsibility in different ways, but with the same successful results. VanCity Savings Credit Union and Husky Injection Molding Systems Ltd. consider a wide variety of stakeholders, including employees, customers, and the community, in their planning and decision-making activities. There are a number of reasons for companies to be concerned about the impact of corporate behaviour on the bottom line. Some CEOs see it as a question of personal ethics. For others, the motivation may be the increased influence of the public through government regulations or watchdog groups.

The public is also having a broader impact on corporate balance sheets through the proliferation of ethical mutual funds. Such funds invest only in companies that meet certain criteria of social responsibility. These criteria include such factors as the level of pollution created by the organization, the nature of the products sold, and the company's hiring and promotion practices.

Socially responsible organizations might also reap benefits that contribute indirectly to profitability. In the same Cone Millennial Study just cited, 79 percent said they wanted to work for a company that cares about how it impacts and contributes to society and 56 percent said they would refuse to work for an irresponsible organization. In addition, good labour relations can reduce absenteeism, prevent costly strikes, and make for smoother operations. A culture of employee empowerment can result in employees who contribute above and beyond the call of duty. And then, of course, there is the issue of customer satisfaction. Although cutting corners on quality and safety might produce short-term profitability, it can kill the chances for long-term profitability.

Sources: Catherine Rockandel, "How to Profit with a Nonprofit Partner," *Marketing Magazine*, 23 February 1998, p. 37; Robert Walker and Susan Flanagan, "The Ethical Imperative: If You Don't Talk About a Wider Range of Values, You May Not Have a Bottom Line," *Financial Post* 500, 1997, pp. 28–36; "Ethical Funds: No Nightmare for Those Who Sleep Lightly," *Financial Post*, 23 January 1997, vol. 9, p. 37; "Civic-Minded Millennials Prepared To Reward Or Punish Companies Based On Commitment To Social Causes," *Cone 2006 Millennial Cause Study*, www.causemarketingforum.com/page.asp?ID=473

world, consumers are legally allowed to inspect credit and medical records. In the online world, this kind of access can be costly and cumbersome, because data are often spread across several computer systems. Despite the technical difficulties, the Canadian government passed the Personal Information Protection and Electronic Documents Act (PIPEDA), which governs the collection, use, and disclosure of personal information. The act requires that companies identify the purposes for the collection of personal information, and obtain consent for and limit its collection and use. In addition the act requires that companies provide disclosure, ensure the accuracy of the information, provide adequate security, provide individuals with access to information about themselves, and give individuals a right to challenge an organization's compliance with the principles set forth in the legislation.

New Employment Relationships

A final significant area of environmental change that is particularly relevant for businesses today involves what we call new employment relationships. While we discuss employment relationships from numerous perspectives in Part 2 of this book, two particularly important areas today involve the management of knowledge workers and the outsourcing of jobs to other businesses, especially when those businesses are in other countries.

The Management of Knowledge Workers

Traditionally, employees added value to organizations because of what they did or because of their experience. However, the impact of the information age in the workplace is that many employees add value simply because of what they know.[21] These employees are usually referred to as **knowledge workers**. How well these employees are managed is seen as a major factor in determining which firms will be successful in the future.[22] Knowledge workers include computer scientists, physical scientists, engineers, product designers, and video game developers. They tend to work in high-technology firms, and are usually experts in some abstract knowledge base. They often believe they have the right to work in an autonomous fashion, and identify more strongly with their profession than any organization—even to the extent of defining performance in terms recognized by other members of their profession.[23]

> **Knowledge workers** are those employees who add value in an organization simply because of what they know.

As the importance of information-driven jobs grows, the need for knowledge workers will grow as well. But these employees require extensive and highly specialized training, and not everyone is willing to make the human capital investment necessary to move into these jobs. In fact, even after knowledge workers are on the job, retraining and training updates are critical so that their skills do not become obsolete. It has been suggested, for example, that the "half-life" for a technical education in engineering is about three years. Further, failure to update the required skills will not only result in the organization losing competitive advantage but will also increase the likelihood that the knowledge worker will go to another firm that is more committed to updating these skills.[24]

Compensation and related policies for knowledge workers must also be specially tailored. For example, in many high-tech organizations, engineers and scientists have the option of entering a technical career path that parallels a management career path. This allows the knowledge worker to continue to carry out specialized work without taking on large management responsibilities, while at the same time offering worker compensation that is equivalent to that available to management. But in other high-tech firms, the emphasis is on pay for performance, with profit sharing based on projects or products developed by the knowledge workers. In addition, most firms employing these workers have tended to reduce the number of levels of the organization to allow the knowledge workers to react more quickly to the external environment and to reduce the need for bureaucratic approval.[25]

Outsourcing

Outsourcing is the practice of hiring other firms to do work previously performed by the organization itself. It is an increasingly popular strategy because it helps firms focus on their core activities and avoid getting sidetracked onto secondary activities.

Outsourcing is the practice of hiring other firms to do work previously performed by the organization itself.

The cafeteria at a large bank may be important to employees and some customers, but running it is not the bank's main line of business and expertise. Bankers need to focus on money management and financial services, not food-service operations. That's why most banks outsource cafeteria operations to food-service management companies whose main line of business is cafeterias. The result, ideally, is more attention to banking by bankers, better food service for cafeteria customers, and formation of a new supplier-client relationship (food-service company/bank). Firms today often outsource numerous activities, including payroll, employee training, facility maintenance, and research and development.

Up to a point, at least, outsourcing makes good business sense in areas that are highly unrelated to a firm's core business activities. However, it has attracted considerable more attention in recent years because of the growing trend toward outsourcing abroad in order to lower labour costs. Many software firms, for example, have found that there is an abundance of talented programmers in India who are willing to work for much lower salaries than their North American counterparts. Likewise, many firms that operate large call centres find that they can handle those operations at much lower costs from other parts of the world. As a result, domestic jobs may be lost. And some firms attract additional criticism when they require their domestic workers— soon to be out of jobs—to train their newly hired foreign replacements! Clearly, there are numerous behavioural and motivational issues involved in practices such as these.

Quality and Productivity

Another competitive challenge that has attracted much attention is quality and productivity. **Quality** is the total set of features and characteristics of a product or service that define its ability to satisfy a stated or implied need of customers or consumers.[26] Quality is an important issue for several reasons.[27] First, more organizations are using quality as a basis for competition. Many companies, for example, pursue accreditation from the International Standards Organization (ISO) as evidence that their products or services meet certain standards for quality.

Quality is the total set of features and characteristics of a product or service that determine its ability to satisfy stated or implied needs.

Second, improving quality tends to increase productivity because making higher-quality products generally results in less waste and rework. Third, enhancing quality lowers costs. Whistler Corporation found that it was using 100 of its 250 employees to repair defective radar detectors that were built incorrectly the first time.[28]

Quality is also important because of its relationship to productivity. Productivity became a major issue for many organizations during the 1980s and continues to this day. In a general sense, **productivity** is an indicator of how much an organization is creating relative to its inputs. For example, if Honda can produce a car for $11,000 whereas General Motors needs $13,000 to produce a comparable car, Honda is clearly more productive.

Productivity is an indicator of how much an organization is creating relative to its inputs.

Productivity in industrial countries, especially Japan and Germany, has grown rapidly in recent decades. To compete with this productivity, experts have suggested numerous techniques and strategies. Many of these centre on increased cooperation and participation on the part of workers. Ultimately, then, managers and workers will need to work in greater harmony and unity of purpose. The implications for organizational behaviour are obvious: The more closely people work together, the more important it is to understand behavioural processes and concepts.

Indeed, many of the things organizations can do to enhance the quality of their products and services depend on the people who work for them. Motivating employees to get involved in quality-improvement efforts, increasing the level of participation throughout the organization, and rewarding people on the basis of contributions to quality are common suggestions—and all rely on human behaviour.[29]

Manufacturing and Service Technology

Technology is the mechanical and intellectual processes used to transform inputs into products and services.

A final environmental challenge confronting managers today is the set of issues involving technology. **Technology** is the set of processes an organization uses to transform resources into goods and services. Traditionally, most businesses were manufacturers—they used tangible resources like raw materials and machinery to create tangible products such as automobiles and steel.

Managing this form of technology requires managers to keep abreast of new forms of technology and to make appropriate investments in the acquisition of new manufacturing equipment. In addition, training employees for this type of work and then evaluating their performance used to be a relatively straightforward undertaking.

More recently, however, the service sector of the economy has become much more important. Indeed, services now account for over two-thirds of the gross domestic product in Canada and play a similarly important role in many other industrialized nations. Service technology involves the use of both tangible resources (such as machinery) and intangible resources (such as intellectual property) to create intangible services (such as a hair cut, insurance protection, or transportation between two cities). Because of the intangible properties associated with services, training and performance evaluation are obviously more complex. Many other managerial activities must also be approached in fundamentally different ways in service-based organizations.[30]

Managing for Effectiveness

Managing an organization for effectiveness involves balancing a number of individual-level, group-level, and organization-level characteristics and outcomes.

Earlier in this chapter we noted that managers work toward various goals. We are now in a position to elaborate on the nature of these goals in detail. In particular, as shown in Figure 2.3, goals—or outcomes—exist at three specific levels in an organization: individual-level outcomes, group-level outcomes, and organizational-level outcomes. Of course, it may sometimes be necessary to make tradeoffs among these different kinds of outcomes, but, in general, each is seen as a critical component of organizational effectiveness. The sections that follow elaborate on these different levels in more detail.

Individual-Level Outcomes

Several outcomes at the individual level are important to managers. Given the focus of the field of organizational behaviour, it should not be surprising that most of these outcomes are directly or indirectly addressed by various theories and models.

Individual Behaviours   First, several individual behaviours result from a person's participation in an organization. One important behaviour is productivity. A person's productivity is an indicator of his or her efficiency and is measured in terms of the

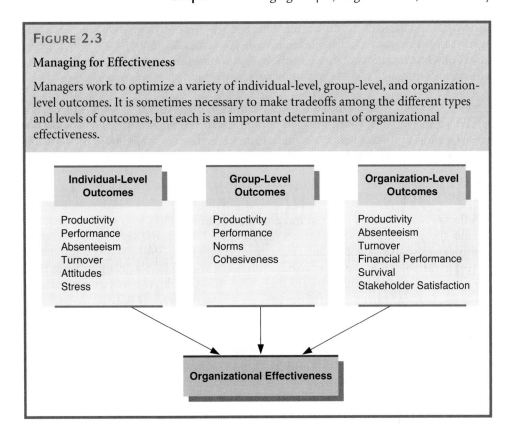

FIGURE 2.3

Managing for Effectiveness

Managers work to optimize a variety of individual-level, group-level, and organization-level outcomes. It is sometimes necessary to make tradeoffs among the different types and levels of outcomes, but each is an important determinant of organizational effectiveness.

Individual-Level Outcomes	Group-Level Outcomes	Organization-Level Outcomes
Productivity	Productivity	Productivity
Performance	Performance	Absenteeism
Absenteeism	Norms	Turnover
Turnover	Cohesiveness	Financial Performance
Attitudes		Survival
Stress		Stakeholder Satisfaction

Organizational Effectiveness

products or services created per unit of input. For example, if Bill makes 100 units of a product in a day and Sara makes only 90 units in a day, then assuming that the units are of the same quality and that Bill and Sara make the same wages, Bill is more productive than Sara.

Performance, another important individual-level outcome variable, is a somewhat broader concept. It is made up of all work-related behaviours. For example, even though Bill is highly productive, it may also be that he refuses to work overtime, expresses negative opinions about the organization at every opportunity, and will do nothing unless it falls precisely within the boundaries of his job. Sara, on the other hand, may always be willing to work overtime, is a positive representative of the organization, and goes out of her way to make as many contributions to the organization as possible. Based on the full array of behaviours, then, we might conclude that Sara actually is the better performer.

Two other important individual-level behaviours are absenteeism and turnover. Absenteeism is a measure of attendance. Although virtually everyone misses work occasionally, some people miss far more than others. Some look for excuses to miss work and call in sick regularly just for some time off; others miss work only when absolutely necessary. The flip side of absenteeism is a phenomenon referred to as presenteeism. Presenteeism occurs when employees show up to work even though they are sick or injured. One poll indicated that 98 percent of respondents admitted to going to work when sick. Employees usually do so because of heavy workload or commitment to the organization or clients. The result, however, is often unproductive work time.[31] Turnover occurs when a person leaves the organization. If the individual who leaves is a good performer or if the organization has invested heavily in training the person, turnover can be costly.

Individual Attitudes   Another set of individual-level outcomes influenced by managers consists of individual attitudes. (We discuss attitudes more fully in Chapter 3.) Levels of job satisfaction or dissatisfaction, organizational commitment, and organizational involvement all play an important role in organizational behaviour.

Stress   Stress, discussed more fully in Chapter 6, is another important individual-level outcome variable. Given its costs, both personal and organizational, it should not be surprising that stress is becoming an increasingly important topic for both researchers in organizational behaviour and practising managers.

Group- and Team-Level Outcomes

Another set of outcomes exists at the group and team level. Some of these outcomes parallel the individual-level outcomes just discussed. For example, if an organization makes extensive use of work teams, team productivity and performance are important outcome variables. On the other hand, even if all the people in a group or team have the same or similar attitudes toward their jobs, the attitudes themselves are individual-level phenomena. Individuals, not groups, have attitudes.

But groups or teams can also have unique outcomes that individuals do not share. For example, as we will discuss in Chapter 8, groups develop norms that govern the behaviour of individual group members. Groups also develop different levels of cohesiveness. Thus, managers need to assess both common and unique outcomes when considering the individual and group levels.

Organization-Level Outcomes

Finally, a set of outcome variables exists at the organization level. As before, some of these outcomes parallel those at the individual and group levels, but others are unique. For example, we can measure and compare organizational productivity. We can also develop organization-level indicators of absenteeism and turnover. But profitability is generally assessed only at the organizational level.

Work teams are increasingly used in a wide variety of organizations. This team, for example, works in a New Balance shoe assembly plant. Its six members have crossed-trained each other so that each team member has a primary job but also knows how to perform other jobs. This allows them to help each other out when somebody gets behind or needs to miss work.

Organizations are also commonly assessed in terms of financial performance: stock price, return on investment, growth rates, and so on. They are also evaluated in terms of their ability to survive and the extent to which they satisfy important constituents such as investors, government regulators, employees, and unions.

Clearly, then, the manager must balance outcomes across all three levels of analysis. In many cases, these outcomes appear to contradict one another. For example, paying workers high salaries can enhance satisfaction and reduce turnover, but it also may detract from bottom-line performance. Similarly, exerting strong pressure to increase individual performance may boost short-term profitability, but increase turnover and job stress. Thus, the manager must look at the full array of outcomes and attempt to balance them optimally. The manager's ability to do this is a major determinant of the organization's success.

Chapter Review

Summary of Key Points

- By its very nature, management requires an understanding of human behaviour to help managers better comprehend those at different levels in the organization, those at the same level, those in other organizations, and themselves.

- The manager's job can be characterized in terms of four functions, three sets of roles, and four skills. The basic managerial functions are planning, organizing, leading, and controlling. The roles consist of three interpersonal roles, three informational roles, and four decision-making roles. Four basic skills necessary for effective management are technical, interpersonal, conceptual, and diagnostic skills.

- Several organizational challenges confront managers. One major organizational challenge is downsizing and cutbacks. Another is increasing workforce diversity. The new workforce also poses significant organizational challenges for managers, as does organization change. Information technology and new ways of organizing are two other important organizational challenges.

- There are also several important environmental challenges to consider. Determining the most effective competitive strategy and matching people to that strategy are important challenges. Today, global competition is one of the most critical environmental challenges. Ethics and social responsibility are significant as well. The manager must also emphasize product and service quality and manage technology successfully.

- Managing for effectiveness involves balancing a variety of individual-level, group- and team-level, and organization-level outcome variables.

Discussion Questions

1. Is it possible for managers to worry too much about the behaviour of their subordinates? Why or why not?

2. The text identifies four basic managerial functions. Based on your own experiences or observations, provide examples of each function.

3. Which managerial skills do you think are among your strengths? Which are among your weaknesses? How might you improve the latter?

4. The text argues that we cannot understand organizations without understanding the behaviour of the people within them. Do you agree or disagree with this assertion? Why?

5. Interview a local manager or business owner to find out his or her views on the importance of individual behaviour to the success of the organization. Report your findings to the class.

6. What advice would you give managers to help them better prepare to cope with changes in workforce demographics?

7. How has information technology changed your role as a student? Have the changes been positive or negative?

8. Identify firms that use each of the three competitive strategies noted in the text.

9. Of the five environmental challenges noted in the text, which do you think is most important? Which is least important? Give reasons for your answers.

10. Are there any businesses that have not been affected by globalization? Explain.

11. What individual-, group-, or organization-level outcome variables of consequence can you identify beyond those noted in the text?

Purpose: To help you develop a deeper and more complete appreciation of the complexities and nuances of managing individual behaviour in organizational settings.

Format: You will first develop a scenario regarding a behaviour problem of your own choosing, along with a recommended course of action. You will then exchange scenarios with a classmate and compare recommendations.

Procedure: Select one of the organizational challenges (downsizing, workforce diversity, the new workforce, change, information technology, or new ways of organizing) or environmental challenges (competitive strategy, global competition, ethics and social responsibility, quality and productivity, or technology) discussed in this chapter. Working alone (perhaps as an outside-of-class assignment, if requested by your instructor), write a brief scenario (one page or less) describing a hypothetical organization facing that challenge. Your scenario should provide a bit of background about the firm, the specific challenge it is facing, and some detail about why that particular challenge is relevant.

On a separate page, recommend a course of action that a manager might take to address that challenge. For example, if your challenge is to cope with a new form of technology or a need to enhance quality, your recommendation might be to form employee advisory groups to help implement the technology or to establish a new employee reward system to improve quality. Try hard to clearly and logically link the scenario to the recommendation, and provide enough detail that the appropriateness of your plan is readily apparent.

Next, exchange scenarios with one of your classmates. Without discussing it, read the classmate's scenario and develop your own recommendations to address it. After you have finished, verbally summarize your recommendations for your colleague and listen to his or her summary of recommendations for your scenario. Then exchange the written recommendations you prepared for your own scenarios and read them. Discuss similarities and differences between the two sets of recommendations. Explain the logic behind the recommendations you originally proposed and listen carefully to the logic your colleague used to develop his or her own recommendations.

Follow-up Questions

1. Were the two sets of recommendations similar or different? Did the discussion alter your view of what should be done?

2. The contingency view, discussed in Chapter 1, would suggest that different courses of action might be equally effective. How likely is it that each of the two sets of recommendations you and your colleague developed might work?

Cross-Cultural Awareness

The following questions are intended to provide insights into your awareness of other cultures. Please indicate the best answers to the questions listed below. There is no passing or failing answer. Use the following scale, recording it in the space before each question.

1 = definitely no
2 = not likely
3 = not sure
4 = likely
5 = definitely yes

____ 1. I can effectively conduct business in a language other than my native language.

____ 2. I can read and write in a language other than my native language with great ease.

____ 3. I understand the proper protocol for conducting a business card exchange in at least two countries other than my own.

____ 4. I understand the role of the keiretsu in Japan or the chaebol in Korea.

____ 5. I understand the differences in manager–subordinate relationships in two countries other than my own.

____ 6. I understand the differences in negotiation styles in at least two countries other than my own.

____ 7. I understand the proper protocols for gift giving in at least three countries.

____ 8. I understand how a country's characteristic preference for individualism versus collectivism can influence business practices.

____ 9. I understand the nature and importance of demographic diversity in at least three countries.

____ 10. I understand my own country's laws regarding giving gifts or favors while on international assignments.

____ 11. I understand how cultural factors influence the sales, marketing, and distribution systems of different countries.

____ 12. I understand how differences in male-female relationships influence business practices in at least three countries.

____ 13. I have studied and understand the history of a country other than my native country.

____ 14. I can identify the countries of the European Union without looking them up.

____ 15. I know which gestures to avoid using overseas because of their obscene meanings.

____ 16. I understand how the communication style practiced in specific countries can influence business practices.

____ 17. I know in which countries I can use my first name with recent business acquaintances.

____ 18. I understand the culture and business trends in major countries in which my organization conducts business.

____ 19. I regularly receive and review news and information from and about overseas locations.

____ 20. I have access to and utilize a cultural informant before conducting business at an overseas location.

____ = Total Score

When you have finished, add up your score and compare it with those of others in your group. Discuss the areas of strengths and weaknesses of the group members. (Note: This brief instrument has not been scientifically validated and is to be used for classroom discussion purposes only.)

Reference: Neal R. Goodman, "Cross-Cultural Training for the Global Executive," in *Improving Intercultural Interactions: Modules for Cross-Cultural Training Programs*, eds. Richard W. Brislin and Tomoko Yoshida, pp. 35–36. Copyright © 1994 by Sage Publications, Inc. Reprinted by permission of Sage Publications, Inc.

Management Skillbuilder

Exercise Overview: Conceptual skills refer to a manager's ability to think in the abstract while diagnostic skills focus on responses to situations. These skills must frequently be used together to better understand the behaviour of others in an organization, as illustrated by the following exercise.

Exercise Background: We can read about creating an organization in which diverse workers are welcomed and included in everyday work activities. However, working with a diverse workforce every day can be more difficult. Consider, for example, the following situation.

You are the office manager for a large call centre in an urban area. You interview applicants, explain the type of work, and give them a short, job-oriented test. At the call centre employees sit at a desk in front of a computer screen and answer calls and inquiries about the products of several different companies. Employees must answer each call, determine the product, access the appropriate screen that contains all of the information about the product, and, if possible, complete the sale of the product and, it is hoped, extend the purchase to related products. Employees must be able to use a computer and speak well. One day you interview and hire a new employee, Sarah Jane. She completes the simple test that involves sitting at the desk, using the computer, and answering mock calls. Consequently, you hire Sarah Jane, who reports to work the next Monday.

About two weeks after her first day, Sarah Jane shows up with her seeing-eye dog. As it turns out, while modestly sighted, Sarah Jane is legally blind and has decided to start walking to work rather than taking a bus. Because the call stations are built to fit a normal-size person in a desk chair in front of a computer, there is no room for her rather large seeing-eye dog. Sarah Jane requests a special accommodation for her dog. Other employees are concerned about having a large dog sitting underneath the workstations and complain to you about the situation.

Exercise Task: Using the scenario previously described as background, do the following:

1. You have to decide what to do and have to write a report to your boss as well as to Sarah Jane and the other employees. What do you decide? Do you fire Sarah Jane because she is legally blind but did not inform you of this? Do you fire Sarah Jane because her dog is bothering the other employees by sitting underneath the workstations? Do you keep her and find her a separate workstation that is larger and would allow her dog to sit under it without bothering the other employees?

2. What role might outsourcing have played in this incident? How might it affect your response?

3. Are there any technologically based solutions you might be able to identify?

Organizational Behaviour Case for Discussion

Breaking the Glass Ceiling

Although women make up approximately 47 percent of the Canadian labour market, only 3.8 percent of the chief executive officers (CEOs) of Canada's top 500 companies are women. Although the number of women in top jobs in Canadian companies is increasing, the pace of change in recent years has been slow. The same is true for senior posts in general. At the corporate officer level, women hold 15.1 percent of positions in Financial Post 500 companies, an increase from 14.4 percent in 2004 and 14.0 percent in 2002. Interestingly, the level of representation varies considerably by industry with the highest proportions of women corporate officers found in insurance services, food distribution, life and health insurance, credit unions, specialty retailing, and banking. On the other side of the equation, the lowest representation of women corporate officers are found in the more traditional "old economy" sectors such as the auto and steel industries, oil and gas, and construction and engineering.

Why have so few women made it to the top? A variety of theories have been advanced. Among the most common are that some people are still guilty of stereotyping women,

that women are excluded from informal networks and other opportunities for getting inside tracks to success, and that many women lack significant managerial experience. Lack of managerial experience certainly is not a characteristic of successful women as many of them worked their way up through the ranks of their respective companies. Yet, it is telling that so few large companies are headed by women. A survey conducted by Environics Communications indicated that a large number of career women believe that an "old boys network" makes success for women difficult in corporations and that opportunities for women are limited. And it appears that stereotypes and biases do exist, even among women themselves. A recent survey found that 76 percent of men and 52 percent of women would rather have a male than a female as their boss.

Another factor that may be contributing to the lack of women heading large organizations is that they are more likely to find leadership opportunities in small organizations or even by starting their own businesses. However, some larger organizations are being more proactive in creating advancement opportunities for women. Scotiabank developed an initiative that was designed to connect and develop its women employees. The representation of women in senior management positions jumped from 18.9 percent in 2003 to 31.0 percent in 2006. Goldman Sachs initiated a program to develop, train, and mentor women. The Senior Women's Initiative resulted in the number of women partners in the firm doubling from 7 to 14 percent over a five-year period.

Case Questions

1. What challenges do women face working in large corporations?

2. What advantages, if any, do you believe would accrue from having diversity among managers?

3. Do you think there is really a glass ceiling in corporations? Why or why not?

Sources: Camilla Cornell, "Preference for Men in the Corner Office," *Financial Post*, 28 February 2007, www.canada.com; Wendy McLellan, "Old Boys' Club Still Thrives," *The Vancouver Province*, 30 June 2006, www.canada.com; Derek Sankey, "Glass Ceiling Has Yet to Be Shattered," *CanWest News Service*, 13 September 2006, www.canada.com; "Catalyst Canada: Latest Count of Women in Canada's Largest Businesses Show Marginal Progress," 4 April 2007, www.catalyst.org.

SELF TEST

You have read the chapter and studied the key terms. Think you're ready to ace the exam? Take this sample test to gauge your comprehension of chapter material and check your answers at the back of the book.

T   F   1. Motivating employees is a fundamental part of the leading function of management.

T   F   2. First-line managers generally require higher levels of conceptual and diagnostic skills than they do technical and interpersonal skills.

T   F   3. The same manager will behave the same way regardless of what cultural settings he or she is in.

T   F   4. One of the primary ethical issues related to advances in information technologies is individual rights to privacy.

T   F   5. Outsourcing an area that is highly unrelated to a firm's core business activity makes good business sense.

T   F   6. Downsizing always leads to positive outcomes for organizations.

T   F   7. The Personal Information Protection and Electronic Documents Act (PIPEDA) prevents companies from collecting online information about people.

8. A manager who designs jobs, groups jobs into manageable units, and establishes patterns of authority among jobs is performing which basic management function?
   a. Leading
   b. Organizing
   c. Planning
   d. Synthesizing
   e. Controlling

9. A manager acting in the role of monitor would do which of the following?
   a. Carefully supervise employees
   b. Check to see that time cards are properly completed
   c. Actively seek information that might be of value to the organization
   d. Upgrade computer systems whenever necessary
   e. Develop central goals and strategies for achieving those goals

10. Martha is a top manager at a large manufacturing firm. Which of the following skills are most likely to help Martha do her job?
    a. Conceptual and technical skills
    b. Technical and interpersonal skills

    c. Interpersonal and financial skills
    d. Financial and diagnostic skills
    e. Diagnostic and conceptual skills

11. One of Hofstede's cultural dimensions is named power distance. Another name for power distance is
    a. assertiveness.
    b. orientation to authority.
    c. uncertainty avoidance.
    d. materialism.
    e. masculinity.

12. In the "information age," many employees add value to organizations simply due to what they know. These workers are known as
    a. minority group members.
    b. majority group members.
    c. knowledge workers.
    d. assimilated workers.
    e. outsourced employees.

13. A large accounting firm in Halifax offers on-site daycare services for its employees with children. Which of the following makes the best business sense for this firm?
    a. Alter the company strategy to support a combined pursuit of accounting/daycare.
    b. Outsource the daycare operation.
    c. Train senior accountants to run the daycare operation.
    d. Train new employees to run the daycare operation.
    e. Require employees to supervise their own children in the daycare facility.

14. The phenomenon of employees showing up to work even though they are sick or injured is referred to as
    a. absenteeism
    b. presenteeism
    c. commitment
    d. masculinity
    e. assimilation

Part 1 Integrative Running Case

The Success of Starbucks

The first time that Howard Schultz walked into a Starbucks Coffee Company store, he fell in love. In 1981, Schultz was in the Seattle store to sell drip coffeemakers. Starbucks was a local three-store chain that sold coffee beans and accessories, but the owners put great care into choosing and roasting the beans and they taught their customers that same appreciation.

Schultz said to himself, "What a great company, what a great city. I'd love to be part of that." He spent a year convincing the owners to hire him as director of marketing. "I was this East Coast person and I had so much drive and energy, I think I might have scared them at first," Schultz admits. He acknowledges that perseverance is one of the most important traits of a successful entrepreneur, adding, "I have a history of people closing doors and me saying, 'No, it's still open.'"

One year later, Schultz was struck by another lightning bolt. After a visit to Italy, he realized that coffee bars there provided a location for socializing and relaxing. Schultz believed that the social aspect would appeal to Americans, fulfilling a need that restaurants and shopping malls failed to address. Back home, Starbucks's owners refused to enter the highly competitive restaurant business. Schultz quit. He founded a successful coffee bar business and, eighteen months later, used the profits to buy Starbucks for $3.8 million.

From that uncertain beginning, Starbucks grew into a retailing powerhouse, with more than 8,000 locations in over thirty countries, 97,000 employees, and annual sales of $5.3 billion. The first Starbucks in Canada opened in 1987 in Vancouver and expanded to the Ontario market following a partnership agreement with the Chapters bookstore chain in 1995. To date, Starbucks Canada has opened more than 400 company-operated outlets and more than 100 licensed concept stores across the country. Starbucks appears on the *Fortune 500* list and dominates the American specialty eateries industry in much the same way that Tim Hortons, with over 3,000 outlets, does in Canada. Dunkin' Donuts, its closest competitor, is part of the gigantic conglomerate Pernod Ricard, but has less than one-tenth the sales of Starbucks. In Canada, Starbucks' closest competitor is Second Cup, a specialty coffee chain that had its beginnings in Canada in 1975 and, like Starbucks, focuses on the entire coffee experience.

Starbucks has grown rapidly without franchising, although it offers licenses in a few locations. Schultz avoids franchising because he believes that quality and image control are vital to success. Starbucks funds growth with current earnings and has locations in thirty-four countries. Sales revenues increase by double digits in many years. Constant innovation is another indicator of the company's effectiveness.

Starbucks has satisfied many stakeholders, including investors, customers, and employees. Stock price has risen from around $25 in mid-2003 to over $50 in mid-2005, signalling that investors are confident. The total market capitalization was $200 million in 1992, when the firm had its initial public offering. Today it's worth $19 billion. The company never advertises nationally. Starbucks's phenomenal sales growth springs from word-of-mouth from satisfied customers. And there are lots of customers—about 30 million weekly. In 2004, Starbucks was named, for the sixth time, to the *Fortune* Best Companies to Work For list. The company was ranked 34th, up from 47th in 2003.

One reason that Starbucks is considered such a good employer is that it does something that many organizations do not: it assesses the company's corporate culture every 18 months with a Partner View Survey. Employees are asked to take 15 minutes to complete the questionnaire asking about things such as job satisfaction and commitment to the company. To increase participation, the employees complete the survey online on company time. In 2006, the most recent Canadian survey, the participation rate exceeded 90 percent. Another reason that participation is so high is that the company actually uses the data to implement changes. "People have seen tangible results from providing us feedback," says Colin

Moore, president of Starbucks Coffee Canada. The result is a turnover rate 40 to 60 percent lower than many other retail chains.

What created this success? One of the most important factors is the management skill and ability of Howard Schultz and the subsequent CEOs, Orin Smith and Jim Donald. Schultz was raised in a Brooklyn housing project, the son of a working-class family. Schultz says about that time, "I saw the fracturing of the American dream . . . My parents didn't have much—and they didn't have much hope." After attending college on a scholarship, Schultz held positions in sales and operations for various firms, ending up as manager of U.S. operations for Hammarplast. By 1985, he owned Starbucks, which went public in 1992. In 2000, Schultz stepped down from the CEO position, although he remains a member of the board of directors. Although he no longer has daily management responsibility, it is his vision that guides Starbucks today.

Orin C. Smith headed the firm from 2000 to 2005, after joining Starbucks in 1990. Smith's background was quite different from Schultz's. Smith has an MBA from Harvard, worked for years at management consulting firm Deloitte & Touche, and served as a top manager in several large firms before joining Starbucks. Smith was an effective manager who turned Schultz's visions into reality. He oversaw a time of rapid growth, innovation, and operational improvements.

In 2005, Starbucks gained its third CEO, Jim Donald. Donald worked as a bag boy in a supermarket during high school; by nineteen he was an assistant manager, making more money than his schoolteacher father. Donald is down-to-earth and folksy, knows everyone's name, and is willing to lend a hand. When Donald was giving a store tour, a customer spilled coffee. Donald grabbed a mop and cleaned the floor himself. "Being a grocery guy means you always know where the cleaning supplies are," he says. Before Starbucks, Donald helped Wal-Mart introduce groceries into their stores in the early 1990s, then aided Pathmark, an ailing grocery chain, in its recovery from bankruptcy.

However, no matter how skilled the managers, a company's success also relies on a number of factors from the business environment. Starbucks appeals to a demographic market segment whose needs have been ignored by the food-service industry. The typical Starbucks customer is affluent, well-educated, and thirty to fifty years old. Traditional fast-food outlets do not appeal to this segment. Above all else, these customers want customization—products that are personalized to their tastes and needs. Anne Saunders, senior vice president of marketing, worked in a Starbucks store when she was first hired, as does every executive. "I waited on hundreds of customers while working the cash registers and was struck by how every single one of them ordered something different," Saunders says. "Every single person coming in here has a different experience, designed the way they want it."

The preference for personalization is so well known that the popular movie *You've Got Mail* gently makes fun of the phenomenon. In the film, Joe (played by Tom Hanks) writes in an email, "The whole purpose of places like Starbucks is for people with no decision-making ability whatsoever to make six decisions just to buy one cup of coffee. People can get . . . an absolutely defining sense of self."

Another opportunity presented by Starbucks's environment is the potential for global expansion. Starbucks has entered thirty-three European, Asian, and Middle Eastern countries, but there are still markets the company could enter. In addition, the number of outlets in each country could be expanded. Starbucks plans to build 15,000 more overseas locations over five years, about half of the expected new stores.

Expansion plans are not stopped by the fear that selling American-style coffee and fast service to European customers, who are used to a more relaxed environment, might be tough. Some brands that are highly identified with the United States (Barbie dolls and AOL, for example) have seen their foreign sales fall recently.

Starbucks's operations become profitable only when there are a sufficient number of locations in a region or a country to gain economies of scale. It takes time for customers to become familiar with the company's products. Also, expenses are higher in Europe. Minimum wage in France, for instance, is $9.92 hourly, almost double the U.S. rate of $5.15. For these reasons, international operations produced adequate revenues but did not become profitable for Starbucks until 2004. Schultz explains the slow start, saying, "We're simply maturing. Not that we're getting close to maturity, because we're just scratching the surface internationally, but the markets are getting larger now."

The environment also presents some threats to Starbucks. Rising costs are a problem. The cost for employee healthcare benefits in the United States is sharply increasing. Schultz remains absolutely committed to providing health insurance for every employee who works twenty hours or more a week. This is a rarity in the restaurant industry, but Schultz believes that it's vital for his company to provide a living wage. Although hourly wages for overseas employees are higher, public health insurance in many countries such as Canada allows Starbucks to save money on benefits.

Starbucks has been targeted by some advocate groups that are critical of the company's policies. While some of the coffee Starbucks sells is organic and shade grown, environmentalists want them to sell more. They also want Starbucks to sell more Fair Trade certified coffee, which guarantees a living wage and safe working conditions for coffee farm workers. Consumer food safety advocates want Starbucks to stop selling milk that contains hormones and other ingredients that are genetically modified.

The company claims that it is as environmentally friendly as is possible. For example, the company buys 200 million pounds of coffee each year, far more than the current worldwide supply of Fair Trade or organic coffee. Starbucks has developed Coffee and Farmer Equity (CAFE), a set of guidelines that includes some of the Fair Trade coffee requirements. The CAFE standards have been adopted by other firms and Starbucks has won awards for its environmentally friendly supplier guidelines.

Even Starbuck's very apparent success opens the company up to criticism. Writer Ruth Rosselson suggests "consumers choose non-chain shops that offer fair-trade coffee. Starbucks . . . puts local companies out of business and with this policy can never be 100 percent ethical." Many agree. On the other hand, studies have shown that when Starbucks enters a city for the first time, coffee consumption increases and local coffee houses experience increased sales. Some local coffee bar chains take advantage of this trend by opening a new store on the same block whenever Starbucks opens one.

For now, Starbucks's continued success seems assured, although skeptics claim there is a limit to the number of $4 cups of coffee people will buy. Among them is venture capitalist and author Geoffrey Moore. "Of course, no chief executive wants to say, 'Yes, our market is saturated.' The notion that 7% market share means he still has a big field to go after is silly," Moore asserts. "His market is not all coffee drinkers. His market is people who buy into an upscale 21st-century café society experience, which is much smaller." For this reason, it is unlikely that Starbucks will ever challenge Tim Hortons' market dominance in Canada.

Yet Moore and other doubters have consistently been proven wrong. Analyst Sandy Sanders believes that customers

> **" Every single person coming in here has a different experience, designed the way they want it. "**
>
> ANNE SAUNDERS, SENIOR VICE PRESIDENT OF MARKETING, STARBUCKS

will continue to indulge. "It's a simple way of rewarding yourself without spending a ton of money," Sanders claims. Schultz is optimistic about the future of Starbucks. "We are in the infant stages of the growth of the business in America," he says. "And now seeing what we've done internationally . . . we are going to shock people in terms of what Starbucks is going to be."

Integrative Case Questions

1. Which managerial skills do Howard Schultz, Orin Smith, and Jim Donald have that allow Starbucks to prosper? How did they develop those skills?

2. What are the organizational-level outcomes experienced by Starbucks Corporation? Based on these outcomes, do you think Starbucks is an effective organization? Why or why not?

3. What forces from the environment are affecting Starbucks? Does the environment present more opportunities or more threats for Starbucks? Explain.

Sources: "Corporate Social Responsibility Report 2004," "International Development," "Starbucks Corporation Board of Directors," Starbucks website, www.starbucks.com on June 25, 2005; "Biography: Howard Schultz, Starbucks," Great Entrepreneurs website, 2000, www.myprimetime.com on June 30, 2005; "Orin Smith," Business Week, January 12, 2004, www.businessweek.com on February 2, 2005; "Specialty Eateries," "Starbucks Corporation," Hoover's, www.hoovers.com on February 2, 2005; "Starbucks Coffee Company to Receive 2005 World Environment Center Gold Medal," World Environment Center website, January 2005, www.wec.org on February 2, 2005; Donna Borak, "Europeans Costing American Companies," The Washington Times, December 27, 2004, www.washtimes.com on June 30, 2005; Stanley Holmes, "Starbucks: An American in Paris," Business Week, December 8, 2003, www.businessweek.com on February 2, 2005; Peter Kafka, "Bean Counter," Forbes, February 28, 2005, www.forbes.com on June 30, 2005; Patricia O'Connell, "A Full-Bodied Talk with Mr. Starbucks," Business Week, November 22, 2004, www.businessweek.com on January 31, 2005; Alison Overholt, "Listening to Starbucks," Fast Company, July 2004, pp. 50–56 (quotation); Sarah Robertson, "Starbucks Under Fire in Europe for Greenwashing," Organic Consumers Association website, January 21, 2004, www.organicconsumers.org on February 2, 2005; Dan Skeen, "Howard Schultz for Hire," My Prime Time website, www.myprimetime.com on June 30, 2005; Amy Tsao, "Starbucks: A Bit Overheated?" Business Week, April 5, 2004, www.businessweek.com on January 31, 2005; Amy Tsao, "Starbucks' Plan to Brew Growth," Business Week, April 5, 2004, www.businessweek.com on January 31, 2005; Eric Wahlgren, "Will Europe Warm to Starbucks?" Business Week, January 24, 2004, www.businessweek.com on June 30, 2005; Calvin Leung, "Culture Club: Effective Corporate Cultures," Canadian Business, October 9–22, 2006, www.canadianbusiness.com on August 21, 2007.

Foundations of Individual Behaviour

CHAPTER 3

After studying this chapter, you should be able to:

▶ **Discuss psychological contracts, the person–job fit, and the nature of individual differences.**

▶ **Define "personality" and describe personality attributes that affect behaviour in organizations.**

▶ **Describe perceptual processes and the role of attributions in organizations.**

▶ **Explain the role of attitudes in organizations and identify specific job-related attitudes that may affect behaviour.**

▶ **Explain how workplace behaviours can directly and indirectly influence organizational effectiveness.**

The Impact of Entrepreneurship

ost Canadians are familiar with Tim Hortons. The ubiquitous coffee and donut chain founded by the former National Hockey League defenceman, Tim Horton, in 1964 in Hamilton, Ontario, seems to be on almost every street corner in the country. However, few people have heard of Ron Joyce, the former police officer who took over the first Tim Hortons franchise in 1965 and then partnered with Horton to build the franchise. After Horton's untimely death in an automobile accident in 1974, Joyce purchased Horton's share of the business from Horton's wife, Lori. At the time, the chain consisted of 40 stores, but Joyce embarked on an aggressive expansion campaign. In 1991, the chain's five-hundredth store was opened in Aylmer, Quebec. By 2007, Tim Hortons was Canada's largest food service operator with over 2,700 outlets, plus more than 300 more in the United States. Tim Hortons has become so ingrained in the Canadian cultural landscape that the term, "double double," referring to a coffee with double cream and double sugar, now appears in the *Canadian Oxford Dictionary*!

Ron Joyce is just one example of a successful Canadian entrepreneur; there are many others as well. Frank Stronach arrived in Canada from his native Austria with $200 in his pocket and started a tool-making business in 1957. Today, Magna International is a multi-billion dollar manufacturer of automobile parts. Jim Pattison started out by acquiring a single Pontiac Buick dealership in Vancouver in 1961. More than four decades later, the Jim Pattison Group of companies comprising over 383 locations worldwide focusing on the automotive, media, packaging, food sales and distribution, magazine distribution, entertainment, export and financial industries. With sales of over $6.1 billion in 2005 and more than 28,000 employees, the Jim Pattison Group is the third largest private company in Canada. What factors made people like Ron Joyce, Frank Stronach, and Jim Pattison so successful?

Although there is no single predictor of success in entrepreneurial ventures, a common thread among those who are successful appears to be related to their personalities. A 2007 survey by Compas Inc. asked CEOs of midsized, entrepreneurial organizations what attributes were important to success in running your own business. Ranked most highly by the CEOs was persistence in the face of difficulty, followed by determination. That CEOs rated personality factors as being so important to the success of entrepreneurs is not surprising. Researchers have also found that conscientiousness, a personality trait that we will discuss later in this chapter, is associated with firm survival. In other words, the personality of the entrepreneur can influence the likely lifespan of the venture. This is an important consideration given that most businesses fail within their first few years of existence. Furthermore, it has been suggested that not everyone is suited to be an entrepreneur. Rather, specific individual traits such as self-efficacy, which we also discuss later in this chapter, create a higher degree of "person-entrepreneurship fit" that increases the chance of success.[1]

Think of human behaviour as a jigsaw puzzle. Puzzles consist of various pieces that fit together in precise ways. And of course, no two puzzles are exactly alike. They have different numbers of pieces, the pieces are of different sizes and shapes, and they fit together in different ways. The same can be said of human behaviour and its determinants. Each of us is a whole picture, like a fully assembled jigsaw puzzle, but the puzzle pieces that define us and the way those pieces fit together are unique. Thus, every person in an organization is fundamentally different from everyone else. To be successful, managers must recognize that these differences exist and attempt to understand them.

In this chapter we explore some of the key characteristics that differentiate people from one another in organizations. We first investigate the psychological nature of individuals in organizations. We then look at elements of people's personalities that can influence behaviour and the role of perception in organizations. Next, we consider individual attitudes and key work-related attitudes such as job satisfaction and organizational commitment as well as the impact of organizational justice in its different forms. We close this chapter with an examination of various kinds of workplace behaviours that affect organizational performance.

People in Organizations

As a starting point for understanding the behaviour of people in organizations, we examine the basic nature of the individual–organization relationship. Understanding this relationship helps us appreciate the nature of individual differences. These differences, in turn, play a critical role in determining various important workplace behaviours of special relevance to managers.

Psychological Contracts

Whenever we buy a car or sell a house, both buyer and seller sign a contract that specifies the terms of the agreement—who pays what to whom, when it's paid, and so forth. A psychological contract resembles a standard legal contract in some ways, but is less formal and well defined. Specifically, a **psychological contract** is a person's overall set of expectations regarding what he or she will contribute to the organization and what the organization will provide in return.[2] Thus, unlike a business contract, a psychological contract is not written on paper, nor are all of its terms explicitly negotiated.

Figure 3.1 illustrates the essential nature of a psychological contract. The individual makes a variety of **contributions** to the organization—such things as effort, skills, ability, time, and loyalty. In return for these contributions, the organization provides **inducements** to the individual. Jill Henderson started at Merrill Lynch at a very competitive salary and has received an attractive salary increase each of the six years she has been with the firm. She has also been promoted twice, and expects another promotion—and perhaps a larger office—in the near future.

In this instance, both Jill Henderson and Merrill Lynch apparently perceive that the psychological contract is fair and equitable. Both will be satisfied with the relationship and will do what they can to continue it. Henderson is likely to continue to work hard and effectively, and Merrill Lynch is likely to continue to increase her salary and give

> A **psychological contract** is a person's set of expectations regarding what he or she will contribute to the organization and what the organization, in return, will provide to the individual.

> An individual's **contributions** to an organization include such things as effort, skills, ability, time, and loyalty.

> Organizations provide **inducements** to individuals in the form of tangible and intangible rewards.

FIGURE 3.1

The Psychological Contract

Psychological contracts govern the basic relationship between people and organizations. Individuals contribute such things as effort and loyalty. Organizations, in turn, offer such inducements as pay and job security.

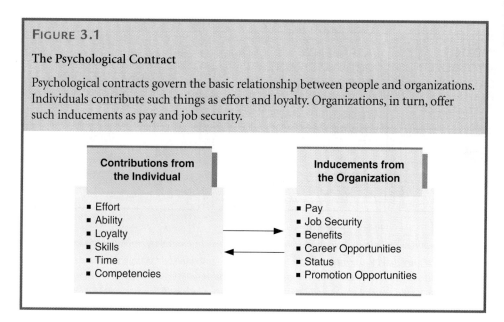

Contributions from the Individual

- Effort
- Ability
- Loyalty
- Skills
- Time
- Competencies

Inducements from the Organization

- Pay
- Job Security
- Benefits
- Career Opportunities
- Status
- Promotion Opportunities

her promotions. In other situations, however, things might not work out as well. If either party sees an inequity in the contract, that party might initiate a change. The employee might ask for a pay raise or promotion, put forth less effort, or look for a better job elsewhere. The organization can also initiate change by training the worker to improve his skills, transferring him to another job, or firing him.

All organizations face the basic challenge of managing psychological contracts. They want value from their employees, and they need to give employees the right inducements. For instance, underpaid employees may perform poorly. Overpaying employees who contribute little to the organization, though, incurs unnecessary costs.

The recent trends of downsizing and cutbacks have complicated the process of managing psychological contracts. For example, many organizations used to offer at least reasonable assurances of job permanence as a fundamental inducement to employees. Now, however, although job permanence is less likely, some organizations take more creative approaches to addressing the psychological contract.[3] The Business of Ethics box describes how some firms, including Spruceland Millworks and the Business Development Bank of Canada, have handled this situation.

Increased globalization of business also complicates the management of psychological contracts. For example, the array of inducements that employees deem to be of value varies across cultures. American workers tend to value individual rewards and recognition, but Japanese workers are more likely to value group-based rewards and recognition. Workers in Mexico and Germany highly value leisure time and may thus prefer more time off from work, whereas workers in China place a lower premium on time off. Several years ago the Lionel Train Company, an American manufacturer of toy electric trains, moved its operations to Mexico to capitalize on cheaper labour. The firm encountered problems, however, when it could not hire enough motivated employees to maintain quality standards and ended up making a costly move back to the United States.

A related problem faced by international businesses is the management of psychological contracts for expatriate managers. In some ways, this process is more like a formal contract than are other employment relationships. Managers selected for a foreign assignment, for instance, are usually given some estimate of the duration of the assignment and receive various adjustments in their compensation package— cost-of-living adjustments, education subsidies for children, personal travel expenses,

DILBERT reprint by permission of United Features Syndication, Inc.

Psychological contracts play an important role in the relationship between an organization and its employees. As long as both parties agree that the contributions provided by an employee and the inducements provided by the organization are balanced, both parties are satisfied and will likely maintain their relationship. But if a serious imbalance occurs, one or both parties may attempt to change the relationship. As illustrated here, for example, an employee who feels sufficiently dissatisfied may even resort to using company assets for his or her own personal gain.

Relationships and . . .  **ETHICS**

Maintaining the Psychological Contract

One of the most fundamental relationships in an organization is the psychological contract between each worker and the organization itself. Because of the recent trends of downsizing and layoffs, many organizations and employees have found that the traditional psychological contract is no longer valid. In the past, one of the primary inducements an organization could offer to its employees was the prospect for stable, steady, long-term employment. But in the age of downsizing, cutbacks, and worker flexibility, job security is constantly threatened.

Despite adversity, some organizations take steps to ensure that the psychological contract with its employees is not violated. A prime example is Spruceland Millworks, a company based in Acheson, Alberta, that makes wooden trim and mouldings. In 1992, the company's main plant burned to the ground. Rather than laying off the workers, owner Ben Sawatzky kept them on the payroll and had them rebuild the plant. Just over three months later, the plant was operational again. Sawatzky didn't stop there. Over the years, he provided employees with low-interest loans allowing them to buy shares in the company. In addition, employees are given a daily production target. If they meet that target in less than the normal eight hour day, they are free to go home with a full day's pay. The company is highly profitable and, when the company recently earned a record profit, Sawatzky chartered a holiday for the entire company to the Mexican Riviera.

Not all organizations follow Spruceland's approach. However, increasingly, forward-looking employers are realizing that they can replace job security as a part of their side of the psychological contract by offering other inducements that can at least partially substitute for job security. For example, the Business Development Bank (BDC) offers its employees flexible benefits that allow employees to choose the benefits that suit their personal needs. Employees are given a pool of money with which to buy benefits and they can choose different levels of life insurance, dental, and medical coverage. They can even use the money to purchase additional vacation days. Not surprisingly, 81 percent of the staff rate BDC as an exceptional place to work.

Sources: Steve Maich "Canada's Top 100 Employers," *Maclean's*, http://www.macleans.ca/topstories/business/article.jsp?content=20061016_134445_134445 on October 13, 2006; Stephanie Whittaker, "BDC Employees Say "Bravo" to Benefit Plan," *The National Post*, http://working.canada.com/toronto/resources/topemployers/story.html?id=ba596707-a27c-49c2-ad11-c0f69c686392&k=63694 on October 18, 2006.

and so forth. When the assignment is over, the manager must then be integrated back into the domestic organization. During the time of the assignment, however, the organization itself may have changed in many ways—new managers, new coworkers, new procedures, new business practices, and so forth. Thus, returning managers may very well come back to an organization that is quite different from the one they left and to a job quite different from what they expected.[4]

The Person–Job Fit

One specific aspect of managing psychological contracts is managing the person–job fit. A good **person–job fit** is one in which the employee's contributions match the inducements the organization offers. In theory, each employee has a specific set of needs that he or she wants fulfilled and a set of job-related behaviours and abilities to contribute. If the organization can take perfect advantage of those behaviours and abilities and exactly fulfil those needs, it will have achieved a perfect person–job fit.[5]

Of course, such a precise person–job fit is seldom achieved. For one thing, hiring procedures are imperfect. Managers can estimate employee skill levels when making hiring decisions and can improve them through training, but even simple performance dimensions are hard to measure objectively and validly. For another, both people and organizations change. An employee who finds a new job stimulating and exciting to begin with may find the same job boring and monotonous a few years later.

Person–job fit is the extent to which the contributions made by the individual match the inducements offered by the organization.

Person–job fit plays an important role in the success of any enterprise. Take NASCAR racing, for instance. Only a handful of people, such as Jacques Villeneuve, have the skills, nerves, and motivation to drive a race car around a narrow track at speeds in excess of 160 km per hour sometimes only a matter of centimetres (or less!) from other cars. While many people find their work to be enjoyable to watch, few spectators would actually want to take their place.

An organization that adopts new technology needs new skills from its employees. Finally, each person is unique. Measuring skills and performance is difficult enough. Assessing attitudes and personality is far more complex. Each of these individual differences makes matching individuals with jobs a difficult and complex process.[6]

Individual Differences

Individual differences are personal attributes that vary from one person to another.

Every individual is unique. **Individual differences** are personal attributes that vary from one person to another. Individual differences may be physical, psychological, and emotional. The individual differences that characterize a specific person make that person unique. As we see in the sections that follow, basic categories of individual differences include perception, personality, and creativity. First, however, we need to note the importance of the situation in assessing the individual's behaviour.

Are the specific differences that characterize a given person good or bad? Do they contribute to or detract from performance? The answer, of course, is that it depends on the circumstances. One person may be dissatisfied, withdrawn, and negative in one job setting but satisfied, outgoing, and positive in another. Working conditions, coworkers, and leadership are just a few of the factors that affect how a person performs and feels about a job. Thus, whenever a manager attempts to assess or account for individual differences among employees, the situation in which behaviour occurs must also be considered.

Because managers strive to achieve optimal fits between people and jobs, they face a major challenge in attempting to understand both individual differences and contributions in relation to inducements and contexts. A good starting point in developing this understanding is to appreciate the role of perception in organizations.

Personality and Organizations

The **personality** is the relatively stable set of psychological attributes that distinguish one person from another.

Personality is the relatively stable set of psychological attributes that distinguish one person from another.[7] A longstanding debate among psychologists—often described

The NFL and . . .   CHANGE

Person–Job Fit for the NFL Commissioner

On September 13, 2001, NFL commissioner Paul Tagliabue announced to the media that he would postpone all of that weekend's professional football games in the wake of the terrorist attacks. Tagliabue said, "[W]e had our priorities straight. We were concerned about the loss of life, not football." Other professional sports including baseball, golf, hockey, and NASCAR followed suit by postponing competitions scheduled for that weekend. *Sporting News* claims, "Tagliabue emerged as a guide. His leadership reached across an entire industry that day, illustrating his influence and command."

Although September 11 required a unique response, Tagliabue was already adept at managing change. A long-term strategic planner, he is known for his thoughtful analysis of trends that shape the sports industry. As the league negotiates contracts with broadcasters, Tagliabue is looking ahead ten, twenty, or even fifty years, evaluating the opportunities in traditional and emerging media such as wireless technology, interactive systems, and video-on-demand.

Another area of considerable change for the league is ethics, where safety, performance-enhancing drugs, and player behaviour off the field are top concerns. One of Tagliabue's responses is an increased emphasis on community service. For example, Will Shields of the Kansas City Chiefs won the Walter Payton Man of the Year Award for community service. Shield's "Will to Succeed" foundation helped 88,000 individuals meet needs ranging from after-school tutoring to sheltering abused women.

The NFL is facing pressure to change from inside and outside. Owners want more revenue, players want more pay, fans want more access. Tagliabue has been effective by building trust and listening. He plans ahead, so that the league is "proactive, not reactive," according to deputy commissioner Roger Goodell. Goodell is happy to see his boss use his power to influence others, saying, "[Tagliabue has] learned how to use his position . . . to drive change."

> *"[Tagliabue has] learned how to use his position . . . to drive change."*
>
> ROGER GOODELL,
> NFL DEPUTY COMMISSIONER

Sources: "Tagliabue, Paul," *Current Biography* (New York: The H. W. Wilson Co., 1996); "Will Shields Named Walter Payton Man of the Year," Join the Team, NFL website, www.jointheteam.com on February 27, 2005; Dennis Dillon, "Guiding Might, 2001," *The Sporting News*, www.sportingnews.com on February 14, 2005; Stuart Miller, "Tagliabue Tops Sporting News' Power 100," *The Sporting News*, January 4, 2005, msn.foxsports.com on February 25, 2005 (quotation).

in terms of *nature versus nurture*—is the extent to which personality attributes are inherited from our parents (the nature argument) or shaped by our environment (the nurture argument). In reality, both biological and environmental factors play important roles in determining our personalities.[8] Although the details of this debate are beyond the scope of our discussion here, managers should strive to understand basic personality attributes and how they can affect people's behaviour in organizational situations, not to mention their perceptions of and attitudes toward the organization.[9]

The Big Five Personality Traits

Psychologists have identified literally thousands of personality traits and dimensions that differentiate one person from another. But in recent years, researchers have identified five fundamental traits that are especially relevant to organizations. Because these five traits are so important and because they are currently receiving so much attention, they are now commonly called the **Big Five personality traits**.[10] Figure 3.2 illustrates these traits.

Agreeableness refers to a person's ability to get along with others.[11] Agreeableness causes some people to be gentle, cooperative, forgiving, understanding, and good-natured

The **Big Five personality traits** are a set of fundamental traits that are especially relevant to organizations.

Agreeableness is the ability to get along with others.

FIGURE 3.2

The Big Personality Framework

The Big Five personality framework is currently very popular among researchers and managers. These five dimensions represent fundamental personality traits presumed to be important in determining the behaviours of individuals in organizations. In general, experts agree that personality traits closer to the left end of each dimension are more positive in organizational settings, whereas traits closer to the right are less positive.

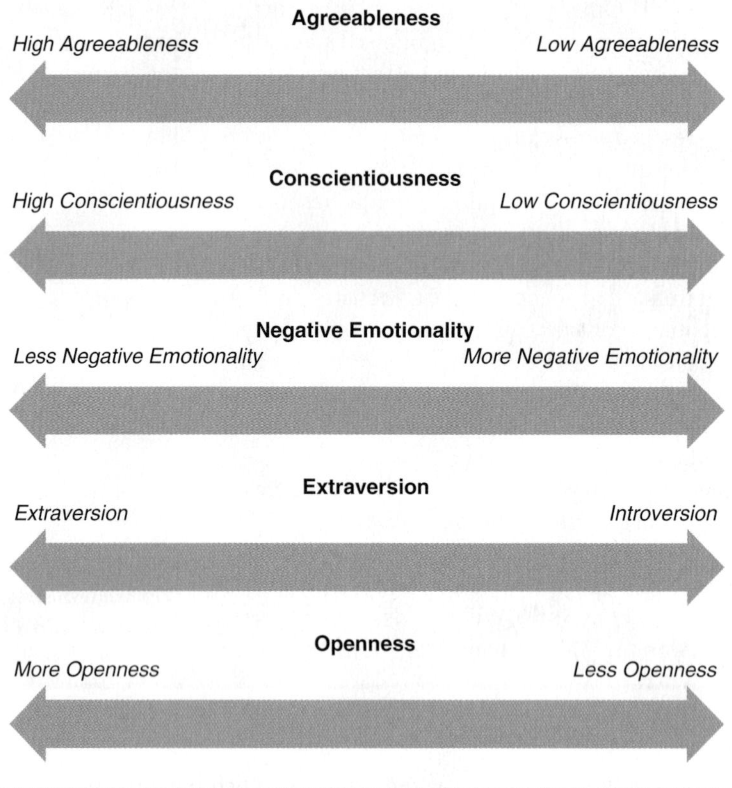

Agreeableness

High Agreeableness   *Low Agreeableness*

Conscientiousness

High Conscientiousness   *Low Conscientiousness*

Negative Emotionality

Less Negative Emotionality   *More Negative Emotionality*

Extraversion

Extraversion   *Introversion*

Openness

More Openness   *Less Openness*

in their dealings with others. But it results in others being irritable, short-tempered, uncooperative, and generally antagonistic toward other people. Researchers have not yet fully investigated the effects of agreeableness, but it seems likely that highly agreeable people are better at developing good working relationships with coworkers, subordinates, and higher-level managers, whereas less-agreeable people are not likely to have particularly good working relationships. The same pattern might extend to relationships with customers, suppliers, and other key organizational constituents.

Conscientiousness refers to the number of goals on which a person focuses. People who focus on a small number of goals at one time are likely to be organized, systematic, careful, thorough, responsible, and self-disciplined. Others, however, tend to pursue a wider array of goals, and, as a result, tend to be more disorganized, careless, and irresponsible, as well as less thorough and self-disciplined. Research has found that more-conscientious people tend to be higher performers than less-conscientious people in a

Conscientiousness refers to the number of goals on which a person focuses.

variety of jobs.[12] This pattern seems logical, of course, because conscientious people take their jobs seriously and approach their jobs in a highly responsible fashion.

The third of the Big Five personality dimensions is **negative emotionality** (also referred to as **neuroticism**) People with less negative emotionality are relatively poised, calm, resilient, and secure; people with more negative emotionality are more excitable, insecure, reactive, and subject to extreme mood swings. People with less negative emotionality might be expected to better handle job stress, pressure, and tension. Their stability might also lead them to be seen as being more reliable than their less-stable counterparts.

Extraversion reflects a person's comfort level with relationships. Extraverts are sociable, talkative, assertive, and open to establishing new relationships. Introverts are much less sociable, talkative, and assertive, and more reluctant to begin new relationships. Research suggests that extroverts tend to be higher overall job performers than introverts, and that they are more likely to be attracted to jobs based on personal relationships, such as sales and marketing positions.

Finally, **openness** reflects a person's rigidity of beliefs and range of interests. People with high levels of openness are willing to listen to new ideas and to change their own ideas, beliefs, and attitudes in response to new information. They also tend to have broad interests and to be curious, imaginative, and creative. People with low levels of openness tend to be less receptive to new ideas and less willing to change their minds. Further, they tend to have fewer and narrower interests and to be less curious and creative. People with more openness might be expected to be better performers due to their flexibility and the likelihood that they will be better accepted by others in the organization. Openness may also encompass a person's willingness to accept change; people with high levels of openness may be more receptive to change, whereas people with little openness may resist change.

The Big Five framework continues to attract the attention of both researchers and managers. The potential value of this framework is that it encompasses an integrated set of traits that appear to be valid predictors of certain behaviours in certain situations. Thus, managers who can both understand the framework and assess these traits in their employees are in a good position to understand how and why they behave as they do.[13] But managers must be careful to not overestimate their ability to assess the Big Five traits in others. Even assessment using the most rigorous and valid measures is likely to be somewhat imprecise. Another limitation of the Big Five framework is that it is primarily based on research conducted in North America. Thus, its generalizability to other cultures presents unanswered questions. Even within North America, a variety of other factors and traits are also likely to affect behaviour in organizations.

Emotional Intelligence

The concept of emotional intelligence has been identified in recent years and provides some interesting insights into personality. **Emotional intelligence**, or **EQ**, refers to the ability to perceive, express, assimilate, understand, and regulate emotions as a means of promoting emotional and intellectual growth. Individuals with high levels of EQ are self-aware, can manage their emotions, can motivate themselves, express empathy for others, and possess social skills.[14] These various dimensions can be described as follows:

Perception of Emotion This is the ability to perceive emotions in oneself and others, as well as in objects, art, and stories.

Emotional Facilitation of Thought This refers to the ability to generate emotions in order to use them in other mental processes.

Negative emotionality is characterized by moodiness and insecurity; those who have little negative emotionality are better able to withstand stress.

Extraversion is the quality of being comfortable with relationships; the opposite extreme, introversion, is characterized by more social discomfort.

Openness is the capacity to entertain new ideas and to change as a result of new information.

Emotional intelligence (EQ) is the the ability to perceive, express, assimilate, understand, and regulate emotions as a means of promoting emotional and intellectual growth.

Understanding Emotion This is the ability to understand and reason about emotional information and how emotions combine and progress through relationship transitions.

Managing Emotions This refers to the ability to be open to emotions and to moderate them in oneself and others.

Preliminary research suggests that people with high EQs may perform better than others, especially in jobs that require a high degree of interpersonal interaction and that involve influencing or directing the work of others. However, EQ remains a hotly debated concept in the organizational behaviour literature and there are different conceptualizations of EQ. Some view EQ as being trait-based whereas others conceive of EQ as an ability.[15] These differences may account for some of the contradictory findings. Research by Arla Day and her colleagues at Saint Mary's University suggests that trait-based measures of EQ tend to be highly correlated with personality measures. Conversely, ability-based measures of EQ have been demonstrated in some studies to be related to performance. In fact, Stéphane Côté and Christopher Miners at the University of Toronto found in a recent study that high levels of EQ can compensate for lower levels of cognitive ability on task performance.[16]

Other Personality Traits at Work

Besides the Big Five, several other personality traits influence behaviour in organizations. Among the most important are locus of control, self-efficacy, authoritarianism, Machiavellianism, self-esteem, and risk propensity.

A person's **locus of control** is the extent to which he or she believes circumstances are a function of either his or her own actions or of external factors beyond his or her control.

Locus of control is the extent to which people believe that their behaviour has a real effect on what happens to them.[17] Some people, for example, believe that if they work hard they will succeed. They may also believe that people who fail do so because they lack ability or motivation. People who believe that individuals are in control of their lives are said to have an *internal locus of control*. Other people think that fate, chance, luck, or other people's behaviour determines what happens to them. For example, an employee who fails to get a promotion may attribute that failure to a politically motivated boss or just bad luck, rather than to her or his own lack of skills or poor performance record. People who think that forces beyond their control dictate what happens to them are said to have an *external locus of control*. Research suggests that people with an internal locus of control are more satisfied with their jobs and more committed to their organizations than are people with an external locus of control. Furthermore, people with an external locus of control are more likely to feel stuck in their jobs than are people with an internal locus of control.[18]

A person's **self-efficacy** is that person's beliefs about his or her capabilities to perform a task.

Self-efficacy is a related but subtly different personality characteristic. A person's self-efficacy is that person's belief about his or her capabilities to perform a task.[19] People with high self-efficacy believe that they can perform well on a specific task, but people with low self-efficacy tend to doubt their ability to perform a specific task. Self-assessments of ability contribute to self-efficacy, but so does the individual's personality. Some people simply have more self-confidence than others. This belief in their ability to perform a task effectively results in their being more self-assured and better able to focus their attention on performance.[20]

Authoritarianism is the belief that power and status differences are appropriate within hierarchical social systems such as organizations.

Another important personality characteristic is **authoritarianism**, the extent to which a person believes that power and status differences are appropriate within hierarchical social systems such as organizations.[21] For example, a person who is highly authoritarian may accept directives or orders from someone with more authority purely because the other person is the boss. Conversely, a person who is not highly authoritarian, although she or he may still carry out reasonable directives from the boss, is more likely to question things, express disagreement with the boss, and even refuse

Risk propensity is the degree to which a person is willing to take chances and make risky decisions. Top managers at Lockheed Martin demonstrated strong risk propensity in their recent quest to earn a $200 billion contract to build the new Joint Strike Fighter shown here. No fewer than three times did they essentially risk the future of the company in order to remain the leader in the bidding. Had they ultimately failed, Lockheed Martin would have suffered serious consequences for years.

to carry out orders if they are for some reason objectionable. A highly authoritarian manager may be relatively autocratic and demanding, and highly authoritarian subordinates are more likely to accept this behaviour from their leader. Conversely, a less authoritarian manager may allow subordinates a bigger role in making decisions, and less authoritarian subordinates respond positively to this behaviour.[22]

Machiavellianism is another important personality trait. This concept is named after Niccolo Machiavelli, a sixteenth-century author. In his book, *The Prince*, Machiavelli explained how the nobility could more easily gain and use power. The term *Machiavellianism* is now used to describe behaviour directed at gaining power and controlling the behaviour of others. Research suggests that the degree of Machiavellianism varies from person to person. More Machiavellian individuals tend to be rational and nonemotional, may be willing to lie to attain their personal goals, put little emphasis on loyalty and friendship, and enjoy manipulating others' behaviour. Less Machiavellian individuals are more emotional, less willing to lie to succeed, value loyalty and friendship highly, and get little personal pleasure from manipulating others.

> People who possess the personality trait of **Machiavellianism** behave to gain power and control the behaviour of others.

Self-esteem is the extent to which a person believes that he or she is a worthwhile and deserving individual.[23] A person with high self-esteem is more likely to seek higher-status jobs, be more confident in her or his ability to achieve higher levels of performance, and derive greater intrinsic satisfaction from accomplishments. In contrast, a person with less self-esteem may be more content to remain in a lower-level job, be less confident of his ability, and focus more on extrinsic rewards.[24] Among the major personality dimensions, self-esteem is the one that has been most widely studied in other countries. Although more research is clearly needed, the published evidence suggests that self-esteem as a personality trait does indeed exist in many countries and that its role in organizations is reasonably important across cultures.[25]

> A person's **self-esteem** is the extent to which that person believes he or she is a worthwhile and deserving individual.

A person's **risk propensity** is the degree to which he or she is willing to take chances and make risky decisions.

Risk propensity is the degree to which a person is willing to take chances and make risky decisions. A manager with a high risk propensity, for example, might experiment with new ideas and gamble on new products. He or she might also lead the organization in new and different directions. This manager might be a catalyst for innovation, or might jeopardize the continued well-being of the organization if the risky decisions prove to be bad ones. A manager with low risk propensity might lead an organization to stagnation and excessive conservatism, or might help the organization successfully weather turbulent and unpredictable times by maintaining stability and calm. Thus, the potential consequences of a manager's risk propensity depend heavily on the organization's environment.

Perception in Organizations

Perception is the set of processes by which an individual becomes aware of and interprets information about the environment.

Perception—the set of processes by which an individual becomes aware of and interprets information about the environment—is another important element of workplace behaviour. If everyone perceived everything the same way, things would be a lot simpler (and a lot less exciting!). Of course, just the opposite is true: People perceive the same things in very different ways.[26] Moreover, people often assume that reality is objective, that we all perceive the same things in the same way. To test this idea, we could ask students at Acadia University and Dalhousie University to describe the most recent hockey game between their schools. We probably would hear two conflicting stories. These differences would arise primarily because of perception. The fans "saw" the same game but interpreted it in sharply contrasting ways.

Because perception plays a role in a variety of workplace behaviours, managers should understand basic perceptual processes. As implied in our definition, perception actually consists of several distinct processes. Moreover, in perceiving, we receive information in many guises, from spoken words to visual images of movements and forms. Through perceptual processes, the receiver assimilates the varied types of incoming information for the purpose of interpreting them.[27]

Basic Perceptual Processes

Figure 3.3 shows two basic perceptual processes that are particularly relevant to managers—selective perception and stereotyping.

Selective perception is the process of screening out information that we are uncomfortable with or that contradicts our beliefs.

Selective Perception   Because we are constantly bombarded with information, we cannot possibly process all of it. **Selective perception** is the process of screening out information that we are uncomfortable with or that contradicts our beliefs. For example, suppose a manager is exceptionally fond of a particular worker. The manager has a very positive attitude about the worker and thinks he or she is a top performer. One day the manager notices that the worker seems to be goofing off. Selective perception may cause the manager to quickly forget the observation. Similarly, suppose a manager has formed a very negative image of a particular worker. The manager thinks this worker is a poor performer who never does a good job. When she or he happens to observe an example of high performance from the worker, it may quickly be forgotten. In one sense, selective perception is beneficial because it allows us to disregard minor bits of information. Of course, the benefit occurs only if our basic perception is accurate. If selective perception causes us to ignore important information, however, it can become quite detrimental.[28]

Stereotyping is the process of categorizing or labelling people on the basis of a single attribute.

Stereotyping   **Stereotyping** is categorizing or labelling people on the basis of a single attribute. Certain forms of stereotyping can be useful and efficient. Suppose, for example, that a manager believes that communication skills are important for a particular job and that speech communication majors tend to have exceptionally good communication skills. As a result, whenever candidates interview for jobs, the manager pays

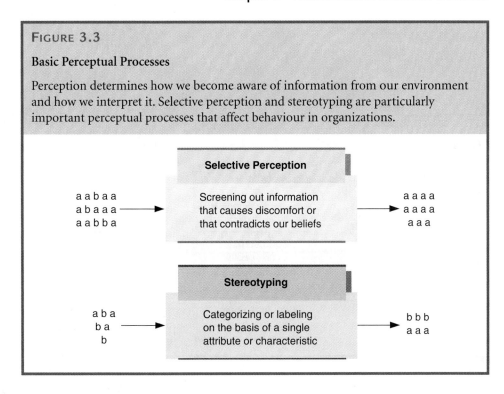

FIGURE 3.3

Basic Perceptual Processes

Perception determines how we become aware of information from our environment and how we interpret it. Selective perception and stereotyping are particularly important perceptual processes that affect behaviour in organizations.

Selective Perception

a a b a a
a b a a a   Screening out information   a a a a
a a b b a   that causes discomfort or   a a a a
                   that contradicts our beliefs   a a a

Stereotyping

a b a
b a   Categorizing or labeling   b b b
b   on the basis of a single   a a a
                  attribute or characteristic

especially close attention to speech communication majors. To the extent that communication skills truly predict job performance and that majoring in speech communication does indeed provide those skills, this form of stereotyping can be beneficial. Common attributes from which people often stereotype are ethnicity, sex, and age. Of course, stereotypes along these lines are inaccurate and can be harmful. For example, suppose a human resource manager forms the stereotype that women can only perform certain tasks and that men are best suited for other tasks. To the extent that this affects the manager's hiring practices, he or she is (1) costing the organization valuable talent for both sets of jobs, (2) violating human rights legislation, and (3) behaving unethically.

Perception and Attribution

Attribution theory has extended our understanding of how perception affects behaviour in organizations.[29] Attribution theory suggests that we observe behaviour and then attribute causes to it. That is, we attempt to explain why people behave as they do. The process of attribution is based on perceptions of reality, and these perceptions may vary widely among individuals.

Figure 3.4 illustrates the basic attribution theory framework. To start the process, we observe behaviour, either our own or someone else's. We then evaluate that behaviour in terms of its degrees of consensus, consistency, and distinctiveness. *Consensus* is the extent to which other people in the same situation behave in the same way. *Consistency* is the degree to which the same person behaves in the same way at different times. *Distinctiveness* is the extent to which the same person behaves in the same way in different situations. We form impressions or attributions about the causes of behaviour based on various combinations of consensus, consistency, and distinctiveness. We may believe the behaviour is caused internally (by forces within the person) or externally (by forces in the person's environment).

For example, suppose you observe one of your subordinates arriving late for work. If you can understand the causes of this behaviour, you may be able to change it. If this

Attribution theory suggests that we attribute causes to behaviour based on our observations of certain characteristics of that behaviour.

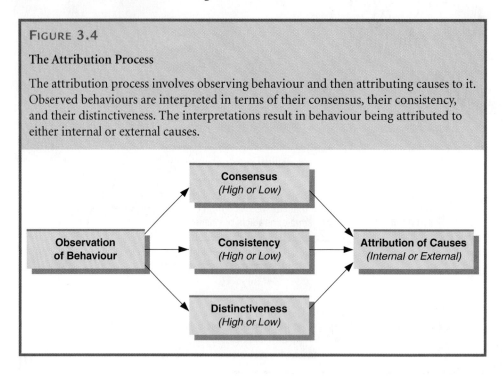

FIGURE 3.4

The Attribution Process

The attribution process involves observing behaviour and then attributing causes to it. Observed behaviours are interpreted in terms of their consensus, their consistency, and their distinctiveness. The interpretations result in behaviour being attributed to either internal or external causes.

employee is the only one who is late for work (low consensus), or is late for work several times each week (high consistency), and if you have seen him or her arrive late in other settings (low distinctiveness), a logical conclusion would be that internal factors are causing this behaviour.

Suppose, however, that you observe a different pattern: Everyone in the person's work group is late (high consensus), this particular employee is typically not late for work (low consistency), and is usually not late in other settings (high distinctiveness). This pattern indicates that something in the situation is causing the behaviour—that is, that the causes of the behaviour are external.

The importance of attributions in organizations is that the manager's response to employee behaviours will likely vary depending on whether the behaviour is attributed to internal or external causes. For example, if a tardy employee's behaviour is attributed to internal causes, the manager may submit the employee to some form of disciplinary action. If, however, the employee is deemed to be late due to external factors, the manager is not likely to punish the employee.

One other interesting aspect of attributions is the fact that individuals are more likely to attribute others' behaviours to internal causes and their own to external causes. This tendency is known as the *fundamental attribution error*.[30] For example, when an employee is late for work, the manager is more likely to attribute that employee's behaviour to internal causes than external causes. This tendency may result in people jumping to conclusions about another's behaviour.

Attitudes in Organizations

Attitudes are a person's complexes of beliefs and feelings about specific ideas, situations, or other people.

Attitudes are complexes of beliefs and feelings that people have about specific ideas, situations, or other people. Attitudes are important because they are the mechanism through which most people express their feelings. People's attitudes also affect their behaviour in organizations. An employee's statement that he or she feels underpaid by the organization reflects feelings about pay. Similarly, when a manager says that she or he likes the new advertising campaign, the manager is expressing feelings about the organization's marketing efforts.

How Attitudes Are Formed

Attitudes are formed by a variety of forces, including our personal values, our experiences, and our personalities. For example, if we value honesty and integrity, we may form especially favourable attitudes toward a manager whom we believe to be very honest and moral. Similarly, if we have had negative and unpleasant experiences with a particular coworker, we may form an unfavourable attitude toward that colleague. Understanding the basic structure of an attitude helps us see how attitudes are formed and can be changed.

Attitude Structure   Attitudes are usually viewed as stable dispositions to behave toward objects in a certain way.[31] For any number of reasons, a person might decide that he or she does not like a particular political figure or a certain restaurant (a disposition). We would expect that person to express consistently negative opinions of the candidate or restaurant and to maintain the consistent, predictable intention of not voting for the political candidate or eating at the restaurant. In this view, attitudes contain three components: affect, cognition, and intention.

A person's **affect** is his or her feelings toward something. In many ways, affect is similar to emotion—it is something over which we have little or no conscious control.[32] For example, most people react to words such as "love," "hate," "sex," and "war" in a manner that reflects their feelings about what those words convey. Similarly, you may like one of your classes, dislike another, and be indifferent toward a third. If the class you dislike is an elective, you may not be particularly concerned. But if it is the first course in your chosen major, your affective reaction may cause you considerable anxiety.

> A person's **affect** is his or her feelings toward something.

Cognition is the knowledge a person presumes to have about something. You may believe you like a class because the textbook is excellent, the class meets at your favourite time, the instructor is outstanding, and the workload is light. This "knowledge" may be true, partially true, or totally false. For example, you may intend to vote for a particular candidate because you think you know where the candidate stands on several issues. In reality, depending on the candidate's honesty and your understanding of his or her statements, the candidate's thinking on the issues may be exactly the same as yours, partly the same, or totally different. Cognitions are based on perceptions of truth and reality, and, as we note later, perceptions agree with reality to varying degrees.

> A person's **cognitions** constitute the knowledge a person presumes to have about something.

Intention guides a person's behaviour. If you like your instructor, you may intend to take another class from him or her next semester. Intentions are not always translated into actual behaviour, however. If the instructor's course next semester is scheduled for 8 A.M., you may decide that another instructor is just as good. Some attitudes, and their corresponding intentions, are much more central and significant to an individual than others. You may intend to do one thing (take a particular class) but later alter your intentions because of a more significant and central attitude (fondness for sleeping late).[33]

> An **intention** is a component of an attitude that guides behaviour.

Cognitive Dissonance   When two sets of cognitions or perceptions are contradictory or incongruent, a person experiences a level of conflict and anxiety called **cognitive dissonance**. Cognitive dissonance also occurs when people behave in a fashion that is inconsistent with their attitudes.[34] For example, a person may realize that smoking and overeating are dangerous, yet continue to do both. Because the attitudes and behaviours are inconsistent with each other, the person probably will experience a

> **Cognitive dissonance** is the anxiety a person experiences when simultaneously possessing two sets of knowledge or perceptions that are contradictory or incongruent.

certain amount of tension and discomfort and may try to reduce these feelings by changing the attitude, altering the behaviour, or perceptually distorting the circumstances. For example, the dissonance associated with overeating might be resolved by continually deciding to go on a diet next week.

Cognitive dissonance affects people in a variety of ways. We frequently encounter situations in which our attitudes conflict with each other or with our behaviours. Dissonance reduction is the way we deal with these feelings of discomfort and tension. In organizational settings, people contemplating leaving the organization may wonder why they continue to stay and work hard. As a result of this dissonance, they may conclude that the company is not so bad after all, that they have no immediate options elsewhere, or that they will leave "soon."

Attitude Change   Attitudes are not as stable as personality attributes. Some attitudes may be more or less resistant to change than others. When individuals have strong attitudes toward an object, it can be very difficult to persuade them to change their minds under any circumstances. If, however, attitudes are less strongly held, there are several factors that can lead to attitude change. For example, new information may change attitudes. A manager may have a negative attitude about a new colleague because of a lack of job-related experience. After working with the new person for a while, however, the manager may come to realize this person is actually very talented and subsequently develop a more positive attitude. Likewise, if the object of an attitude changes, a person's attitude toward that object may also change. Suppose, for example, that employees feel underpaid and, as a result, have negative attitudes toward the company's reward system. A big salary increase might cause these attitudes to become more positive.

Attitudes can also change when the object of the attitude becomes less important or less relevant to the person. For example, suppose an employee has a negative attitude about the company's dental insurance plan. When his or her spouse gets a new job with an organization that has outstanding dental benefits, his or her attitude toward dental insurance may become more moderate simply because he or she no longer has to worry about it. Finally, as noted earlier, individuals may change their attitudes as a way to reduce cognitive dissonance.

Key Work-Related Attitudes

People in organizations form attitudes about many different things. Employees are likely to have attitudes about their salary, their promotion possibilities, their boss, employee benefits, the food in the company cafeteria, and the colour of the company baseball team uniforms. Of course, some of these attitudes are more important than others. Especially important attitudes are job satisfaction and organizational commitment.

Job satisfaction is the extent to which a person is gratified or fulfilled by his or her work.

Job Satisfaction   **Job satisfaction** reflects the extent to which people find gratification or fulfilment in their work. When we ask people if they are satisfied with their jobs, there are two approaches they can take to responding. Job satisfaction can reflect an overall attitude about the job, which is referred to as global job satisfaction. Therefore, an employee might say that, "I am satisfied with this job." Alternatively, job satisfaction can reflect different facets of a job, such as pay, coworkers, supervision, and working conditions. When approached this way, it is possible for employees to have a positive attitude about some facets of the job, but not others. For example, an employee might say, "I am not happy with my level of pay, but I like my boss and coworkers."

Job satisfaction is probably the most frequently studied work attitude because for many years it was assumed that job satisfaction was linked to important organizational variables such as absenteeism, turnover, and performance/productivity. In general, a satisfied employee tends to be absent less often, to make positive contributions, and to stay with the organization.[35] In contrast, a dissatisfied employee may be absent more often, may experience stress that disrupts coworkers, and may be continually looking for another job. However, the impact of job satisfaction on withdrawal behaviours such as absenteeism and turnover are not as strong as one might expect. That is because there are many other variables that also influence absenteeism, such as work-related norms (see Chapter 8 for a discussion of group norms), attendance control policies, or even legitimate illnesses. And turnover can also be influenced by economic conditions and the availability of alternative employment opportunities.

Furthermore, contrary to what a lot of managers believe, high levels of job satisfaction do not necessarily lead to higher levels of performance. Although job satisfaction may make an employee more inclined to work hard, the link between job satisfaction and performance is not as direct and strong as one might think. Performance is influenced by a variety of factors such as ability, motivation (see Chapters 4 and 5 for a discussion of work motivation), and situational constraints. Although a satisfied employee may be more motivated to perform, that employee might not have the requisite skill or may be faced with situational factors that impede performance.

What factors determine whether employees will be satisfied with their jobs? One theory is that it is the discrepancy between what one wants and what one gets on the job that will influence how satisfied that employee will be. That is, if an employee is getting less of a valued benefit than she or he desires, that will contribute to job dissatisfaction. Larger negative discrepancies result in higher levels of job dissatisfaction. Conversely, according to this discrepancy theory of job satisfaction, employees who receive as much or more of valued outcomes than they want will be satisfied.

Some research also suggests that personality can influence job satisfaction. There are several findings that contribute to this notion. First, there is evidence that job satisfaction tends to be fairly stable over time, even when individuals change jobs. Second, studies of identical twins reared apart suggest that their job satisfaction levels are similar. More recently, studies examining links between the Big Five personality characteristics (described earlier in this chapter) and job satisfaction suggest that individuals with a higher degree of negative emotionality tend to be less satisfied with their jobs whereas individuals with higher levels of conscientiousness and extraversion tend to be more satisfied.[36]

Surveys of Canadian workers on workopolis.ca and jobquality.ca show that the vast majority are satisfied with their jobs. These findings are consistent with those reported in surveys conducted in earlier years. However, some differences exist across different types of jobs. For example, one survey demonstrated that the least satisfying jobs in Canada were assembly worker, customer service representative, auditor, accounting clerk, and warehouse manager. It appears then that factors such as low pay, lack of challenge, lack of control, job insecurity, and stress all contribute to job dissatisfaction. Not surprisingly, high level managers who enjoy high pay and autonomy were among the most satisfied workers. Even then, executives reported that they would like to have greater work-life balance if they could change anything about their jobs.[37]

Organizational Commitment

Organizational Commitment   **Organizational commitment**, sometimes called job commitment, reflects an individual's identification with and attachment to the organization. Highly committed people will probably see themselves as true members of the firm (for example, referring to the organization in personal terms such as "we make high-quality products"), overlook minor sources of dissatisfaction, and remain members of the organization. In contrast, less-committed people are more likely to see themselves as outsiders (for example, referring to the organization in less personal terms like "they don't pay their employees very well"), to express more dissatisfaction about things, and to not see themselves as long-term members of the organization.[38]

Organizational commitment is a person's identification with and attachment to an organization.

Employee attitudes such as job satisfaction and organizational commitment contribute to organizational effectiveness in a variety of works. Consequently, firms often seek ways to make their employees enjoy coming to work and to make them reluctant to consider leaving for a different job. The Oriental Trading Company warehouse in Nebraska, for instance, has set up this "cash machine." When someone makes an especially noteworthy contribution to the firm, that employee gets to spend some time in the machine catching bills as they are blown about.

Although this unidimensional view of organizational commitment has dominated research for many years, John Meyer and Natalie Allen of the University of Western Ontario have suggested that an employee's commitment to an organization can take several forms. An employee who has high levels of *affective commitment* has an emotional attachment to the organization, identifies with the organization, and is involved with the organization. These individuals remain with the organization because they want to. Affective commitment is very similar to the definition of organizational commitment described previously. *Continuance commitment* refers to an employee's perceptions of the costs associated with leaving the organization. Individuals with high levels of continuance commitment remain with their organization because they feel they need to. Finally, *normative commitment* reflects an employee's perceived obligation to remain with the organization. Individuals with high levels of normative commitment remain with their organization because they believe they ought to.[39]

The importance of Meyer and Allen's model of organizational commitment lies in the fact that the various forms of commitment develop in different ways and also have different consequences. Affective commitment develops primarily as a result of employees' experiences on the job, particularly early in the employee–organization relationship. For example, the extent to which the job provides challenge, autonomy, and the opportunity to use a variety of skills has been positively linked with affective commitment, as have positive relationships with supervisors. Employees develop continuance commitment as a result of investments in their organization. These investments refer to things of value that would be lost by leaving the organization such as time, money, and effort in developing organization-specific skills or the expense and personal cost of relocating the family to another city.

Continuance commitment may also develop when employees perceive that they have few, if any, employment alternatives outside of their current organization. Normative commitment, or feelings of obligation to the organization, may develop as a result of employer investments in the employee. For example, many organizations, such as Toronto-based information technology consulting firm, Sapient, provide tuition reimbursements to employees who upgrade their skills. Reciprocity norms may provide these employees with a sense of obligation to their benefactor employers. Normative commitment may also develop as a result of either cultural or organizational socialization experiences. For example, an individual may remain with the family business out of a sense of familial obligation.

Not only do the different forms of commitment have different antecedents, they also have different consequences. Although all three forms of commitment reduce the likelihood of employee turnover, Meyer and Allen argue that affective commitment is positively associated with work performance and organizational citizenship behaviours. Conversely, continuance commitment has been found to be either unrelated or negatively related with performance.[40] To this point, little research has focused on relations between normative commitment and various organizational behaviours, but what research has been done suggests that these relations are similar to those found with affective commitment, albeit somewhat weaker.[41] Given the pattern of relations between the various forms of commitment and organizational behaviours, it would seem that organizations would benefit more by focusing on developing affective commitment in their employees rather than continuance commitment.

Although we have so far discussed commitment to organizations themselves, individuals may be committed to other entities either inside or outside organizations. For example, people may develop commitment to their supervisors, their careers, or their professions. Meyer and Allen's three-component model of organizational commitment has been found to apply to occupational commitment across a variety of occupations.[42]

Organizations can do few definitive things to promote satisfaction and commitment, but some specific guidelines are available. For one thing, if the organization treats its employees fairly and provides reasonable rewards and job security, its employees are more likely to be satisfied and committed. Allowing employees to have a say in how things are done can also promote these attitudes. Designing jobs so that they are stimulating can enhance both satisfaction and commitment. Research suggests that some of the factors that may lead to commitment, including extrinsic rewards, role clarity, and participative management, are the same across different cultures.[43]

Affect and Mood in Organizations

Researchers have recently started to renew their interest in the affective component of attitudes. Recall from our discussion above that the affect component of an attitude reflects our emotions. Managers once believed that emotion and feelings varied among people from day to day, but research now suggests that although some short-term fluctuation does indeed occur, there are also underlying stable predispositions toward fairly constant and predictable moods and emotional states.[44]

Some people, for example, tend to have a higher degree of **positive affectivity**. This means that they are relatively upbeat and optimistic, that they have an overall sense of well-being, and that they usually see things in a positive light. Thus, they always seem to be in a good mood. People with more **negative affectivity** are just the opposite. They are generally downbeat and pessimistic and they usually see things in a negative way. They seem to be in a bad mood most of the time.

> People who possess **positive affectivity** are upbeat and optimistic, have an overall sense of well-being, and see things in a positive light.

> Those characterized by **negative affectivity** are generally downbeat and pessimistic, see things in a negative way, and always seem to be in a bad mood.

Of course, as noted above, short-term variations can occur among even the most extreme types. People with a lot of positive affectivity, for example, may still be in a bad mood if they have just been passed over for a promotion, received extremely negative performance feedback, or been laid off or fired, for instance. Similarly, those with negative affectivity may be in a good mood—at least for a short time—if they have just been promoted, received very positive performance feedback, or had other good things befall them. After the initial impact of these events wears off, however, those with positive affectivity generally return to their normal positive mood, whereas those with negative affectivity gravitate back to their normal bad mood.

Organizational Justice

Organizational justice is an important phenomenon that has recently been introduced into the study of organizations. Justice can be discussed from a variety of perspectives, including motivation, leadership, and group dynamics. We choose to discuss it here because it has a very powerful impact on employee attitudes and behaviours in

Organizational justice refers to the perceptions of people in an organization regarding fairness.

organizations. **Organizational justice** essentially refers to the perceptions of people in an organization regarding fairness.[45] As illustrated in the cartoon , there are four basic forms of organizational justice.

Distributive Justice

Distributive justice refers to people's perceptions of the fairness with which rewards and other valued outcomes are distributed within the organization. Obviously related to the equity theory of motivation that will be discussed in Chapter 4, distributive justice takes a more holistic view of reward distribution than simply a comparison between one person and another. For instance, the compensation paid to top managers (especially the CEO), to peers and colleagues at the same level in an organization, and even entry-level hourly workers can all be assessed in terms of their relative fairness vis-à-vis anyone else in the organization.

Perceptions of distributive justice affect individual satisfaction with various work-related outcomes such as pay, work assignments, recognition, and opportunities for advancement. Specifically, the more people see rewards to be distributed as just, the more satisfied they will be with those rewards; the more they see rewards to be distributed as unjust, the less satisfied they will be. Moreover, individuals who feel that rewards are not distributed justly may be inclined to attribute such injustice to misuse of power and/or to political agendas.

Procedural Justice

Another important form of organizational justice is *procedural justice*—individual perceptions of the fairness used to determine various outcomes. For instance, suppose an employee's performance is evaluated by someone very familiar with the job being performed. Moreover, the evaluator clearly explains the basis for the evaluation and then discusses how that evaluation will translate in other outcomes such as promotions and

Perceptions of distributive justice play an important role in organizations. The extent to which managers make reward decisions that are seen as fair and just can have an impact on satisfaction, motivation, and other key outcomes. Following principles of fairness and equity is therefore very important, a lesson that this executive no doubt still needs to learn!

"I'm making this decision on principle, just to see how it feels."

pay increases. The individual will probably see this set of procedures as being fair and just. But if the evaluation is conducted by someone unfamiliar with the job and who provides no explanation as to how the evaluation is being done nor what it will mean, the individual is likely to see that process as less fair and just.

When workers perceive a high level of procedural justice, they may be motivated to participate in activities, to follow rules, and to accept relevant outcomes as being fair. But if workers perceive procedural injustice, they tend to withdraw from opportunities to participate, to pay less attention to rules and policies, and to see relevant outcomes as being unfair. In addition, perceptions of procedural injustice may be accompanied by interpretations based on the power and political behaviours of others.

Interpersonal Justice

Interpersonal justice relates to the degree of fairness people see in how they are treated by others in their organization. For instance, suppose an employee is treated by his boss with dignity and respect. The boss also provides information on a timely basis and is always open and honest in her dealings with the subordinate. The subordinate will express high levels of interpersonal justice. But if the boss treats her subordinate with disdain and a clear lack of respect, withholds important information, and is often ambiguous or dishonest in her dealings with the subordinate, he will experience more interpersonal injustice.

Perceptions of interpersonal justice will most affect how individuals feel about those with whom they interact and communicate. If they experience interpersonal justice, they are likely to reciprocate by treating others with respect and openness. But if they experience interpersonal injustice, they may be less respectful in turn, and may be less inclined to follow the directives of their leader. Power and political behaviours are also likely to be seen as playing roles in interpersonal justice.

Informational Justice

Finally, *informational justice* refers to the perceived fairness of information used to arrive at decisions. If someone feels that a manager made a decision based on relatively complete and accurate information, and that the information was appropriately processed and considered, the person will likely experience informational justice even if she or he doesn't completely agree with the decision. But if the person feels that the decision was based on incomplete and inaccurate information and/or that important information was ignored, the individual will experience less informational justice. Interpersonal and informational justice are sometimes combined and referred to as *interactional justice*.

As we see in the Employees and . . . Research box, the various forms of organizational justice can affect employee attitudes and behaviours in both positive and negative ways, depending on whether one feels fairly or unfairly treated. We can also think of perceived injustice as a form of stress (see Chapter 6 for a more thorough discussion of stress and its implications for organizational behaviour). In a recent study of Canadian government employees conducted by Lori Francis of Saint Mary's University and Julian Barling of Queen's University, the different forms of organizational injustice predicted symptoms of psychological strain, which are the consequences of being exposed to stress. Examples of symptoms of psychological strain include anxiety and depression.[46]

Types of Workplace Behaviour

Now that we have looked closely at how individual differences can influence behaviour in organizations, let's turn our attention to what we mean by workplace behaviour. **Workplace behaviour** is a pattern of action by the members of an organization that

Workplace behaviour is a pattern of action by the members of an organization that directly or indirectly influences organizational effectiveness.

Employees and . . .   **RESEARCH**

Employees Respond to Unfair Treatment

One of the reasons organizational behaviour researchers are so interested in organizational justice is that employees may react to perceived unfair treatment in many ways, sometimes very destructively. Dan Skarlicki of the University of British Columbia and his colleagues have been studying some of the negative effects of injustice in the workplace for over a decade. In one of the earlier studies, Skarlicki and Robert Folger examined the conditions under which employees would retaliate against the organization as a result of unfair treatment at the hands of the organization and its agents. Skarlicki and Folger defined Organizational Retaliatory Behaviours (ORBs) as negative behaviours, such as damaging equipment, stealing supplies, spreading nasty rumours, or intentionally working slower, that are designed to punish the organization for what the employee views as unfair treatment. Although we sometimes believe that employees respond most negatively to distributive injustices (unfair outcomes), Skarlicki and Folger found that employees were more likely to retaliate when they were also treated unfairly by supervisors or believed that the organization invoked unfair policies.

Skarlicki's work was extended more recently in studies with his former graduate students, Laurie Barclay (now at Wilfrid Laurier University) and David Jones. Barclay, Skarlicki, and Douglas Pugh examined the role of emotions in the relations between injustice perceptions and retaliation. These authors distinguished between inward-focused emotions, such as shame or guilt, and outward-focused emotions, such as anger and hostility. In a study of former employees who had been laid off, they found that individuals were more likely to retaliate against their former employers when the employees perceived low levels of

interactional justice and reacted to that unfair treatment with outward-focused emotions. However, even inward-focused emotions could result in retaliation when the employees shifted the blame for the layoffs from themselves to the organization. This study demonstrated how emotions and attributions can interact with perceptions of injustice to create a situation where employees (or former employees, in this case) can lash out at the organization.

Jones and Skarlicki focused on the impact that social cues from peers has on an individual's interpretation of, and reactions to, subsequent treatment by an authority figure. Study participants heard from peers that the authority figure in question was either fair, unfair, or no information was provided. The participants were more likely to retaliate against the authority figure when they were led to believe that they would receive fair treatment, but instead received unfair treatment. These results suggest that managers who have a reputation as being fair can elicit even stronger negative reactions from employees who feel they have been unfairly treated by that manager. Taken together, these studies suggest that it is important for managers to be vigilant about treating employees as fairly as possible in all circumstances.

Sources: Laurie J. Barclay, Daniel P. Skarlicki, and S. Douglas Pugh, "Exploring the Role of Emotions in Injustice Perceptions and Retaliation," *Journal of Applied Psychology*, 2005, vol. 90, no. 4, pp. 629–643; David A. Jones and Daniel P. Skarlicki, "The Effects of Overhearing Peers Discuss an Authority's Fairness Reputation on Reactions to Subsequent Treatment," *Journal of Applied Psychology*, 2005, vol. 90, no. 2, pp. 363–372; Daniel P. Skarlicki and Robert Folger, "Retaliation in the Workplace: The Roles of Distributive, Procedural, and Interactional Justice," *Journal of Applied Psychology*, 1997, vol. 82, no. 3, pp. 434–443.

directly or indirectly influences the organization's effectiveness. One way to talk about workplace behaviour is to describe its impact on performance and productivity, absenteeism and turnover, and organizational citizenship. Unfortunately, employees can exhibit dysfunctional behaviours as well.

Performance behaviours are all of the total set of work-related behaviours that the organization expects the individual to display.

Performance Behaviours

Performance behaviours are the total set of work-related behaviours that the organization expects the individual to display. You might think of these as the "terms" of the psychological contract. For some jobs, performance behaviours can be narrowly defined and easily measured. For example, an assembly-line worker who sits by a moving conveyor and attaches parts to a product as it passes by has relatively few performance behaviours. He or she is expected to remain at the work station and correctly attach the parts. Performance can often be assessed quantitatively by counting the percentage of parts correctly attached.

For many other jobs, however, performance behaviours are more diverse and much more difficult to assess. For example, consider the case of a research-and-development scientist at Biovail Pharmaceuticals. The scientist works in a lab trying to make scientific breakthroughs that have commercial potential. The scientist must apply knowledge learned in graduate school and experience gained from previous research. Intuition and creativity are also important. The desired breakthrough can take months or even years to accomplish. Organizations rely on a number of methods to evaluate performance. The key, of course, is to match the evaluation mechanism with the job being performed.

Dysfunctional Behaviours

Some work-related behaviours are dysfunctional in nature; that is, they detract from, rather than contribute to, organizational performance. Dysfunctional behaviours can take many forms and can be directed either at the organization or coworkers. Sandra Robinson of the University of British Columbia developed a typology of deviant workplace behaviours that vary along two dimensions: *organizational* versus *interpersonal* and *minor* versus *serious*.[47] Behaviours that are serious and organizational in nature include such things as stealing from the company and sabotaging equipment. Examples of serious interpersonal behaviours include sexual harassment and verbal abuse. Researchers have speculated on the reasons why employees would engage in such behaviours. Some have suggested that these behaviours are sometimes acts of retaliation for perceived unfair treatment within the organization (see the Employees and . . . Research box).[48]

Although these deviant behaviours have serious consequences for organizations, they occur relatively infrequently. Some dysfunctional work-related behaviours may seem less serious, but occur more frequently and also have an important impact on organizational effectiveness. Two of the more common ones are absenteeism and turnover. **Absenteeism** occurs when an employee does not show up for work. Some absenteeism has a legitimate cause, such as illness, jury duty, or death or illness in the family. At other times, the employee may report a feigned legitimate cause that's actually just an excuse to attend to nonwork-related interests or responsibilities. When an employee is absent, legitimately or not, her or his work does not get done at all or a substitute must be hired to do it. In either case, the quantity or quality of actual output is likely to suffer. Obviously, some absenteeism is expected, but organizations strive to minimize feigned absenteeism and reduce legitimate absences as much as possible.

> **Absenteeism** occurs when an individual does not show up for work.

What are some of the factors that affect absenteeism? This question has been the topic of OB research for many years. Some of the factors believed to be important include personal characteristics such as age and organizational tenure, work attitudes such as job satisfaction and organizational commitment, and organizational or group factors such as absenteeism norms. Gary Johns of Concordia University has suggested that work groups develop an *absence culture* that develops over time. This absence culture results in perceptions of work group members concerning how much absenteeism will be tolerated by managers and coworkers. Research by Ian Gellatly of the University of Alberta confirmed this notion and also provided evidence to suggest that people with higher levels of affective organizational commitment are absent less often than employees with low levels of affective commitment.[49]

Although most organizations strive to reduce absenteeism levels, there are times when an employee's attendance at work can lead to problems. One of the assumptions underlying absenteeism reduction is that employees will be productive when they are at work. However, this might be a faulty assumption. **Presenteeism** occurs when employees show up to work even though they are sick or injured. According to UK

> **Presenteeism** occurs when employees show up to work even though they are sick or injured.

organizational psychology professor, Cary Cooper, who is credited with popularizing the term, presenteeism is the result of insecurity and fear of job loss.

Turnover occurs when people leave the organization. Turnover may be voluntary (the employee quits) or involuntary (the employee is laid off or fired). Most OB research concerns voluntary turnover because an organization usually incurs costs in replacing workers who have quit, and if turnover involves especially productive people, it is even more costly. Turnover seems to result from a number of factors, including aspects of the job, the organization, the individual, the labour market, and family influences. Generally, a poor person–job fit is also a cause of turnover. Sometimes turnover results from increasing workforce diversity. As described in the Canadian Companies and . . . Diversity box, for example, people may be prone to leave an organization if its inflexibility makes it difficult to manage family and other personal matters and may be more likely to stay if an organization provides sufficient flexibility to make it easier to balance work and nonwork considerations.

> **Turnover** occurs when people quit their jobs.

Other forms of dysfunctional behaviour may be even more costly for an organization. Theft and sabotage, for example, result in direct financial costs for an organization. Sexual and racial harassment also cost an organization, both indirectly (by lowering morale, producing fear, and driving off valuable employees) and directly (through financial liability if the organization responds inappropriately). Workplace violence is also a growing concern in many organizations. Violence by disgruntled workers or former workers results in dozens of deaths and injuries each year.[50]

Organizational Citizenship

Managers strive to minimize dysfunctional behaviours while trying to promote organizational citizenship. **Organizational citizenship** refers to the behaviour of individuals who make a positive overall contribution to the organization.[51]

> A person's degree of **organizational citizenship** is the extent to which his or her behaviour makes a positive overall contribution to the organization.

Consider, for example, an employee who does work that is acceptable in terms of both quantity and quality. However, that employee refuses to work overtime, won't help newcomers learn the ropes, and is generally unwilling to make any contribution beyond the strict performance of the job. This person may be seen as a good performer, but is not likely to be seen as a good organizational citizen. Another employee may exhibit a comparable level of performance. In addition, however, he or she always works late when the boss asks, takes time to help newcomers learn their way around, and is perceived as being helpful and committed to the organization's success. That employee is likely to be seen as a better organizational citizen.

Turnover in industry, including high-tech industries, can be exceedingly high. As a result, managers have to spend time recruiting new employees. If firms can find ways to lower turnover, managers can devote more of their time to other important activities.

Canadian Companies and . . .   **DIVERSITY**

Flexible Canadian Companies

The Royal Bank is the largest bank in Canada. Like many firms, the Royal Bank offered one basic employment relationship to all employees. This relationship included standardized work schedules, benefit programs, and so forth. But like many corporations, the Royal Bank has become interested in ways to more easily and more effectively provide for other needs of its employees.

A survey of 1700 employees of the RBC Financial Group, which includes the Royal Bank and Royal Trust, revealed that managers were embracing the notion of flexible work arrangements. The managers recognized that such arrangements better enabled their employees to cope with the stress of juggling multiple responsibilities at work and at home. For their part, employees reported that the flexible work arrangements increased morale, efficiency, and customer service, while reducing absenteeism.

The Royal Bank first introduced its flex-work initiative in 1990 and by 1998 it was estimated that 30 percent of Royal Bank Financial Group employees were participating in some form of flexible work arrangement. Some of the options available to employees include job sharing, flexiplace (working outside the office or from home), flextime (flexible start and finish times), modified work weeks, compressed work weeks, and variable hours (working fewer than the standard 37.5 hours per week).

The bank introduced these measures because it recognized the importance of balancing work and home demands, particularly for single-parent households. It is estimated that close to three-quarters of working Canadians have responsibilities that include either childcare or care for aging parents. The flexible work arrangements program has been very well received by employees. By 2005 the number of job shares at RBC across Canada exceeded 1000. The response from customers has been very positive with many clients reporting receiving better service from having two individuals familiar with their accounts. In addition to flexible work schedules, RBC introduced an Emergency Backup Childcare program for staff in the downtown Toronto area. This program was designed to provide emergency childcare for employees whose primary childcare options were unexpectedly unavailable. Over 200 employees used the service in the first year.

Of course, RBC is not the only Canadian organization to embrace flexible work policies. A 2003 survey conducted by Human Resources Development Canada (HRDC) noted that 4 percent of the 24,000 employees who responded utilized some sort of flextime arrangements. One popular approach to flexible work arrangements that is made more viable because of advances in communications technology is telecommuting, in which employees work from home or some other remote location. Approximately 20 percent of IBM Canada's workforce telecommutes. The company suggests that this practice has been highly successful with employees being as much as 50 percent more effective in their jobs. The reaction of employees to telecommuting has been positive as well. A 2002 Royal Bank study of 742 telecommuters indicated that 77 percent of respondents were more satisfied with their jobs as a result.

Source: <http://jobb.oomcc.canoe.ca/News/2003/07/16/1225259-sun.html>; <http://www.rbc.com/newsroom/20050511coffey.html>.

A complex mosaic of individual, social, and organizational variables determines organizational citizenship behaviours. For example, the personality, attitudes, and needs (discussed in Chapter 4) of the individual must be consistent with citizenship behaviours. Similarly, the social context, or work group, in which the individual works must facilitate and promote such behaviours (we discuss group dynamics in Chapter 8). And the organization itself, especially its culture, must be capable of promoting, recognizing, and rewarding these types of behaviours if they are to be maintained.[52] The study of organizational citizenship is still in its infancy, but preliminary research suggests that it may play a powerful role in organizational effectiveness. In addition, organizational citizenship may provide the key link between satisfaction and performance. Although numerous studies have found weak correlations between job satisfaction and traditional measures of performance, recent research suggests that, when performance is defined in terms of organizational citizenship behaviours, the correlation between satisfaction and performance is much stronger.[53]

Summary of Key Points

- Understanding individuals in organizations is important for all managers. A basic framework for facilitating this understanding is the psychological contract—people's expectations regarding what they will contribute to the organization and what they will get in return. Organizations strive to achieve an optimal person–job fit, but this process is complicated by the existence of individual differences.

- Personalities are the relatively stable sets of psychological and behavioural attributes that distinguish one person from another. The Big Five personality traits are agreeableness, conscientiousness, negative emotionality, extroversion, and openness. Other important personality traits include locus of control, self-efficacy, authoritarianism, Machiavellianism, self-esteem, and risk propensity.

- Perception is the set of processes by which a person becomes aware of and interprets information about the environment. Basic perceptual processes include selective perception and stereotyping. Perception and attribution are also closely related.

- Attitudes are based on emotion, knowledge, and intended behaviour. Cognitive dissonance results from contradictory or incongruent attitudes, behaviours, or both. Job satisfaction or dissatisfaction and organizational commitment are important work-related attitudes. Employees' moods, assessed in terms of positive or negative affectivity, also affect attitudes in organizations. Employees' perceptions of organizational justice (distributive, procedural, interpersonal, informational) can influence both their attitudes and behaviours.

- Workplace behaviour is a pattern of action by the members of an organization that directly or indirectly influences organizational effectiveness. Performance behaviours are the set of work-related behaviours the organization expects the individual to display to fulfil

the psychological contract. Dysfunctional behaviours include absenteeism and turnover, as well as theft, sabotage, and violence. Organizational citizenship entails behaviours that make a positive overall contribution to the organization.

Discussion Questions

1. What is a psychological contract? Why is it important? What psychological contracts do you currently have?

2. Sometimes people describe an individual as having no personality. What is wrong with this statement? What does this statement actually mean?

3. Describe how the Big Five personality attributes might affect a manager's own behaviour in dealing with subordinates.

4. How does perception affect behaviour?

5. What stereotypes do you form about people? Are they good or bad?

6. What are the components of an individual's attitude?

7. Think of a person that you know who seems to have positive affectivity. Think of another who has more negative affectivity. How constant are they in their expressions of mood and attitude?

8. Think of a time when you feel like you have been treated unfairly on the job. What was the basis of the unfair treatment and how did you respond?

8. Identify and describe several important workplace behaviours.

9. As a manager, how would you go about trying to make someone a better organizational citizen?

Purpose: This exercise will give you insights into the importance of personality in the workplace and into some of the difficulties associated with assessing personality traits.

Format: You will first try to determine which personality traits are most relevant to different jobs. You will then write a series of questions to help assess or measure those traits in prospective employees.

Procedure: First, read each of the job descriptions below.

Sales Representative. This position involves calling on existing customers to ensure that they continue to be happy with your firm's products. The sales representative also works to get customers to buy more of your products and to attract new customers. A sales representative must be aggressive, but not pushy.

Office Manager. The office manager oversees the work of a staff of 20 secretaries, receptionists, and clerks. The manager hires them, trains them, evaluates their performance, and sets their pay. The manager also schedules working hours and, when necessary, disciplines or fires workers.

Warehouse Worker. Warehouse workers unload trucks and carry shipments to shelves for storage. They also pull orders for customers from shelves and take products for packing. The job requires that workers follow orders precisely; there is little room for autonomy or interaction with others during work.

Working alone, think of a single personality trait that you think is especially important for a person to be able to effectively perform each of these three jobs. Next, write five questions that will help you assess how an applicant scores on that particular trait. These questions should be of the type that can be answered on five-point scales (i.e., strongly agree, agree, neither agree nor disagree, disagree, strongly disagree).

After completing your questions, exchange them with one of your classmates. Pretend you are a job applicant. Provide honest and truthful answers to your partner's questions. After you have both finished, discuss the traits each of you identified for each position and how well you think your classmate's questions actually measure those traits.

Follow-up Questions

1. How easy is it to measure personality?

2. How important do you believe it is for organizations to consider personality in hiring decisions?

3. Do perceptions and attitudes affect how people answer personality questions?

Management Skillbuilder

Assessing Your Locus of Control

Read each pair of statements below and indicate whether you agree more with statement A or with statement B. There are no right or wrong answers. In some cases, you may agree somewhat with both statements; choose the one with which you agree more.

_____ 1. **A.** Making a lot of money is largely a matter of getting the right breaks.

        B. Promotions are earned through hard work and persistence.

_____ 2. **A.** There is usually a direct correlation between how hard I study and the grades I get.

        B. Many times the reactions of teachers seem haphazard to me.

_____ 3. **A.** The number of divorces suggests that more and more people are not trying to make their marriages work.

        B. Marriage is primarily a gamble.

_____ 4. **A.** It is silly to think you can really change another person's basic attitudes.

        B. When I am right, I can generally convince others.

_____ 5. **A.** Getting promoted is really a matter of being a little luckier than the next person.

        B. In our society, a person's future earning power is dependent upon her or his ability.

_____ **6. A.** If one knows how to deal with people, they are really quite easily led.

B. I have little influence over the way other people behave.

_____ **7. A.** The grades I make are the result of my own efforts; luck has little or nothing to do with it.

B. Sometimes I feel that I have little to do with the grades I get.

_____ **8. A.** People like me can change the course of world affairs if we make ourselves heard.

B. It is only wishful thinking to believe that one can readily influence what happens in our society at large.

_____ **9. A.** A great deal that happens to me probably is a matter of chance.

B. I am the master of my life.

_____ **10. A.** Getting along with people is a skill that must be practised.

B. It is almost impossible to figure out how to please some people.

Give yourself 1 point each if you chose the following answers: 1B, 2A, 3A, 4B, 5B, 6A, 7A, 8A, 9B, 10A.

Sum your scores and interpret them as follows:

8–10 = high internal locus of control

6–7 = moderate locus of control

5 = mixed internal and external locus of control

3–4 = moderate external locus of control

1–2 = high external locus of control

Note: This is an abbreviated version of a longer instrument. The scores obtained here are only an approximation of what your score might be on the complete instrument.

Source: Adapted from J. B. Rotter, "External Control and Internal Control," *Psychology Today*, June 1971, p. 42. Reprinted with permission from *Psychology Today* magazine. Copyright © 1971 (Sussex Publishers, Inc.).

Organizational Behaviour Case for Discussion

Differing Perceptions at Clarkston Industries

Susan Harrington continued to drum her fingers on her desk. She had a real problem and wasn't sure what to do next. She had a lot of confidence in Jack Reed, but she suspected she was about the last person in the office who did. Perhaps if she ran through the entire story again in her mind she would see the solution.

Susan had been distribution manager for Clarkston Industries for almost 20 years. An early brush with the law and a short stay in prison had made her realize the importance of honesty and hard work. Henry Clarkston had given her a chance despite her record, and Susan had made the most of it. She now was one of the most respected managers in the company. Few people knew her background.

Susan had hired Jack Reed fresh out of prison six months ago. Susan understood how Jack felt when Jack tried to explain his past and asked for another chance. Susan decided to give him that chance just as Henry

Clarkston had given her one. Jack eagerly accepted a job on the loading docks and could soon load a truck as fast as anyone in the crew.

Things had gone well at first. Everyone seemed to like Jack, and he made several new friends. Susan had been vaguely disturbed about two months ago, however, when another dock worker reported his wallet missing. She confronted Jack about this and was reassured when Jack understood her concern and earnestly but calmly asserted his innocence. Susan was especially relieved when the wallet was found a few days later.

The events of last week, however, had caused serious trouble. First, a new personnel clerk had come across records about Jack's past while updating employee files. Assuming that the information was common knowledge, the clerk had mentioned to several employees what a good thing it was to give ex-convicts like Jack a chance. The next day, someone in bookkeeping discovered some money missing from petty cash. Another worker claimed to have seen Jack in the area around the office strongbox, which was open during working hours, earlier that same day.

Most people assumed Jack was the thief. Even the worker whose wallet had been misplaced suggested that perhaps Jack had indeed stolen it but had returned it when questioned. Several employees had approached Susan and requested that Jack be fired. Meanwhile, when Susan had discussed the problem with Jack, Jack had been defensive and sullen and said little about the petty-cash situation other than to deny stealing the money.

To her dismay, Susan found that rethinking the story did little to solve her problem. Should she fire Jack? The evidence, of course, was purely circumstantial, yet everybody else seemed to see things quite clearly. Susan feared that if she did not fire Jack, she would lose everyone's trust and that some people might even begin to question her own motives.

Case Questions

1. Explain the events in this case in terms of perception and attitudes. Does personality play a role?

2. What should Susan do? Should she fire Jack or give him another chance?

SELF TEST

You have read the chapter and studied the key terms. Think you're ready to ace the exam? Take this sample test to gauge your comprehension of chapter material and check your answers at the back of the book. Want more test questions? Take the ACE quizzes found on the student website: www.hmco.ca/ob.

T F 1. Managers should make sure their psychological contract is written down.

T F 2. One reason precise person–job fit is seldom achieved is hiring procedures are imperfect.

T F 3. Negative emotionality is a personality dimension that reflects how much an employee complains.

T F 4. Managers with high emotional intelligence can motivate themselves and express empathy for other people.

T F 5. A high Machiavellian manager would be interested in gaining power and controlling the behaviour of other people.

T F 6. A worker who hates the work he does, but loves the salary he receives is likely to experience cognitive dissonance.

T F 7. If one of your employees who is always on time shows up late for work one day, you are likely to make an internal attribution.

8. Which of the following is not a contribution an individual makes in a psychological contract?
   a. Effort
   b. Skills
   c. Salary
   d. Ability
   e. Loyalty

9. Achieving a good person–job fit is difficult for all of the following reasons, except
   a. people change.
   b. organizations change.
   c. hiring procedures are imperfect.
   d. each person is unique.
   e. achieving a good person–job fit is difficult for all of the above reasons.

10. Which of the following "big five" personality dimensions has been linked to higher job performance?
   a. Sensing
   b. Conscientiousness
   c. Intuition
   d. Judging
   e. Perception

11. Janice believes she can do well on the exam if she studies enough. William believes it won't really matter how much or little he studies—his performance all depends on how hard the professor makes the test. Janice and William differ in their
   a. authoritarianism.
   b. Machiavellianism.
   c. self-esteem.
   d. locus of control.
   e. risk propensity.

12. Adam is an ambitious employee who loves his job and intends to keep it, but he knows it offers little, if any, advancement potential. Adam is likely to experience
   a. negative affectivity.
   b. self-efficacy.
   c. openness to experience.
   d. cognitive dissonance.
   e. negative emotionality.

13. Managers ought to expect all of the following from satisfied employees, except
   a. lower absenteeism.
   b. higher levels of productivity.
   c. lower turnover.
   d. positive contributions.
   e. Managers ought to expect all of the above from satisfied employees.

14. Jennifer believes her manager is incompetent. Even when her manager makes a good decision, Jennifer is likely to screen out that information through a process called
   a. selective perception.
   b. stereotyping.
   c. attribution.
   d. distinctiveness.
   e. organizational citizenship.

15. In general, poor person–job fit will likely cause higher
   a. negative affectivity.
   b. self-efficacy.
   c. turnover.
   d. performance.
   e. stereotyping.

Perspectives on Motivation

After studying this chapter, you should be able to:

▶ **Explain the concept of needs and describe the basic motivational process.**

▶ **Describe several historical perspectives on motivation.**

▶ **Discuss important need theories of motivation.**

▶ **Describe the equity theory of motivation.**

▶ **Identify and summarize the components of expectancy theory.**

▶ **Understand the importance of social learning processes and self-efficacy.**

Vancity Credit Union Sees Employee Happiness as a Key to Success

What does it take to be named the top employer in Canada? Making sure that employees are well treated is a key ingredient, according to Vancity. Vancity is Canada's largest credit union. It is located in British Columbia and was named as the best place to work in Canada by both *Canadian Business* and *MacLean's* magazines in 2006.

Vancity uses a number of practices and programs to promote employee satisfaction, commitment, and motivation. One seemingly simple practice is that it pays its employees at rates that are slightly higher than the major Canadian banks that are Vancity's main competitors not only for customers, but also for employees. While it may seem like a common sense approach, it is striking to consider that although Vancity is large for a credit union, it is tiny when compared to the major banks. It is very important to Vancity employees to know they are paid fairly compared with other professionals in their industry.

Employees are also expected to be engaged in the operations of the firm, and in their communities. Vancity uses surveys to gather employee opinions on operations and their level of satisfaction and engagement. It even established a program called "Courageous Conversations" to get more critical feedback from its employees. Vancity also makes significant cash and volunteer investments into a wide variety of community projects, which employees actively support.

Additionally, Vancity has a number of progressive benefits. These include three weeks of vacation each year, the option to swap unused cash-based benefits to take additional time off, employee tuition support to help them further their education, and low-interest mortgage loans.

Slightly less tangible is a program where managers are given a number of gift certificates to Starbuck's Coffee shops. Managers distribute these to employees as an informal way to recognize good effort and performance. Managers also occasionally call the spouses of employees who have put in overtime hours to say thanks to the family.

The fact that executive compensation is in part determined by the results of employee surveys demonstrates the importance Vancity places on employee satisfaction. Why does Vancity put so much time, effort, and resources into their employees? One of the reasons is that Vancity is sincere in its corporate social responsibility efforts. One aspect of being a responsible corporate citizen is to treat employees well. Another reason is simply the bottom line. Dave Mowat, the former CEO of Vancity clearly believes that there is a direct relationship between employee happiness and the firm's profitability.[1]

People work for a wide variety of different reasons. Vancity's workers want money, fair pay, security, and their performance to be acknowledged. Additionally, Vancity realizes that its employees are also motivated to improve their lives outside of work, which is why it provides tuition support and low-interest mortgage loans. This recognizes that people within the same organization have a wide array of needs and motives. Some people want money, some want challenge, and some want to make a contribution. What each unique person in an organization wants from work plays an instrumental role in determining that person's motivation to work.

As we see in this chapter, motivation is vital to all organizations. Often the difference between highly effective organizations and less effective ones lies in the motivations of their members. Thus, managers need to understand the nature of individual motivation, especially as it applies to work situations. This is the first of two chapters dealing with employee motivation. This chapter considers the historical and current perspectives on motivation. Applied motivational techniques will be discussed in the next chapter.

> **Motivation** is the set of forces that leads people to behave in particular ways.

The Nature of Motivation

Motivation is the set of forces that causes people to engage in one behaviour rather than an alternative behaviour.[2] Students who stay up all night to ensure that their term papers are the best they can be, salespersons who work on Saturdays to get ahead, and doctors who make follow-up phone calls to patients to check on their condition are all motivated people. Of course, students who avoid the term paper by spending the day at the beach, salespersons who go home early to escape a tedious sales call, and doctors who skip follow-up calls to have more time for golf are also motivated, but their goals are different. From the manager's viewpoint, the objective is to motivate people to behave in ways that are in the organization's best interest.[3]

The Importance of Motivation

Managers strive to motivate people in the organization to perform at high levels. This means getting them to work hard, to come to work regularly, and to make positive contributions to the organization's mission. But job performance depends on ability and environment as well as motivation. The relationship can be stated as follows:

$$P = M + A + E$$

where P = performance, M = motivation, A = ability, and E = environment.

Motivation is important in organizations because, in conjunction with ability and environment, it determines performance.

To reach high levels of performance, an employee must want to do the job (motivation), must be able to do the job

Motivating performance is an important role for any manager, regardless of the circumstance. Take Lance Armstrong, for instance. During his unprecedented string of victories in the Tour de France, he had to inspire and motivate his team members to do their best each and every day as they pushed forward to victory. And they had to excel under arduous conditions and with no hope of winning—since their job was to help Armstrong!

(ability), and must have the materials, resources, and equipment to do the job (environment). A deficiency in any one of these areas hurts performance. A manager should thus strive to ensure that all three conditions are met.[4]

Motivation is the most difficult factor to manage. An employee who lacks the ability to perform can be sent to training programs to learn new job skills. An employee who cannot learn new skills can be transferred to a simpler job and replaced with a more skilled worker. If an employee lacks materials, resources, or equipment, the manager can take steps to provide them. For example, if a worker cannot complete a project without sales forecast data from marketing, the manager can contact marketing and request that information. But if motivation is deficient, the manager faces the more complex situation of determining what will motivate the employee to work harder.

The Motivational Framework

We can begin to understand motivation by recognizing that it is a complex process with many components and is approached from a variety of different points of view. One attempt to capture the various facets of motivation was developed by Edwin Locke, and is shown in Figure 4.1.

The motivation process begins with a set of needs or drives that lead to what Locke labelled the motivation core of values and motives. For our purposes, the main values and motives contained in the motivation core are best explained by equity theory and expectancy theory, which are discussed in more depth later in this chapter. The basic premise of equity theory is quite simple: people want to feel fairly treated. They want a balance between outcomes they desire from work, inputs they provide to their work, and to be treated fairly compared to other people. Expectancy theory is slightly more complex. Similar to equity theory, it suggests that people have valued outcomes. It also suggests that people will work toward those outcomes if they feel that they can reach an acceptable level of performance, and if they feel that their performance will lead to the valued outcomes they desire.

The central features of the motivation hub are goals and intentions for action. Figure 4.1 demonstrates that once proper conditions of the motivation core are present, once individuals predict fair treatment and expect successful performance with desired outcomes, people will set goals to attain specific levels of performance. However, goals are also affected by individuals' perceived self-efficacy. Self-efficacy is the belief in oneself that a particular level of task performance is doable. Goals and intentions are also affected by expectancies for success and for positive outcomes to follow goal achievement. The sequence concludes with rewards following performance.

At this point, two important psychological processes occur. One is that equity theory re-enters the process, because the rewards are judged by the recipient on whether they seem to be fair. The other is that the recipients will, under proper conditions, perceive a link between their performance and rewards. Finally, satisfaction may occur, again from a variety of sources, which if present will serve as a positive feedback loop to motivate future performance.

This chapter will look extensively at the theoretical approaches that are included in the motivation sequence, focusing mainly on the motivation hub and on self-efficacy, which supports the motivation core. Needs will be considered briefly in the next section of this chapter, Historical Approaches on Motivation. Goal setting, the application technique that directly affects the motivation core and job design, and a theory and set of practices that affect satisfaction will be addressed in the next chapter "Applied Motivation Techniques and Job Design."

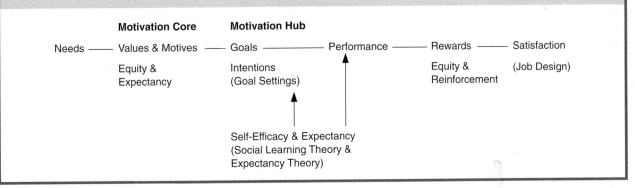

FIGURE 4.1

The Motivation Sequence, Hub, and Core

Locke's model demonstrates that motivation is a very complex process encompassing a variety of components and concepts. Moreover, all of the components of the model are in themselves fairly complex. This chapter and the next discuss the main components of the process to provide a comprehensive understanding of motivation.

Source: Adapted from Edwin A. Locke, "The Motivation Sequence, the Motivation Hub, and the Motivation Core," *Organizational Behavior and Human Decision Processes*, 1991, vol. 50, pp. 288–299.

Motives in Organizations

Individuals in organizations are motivated by a variety of factors. This is not surprising, given the complexity of the motivation sequence shown in Figure 4.1, and given our everyday experience. We probably all know some people who are working at jobs for less pay than they could otherwise earn because they are interested in the job itself or like the flexibility that the job affords. We also probably know people who are primarily if not exclusively motivated by how much money they can make. The key point is that, with so many factors involved, different people will be motivated by different forces.

We may also know people, or have experienced ourselves, situations where jobs that were interesting have become boring, or situations where pay and other working conditions once seen as fair are now perceived as being unfair. It is important to note that not only do people differ in terms of motivating factors, but also that their **motives** can change with time. When you graduate and accept a new job, you may be very satisfied with your compensation. But if you do not receive a raise for several years, you will eventually become quite dissatisfied. Thus, efforts designed to motivate employees to behave in a certain way may lose their effectiveness as employees satisfy one set of valued outcomes, and begin to identify another set. The variety of programs used by Vancity discussed in the opening of this chapter describes how one company recognized that motives differ across employees and can change over time.

A **motive** is a factor that determines a person's choice of one course of behaviour from among several possibilities.

Historical Perspectives on Motivation

Historical views on motivation, although not always accurate, are of interest for several reasons. For one thing, they provide a foundation for contemporary thinking about motivation. For another, because they generally were based on common sense and intuition, an appreciation of their strengths and weaknesses can help managers gain useful insights into employee motivation in the workplace.

Early Views of Motivation

One early view of motivation was based on the concept of **hedonism**: the notion that people seek pleasure and comfort and avoid pain and discomfort.

The concept of hedonism—the idea that people seek pleasure and comfort and try to avoid pain and discomfort—dominated early thinking on human motivation.[5] Although this seems reasonable, there are many kinds of behaviour that it cannot explain. For example, why do recreational athletes exert themselves willingly and regularly, whereas a hedonist would prefer to relax? Why do volunteers work tirelessly to collect money for charitable causes? Why do some employees work extra hard, when a hedonist would prefer to loaf? As experts recognized that hedonism is an extremely limited—and often incorrect—view of human behaviour, other perspectives emerged.

The Scientific Management Approach

As noted in Chapter 1, Frederick W. Taylor, the chief advocate of scientific management, assumed that employees are economically motivated and work to earn as much money as they can.[6] Taylor once used the case of a Bethlehem Steel worker named Schmidt to illustrate the importance of money in motivation. Schmidt's job was to move heavy pieces of iron called "pigs" from one pile to another. He appeared to be doing an adequate job and regularly met the standard of 1100 kg per day. Taylor, however, believed that Schmidt was strong enough to do much more. To test his ideas, Taylor designed a piece-rate pay system that would award Schmidt a fixed sum of money for each ton of iron he loaded. Then he had the following conversation with Schmidt and observed his work:

Taylor: "Schmidt, are you a high-priced man?"

Schmidt: "Well, I don't know what you mean."

[Several minutes of conversation ensue.]

Taylor: "Well, if you are a high-priced man, you will do exactly as this [supervisor] tells you tomorrow, from morning until night. When he tells you to pick up [a piece of iron] and walk, you pick it up and walk, and when he tells you to sit down and rest, you sit down and rest. You do that right straight through the day. And what's more, no back talk. Do you understand that?"

Scientific management assumed that employees are motivated by money.

The human relations approach to motivation suggested that favourable employee attitudes result in motivation to work hard.

The next day Schmidt started to work, and all day long and at regular intervals was told by the supervisor who stood over him with a watch, "Now pick up a pig and walk. Now sit down and rest. Now walk, now rest." He worked when he was told to work, rested when he was told to rest, and by half-past five in the afternoon had loaded 4300 kg on the car. And he practically never failed to work at this pace and do the task that was set him during the three years Taylor was at Bethlehem.[7]

Recent evidence suggests that Taylor may have fabricated the conversation just related; Schmidt himself may have been an invention.[8] If so, Taylor's willingness to lie shows just how strongly he believed in his economic view of human motivation and in the need to spread the doctrine. But researchers soon recognized that scientific management's assumptions about motivation could not always explain complex human behaviour. The next perspective on motivation to emerge was the human relations approach.

The Human Relations Approach

The human relations approach, which we also discussed in Chapter 1, arose from the Hawthorne studies.[9] Douglas McGregor's popular Theory X and Theory Y, for example, exemplified this view of employee motivation. The human relations perspective suggested that people are motivated by things other than money; in particular, employees are motivated by and respond to their social environment at work. Favourable employee attitudes, such as job satisfaction, were presumed to result in improved employee performance. In Chapter 5, we explore this relationship in more detail. At this point it is sufficient to say, as we did in Chapter 1, that the human relations approach left many questions about human behaviour unanswered. However, one of the primary theorists associated with this movement, Abraham Maslow, helped develop an important need theory of motivation.

Need Theories of Motivation

Need theories represent the starting point for most contemporary thought on motivation,[10] although these theories too attracted critics.[11] The basic premise of need theories is that humans are motivated primarily by deficiencies in one or more important needs or need categories. Need theorists have attempted to identify and categorize the needs that are most important to people. The best-known need theories are the hierarchy of needs and the ERG theory.

> **Need theories** of motivation assume that need deficiencies cause behaviour.

The Hierarchy of Needs   The **hierarchy of needs**, developed by psychologist Abraham Maslow in the 1940s, is the best-known need theory.[12] Influenced by the human relations school, Maslow argued that human beings have innate desires to satisfy a given set of needs. Furthermore, Maslow believed that these needs are arranged in a hierarchy of importance, with the most basic needs at the foundation of the hierarchy.

> Maslow's **hierarchy of needs** theory assumes that human needs are arranged in a hierarchy of importance.

Figure 4.2 shows Maslow's hierarchy of needs. The most basic needs in the hierarchy are *physiological needs*. They include the needs for food, sex, and air. Next in the hierarchy are *security needs*: things that offer safety and security, such as adequate housing and clothing and freedom from worry and anxiety. *Belongingness needs*, the third level in the hierarchy, are primarily social. Examples include the need for love and affection and the need to be accepted by peers. The fourth level, *esteem needs*, actually encompasses two slightly different kinds of needs: the need for a positive self-image and self-respect and the need to be respected by others. At the top of the hierarchy are *self-actualization needs*. These involve realizing our full potential and becoming all that we can be.

Maslow believed that each need level must be satisfied before the level above it becomes important. Thus, once physiological needs have been satisfied, their importance diminishes, and security needs emerge as the primary sources of motivation. This escalation up the hierarchy continues until the self-actualization needs become primary motivators.

Maslow's needs hierarchy makes a certain amount of intuitive sense. And because it was the first motivation theory to be popularized, it is also one of the best known among practising managers. Yet research has revealed a number of deficiencies in the theory. For example, five levels of needs are not always present, the actual hierarchy of needs does not always conform to Maslow's model, and need structures are more unstable and variable than the theory would lead us to believe.[13] Thus, the theory's primary contribution seems to lie in the conceptual legacy that has influenced many modern motivation theories. As we will see later in this chapter, Maslow's humanistic philosophy, particularly his notions of esteem and self-actualization needs, continue to shape the field.

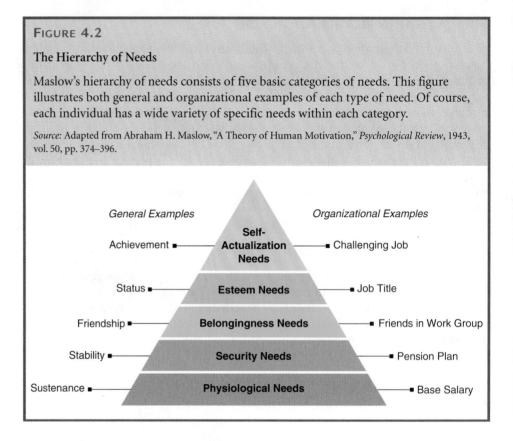

FIGURE 4.2

The Hierarchy of Needs

Maslow's hierarchy of needs consists of five basic categories of needs. This figure illustrates both general and organizational examples of each type of need. Of course, each individual has a wide variety of specific needs within each category.

Source: Adapted from Abraham H. Maslow, "A Theory of Human Motivation," *Psychological Review*, 1943, vol. 50, pp. 374–396.

The **ERG theory** represents an extension and refinement of the needs hierarchy theory. It describes **existence, relatedness** and **growth needs.** It suggests that if people become frustrated trying to satisfy one set of needs, they will regress to the previously satisfied set of needs.

ERG Theory   The **ERG theory,** developed by Yale psychologist Clayton Alderfer, extends and refines Maslow's needs hierarchy concept, although there are several important differences between the two.[14] The E, R, and G stand for three basic need categories: existence, relatedness, and growth. **Existence needs**—those necessary for basic human survival—roughly correspond to the physiological and security needs of Maslow's hierarchy. **Relatedness needs,** involving the need to relate to others, are similar to Maslow's belongingness and esteem needs. Finally, **growth needs** are analogous to Maslow's needs for self-esteem and self-actualization.

In contrast to Maslow's approach, ERG theory suggests that more than one kind of need, for example, relatedness and growth needs, motivates a person at the same time. A more important difference from Maslow's hierarchy is that ERG theory includes a satisfaction-progression component and a frustration-regression component (see Figure 4.3). The satisfaction-progression concept suggests that after satisfying one category of needs, a person progresses to the next level. On this point, the need hierarchy and ERG theory agree. The need hierarchy, however, assumes the individual remains at the next level until the needs at that level are satisfied. In contrast, the frustration-regression component of ERG theory suggests that a person who is frustrated in trying to satisfy a higher level of needs eventually will regress to the preceding level.[15]

The **dual-structure theory** identifies motivation factors, which affect satisfaction, and hygiene factors, which determine dissatisfaction.

Hygiene factors are extrinsic to the work itself and include factors such as pay and job security.

Dual-Structure Theory   Frederick Herzberg and his associates developed the **dual-structure theory** in the late 1950s and early 1960s.[16] Herzberg proposed that jobs consist of two factors. One is the work context, or **hygiene factor**. Elements of the hygiene factor include pay, job security, supervisors, and working conditions.

FIGURE 4.3

The ERG theory

The ERG theory includes an important process missing from other need hierarchies—the frustration-regression component, which suggests that if a person becomes frustrated attempting to satisfy one level of needs, he or she may regress to a need level that was previously satisfied. Only if a need level is satisfied does the person progress to a higher level.

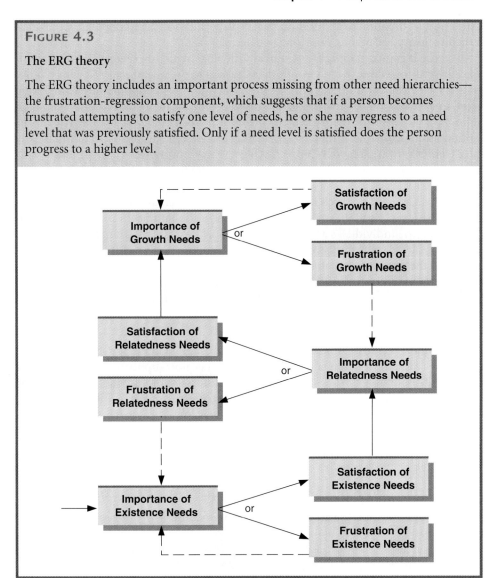

Generally, the hygiene factor addresses lower-order needs. If seen as inadequate, these lead to feelings of dissatisfaction. When these factors are considered acceptable, however, a person may still not necessarily be satisfied; rather, he or she may simply be not dissatisfied.[17] The second, the **motivation factor**, includes such aspects as achievement and recognition that were thought to be primary causes of satisfaction and motivation. Motivators operate on growth-oriented needs. When present in a job, these factors apparently could cause satisfaction and motivation; when they were absent, the result was feelings of no satisfaction rather than dissatisfaction.

To use the dual-structure theory in the workplace, Herzberg recommended a two-stage process. First, the manager should try to eliminate situations that cause dissatisfaction, which Herzberg assumed to be the more basic of the two dimensions. Once this is accomplished, motivators should be improved through a technique called *job enrichment* for structuring employee tasks.[18] (We discuss job enrichment in Chapter 5.)

Motivation factors are intrinsic to the work itself and include factors such as achievement and recognition.

This unusual attention to application may explain the widespread popularity the dual-structure theory had among practising managers.

Because it gained popularity so quickly, the dual-structure theory has been scientifically scrutinized more than most other theories in organizational behaviour.[19] The results have been contradictory, to say the least. Studies that use methods other than Herzberg's measures of satisfaction and dissatisfaction usually find results that fail to support the dual-factor theory.[20] If the theory is *method bound*, as it appears to be, its validity is questionable. Other critics say that Herzberg's sample of accountants and engineers from which he developed the theory may not represent the general working population. Furthermore, they maintain that the theory fails to account for individual differences.

Also, subsequent research has found that a factor such as pay may affect satisfaction in one sample and dissatisfaction in another, and that the effect of a given factor depends on the individual's age and organizational level. In addition, the theory does not define the relationship between satisfaction and motivation.[21] It is not surprising, then, that the dual-structure theory is no longer held in high esteem by organizational behaviour researchers.[22] Indeed, the field has since adopted far more complex and valid conceptualizations of motivation, most of which we discuss here and in Chapter 5.

Need-Based Theories: Concluding Thoughts

Craig Pinder of the University of Victoria notes that although research has not supported need hierarchy theories, it is not appropriate to completely abandon the underlying concepts of the approach. He suggests that "there are predictable patterns among people at various life and career stages in the desires they express on their jobs."[23] Generally speaking, all of the need-based approaches are historically important. Like Maslow's need hierarchy, they contributed to the way that we think about motivation.

Reinforcement Theory and Behaviour Modification

Another important historical foundation for motivation is organizational behaviour modification (OB mod). This approach was popular during the 1970s, but has more recently been displaced by social-cognitive theory, which is discussed later in this chapter. OB mod was based on principles of operant learning, particularly, reinforcement theory.

Reinforcement theory is based on the idea that behaviour is a function of its consequences.

Reinforcement theory (also called operant conditioning) is generally associated with the work of B. F. Skinner.[24] In its simplest form, **reinforcement theory** suggests that behaviour is a function of its consequences.[25] Behaviour that results in pleasant consequences is more likely to be repeated (the employee will be motivated to repeat the current behaviour), and behaviour that results in unpleasant consequences is less likely to be repeated (the employee will be motivated to engage in different behaviours). Reinforcement theory also suggests that in any given situation, people explore a variety of possible behaviours. Future behavioural choices are affected by the consequences of earlier behaviours.

Reinforcement is the consequence of behaviour.

Types of Reinforcement in Organizations

The consequences of behaviour are called **reinforcement**. Managers can use various kinds of reinforcement to affect employee behaviour. The four basic forms of reinforcement—positive reinforcement, avoidance, extinction, and punishment—are summarized in Figure 4.4.

Positive reinforcement is a reward or other desirable consequence that a person receives after exhibiting behaviour.

Positive reinforcement is a reward or other desirable consequence that follows behaviour. Providing positive reinforcement after a particular behaviour motivates employees to maintain or increase the frequency of that behaviour.[26] A compliment

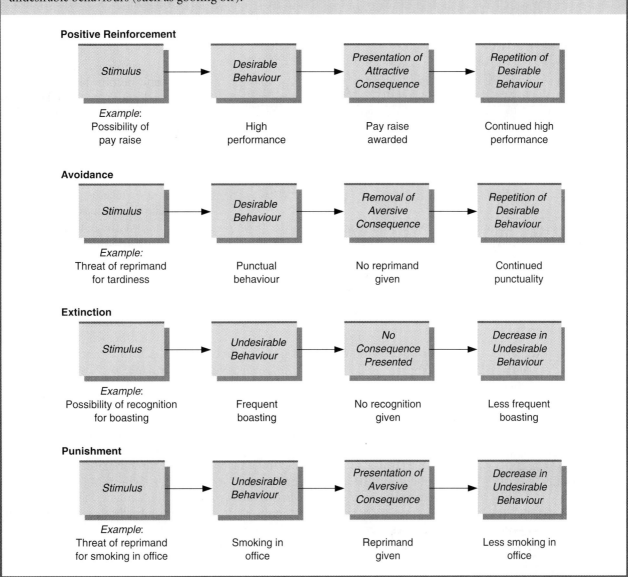

FIGURE 4.4

Kinds of Reinforcement

The four basic kinds of reinforcement managers can use to motivate employee behaviour. The first two, positive reinforcement and avoidance, can be used to motivate employees to continue to engage in desirable behaviours (such as working hard). The other two, extinction and punishment, might be used to motivate employees to change undesirable behaviours (such as goofing off).

from the boss after completing a difficult job and a salary increase following a period of high performance are examples of positive reinforcement.

Avoidance, also known as negative reinforcement, is another means of increasing the frequency of desirable behaviour. Rather than receiving a reward following a desirable behaviour, the person is given the opportunity to avoid an unpleasant consequence. For example, suppose that a boss habitually criticizes employees who dress

Avoidance, or **negative reinforcement**, is the opportunity to avoid or escape from an unpleasant circumstance after exhibiting behaviour.

Positive reinforcement, of course, can be a powerful force in organizations and can help sustain motivated behaviours. But in order to really work, reinforcement should be of value to the individual and conform to one of the five schedules, as discussed in the text. However, if someone is truly desperate for a pat on the back, a simple device such as the one shown here might have some hidden market potential!

casually. To avoid criticism, an employee may routinely dress to suit the supervisor's tastes. The employee is motivated to engage in desirable behaviour (at least from the supervisor's viewpoint) to avoid an unpleasant, or aversive, consequence.

Extinction decreases the frequency of behaviour, especially behaviour that was previously rewarded. If rewards are withdrawn for behaviours that were previously reinforced, the behaviours will probably become less frequent and eventually die out. For example, a manager with a small staff may encourage frequent visits from subordinates as a way to keep in touch with what is going on. Positive reinforcement might include cordial conversation, attention to subordinates' concerns, and encouragement to come in again soon. As the staff grows, however, the manager may find that such unstructured conversations make it difficult to get his or her own job done. The manager then might brush off casual conversation and reward only to-the-point business conversations. Withdrawing the rewards for casual chatting will probably extin-

> **Extinction** decreases the frequency of behaviour by eliminating a reward or desirable consequence that follows that behaviour.

guish that behaviour. We should also note that if managers, inadvertently or otherwise, cease to reward valuable behaviours such as good performance and punctuality, those behaviours too may become extinct.[27]

Punishment, like extinction, also tends to decrease the frequency of undesirable behaviours. **Punishment** is an unpleasant, or aversive, consequence of a behaviour.[28] Examples of punishment are verbal or written reprimands, pay cuts, loss of privileges, layoffs, and termination. Many experts question the value of punishment and believe that managers use it too often and use it inappropriately. In some situations, however, punishment may be an appropriate tool for altering behaviour. Many instances of life's unpleasantness teach us what to do by means of punishment. Falling off a bike, drinking too much, or going out in the rain without an umbrella all lead to punishing consequences (getting bruised, suffering a hangover, and getting wet), and we often learn to change our behaviour as a result. Furthermore, certain types of undesirable behaviour may have far-reaching negative effects if they go unpunished. For instance, an employee who sexually harasses a coworker, a clerk who steals money from the petty cash account, and an executive who engages in illegal stock transactions all deserve punishment.

> **Punishment** is an unpleasant, or aversive, consequence that results from behaviour.

Behaviour Modification in Organizations

Organizational behaviour modification, or **OB mod**, is the application of reinforcement theory to people in organizational settings.[29] Reinforcement theory says that we can increase the frequency of desirable behaviours by linking those behaviours with positive consequences and decrease undesirable

> **Organizational behaviour modification**, or **OB mod**, is the application of reinforcement theory to people in organizational settings.

behaviours by linking them with negative consequences. OB mod characteristically uses positive reinforcement to encourage desirable behaviours in employees. Figure 4.5 illustrates the basic steps in OB mod.

The first step is to identify performance-related behavioural events—that is, desirable and undesirable behaviours. A manager of an electronics store might decide that the most important behaviour for salespeople working on commission is to greet customers warmly and show them the exact merchandise they came in to see. Note in Figure 4.5 that three kinds of organizational activity are associated with this behaviour: the behavioural event itself, the performance that results, and the organizational consequences that befall the individual.

Next, the manager measures baseline performance—the existing level of performance for each individual. This usually is stated in terms of a percentage frequency across different time intervals. For example, the electronics store manager may observe that a particular salesperson presently is greeting around 40 percent of the customers each day as desired.

The third step is to identify the existing behavioural contingencies, or consequences, of performance; that is, what happens now to employees who perform at various levels? If an employee works hard, does he or she get a reward or just get tired? The electronics store manager may observe that when customers are greeted warmly and assisted competently, they buy something 40 percent of the time, whereas customers who are not properly greeted and assisted make a purchase only 20 percent of the time.

At this point, the manager develops and applies an appropriate intervention strategy. In other words, some element of the performance-reward linkage—structure, process, technology, groups, or the task—is changed to make high-level performance more rewarding. Various kinds of positive reinforcement are used to guide employee behaviour in desired directions. The electronics store manager might offer a sales commission plan whereby salespeople earn a percentage of the dollar amount taken in by each sale. The manager might also compliment salespeople who give appropriate greetings and ignore those who do not. The reinforcement helps shape the behaviour of salespeople. In addition, an individual salesperson who does not get reinforced may imitate the behaviour of more successful salespersons.[30] In general, this step relies on the reward system in the organization, as discussed previously.

After the intervention step, the manager again measures performance to determine whether the desired effect has been achieved. If not, the manager must redesign the intervention strategy or repeat the entire process. For instance, if the salespeople in the electronics store are still not greeting customers properly, the manager may need to look for other forms of positive reinforcement—perhaps a higher commission.

If performance has increased, the manager must try to maintain the desirable behaviour through some schedule of positive reinforcement. For example, higher commissions might be granted for every other sale, for sales over a certain dollar amount, and so forth.

Finally, the manager looks for improvements in individual employees' behaviour. Here the emphasis is on offering significant longer-term rewards, such as promotions and salary adjustments, to sustain ongoing efforts to improve performance.

Criticisms of OB Mod   A number of criticisms have been levelled at OB mod. From a practical point of view, it is frequently difficult to implement. OB mod works best when the target behaviour is easily measurable and has been successfully used to improve safety practices or reduce absenteeism.[31] It does not work when measurements are unreliable. Furthermore, it is also sometimes difficult to find effective reinforcers, because not all people will respond to the same outcomes.[32] It has also been questioned

FIGURE 4.5

Steps in Organizational Behaviour Modification

Organizational behaviour modification involves using reinforcement theory to motivate employee behaviour. By employing the steps shown here, managers can often isolate behaviours they value and then link specific rewards to those behaviours. As a result, employees will be more likely to engage in those behaviours in the future.

Source: "The Management of Behavioural Contingencies," by Fred Luthans et al. Reprinted from *Personnel,* July–August 1974, by permission of American Management Association, New York. © 1974.

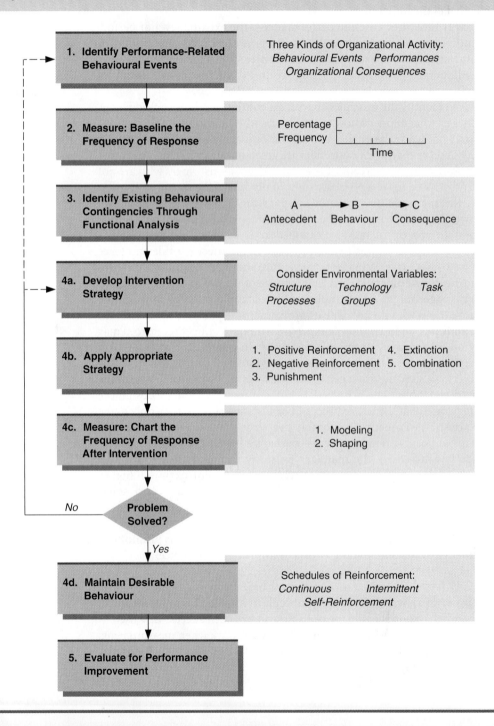

on ethical grounds. Measurement can be unethical if it is overly intrusive or secretive. Other critics question the ethicality of OB mod because it is seen as being overtly manipulative and dehumanizing.

OB mod has also been questioned based on its theoretical underpinnings. In particular, although not completely fair, some critics argued that OB mod is based on "environmental determinism," which discounts the role of thought processes in motivation. Pinder notes that by the mid-1980s there was a "decline of the behaviourist camp," and that the field progressed to recognize a balance between cognitive processes and reinforcers.[33] Latham and Pinder recently noted that little attention has been given to behaviourism over the past couple of decades, and it has largely been replaced by interest in social-cognitive theory, discussed later in this chapter.[34] Still, reinforcement theory and OB mod have had important influences on our understanding of learning and motivation. As we will see later, rewards and punishments, and especially how they are perceived to be linked to performance are key features of social-cognitive theory. With this in mind, we now turn to more current theories of motivation.

Current Approaches to Motivation

Organizational Justice

Recall from Figure 4.1 that part of the "motivation core" is the notion of equity, which recognizes that people in organizations want to be treated fairly. Equity theory was developed in the late 1950s and early 1960s. This research focused on the fairness of how a variety of outcomes, such as pay, job titles, and other benefits are distributed. Equity theory is considered one facet of organizational justice and is now considered an aspect of "distributive justice." Researchers noted that while distributive justice plays an important role in overall perceived fairness, other forms of justice are also important. One additional factor is procedural justice, which deals with the fairness of processes that are used in distributing outcomes. Interactional justice, or the degree to which employees feel they are treated with dignity and respect is another important determinant of fairness.[35] Although organizational justice was discussed in Chapter 3 as an important determinant of attitudes, we will revisit it here within the framework of motivation, and begin this discussion of justice with the equity theory of motivation.

The Equity Theory of Motivation
The **equity theory** of motivation, one of the components of the motivation core in Figure 4.1, is based on the relatively simple premise that people in organizations want to be treated fairly.[36] The theory defines **equity** as the belief that we are being treated fairly compared with others and **inequity** as the belief that we are being treated unfairly compared with others. Equity theory is just one of several theoretical formulations derived from social comparison processes.[37] Social comparisons involve evaluating our own situation in terms of others' situations. We focus now mainly on equity theory because it is the most highly developed of the social comparison approaches and the one that applies most directly to the work motivation of people in organizations.

> **Equity theory** focuses on people's desire to be treated with what they perceive as equity and to avoid perceived inequity.

> **Equity** is the belief that we are being treated fairly in relation to others; **inequity** is the belief that we are being treated unfairly in relation to others.

Forming Equity Perceptions
People in organizations form perceptions of the equity of their treatment through a four-step process. First, they evaluate how they are being treated by the firm. Second, they form a perception of how a comparison-other is being treated. The comparison-other might be a person in the same work group, someone in

another part of the organization, or even a composite of several people scattered throughout the organization. Third, they compare their own circumstances with those of the comparison-other, and this comparison is the basis for a perception of either equity or inequity. Fourth, depending on the strength of this feeling, the person may choose to pursue one or more of the alternatives discussed in the next section.

Equity theory describes the equity comparison process in terms of an input-to-outcome ratio. Inputs are an individual's contributions to the organization—such factors as education, experience, effort, and loyalty. Outcomes are what the person receives in return—pay, recognition, social relationships, intrinsic rewards, and similar things. Thus, this part of the equity process is essentially a personal assessment of one's psychological contract. A person's assessments of inputs and outcomes for both self and others are based partly on objective data (for example, the person's own salary) and partly on perceptions (such as the comparison-other's level of recognition). The equity comparison thus takes the following form:

> People form perceptions of equity or inequity by comparing what they give to the organization to what they get back and by comparing this ratio to the ratio they perceive others as receiving.

$$\frac{\text{Outcomes (self)}}{\text{Inputs (self)}} \quad \text{compared with} \quad \frac{\text{Outcomes (other)}}{\text{Inputs (other)}}$$

If the two sides of this psychological equation are in balance, the person experiences a feeling of equity; if the two sides do not balance, a feeling of inequity results. We should stress, however, that a perception of equity does not require that the perceived outcomes and inputs be equal, but only that their ratios be the same. A person may believe that his or her comparison-other deserves to make more money because she or he works harder, thus making the higher ratio of outcome to input acceptable. Only if the other person's outcomes seem disproportionate to inputs does the comparison provoke a perception of inequity. The Employment Equity and . . . Ethics box highlights some ethical considerations pertaining to employment equity in Canada. Advocates of employment equity argue that historic discrimination against women, people with disabilities, aboriginal peoples, and visible minorities must be eliminated through legislation. Critics of the policy counter by suggesting that the law causes reverse discrimination, detracts from merit-based systems, and that demographic and accompanying social changes will remedy past discrimination.

Responses to Equity and Inequity   Figure 4.6 summarizes the results of an equity comparison. The perception of equity generally motivates the person to maintain the status quo. She continues to provide the same level of input to the organization as long as her outcomes do not change and the inputs and outcomes of the comparison-other do not change. A person who perceives inequity, however, is motivated to reduce it, and the greater the inequity, the stronger the level of motivation.

> People may have a variety of responses in an effort to maintain perceived equity or reduce perceived inequity.

People use one of six common methods to reduce inequity.[38] First, we may change our own inputs. Thus, we may put more or less effort into the job, depending on which way the inequity lies, as a way to alter our ratio. If we believe we are being underpaid, for example, we may decide not to work as hard.

Second, we may change our own outcomes. We might, for example, demand a pay raise, seek additional avenues for growth and development, or even resort to stealing as a way to get more from the organization. Or we might alter our perceptions of the value of our current outcomes, say by deciding that our present level of job security is greater and more valuable than we originally thought.

A third, more complex response is to alter our perceptions of ourselves and our behaviour. After perceiving an inequity, for example, we may change our original self-assessment and thus decide that we are really contributing less but receiving more than we originally believed. For example, we might decide that we are not really working as many hours as we first thought—that some of the time spent in the office is really just socializing.

Fourth, we may alter our perception of the other's inputs or outcomes. After all, much of our assessment of other people is based on perceptions, and perceptions can be changed. For example, if we feel under-rewarded, we may decide that our comparison-other is working more hours than we originally believed—say by coming in on weekends and taking work home at night.

Fifth, we may change the object of comparison. We may conclude, for instance, that the current comparison-other is the boss's personal favourite, is unusually lucky, or has special skills and abilities. A different person would thus provide a more valid basis for comparison. Indeed, we might change comparison-others fairly often.

Finally, as a last resort, we may simply leave the situation. That is, we might decide that the only way to feel better about things is to be in a different situation altogether.

> ### FIGURE 4.6
>
> **Responses to Perceptions of Equity and Inequity**
>
> People form equity perceptions by comparing their situation with that of someone else. If they experience equity, they are motivated to maintain the current situation. If they experience inequity, they are motivated to use one or more of the strategies shown to reduce the inequity.
>
>
> Comparison of Self with Other
>
> Inequity
>
> Equity
>
> Motivation to Reduce Inequity:
> 1. Change Inputs
> 2. Change Outcomes
> 3. Alter Perceptions of Self
> 4. Alter Perception of Other
> 5. Change Comparisons
> 6. Leave Situation
>
> Motivation to Maintain Current Situation

Transferring to another department or seeking a new job may be the only way to reduce inequity.

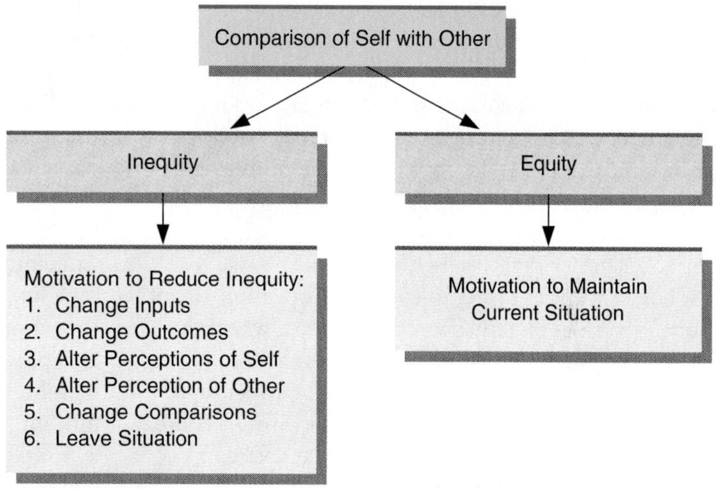

An interesting example of how equity theory works in practice is the 1998 strike of the pilots at Air Canada. When the pilots went out on strike, one of their main complaints was that their wages were 20 percent to 30 percent lower than pilots working for major American-based airlines. Officials from Air Canada argued that they could not afford to pay those kinds of salaries, and that the Air Canada pilots should be comparing themselves with pilots from other Canadian airlines. It is clear that the Air Canada pilots felt they were underpaid and they used American pilots as the comparison-other. Air Canada used a comparison point of their own budget and suggested that the pilots should compare themselves to a different group.[39]

Evaluation and Implications Much of the earliest research on equity theory was narrowly focused, dealing with only one ratio, between pay (hourly and piece-rate) and the quality or quantity of worker output given overpayment and underpayment.[40] Findings support the predictions of equity theory quite consistently, especially when the worker feels underpaid. When people being paid on a piece-rate basis experience inequity, they tend to reduce their inputs by decreasing quality and to increase their outcomes by producing more units of work. When a person paid by the hour experiences inequity, the theory predicts an increase in quality and quantity if the person feels overpaid and a decrease in quality and quantity if the person feels underpaid. Research provides stronger support for responses to underpayment than for responses to overpayment, but overall, most studies appear to uphold the basic premises of the

Employment Equity and . . .  **ETHICS**

Employment Equity in Canada

The 1995 Employment Equity Act requires that many private- and public-sector organizations take actions to eliminate practices that discriminate against women, aboriginal peoples, people with disabilities, and visible minorities. The goal of the legislation is to have representation of these designated groups in all occupational categories proportional to their representation in the Canadian workforce, or identifiable subsections of the workforce. This latter clause is in recognition that it may not be possible in some cases to achieve representation proportional to the population if too few people in the designated groups possess the necessary qualifications, such as levels of education, professional licenses, and the like.

The Act requires that employers develop employment equity plans that identify occupational areas where the designated groups are currently underrepresented, then develop strategies through which to reach proper representation. Employers must document the hiring, training, promotion, and retention practices used to overcome underrepresentation of people in the designated groups. They must also report salary ranges for all occupational groups, and the number of people from the designated groups who hold positions within each occupation.

Employment Equity is a good name for the act, because it is clear that the intention is to apply concepts similar to those included in the equity theory of motivation. The Act attempts to get employers to focus on inputs that are important for job performance, such as skills, education, and abilities, and forbids employers to make decisions based on inconsequential inputs of gender, ethnicity, skin colour, or disability. Furthermore, the Act attempts to ensure that outcomes, such as promotions and pay levels, reflect proper inputs.

Debates about the Act have been fierce. Supporters argue that employment equity legislation and voluntary programs help to reduce the wage gap between white males and all other groups. They also contend that employment equity can be achieved without diminishing merit. Indeed, the 1995 Act expressly notes that employers are not required to hire or promote unqualified people or without regard to merit. Nonetheless, detractors of the legislation claim that this type of legislation lowers employment standards, hires and promotes people for who or what they are rather than the skills that they possess, creates reverse discrimination, and costs too much money to implement. Furthermore, some critics suggest that the existing wage gap is an artifact resulting because white males have been in the workforce at higher rates for a longer period of time than the designated groups, so their average salaries are naturally higher. Designated groups will catch up on their own, they suggest, because members of the designated groups now constitute a significant portion of the labour force.

Employers cannot ignore such a significant component of the labour force, and will have to pay people from the designated groups higher wages to maintain skilled employees. However, Jean Helms Mills of Saint Mary's University in Halifax noted that actual changes in employment practices have been slow despite the legislation. She argues that organizational cultures must significantly change if employment equity is to become a reality.

Clearly, the debate will continue for years to come.

Sources: Employment Equity Act, Government of Canada website: <canada.justicce.gc.ca>. Joanne D. Leck and Sylvie St. Onge, "Wage Gap Changes Among Organizations Subject to the Employment Equity Act," *Canadian Journal of Public Policy*, 1995, vol. 21, pp. 387–401; Dave Cunningham, "Big Wins for Women and Minorities," *Alberta Report*, 11 August 1997. Jean Helms Mills, "Organizational Change and Representations of Women in a North American Utility Company," *Gender, Work and Organization*. Vol. 12 No. 3 May 2005 pp. 242–269.

theory.[41] Later research successfully demonstrated equity theory's predictions using non-monetary outcomes such as job titles and office size, and perceived fairness in performance evaluations.[42]

However, other researchers have found that not everyone responds the same to either equitable or inequitable situations. Rather, some people are more sensitive than others to perceptions of inequity. That is, some people pay a good deal of attention to their relative standing in the organization. Others focus more on their own situation without considering the situations of others.[43]

Social comparisons clearly are a powerful factor in the workplace.[44] For managers, the most important implication of equity theory concerns organizational rewards and reward systems. Because *formal* organizational rewards (pay, task assignments, and so forth) are more easily observable than *informal* rewards (intrinsic satisfaction, feelings of accomplishment, and so forth), they are often central to a person's perceptions of equity.

Procedural and Interactional Justice   Although equity theory is useful in understanding perceptions of justice, it does not explain all aspects of fairness. Recall from the introduction to this topic that equity theory focuses on the distribution of outcomes. Research on equity theory has demonstrated that people are responsive to the fairness of the distribution outcomes. But perceived justice is affected by other considerations beyond how much of something someone receives.

Consider a case, for example, where an employee received an unexpected promotion. When the employee asks why the promotion was granted, it is explained that the decision was made based on a random draw of people with equal seniority. Although the promoted employee might be happy with the outcome (the distribution), he or she may not feel that the decision-making process was fair. And most certainly, other employees who did not receive the promotion will be dissatisfied with both the outcome and the process.

Let's add one more dimension to this scene. Suppose when the promoted employee asked why he or she was promoted, the answer was: "Well, John, the previous manager, just up and left. We were in a jam. Somebody's got to do the job, so we threw your names in a hat and picked you. We figured you'd probably be no worse than anyone else. You gotta problem with that?" Compare that with another possible response: "John suddenly quit. Since this is the busy time of the year for us, we wanted to fill the position quickly. We figured that all of you who reported to John were equally qualified, so we thought the fairest and quickest solution was a random draw. I'm sure you can do the job." The first response is low on interactional justice, while the second is better.

Procedural Justice   Procedural justice is perceived when decision-making methods, including the distribution of outcomes, are thought to be fair. One framework describes six components of procedural justice. They are: 1) consistency, that the same criteria are used to make decisions in similar cases; 2) bias-suppression, that individuals will not make self-serving decisions; 3) accuracy, that accurate information or data are used to arrive at a decision; 4) correctability, that there is a way to appeal and, if necessary, change incorrect decisions; 5) ethicality, that the process is generally believed to be moral or ethical; and 6) representativeness, that all parties believe their views have been considered in the decision-making process.[45] Generally speaking, procedures are fairest if they cover all components. Procedural injustice can be felt if even one of the components is missing. See the Justice and . . . Research box for an example of how procedural justice can work in organizations.

Interactional Justice   Interactional justice is the question of whether a person feels that he or she has been treated with respect. Important determinants of inteactional justice are whether decisions have been fully explained, if the person delivering the message is sincere, and if the messenger appears to care about the other party.[46]

The three forms of justice often interact. Unfavourable outcomes, or low distributive justice, frequently triggers considerations about procedural and interactional justice. Some research has shown that unfavourable outcomes are relatively more acceptable if they were thought to be the result of fair procedures, and delivered with

Procedural Justice in Action

In the mid-1990s the government of Canada decided to privatize the Canadian Air Navigation System (ANS). A team of researchers was invited to examine the process in the Atlantic Region as the ANS was moved from being a subsection of Transport Canada to a fee-standing, not-for-profit organization that became known as NavCan. Two of the authors of this book, Dan Coleman, of the University of New Brunswick (Fredericton), and Greg Irving, now of Wilfred Laurier University, were the lead researchers. At various times, Jim Tolliver, also of UNB, Christine Cooper, now of Susquehanna University in Selinsgrove, Pennsylvania, and Ramona Bobacel of the University of Waterloo took part in the research.

The perceptions of procedural justice were collected using surveys from employees who were experiencing a fundamental change in organizational structure. Specifically, the ANS was being "commercialized" (that is, sold to private sector interests to be run as a not-for-profit agency) at the time of the study. While Transport Canada headquarters—located in Ottawa—established many of the policies through which the change was to be implemented, regional "implementation teams" were also established to conduct some planning, make decisions about who would be assigned to NavCan and who would stay with Transport Canada, and communicate with the employees as decisions and changes were made.

During the time of the data collection many decisions were being made, such as the assignment of jobs and individuals to the new entity, pension portability, whether employees would receive severance pay upon being released by the Canadian Government to the new entity, and so on. The change itself, although creating painful uncertainties for the affected employees, could not be labelled as either blatantly positive or negative. As a matter of fact, focus groups held with some employees revealed that most were looking forward to the change.

The researchers chose to focus on a key aspect of the change: the assignment of specific jobs to Transport Canada or to the new agency. These job assignments had significant personal and professional implications for

those who would stay with Transport Canada or go to the new entity. One set of data was collected one full year before the actual ownership change took place, shortly after the assignments were made official, but before the form of the new entity was finalized.

In addition to conducting a survey, members of the implementation team were interviewed, archival sources were examined, and discussions with a focus group of employees affected by the changes were held. Information from these sources suggests that the policies guiding the change—particularly about how or whether to assign jobs to the new entity—followed most of Leventhal's (1980) procedural justice rules.

A "consistent set of rules" was provided by a policy manual on how or whether jobs were to be assigned to the new entity; these rules should have led to "bias suppression." Specifically, positions were assigned to the new entity based upon the amount of time that the incumbents dedicated directly to the ANS. For example, air traffic controllers (by definition) dedicated 100 percent of their time to ANS. However, support staff such as human resources and finance, dedicated more or less time directly to ANS. The organization went to great lengths to gather accurate information regarding the amount of time each incumbent's position was dedicated to ANS. Information was requested from and supplied by supervisors and incumbents. An appeal process was established so job assignments could be reconsidered (Leventhal's "correctability" and "representativeness" rules). In sum these aspects of the change generally led to perceptions of "ethicality."

The start-up of NavCan was not without its difficulties. However, it is clear that Transport Canada and the Atlantic Regional management team did a very good job in making the transition as procedurally fair as was possible.

Sources: P. Gregory Irving, Daniel F. Coleman, and Ramona Bobacel, "Exploring the moderating effect of negative affectivity in the procedural justice-job satisfaction relation" *Canadian Journal of Behavioural Science*, 2005, Vol. 37, pp. 20–32; Daniel F. Coleman, James M. Tolliver, and P. Gregory Irving, "Work locus of control and procedural justice in a case of privatization," Proceedings of the Seventh International Conference of the Eastern Academy of Management, 1997, 165–169.

dignity and respect for the recipients.[47] Other research has demonstrated that breaches of procedural or interactional justice themselves can cause negative emotions and actions.[48]

Summary of Approaches to Organizational Justice   Equity theory offers managers three messages. First, everyone in the organization needs to understand the basis for rewards. If people are to be rewarded more for high-quality work than for quantity of work, for instance, that fact needs to be clearly communicated to everyone. Second, people tend to take a multifaceted view of their rewards; they perceive and experience a variety of rewards, some tangible and others intangible. Finally, people base their actions on their perceptions of reality. If two people make exactly the same salary but each thinks the other makes more, they base their experience of equity on the perception, not the reality. Hence, even if a manager believes two employees are being fairly rewarded, the employees themselves may not necessarily agree if their perceptions differ from the manager's. Procedural justice offers the additional consideration that not only must distribution of outcomes be fair, but so must also the procedures that guide the decisions about how outcomes are to be distributed. Finally, interactive justice tells managers that regardless of other considerations, time must be spent to fully communicate decisions, and to do so with respect and consideration for employees.

The Expectancy Theory of Motivation

Expectancy theory is a more encompassing model of motivation than equity theory. Over the years since its original formulation, the theory's scope and complexity have continued to grow.

The Basic Expectancy Model

The basic expectancy theory model emerged from the work of Edward Tolman and Kurt Lewin.[49] Canadian-born Victor Vroom, however, is generally credited with first applying the theory to motivation in the workplace.[50] The theory attempts to determine how individuals choose among alternative behaviours. The basic premise of **expectancy theory** is that motivation depends on how much we want something and how likely we think we are to get it.

A simple example illustrates this premise. Suppose a recent university graduate is looking for her first managerial job. While scanning the want ads, the graduate sees that CIBC is seeking a new executive vice-president to oversee its foreign operations. The starting salary is in the hundreds of thousands of dollars. The graduate would love the job, but does not bother to apply because she recognizes that there is no chance of getting it. Reading on, she or he sees a position that involves scraping bubble gum from underneath desks in university classrooms. The starting pay is $6.00 an hour, and no experience is necessary. Again, the graduate is unlikely to apply—even though she thinks she could get the job, she does not want it.

Then the graduate comes across an advertisement for a management training position with a large company. No experience is necessary, the primary requirement is a university degree, and the starting salary is $28 000. The graduate will probably apply for this position because (1) she wants it, and (2) she thinks there is a reasonable chance of getting it. (Of course, this simple example understates the true complexity of most choices. Job-seeking students may have strong geographic preferences, have other job opportunities, and be considering graduate school. Most decisions, in fact, are quite complex.)

Expectancy theory suggests that people are motivated by how much they want something and the likelihood they perceive of getting it.

Figure 4.7 summarizes the basic expectancy model. The model's general components are effort (the result of motivated behaviour), performance, and outcomes. Expectancy theory emphasizes the linkages among these elements, which are described in terms of expectancies and valences.

Effort-to-performance expectancy is a person's perception of the probability that effort will lead to performance.

Effort-to-Performance Expectancy   **Effort-to-performance expectancy** is a person's perception of the probability that effort will lead to successful performance. If we believe our effort will lead to higher performance, this expectancy is very strong, perhaps approaching a probability of 1.0, where 1.0 equals absolute certainty that the outcome will occur. If we believe our performance will be the same no matter how much effort we make, our expectancy is very low—perhaps as low as 0, meaning that there is no probability that the outcome will occur. A person who thinks there is a moderate relationship between effort and subsequent performance—the normal circumstance—has an expectancy somewhere between 1.0 and 0.

Performance-to-outcome expectancy is the individual's perception of the probability that performance will lead to certain outcomes.

Performance-to-Outcome Expectancy   **Performance-to-outcome expectancy** is a person's perception of the probability that performance will lead to certain other outcomes. If a person thinks a high performer is certain to get a pay raise, this expectancy is close to 1.0. At the other extreme, a person who believes raises are entirely independent of performance has an expectancy close to 0. Finally, if a person thinks performance has some bearing on the prospects for a pay raise, expectancy is somewhere between 1.0 and 0. In a work setting, several performance-to-outcome expectancies are relevant because, as Figure 4.7 shows, several outcomes might logically result from performance. Each outcome then has its own expectancy.

An **outcome** is anything that results from performing a particular behaviour.

Outcomes and Valences   An **outcome** is anything that might potentially result from performance. High-level performance conceivably might produce such

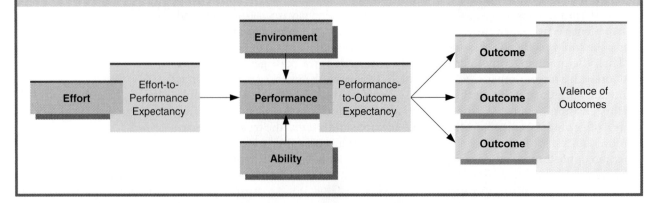

FIGURE 4.7

The Expectancy Theory of Motivation

The expectancy theory is the most complex model of employee motivation in organizations. As shown here, the key components of expectancy theory are effort-to-performance expectancy, performance-to-outcome expectancy, and outcomes, each of which has an associated valence. These components interact with effort, the environment, and ability to determine an individual's performance.

Graduate Eric Weese of Lisgar Collegiate in Ottawa, holds up his Governor General's Academic Medal that he received from the Governor General during a graduation ceremony. As described by Expectancy Theory, he has worked hard in his studies in the knowledge that his effort would lead to certain outcomes.

outcomes as a pay raise, a promotion, recognition from the boss, fatigue, stress, or less time to rest, among others. The **valence** of an outcome is the relative attractiveness or unattractiveness—the value—of that outcome to the person. Pay raises, promotions, and recognition might all have positive valences, whereas fatigue, stress, and less time to rest might all have negative valences.

Valence is the degree of attractiveness or unattractiveness a particular outcome has for a person.

People vary in the strength of their outcome valences. Work-related stress may be a significant negative factor for one person, but only a slight annoyance to another. Similarly, a pay increase may have a strong positive valence for someone desperately in need of money, a slight positive valence for someone interested mostly in getting a promotion—or, for someone in an unfavourable tax position, even a negative valence!

The basic expectancy framework suggests that three conditions must be met before motivated behaviour occurs. First, the effort-to-performance expectancy must be well above zero. That is, the worker must reasonably expect that exerting effort will produce high levels of performance. Second, the performance-to-outcome expectancies must be well above zero. Thus, the person must believe that performance will realistically result in valued outcomes. Third, the sum of all the valences for the potential outcomes relevant to the person must be positive. One or more valences may be negative so long as the positives outweigh the negatives. For example, stress and fatigue may have moderately negative valences, but if pay, promotion, and recognition have very high positive valences, the overall valence of the set of outcomes associated with performance will still be positive.

Conceptually, the valences of all relevant outcomes and the corresponding pattern of expectancies are assumed to interact in an almost mathematical fashion to determine a person's level of motivation. Most people do assess the likelihood of and preferences for various consequences of behaviour, but they seldom approach them in such a calculating manner.

The Porter-Lawler Model   The original presentation of expectancy theory placed it in the mainstream of contemporary motivation theory. Since then, the model has been refined and extended many times. Most modifications have focused on identifying and measuring outcomes and expectancies. An exception is the variation of expectancy theory developed by Porter and Lawler. These researchers used expectancy theory to develop a novel view of the relationship between employee satisfaction and performance.[51] Although the conventional wisdom was that satisfaction leads to performance, Porter and Lawler argued the reverse: if rewards are adequate, high levels of performance may lead to satisfaction.

The Porter-Lawler model appears in Figure 4.8. Some of its features are quite different from the original version of expectancy theory. For example, the extended model includes abilities, traits, and role perceptions. At the beginning of the motivational cycle, effort is a function of the value of the potential reward for the employee (its valence) and the perceived effort-reward probability (an expectancy). Effort then combines with abilities, traits, and role perceptions to determine actual performance.

Performance results in two kinds of rewards. Intrinsic rewards are intangible—a feeling of accomplishment, a sense of achievement, and so forth. Extrinsic rewards are tangible outcomes such as pay and promotion. The individual judges the value of his or her performance to the organization and uses social comparison processes (as in equity theory) to form an impression of the equity of the rewards received. If the rewards are regarded as equitable, the employee feels satisfied. In subsequent cycles, satisfaction

FIGURE 4.8

The Porter-Lawler Model

The Porter and Lawler expectancy model provides interesting insights into the relationship between satisfaction and performance. As illustrated here, this model predicts that satisfaction is determined by the perceived equity of intrinsic and extrinsic rewards for performance. That is, rather than satisfaction causing performance, which many people might predict, this model argues that it is actually performance that eventually leads to satisfaction.

Source: Figure from Lyman W. Porter and Edward E. Lawler, *Managerial Attitudes and Performance*. Copyright 1968. Reproduced by permission of the author.

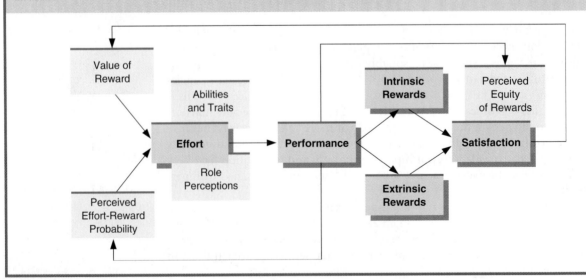

with rewards influences the value of the rewards anticipated, and actual performance following effort influences future perceived effort-reward probabilities.

Evaluation and Implications   Expectancy theory has been tested by many researchers in a variety of settings and using a variety of methods.[52] As noted earlier, the complexity of the theory has been both a blessing and a curse.[53] Nowhere is this double-edged quality more apparent than in the research undertaken to evaluate the theory. Several studies have supported various parts of the theory. For example, both kinds of expectancy and valence have been found to be associated with effort and performance in the workplace.[54] Research has also confirmed expectancy theory's claims that people will not engage in motivated behaviour unless they (1) value the expected rewards, (2) believe their efforts will lead to performance, and (3) believe their performance will result in the desired rewards.[55]

However, expectancy theory is so complicated that researchers have found it quite difficult to test.[56] In particular, the measures of various parts of the model may lack validity, and the procedures for investigating relationships among the variables have often been less scientific than researchers would like. Moreover, people are seldom as rational and objective in choosing behaviours as expectancy theory implies. Still, the logic of the model, combined with the consistent, albeit modest, research support for it, suggests that the theory has much to offer.[57]

Research also suggests that expectancy theory is more likely to explain motivation in North America than in other countries. People from Canada and the United States tend to be very goal-oriented and to think that they can influence their own success. Thus, under the right combinations of expectancies, valences, and outcomes they will be highly motivated. But different patterns may exist in other countries. For example, many people from Muslim countries think that God determines the outcome of every behaviour, so the concept of expectancy is not applicable.[58]

> The Porter-Lawler model suggests that a high performance level, if followed by equitable rewards, may lead to increased satisfaction.

Because expectancy theory is so complex, it is difficult to apply directly in the workplace. A manager would need to figure out what rewards each employee wants and how valuable those rewards are to each person, measure the various expectancies, and finally adjust the relationships to create motivation. Nevertheless, expectancy theory offers several important guidelines for the practising manager. Some of the more fundamental guidelines include:

1. Determine the primary outcomes each employee wants.
2. Decide what levels and kinds of performance are needed to meet organizational goals.
3. Make sure the desired levels of performance are possible.
4. Link desired outcomes and desired performance.
5. Analyze the situation for conflicting expectancies.
6. Make sure the rewards are large enough.
7. Make sure the overall system is equitable for everyone.[59]

Social Learning and Motivation

Social learning is another key component in employee motivation. In any organization, employees quickly learn which behaviours are rewarded and which are ignored or punished. Thus, learning plays a critical role in maintaining motivated behaviour. **Learning** is a relatively permanent change in behaviour or behavioural potential that results from direct or indirect experience.[60] For example, we can learn to use a new software application program by practising and experimenting with its various functions and options.

> **Learning** is a relatively permanent change in behaviour or behavioural potential resulting from direct or indirect experience.

How Learning Occurs

Learning as a Social-Cognitive Process   Although it is not tied to a single theory or model, contemporary learning theory generally views learning as a social-cognitive process; that is, it assumes that people are conscious, active participants in how they learn.[61] Figure 4.9 illustrates some underpinnings of the social-cognitive view of learning.[62]

Albert Bandura, one of the main proponents of the social-cognitive view suggests that people learn through the interaction of three determinants: the thinking (cognitive) self, behaviour in which the person engages, and the environment.[63] The thinking self determinant means that people can plan and actively decide how they will attempt to influence their environment. Behaviours are the actions that people make to try to change their environment. The environment may or may not be successfully altered. The thinking self then evaluates the success or failure of the behaviour and forms strategies for the future.

Although these terms may seem ambiguous, the basic processes that they describe are fairly simple. Suppose, for example, you start a new job. You want to do well at the new job. You will not, however, merely engage in a set of hit or miss actions. Your thinking self will plan the actions that you will take. You may decide, for example, that you will put in a lot of effort, take additional training, or find a mentor to show you the ropes. In this case, the environment that you are trying to alter is to create quality work and, equally important in real organizations, be seen by others as producing quality work. You then execute the planned behaviours. After some time has passed, you will evaluate the success of your behaviours in terms of whether you have had the effect on the environment that you had planned. Was your work of high quality? Did your supervisors give you positive feedback? Depending on your self-evaluation, you may decide to continue the actions you used, if they were successful, or change them if they were not.

Social-cognitive theory has its roots in two schools of thought. One is reinforcement theory discussed earlier in this chapter. This is recognized in Figure 4.10 in the link between behaviour and environment. It also has a cognitive component, as recognized by the role of the person as planner and evaluator of actions, similar to expectancy theory. Thus, social-cognitive theory goes beyond reinforcement theory by explicitly recognizing thinking processes, and rejecting environmental determinism.

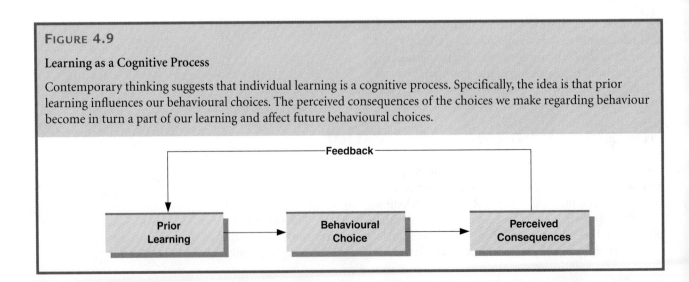

FIGURE 4.9

Learning as a Cognitive Process

Contemporary thinking suggests that individual learning is a cognitive process. Specifically, the idea is that prior learning influences our behavioural choices. The perceived consequences of the choices we make regarding behaviour become in turn a part of our learning and affect future behavioural choices.

Self-Efficacy

The underlying motivational mechanism in social-cognitive theory is **self-efficacy**. Bandura says that "[p]erceived self-efficacy refers to beliefs in one's capabilities to organize and execute the courses of action required to produce given attainments."[64] People must believe in their ability to accomplish their objectives. If self-efficacy is high, then people will exert effort to produce results; if it is low, they will not even try. Self-efficacy is a key to motivation for this reason, and it is also a key to performance outcomes. People with higher levels of self-efficacy perform better on a task than others with the same objective level of ability with lower levels of self-efficacy.

There are two additional assumptions to social-cognitive theory that are important for understanding work motivation. The first is that people seek control and mastery over their environments. This assumption is similar to the notion of self-actualization as described in Maslow's theory discussed earlier in this chapter. However, the assumption is different in social-cognitive theory because here we do not assume that the drive for mastery is an inborn characteristic of human beings. Rather, people seek control and mastery not as outcomes in themselves, but because they yield benefits, which act as incentives. Thus, the exercises of control and mastery-seeking are learned, and can be developed. For example, if you are trying to do well in a course, you will study hard to try to learn the material. These activities assert control over the environment in the sense that your learning the material should remove your performance on tests and exams from beyond the realm of chance. Your mastery of the material may be inherently stimulating (depending on the subject matter!), but mastery also yields praise, self-respect, good marks, and potentially a better job in the future.

The second important assumption in social-cognitive theory is that most people are not content to stay at a particular level of mastery. Rather, people are creative, proactive, and have a generative capacity.[65] People with high levels of self-efficacy will set high performance goals, and give high levels of effort to achieve those goals. Additionally, when a given level of performance or mastery is attained, new goals frequently will be set. Consider, for example, someone who is just learning how to play golf. The person may begin with the goals of learning proper club selection, swing techniques, and just surviving 18 holes without dying of embarrassment. If the person possesses adequate self-efficacy once the basics are mastered, she or he may then set a goal of breaking 100. But if you know any golf addict, you know that once this goal is attained, new goals are set (to break 90, 80, and, for many people, to shoot par). Now, consider a parallel to worklife: an entry-level job is not satisfying to most people once the tasks have been mastered. New responsibilities that require new skills and new levels of effort are sought.

Taken together, the motivational implications are considerable. Basic levels of self-efficacy must be present for people to be motivated to try to accomplish a task. High levels of self-efficacy will lead to higher performance. People will not be satisfied to remain in a position that they have mastered; they will seek new challenges even if it requires more effort.

> **FIGURE 4.10**
>
> **Interaction Between Behaviour, Cognition, and Environment in Social-Cognitive Theory**
>
> Social-cognitive theory recognizes that people learn through an interaction of thinking about their behaviour (cognition), the behaviour they exhibit, and the environment in which the behaviour occurs. Interactions are present, for example, in the extent to which people self-observe and self-evaluate the relationships between their behaviour and the environment.
>
> *Source:* Adapted from Albert Bandura, *Social Foundations of Thought and Action: A Social Cognitive Theory.* Englewood Cliffs, New Jersey, Prentice-Hall, 1986.

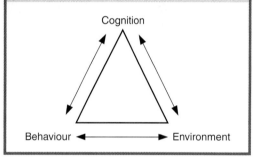

> Our **self-efficacy** is the extent to which we believe we can accomplish our goals even if we failed to do so in the past.

Evaluation and Implications

Social cognitive theory is now regarded as one of the three dominant theories of motivation, along with organizational justice and goal setting theory (which will be discussed

People can be motivated by a wide variety of factors. Jay Schwartz provides a vivid example. After a distinguished and lucrative career as Director of Institutional Financial Strategies for a major insurance company, he decided to seek greater fulfillment as a high school math teacher in the Bronx. Mr. Schwartz is shown here with 9000 of his new colleagues filling out orientation forms before their school year opens.

in the next chapter).[66] Self-efficacy has been found to be an important predictor of motivation and performance, as well as how well people adapt to new jobs.[67]

Self-efficacy, according to Bandura, is developed through a number of mechanisms. The strongest source is called enactive mastery, which means that people learn best through direct hands-on experience with a task. The next most powerful way to develop self-efficacy is through observation of a model performing the task. The third is by telling people how to do the task, while the weakest form is through emotional arousal—cheerleading, in a sense. Think about this in your own experience. You may have had classroom instruction on how to operate a piece of software (telling), but you would learn the software more effectively if you sat next to someone and watched that person operate it (observational learning). However, you will learn it best once you get in front of a monitor and start banging away on the keyboard yourself.

Organizations can use this knowledge to help employees develop. Training is important, and has been recognized as such for many years. However, self-efficacy theory tells us that training should be as hands-on as possible. Other aspects of social learning and self-efficacy tell us that true efficacy is established if employees are presented with challenging, but achievable goals. That is, efficacy is not developed if the task is overly simple. Finally, because mastery levels are not static, individuals constantly need new challenges to remain fully motivated. This last implication is probably the reason that employee empowerment programs are effective and growing in popularity. We will discuss these programs in a later chapter.

Summary of Key Points

- Motivation is the set of forces that cause people to behave as they do. Motivation starts with a need. People search for ways to satisfy their needs and then behave accordingly. Their behaviour results in rewards or punishment. To varying degrees, an outcome may satisfy the original need.

- The earliest view of motivation was based on the concept of hedonism, the idea that people seek pleasure and comfort and try to avoid pain and discomfort. Scientific management extended this view, asserting that money is the primary human motivator in the workplace. The human relations view suggested that social factors are primary motivators.

- According to Abraham Maslow, human needs are arranged in a hierarchy of importance, from physiological to security to belongingness to esteem and, finally, to self-actualization. The ERG theory is a refinement of Maslow's original hierarchy that includes a frustration-regression component.

- Herzberg's dual-structure theory attempted to explain work motivation as a consequence of hygiene factors, which are related to dissatisfaction, and motivator factors, which are related to job satisfaction.

- Need-based theories, although no longer as popular as they once were, have contributed to the way we think about motivation.

- Learning also plays a role in employee motivation. Various kinds of reinforcement can increase or decrease motivated behaviour.

- Organizational behaviour modification is a strategy for using learning and reinforcement principles to enhance employee motivation and performance. This strategy relies heavily on the effective measurement of performance and the provision of rewards to employees performing at a high level.

- Organizational justice is important for motivation and has several facets. The equity theory of motivation based on a form of distributive justice assumes that people want to be treated fairly. It hypothesizes that people compare their own input-to-outcome ratio in the organization to the ratio of a comparison-other. If they feel their treatment is inequitable, they take steps to reduce the inequity. Procedural justice highlights the importance of fair decision-making processes in organizations, while interactional justice reminds us that people want to be treated with compassion, dignity, and respect.

- Expectancy theory, a somewhat more complicated model, follows from the assumption that people are motivated to work toward a goal if they want it and think they have a reasonable chance of achieving it. Effort-to-performance expectancy is the belief that effort will lead to performance. Performance-to-outcome expectancy is the belief that performance will lead to certain outcomes. Valence is the desirability to the individual of the various possible outcomes of performance. The Porter-Lawler version of expectancy theory provides useful insights into the relationship between satisfaction and performance. This model suggests that performance may lead to a variety of intrinsic and extrinsic rewards. When perceived as equitable, these rewards lead to satisfaction.

- Social learning theory assumes that people learn through the interaction of the thinking self, behaviour that people exhibit, and the social environment. Self-efficacy, which is one's belief in one's own ability, is a key to motivation. People are motivated to take part in activities in which they can succeed, and enjoy challenge and growth.

Discussion Questions

1. Is it possible for someone to be unmotivated, or is all behaviour motivated?

2. In what meaningful ways might the motivational process vary in different cultures?

3. Is it useful to characterize motivation in terms of a deficiency? Why or why not? Is it possible to characterize motivation in terms of excess? If so, how?

4. When has your level of performance been directly affected by your motivation? By your ability? By the environment?

5. Think of occasions on which you experienced each of the four types of reinforcement.

6. Have you ever experienced inequity in a job or a class? How did it affect you?

7. Which is likely to be a more serious problem, perceptions of being underrewarded or perceptions of being overrewarded?

8. What are some of the managerial implications of equity theory beyond those discussed in the chapter?

9. Do you think expectancy theory is too complex for direct use in organizational settings? Why or why not?

10. Do the relationships between performance and satisfaction suggested by Porter and Lawler seem valid? Cite examples that both support and refute the model.

11. How has your perception of your self-efficacy affected your choice and performance of activities, either at work, school, or leisure?

Experiencing Organizational Behaviour

Purpose: This exercise asks you to apply the theories discussed in the chapter to your own needs and motives.

Format: First, you will develop a list of things you want from life. Then you will categorize them according to one of the theories in the chapter. Next, you will discuss your results with a small group of classmates.

Procedure: Prepare a list of approximately 15 things you want from life. These can be very specific (such as a new car) or very general (such as a feeling of accomplishment in school). Try to include some things you want right now and other things you want later in life. Next, choose the one motivational theory discussed in this chapter that best fits your set of needs. Classify each item from your "wish list" in terms of the need or needs it might satisfy.

Your instructor will then divide the class into groups of three. Spend a few minutes in the group discussing

each person's list and its classification according to needs.

After the small-group discussions, your instructor will reconvene the entire class. Discussion should centre on the extent to which each theory can serve as a useful framework for classifying individual needs. Students who found that their needs could be neatly categorized and those who found little correlation between their needs and the theories are especially encouraged to share their results.

Follow-up Questions

1. As a result of this exercise, do you now have more or less trust in need theories as viable management tools?

2. Could a manager use some form of this exercise in an organizational setting to enhance employee motivation?

Self-Assessment Exercises

Assessing Your Equity Sensitivity

The questions that follow are intended to help you understand your equity sensitivity. Answer each question on the scales by circling the number that best reflects your personal feelings.

1. I think it is important for everyone to be treated fairly.

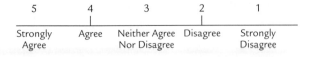

5	4	3	2	1
Strongly Agree	Agree	Neither Agree Nor Disagree	Disagree	Strongly Disagree

2. I pay a lot of attention to how I am treated, in comparison to how others are treated.

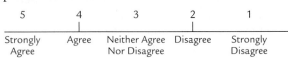

5	4	3	2	1
Strongly Agree	Agree	Neither Agree Nor Disagree	Disagree	Strongly Disagree

3. I get really angry if I think I'm being treated unfairly.

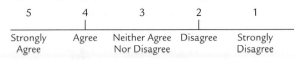

5	4	3	2	1
Strongly Agree	Agree	Neither Agree Nor Disagree	Disagree	Strongly Disagree

4. It makes me uncomfortable if I think someone else is not being treated fairly.

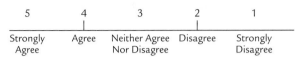

5. If I thought I was being treated unfairly, I would be very motivated to change things.

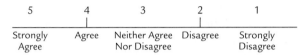

6. It doesn't really bother me if someone else gets a better deal than me.

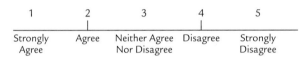

7. It is impossible for everyone to be treated fairly all the time.

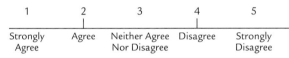

8. When I'm a manager, I'll make sure that all of my employees are treated fairly.

9. I would quit my job if I thought I was being treated unfairly.

10. Short-term inequities are okay, because things all even out in the long run.

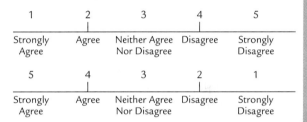

Instructions: Add up your total points (note that some items have a reversed numbering arrangement). If you scored 35 or above, you are highly sensitive to equity and fairness; 15 or less, you have very little sensitivity to equity and fairness; between 35 and 15, you have moderate equity sensitivity.

Organizational Behaviour Case for Discussion

Motivational Problems at the Mine

Paul LaForge was reviewing productivity reports for the last quarter at the Northern Ontario Coal Mine (NOCM). He was very depressed because the work records in both areas of his responsibility showed another decline. This was the fifth quarter in a row where performance had dropped.

LaForge was the site supervisor for the mine. He was responsible for the actual mining of the coal, which was an open-pit operation. He was also responsible for land reclamation, which was the process of restoring the landscape after mining to being fairly close to the original contour and vegetation level it was in before the coal was extracted.

The coal production was off another 5000 tonnes from the previous quarter, and similarly 100 fewer

hectares of mined land had been reclaimed compared to the last report. He had a good idea why production and reclamation was slowing, but he decided to talk to a few of his workers to see if his assumptions were correct. He called in Kevin Marcus, one of the lead hands in the reclamation unit.

"Kevin, look at these records from last quarter," LaForge said. "What do you make of this? What are the guys in the field saying?"

"Well, it's pretty obvious, isn't it?" replied Marcus. "Everyone knows that the coal seams are running out around here. The faster we work, the quicker the coal will be gone, and the sooner we'll all be out of work. There is no incentive to work fast."

Marcus continued: "The same goes for reclamation. When the mine was expanding and finding new seams of coal, we used to work fast on the reclamation because it looked like the work would go on forever. Now, with production nearing an end, we know that the faster we work to reclaim the land, the sooner the work will be gone completely."

LaForge talked to a few other lead hands and field workers. The explanations were not always as clear and blunt as Marcus', but they were fairly consistent. The biggest problem for LaForge was that it was all true—the seams were being exhausted, the mine had a limited future, and most of the reclamation work, once done, would result in most of the workers being laid off or retired.

LaForge did not know what to do. The mine was a Crown corporation, owned by the province. The provincial government was increasing its monitoring of the mine's performance. It would not tolerate decreased efficiencies for very long. LaForge was concerned that unless both production and reclamation activities increased that the government might prematurely close the NOCM even before it depleted its remaining reserves.

LaForge then consulted with Mike Kimmit, the mining engineer who was responsible for designing mining and reclamation plans. "Mike, I don't know what to do," LaForge said. "The workers are absolutely right, the faster they work, the faster they'll be out of a job."

Kimmit thought about it for a couple of days, and then an idea struck him that he shared with LaForge: "Paul, you're almost right about this, but you are missing one important consideration. When the mining is done, the government is going to sell the property to a private company. There's no way that the land reclamation will be finished before the mining operation shuts down. There will be years and years of reclamation work that the private company will be doing on government contracts. Even when that is done, there will be a few environmental monitoring positions for a long time to make sure that there is no seepage of pollutants from the old mine site. So, there are going to be some jobs around here for a long time."

"I know that" replied LaForge. "But the private operator is only going to need less than half of our current workforce. How do I get our crews to work harder now?"

Case Questions

1. Which motivation theories best explain what has happened at NOCM?

2. If you were running NOCM today, how would you convince your employees to remain motivated?

**Organizational Behaviour
Case for Discussion**

Self-Efficacy in Academia

"What a mess", thought George Rhodes, the Dean of the Faculty of Management at Upper Ontario University, "our student retention rate is close to crisis levels."

Rhodes was reviewing first year student performance records from the previous academic year. The data showed that almost 40 percent of first year students were in "academic jeopardy" (that is, have Grade Point Averages of less than 2.0) after their first academic year.

Rhodes instructed Sam Aaron, the Undergraduate Student Advisor, to do an analysis of incoming high school averages, and their correlation with first year student performance. When the analysis was complete, the following discussion took place between Rhodes and Aaron: "Sam, the numbers tell the story," began Rhodes, "We require a 70% high school average to be admitted to our program. Your analysis shows that a full 80% of students with high school averages between 70 and 75 are in jeopardy, 60 percent of students with high school averages between 75 and 80 percent are in jeopardy, but only 20% of students with high school averages above 80% are in jeopardy. Clearly, we have to raise our high school admission average to 80 percent. Right now, what we are doing is unethical; we are accepting students into the program we know will have little chance of success. We take them in, take their money, stamp 'loser' on their foreheads, and chuck them out the door. They would be better served, and we could use our scant resources better if they were not admitted in the first place. They are doomed to failure." "George, I am really disappointed in you," countered Aaron, "What I see here is a self-fulfilling prophecy. Our instructors assume that the students are unable, treat them like idiots, which alienates the students, leading to poor performance. I've been the advisor for 10 years now, and you've been the dean for seven years. Let me ask you this question: In your experience, how many of the students who do poorly in our program are truly unable to do the work? In my experience, there are very few who are unable, but a lot who have poor study skills, are stressed, or are not highly motivated."

Rhodes agreed, "Sam, that is my experience too. The weaker students are not stupid, they just don't do the work."

"Bingo!" said Aaron. "But we don't do anything about it. We just toss the weaker students into the program, and see if they 'sink or swim'. Now George, you are a professor of organizational behaviour, and an expert in motivation. So, to put a fine point on this, 'Physician, heal thyself': clearly, you should be able to develop a program, based on solid principles of motivation, to help these weaker students to succeed."

Case Question

1. Using the principles of self-efficacy, what sort of program should be designed to help the type of students who are currently performing poorly?

SELF TEST

You have read the chapter and studied the key terms. Think you're ready to ace the exam? Take this sample test to gauge your comprehension of chapter material and check your answers at the back of the book. Want more test questions? Take the ACE quizzes found on the student website: www.hmco.ca/ob

T   F   1. Motivation is the only factor that influences employee performance.

T   F   2. According to Alderfer's ERG theory, a person who is frustrated by trying to satisfy a higher-level need will eventually regress to the preceding level.

T   F   3. Reinforcement theory suggests behaviour is a function of its consequences.

T   F   4. According to equity theory, if you feel you are being underpaid, you will work harder.

T   F   5. Expectancy theory suggests that people will always work to achieve the outcomes with the highest valence.

T   F   6. Self-efficacy is an individual's belief that a task can be accomplished.

7. Performance is a function of all of the following except
   a. motivation.
   b. ability.
   c. environment.
   d. organizational behaviour.
   e. All of the above influence performance.

8. The easiest needs for managers to evaluate and meet are
   a. physiological needs.
   b. safety needs.
   c. belongingness needs.
   d. self-actualization needs.
   e. social needs

9. The basis of equity theory is
   a. people in organizations want to be treated equally.
   b. different factors influence dissatisfaction and satisfaction.
   c. the psychological contract is irrelevant once employment begins.
   d. people in organizations want to be treated fairly.
   e. managers must focus on motivation, ability, and environment to enhance performance.

10. Samantha needs to motivate her employees to perform a difficult task. According to Vroom's expectancy theory, Samantha needs to make sure her employees believe which of the following?
    a. Outcomes will be distributed fairly.

    b. Performing the task will result in valued outcomes.
    c. High levels of performance will reduce dissatisfaction.
    d. The task satisfies self-actualization needs.
    e. Rewards for performance will increase satisfaction.

11. During the regular staff briefing each morning, Mike makes jokes at the back of the room. If Mike's manager were to use extinction to decrease the frequency of this behaviour, he might
    a. send Mike out of the room the next time he made a joke.
    b. ask the other employees not to laugh at Mike's jokes.
    c. give Mike a bonus for not making jokes.
    d. glare at Mike until he stopped making jokes.
    e. ask the other employees to sit closer to Mike.

12. Organizational Behaviour modification, or OB mod, uses _____ to encourage desirable behaviours in employees.
    a. punishment
    b. extinction
    c. avoidance
    d. social learning
    e. positive reinforcement

13. The primary ethical dilemma regarding Organizational Behaviour modification, or OB mod, is
    a. outcomes typically exceed inputs when managers use OB mod.
    b. behaviours that promote personal growth and development are overrewarded.
    c. use of OB mod compromises individual freedom of choice.
    d. OB mod fails to link valued outcomes with desired levels of performance.
    e. lower-level needs are left unsatisfied.

14. Self-efficacy is best developed by:
    a. enactive mastery
    b. observational learning
    c. listening to a lecture
    d. listening to an inspirational speech
    e. All of the above are equally effective

Applied Motivation Techniques and Job Design

CHAPTER 5

After studying this chapter, you should be able to:

- ▶ **Describe how goal setting can enhance motivation and performance.**
- ▶ **Discuss how motivation gets translated into actual employee performance.**
- ▶ **Summarize the evolution of job design and evaluate early approaches to job design.**
- ▶ **Discuss and evaluate the job characteristics approach to job design.**
- ▶ **Discuss participation and empowerment and how they relate to motivation.**
- ▶ **Identify and summarize various alternative work arrangements.**

Keeping Employees Motivated at WestJet

WestJet Airlines Ltd. based in Calgary, Alberta, uses a number of unique practices to motivate their "people." The first striking technique is the very term "people" that WestJet uses to describe what other companies would call "employees." WestJet does not refer to its "people" as employees, associates, or other such term. This reflects one of their strong company values, that everyone is an individual with his or her own attitudes, talents, and personalities. So, they are "people."

Another core value that permeates the WestJet culture is that the work should be fun. This is demonstrated in a number of ways. The clearest example is the admittedly "corny" jokes that flight attendants tell on most WestJet flights. As a matter of fact, there is a committee of flight attendants responsible for writing the material that goes into the WestJet joke book that is standard equipment on every airplane in the WestJet fleet.

WestJet clearly uses a "people first" philosophy. Not only are individuals respected for who they are, but there are financial rewards as well. Employees can take up to 20 percent of their salaries in stock options, which the company matches 100 percent. As one of WestJet's advertising campaigns noted, everyone at WestJet is an owner. There is also a significant profit-sharing plan.

Beyond the financial benefits, WestJet employees are frequently consulted about the company's operations. This takes place both in formal committees as well as a very open communication system. The "people" are expected to take an active part in helping the organization to succeed. The joke committee mentioned above is one such example. Even more striking is the fact that a proposed advertising campaign that was designed by WestJet's newly hired ad agency was abandoned—as was the agency—in large part due to objections by employees. Another specific example of WestJet's emphasis on personal responsibility is that its call centre operators have the discretion to reroute, rebook, and sometimes waive fees and override standard fares without consulting managers.

Pilots and the founder and former CEO Clive Beddoe were known for helping to clean the airplanes after flights. This not only strengthens the egalitarian atmosphere of the company, but also helps pragmatically in reducing flight turn-around times. WestJet "people" are seen to be friendly and helpful, particularly on the front line, which clearly distinguishes it from major competitors.

The results of its approach are also striking. WestJet was founded in 1996, with just a few planes and routes mostly in Western Canada. Today, it is Canada's third largest airline (behind Air Canada and Air Canada Jazz), and operates from across Canada and into the United States. Beddoe was named Canadian Business CEO of the year in 2004; it was recently voted as having the best corporate culture in Canada, and one of the ten best managed brands in Canada. It also appears to work on the bottom line: it recently had the highest seat occupancy and its most profitable year in its history.[1]

This chapter addresses the strategies managers use to optimize the performance of their employees. We begin with a discussion of goal setting, one of the most well-researched motivational techniques. We then turn to job design, starting with a look at historical approaches to job design. Then we discuss an important contemporary perspective on jobs, the job characteristics theory. Next, we describe how social information affects job design, and cover the importance of employee participation and empowerment. Finally, we discuss alternative work arrangements that can be used to enhance motivation and performance.

Motivation and Employee Performance

Chapter 4 described a variety of perspectives on motivation. Those discussions focused on theories included in the *motivation core* in Figure 4.1. In this chapter, we will look at the goal-setting aspect of the *motivation hub*, and at job design techniques that contribute to *satisfaction* in Figure 4.1. The last part of this chapter looks at alternative work schedules, which are also used in many organizations to increase satisfaction among employees. It is important to realize, however, that no single theory or model described here or in the previous chapter can completely explain motivation—each covers only some of the factors that actually cause motivated behaviour. Moreover, even if one theory was applicable in a particular situation, a manager might still need to translate that theory into operational terms. Thus, while using the actual theories as tools, managers need to understand various operational procedures, systems, and methods for enhancing motivation and performance.

This recognition is important when considering the contents of this chapter. The two main applied motivational techniques described here take widely different perspectives. Goal setting, as its name implies, concerns how to set objectives to stimulate performance. Job design focuses on the contents of work to improve workers' levels of satisfaction.

Goal Setting and Motivation

Goal setting is a useful method of enhancing employee performance. From a motivational perspective, a **goal** is a desirable objective. Goals serve two purposes in most organizations. First, they provide a useful framework for managing motivation. Managers and employees can set goals for themselves and then work toward them. Thus, if the organization's goal is to increase sales by 10 percent, a manager can use individual goals to help attain an overall goal. Second, goals are an effective control device; control is monitoring by management of how well the organization is performing. Comparing people's short-term performances with their goals can be an effective way to monitor the organization's long-run performance.

Social learning theory, discussed in the previous chapter, perhaps best describes the role and importance of goal setting in organizations.[2] This perspective suggests that feelings of pride or shame about performance are a function of the extent to which people achieve their goals. A person who achieves a goal will be proud of having done so, whereas a person who fails to achieve a goal will feel personal disappointment, and perhaps even shame. People's degree of pride or disappointment is affected by their *self-efficacy*, the extent to which they feel that they can still meet their goals even if they failed to do so in the past.

> A **goal** is a desirable objective.

The Goal-Setting Theory

Social learning theory provides insights into why and how goals can motivate behaviour. It also helps us understand how different people cope with failure to reach their goals. It is the research of Edwin Locke and his associates that most decisively showed the utility of goal-setting theory in a motivational context.[3]

Locke's goal-setting theory of motivation assumes that behaviour is a result of conscious goals and intentions. By setting goals for people in the organization, a manager should be able to influence their behaviour. Given this premise, the challenge is to develop a thorough understanding of the processes by which people set goals and then work to reach them. In the original version of goal-setting theory, two specific goal characteristics—goal difficulty and goal specificity—were expected to shape performance.

Goal Difficulty   **Goal difficulty** is the extent to which a goal is challenging and requires effort. If people work to achieve goals, it is reasonable to assume they will work

> **Goal difficulty** is the extent to which a goal is challenging and requires effort.

harder to achieve more difficult goals. But a goal must not be so difficult that it is unattainable. If a new manager asks her sales force to increase sales by 300 percent, the group may become disillusioned. A more realistic but still difficult goal—perhaps a 50 percent increase—would be a better incentive. A substantial body of research supports the importance of goal difficulty.[4] In one study, managers at Weyerhauser set difficult goals for truck drivers hauling loads of timber from cutting sites to wood yards. Over a nine-month period, the drivers increased the quantity of wood they delivered by an amount that would have required $250 000 worth of new trucks at the previous per-truck average load.[5]

Goal specificity is the clarity and precision of a goal.

Goal Specificity   **Goal specificity** is the clarity and precision of the goal. A goal of increasing productivity is not very specific; a goal of increasing productivity by 3 percent in the next six months is quite specific. Some goals, such as those involving costs, output, profitability, and growth, are readily specified. Other goals, such as improving employee job satisfaction and morale, company image and reputation, ethics, and socially responsible behaviour, are much harder to state in specific terms.

Like difficulty, specificity has been shown to be consistently related to performance.[6] The study of timber truck drivers mentioned above also examined goal specificity. The initial loads the truck drivers were carrying were found to be 60 percent of the maximum weight each truck could haul. The managers set a new goal for drivers of 94 percent, which the drivers were soon able to reach. Thus, the goal was quite specific as well as difficult.

Locke's theory attracted much widespread interest and research support from both researchers and managers, so Locke, together with Gary Latham, now at the University of Toronto, eventually proposed an expanded model of the goal-setting process. The expanded model, shown in Figure 5.1, attempts to capture more fully the complexities of goal setting in organizations.

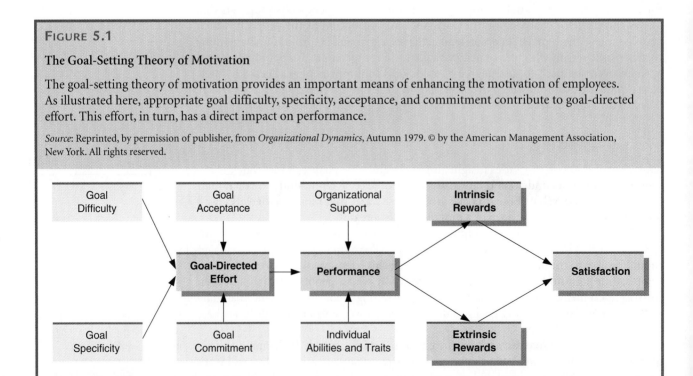

FIGURE 5.1

The Goal-Setting Theory of Motivation

The goal-setting theory of motivation provides an important means of enhancing the motivation of employees. As illustrated here, appropriate goal difficulty, specificity, acceptance, and commitment contribute to goal-directed effort. This effort, in turn, has a direct impact on performance.

Source: Reprinted, by permission of publisher, from *Organizational Dynamics*, Autumn 1979. © by the American Management Association, New York. All rights reserved.

The expanded theory argues that goal-directed effort is a function of four goal attributes: difficulty and specificity, which we already discussed, and acceptance and commitment. **Goal acceptance** is the extent to which a person accepts a goal as his or her own. **Goal commitment** is the extent to which he or she is personally interested in reaching the goal. The manager who vows to take whatever steps are necessary to cut costs by 10 percent has made a commitment to achieve the goal. Factors that can foster goal acceptance and commitment include participating in the goal-setting process, making goals challenging but realistic, and believing that goal achievement will lead to valued rewards.[7]

The interaction of goal-directed effort, organizational support, and individual abilities and traits determines actual performance. Organizational support is everything the organization does to help or hinder performance. Positive support might mean making enough personnel and raw materials available to meet the goal; negative support might mean failing to fix damaged equipment. Individual abilities and traits are the skills and other personal characteristics necessary to do a job. As a result of performance, a person receives various intrinsic and extrinsic rewards, which in turn influence satisfaction. Note that the latter stages of this model are quite similar to those of the Porter and Lawler expectancy model discussed in Chapter 4.

Vancity, a credit union in British Columbia, uses goal setting as part of its executive compensation program. Executives' compensation is tied to specific performance goals around profitability, membership (customer) growth, customer satisfaction, and employee satisfaction.[8] An example of how different types of goal setting can be used to affect students in university programs is shown in the Goal Setting and . . . Research box.

> **Goal acceptance** is the extent to which a person accepts a goal as his or her own.

> **Goal commitment** is the extent to which a person is personally interested in reaching the goal.

Broader Perspectives on Goal Setting

Some organizations undertake goal setting from the somewhat broader perspective of **management by objectives**, or **MBO**.[9] MBO is essentially a collaborative goal-setting process through which organizational goals systematically cascade down through the organization. Our discussion describes a generic approach, but many organizations adapt MBO to suit their own purposes.

A successful MBO program starts with top managers establishing overall goals for the organization.[10] After these goals are set, managers and employees throughout the organization collaborate to set subsidiary goals. First, the overall goals are communicated to everyone. Then each manager meets with each subordinate. During these meetings, the manager explains the unit goals to the subordinate and the two determine together how the subordinate can contribute to the goals most effectively. The manager acts as a counsellor and helps ensure that the subordinate develops goals that are verifiable. For example, a goal of cutting costs by 5 percent is verifiable, whereas a goal of doing your best is not. Finally, manager and subordinate ensure that the subordinate has the resources needed to reach the goals. The entire process spirals downward as each subordinate meets with his or her own subordinates to develop their goals. Thus, as we noted earlier, the initial goals set at the top cascade down through the entire organization.

During the time frame set for goal attainment (usually one year), the manager periodically meets with each subordinate to check progress. It may be necessary to modify goals in light of new information, to provide additional resources, or to take some other action. At the end of the specified period, managers hold a final evaluation meeting with each subordinate. At this meeting, manager and subordinate assess how well goals were met and discuss why. This meeting often serves as the annual performance review as well, determining salary adjustments and other rewards based on reaching goals. This meeting may also serve as the initial goal-setting meeting for the next year's cycle.

> **Management by objectives (MBO)** is a collaborative goal-setting process through which organizational goals cascade down throughout the organization.

Goal Setting and . . .   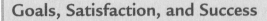 **RESEARCH**

Goals, Satisfaction, and Success

Gary Latham of the University of Toronto and Travor Brown of the Memorial University of Newfoundland did a study on the effects that different types of goal setting have on MBA students. They examined four different types of goal setting and their influence on students' self-efficacy in performing in an MBA program, satisfaction with the MBA program, and their grade point average (GPA).

The participants were 125 MBA students at a Canadian university. The goal setting exercise was done very early in the first term of the first year of the program. Students were assigned to one of four groups:

1. *Distal goals:* students in this group were asked to set goals they would like to accomplish by the end of their first year of study in the MBA program. Typical goals that were set by students in this group were focused on year-end GPA, summer employment objectives, or salary for a summer job.
2. *Distal and proximal goals:* participants in this condition were asked to set distal goals similar to the first group, as well as some proximal (shorter term) goals. The proximal goals set by students in this group included targets for mid-term and semester marks, the number of job opportunities identified, and the like.
3. *Learning goals:* students in this group were asked to identify specific strategies or processes that would assist them to be satisfied with their MBA program at the end of their first year. Developing learning strategies to overcome initial fear or dislike of course material, developing networking skills, and enhancing understanding of others' opinions were goals set by students in this group.
4. *"Do your best":* Students in this group were not asked to set any type of goal. They did have a discussion of why they entered the MBA program, and were simply told to think of ways they could get the most out of the program.

The dependent variables were: a) a task-specific measure of self-efficacy (see chapter 4) about students' belief that they could attain their MBA program goals, which was assessed immediately after the goal condition at the start of the first term, and again toward the end of the second term; b) a measure of satisfaction with the program, which was taken at the end of the first and second terms, and; c) students' year-end GPA.

Latham and Brown found that those students who had set learning goals, or were in the "do your best" group had higher levels of self-efficacy at the beginning of the academic year than did the other two groups. However, those differences in self-efficacy disappeared by year end.

Satisfaction with the MBA program showed a different pattern. There were no differences across goal setting groups in satisfaction after the first term. However, at the end of the second term, students in the learning goal group had higher levels of satisfaction than those in the "do your best group." There were no differences, on the other hand, between the learning goal and other goal setting groups.

The results for year-end GPA showed an interesting pattern. The groups that set either distal *and* proximal goals *or* learning goals had approximately equal GPAs. These groups had higher GPA scores than did the distal goal only group, which in turn had higher averages than the "do your best" group.

The practical implications for students and program administrators are clear. A focus on only long range goals such as what will happen a year away or a "do your best" orientation will not yield optimal satisfaction or performance. On the other hand, it appears that long-range and shorter term goals, as well as learning goals can help to improve satisfaction with a program and student performance.

Source: Gary P. Latham and Travor C. Brown, "The Effect of Learning vs. Outcome Goals on Self-Efficacy, Satisfaction and Performance in an MBA Program," *Applied Psychology: An International Review*, 2006, vol. 55, pp. 606–623.

Evaluation and Implications

Goal-setting theory has been widely tested in a variety of settings. Research has demonstrated fairly consistently that goal difficulty and specificity are closely associated with performance. Other elements of the theory, such as acceptance and commitment, have been studied less frequently. A few studies have shown the importance of acceptance and commitment, but little is currently known about how people accept and become committed to goals. Goal-setting theory may also focus too much attention on the short run at the expense of long-term considerations. Additionally, one study that used scientists and professionals as subjects found negative relationships between goal difficulty and performance, contrary to the theory. This led the authors to suggest that goal setting might not work well in organizations where the work is extremely complex.[11] Despite these questions, however, goal setting is clearly very well researched and proven to work in a wide variety of situations. It is an important way for managers to convert motivation into actual improved performance in many contexts.[12]

From the broader perspective, MBO is also a very successful technique. Alcoa, Tenneco, Black & Decker, General Foods, and Du Pont, for example, have used it extensively. MBO's popularity stems in part from its many strengths. For one thing, MBO clearly has the potential to motivate employees because it helps implement goal-setting theory on a systematic basis throughout the organization. It also clarifies the basis for rewards, and it can spur communication. Performance appraisals are easier and more clear-cut under MBO. Further, managers can use the system for control purposes.[13]

However, using MBO also presents pitfalls. Research has shown that top management commitment is essential for MBO programs to work.[14] Sometimes top managers do not really participate; that is, the goals really start in the middle of the organization and may not reflect the real goals of top management. If employees believe this to be true, they may become cynical, interpreting the lack of participation by top management as a sign that the goals are not important and that their own involvement is therefore a waste of time. MBO also has a tendency to overemphasize quantitative goals to enhance verifiability. Another potential liability is that an MBO system requires a great deal of paperwork and record keeping, since every goal must be documented. Finally, some managers do not really let subordinates participate in goal setting, merely assigning goals and ordering subordinates to accept them.

On balance, MBO is often an effective and useful system for managing goal setting and enhancing performance in organizations. Research suggests that it can actually do many of the things its advocates claim, but that it must also be handled carefully. In particular, most organizations need to tailor it to their own circumstances. Properly used, MBO can also be an effective approach to managing an organization's reward system. It requires, however, individual, one-on-one interactions between each supervisor and each employee, and these one-on-one interactions can be difficult because of the time they take and the likelihood that at least some of them will involve critical assessments of unacceptable performance.

Job Design

Whereas goal setting and MBO programs successfully motivate workers to perform, the actual content of jobs also has a major effect on motivation and satisfaction. How can the work itself be made more interesting and motivating? Job design is an important method that managers can use to enhance employee performance. **Job design** is how organizations define and structure jobs. As we will see, properly designed jobs can have a positive impact on the motivation, performance, and job satisfaction of those who perform them. On the other hand, poorly designed jobs can impair motivation, performance, and job satisfaction. Before we get to that discussion however, we will explain a number of job design assumptions and approaches that have been developed over the last two centuries.

Job design is how organizations define and structure jobs.

The Evolution of Job Design

Until the nineteenth century, many families grew the things they needed, especially food. General craft jobs arose as people ceased or reduced their own food production, used their labour to produce other goods such as clothing and furniture, and traded these goods for food and other necessities. Over time, people's work became increasingly specialized as they followed this general pattern. For example, the general craft of clothing production splintered into specialized craft jobs such as weaving, tailoring, and sewing. This evolution toward specialization accelerated as the Industrial Revolution swept Europe in the 1700s and 1800s, followed by North America in the later 1800s.

The trend toward specialization eventually became a subject of formal study. The two most influential students of specialization were Adam Smith and Charles Babbage. Smith, an eighteenth-century Scottish economist, originated the phrase *division of labour* in his classic book *An Inquiry into the Nature and Causes of the Wealth of Nations* published in 1776.[15] The book tells the story of a group of pin-makers who specialized their jobs to produce many more pins per person in a day than each could have made by working alone.

In Smith's time, pin-making, like most other production work, was still an individual job. One person would perform all of the tasks required: drawing out a strip of wire, clipping it to the proper length, sharpening one end, attaching a head to the other end, and polishing the finished pin. With specialization, one person did nothing but draw out wire, another did the clipping, and so on. Smith attributed the dramatic increases in output to factors such as increased dexterity owing to practice, decreased time changing from one production operation to another, and the development of specialized equipment and machinery. The basic principles described in *The Wealth of Nations* provided the foundation for the assembly line.

Charles Babbage wrote *On the Economy of Machinery and Manufactures* in 1832.[16] Extending Smith's work, Babbage cited several additional advantages of job specialization: Relatively little time was needed to learn specialized jobs, waste decreased, workers needed to make fewer tool and equipment changes, and workers' skills improved through frequent repetition of tasks.

As the Industrial Revolution spread to North America from Europe, job specialization proliferated throughout industry. It began in the mid-1880s and reached its peak with the development of scientific management in the early 1900s.

Job Specialization

Job specialization, as advocated by scientific management, can help improve efficiency, but it can also promote monotony and boredom.

Frederick W. Taylor, the chief proponent of **job specialization**, argued that jobs should be scientifically studied, broken down into small component tasks, and then standardized across all workers doing the jobs.[17] (Recall our discussion of scientific management in Chapter 1.) Taylor's view was consistent with the premises of division of labour as discussed by Smith and Babbage. In practice, job specialization generally brought most, if not all, of the advantages its advocates claimed. Specialization paved the way for large-scale assembly lines and was at least partly responsible for the dramatic gains in output that North American industry achieved for several decades after the turn of the twentieth century.

On the surface, job specialization appears to be a rational and efficient way to structure jobs. In practice, however, performing those jobs can cause problems, foremost among them the extreme monotony of highly specialized tasks. Consider the job of assembling toasters. A person who does the entire assembly may find the job complex and challenging, albeit inefficient. If the job is specialized so that the worker simply inserts a heating coil into the toaster as it passes along on an assembly line, the process may be efficient, but it is unlikely to interest or challenge the worker. A worker numbed by boredom and monotony may be less motivated to work hard and more inclined to do poor-quality work or to complain about the job. For these reasons, managers began to search for job design alternatives to specialization.

One of the primary catalysts for this search was a famous 1952 study of jobs in the automobile industry. The purpose of this study was to assess how satisfied automobile workers were with various aspects of their jobs.[18] The workers indicated that they were reasonably satisfied with their pay, working conditions, and the quality of their supervision. However, they expressed extreme dissatisfaction with the actual work they did. The plants were very noisy, and the moving assembly line dictated a rigid, gruelling pace. Jobs were highly specialized and standardized.

The workers complained about six facets of their jobs: mechanical pacing by an assembly line, repetitiveness, low skill requirements, involvement with only a portion of the total production cycle, limited social interaction with others in the workplace, and lack of control over the tools and techniques used in the job. These sources of dissatisfaction were a consequence of the job design prescriptions of scientific management. Thus, managers began to recognize that although job specialization might lead to efficiency, if carried too far, it would have a number of negative consequences.[19]

Job specialization has been a common method for structuring jobs for over a hundred years. Take this young woman, for instance. She works in a Samsung electronics assembly plant in northern Mexico. The plant manufactures, among many other things, video tuning devices. Her job involves inserting tiny electronic components into the tuners as they pass along an assembly line. While specialization allows her to work quickly and efficiently, her job is also very monotonous.

Early Alternatives to Job Specialization

In response to the automobile plant study, other reported problems with job specialization, and a general desire to explore ways to create less monotonous jobs, managers began to seek alternative ways to design jobs. The Job Design and . . . Technology box describes some of the efforts made in other countries. In the United States, managers formulated two alternative approaches: job rotation and job enlargement.

Job Rotation   **Job rotation** involves systematically shifting workers from one job to another to sustain their motivation and interest. Figure 5.2 contrasts job rotation and job specialization. Under specialization, each task is broken down into small parts. For example, assembling pens might involve four discrete steps: testing the ink cartridge, inserting the cartridge into the barrel of the pen, screwing the cap onto the barrel, and inserting the assembled pen into a box. One worker performs each of these four tasks.

Job rotation is systematically moving workers from one job to another in an attempt to minimize monotony and boredom.

The Tavistock Institute of London conducted early studies on work arrangements. When job rotation is introduced, the tasks themselves stay the same. However, as Figure 5.2 shows, the workers who perform them are systematically rotated across the various tasks. White, for example, starts out with job 1 (testing ink cartridges). On a regular basis—perhaps weekly or monthly—she or he is systematically rotated to job 2, to job 3, to job 4, and back to job 1. LeBlanc, who starts out on job 2 (inserting cartridges into barrels), rotates ahead of White to jobs 3, 4, 1, and back to 2.

Numerous firms have used job rotation, including American Cyanamid, Baker International, Ford, Prudential Insurance, and Canada Post. Job rotation did not entirely live up to expectations, however.[20] The problem again was narrowly defined, routine

Job Design and . . . **TECHNOLOGY**

Job Design at Volvo

Many contemporary breakthroughs and innovations in job design were developed and pioneered abroad. As far back as 1951, for example, researchers at London's Tavistock Institute conducted important pioneering studies of jobs in the coal-mining industry in England. They examined a wide variety of work arrangements and found that flexibility in how jobs were performed and improved interpersonal relationships among employees could be a critical part of organizational effectiveness. Other research, conducted in textile mills in India, focused on the relationship between people and technology. The findings led managers to better appreciate the importance of both technical systems and social systems in organizations.

But perhaps the most ambitious experiment in job design took place in Sweden. In the early 1970s, Volvo was planning to build a new automobile assembly plant near the town of Kalmar. In designing the new factory, the firm's managers decided to see if they could change the traditional approach to jobs in the automobile industry to offset many of the negative factors associated with traditional assembly-line work. They constructed the entire facility to promote better job design and a more pleasant work environment for Volvo employees. For example, each worker was assigned a space that felt like a small workshop rather than a large factory. Natural lighting was emphasized, and each bay had separate lounge and rest facilities for the workers assigned there.

Instead of using a traditional automobile assembly line, the firm installed computer-guided trolleys that rolled along the floor. Workers moved around the trolleys to perform their tasks rather than standing stationary while the car moved past them. This gave them the flexibility to move the trolley off the line when a serious problem arose with the car on that particular trolley; thus, the problem could be attended to without slowing down the entire line.

While the factory cost about 10 percent more to construct than a traditional automobile plant, Volvo management believed that improvements in the quality of both worklife and the products that resulted compensated for at least some of the additional cost.

Sources: William Bridges, "The End of the Job," *Fortune*, 19 September 1994, pp. 62–74; Ricky W. Griffin, *Task Design: An Integrative Approach* (Glenview, Illinois: Scott, Foresman, 1982); Ricky W. Griffin and Gary C. McMahan, "Motivation Through Job Design," in Jerald Greenberg (ed.), *Organizational Behavior: State of the Science* (New York: Lawrence Erlbaum and Associates, 1994), pp. 23–44.

jobs. If a rotation cycle takes workers through the same old jobs, the workers simply experience several routine and boring jobs instead of just one. Although a worker may begin each job shift with a bit of renewed interest, the effect usually is short-lived.

Rotation can also decrease efficiency. For example, it clearly sacrifices the proficiency and expertise that grow from specialization. At the same time, job rotation is an effective training technique because a worker rotated through a variety of related jobs acquires a larger set of job skills. Thus, there is increased flexibility in transferring workers to new jobs. Many firms now use job rotation for training or other purposes, but few rely on it to motivate workers.

Job enlargement involves giving workers more tasks to perform.

Job Enlargement   **Job enlargement**, or horizontal job loading, expands a worker's job to include tasks previously performed by other workers. This process is also illustrated in Figure 5.2. Before enlargement, workers perform a single, specialized task; afterward, they have a larger job to do. Thus, after enlargement White and the other workers each does a bigger job than he or she did previously. Thus, assembling the pens has been redefined as two tasks rather than four. White and LeBlanc do the first task, while Chen and Goodleaf do the other. The logic behind this change is that the increased number of tasks in each job reduces monotony and boredom.

Maytag was one of the first companies to use job enlargement.[21] In the assembly of washing machine water pumps, for example, jobs done sequentially by six workers at a

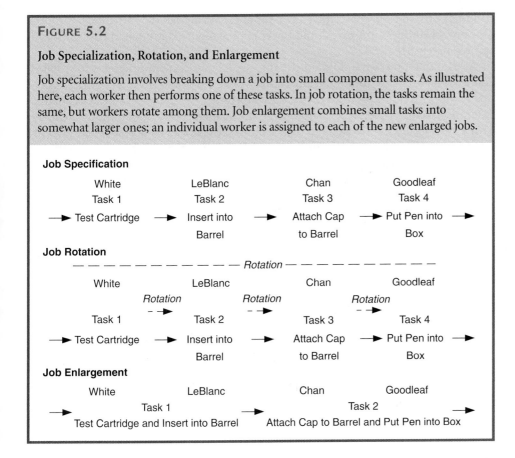

FIGURE 5.2

Job Specialization, Rotation, and Enlargement

Job specialization involves breaking down a job into small component tasks. As illustrated here, each worker then performs one of these tasks. In job rotation, the tasks remain the same, but workers rotate among them. Job enlargement combines small tasks into somewhat larger ones; an individual worker is assigned to each of the new enlarged jobs.

conveyor belt were modified so that each worker completed an entire pump alone. Other organizations that implemented job enlargement included AT&T, the U.S. Civil Service, and Colonial Life Insurance Company.

Unfortunately, job enlargement also failed to have the desired effects. Generally, if the entire production sequence consisted of simple, easy-to-master tasks, merely doing more of them did not significantly change the worker's job. If the task of putting two bolts on a piece of machinery was enlarged to putting on three bolts and connecting two wires, for example, the monotony of the original job essentially remained.

Job Enrichment

Job rotation and job enlargement seemed promising, but eventually disappointed managers seeking to counter the ill effects of extreme specialization. They failed partly because they were intuitive, narrow approaches rather than fully developed, theory-driven methods. Consequently, a new, more complex approach to task design—job enrichment—was developed. **Job enrichment** was initially based on the dual-structure theory of motivation, as discussed in Chapter 4. That theory contended that employees could be motivated by positive job-related experiences such as feelings of achievement, responsibility, and recognition. To achieve this, job enrichment relies on vertical job loading—not only adding more tasks to a job, as in horizontal loading, but giving the employee more control over those tasks.[22]

Texas Instruments used job enrichment to improve janitorial jobs. The company gave janitors more control over their schedules and let them sequence their own

Job enrichment entails giving workers more tasks to perform and more control over how to perform them.

cleaning jobs and purchase their own supplies. What was the outcome? Turnover dropped, cleanliness improved, and the company reported estimated cost savings of approximately $103 000.[23]

At the same time, we should note that many job enrichment programs have failed. Some companies have found job enrichment to be cost ineffective, and others believe that it simply did not produce the expected results.[24] Several programs at Prudential Insurance, for example, were abandoned because managers believed they were benefitting neither employees nor the firm. Some of the criticism is associated with the dual-structure theory of motivation, on which job enrichment is based. In Chapter 4, we reviewed the major objections: the theory confuses employee satisfaction with motivation, is fraught with methodological flaws, ignores situational factors, and is not convincingly supported by research.[25]

Because of these and other problems, job enrichment fell into disfavour among managers. Yet some valuable aspects of the concept can be salvaged. The efforts of managers and academic theorists ultimately have led to more complex and sophisticated viewpoints. Many of these advances are evident in the job characteristics approach, which we consider next.

The Job Characteristics Approach

The **job characteristics approach** focuses on the specific motivational properties of jobs. The most current view is the job characteristics theory. The theory also suggests that social information affects job design properties.

The Job Characteristics Theory

The **job characteristics theory**, diagrammed in Figure 5.3, was developed by Hackman and Oldham.[26] At the core of the theory is the idea of critical psychological states. These states are presumed to determine the extent to which characteristics of the job enhance employee responses to the task. The three critical psychological states are:

1. *Experienced meaningfulness of the work*—the degree to which the individual experiences the job as generally meaningful, valuable, and worthwhile.
2. *Experienced responsibility for work outcomes*—the degree to which individuals feel personally accountable and responsible for the results of their work.
3. *Knowledge of results*—the degree to which individuals continually understand how effectively they are performing the job.[27]

If employees experience these states at sufficiently high levels, they are likely to feel good about themselves and to respond favourably to their jobs. Hackman and Oldham suggest that the three critical psychological states are triggered by five characteristics of the job, or core job dimensions:

1. Skill variety—the degree to which the job requires a variety of activities that involve different skills and talents.
2. Task identity—the degree to which the job requires completion of a whole and an identifiable piece of work; that is, the extent to which a job has a beginning and an end with a tangible outcome.
3. Task significance—the degree to which the job affects the lives or work of other people, both in the immediate organization and in the external environment.

The job characteristics theory identifies three critical psychological states: experienced meaningfulness of the work, experienced responsibility for work outcomes, and knowledge of results.

The **job characteristics approach** focuses on the motivational attributes of jobs.

The **job characteristics theory** identifies five core job dimensions: skill variety, task identity, task significance, autonomy, and feedback.

FIGURE 5.3

The Job Characteristics Theory

The job characteristics theory is an important contemporary model of how to design jobs. By using five core job characteristics, managers can enhance three critical psychological states. These states, in turn, can improve a variety of personal and work outcomes. Individual differences also affect how the job characteristics affect people.

Source: J. R. Hackman and G. R. Oldham, "Motivation Through the Design of Work: Test of a Theory," *Organizational Behavior and Human Performance*, 1976, vol. 16, pp. 250–279. Copyright 1976 by Academic Press, Inc. Used with permission of the publisher and author.

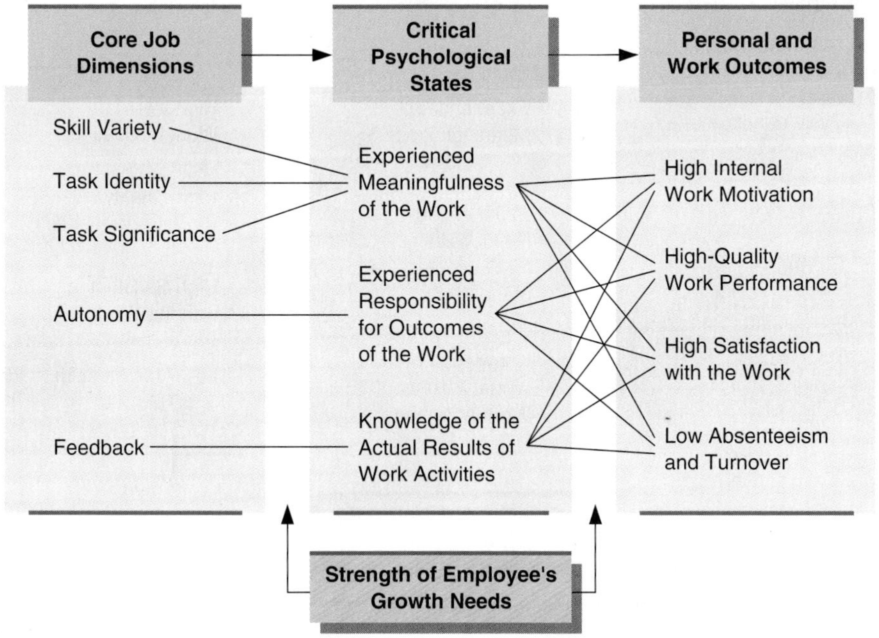

4. Autonomy—the degree to which the job allows the individual substantial freedom, independence, and discretion to schedule the work and determine the procedures for carrying it out.
5. Feedback—the degree to which the job activities give the individual direct and clear information about the effectiveness of his or her performance.

Figure 5.3 shows that these five job characteristics, operating through the critical psychological states, affect a variety of personal and work outcomes: high internal work motivation (that is, intrinsic motivation), high-quality work performance, high satisfaction with the work, and low absenteeism and turnover. The figure also suggests that individual differences play a role in job design. People with strong needs for personal growth and development will be especially motivated by the five core job characteristics. On the other hand, people with weaker needs for personal growth and development are less likely to be motivated by the core job characteristics.

Figure 5.4 expands the basic job characteristics theory by incorporating general guidelines to help managers implement it.[28] Managers can use such means as forming natural work units (that is, grouping similar tasks together), combining existing tasks into more complex ones, establishing direct relationships between workers and clients,

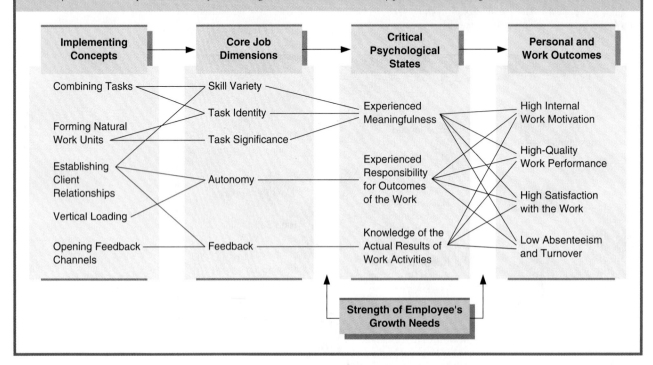

FIGURE 5.4

Implementing the Job Characteristics Theory

Managers should use a set of implementation guidelines if they want to apply the job characteristics theory in their organization. This figure shows some of these guidelines. For example, managers can combine tasks, form natural work units, establish client relationships, vertically load jobs, and open feedback channels.

Source: J. R. Hackman, G. R. Oldham, R. Janson, and K. Purdy, "A New Stage for Job Enrichment." Copyright © 1975 by the Regents of the University of California. Reprinted from *California Management Review*, vol. 17, no. 4, by permission of the Regents.

increasing worker autonomy through vertical job loading, and opening feedback channels. Theoretically, such actions should enhance the motivational properties of each task. Using these guidelines, sometimes in adapted form, several firms have successfully implemented job design changes, including 3M, Volvo, AT&T, Xerox, Motorola,[29] and the Michelin Tire plants in Nova Scotia.

Much research has been devoted to this approach to job design.[30] This research has generally supported the theory, particularly in demonstrating relationships between job characteristics and psychological outcomes such as satisfaction and motivation. However, the relationship between job characteristics and performance is generally weaker.[31] Several apparent weaknesses in the theory have also come to light. First, the measures used to test the theory are not always as valid and reliable as they should be.[32] Further, the role of individual differences frequently has not been supported by research. Finally, guidelines for implementation are not specific and managers usually tailor them to their own specific circumstances.[33] Still, the theory remains a popular perspective on studying and changing jobs.[34]

Social Information and Job Design

Research has also suggested that social information in the workplace may influence how individuals perceive and react to job characteristics.[35] For example, if a newcomer to the organization is told, "You're really going to like it here because everybody gets along so well," that person may assume that the job should be evaluated in terms of social interactions and that those interactions are satisfactory. But if the message is "You won't like it here because the boss is lousy and the pay is worse," the newcomer may think that the job's most important aspects are pay and interactions with the boss and that both areas are deficient.[36]

This view has received mixed support from empirical research.[37] Indeed, research suggests that how people perceive their jobs is determined by a complex combination of both objective task characteristics and social information about those characteristics.[38] For example, positive social information and a well-designed job may produce more favourable results than either positive information or a well-designed job alone. Conversely, negative information and a poorly designed job may produce more negative reactions than either negative social information or a poorly designed job would by itself. In situations where social information and job characteristics do not reinforce each other, they can cancel each other out. For example, negative social information can diminish the positive effects of a well-designed job, whereas positive information may at least partly offset the negative consequences of a poorly designed job.

Participation, Empowerment, and Motivation

Participative management and empowerment are two additional methods managers can use to enhance employee motivation. In a sense, participation and empowerment are extensions of job design, because each fundamentally alters how employees in an organization perform their jobs. **Participation** occurs when employees have a voice in decisions about their own work. **Empowerment** is the process of enabling workers to set their own work goals, make decisions, and solve problems within their spheres of responsibility and authority. Thus, empowerment is a somewhat broader concept that promotes participation in a wide variety of areas, including, but not limited to, work itself, work context, and work environment.[39]

> **Participation** entails giving employees a voice in making decisions about their own work.

> **Empowerment** is the process of enabling workers to set their own work goals, make decisions, and solve problems within their sphere of responsibility and authority.

Early Perspectives on Participation and Empowerment

The human relations movement, in vogue from the 1930s through the 1950s (see Chapter 1), assumed that employees who are happy and satisfied will work harder. This view stimulated management interest in having workers participate in a variety of organizational activities. Managers hoped that if employees had a chance to participate in decision making concerning their work environment, they would be satisfied, and this satisfaction would supposedly result in improved performance. But managers tended to see employee participation merely as a way to increase satisfaction, not as a source of potentially valuable input. Eventually, managers began to recognize that employee input was useful in itself, apart from its presumed effect on satisfaction. In other words, they came to see employees as valued human resources who can contribute to organizational effectiveness.[40]

The role of participation and empowerment in motivation can be expressed in terms of the expectancy theory discussed in Chapter 4. Employees who participate in decision making may be more committed to executing decisions properly. Furthermore, successfully making a decision, executing it, and then seeing the positive consequences can help provide recognition and responsibility, and enhance self-esteem and self-efficacy. Simply being asked to participate in organizational decision making may also

Autonomous work teams have become an increasingly popular form of work design in organizations. This team works at the NASA Jet Propulsion Laboratory in Pasadena. The team is working on a rover device used to explore Mars. The team is accountable for meeting NASA performance goals and expectations, but also has considerable autonomy over how it does its work.

enhance an employee's self-esteem. In addition, participation should help clarify expectancies; that is, by participating in decision making, employees may better understand the linkage between their performance and the rewards they want most.

Areas of Participation

At one level, employees can participate in addressing questions and making decisions about their own jobs. Instead of just telling them how to do their jobs, for example, managers can ask employees to make their own decisions about how to do them. Based on their own expertise and experience with their tasks, workers might be able to improve their own productivity. In many situations, they might also be well qualified to make decisions about what materials to use, what tools to use, and so forth. The example at the opening of this chapter of the freedom of people at WestJet to participate in management decisions is an illustration of this type of empowerment in the service sector.

It might also help to let workers make decisions about administrative matters, such as work schedules. If jobs are relatively independent of one another, employees might decide when to change shifts, take breaks, go to lunch, and so forth. A work group or team might also be able to schedule vacations and days off for all of its members. Furthermore, employees are getting increasingly more opportunities to participate in broader issues of product quality. Participation of this type has become a hallmark of successful Japanese and other international firms, and many North American companies have followed suit.[41]

Techniques and Issues in Empowerment

In recent years many organizations have actively sought ways to extend participation beyond the traditional areas. Simple techniques such as suggestion boxes and question-and-answer meetings allow a certain degree of participation, for example. The basic motive has been to better capitalize on the assets and capabilities inherent in all employees. Thus, many managers today prefer the term *empowerment* to *participation* because it implies a more comprehensive involvement.

One method some firms use to empower their workers is the use of work teams. This method grew out of early attempts to use what Japanese firms call *quality circles*. A quality circle is a group of employees who voluntarily meet regularly to identify and propose solutions to problems related to quality. This use of quality circles quickly grew to encompass a wider array of work groups, now generally called *work teams*. These teams are collections of employees empowered to plan, organize, direct, and control their own work. Their supervisor, rather than being a traditional boss, plays more the role of a coach. We discuss work teams more fully in Chapter 8.

The other method some organizations use to facilitate empowerment is to change their overall method of organizing. The basic pattern is for an organization to eliminate layers from its hierarchy, thereby becoming much more decentralized. Power, responsibility, and authority are delegated as far down the organization as possible, so control of work is squarely in the hands of those who actually do it. Chapter 13 addresses these trends in more detail.

Regardless of the specific technique used, however, empowerment only enhances organizational effectiveness if certain conditions exist. First, the organization must be sincere in its efforts to spread power and autonomy to lower levels of the organization. Token efforts to promote participation in just a few areas are unlikely to succeed. Second, the organization must be committed to maintaining participation and empowerment. Workers will be resentful if they are given more control, only to later have it reduced or taken away altogether. Third, the organization must be systematic and patient in its efforts to empower workers. Turning over too much control too quickly can spell disaster. Finally, the organization must be prepared to increase its commitment to training. Employees being given more freedom concerning how they work are likely to need additional training to help them exercise that freedom most effectively.

Alternative Work Arrangements

Beyond the actual design of jobs and the use of participation and empowerment, many organizations today are experimenting with a variety of alternative work arrangements. These arrangements are generally intended to enhance employee motivation and performance by giving them more flexibility about how and when they work. Among the more popular alternative work arrangements are variable work schedules, flexible work schedules, job sharing, and telecommuting.[42]

Variable Work Schedules

There are many exceptions, of course, but the traditional work schedule in Canada has long been days that start at 8:00 or 9:00 in the morning and end at 5:00 in the evening, five days a week (and of course, managers often work many additional hours outside of these times). Although the exact starting and ending times vary, most companies in other countries have also used a well-defined work schedule. But this schedule makes it difficult to attend to routine personal business—going to the bank, seeing a doctor or dentist, having a parent–teacher conference, getting an automobile serviced, and so forth. Employees locked into this work schedule may find it necessary to take a sick or vacation day to handle these activities. On a more psychological level, some people may feel so powerless and constrained by their job schedules that they grow resentful and frustrated.

To help counter these problems, one alternative some businesses use is a compressed work schedule.[43] An employee following a **compressed workweek** schedule works a full 40-hour week in fewer than the traditional five days. Most typically, this schedule involves working 10 hours a day for four days, leaving an extra day off. Another alternative

In a **compressed workweek**, employees work a full 40-hour week in fewer than the traditional five days.

Job sharing is an alternative work arrangement in which two part-time employees share one full-time job. For example, Amy Frank (left) and Denise Brown share the job of vice president of fixed-income sales at Bank of America. Frank works 9:00 to 5:00 Monday and Tuesday, and 9:00 to noon on Wednesday, while Brown works Wednesday afternoon, and all day on Thursday and Friday. This arrangement allows each of them to pursue a career, earn a reasonable income, and spend time at home with their children.

is for employees to work slightly less than 10 hours a day, but to complete the 40 hours by lunchtime on Friday. And a few firms have tried having employees work 12 hours a day for three days, followed by four days off. Canadian organizations that have used these forms of compressed work weeks include the nursing staffs at many hospitals and regional 911 operators. One problem with this schedule is that if everyone in the organization is off at the same time, the firm may have no one on duty to handle problems or deal with outsiders on the off day. But if the days off are staggered across the workforce, people who don't get the more desirable days off (Monday and Friday, for most people) may be jealous or resentful. Another problem is that when employees put in too much time in a single day, they tend to get tired and perform at a lower level later in the day. However, the examples of nurses and 911 operators demonstrate that these schedules can be used even when workstations must always be covered. Potential coverage problems and jealousy are avoided by the use of rotating schedules to ensure that everyone periodically gets desirable days off.

A popular schedule some organizations are beginning to use is called a "nine-eighty" schedule. Under this arrangement, an employee works a traditional schedule one week and a compressed schedule the next, getting every other Friday off. That is, they work 80 hours (the equivalent of two weeks of full-time work) in nine days. By alternating the regular and compressed schedules across half of its workforce, the organization is fully staffed at all times and still gives employees two additional full days off each month.

Flexible Work Schedules

Flexible work schedules, or **flextime**, give employees more personal control over the hours they work each day.

Another promising alternative work arrangement is **flexible work schedules**, sometimes called **flextime**. The compressed work schedules discussed above give employees time off during regular working hours, but they must still follow a regular and defined schedule on the days they do work. Flextime, however, usually gives employees less say over what days they work, but more personal control over when they work on those days.

Figure 5.5 illustrates how flextime works. The workday is broken down into two categories: flexible time and core time. All employees must be at their workstations

---

FIGURE 5.5

Flexible Work Schedules

Flexible work schedules are an important new work arrangement used in some organizations today. All employees must be at work during "core time." In the hypothetical example shown here, core time is from 9 to 11 A.M. and 1 to 3 P.M. The other time is flexible—employees can come and go as they please during this time, as long as the total time spent at work meets organizational expectations.

6:00 A.M.	9:00 A.M. – 11:00 A.M.		1:00 P.M. – 3:00 P.M.	6:00 P.M.
Flexible Time	Core Time	Flexible Time	Core Time	Flexible Time

---

during core time, but they can choose their own schedules during flexible time. Thus, one employee may choose to start work early in the morning and leave in mid-afternoon, another to start in the late morning and work until late afternoon, and a third to start early in the morning, take a long lunch break, and work until late afternoon.

The major advantage of this approach, as already noted, is that workers get to tailor their workday to fit their personal needs. A person who needs to visit the dentist in the late afternoon can just start work early. A person who stays out late one night can start work late the next day. And the person who needs to run some errands during lunch can take a longer midday break. On the other hand, flextime is more difficult to manage, because others in the organization may not be sure when a person will be available for meetings other than during the core time. Expenses such as utilities will also be higher, since the organization must remain open for a longer period each day.

Some organizations have experimented with a plan in which workers set their own hours, but then must follow that schedule each day. Others allow workers to modify their own schedule each day. Organizations that have used the flexible work schedule method for arranging work include most of the major banks in Canada, such as the Bank of Montreal, the Royal Bank of Canada, TD CanadaTrust, CIBC, and Scotiabank. The TD CanadaTrust and . . . Change box gives examples of flexible job schedules at TD CanadaTrust and other organizations.

Job Sharing

Yet another potentially useful alternative work arrangement is **job sharing**. In job sharing, two part-time employees share one full-time job. One person may perform the job from 8 A.M. to noon and the other from 1 to 5 P.M. Job sharing may be desirable for people who want to work only part-time or when job markets are tight. For its part, the organization can accommodate the preferences of a broader range of employees and may benefit from the talents of more people. Although job sharing has not been scientifically evaluated, it appears to be a useful alternative to traditional work scheduling.

Another work scheduling variation is the increasing movement toward permanent part-time, or contingent, workers. Organizations often do not have to pay benefits to part-time workers and can use them to more easily cut back or expand the workforce as needed.

In **job sharing**, two or more part-time employees share one full-time job.

Telecommuting

Telecommuting is a work arrangement in which employees spend part of their time working off-site.

A relatively new approach to alternative work arrangements is **telecommuting**—allowing employees to spend part of their time working off-site, usually at home. By using e-mail, computer networks, and other technology, many employees can maintain close contact with their organization and do as much work at home as they could in their office. The increased power and sophistication of modern communication technology is making telecommuting easier and easier. Oracle Corporation of Canada, and the major Canadian banks offer telecommuting options to some of their employees.

TD CanadaTrust and . . .   CHANGE

Flexible Work Arrangements

Flexible work arrangements—simply described as any work schedule other than the typical 9 to 5 Monday–Friday routine—have been used by organizations for roughly 40 years, and they continue to increase in popularity. People seek flexible schedules for many reasons. Some need flexibility to handle family obligations; some to help avoid peak rush hour traffic; others as a convenience or lifestyle choice.

Many Canadian organizations and their employees are using flexible work arrangements. One Government of Canada study found that one-third of Canadian workers have some form of flexible work schedules, and one-fifth can work from home, or telecommute. And further growth is predicted. A survey done for CareerBuilder.ca, a job posting site, found that slightly more than 25 percent of hiring managers were willing or extremely willing to offer flexible arrangements to future hires. The same

survey found that 16 percent of hiring managers would be willing to extend telecommuting as an option.

TD CanadaTrust offers a wide variety of flexible work arrangements. *Flextime* allows employees to work regular hours that combine to be less than 37.5 hours per week. This can be accomplished by working fewer scheduled hours per day, or fewer scheduled days per week. *Flexhours* occur when an employee and manager establish a flexible schedule that allows employees to work the full number of daily scheduled hours at some point during the day. *Flexweek* offers employees an opportunity to work a standard amount of hours over a greater or less number of days. *Flexplace* provides the employee with the freedom to work at a location other than the main office, typically from home, for all or part of the week. *Flexjob* allows two employees to share a full-time position. The number of hours worked by each employee can vary, but both partners are equally responsible for the results of the position. Finally, *Flexreturn* is a gradual return to normal duties that is available to all employees, male or female, who are returning from a childcare leave.

Similarly, the Royal Bank of Canada offers flextime, job sharing, telecommuting, and modified work weeks to employees. It even has a special program for Canadian Olympians and Paralympians whereby they can work flexible hours to accommodate their training schedules!

Sources: "Control Over Time and Work-Life Balance: An Empirical Analysis," *Federal Labour Standards Review,* prepared by Graham Lowe; www.fls-ntf.gc.ca/en/re-exsum-15.asp on Feb 12, 2007; "Top Job Trends for 2007." Remy Piazza, Managing Director of CareerBuilder.ca; www.careerbuilder.ca, on Feb 12, 2007; Toronto Dominion, http://www.td.com/hr/balance.jsp on Feb 12, 2007; RBC website for all employees http://www.rbc.com/uniquecareers/meetrbc/workplace.html, and about the athletes http://www.rbc.com/newsroom/20060612athletes.html

On the plus side, many employees like telecommuting because it gives them added flexibility. By spending one or two days a week at home, for instance, they have the same kind of flexibility to manage personal activities as is afforded by flextime or compressed schedules. Some employees also feel that they get more work done by staying at home, because they are less likely to be interrupted. Organizations can also benefit: (1) they can reduce absenteeism and turnover, since employees need to take less *formal* time off, and (2) they can save on facilities such as parking spaces, because fewer people are at work on any given day.

On the other hand, although many employees thrive under this arrangement, others do not. Some feel isolated and miss the social interaction of the workplace. And some people simply lack the self-discipline to walk from the breakfast table to their desk and start working. Managers may also encounter coordination difficulties in scheduling meetings and other activities that require face-to-face contact. Still, given the boom in communication technology and the pressures for flexibility, many more organizations will no doubt be using telecommuting in the years to come.

Chapter Review

Summary of Key Points

■ Managers seek to enhance employee performance by capitalizing on the potential for motivated behaviour intended to improve performance. Methods often used to translate motivation into performance involve goal setting, management by objectives, job design, participation and empowerment, and alternative work arrangements.

■ A goal is a desirable objective. The goal-setting theory of motivation suggests that appropriate goal difficulty, specificity, acceptance, and commitment will result in higher levels of motivated performance. Management by objectives, or MBO, extends goal setting throughout an organization by cascading goals down from the top of the firm to the bottom.

■ Job design is how organizations define and structure jobs. Historically, there was a general trend toward increasingly specialized jobs, but more recently the movement has consistently been away from extreme specialization. Two early alternatives to specialization were job rotation and job enlargement. Job enrichment approaches stimulated considerable interest in job design.

■ The job characteristics theory grew from early work on job enrichment. One basic premise of this theory is that jobs can be described in terms of a specific set of motivational characteristics. Another is that managers should work to enhance the presence of those motivational characteristics in jobs, but should also take individual differences into account. Today the emerging opinion is that employees' job perceptions and attitudes are jointly determined by objective task properties and social information.

■ Participative management and empowerment can help improve employee motivation in many business settings. New management practices, such as the use of various kinds of work teams and of flatter, more decentralized methods of organizing, are each intended to empower employees throughout the organization. Organizations that want to empower their employees need to understand a variety of issues as they go about promoting participation.

■ Alternative work arrangements are commonly used today to enhance motivated job performance. Among the more popular alternative arrangements are compressed work weeks, flexible work schedules, job sharing, and telecommuting.

Discussion Questions

1. Critique the goal-setting theory of motivation.

2. Develop a framework whereby an instructor could use goal setting in running a class such as this one.

3. What are the primary advantages and disadvantages of job specialization? Were they the same in the early days of mass production?

4. Under what circumstances might job enlargement be especially effective? Especially ineffective? How about job rotation?

5. Do any trends today suggest a return to job specialization?

6. What are the strengths and weaknesses of job enrichment? When might it be useful?

7. Do you agree or disagree that individual differences affect how people respond to their jobs? Explain.

8. What are the primary similarities and differences between job enrichment and the approach proposed by job characteristics theory?

9. Can you recall any instances in which social information affected how you perceived or felt about something?

10. What are the motivational consequences of participative management from the frame of reference of expectancy and equity theories?

11. Which form of alternative work schedule might you prefer?

12. How do you think you would like telecommuting?

Purpose: This exercise will help you assess the processes involved in designing jobs to make them more motivating.

Format: Working in small groups, you will diagnose the motivating potential of an existing job, compare its motivating potential to that of other jobs, suggest ways to redesign the job, and then assess the effects of your redesign suggestions on other aspects of the workplace.

Procedure: Your instructor will divide the class into groups of three or four people each. In assessing the characteristics of jobs, use a scale value of 1 ("very little") to 7 ("very high").

1. Using the scale values, assign scores on each core job dimension used in the job characteristics theory (see page 140) to the following jobs: secretary, professor, food server, auto mechanic, lawyer, short-order cook, department store clerk, construction worker, and newspaper reporter.

2. Researchers often assess the motivational properties of jobs by calculating their motivating potential score (MPS). The usual formula for MPS is:

$$(\text{Variety} + \text{Identity} + \text{Significance})/3 \times \text{Autonomy} \times \text{Feedback}.$$

Use this formula to calculate the MPS for each job in step 1.

3. Your instructor will now assign your group one of the jobs from the list. Discuss how you might reasonably go about enriching the job.

4. Calculate the new MPS score for the redesigned job, and check its new position in the rank ordering.

5. Discuss the feasibility of your redesign suggestions. In particular, look at how your recommended changes might necessitate changes in other jobs, in the reward system, and in the selection criteria used to hire people for the job.

6. Briefly discuss your observations with the rest of the class.

Follow-up Questions

1. How might the social-information-processing model explain some of your own perceptions in this exercise?

2. Are some jobs simply impossible to redesign?

The Job Characteristics Inventory

The questionnaire below was developed to measure the central concepts of the job characteristics theory. Answer the questions in relation to the job you currently hold or the job you most recently held.

Skill Variety

1. How much *variety* is there in your job? That is, to what extent does the job require you to do many different things at work, using a variety of your skills and talents?

1	2	3	4	5	6	7
Very little; the job requires me to do the same routine things over and over again.			Moderate variety			Very much; the job requires me to do many different things, using a number of different skills and talents.

2. The job requires me to use a number of complex or high-level skills.

How accurate is the statement in describing your job?

1	2	3	4	5	6	7
Very inaccurate	Mostly inaccurate	Slightly inaccurate	Uncertain	Slightly accurate	Mostly accurate	Very accurate

3. The job is quite simple and repetitive.*

How accurate is the statement in describing your job?

1	2	3	4	5	6	7
Very inaccurate	Mostly inaccurate	Slightly inaccurate	Uncertain	Slightly accurate	Mostly accurate	Very accurate

Task Identity

1. To what extent does your job involve doing a *"whole" and identifiable piece of work*? That is, is the job a complete piece of work that has an obvious beginning and end? Or is it only a small *part* of the overall piece of work, which is finished by other people or by automatic machines?

1	2	3	4	5	6	7
My job is only a tiny part of the overall piece of work; the results of my activities cannot be seen in the final product or service.			My job is a moderate-sized "chunk" of the overall piece of work; my own contribution can be seen in the final outcome.			My job involves doing the whole piece of work, from start to finish; the results of my activities are easily seen in the final product or service.

2. The job provides me a chance to completely finish the pieces of work I begin.

How accurate is the statement in describing your job?

1	2	3	4	5	6	7
Very inaccurate	Mostly inaccurate	Slightly inaccurate	Uncertain	Slightly accurate	Mostly accurate	Very accurate

3. The job is arranged so that I do *not* have the chance to do an entire piece of work from beginning to end.*

How accurate is the statement in describing your job?

1	2	3	4	5	6	7
Very inaccurate	Mostly inaccurate	Slightly inaccurate	Uncertain	Slightly accurate	Mostly accurate	Very accurate

Task Significance

1. In general, how significant or important is your job? That is, are the results of your work likely to significantly affect the lives or well-being of other people?

1	2	3	4	5	6	7
Not very significant; the outcomes of my work are *not* likely to have important effects on other people.			Moderately significant			Highly significant; the outcomes of my work can affect other people in very important ways.

2. This job is one where a lot of people can be affected by how well the work gets done.

How accurate is the statement in describing your job?

1	2	3	4	5	6	7
Very inaccurate	Mostly inaccurate	Slightly inaccurate	Uncertain	Slightly accurate	Mostly accurate	Very accurate

3. The job itself is *not* very significant or important in the broader scheme of things.*

How accurate is the statement in describing your job?

1	2	3	4	5	6	7
Very inaccurate	Mostly inaccurate	Slightly inaccurate	Uncertain	Slightly accurate	Mostly accurate	Very accurate

Autonomy

1. How much *autonomy* is there in your job? That is, to what extent does your job permit you to decide *on your own* how to go about doing your work?

1	2	3	4	5	6	7
Very little; the job gives me almost no personal "say" about how and when the work is done.			Moderate autonomy; many things are standardized and not under my control, but I can make some decisions about the work.			Very much; the job gives me almost complete responsibility for deciding how and when the work is done.

2. The job gives me considerable opportunity for independence and freedom in how I do the work.

How accurate is the statement in describing your job?

1	2	3	4	5	6	7
Very inaccurate	Mostly inaccurate	Slightly inaccurate	Uncertain	Slightly accurate	Mostly accurate	Very accurate

3. The job denies me any chance to use my personal initiative or judgment in carrying out the work.*

How accurate is the statement in describing your job?

1	2	3	4	5	6	7
Very inaccurate	Mostly inaccurate	Slightly inaccurate	Uncertain	Slightly accurate	Mostly accurate	Very accurate

Feedback

1. To what extent does *doing the job itself* provide you with information about your work performance? That is, does the actual *work itself* provide clues about how well you are doing—aside from any "feedback" coworkers or supervisors may provide?

1	2	3	4	5	6	7
Very little; the job itself is set up so I could work forever without finding out how well I am doing.			Moderately; sometimes doing the job provides "feedback" to me; sometimes it does not.			Very much; the job is set up so that I get almost constant "feedback" as I work about how well I am doing.

2. Just doing the work required by the job provides many chances for me to figure out how well I am doing.

How accurate is the statement in describing your job?

1	2	3	4	5	6	7
Very inaccurate	Mostly inaccurate	Slightly inaccurate	Uncertain	Slightly accurate	Mostly accurate	Very accurate

3. The job itself provides very few clues about whether or not I am performing well.*

How accurate is the statement in describing your job?

1	2	3	4	5	6	7
Very inaccurate	Mostly inaccurate	Slightly inaccurate	Uncertain	Slightly accurate	Mostly accurate	Very accurate

Scoring: Responses to the three items for each core characteristic are averaged to yield an overall score for that characteristic. Items marked with a "*" should be scored as follows: 1 = 7; 2 = 6; 3 = 3; 6 = 2; 7 = 1

$$\text{Motivating potential score} = \frac{\text{Skill variety} + \text{Task identity} + \text{Task Significance}}{3} \times \text{Autonomy} \times \text{Feedback}$$

Source: J. R. Hackman and G. R. Oldham, *Work Redesign* (adapted from pages 275–294). © 1980. Reprinted by permission of Pearson Education, Inc., Upper Saddle River, NJ.

Management Skillbuilder

Exercise Overview: Conceptual skills refer to a person's abilities to think in the abstract. This exercise will help you develop your conceptual skills as they relate to designing jobs.

Exercise Background: Begin by thinking of three different jobs, one that appears to have virtually no enrichment, one that seems to have moderate enrichment, and one that appears to have a great deal of enrichment. These jobs might be ones that you have personally held or ones that you have observed and about which you can make some educated or informed judgments.

Evaluate each job along the five dimensions described in the job characteristics theory. Next, see if you can identify ways to improve each of the five dimensions for each job. That is, see if you can determine how to enrich the jobs by using the job characteristics theory as a framework.

Finally, meet with a classmate and share results. See if you can improve your job enrichment strategy based on the critique offered by your classmate.

Exercise Task: Using the background information about the three jobs you examined as context, answer the following questions.

1. What job qualities make some jobs easier to enrich than others?

2. Can all jobs be enriched?

3. Even if a particular job can be enriched, does that always mean that it should be enriched?

4. Under what circumstances might an individual prefer to have a routine and unenriched job?

Organizational Behaviour Case for Discussion

No More Dawdling over Dishes

Andy Davis was proud of his restaurant, The Golden Bow. Its location was perfect, its decor tasteful, its clientele generous and distinguished. When he first took over the business a year ago, Davis had worried that the local labour shortage might make it difficult to hire good workers. But he had made some contacts at a local college and hired a group of servers who worked well with customers and with one another. The only problem he still had not solved was the dishwasher.

At first Davis felt lucky when he found Eddie Munz, a local high-school dropout who had some experience washing dishes. Davis could not afford to pay a dishwasher more than $7.25 an hour, but Eddie did not seem to mind that. Moreover, Eddie seemed to get the dishes clean. But he was so slow! Davis originally thought Eddie just was not quick about anything, but he changed his mind as he observed his behaviour in the kitchen. Eddie loved to talk to the cooks, often turning his back on the dishes for minutes at a time to chitchat. He also nibbled desserts off of dirty plates and sprayed the servers with water whenever they got near him. The kitchen was always a mess, and so many dishes piled up that often two hours after closing time, when everything else was ready for the next day, Eddie would still be scraping and squirting and talking. Davis began to wonder if there was a method to Eddie's madness: he was getting paid by the hour, so why should he work faster? But Davis did not like having a constantly sloppy kitchen, so he decided to have a talk with Eddie.

Davis figured out that Eddie had been making $50.75 on his reasonably efficient nights and then met with Eddie and made him a proposal. First he asked Eddie how soon he thought he could finish after the last customer left. Eddie said an hour and a quarter. When Davis asked if he would be interested in getting off forty-five minutes earlier than he had been, Eddie seemed excited. And when he offered to pay Eddie the $50.75 for a complete job every night, regardless of when he finished, Eddie could hardly contain himself. It turned out he did not like to work until 2:00 A.M., but he needed every dollar he could get.

The next week, a new chalkboard appeared next to the kitchen door leading out to the dining room. On top it read, "Eddie's Goal for a Record Time." By the end of the first week, Davis had printed on the bottom "1 hour."

Davis began inspecting the dishes more often than usual, but he found no decrease in the quality of Eddie's work. So on Sunday, he said to Eddie, "Let's try for an hour."

A month later, the board read "42 minutes." The situation in the kitchen had changed radically. The former "Eddie the Slob" had become "Eddie the Perfectionist." His area was spotless, he was often waiting when someone came from the dining room with a stack of dirty plates, and he took it as a personal affront if anyone found a spot on a plate he had washed. Instead of complaining about Eddie squirting them, the servers kidded him about what a worker he had become, and they stacked the plates and separated the silver to help him break his record. And the first time Eddie got done at 12:42, they all went out for an hour on the town together.

Case Questions

1. What did Andy Davis do to change Eddie's behaviour?

2. Which elements of goal setting and job design did Davis use?

3. Could Davis have used a different system of rewards to get the same results from Eddie?

Organizational Behaviour Case for Discussion

Allen's Insurance

Allen's Insurance is a small insurance company located in Meductic, New Brunswick. The entire agency employs six people: the owner/manager/agent, and five clerical staff who perform all of the paperwork (new policies, renewals, claims processing, etc.) required for the agency. The current owner, Jean Allen, took over the business after her father, the founder, died. Jean had a business degree, but no previous experience in insurance prior to inheriting the company. When she became president five years ago, she quickly realized that the company was nearly bankrupt.

Her father had been in poor health for several years prior to his death. He prided himself on being a "people person" who did not like to turn anyone away. These two factors—poor health (and the apparent consequent lack of attention to the business) coupled with an overly generous spirit, led the company to write a number of overly risky policies. The poor risks turned out to be very poor risks indeed. When Jean took over, the company was severely strapped for cash. So, Jean took charge. Her first action was to initiate the practice that every policy-writing decision had to be approved by her. Like her father before her, Jean was the only official agent in the company, so she was the only person who could actually write policies. However, her father had over the years developed the practice of allowing the clerical staff to handle much of the routine business. They contacted current clients with renewal notices, negotiated rates (within guidelines), and did most of the claims work. Jean's father, for the most part, simply signed the papers after the clerical staff had completed them.

Jean thought that part of the reason for the agency's poor financial health when she took over was that the clerks had too much freedom. So, the first action she took upon taking over was to demand that every decision regarding policies be made by her, even the most straightforward renewals. Jean's hard-nosed approach of not renewing high risk policies, then slowly adding more lucrative policies, especially in commercial insurance, to the company's client base, succeeded in turning the company around.

There were some hard feelings at first. Since Allen's operates in a small community, it seemed like everyone knew someone who had a policy either cancelled or not renewed by Jean. However, over time, Jean was able to restore good will in the community by telling her remaining and new clients the reason for her actions. In short, she told them that the high risk policies put the low risk policy holders into jeopardy. If Allen's went under because of the poor risks, everyone would suffer.

There were also hard feelings within the company. The clerks had been fairly free to do pretty much whatever they thought was right during the last few years that Jean's father ran the company. The staff had a good feel for the company's operating philosophy. After Jean took over, however, every action had to be justified. The staff felt stifled. However, the staff seemed to come around after a while, when Jean explained the poor shape that the company was in, and why she needed complete control of operations. She told the employees the same message that she told the clients. Change was necessary. The old way of doing business almost killed the company. Although the staff might not like the new methods, at least they still had jobs. After that, things ran relatively smoothly for a couple of years.

However, about one and a half years ago, everyone at the agency felt that something was wrong. Jean was starting to feel stretched and stressed. The client base that she restored and built was hard for her to maintain, since she had to review every policy decision. Added to that was the increased complexity of the agency's client base. Since Jean took over, the commercial side of the agency's business had grown to the point that it represented about 35 percent of revenues. This was on top of the residential insurance that historically had been the agency's bread and butter. Jean was having a hard time keeping up with regulatory and product changes in commercial and residential insurance. She wanted to offer a wider variety of commercial products to attract larger policies, but she realized that the company had no room for growth given its current operating system.

The staff's morale also had plummeted. They could no longer respond to client's inquiries or claims directly, since they had learned to refer all decisions to Jean. They were reduced to a purely mechanical function of filling and filing forms that Jean had drafted. Since they had insurance experience ranging between 9–25 years, they felt that they were not being used to their potential. They occasionally discussed their feelings among themselves, and some even talked about quitting, but since jobs were scarce in the community, there were not any real opportunities to leave.

The crunch came about six months ago, when a couple of large commercial clients and a few longstanding residential clients opted not to renew their policies. Jean was savvy enough to call the clients who had left to determine why they left and to try to get them back. The responses she got from all of the clients, both commercial and residential were nearly identical. Mike Kraft, who had been a residential client with the agency for almost twenty years, gave a typical response:

"Well, y'know Jeannie, I liked doing business with your father. I knew all the girls, and your dad knew me. Things ran pretty smooth. But now, it seems like I don't know anyone there. When I call with a question, it's still the same girls, but they act like they don't know anything about me or about anything at all. They tell me that only you can give the answer, but it seems like I never got to talk to you—you were always with another client or busy with something else. Anyway, it seems like I was always getting a runaround and it took forever to get a simple question answered. The last straw came late last year, when I filed my first claim ever. It took about four months to get a settlement. That's way too slow.

"So, I took my business to the big All Farm agency down in Fredericton. The rates are a little cheaper, and I don't know anyone there either, but so far, I always get fast service. I like you and all that, and know you're doing the best you can, but I can't afford another long wait if I have to file another claim. Sorry, but good luck to you, and say 'hi' to your mom for me."

Jean was floored. She had already given up on the idea of growing the business because of the workload. Now, it looked like she was going to start losing clients for the same reason. She didn't know what to do. She couldn't afford to add another agent, especially if she was losing clients, and if things went really bad, she might have to lay some staff off, which could only lead to a downward spiral of losing business, layoffs, lose more business because service would deteriorate, which would result in more layoffs . . .

Case Questions

1. How can the work be redesigned to resolve the problems?

Look back to the "Implementing Concepts" in the discussion of the job characteristics approach for hints on how to approach the question.

SELF TEST

You have read the chapter and studied the key terms. Think you're ready to ace the exam? Take this sample test to gauge your comprehension of chapter material and check your answers at the back of the book. Want more test questions? Take the ACE quizzes found on the student website: www.hmco.ca/ob

T F 1. Goals are effective control devices.

T F 2. Research shows "do your best" goals are the most effective.

T F 3. Job specialization is a technique in which managers assign certain high-performing employees to the best jobs in the company.

T F 4. Many organizations today rely on job rotation to motivate employees.

T F 5. Job enrichment adds more tasks to a job and gives employees more control over those tasks.

T F 6. According to job characteristics theory, all individuals are equally motivated by core job characteristics.

7. Which of the following best describes management by objectives (MBO)?
a. Market forces determine organizational goals.
b. Top managers determine goals for each employee in the organization.
c. Objective performance goals are set for the organization as a whole, but not for individual employees.
d. Managers and subordinates meet and jointly determine goals for the subordinate.
e. Subordinates are trained to set personal goals without the help of managers.

8. Which of the following is not true about job specialization?
a. Jobs are broken down into small component tasks.
b. Specialization paved the way for large-scale assembly lines.
c. Specialization typically raises employees' job motivation.
d. Specialization increases efficiency.
e. Problems with specialization led to the study of alternative job designs.

9. Job enrichment combines job enlargement with
a. a piece-rate incentive system.
b. commission-based wages.
c. hygiene factors from dual-structure theory.
d. greater employee control over their tasks.
e. job characteristics theory.

10. Which of the following is not a core job dimension in job characteristics theory?
a. Feedback
b. Specialization
c. Skill variety
d. Task identity
e. Autonomy

11. Larry has a strong need for personal growth and development. According to job characteristics theory
a. Larry will be especially motivated by the five core job dimensions.
b. Larry will thrive in an environment of high specialization.
c. Larry will seek knowledge of results but avoid responsibility for work outcomes.
d. high levels of task identity and task significance will potentially lower Larry's motivation.
e. the core job dimensions will be only minimally motivating to Larry.

12. Allison's manager solicits her participation when making decisions in the department. Allison's participation is likely to lead to her
a. eventual turnover.
b. increased commitment to executing the decisions properly.
c. frustration in trying to satisfy her need for achievement and recognition.
d. belief that job specialization is a superior job design.
e. ability to separate her work life from her private life.

13. Matthew drives a delivery truck and works a full forty-hour week in four ten-hour days. Matthew's schedule is called
a. telecommuting.
b. job sharing.
c. flextime.
d. core time.
e. a compressed work week.

CHAPTER 6

Managing Stress and the Work–Life Balance

- ▶ **Discuss the meaning and nature of work stress.**
- ▶ **Describe how basic individual differences affect stress.**
- ▶ **Identify and discuss several common causes of stress.**
- ▶ **Identify and discuss several common consequences of stress.**
- ▶ **Explain ways that individuals and organizations can better manage stress.**
- ▶ **Describe work–life linkages and how they relate to stress.**

The Stress of Nursing

Although burnout is a reality in many professions, some are hit harder than others. There is no doubt that nursing is a stressful profession. Nurses deal with medical emergencies on a daily basis and are charged with providing care for individuals with a wide variety of illnesses, including terminal ones. At the same time, they are afforded little opportunity to exercise their professional judgment in diagnoses and treatment decisions.

Not surprisingly, nurses are susceptible to burnout, especially in an era in which hospitals are experiencing significant decreases in government funding and increasing workloads. And though burnout hits nurses at all career stages, it seems that it particularly affects younger nurses. A recent survey of 225 junior nurses across Ontario by researchers at the University of Western Ontario indicated that 66 percent reported symptoms of burnout, such as emotional exhaustion and depression.

These findings were borne out by a National Survey of the Work and Health of Nurses conducted by Statistics Canada. This large scale survey of nearly 19 000 nurses across the country revealed that depression rates were higher among nurses than in the general working population. Burnout also has implications for the organization because of higher levels of absenteeism among those individuals experiencing job strain. According to the study findings, 17 percent of nurses who reported high levels of job strain reported 20 or more sick days in the previous year.

Insurance claim information provided by the Quebec Provincial Association of Teachers indicates that burnout is taking its toll in the teaching profession as well. According to these figures, 31 percent of the Quebec teachers who go on long-term leave do so because of stress-related illnesses. And, as with nurses, burnout seems to hit younger teachers harder. Most of those teachers suffering from burnout have been in the profession fewer than 10 years. In addition to an increased workload, a major contributing factor to burnout is the lack of physical and emotional resources to do the job. With tighter government budgets, teachers face larger class sizes and more special-needs children in classrooms without assistance provided for the teachers. According to Michael Leiter, Canada Research Chair in Occupational Health and Well-Being at Acadia University, the amount of influence one has on the decisions about one's work is the most important determinant of burnout.[1]

Nurses and teachers, of course, are not the only people who experience the negative impact of a stressful workplace. Many people today work long hours, face constant deadlines, and are pressured to produce more and more. Organizations and the people who run them are under constant pressure to increase income while keeping costs in check. To do things faster and better—but with fewer people—is the goal of many companies. An unfortunate effect of this trend is that it puts too much pressure on people, such as operating employees and other managers. The results can indeed be increased performance, higher profits, and faster growth. But stress, burnout, turnover, aggression, and other unpleasant side effects can also occur.

In this chapter, we examine how and why stress occurs in organizations and how to better understand and control it. First, we explore the nature of stress. Then we look at such important individual differences as Type A and B personality profiles and their role in stress. Next, we discuss a number of causes of stress and consider the potential consequences of stress. We then highlight several things people and organizations can do to manage stress at work. Finally, we discuss an important factor related to stress-work-life linkages.

The Nature of Stress

Many people think of stress as a simple problem. In reality, however, stress is complex and often misunderstood. To learn how job stress truly works, we must first define it and then describe the process through which it develops.

Stress Defined

Stress is a person's adaptive response to a stimulus that places excessive psychological or physical demands on that person.

Stress has been defined in many ways, but most definitions say that stress is caused by a stimulus, that the stimulus can be either physical or psychological, and that the individual responds to the stimulus in some way.[2] We define **stress** as a person's adaptive response to a stimulus that places excessive psychological or physical demands on him or her.

Given the underlying complexities of this definition, we need to examine its components carefully. First is the notion of adaptation. As we discuss presently, people adapt to stressful circumstances in any of several ways. Second is the role of the stimulus. This stimulus, generally called a stressor, is anything that induces stress. Third, stressors can be either psychological or physical. Fourth, the demands the stressor places on the individual must be excessive for stress to result. Of course, what one person finds excessive, another may find perfectly tolerable. The point is simply that a person must perceive the demands as excessive or stress will not result.

The Stress Process

Much of what we know about stress today can be traced to the pioneering work of Dr. Hans Selye.[3] Among Selye's most important contributions were his identification of the general adaptation syndrome and the concepts of eustress and distress.

The **general adaptation syndrome (GAS)** identifies three stages of response to a stressor: alarm, resistance, and exhaustion.

General Adaptation Syndrome   Figure 6.1 graphically shows the **general adaptation syndrome (GAS)**. According to this model, each of us has a normal level of resistance to stressful events. Some of us can tolerate a great deal of stress and others much less, but we all have a threshold at which stress starts to affect us.

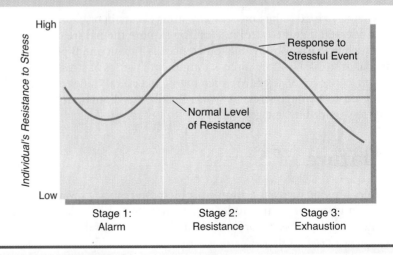

FIGURE 6.1

The General Adaptation Syndrome

The general adaptation syndrome (GAS) perspective describes three stages of the stress process. The initial stage is called alarm. As illustrated here, a person's resistance often dips slightly below the normal level during this stage. Next comes actual resistance to the stressor, usually leading to an increase above the person's normal level of resistance. Finally, in stage 3, exhaustion may set in and the person's resistance declines sharply below normal levels.

The GAS begins when a person first encounters a stressor. The first stage is called *alarm*. At this point, the person may feel some degree of panic and begin to wonder how to cope. The individual may also have to resolve a *fight-or-flight* question: "Can I deal with this, or should I run away?" For example, suppose a manager is assigned to write a lengthy report overnight. His or her first reaction may be "How will I ever get this done by tomorrow?"

If the stressor is too extreme, the person may simply be unable to cope with it. In most cases, however, the individual gathers his or her strength (physical or emotional) and begins to resist the negative effects of the stressor. The manager with the long report to write may calm down, call home to tell the kids that she or he is working late, roll up her or his sleeves, order out for dinner, and get to work. Thus, at stage 2 of the GAS, the person is *resisting* the effects of the stressor.

Often, the resistance phase ends the GAS. If the manager completes the report earlier than expected, she or he may drop it in a briefcase, smile, and head home tired but happy. On the other hand, prolonged exposure to a stressor without resolution may bring on phase 3 of the GAS: *exhaustion*. At this stage, the person literally gives up and can no longer fight the stressor. For example, the manager may fall asleep at her or his desk at 3 A.M. and fail to finish the report.

Distress and Eustress   Selye also pointed out that the sources of stress need not be bad.[4] For example, receiving a bonus and then having to decide what to do with the money can be stressful. So can getting a promotion, gaining recognition, getting married, and similar good things. Selye called this type of stress **eustress**. As we will see later, eustress can lead to a number of positive outcomes for the individual.

> **Eustress** is the pleasurable stress that accompanies positive events.

Of course, there is also negative stress. Called **distress**, this is what most people think of when they hear the word stress. Excessive pressure, unreasonable demands on our time, and bad news all fall into this category. As the term suggests, this form of stress generally results in negative consequences for the individual.

> **Distress** is the unpleasant stress that accompanies negative events.

For purposes of simplicity, we will continue to use the simple term stress throughout this chapter. But as you read and study the chapter, remember that stress can be either good or bad. It can motivate and stimulate us, or it can lead to any number of dangerous side effects.

Individual Differences and Stress

We have already alluded to the fact that stress affects people in different ways. Given our earlier discussion of individual differences back in Chapter 3, of course, this should come as no surprise. The most fully developed individual difference relating specifically to stress is the distinction between Type A and Type B personality profiles.

Type A and B Personality Profiles

Type A and Type B profiles were first observed by two cardiologists, Meyer Friedman and Ray Rosenman.[5] They first got the idea when a worker repairing the upholstery on their waiting-room chairs noted that many of the chairs were worn only on the front. This suggested to the two cardiologists that many heart patients were anxious and had a hard time sitting still—they were literally sitting on the edges of their seats!

Using this observation as a starting point, they began to study the phenomenon more closely. They eventually concluded that their patients were exhibiting one of two very different types of behaviour patterns. Their research also led them to conclude that the differences were personality based. They labelled these two behaviour patterns Type A and Type B.

The extreme **Type A** individual is extremely competitive, very devoted to work, and has a strong sense of time urgency. Moreover, this person is likely to be aggressive, impatient, and highly work oriented. He or she has a lot of drive and motivation and wants to accomplish as much as possible in as short a time as possible.

The extreme **Type B** person, in contrast, is less competitive, is less devoted to work, and has a weaker sense of time urgency. This person feels less conflict with either people or time and has a more balanced, relaxed approach to life. She or he has more confidence and is able to work at a constant pace.

A common-sense expectation might be that Type A people are more successful than Type B people. In reality, however, this is not necessarily true—the Type B person is not necessarily any more or less successful than the Type A. There are several possible explanations for this. For example, Type A people may alienate others because of their drive and they may miss out on important learning opportunities in their quest to get ahead. Type Bs, on the other hand, may have better interpersonal reputations and may learn a wider array of skills.

Friedman and Rosenman pointed out that people are not purely Type A or Type B; instead, people tend toward one or the other type. For example, an individual might exhibit marked Type A characteristics much of the time but still be able to relax once in a while and even occasionally forget about time.

Friedman and Rosenman's initial research on the Type A and Type B profile differences yielded some alarming findings. In particular, they suggested that Type As were much more likely to get coronary heart disease than were Type Bs.[6] In recent years, however, follow-up research by other scientists has suggested that the relationship between Type A behaviour and the risk of coronary heart disease is not all that straightforward.[7]

Although the reasons are unclear, recent findings suggest that Type As are much more complex than originally believed. For example, in addition to the characteristics already noted, they are likely to be depressed and hostile. Any one of these characteristics or a combination of them can lead to heart problems. Moreover, different approaches to measuring Type A tendencies have yielded different results. In one study that found Type As to actually be less susceptible to heart problems than Type Bs, the researchers offered an explanation consistent with earlier thinking: Because Type As are compulsive, they seek treatment earlier and are more likely to follow their doctors' orders![8]

Hardiness and Optimism

Two other important individual differences related to stress are hardiness and optimism. Research suggests that some people have what are termed hardier personalities than others.[9] **Hardiness** is a person's ability to cope with stress. People with hardy personalities have an internal locus of control, are strongly committed to the activities in their lives, and view change as an opportunity for advancement and growth. Such people are seen as relatively unlikely to suffer illness if they experience high levels of pressure and stress. On the other hand, people with low hardiness may have more difficulties in coping with pressure and stress.

Another potentially important individual difference is optimism. **Optimism** is the extent to which a person sees life in positive or negative terms. A popular expression used to convey this idea concerns the glass half filled with water. A person with a lot of optimism will tend to see it as half full, whereas a person with less optimism (a pessimist) will often see it as half empty. Optimism is also related to positive and negative affectivity, as discussed earlier in Chapter 3. In general, optimistic people tend to handle stress better. They will be able to see the positive characteristics of the situation and

---

Type A people are extremely competitive, highly committed to work, and have a strong sense of time urgency.

Type B people are less competitive, less committed to work, and have a weaker sense of time urgency.

Hardiness is a person's ability to cope with stress.

Optimism is the extent to which a person sees life in relatively positive or negative terms.

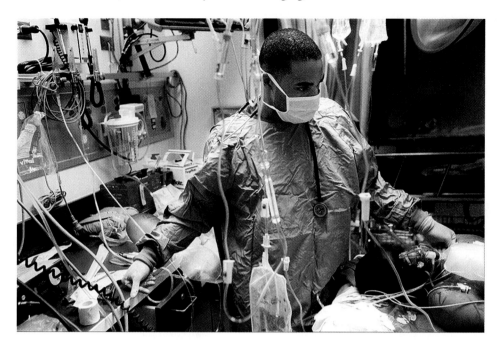

Considerable hardiness is required for many high-stress jobs. Dr. Chris Ervin is a third-year emergency medicine resident in Chicago's Cook County Hospital trauma unit. As part of his four-week rotation, he must work a 24-hour shift every three days, plus four to six hours on the other days. Fortunately, the stressful demands of the job are offset by his motivation to become a physician.

recognize that things may eventually improve. In contrast, less optimistic people may focus more on the negative characteristics of the situation and expect things to get worse, not better.

Other research suggests that women are perhaps more prone to experience the psychological effects of stress, whereas men may report more physical effects.[10] Finally, some studies suggest that people who see themselves as complex individuals are better able to handle stress than people who view themselves as relatively simple.[11] We should add, however, that the study of individual differences in stress is still in its infancy. It would be premature to draw rigid conclusions about how different types of people handle stress.

Common Causes of Stress

Many things can cause stress.[12] Figure 6.2 shows two broad categories: *organizational stressors* and *life stressors*. It also shows three categories of stress consequences: *individual consequences*, *organizational consequences*, and *burnout*.

Organizational Stressors

Organizational stressors are various factors in the workplace that can cause stress. Four general sets of organizational stressors are *task demands, physical demands, role demands*, and *interpersonal demands*.[13]

Task Demands   **Task demands** are stressors associated with the specific job a person performs. Some occupations are by nature more stressful than others. The jobs of surgeons, air traffic controllers, and professional hockey coaches are more stressful than those of general practitioners, airplane baggage loaders, and hockey team equipment managers.

Organizational stressors are factors in the workplace that can cause stress.

Task demands are stressors associated with the specific job a person performs.

FIGURE 6.2

Causes and Consequences of Stress

The causes and consequences of stress are related in complex ways. As shown here, most common causes of stress can be classified as either organizational stressors or life stressors. Similarly, common consequences include individual and organizational consequences, as well as burnout.

Source: Adapted, with permission, from James C. Quick and Jonathan D. Quick, *Preventive Stress Management in Organizations*, pp. 22, 66, and 96. Copyright © 1997 by the American Psychological Association.

Organizational Stressors
Task Demands
▪ Occupation
▪ Security
▪ Overload
Physical Demands
▪ Temperature
▪ Office Design
Role Demands
▪ Ambiguity
▪ Conflict
Interpersonal Demands
▪ Group Pressures
▪ Leadership Style
▪ Personalities
Life Stressors
Life Change
Life Trauma
Individual Consequences
Behavioural
▪ Alcohol and Drug Abuse
▪ Violence
Psychological
▪ Sleep Disturbances
▪ Depression
Medical
▪ Heart Disease
▪ Headaches
Organizational Consequences
Decline in Performance
Absenteeism and Turnover
Decreased Motivation and Satisfaction
Burnout

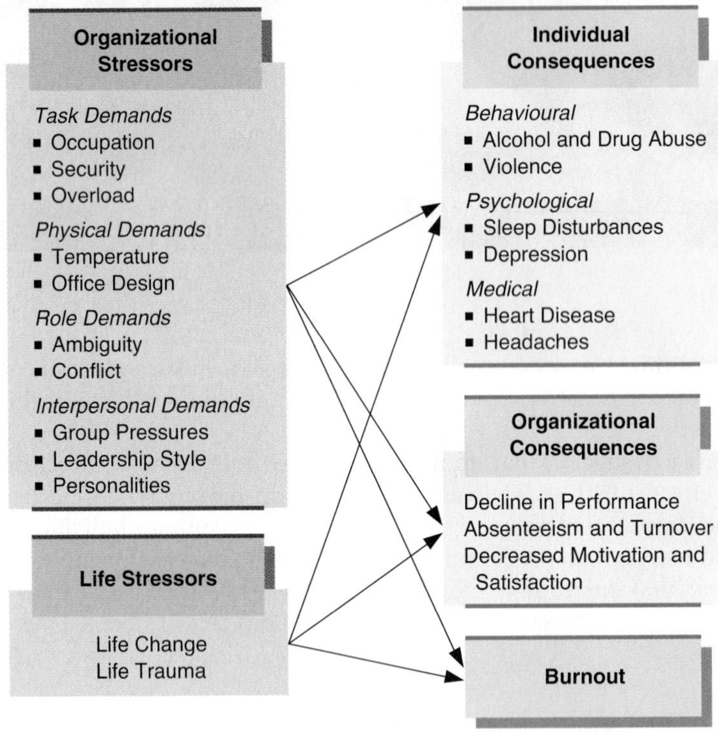

Beyond specific task-related pressures, other aspects of a job can pose physical threats to a person's health. Unhealthy conditions exist in occupations such as coal mining and toxic waste handling. Security is another task demand that can cause stress. Someone in a relatively secure job is not likely to worry unduly about losing that position. Threats to job security can increase stress dramatically.

A final task demand stressor is overload. Overload occurs when a person simply has more work than he or she can handle. The overload can be either quantitative (the person has too many tasks to perform or too little time to perform them) or qualitative (the person may believe he or she lacks the ability to do the job). Downsizing can have an impact on overload as well. For example, at the same time that St. Michael's Hospital in Toronto had its staff reduced from 2900 to 2200 over a period of six years, inpatient admissions went from 18 000 to 19 000 and outpatient visits increased from 200 000 to 290 000 annually. In a study of 12 Ontario hospitals experiencing similar re-engineering efforts conducted by researchers at the Richard Ivey School of Business at the University of Western Ontario, employees reported high levels of stress. Other organizations have reported increases in disability claims after downsizing.[14] We should note that the opposite of overload is also undesirable. As Figure 6.3 shows, low task demands can result in boredom and apathy just as overload can cause tension and anxiety. Thus, a moderate degree of workload-related stress is optimal, because it leads to high levels of energy and motivation.

Physical Demands   The **physical demands** of a job are its physical requirements on the worker; these demands are a function of the physical characteristics of the setting and the physical tasks the job involves. One important element is temperature. Working outdoors in extreme temperatures can result in stress, as can working in an improperly heated or cooled office. Strenuous labour such as loading heavy cargo or lifting packages can lead to similar results. Office design also can be a problem. A poorly designed office can make it difficult for people to have privacy or promote too much or too little social interaction. Too much interaction can distract a person from his or her task, whereas too little can lead to boredom or loneliness. Likewise, poor lighting, inadequate work surfaces, and similar deficiencies can create stress.[15]

> **Physical demands** are stressors associated with the job's physical setting, such as the adequacy of temperature and lighting and the physical requirements the job makes on the employee.

Role Demands   **Role demands** also can be stressful to people in organizations. A **role** is a set of expected behaviours associated with a particular position in a group or organization. As such, it has both formal (i.e., job-related and explicit) and informal (i.e., social and implicit) requirements. People in an organization or work group expect a person in a particular role to act in certain ways. They transmit these expectations both formally and informally. Individuals perceive role expectations with

> **Role demands** are stressors associated with the role a person is expected to play.

FIGURE 6.3

Workload, Stress, and Performance

Too much stress is clearly undesirable, but too little stress can also lead to unexpected problems. For example, too little stress can result in boredom and apathy and be accompanied by low performance. And although too much stress can cause tension, anxiety, and low performance, for most people there is an optimal level of stress that results in high energy, motivation, and performance.

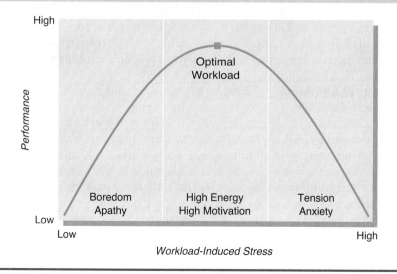

varying degrees of accuracy, and then attempt to enact that role. However, errors can creep into this process, resulting in stress-inducing problems called role ambiguity, role conflict, and role overload.[16]

Role ambiguity arises when a role is unclear. If your instructor tells you to write a term paper but refuses to provide more information, you will probably experience ambiguity. You do not know what the topic is, how long the paper should be, what format to use, or when the paper is due. In work settings, role ambiguity can stem from poor job descriptions, vague instructions from a supervisor, or unclear cues from coworkers. The result is likely to be a subordinate who does not know what to do. Role ambiguity can thus be a significant source of stress.

Role conflict occurs when the messages and cues from others about the role are clear but contradictory or mutually exclusive.[17] One common form is interrole conflict—conflict between roles. For example, if a person's boss says that to get ahead you must work overtime and on weekends, and your spouse says that more time is needed at home with the family, conflict can result.[18]

Intrarole conflict may occur when the person gets conflicting demands from different sources within the context of the same role. A manager's boss may say that he or she needs to put more pressure on subordinates to follow new work rules. At the same time, the subordinates may indicate that they expect the manager to get the rules changed. Thus, the cues are in conflict, and the manager may be unsure about which course to follow.

Intrasender conflict occurs when a single source sends clear but contradictory messages. This might occur if the boss says one morning that there can be no more overtime for the next month but after lunch tells someone to work late that same evening. Person–role conflict results from a discrepancy between role requirements and an individual's personal values, attitudes, and needs. If a person is told to do something unethical or illegal, or if the work is distasteful (for example, firing a close friend), person–role conflict is likely. Role conflict of all varieties is of particular concern to managers. Research has shown that conflict can occur in a variety of situations and lead to a variety of adverse consequences, including stress, poor performance, and rapid turnover.[19]

A final consequence of a weak role structure is **role overload**, which occurs when expectations for the role exceed the individual's capabilities. When a manager gives an employee several major assignments at once while increasing the person's regular workload, the employee will probably experience role overload. Role overload can also result when an individual takes on too many roles at one time. For example, a person trying to work extra hard at work, run for election to the school board, serve on a committee in church, coach minor hockey, maintain an active exercise program, and be a contributing member to his or her family will probably encounter role overload.

Interpersonal Demands   A final set of organizational stressors consists of three **interpersonal demands**: group pressures, leadership, and interpersonal conflict. Group pressures may include pressure to restrict output, pressure to conform to the group's norms, and so forth. For instance, as we have noted before, it is quite common for a work group to arrive at an informal agreement about how much each member will produce. Individuals who produce much more or much less than this level may be pressured by the group to get back in line. An individual who feels a strong need to vary from the group's expectations (perhaps to get a pay raise or promotion) will experience a great deal of stress, especially if acceptance by the group is also important to him or her.

Leadership style also can cause stress. Suppose an employee needs a great deal of social support from his leader. The leader, however, is quite brusque and shows no

Role ambiguity arises when a role is unclear.

Role conflict occurs when the messages and cues constituting a role are clear but contradictory or mutually exclusive.

Role overload occurs when expectations for the role exceed the individual's capabilities.

Interpersonal demands are stressors associated with group pressures, leadership, and personality conflicts.

concern or compassion. This employee will probably feel stressed. Similarly, assume an employee feels a strong need to participate in decision making and to be active in all aspects of management. Her or his boss is very autocratic and refuses to consult subordinates about anything. Once again stress is likely to result.[20]

Finally, conflicting personalities and behaviours may cause stress. Conflict can occur when two or more people must work together even though their personalities, attitudes, and behaviours differ. For example, a person with an internal locus of control—that is, who always wants to control how things turn out—might get frustrated working with an external person who likes to wait and just let things happen.[21]

Another example of how interpersonal demands can result in stress is sexual harassment, which in most, but not all, cases is a situation in which a woman is a target of a man's unwanted approaches, touching, or verbal statements. While sexual harassment complaints are on the increase, this might be partly explained by an increased willingness of organizations to acknowledge such problems, and to not disregard employees who come forward with a complaint. It is certainly in an organization's interest to deal with such situations, not only because of the potential legal issues involved, but also because employees who are the targets of harassment are subjected to an extremely high level of stress each day.

Life Stressors

Stress in organizational settings also can be influenced by events that take place outside the organization. Life stressors generally are categorized in terms of life change and life trauma.[22]

Life Change   Thomas Holmes and Richard Rahe first developed and popularized the notion of life change as a source of stress.[23] A **life change** is any meaningful change in a person's personal or work situation. Holmes and Rahe reasoned that major changes in a person's life can lead to stress and eventually to disease. Table 6.1 summarizes their

A **life change** is any meaningful change in a person's personal or work situation; too many life changes can lead to health problems.

Life stressors can be addressed by different people in different ways. Take Brian Benavidez, for example. After being laid off from his job as an investment banker during the 2002 recession, Benavidez spent his days watching television. One day he watched a documentary about—of all things—hot dogs. But he also noticed that everyone engaged in the process of making, selling, and eating hot dogs seemed to be happy! So rather than trying to get back into the corporate rat race, he has decided to open his own hot dog stand.

TABLE 6.1

Life Changes and Life
Change Units

Rank	Life Event	Mean
1	Death of spouse	100
2	Divorce	73
3	Marital separation	65
4	Jail term	63
5	Death of close family member	63
6	Personal injury or illness	53
7	Marriage	50
8	Fired at work	47
9	Marital reconciliation	45
10	Retirement	45
11	Change in health of family member	44
12	Pregnancy	40
13	Sex difficulties	39
14	Gain of new family member	39
15	Business readjustment	39
16	Change in financial state	38
17	Death of close family friend	37
18	Change to different line of work	36
19	Change in number of arguments with spouse	35
20	Mortgage over $10 000*	31
21	Foreclosure of mortgage or loan	30
22	Change in responsibilities of work	29
23	Son or daughter leaving home	29
24	Trouble with in-laws	29
25	Outstanding personal achievement	28
26	Spouse beginning or starting work	26
27	Beginning or ending school	26
28	Change in living conditions	25
29	Revision of personal habits	24
30	Trouble with boss	23
31	Change in work hours or conditions	20
32	Change in residence	20
33	Change in schools	20
34	Change in recreation	19
35	Change in church activities	19
36	Change in social activities	18
37	Mortgage or loan less than $10 000*	17
38	Change in sleeping habits	16
39	Change in the number of family get-togethers	15
40	Change in eating habits	15
41	Vacation	13
42	Christmas	12
43	Minor violations of the law	11

The amount of life stress that a person has experienced in a given period of time, say one year, is measured by the total number of life change units (LCUs). These units result from the addition of the values (shown in the right column) associated with events that the person has experienced during the target time period.

*With inflation, the value of a mortgage that produces stress may be nearer to $100 000; however, no research confirms this figure.

Source: Reprinted with permission from *Journal of Psychosomatic Research*, 11 (2), Thomas H. Holmes and Richard H. Rahe, "The Social Adjustment Rating Scale," 1967. Elsevier Science, Inc.

findings on major life change events. Note that several of these events relate directly (fired from work, retirement) or indirectly (change in residence) to work.

Each event's point value supposedly reflects the event's impact on the individual. At one extreme, a spouse's death, assumed to be the most traumatic event considered, is assigned a point value of 100. At the other extreme, minor violations of the law rank only 11 points. The points themselves represent life change units, or LCUs. Note also that the list includes negative events (divorce and trouble with the boss) as well as positive ones (marriage and vacations).

Holmes and Rahe argued that a person can handle a certain threshold of LCUs, but beyond that level problems can set in. In particular, they suggest that people who encounter more than 150 LCUs in a given year will experience a decline in their health the following year. A score of between 150 and 300 LCUs supposedly carries a 50 percent chance of major illness, while the chance of major illness is said to increase to 70 percent if the number of LCUs exceeds 300. These ideas offer some insight into the potential impact of stress and underscore our limitations in coping with stressful events. However, research on Holmes and Rahe's suggestions has provided only mixed support.

Life Trauma   Life trauma is similar to life change, but it has a narrower, more direct, and shorter-term focus. A *life trauma* is any upheaval in an individual's life that alters his or her attitudes, emotions, or behaviours. To illustrate, according to the life change view, a divorce adds to a person's potential for health problems in the following year. At the same time, the person will obviously also experience emotional turmoil during the actual divorce process. This turmoil is a form of life trauma and will clearly cause stress, much of which can spill over into the workplace.[24]

Major life traumas that may cause stress include marital problems, family difficulties, and health problems initially unrelated to stress. For example, suppose a person learns she or he has developed arthritis that will limit a favourite activity, skiing. Dismay over the news may translate into stress at work. Similarly, a worker going through a family breakup will almost certainly go through difficult periods, some of which will affect his or her job performance.

Consequences of Stress

Stress can have a number of consequences. As we already noted, if the stress is positive, the result may be more energy, enthusiasm, and motivation. Of more concern, of course, are the negative consequences of stress. Referring back to Figure 6.2, we see that stress can produce individual consequences, organizational consequences, and burnout.[25]

We should first note that many of the factors listed are obviously interrelated. For example, alcohol abuse is shown as an individual consequence, but it also affects the organization the person works for. An employee who drinks on the job might perform poorly and create a hazard for others. If the category for a consequence seems somewhat arbitrary, be aware that each consequence is categorized according to the area of its primary influence.

Individual Consequences

The *individual consequences* of stress, then, are the outcomes that affect mainly the individual. The organization also may suffer, either directly or indirectly, but it is the individual who pays the real price. Stress may produce behavioural, psychological, and medical consequences.

Behavioural Consequences   The *behavioural consequences* of stress may harm the person under stress or others. One such behaviour is smoking. Research has clearly documented that people who smoke tend to smoke more when they experience stress. There is also evidence that alcohol and drug abuse are linked to stress, although this relationship is less well documented.[26] Other possible behavioural consequences are accident proneness, violence, and appetite disorders.

Psychological Consequences   The *psychological consequences* of stress relate to a person's mental health and well-being. When people experience too much stress at work, they may become depressed or find themselves sleeping too much or not enough. Stress can also lead to family problems and sexual difficulties. Research by Julian Barling of Queen's University and his colleagues have demonstrated that work-related stress can have a negative impact on marital functioning as well as interpersonal functioning on the job.[27]

Medical Consequences   The *medical consequences* of stress affect a person's physical well-being. Heart disease and stroke, among other illnesses, have been linked to stress. Other common medical problems resulting from too much stress include headaches, backaches, ulcers and related stomach and intestinal disorders, and skin conditions such as acne and hives.[28]

Organizational Consequences

Clearly, any of the individual consequences just discussed can also affect the organization. Other results of stress have even more direct consequences for organizations. These include decline in performance, withdrawal, and negative changes in attitudes.

Performance   One clear organizational consequence of too much stress is a decline in *performance*. For operating workers, such a decline can translate into poor-quality work or a drop in productivity. For managers, it can mean faulty decision making or disruptions in working relationships as people become irritable and hard to get along with.

Withdrawal   *Withdrawal* behaviours also can result from stress. The two most significant forms of withdrawal behaviour in an organization are absenteeism and quitting. People who are having a hard time coping with stress in their jobs are more likely to call in sick or consider leaving the organization for good. Stress can also produce other, more subtle forms of withdrawal. A manager might start missing deadlines or taking longer lunch breaks. An employee might withdraw psychologically by ceasing to care about the organization and the job.[29] Employee violence is a potential individual consequence of stress. This also has obvious organizational implications, especially if the violence is directed at an employee or at the organization in general.[30]

Attitudes   Another direct organizational consequence of employee stress relates to *attitudes*. As we just noted, job satisfaction, morale, and organizational commitment can all suffer, along with motivation to perform at high levels. As a result, people may be more prone to complain about unimportant things, do only enough work to get by, and so forth.

Burnout is a general feeling of exhaustion that develops when an individual simultaneously experiences too much pressure and has too few sources of satisfaction.

Burnout   As we stated at the outset of this chapter, burnout, another consequence of stress, has clear implications for both people and organizations. **Burnout** is a general feeling of exhaustion that develops when a person simultaneously experiences too much pressure and has too few sources of satisfaction.[31]

Burnout generally develops in the following way.[32] First, people with high aspirations and strong motivation to get things done are prime candidates for burnout under certain conditions. They are especially vulnerable when the organization suppresses or limits their initiative while constantly demanding that they serve the organization's own ends.

In such a situation, the individual is likely to put too much of himself or herself into the job. In other words, the person may well keep trying to meet his or her own agenda while simultaneously trying to fulfil the organization's expectations. The most likely effects of this situation are prolonged stress, fatigue, frustration, and helplessness under the burden of overwhelming demands. The person literally exhausts his or her aspirations and motivation, much as a candle burns itself out. Loss of self-confidence and psychological withdrawal follow. Ultimately, burnout results. At this point, the individual might start dreading going to work in the morning, put in longer hours but accomplish less than before, and generally display mental and physical exhaustion.

Burnout consists of three dimensions: *emotional exhaustion*, *depersonalization*, and *diminished personal accomplishment*. Emotional exhaustion is a strain brought on by too many demands. Depersonalization (that is, emotional distance from others) is a defensive means of coping that results from not having enough resources to cope with the demands. The lack of resources also affects one's ability to accomplish tasks. Michael Leiter of Acadia University and his colleagues have developed and revised models of burnout over the past decade or so, and they suggest that emotional exhaustion and depersonalization develop simultaneously rather than sequentially.[33]

Raymond Lee of the University of Manitoba and Blake Ashforth, formerly of Concordia University, conducted a review of studies examining burnout. These authors found that higher levels of emotional exhaustion and depersonalization were strongly associated with increased turnover intentions and decreased organizational commitment.[34]

Managing Stress in the Workplace

Given that stress is widespread in and so potentially disruptive to organizations, it follows that people and organizations should be concerned about how to manage it more effectively. And in fact they are. Many strategies have been developed to help manage stress in the workplace. Some are for individuals and others are geared toward organizations.[35]

Individual Coping Strategies

Many strategies for helping individuals manage stress have been proposed. Figure 6.4 lists five of the more popular.

Exercise   Exercise is one method of managing stress. People who exercise regularly are less likely to have heart attacks than inactive people. More directly, research has suggested that people who exercise regularly feel less tension and stress, are more self-confident, and show greater optimism. People who do not exercise regularly feel more stress, are more likely to be depressed, and experience other negative consequences.[36]

Relaxation   A related method of managing stress is relaxation. We noted at the beginning of the chapter that coping with stress requires adaptation. Proper relaxation is an effective way to adapt. Relaxation can take many forms. One way to relax is to take regular vacations. A recent study found that people's attitudes toward a variety of

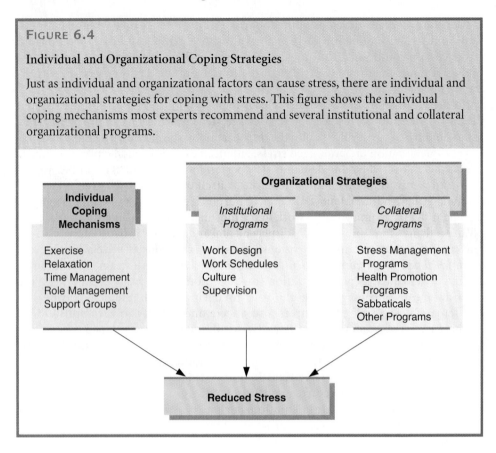

FIGURE 6.4

Individual and Organizational Coping Strategies

Just as individual and organizational factors can cause stress, there are individual and organizational strategies for coping with stress. This figure shows the individual coping mechanisms most experts recommend and several institutional and collateral organizational programs.

workplace characteristics improved significantly following a vacation.[37] People can also relax while on the job. For example, it has been recommended that people take regular rest breaks during their normal workday. A popular way of resting is to sit quietly with closed eyes for 10 minutes every afternoon. (Of course, it might be necessary to have an alarm clock handy!)

Time Management   Time management is often recommended for managing stress. The idea is that many daily pressures can be eased or eliminated if a person does a better job of managing time. One popular approach to time management is to make a list every morning of the things to be done that day. Then you group the items on the list into three categories: critical activities that must be performed, important activities that should be performed, and optional or trivial things that can be delegated or postponed. Then, of course, you do the things on the list in their order of importance. This strategy helps people get more of the important things done every day. It also encourages delegation of less important activities to others. The Stress and . . . Technology box that follows illustrates how managers can better manage their time by not allowing technology to rule their lives.

Role Management   Somewhat related to time management is the idea of role management, in which the individual actively works to avoid overload, ambiguity, and conflict. For example, if you do not know what is expected of you, you should not sit and worry about it. Instead, ask for clarification from your boss. Another role management strategy is to learn to say "no." As simple as saying "no" might sound, a lot of

Stress and . . . TECHNOLOGY

Technostress: The New Organizational Stressor

Advances in information technology have made our work lives easier in many ways. Computers are now faster and more powerful than ever. The advent of cellular phones has given many managers an opportunity to become considerably more productive. It's easier for them to make telephone calls on the road, to stay in touch with clients and customers, and to maintain contact with their offices. Of course, these innovations in the working world have not arrived without cost. A significant number of people are now experiencing some form of technology-related stress, or technostress. Some symptoms of technostress are similar to other stress-related problems, such as chronic anxiety, sleep difficulties, and irritability. However, technostress also involves some unique symptoms, such as the compulsive need to check electronic and voicemail messages, and technology dependency. The ubiquitous BlackBerry wireless device developed by Waterloo-based Research in Motion has been jokingly referred to as "CrackBerry" because of its seemingly addictive qualities.

What causes technostress? Many people now feel that technology has encroached on all aspects of their lives to the point where the new work schedule is 24/7. A 2006 survey conducted by Desjardin Financial Security found that more than 80 percent of Canadian employees who use mobile technology report added stress to their lives as a result. In some cases, employees can develop technology addictions that can cause their personal lives to suffer. Particularly susceptible to technostress are people with home offices, such as small business operators and telecommuters. The boundary between home and

work–life is much less distinct for those who live and work in the same place. Consequently, the line between work and leisure is often blurred and one gets the feeling of being always on call. In the past decade, the number of Canadians who regularly work overtime hours on the weekend rose from 11 percent to 18.5 percent, primarily because of the availability of technology.

The key to dealing with technostress is to control the technology rather than allow the technology to control you. For example, people with home offices should set strict work hours and stick to them. All work-related technology should be turned off during nonwork hours. That way, a psychological distinction between home and work is maintained. Of course, the news is not bad for employees at all levels. One large scale study of executives found that, although a third of the respondents believed they spent too much time connected to communications devices, more than three quarters said that they believed the communications devices enhanced rather than harmed their work–life balance.

Sources: Krista Foss, "Stressed Out? Blame Technology," *The Globe and Mail*, 29 May 1998, p. C8; Paula Brook, "Slaves To Our Technology, Burdens On Each Other," *Vancouver Sun*, 8 July 2006, http://www.canada.com/topics/finance/story.html?id=e8417c89-883e-4551-8e8b-5d3a5b709b8e&p=3 accessed on February 20, 2007; Susan Semenak, "The Age of Overwork," *CanWest News Service*, 25 January 2007, http://www.canada.com/topics/technology/story.html?id=0b3200f1-371d-47cd-960f-0ed64e75a0be on February 20, 2007; Reuters, "Unable To Unplug, Tech Addicts May Sue, Professor Says," *The Edmonton Journal* 28 August 2006, http://www.canada.com/edmontonjournal/news/business/story.html?id=34d339b1-3504-45a6-ad74-ad6f09ca2617 on February 20, 2007.

people create problems for themselves by always saying "yes." Besides working in their regular jobs, they agree to serve on committees, volunteer for extra duties, and accept extra assignments. Sometimes, of course, we have no choice but to accept an extra obligation (if our boss tells us to complete a new project, we will probably have to do it). In many cases, however, saying "no" is an option.[38]

Support Groups A final method for managing stress is to develop and maintain support groups. A support group is simply a group of family members or friends with whom a person can spend time. Going out after work with a couple of coworkers to a basketball game, for example, can help relieve the stress that builds up during the day.

Supportive family and friends can help people deal with normal stress on an ongoing basis. Support groups can be particularly useful during times of crisis. For example, suppose an employee has just learned that she or he did not get the promotion she has been working toward for months. It may help tremendously if she or he has good friends to lean on, be it to talk to or to yell at.[39]

Organizational Coping Strategies

Organizations are also increasingly realizing that they should be involved in managing their employees' stress. There are two different rationales for this view. One is that because the organization is at least partly responsible for creating the stress, it should help relieve it. The other is that workers experiencing lower levels of harmful stress will function more effectively. Two basic organizational strategies for helping employees manage stress are institutional programs and collateral programs.

Institutional Programs   *Institutional programs* for managing stress are undertaken through established organizational mechanisms.[40] For example, properly designed jobs (discussed in Chapter 5) and work schedules (also discussed in Chapter 5) can help ease stress. Shift work, in particular, can cause major problems for employees, because they constantly have to adjust their sleep and relaxation patterns. Thus, the design of work and work schedules should be a focus of organizational efforts to reduce stress.[41]

The organization's culture (covered in Chapter 14) also can be used to help manage stress. In some organizations, for example, there is a strong norm against taking time off or going on vacation. In the long run, such norms can cause major stress. Thus, the organization should strive to foster a culture that reinforces a healthy mix of work and nonwork activities.

Finally, supervision can play an important institutional role in managing stress. A supervisor can be a major source of overload. If made aware of their potential for assigning stressful amounts of work, supervisors can do a better job of keeping workloads reasonable.

Collateral Programs   In addition to institutional efforts aimed at reducing stress, many organizations are turning to *collateral programs*. A collateral stress program is an organizational program specifically created to help employees deal with stress. Organizations have adopted stress management programs, health promotion programs, and other kinds of programs for this purpose. More and more companies are developing their own programs or adopting existing programs of this type.[42]

Many firms today also have employee fitness programs. These programs attack stress indirectly by encouraging employees to exercise, which is presumed to reduce stress. On the negative side, this kind of effort costs considerably more than stress management programs, because the firm must invest in physical facilities. Still, more and more companies are exploring this option.[43]

Finally, organizations try to help employees cope with stress through other kinds of programs. For example, existing career development programs, like the one at General Electric, are used for this purpose. Other companies use programs promoting everything from humour to massage as antidotes for stress.[44] Of course, little or no research supports some of the claims made by advocates of these programs. Thus, managers must take steps to ensure that any organizational effort to help employees cope with stress is at least reasonably effective.

The Workplace and . . .   CHANGE

Top Employers Take Action to Fight Employee Stress

If you peruse the annual list of the Top 100 Employers in Canada, it becomes readily apparent that many of these most sought after employers are very aware of the toll that stress takes on their employees. And given the negative impact that stress can have on productivity, it is not surprising to note that a lot of these organizations take a proactive approach to helping their employees deal with stress. In some cases, the focus is on collateral programs. For example, Calgary-based Enmax Energy Corp. provides its employees with fitness facility memberships as well as a number of on-site services and facilities designed to maintain employee health. These include a wellness professional on-site, weekly massages, yoga classes, and even sleep and healthy eating clinics. In addition to on-site exercise classes, Winnipeg-based Ceridian provides influenza immunizations and cardiovascular screening programs.

As well as the collateral programs discussed above, many of the top Canadian employers utilize institutional programs that focus on developing a positive organizational culture and providing employees with flexibility and work–life balance. In order to enhance the social atmosphere at work, General Dynamics

Canada Ltd. built an outdoor hockey rink at its Ottawa head office and organized a company hockey league. MBNA Canada Bank allows employees to pool their vacation and sick days, so that employees can use days as regular sick days or as vacation days. As a result, even entry-level employees can have up to four weeks of vacation. Finally, many organizations now recognize the importance of work–family balance by providing topped up parental leave and compassionate leave benefits. One example is Dartmouth, Nova Scotia, consulting engineering firm Jacques Whitford Ltd., which tops up parental leave benefits to 75 percent of salary for a year.

Sources: Murray McNeill, "City Firms Among Best Employers," *Winnipeg Free Press*, 24 December 2005, p. B7; Carrie Tait, "Perks With A Personal Touch," *Financial Post*, 18 October 2006 http://www.canada.com/nationalpost/news/story.html?id=c316f829-de80-47bd-8a3c-ce2e21d294f3 on December 11, 2006; Peter Koven, "Seven Criteria Determine Canada's Best Employers," *Edmonton Journal*, 14 October 2006, http://www.canada.com/edmontonjournal/story.html?id=c08f1916-d2d1-4705-91e7-1b960ca7dfe3 on 1 November 2006; Derek Sankey, "City Firms Dominate Provincial Ranks," *Calgary Herald*, 14 October 2006, http://www.canada.com/calgaryherald/news/working/story.html?id=b22d9d36-4070-448a-8dd6-5a384d503015 on November 1, 2006.

Work–Life Linkages

At numerous points in this chapter we have alluded to relationships between a person's work and life. In this final brief section we will make these relationships a bit more explicit.

Fundamental Work–Life Relationships

Work–life relationships can be characterized in any number of ways.[45] Consider, for example, the basic dimensions of the part of a person's life tied specifically to work. Common dimensions would include such things as an individual's current job (including working hours, job satisfaction, and so forth), his or her career goals (the person's aspirations, career trajectory, and so forth), interpersonal relations at work (with the supervisor, subordinates, coworkers, and others), and job security.

Part of each person's life is also distinctly separate from work. These dimensions might include the person's spouse or life companion, dependants (such as children or elderly parents), personal life interests (hobbies, leisure time interests, religious affiliations, community involvement), and friendship networks.

Work–life relationships are interrelationships between a person's work life and personal life.

Work–life relationships, then, include any relationships between dimensions of a person's worklife and the person's personal life. For example, a person with numerous dependants (a nonworking spouse, dependent children, dependent parents, etc.) might prefer a job with a relatively high salary, fewer overtime demands, and less travel. A person with no dependants may be less interested in salary, more receptive to overtime, and enjoy job-related travel.

Stress will occur when there is a basic inconsistency or incompatibility between a person's work and life dimensions. For example, if a person is the sole care provider for a dependent elderly parent but has a job that requires considerable travel and evening work, stress is likely to result. Such stress develops as a result of a role conflict between demands in the home and at work.

Balancing Work–Life Linkages

Balancing work–life linkages is, of course, no easy thing to do. Demands from both sides can be extreme, and people may need to be prepared to make tradeoffs. The important thing is to recognize the potential tradeoffs in advance so that they can be carefully weighed and a comfortable decision made. Some of the strategies for doing this were discussed earlier. For example, working for a company that offers flexible work schedules could be an attractive option.

Individuals must also recognize the importance of long-term versus short-term perspectives in balancing their work and personal lives. For example, people may have to respond a bit more to work than to life demands in the early years of their careers. In mid career, they may be able to achieve a more comfortable balance. In later career stages, they may be able to put life dimensions first, by refusing to relocate, by working shorter hours, and so forth.

People also have to decide for themselves what they value and what tradeoffs they are willing to make. For instance, consider the dilemma faced by a dual-career couple when one partner is transferred to another city. One option is for one of the partners

Managing work–life relationships can be a complicated activity, especially when people are working highly demanding jobs and/or jobs that require a lot of travel. The first marriage of racing driver Michael Andretti ended in divorce. But he has taken active steps to avoid problems in the future. For example, he is shown here with his second wife, Leslie Andretti. Leslie travels with Michael and the couple tries to spend as much time together as possible.

Conflict and . . . 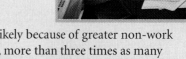 **RESEARCH**

Work–Family Conflicts

The rise in dual-income and dual-career families is heightening a problem that has long existed in the Canadian workforce. Many people experience work–family conflict as they attempt to fill multiple roles as employees, spouses, and parents. Conflict occurs when fulfilling one role interferes with one's ability to fulfil other roles. Linda Duxbury of Carleton University and Christopher Higgins of the University of Western Ontario have studied the causes and consequences of work–family conflict for a number of years. Duxbury and Higgins recently completed a study that involved surveying 31 571 Canadian employees from 100 companies. The results of this survey suggested that the vast majority of employees who responded experienced at least moderate levels of role overload and that the proportion that have experienced high levels of role overload has increased over the previous decade. The survey also revealed that a significant number of employees were experiencing difficulty in balancing work and life demands. This was especially true for employees with dependent care responsibilities (child or elder care). Of those employees who were better able to balance work and life demands, a key factor was the ability to control their time at work. It was also evident from the study that women experienced greater levels of work–life conflict. Female employees reported both higher levels of role overlead and caregiver strain than

did male employees, likely because of greater non-work responsibilities. In all, more than three times as many employees reported high levels of job stress than they did in a similar survey a decade earlier.

The increase in stress reported by employees comes with a cost for employers. In addition to declining job satisfaction and organizational commitment, the stress resulted in higher levels of absenteeism and a greater likelihood of turnover. Based on their findings, Duxbury and Higgins estimated the direct costs of absenteeism due to high work–life conflict to be approximately $3 to $5 billion per year. Although there is no "one size fits all" solution to these problems, Duxbury and Higgins provided a number of recommendations designed to mitigate the negative impact of work–life conflict. For example, organizations could take steps to reduce employee workloads, ensure that the organization is not understaffed, make alternative work arrangements available to employees, provide caregiver leave, and develop etiquette around the use of office technologies such as e-mail and cellphones.

Source: Linda Duxbury and Christopher Higgins, "Work–Life Conflict in Canada in the New Millennium: A Status Report," Public Health Agency of Canada, 2003, www.phac_aspc.gc.ca/publicat/work-travail/pdf/rprt_2_e.pdf on November 1, 2006.

to subordinate her or his career for the other partner, at least temporarily. For example, the partner being transferred can turn it down, risking a potential career setback or the loss of the job. Or the other partner can resign from his or her current position and seek another one in the new location. The couple might also decide to live apart, with one moving and the other staying. The partners might also come to realize that their respective careers are more important to them than their relationship and decide to go their separate ways.

Chapter Review

Summary of Key Points

- Stress is a person's adaptive response to a stimulus that places excessive psychological or physical demands on that person. According to the general adaptation syndrome (GAS) perspective, the three stages of response to stress are alarm, resistance, and exhaustion. Two important forms of stress are eustress and distress.

- Type A personalities are more competitive and time-driven than Type B personalities. Initial evidence suggested that Type As are more susceptible to coronary heart disease, but recent findings provide less support for this idea. Hardiness, optimism, cultural context, and gender may also affect stress.

- Stress can be caused by many factors. Major organizational stressors are task demands, physical demands, role demands, and interpersonal demands. Life stressors include life change and life trauma.

- Stress has many consequences. Individual consequences can include behavioural, psychological, and medical problems. On the organizational level, stress can affect performance and attitudes or cause withdrawal. Burnout is another possibility.

- Primary individual mechanisms for managing stress are exercise, relaxation, time management, role management, and support groups. Organizations use both institutional and collateral programs to control stress.

- People have numerous dimensions to their work and personal lives. When these dimensions are interrelated, individuals must decide for themselves which are more important and how to balance them.

Discussion Questions

1. Describe one or two recent times when stress had both good and bad consequences for you.

2. Describe a time when you successfully avoided stage 3 of the GAS and another time when you got to stage 3.

3. Do you consider yourself a Type A or a Type B person? Why?

4. Can a person who is a Type A change? If so, how?

5. What are the major stressors for a student?

6. Is an organizational stressor or a life stressor likely to be more powerful?

7. What consequences are students most likely to suffer as a result of too much stress?

8. Do you agree that a certain degree of stress is necessary to induce high energy and motivation?

9. What can be done to prevent burnout? If someone you know is suffering burnout, how would you advise that person to recover from it?

10. Do you practise any of the stress-reduction methods discussed in the text? Which ones? Do you use others not mentioned in the text?

11. Has the work–life balance been an issue in your life?

Experiencing Organizational Behaviour

Purpose: To help you develop a better understanding of how stress affects you.

Format: Following is a set of questions about your job. If you work, respond to the questions in terms of your job. If you do not work, respond to the questions in terms of your role as a student.

Procedure: This quiz will help you recognize your level of stress on the job. Take the test, figure your score, and

then see if your stress level is normal, beginning to be a problem, or dangerous. Answer the following statements by putting a number in front of each:

1 = seldom true
2 = sometimes true
3 = mostly true

_____ 1. Even over minor problems, I lose my temper and do embarrassing things, like yell or kick a garbage can.

_2_   2. I hear every piece of information or question as criticism of my work.

_2_   3. If someone criticizes my work, I take it as a personal attack.

_1_   4. My emotions seem flat whether I'm told good news or bad news about my performance.

_1_   5. Sunday nights are the worst time of the week.

_1_   6. To avoid going to work, I'd even call in sick when I'm feeling fine.

_2_   7. I feel powerless to lighten my work load or schedule, even though I've always got far too much to do.

_1_   8. I respond irritably to any request from coworkers.

_1_   9. On the job and off I get highly emotional over minor accidents such as typos or spills.

_2_ 10. I tell people about sports or hobbies that I'd like to do but say I never have time because of the hours I spend at work.

_1_ 11. I work overtime consistently, yet never feel caught up.

_1_ 12. My health is running down; I often have headaches, backaches, stomachaches.

_2_ 13. If I even eat lunch, I do it at my desk while working.

_2_ 14. I see time as my enemy.

_1_ 15. I can't tell the difference between work and play; it all feels like one more thing to do.

_1_ 16. Everything I do feels like a drain on my energy.

_1_ 17. I feel like I want to pull the covers over my head and hide.

_1_ 18. I seem off centre, distracted—I do things like walk into mirrored pillars in department stores and excuse myself.

_1_ 19. I blame my family—because of them, I have to stay in this job and location.

_1_ 20. I have ruined my relationship with coworkers whom I feel I compete against.

Scoring: Add up the points you wrote beside the questions; interpret your score as follows:

20–29 = Normal amounts of stress.

30–49 = Stress is becoming a problem; you should try to identify its source and manage it.

50–60 = Stress is at dangerous levels; you should seek help or it could result in worse symptoms, such as alcoholism or illness.

Follow-up Questions

1. How valid do you think your score is?

2. Is it possible to anticipate stress ahead of time and plan ways to help manage it?

Source: "Stress on the Job? Ask Yourself," _USA Today,_ 16 June 1987. Copyright 1987, _USA Today._ Reprinted with permission.

Self-Assessment Exercise

Are You Type A or Type B?

This test will help you develop insights into your own tendencies toward Type A or Type B behaviour patterns. Answer the questions honestly and accurately about either your job or your school, whichever requires the most time each week. Then calculate your score according to the instructions that follow the questions. Discuss your results with a classmate. Critique each other's answers and see if you can help each other develop a strategy for reducing Type A tendencies.

Choose from the following responses to answer the questions below:

a. Almost always true

b. Usually true

c. Seldom true

d. Never true

_B_ 1. I do not like to wait for other people to complete their work before I can proceed with mine.

_A_ 2. I hate to wait in most lines.

_C_ 3. People tell me that I tend to get irritated too easily.

_B_ 4. Whenever possible I try to make activities competitive.

_C_ 5. I have a tendency to rush into work that needs to be done before knowing the procedure I will use to complete the job.

_C_ 6. Even when I go on vacation, I usually take some work along.

_B_ 7. When I make a mistake, it is usually because I have rushed into the job before completely planning it through.

_C_ 8. I feel guilty about taking time off from work.

_C_ 9. People tell me I have a bad temper when it comes to competitive situations.

_B_ 10. I tend to lose my temper when I am under a lot of pressure at work.

_B_ 11. Whenever possible, I will attempt to complete two or more tasks at once.

_B_ 12. I tend to race against the clock.

_A_ 13. I have no patience with lateness.

_B_ 14. I catch myself rushing when there is no need.

Score your responses according to the following key:

■ *An intense sense of time urgency* is a tendency to race against the clock, even when there is little reason to. The person feels a need to hurry for hurry's sake alone, and this tendency has appropriately been called *hurry sickness.* Time urgency is measured by items 1, 2, 8, 12, 13, and 14. Every A or B answer to these six questions scores one point.

■ *Inappropriate aggression and hostility* reveals itself in a person who is excessively competitive and who cannot do anything for fun. This inappropriately aggressive behaviour easily evolves into frequent displays of hostility, usually at the slightest provocation or frustration. Competitiveness and hostility is measured by items 3, 4, 9, and 10. Every A or B answer scores one point.

■ *Polyphasic behaviour* refers to the tendency to undertake two or more tasks simultaneously at inappropriate times. It usually results in wasted time due to an inability to complete the tasks. This behaviour is measured by items 6 and 11. Every A or B answer scores one point.

■ *Goal directedness* without proper planning refers to the tendency of an individual to rush into work without really knowing how to accomplish the desired result. This usually results in incomplete work or work with many errors, which in turn leads to wasted time, energy, and money. Lack of planning is measured by items 5 and 7. Every A or B response scores one point.

TOTAL SCORE = 9

If your score is 5 or greater, you may possess some basic components of the Type A personality.

Stress Takes Its Toll

Larry Field had a lot of fun in high school. He was a fairly good student, especially in math, he worked harder than most of his friends, and somehow he ended up going steady with Alice Shiflette, class valedictorian. He worked summers for a local surveyor, William Loude, and when he graduated, Mr. Loude offered him a job as number-three man on one of his survey crews. The pay wasn't very high, but Field already was good at the work, and he believed all he needed was a steady job to boost his confidence to ask Alice to marry him. Once he did, events unfolded rapidly. He started work in June, he and Alice were married in October, Alice took a job as a secretary in a local company that made business forms, and a year later they had their first child.

The baby came as something of a shock to Field. He had come to enjoy the independence his own paycheque gave him every week. Food and rent took up most of it, but he still enjoyed playing basketball a few nights a week with his high school buddies and spending Sunday afternoons on the softball field. When the baby came, however, Field's brow began to furrow a bit. He was only 20 years old, and he still wasn't making much money. He asked Mr. Loude for a raise and got it—his first.

Two months later, one of the crew chiefs quit just when Mr. Loude's crews had more work than they could handle. Mr. Loude hated to turn down work, so he made Larry Field a crew chief, giving his crew some of the old instruments that weren't good enough for the precision work of the top crews, and assigned him the easy title surveys in town. Because it meant a jump in salary, Field had no choice but to accept the crew chief position. But it scared him. He had never been very ambitious or curious, so he'd paid little attention to the training of his former crew chief. He knew how to run the instruments—the basics, anyway—but every morning he woke up terrified that he would be sent on a job he couldn't handle.

During his first few months as a crew chief, Field began doing things that his wife thought he had outgrown. He frequently talked so fast that he would stumble over his own words, stammer, turn red in the face, and have to start all over again. He began smoking, too, something he had not done since they had started dating. He told his two crew members that smoking kept his hands from shaking when he was working on an instrument. Neither of them smoked, and when Field began lighting up in the truck while they were waiting for the rain to stop, they would become resentful and complain that he had no right to ruin their lungs.

Field found it particularly hard to adjust to being the boss, especially since one of his workers was getting an engineering degree at night school and both crew members were the same age as he. He felt sure that Alfonso Reyes, the scholar, would take over his position in no time. He kept feeling that Alfonso was looking over his shoulder and began snapping any time they worked close together.

Things were getting tense at home, too. Alice had to give up her full-time day job to take care of the baby, so she had started working nights. They hardly ever saw each other, and it seemed as though her only topic of conversation was that they should move to Alberta, where she had heard that surveyors were paid five times what Field made. Field knew his wife was dissatisfied with her work and believed her intelligence was being wasted, but he didn't know what he could do about it. He was disconcerted when he realized that drinking and worrying about the next day at work while sitting at home with the baby at night had become a pattern.

Case Questions

1. What signs of stress was Larry Field exhibiting?

2. How was Larry Field trying to cope with his stress? Can you suggest more effective coping strategies?

SELF TEST

You have read the chapter and studied the key terms. Think you're ready to ace the exam? Take this sample test to gauge your comprehension of chapter material and check your answers at the back of the book. Want more test questions? Take the ACE quizzes found on the student website: www.hmco.ca/ob.

T F   1. Stress is an adaptive response.

T F   2. A Type B person is very competitive, devoted to work, and has a strong sense of time urgency.

T F   3. Overload can occur if a person believes he or she lacks the ability to do the job.

T F   4. Negative and positive life events may both be sources of stress.

T F   5. Burnout is a general feeling of exhaustion when a person has too few positive sources of stress.

T F   6. Collateral stress programs focus on repairing the damage stress does to those outside the organization.

T F   7. Flexible work schedules may help employees balance work–life linkages.

8. For an employee to experience stress
   a. the demands on the employee must be physical.
   b. the demands on the employee must be psychological.
   c. the demands must prevent the employee from adapting.
   d. the demands on the employee must be excessive.
   e. the demands must be greater than the employee has experienced in the past.

9. Which of the following does not describe a Type A person as compared to a Type B person?
   a. Impatient
   b. Confident
   c. Strong sense of time urgency
   d. Very devoted to work
   e. Extremely competitive

10. Studies suggest that which of the following is the most stressful job:
   a. broadcast technician.
   b. mechanical engineer.
   c. actuary.
   d. bank officer.
   e. prime minister.

11. Thomas believes in always telling the truth. His manager asks him to "bend" the truth when discussing the technical specifications of the machinery they are selling because the customers will really

never know the difference. Thomas is likely to experience
   a. intrasender conflict.
   b. intersender conflict.
   c. role ambiguity.
   d. person–role conflict.
   e. role overload.

12. According to research by Holms and Rahe, excessive life changes are expected to result in
   a. a decline in the person's health.
   b. a sensation of accomplishment.
   c. a tendency to become a Type A person.
   d. a tendency to become a Type B person.
   e. increased role overload.

13. Too much stress at work can be expected to have all the following consequences for organizations except
   a. a decline in performance.
   b. withdrawal behaviours.
   c. employees spending more time at work.
   d. lower organizational commitment.
   e. burnout.

14. One of your subordinates tells you she is experiencing a lot of stress. There doesn't seem to be anything wrong with the organization, so you assume an individual coping strategy might help her the most. Which of the following would you not recommend?
   a. Exercise
   b. Role management
   c. Relaxation
   d. Time management
   e. All of the above are individual coping strategies you might recommend.

15. Balancing work–life linkages sometimes requires people to make tradeoffs. Which of the following best describes the process to make these tradeoffs?
   a. Always respond to work demands early in your career.
   b. Always respond to life demands later in your career.
   c. Always subordinate your career for your partner's career.
   d. Never subordinate your career for your partner's career.
   e. Decide for yourself what you value and what tradeoffs you are willing to make.

The Success of Individuals at Starbucks

Starbucks sells food and drinks, but the most important component of a customer's purchase is the service. Customers demand high-quality service that is personal, friendly, fast, and accurate. They want a relaxing and social store atmosphere. Customer satisfaction is crucial to generating profitable repeat buyers, as the most loyal customers visit Starbucks eighteen times a month or more. "When … the person behind the counter says hello and maybe greets you by name, you feel a connection you don't find with most retailers anymore. It makes you feel welcome and it makes you want to come back," says Dave Pace, executive vice president. To offer that level of service and atmosphere, Starbucks depends on its 97 000 worldwide employees.

Success starts with choosing workers, called "baristas" (from the Italian word for barkeeper), for front-line positions. A good person–job fit is created by selecting individuals with the right skills and personality. Baristas must be knowledgeable about the various items that Starbucks sells. They are constantly on their feet, must lift heavy items frequently, use dangerously hot machinery, and communicate and cooperate with their coworkers. Most importantly, they must provide a satisfying, personal interaction to hundreds of customers each day. "Our baristas are the foundation of our business," claims the company. "Baristas deliver legendary customer service to all customers by acting with a 'customer comes first' attitude and connecting with the customer. They discover and respond to customer needs." To meet high customer expectations, Starbucks "looks for people who are adaptable, self-motivated, passionate, creative team players."

It's not hard to find individuals with the minimal skills needed for entry-level jobs. However, it's more difficult to identify who can contribute the most and who is most likely to stay. Applicants undergo interviews with two managers, to assess complex abilities such as social and communication skills. Each applicant completes a behavioural assessment designed to measure cooperativeness, extroversion, honesty, and conscientiousness.

"It's not hard to recruit at this company," claims vice president Sheri Southern. "People want to work here. We're very fortunate that way." The company has a reputation for being a great employer. A 2004 survey found that 82 percent of employees were satisfied or very satisfied. In January 2005, Starbucks was named #2 on *Fortune* magazine's list of best large employers. One tangible measure of the good person–job fit at Starbucks is the low annual turnover rate among baristas—80 percent—compared to 200 percent for the quick-serve food industry. Starbucks CEO Jim Donald is intensely interested in generating enough applicants to keep up with growth while maintaining the quality of personnel. The company must hire 200 new workers each day, for vacancies at existing stores and for new locations. "My biggest fear isn't the competition, although I respect it," Donald says. "It's having a robust pipeline of people to open and manage the stores who will also be able to take their next steps with the company."

Although Starbucks's baristas are generally satisfied, their jobs can be stressful. There are the physical demands of constant standing and walking. At the same time, baristas must properly prepare orders and work in a constrained physical space with others. Interpersonal stress can also be high. It is difficult to establish a personal and positive relationship with a stranger in just a few seconds, and baristas must do this over and over again for hours. As in any job with heavy customer contact, there is the potential for unpleasant interactions and encounters with difficult customers. For example, some of Starbucks's customers are irritated by the language the company uses. Although customers may order Starbucks's products by using the words "small, medium, large," the baristas are required by the company to respond with the official terms of "tall, grande, venti." "Customers will mock the drink sizes and get snippy with the barista over how they think it's stupid to not just use small, medium, and large. And that's when I find myself tempted to be rude. To simply say, 'Oh, thank you, mister! I'm so glad you're taking on the corporate dominance of Starbucks by irritating an hourly employee!'" says one barista.

Another factor in creating success through the efforts of individuals is to properly design the work. The job of barista combines physical production, personal interaction, and planning and time management. Therefore, workers use a variety of skills and switch tasks frequently, reducing boredom and fatigue. The barista participates in the entire process, from the time the customer enters the store through payment. Baristas receive constant feedback from customers about their performance. Based on Hackman and Oldham's job characteristics theory, these qualities of the barista job should result in higher satisfaction and motivation. On the other hand, baristas do not have a lot of autonomy. The products must be prepared consistently, reducing creative opportunities. Also, although providing good customer service is a priority, baristas may feel that their job does not have a significant impact on others. These factors would tend to reduce satisfaction and motivation.

Another important aspect of job design at Starbucks is work scheduling. The majority of Starbucks' workers have part-time work schedules. Operating hours for each Starbucks location is determined by local demand; however, many stores open as early as 6:00 A.M. and remain open until 11:00 P.M. The busiest hours at most stores are between 8:00 A.M. and 10:00 A.M. Clearly then, work scheduling is a complex task. Stores use a flexible scheduling approach. Many baristas appreciate the part-time and flexible nature of their work hours, so they can attend school or meet other needs. Some workers, however, would prefer a more predictable schedule. In addition, the total number of hours worked per week has a significant impact on income and benefits eligibility, so some workers are displeased when their hours vary.

From 2000 to 2005, then CEO Orin Smith concentrated on improving operational effectiveness. Automated espresso machines were introduced to speed up coffee production, which now takes about one minute per cup, down from three minutes. The taste of the machine-made drinks is as good as those made by hand, an important point for quality-conscious Starbucks. Another factor in the decision to adopt espresso machines was worker safety. Overall, Starbucks is a very safe employer. Workers sustain injuries at about half the rate of other companies in the industry. However, burns are the most frequent injuries sustained by baristas and are a concern. Automated machines reduce baristas' burn rate by 50 percent. Workers must learn new skills in order to operate the new machinery.

Finally, success based on individual employees comes from motivating workers to perform at high levels, coupled with meaningful and appropriate rewards. CEO Donald role-models motivation skills. Every morning, he calls five store managers for a personal chat. Then he calls three hourly workers. Donald says, "We've got to be able to reach into this organization and say, 'How's it going?' and 'Good job!' If any company doesn't have the time to talk to people on the front lines, then you might as well close it up, because it's not going anywhere."

Motivation at Starbucks is accomplished through the use of rewards to meet the needs of employees. An important motivator is base pay, which at Starbucks is about average for the fast-food industry. In Canada, the median salary for full time supervisors and store managers is $36 171. Starbucks also offers above-average benefits to most workers.

All employees (including those in Canada) who work 20 hours per week or more can receive healthcare benefits, including medical, drug, vision, dental, as well as a stock option purchase plan, and discounted Starbucks merchandise. And all partners get a pound of coffee each week! In its list of the Best Companies to Work For published in January of 2005, *Fortune* magazine said about Starbucks: "The coffee behemoth is justly famous for its generous benefits. One example: Part-timers and their same-sex or opposite-sex partners receive comprehensive health coverage. Hypnotherapy? Covered. Naturopathy? Ditto." The company pays between 50 percent and 80 percent of the cost of the care for workers and family members.

A stock purchase plan allows employees to buy shares of Starbucks at a 15 percent discount. Another program, called "Bean Stock," grants stock options to almost every employee, allowing them to purchase stock at even deeper discounts. The stock options are awarded based on an individual's pay, length of employment, and even more importantly, Starbucks's overall corporate performance. Stock ownership is seen as a way to increase wealth for hourly workers, while also helping to align their interests with those of the company. "Share success with the people who make it happen," says vice president Emily Ericsen. "It makes everybody think like an owner, which helps them build long-term relationships with customers and influences them to do things in an efficient way."

Starbucks also offers a variety of miscellaneous benefits, including reimbursement for college tuition and adoption expenses. Time-off benefits include paid vacation for full-time employees, and personal days and time-and-a-half pay for holiday work. Extensive training improves employees' skills and prepares them for positions of greater responsibility. Finally, the benefits package is flexible. Under the Starbucks's program, called "Your Special Blend," employees can shift benefits dollars between the various components of the total pay package, customizing their compensation. Each worker can use their benefit dollars in the way that provides the best value.

In addition to above-average benefits, Starbucks has responded to employee concerns about career development. One issue that arose as a result of the Partner View Surveys was the lack of understanding on the part of employees about career progression within the organization. Although most baristas know the process involved to become a store manager, many did not know how to secure jobs at the Starbucks Coffee Canada head office in Toronto or at the various regional offices. Starbucks Coffee Canada's president Colin Moore responded by holding career fairs in Vancouver, Calgary, and Toronto. Says Moore, "we rented halls and staffed them with our department heads and other people across the country who spoke about their roles and job opportunities within the organization."

With its emphasis on appropriate recruiting, job design, and motivation, Starbucks is fulfilling its mission statement, which states, "[We will] provide a great work environment and treat each other with respect and dignity." Many employees realize that Starbucks, while not perfect, is clearly one of the best employers. When a barista posted negative comments on the Internet, one employee replied with: "Starbucks work isn't much different from that of any other foodservice job. Yet employees show more loyalty and support for Starbucks than they do for any other similar employer." Another

> **❝ If any company doesn't have the time to talk to people on the front lines, then you might as well close it up, because it's not going anywhere. ❞**
> *JIM DONALD, CEO, STARBUCKS*

also defended the firm, writing, "Starbucks does more for its employees than any other food service or retail business. Perhaps not as good as a company where everyone has their Masters degrees, but it's a lot better than the McDonald's and Wal-Mart's of the world."

Sources: "Application for Employment," "Barista," "Career Paths," "Corporate Social Responsibility Report 2004," "Retail Careers," "Starbucks Mission Statement," Starbucks website, www.starbucks.com on June 30, 2005; "Man Orders a 'Medium' Starbucks Coffee," Starbucks Gossip website, starbucksgossip.typepad.com on June 30, 2005; "100 Best Companies to Work For 2005," *Fortune*, January 2005, www.fortune.com on June 30, 2005; "Ideas and Inspirations," November 25, 2003, The Employee Involvement Association website, www.eianet.org on June 30, 2005; "Industry Solutions: Taleo for Foodservice," Taleo website, www.taleo.com on June 30, 2005; Gretchen Weber, "Preserving the Starbucks' Counter Culture," *Workforce Management*, February 2005, pp. 28–34 (quotation) ; Calvin Leung, "Culture Club: Effective Corporate Cultures," Canadian Business, October 9–22, 2006, www.canadianbusiness.com on August 21, 2007; www.payscale.com/research/CA/Employer=Starbucks_Corp/Salary on October 23, 2007.

Integrative Case Questions

1. Describe the psychological contract for baristas working at Starbucks. What are the inducements? What are the contributions? In your opinion, is this a reasonable and fair exchange? If so, explain why. If not, tell how it could be improved.

2. How do alternative work arrangements contribute to the motivation of baristas at Starbucks? Are there any potential limitations or drawbacks of the alternative work arrangements?

3. Consider all of the significant stakeholders of Starbucks: investors, employees, customers, and local communities. Do the generous rewards offered to baristas help or hinder each of these groups in reaching their goals? Explain.

CHAPTER 7

Communication in Organizations

Chapter Outline

eBay Manages Communication Challenges

Bay, the online auction company, faces many challenges. Although providing an online space for buyers and sellers to exchange information might sound simple, the communication demands of such a business are staggering.

There are 100 million registered members of eBay worldwide. There are 430 000 people who earn their primary living as eBay sellers.

> **"** *Make your complaints in the open. Better yet, give your praise in the open.* **"**
>
> PIERRE OMIDYAR, FOUNDER, eBAY

If eBay sellers constituted a single organization, the firm would be the sixth-largest American employer, after the civil service, Wal-Mart, McDonald's, the military, and the post office. Communication is essential for eBay, both between individuals and between individuals and the firm.

eBay's online system allows sellers to post descriptive text and images, name prices, and set terms. The system provides a mechanism for online auctioning—including monitoring the time limit, number of bids, reserve price, and other auction details. Buyers search items by categories, view items, and submit bids.

The system also provides many additional capabilities. One of the most important features of eBay is the feedback feature. Every eBay member has an online profile that reports comments and scores from previous transactions. According to the eBay website, "Learning to trust a member of the community has a lot to do with what their past customers or sellers have to say!" eBay founder Pierre Omidyar believes that feedback provides a policing mechanism that enhances the organization's sense of community. He says, "Some people are dishonest. Or deceptive . . . But here, those people can't hide. We'll drive them away . . . Make your complaints in the open. Better yet, give your praise in the open . . . Deal with others the way you would have them deal with you." By April of 2005, eBay members had posted 3 billion feedback messages.

To further encourage communication, eBay creates online discussion boards for item categories, such as dolls or motorcycles, and help topics. A more sophisticated community discussion tool is the group—hundreds of classifications based on regions, items, or interests. The group allows for online discussion and adds the capability of taking opinion polls, posting photos, and setting up online "meetings."

eBay doesn't neglect more traditional forms of online communication. The company sponsors chat rooms, frequently asked questions (FAQs) lists, and an online and e-mail newsletter. Online town hall meetings with eBay managers are conducted through streaming audio and allow members to submit questions in advance or during the event. Workshops on various topics also rely on streaming audio.

eBay's communication systems, based on trust and the voluntary involvement of millions of people, do not always work smoothly. Feedback ratings can be maliciously manipulated or just neglected, reducing the system's effectiveness. Frequent users complain that the firm's democratic system fails to provide extra communication channels for the firm's most profitable customers. Yet some things clearly work—the hardware supporting millions of daily transactions crashes on average for just three seconds per month.

eBay's online communication system is necessary for the firm's survival. With that in mind, the company works hard to ensure that the system performs effectively. See the boxed insert on page 191 titled eBay and . . . Globalization for more about eBay's international communication challenges.[1]

Communication is something that most of us take for granted—we have been communicating for so long that we really pay little attention to the actual process. Even at work, we often focus primarily on doing our jobs and pay little attention to how we communicate about those jobs. However, since methods of communication play such a pervasive role in affecting behaviour in organizations and represent another vital underpinning of interpersonal processes, we need to pay more attention to the effective processes that link what we do to others in the organization. In this chapter, we focus on the important processes of interpersonal communication and information processing. Communication is important for all phases of organizational behaviour, but it is especially crucial in decision making, performance appraisal, motivation, and ensuring that the organization functions effectively. First, we discuss the importance of communication in organizations and some important aspects of international communication in organizations. Next, we describe the methods of organizational communication and examine the basic communication process. Then we examine the potential effects of computerized information processing and telecommunications. Next, we explore the development of communication networks in organizations. Finally, we discuss several common problems of organizational communication and methods of managing communication.

The Nature of Communication in Organizations

Communication is the social process in which two or more parties exchange information and share meaning.

Communication is the social process in which two or more parties exchange information and share meaning.[2] Communication has been studied from many perspectives. In this section, we provide an overview of the complex and dynamic communication process and discuss some important issues relating to international communication in organizations.

The Purposes of Communication in Organizations

Communication among individuals and groups is vital in all organizations. Some of the purposes of organizational communication are shown in Figure 7.1. The primary purpose is to achieve coordinated action.[3] Just as the human nervous system responds to stimuli and coordinates responses by sending messages to the various parts of the body, communications coordinate the actions of the parts of an organization. Without communication, an organization would be merely a collection of individual workers doing separate tasks. Organizational action would lack coordination and be oriented toward individual rather than organizational goals.

A second purpose of communication is information sharing. The most important information relates to organizational goals, which give members a sense of purpose and direction. Another information-sharing function of communication is to give specific task directions to individuals. Whereas information on organizational goals gives employees a sense of how their activities fit into the overall picture, task communication tells them what their job duties are and are not. Employees must also receive information on the results of their efforts, as in performance appraisals.

Communication is essential to the decision-making process as well, as we discuss in Chapter 9. Information, and thus information sharing, are needed to define problems, generate and evaluate alternatives, implement decisions, and control and evaluate results.

Finally, communication expresses feelings and emotions. Organizational communication is far from a collection of facts and figures. People in organizations, like people anywhere else, often need to communicate emotions such as happiness, anger, displeasure, confidence, and fear.

Despite the importance of communication between management and employees for the smooth operation of organizations, the effectiveness of this communication is

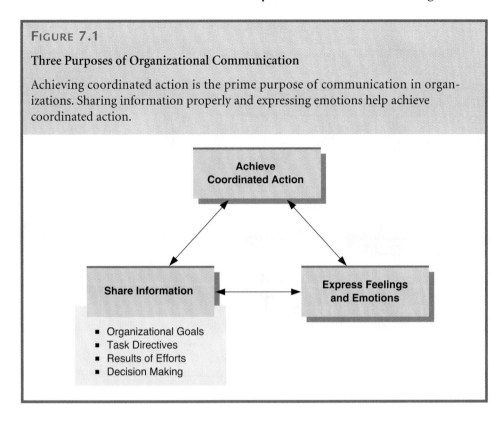

FIGURE 7.1

Three Purposes of Organizational Communication

Achieving coordinated action is the prime purpose of communication in organizations. Sharing information properly and expressing emotions help achieve coordinated action.

Achieve Coordinated Action

Share Information

Express Feelings and Emotions

- Organizational Goals
- Task Directives
- Results of Efforts
- Decision Making

the source of disagreement between these groups. A survey of 2039 Canadians in six industrial and service categories conducted by Watson Wyatt Worldwide revealed wide gaps in the perceived effectiveness of communication by senior management. The survey shows 61 percent of senior executives feel they are doing a good job of communicating with employees, but only 33 percent of the managers and department heads who report to them agree. At lower levels in the organization, even fewer employees agree that senior management communicates well with employees. Only 22 percent of hourly workers, 27 percent of clerical employees, and 22 percent of professional staff agreed that senior executives communicate well with them.[4]

Communication Across Cultures

Communication is an aspect of interpersonal relations that obviously is affected by the international environment, partly because of language issues and partly due to coordination issues.

Language and Nonverbal Communication   One of the factors that complicates communication between cultures is the use of different languages. Because Canada has two official languages, English and French, the possibilities for miscommunication are increased. Many key positions in the federal government (and some provincial governments) stipulate bilingualism as a condition of employment. Given that French is the native language of approximately 25 percent of Canadians, it is not surprising that many organizations sponsor employees who wish to learn a second language.

Even when people speak the same language, there can be regional differences in usage. Differences in languages are compounded by the fact that the same word can mean different things in different cultures. For example, "Coca-Cola" means "bite the head of a

Understanding communication dynamics across cultures is a challenging but important business necessity. Tyson Foods, for instance, is trying to learn more about the kinds of products and product packaging that work best in different cultures. During a recent agricultural conference in Havana, Cuba, Tyson sent a sales representative out to a local market to observe how consumers assessed and made purchase decisions about poultry products.

dead tadpole" in Chinese. Chevrolet once tried to export a line of cars to Latin America that it called the Nova in North America, but then discovered that "no va" is Spanish for "doesn't go"—not the best name for an automobile!

Note that elements of nonverbal communication also vary across cultures. Colours and body language can convey quite a different message in one culture than in another. For example, the sign for "OK" in Canada (making a loop with thumb and first fingers) is considered rude in Spain and vulgar in Brazil. Managers should be forewarned so that they can take nothing for granted in dealing with people from other cultures. They must take the time to become as fully acquainted as possible with the verbal and non-verbal languages of that culture. And indeed, newer forms of communication technology such as e-mail and internet messaging are actually changing language itself.

Coordination   International communication is closely related to issues of coordination. For example, a Canadian manager who wants to talk with his or her counterpart in Hong Kong or Singapore must contend not only with differences in language but also with a time difference of many hours. When the Canadian manager needs to talk on the telephone, the Hong Kong executive may be asleep at home. Organizations are finding increasingly innovative methods for coordinating their activities in scattered parts of the globe. Merrill Lynch, for example, has developed its own satellite-based telephone network to monitor and participate in the worldwide money and financial markets.[5] The eBay and . . . Globalization box discusses some of eBay's successes—and failures—regarding communication across cultures.

Methods of Communication

The three primary methods of communicating in organizations are written, oral, and nonverbal. Often the methods are combined. Considerations that affect the choice of

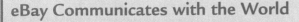
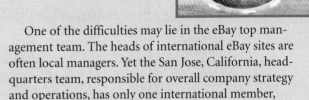

eBay and . . . GLOBALIZATION

eBay Communicates with the World

eBay communicates globally through 26 international websites, representing countries in the Americas, Asia, and Europe. About $1.4 billion, or 15 percent of the firm's total business, comes from outside of the United States.

International eBay websites all look the same. On each site, the navigation toolbar lists categories of items. Categories are similar, including items such as computers, autos, and jewelry. In 2002, eBay purchased PayPal, a company that provides a secure online payment method. PayPal enables members from around the world to trade with each other, managing the currency translation for both buyers and sellers.

In other aspects, the websites are tailored to local communication needs—Bollywood memorabilia on eBay India, for example. While sites for Italy, Korea, and Argentina are translated into their country's primary language, sites for India, the Philippines, and Sweden use English. Each site lists prices in the local currency.

eBay is aggressively expanding overseas but is not equally successful everywhere. In Japan, for example, eBay entered the online auction business after competitors had established strong market positions, charged higher fees, and failed to establish a relationship with users. "When we arrived last year, the 800-pound gorilla was already positioned," says eBay Japan president Merle Okawara. The company ceased Japanese operations in 2003.

One of the difficulties may lie in the eBay top management team. The heads of international eBay sites are often local managers. Yet the San Jose, California, headquarters team, responsible for overall company strategy and operations, has only one international member, Rajiv Dutta, the Chief Financial Officer.

As the online auction industry becomes more profitable, it will attract stronger competitors. Focusing on communication with diverse international users can lead eBay to increased success and competitive victory.

> *"When we arrived last year, the 800-pound gorilla was already positioned."*
>
> MERLE OKAWARA, PRESIDENT, eBAY JAPAN

Sources: "eBay Profits Miss the Mark," *CNN Money,* January 19, 2005, money.cnn.com on April 20, 2005; "Global Trade," "Welcome to eBay," eBay website, www.ebay.com on April 20, 2005; Ken Belson, "How Yahoo! Japan Beat eBay at Its Own Game," *Business Week,* June 4, 2001, www.businessweek.com on April 20, 2005 (quotation); Bambi Francisco, "All Eyes on eBay," *Market Watch,* www.marketwatch.com on April 20, 2005; Troy Wolverton, "eBay Readies Execs for Merger," *C/Net,* September 5, 2002, news.com on April 20, 2005.

method include the audience (whether it is physically present), the nature of the message (its urgency or secrecy), and the costs of transmission. Figure 7.2 shows various forms each method can take.

Written Communication

Organizations typically produce a great deal of written communication of many kinds. A letter is a formal means of communicating with an individual, generally someone outside the organization. Probably the most common form of written communication in organizations is the office memorandum, or memo. Memos usually are addressed to a person or group inside the organization.[6] They tend to deal with a single topic and are more impersonal (as they often are destined to more than one person) but less formal than letters. Most e-mail is similar to the traditional memo, although it is even less formal.

Other common forms of written communication include reports, manuals, and forms. Reports generally summarize the progress or results of a project and often provide information to be used in decision making. Manuals have various functions in

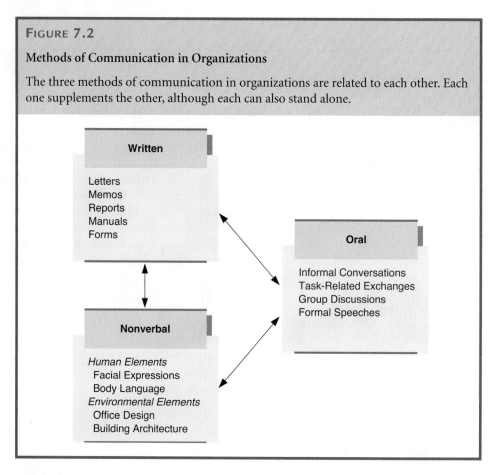

FIGURE 7.2

Methods of Communication in Organizations

The three methods of communication in organizations are related to each other. Each one supplements the other, although each can also stand alone.

organizations. Instruction manuals tell employees how to operate machines; policy and procedures manuals inform them of organizational rules; operations manuals describe how to perform tasks and respond to work-related problems. Forms are standardized documents on which to report information. As such, they represent attempts to make communication more efficient and information more accessible. A performance appraisal form is an example. We should also note that although many of these forms of written communication have historically been used in a paper-based environment, they are increasingly being put on websites and intranets in many larger companies.

Oral Communication

The most prevalent form of organizational communication is oral. Oral communication takes place everywhere—in informal conversations, in the process of doing work, in meetings of groups and task forces, and in formal speeches and presentations. Recent studies identified oral communication skills as the number one criterion for hiring new college graduates.[7] Business school leaders have also been urged by industry to develop better communication skills in their graduates.[8] Even in Europe, employers have complained that the number one problem with current graduates is the lack of oral communication skills, citing cultural factors and changes in the educational process as primary causes.[9]

Oral forms of communication are particularly powerful because they include not only speakers' words but also their changes in tone, pitch, speed, and volume. As listeners, people use all of these cues to understand oral messages. Try this example with a friend or work colleague. Say this sentence several times, each time placing the emphasis on a different word: "The boss gave Joe a raise." See how the meaning changes depending on the emphasis! Moreover, receivers interpret oral messages in the context of previous communications and, perhaps, the reactions of other receivers. (Try saying another sentence before saying the phrase about the boss—such as "Joe is so lazy" or "Joe is such a good worker.") Quite often the top management of an organization sets the tone for oral communication throughout the organization.

Voicemail has all the characteristics of traditional verbal communication except that there is no feedback. The sender just leaves a message on the machine or network with no feedback or confirmation that the message was, or will be, received. With no confirmation, the sender does not know for sure whether the message will be received as he or she intended it. Therefore, it may be wise for the receiver of a voicemail to quickly leave a message on the sender's voicemail acknowledging that the original message was received. But then the "great voicemail phone tag" is at its worst! Also, the receiver then has an excuse in the event that something goes wrong later and can always say that a return message was left on the sender's voicemail! The receiver could also pass the blame by saying that no such voice message was received. The lack of confirmation, or two-way communication, can lead to several problems, as will be discussed in later sections of this chapter.

Nonverbal Communication

Nonverbal communication includes all the elements associated with human communication that are not expressed orally or in writing. Sometimes it conveys more meaning than words. Human elements include facial expressions and physical movements, both conscious and unconscious. Facial expressions have been categorized as (1) interest-excitement, (2) enjoyment-joy, (3) surprise-startle, (4) distress-anguish, (5) fear-terror, (6) shame-humiliation, (7) contempt-disgust, and (8) anger-rage.[10] The eyes are the most expressive component of the face.

Physical movements and body language are also highly expressive human elements. Body language includes both actual movement and body positions during communication. The handshake is a common form of body language. Other examples include making eye contact, which expresses a willingness to communicate; sitting on the edge of a chair, which may indicate nervousness or anxiety; and sitting back with arms folded, which may convey an unwillingness to continue the discussion.

Environmental elements such as buildings, office space, and furniture can also convey messages. A spacious office, expensive draperies, plush carpeting, and elegant furniture can combine to remind employees or visitors that they are in the office of the president and CEO of the firm. The small metal desk set in the middle of the shop floor accurately communicates the organizational rank of a first-line supervisor. Thus, office arrangements convey status, power, and prestige and create an atmosphere for doing business. Some organizations such as Alberta-based Palliser Lumber, however, consciously attempt to minimize the distinction between management and employees. The physical setting can also be instrumental in the development of communication networks, because a centrally located person can more easily control the flow of task-related information.[11]

Most forms of communication, including written and oral, usually are associated with some form of nonverbal communication.

The Communication Process

Communication is a social process in which two or more parties exchange information and share meaning. The process is social because it involves two or more people. It is a two-way process and takes place over time rather than instantaneously. The communication process illustrated in Figure 7.3 shows a loop between the source and the receiver.[12] Note the importance of the feedback portion of the loop; upon receiving the message, the receiver responds with a message to the source to verify the communication. Each element of the basic communication process is important. If one part is faulty, the message may not be communicated as it was intended. A simple organizational example might be when a manager attempts to give direction to an employee regarding the order in which to do two tasks. (We refer to this example again in later discussions.) The manager wants to send a message and have the employee understand precisely the meaning the manager intends. Each part of the communication process is described below.

Source

The **source** is the individual, group, or organization interested in communicating something to another party.

The **source** is the individual, group, or organization interested in communicating something to another party. In group or organizational communication, an individual might send the message on behalf of the organization. The source is responsible for preparing the message, encoding it, and entering it into the transmission medium. In some cases, the receiver chooses the source of information, as when a decision maker seeks information from trusted and knowledgeable individuals.[13] The source in organizational communication is often the manager giving directions to employees.

Encoding

Encoding is the process by which the message is translated from an idea or thought into transmittable symbols.

Encoding is the process by which the message is translated from an idea or thought into symbols that can be transmitted. The symbols may be words, numbers, pictures, sounds, or physical gestures and movements. In a simple example, the manager may use words

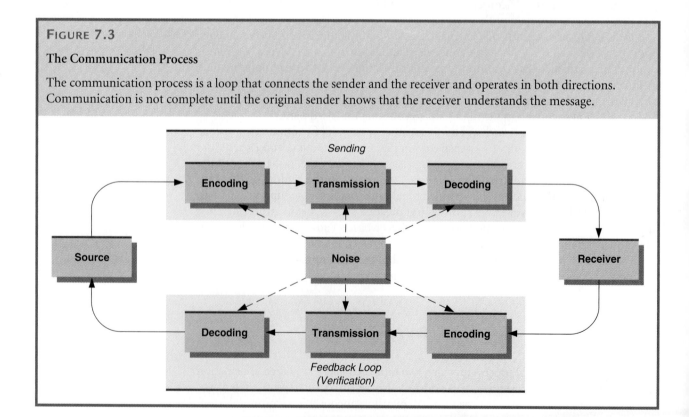

Figure 7.3

The Communication Process

The communication process is a loop that connects the sender and the receiver and operates in both directions. Communication is not complete until the original sender knows that the receiver understands the message.

in English as the symbols, usually spoken or written. The source must encode the message in symbols that the receiver can decode properly; that is, the source and the receiver must attach the same meaning to the symbols. When we use the symbols of a common language, we assume those symbols have the same meaning to everyone who uses them. Yet the inherent ambiguity of symbol systems can lead to decoding errors. In verbal communication, for example, some words have different meanings for different people. Parents and children often use the same word, but the differences in their positions and ages can lead them to interpret words quite differently. If the manager only speaks French and the employee only speaks English, the message is unlikely to be understood. The meanings of words used by the sender may differ depending on the nonverbal cues, such as facial expression, that the sender transmits along with them.

Transmission

Transmission is the process through which the symbols that carry the message are sent to the receiver. The **medium** is the channel or path of transmission. The medium for face-to-face conversation is sound waves. The same conversation conducted over the telephone involves not only sound waves but also electrical impulses and the line that connects the two phones. To tell the employee in what order to do tasks, the manager could tell the employee face to face or use the telephone, a memo, an e-mail, or voicemail.

Communications media range from an interpersonal media, such as talking or touching, to mass media, such as newspapers, magazines, or television broadcasts. Different media have different capacities for carrying information. For example, a face-to-face conversation generally has more carrying capacity than a letter, because it allows the transmission of more than just words.[14] In addition, the medium can help determine the effect the message has on the receiver. Calling a prospective client on the telephone to make a business proposal is a more personal approach than sending a letter and is likely to elicit a different response. It is important that a manager choose the medium that is most likely to correspond to the type of message that needs to be sent and understood.[15]

> **Transmission** is the process through which the symbols that represent the message are sent to the receiver.

> The **medium** is the channel or path through which the message is transmitted.

Decoding

Decoding is the process by which the receiver of the message interprets its meaning. The receiver uses knowledge and experience to interpret the symbols of the message; in some situations, he or she may consult an authority such as a dictionary or a code book. Up to this point the receiver has been relatively inactive, but the receiver becomes more active in the decoding phase. The meaning the receiver attaches to the symbols may be the same as or different from the meaning intended by the source. If the meanings differ, of course, communication breaks down, and misunderstanding is likely. In our example, if the employee does not understand the language or a particular word, the employee will not perceive the same meaning as the sender (manager) and may do the tasks in the wrong order or not do them at all.

> **Decoding** is the process by which the receiver of the message interprets the message's meaning.

Receiver

The **receiver** of the message can be an individual, a group, an organization, or an individual acting as the representative of a group. The receiver decides whether to decode the message, whether to make an effort to understand it, and whether to respond. The intended receiver might not get the message at all, whereas an unintended receiver might get it, depending on the medium and symbols used by the source and the attention level of potential receivers. An employee might share the same language (know the symbols) used by the manager, but not want to get the sender's meaning.

> The **receiver** is the individual, group, or organization that perceives the encoded symbols and may or may not decode them and try to understand the intended message.

The key skill for proper reception of the message is good listening. The receiver may not concentrate on the sender, the message, or the medium so the message is lost. Listening is an active process that requires as much concentration and effort from the receiver as sending the message does for the sender. The expression of emotions by the sender and receiver enters the communication process at several points. First, the emotions could be part of the message, entering into the encoding process. For example, if the manager's directions are consistent with a sense of urgency in his or her emotions, like a high-pitched or loud voice, the employee may move quickly to follow directions. However, if the message is urgent, but the tone of voice is low and does not send the same signals, employees may not engage in quick action. Second, as the message is decoded, the receiver may let his or her emotions perceive a message different from what the sender intended. Third, emotion-filled feedback from the intended receiver can cause the sender to modify her or his subsequent message.[16]

Feedback

Feedback is the process in which the receiver returns a message to the sender that indicates the receiver received and understood the message.

Feedback is the receiver's response to the message. Feedback verifies the message by telling the source whether the receiver received and understood the message. The feedback can be as simple as a phone call from the prospective client expressing interest in the business proposal or as complex as a written brief on a complicated point of law sent from an attorney to a judge. In our example, the employee can respond to the manager's directions by a verbal or written response indicating that he or she does or does not understand the message. Feedback could also be nonverbal, as when, in our example, the employee does not do either task. With typical voicemail, the feedback loop is missing, which can lead to many communication problems.

Noise

Noise is any disturbance in the communication process that interferes with or distorts communication.

Noise is any disturbance in the communication process that interferes with or distorts communication. Noise can be introduced at virtually any point in the communication

Information overload can serve as a major source of noise in the communication process. This harried manager, for example, seems overwhelmed with the vast amount of information spread before him. His feelings of stress will no doubt affect his ability to effectively cope with the tasks he needs to accomplish. Unfortunately, advances in electronic communication seem likely to make this problem even worse in the future.

process. The principal type, called **channel noise**, is associated with the medium.[17] Radio static and ghost images on television are examples of channel noise. When noise interferes with the encoding and decoding processes, poor encoding and decoding can result. An employee may not hear the directions given by the manager due to noisy machinery on the shop floor or competing input from other people. Emotions that interfere with an intended communication may also be considered a type of noise.

> **Channel noise** is a disturbance in communication that is primarily a function of the medium.

Effective communication occurs when information or meaning has been shared by at least two people. Therefore, communication must include the response from the receiver back to the sender. The sender cannot know if the message has been conveyed as intended if there is no feedback from the receiver. Both parties are responsible for the effectiveness of the communication. The evolution of new technology in recent years presents novel problems in ensuring that communications work as sender and receiver expect them to.

Electronic Information Processing and Telecommunications

Changes in the workplace are occurring at an astonishing rate. Many innovations are based on new technologies—computerized information-processing systems, new types of telecommunication systems, the Internet, organizational intranets and extranets, and various combinations of these technologies. Experts have estimated that performance of new information technology (at the same cost) doubles every 18 months.[18] Managers can now send and receive memos and other documents to and from one person or a group scattered around the world from their computers using the Internet, and they can do so in their cars or via their notebook computers and cellular phones on the commuter train. Wireless devices such as PDAs and so-called Wi-Fi hotspots are making these activities even more commonplace. Indeed, many employees are now telecommuting from home rather than going to the office every day. And whole new industries are developing around information storage, transmission, and retrieval that were not even dreamed of a few years ago.

> New information-processing and transmission technologies have created new media, symbols, message transmission methods, and networks for organizational communication.

The office of the future is here. It just may not be in a typical office building. Virtually every office now has a facsimile (fax) machine, a copier, and personal computers, most of them linked into a single integrated system and to numerous databases and electronic mail systems. Automobile companies advertise that their cars and trucks have equipment for your cellular telephone, computer, and fax machine. The electronic office links managers, clerical employees, professional workers, sales personnel, and, often, suppliers and customers in a worldwide communication network that uses a combination of computerized data storage, retrieval, and transmission systems.

In fact, the computer-integrated organization is commonplace. Some organizations boast totally computer-integrated operations in which all major functions—sales, marketing, finance, distribution, and manufacturing—exchange operating information quickly and continuously via computers. For example, product designers can send specifications directly to machines on the factory floor, and accounting personnel receive on-line information about sales, purchases, and prices instantaneously. The computer system parallels and greatly speeds up the entire process.

Computers are facilitating the increase in telecommuting across North America and reducing the number of trips to the office to get work done. A number of years ago IBM provided many of their employees with notebook computers and told them to not come to the office but to use the computers to do the work out in the field and send it in electronically.[19] Other companies, such as the Royal Bank and Bell Canada, have encouraged such telecommuting by employees. Employees report increased productivity,

While electronic communication technology may be dysfunctional in some cases, it can also help promote new methods of working, such as telecommuting. Rather than making the one-hour commute to and from work each day, this employee works from her home office two or three days a week. This arrangement helps her be more productive and to simultaneously better balance some of the demands of work and home.

less fatigue caused by commuting, reduced commuting expenses, and increased personal freedom. In addition, telecommuting may reduce air pollution and overcrowding. Some employees have reported, however, that they miss the social interaction of the office. Some managers have also expressed concerns about the quantity and quality of the work telecommuting employees do when away from the office.

Research conducted among office workers using a new electronic office system indicated that attitudes toward the system were generally favourable. On the other hand, reduction of face-to-face meetings may depersonalize the office. Some observers are concerned that companies are installing electronic systems with little consideration for the social structures of the office. As departments adopt computerized information systems, the activities of work groups throughout the organization are likely to become more interdependent, a situation that may alter power relationships among the groups.[20] Most employees quickly learn the system of power, politics, authority, and responsibility in the office. A radical change in work and personal relationships caused by new office technology may disrupt normal ways of accomplishing tasks, thereby reducing productivity. Other potential problems include information overload, loss of records in a paperless office, and the dehumanizing effects of electronic equipment. In effect, new information processing and transmission technologies have resulted in new media, symbols, message transmission methods, and networks for organizational communication.

The real increases in organizational productivity due to information technology may come from the ability to communicate in new and different ways rather than from simply speeding up existing communication patterns. For example, to remain competitive in a challenging global marketplace, companies will need to generate, disseminate, and implement new ideas with increasing speed and effectiveness.[21] In effect, organizations will become knowledge-based learning organizations that are continually generating new ideas to improve themselves. This can only occur when expert knowledge is communicated and available throughout the organization.

One of these new ways of communicating is idea sharing, or knowledge sharing, by sharing information on what practices work best. A computer-based system is necessary to store, organize, and then make available to others the best practices from throughout the company.[22] For example, Petro-Canada found that its intranet system was becoming too unwieldy. The company grew to over 5000 employees world wide. In addition to its retail locations across Canada, the company is involved in energy exploration and production in the Alberta oil sands and drilling rigs in Europe, North Africa, and Latin America. With the growth in the number of employees came a growth in the company intranet to nearly 150 sites. To streamline the flow of information within the company, Petro-Canada moved to a single portal that provided all users with a common information platform.[23] Electronic information technology is, therefore, speeding up existing communication and developing new types of organizational communication processes with potential new benefits and problems for managers.

Communication Networks

Communication links individuals and groups in a social system. Initially, task-related communication links develop in an organization so that employees can get the information they need to do their jobs and coordinate their work with that of others in the system. Over a long period, these communication relationships become a sophisticated

Family-Run Businesses and . . . DIVERSITY

Minority Family Businesses and Communication

Communication in family-owned businesses presents opportunities and challenges. Yet family businesses owned by visible minority families offer unique communication patterns and complications.

According to professors Young-Ho Nam and James I. Herbert, Korean and Chinese ethnic cultures place high value on family and kinship. Therefore, Asian family businesses experience little conflict or disagreement. Communication between family members is clear, even across generations. There is a strong preference for hiring family members, which tends to reduce conflict and enhance communication. However, most Korean and Chinese families do not emphasize the importance of passing the business onto their children. Rather, many hope that their children will have very different careers. This cultural value is supported by the traditional Korean saying, "Inherited wealth is difficult to transfer through three generations."

Many of the values shared by Asian families are present in other visible minority families. Family is an important value and most employees are family members. There are some differences. For example, there is less emphasis on communications that increase family harmony and more tolerance for challenging or creative statements. Unlike many Asian families, families from other cultural backgrounds often intend that the family business be a source of income for many generations. Communication about succession is therefore a high priority.

Family communication skills are vitally important to the success of a family-owned business. Yet differences in family heritage and values can have significant impact on the way in which families communicate at home and at work.

> *"Inherited wealth is difficult to transfer through three generations."*
>
> *TRADITIONAL KOREAN SAYING*

Sources: "Competing with the Big Dogs," Making It! Minority Success Stories, March 6, 2005, www.makingittv.com on April 25, 2005; "LuLu's Journey," "LuLu's Philosophy," LuLu's Desserts website, www.lu-lusdessert.com on April 25, 2005; Young-Ho Nam and James I. Herbert, "Characteristics and Key Success Factors in Family Business: The Case of Korean Immigrant Businesses in Metro-Atlanta," Kennesaw State University website, www.kennesaw.edu on April 25, 2005 (quotation).

social system composed of both small-group communication networks and a larger organizational network. These networks structure both the flow and the content of communication and support the organizational structure.[24] The pattern and content of communication also support the culture, beliefs, and value systems that enable the organization to operate. The Family-Run Businesses and . . . Diversity box on page 199 previews the role of communication networks in family-owned businesses.

Small-Group Networks

To examine interpersonal communication in a small group, we can observe the patterns that emerge as the work of the group proceeds and information flows from some people in the group to others. Four such patterns are shown in Figure 7.4. The lines identify the communication links most frequently used in the groups.

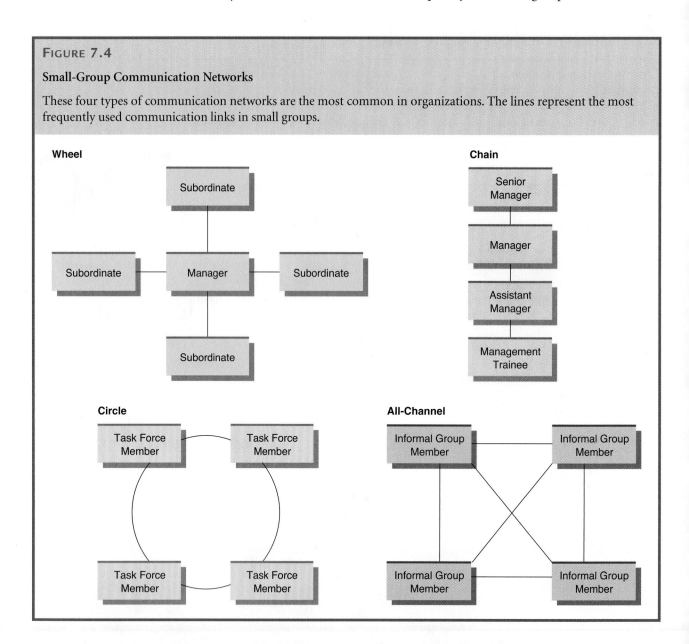

FIGURE 7.4

Small-Group Communication Networks

These four types of communication networks are the most common in organizations. The lines represent the most frequently used communication links in small groups.

A **wheel network** is a pattern in which information flows between the person at the end of each spoke and the person in the middle. Those on the ends of the spokes do not directly communicate with each other. The wheel network is a feature of the typical work group, where the primary communication occurs between the members and the group manager. In a **chain network**, each member communicates with the person above and below, except for the individuals on each end, who communicate with only one person. The chain network is typical of communication in a vertical hierarchy, in which most communication travels up and down the chain of command. Each person in a **circle network** communicates with the people on both sides but not with anyone else. The circle network often is found in task forces and committees. Finally, in an **all-channel network**, all the members communicate with all the other members. The all-channel network often is found in informal groups that have no formal structure, leader, or task to accomplish.

Communication may be more easily distorted by noise when much is being communicated or when the communication must travel a great distance.[25] Improvements in electronic communication technology, such as computerized mail systems and intranets, are reducing this effect. A relatively central position gives a person an opportunity to communicate with all of the other members, so a member in a relatively central position can control the information flow and may become a leader of the group. This leadership position is separate and distinct from the formal group structure, although a central person in a group could also emerge as a formal group leader over a long period.

Communication networks form spontaneously and naturally as interactions among workers continue. They are rarely permanent, since they change as the tasks, interactions, and memberships change. The patterns and characteristics of small-group communication networks are determined by the factors summarized in Table 7.1. The task is crucial in determining the pattern of the network. If the group's primary task is decision making, an all-channel network may develop to provide the information needed to evaluate all possible alternatives. If, however, the group's task mainly involves the sequential execution of individual tasks, a chain or wheel network is more likely, because communication among members may not be important to the completion of the tasks.

The environment (the type of room in which the group works or meets, the seating arrangement, the placement of chairs and tables, the geographical dispersion, and other aspects of the group's setting) can affect the frequency and types of interactions among members. For example, if most members work on the same floor of an office building, the members who work three floors down may be considered outsiders and develop weaker communication ties to the group. They might even form a separate communication network.

Personal factors also influence the development of the communication network. These include technical expertise, openness, speaking ability, and the degree to which members are acquainted with one another. For example, in a group concerned mainly

In a **wheel network**, information flows between the person at the end of each spoke and the person in the middle.

In a **chain network**, each member communicates with the person above and below, but not with the individuals on each end.

In a **circle network**, each member communicates with the people on both sides but with no one else.

In an **all-channel network**, all the members communicate with all the other members.

Communication networks form spontaneously and naturally as the interactions among workers continue over time.

Factor	Example
Task	Decision making
	Sequential production
Environment	Type of room, placement of chairs and tables, dispersion of members
Personal Characteristics	Expertise, openness, speaking ability, degree of familiarity among group members
Group Performance Factors	Composition, size, norms, cohesiveness

TABLE 7.1

Factors Influencing the Development of Small-Group Networks

Communication networks structure both the flow and the content of communication in organizations. When Clive Beddoe, Chairman and CEO of WestJet Airlines, speaks during the company's annual general meeting held in the airline's hangar at Calgary, the networks become more formalized. The information from this meeting will then be taken back by the managers who attend the meeting to their staffs.

with highly technical problems, the person with the most expertise might dominate the communication flow during a meeting.

The group performance factors that influence the communication network include composition, size, norms, and cohesiveness. For example, group norms in one organization may encourage open communication across different levels and functional units, whereas the norms in another organization may discourage such lateral and diagonal communication. These performance factors are discussed in Chapter 8.

Because the outcome of the group's efforts depends on the coordinated action of its members, the communication network strongly influences group effectiveness. Thus, to develop effective working relationships in the organization, managers need to make a special effort to manage the flow of information and the development of communication networks. Managers can, for example, arrange offices and work spaces to foster communication among certain employees. Managers may also attempt to involve members who typically contribute little during discussions by asking them direct questions such as "What do you think, Denis?" or "Harjinder, please tell us how this problem is handled in your district." Methods such as the nominal group technique, discussed in Chapter 8, can also encourage participation.

One other factor that is becoming increasingly important in the development of communication networks is the advent of electronic groups, fostered by electronic distribution lists, chat rooms, discussion boards, and other computer networking systems. This form of communication results in a network of people who may have little or no face-to-face communication, but still may be considered a group communication network.

For example, your professor is probably a member of an electronic group of other professors who share an interest in the topic of this course. Through the electronic group, they keep up with new ideas in the field. Many universities now use web-based interfaces such as WebCT to allow communication among class members and faculty outside of regularly scheduled class time.

Organizational Communication Networks

An organization chart shows reporting relationships from the line worker up to the CEO of the firm. The lines of an organization chart may also represent channels of communication through which information flows, yet communication may also follow paths that cross traditional reporting lines. Information moves not only from the top down—from CEO to group members—but upward from group members to the CEO.[26] In fact, a good flow of information to the CEO is an important determinant of the organization's success.[27]

Several companies have realized that the key to their continuing success is improved internal communication. General Motors was known for its extremely formal, top-down communication system. In the mid 1980s, however, the formality of its system came under fire from virtually all its stakeholders. GM's response was to embark on a massive communication improvement program that included sending employees to public-speaking workshops, improving the more than 350 publications it sends out, providing videotapes of management meetings to employees, and using satellite links between headquarters and field operations to establish two-way conversations around the world.[28]

Downward communication generally provides directions or feedback concerning employee performance. Upward communication provides feedback to top management concerning problems or progress toward goals. Communication that flows horizontally or crosses traditional reporting lines usually is related to task performance. For example, a design engineer, a manufacturing engineer and a quality engineer may communicate about the details of a particular product design that makes it easier to manufacture and inspect. Horizontal communication often travels faster than vertical communication, because it need not follow organizational protocols and procedures.

Organizational communication networks may diverge from reporting relationships as employees seek better information with which to do their jobs. Employees often find that the easiest way to get their jobs done or to obtain the necessary information is to go directly to employees in other departments rather than through the formal channels shown on the organization chart. Figure 7.5 shows a simple organization chart and the organization's real communication network. The communication network links the individuals who most frequently communicate with one another; the firm's CEO, for example, communicates most often with employee 5. (This does not mean that individuals not linked in the communication network never communicate, but only that their communications are relatively infrequent.) Perhaps the CEO and the employee interact frequently outside of work, in church, or service organizations such as Kiwanis, or at sporting events. Such interactions can lead to close friendships that carry over into business relationships. The figure also shows that the group managers do not have important roles in the communication network, contrary to common-sense expectations. There is evidence that communication networks have an influence on employee satisfaction and productivity. For example, formal upward communication procedures have been found to lead to greater satisfaction and productivity, although many organizations do not implement such procedures. The problem may lie in the fact that management and employees often have different views about what formal upward communication procedures should be used for.

The roles that people play in organizational communication networks can be analyzed in terms of their contribution to the functioning of the network.[29] The most important roles are labelled in the bottom portion of Figure 7.5. A **gatekeeper** (employee 5) has a strategic position in the network that allows him or her to control information moving in either direction through a channel. A **liaison** (employee 15) serves as a bridge between groups, tying groups together and facilitating the communication flow needed to integrate group activities. Employee 13 performs the interesting function of **cosmopolite**, who links the organization to the external environment by, for instance, attending conventions and trade shows, keeping up with outside technological innovations, and having more frequent contact with sources outside the organization. This person may also be an opinion leader in the group. Finally, the **isolate** (employee 3)

A free flow of information to the CEO or president of the organization is essential to the organization's success.

The **gatekeeper** has a strategic position in the network that allows him or her to control information moving in either direction through a channel.

The **liaison** serves as a bridge between groups, tying groups together and facilitating communication flow needed to integrate group activities.

The **cosmopolite** links the organization to the external environment and may also be an opinion leader in the group.

The **isolate** and the **isolated dyad** tend to work alone and to interact and communicate little with others.

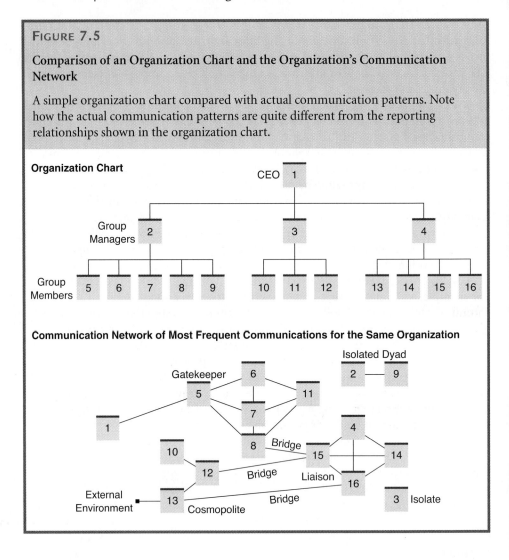

FIGURE 7.5

Comparison of an Organization Chart and the Organization's Communication Network

A simple organization chart compared with actual communication patterns. Note how the actual communication patterns are quite different from the reporting relationships shown in the organization chart.

and the **isolated dyad** (employees 2 and 9) tend to work alone and to interact and communicate little with others.

Each of these roles and functions plays an important part in the overall functioning of the communication network and in the organization as a whole. Understanding these roles can help both managers and group members facilitate communication. For instance, the manager who wants to be sure that the CEO receives certain information is well advised to go through the gatekeeper. If the employee who has the technical knowledge necessary for a particular project is an isolate, the manager can take special steps to integrate the employee into the communication network for the duration of the project.

Research has indicated some possible negative impacts of communication networks. Employee turnover has been shown to occur in clusters related to employee communication networks.[30] That is, employees who communicate regularly in a network may share feelings about the organization and thus influence one another's intentions to stay or quit. Communication networks, therefore, can have both positive and negative consequences.

As we discuss in Chapters 12 and 13, a primary function of organizational structure is to coordinate the activities of many people doing specialized tasks. Communication

Gender Differences in Communication and ...  RESEARCH

Men Are from Mars, Women Are from Venus: or Are They?

In recent decades, we have seen an increase in the number of women in the workforce. This has resulted in greater number of mixed gender work groups. In the early 1990s, relationship therapist John Gray published his best-selling book, *Men Are from Mars, Women Are from Venus*, to assist men and women in improving their understanding of communication styles and emotional needs in the opposite sex. A decade later, Gray published *Mars and Venus in the Workplace*, which examined the communication gap between men and women at work. According to Gray, when a woman seeks others' opinions about a work-related problem, men interpret that to mean that she is not competent to solve the problem herself. On the contrary, men tend to isolate themselves when solving a problem, which can be interpreted by women as exclusionary. Georgetown University sociolinguist Deborah Tannen has also suggested that men and women have different speaking styles that, when used with the opposite sex, can lead to breakdowns in communication.

Recent research by York University professors Leonard Karakowsky and Kenneth McBey and Diane Miller from Brock University suggests that context can have an influence on the extent to which men and women engage in stereotypical communication behaviours. These researchers examined the extent to which verbal interruptions, a mechanism of power and dominance in conversation typically used by men in same gender peer groups, is used when men find themselves in different contexts. One aspect of context reflected their gender majority/minority status within the group. The other aspect of context concerned the gender orientation of the task in which the group was engaged. These authors found that men were more likely than women to engage in verbal power displays in same gender groups. In addition, they found some support for their hypothesis that men were less likely to engage in these behaviours when they found themselves in female-dominated groups. The gender orientation of the task also had a small effect on interruption behaviours. These behaviours decreased when individuals found themselves completing tasks that were more stereotypical of the opposite gender.

Overall the results suggested that power displays among men and women are not solely due to differences in gender-role socialization. It appears that men and women are sensitive to contextual factors such as perceptions of expertise and relative representation. Perhaps it is not true after all that men are from Mars and women are from Venus!

Source: Leonard Karakowsky, Kenneth McBey, and Diane L. Miller, "Gender, Perceived Competence, and Power Displays: Examining Verbal Interruptions in a Group Context," *Small Group Research*, August 2004, pp. 407–439.

networks in organizations provide this much-needed integration.[31] In fact, in some ways, communication patterns influence organizational structure.[32] Some companies are finding that the need for better communication forces them to create smaller divisions. The fewer managerial levels and improved team spirit of these divisions tend to enhance communication flow.[33]

Managing Communication

As simple as the process of communication may seem, messages are not always understood. The degree of correspondence between the message intended by the source and the message understood by the receiver is called **communication fidelity**.[34] Fidelity can be diminished anywhere in the communication process, from the source to the feedback. Moreover, organizations have characteristics that might impede the flow of information. Table 7.2 summarizes the most common types of breakdowns and barriers in organizational communication.

Communication fidelity is the degree of correspondence between the message intended by the source and the message understood by the receiver.

Root of the Problem	Type of Problem
Source	Filtering
Encoding and Decoding	Lack of common experience
	Semantics, jargon
	Medium problems
Receiver	Selective attention
	Value judgments
	Lack of source credibility
	Overload
Feedback	Omission
Organizational Factors	Noise
	Status differences
	Time pressures
	Overload
	Communication structure

Improving the Communication Process

To improve organizational communication one must understand potential problems. Using the basic communication process, we can identify several ways to overcome typical problems.

Source   The source may intentionally withhold or filter information on the assumption that the receiver does not need it to understand the communication. Withholding information, however, may render the message meaningless or cause an erroneous interpretation. For example, during a performance appraisal interview, a manager may not tell the employee all of the sources of information being used to make the evaluation, thinking that the employee does not need to know them. If the employee knew, however, he or she might be able to explain certain behaviours or otherwise alter the manager's perspective of the evaluation and thereby make it more accurate. Selective filtering can cause a breakdown in communication that cannot be repaired, even with good follow-up communication.[35]

To avoid filtering, the communicator needs to understand why it occurs. Filtering can result from lack of understanding of the receiver's position, from the sender's need to protect his or her own power by limiting the receiver's access to information, or from doubts about what the receiver might do with the information. The sender's primary concern, however, should be the message. In essence, the sender must determine exactly what message he or she wants the receiver to understand, send the receiver enough information to understand the message but not enough to create an overload, and trust the receiver to use the information properly.

Encoding and Decoding   Encoding and decoding problems occur as the message is translated into or from the symbols used in transmission. Such problems can relate to the meaning of the symbols or to the transmission itself. Encoding and decoding problems include lack of common experience between source and receiver, problems related to semantics and the use of jargon, and difficulties with the medium.

Clearly, the source and the receiver must share a common experience with the symbols that express the message if they are to encode and decode them in exactly the same way. People who speak different languages or come from different cultural backgrounds can experience problems of this sort. But even people who speak the same language can misunderstand each other. **Semantics** is the study of language forms, and semantic problems occur when people attribute different meanings to the same words or language forms. For example, when discussing a problem employee, the division head may tell her assistant, "We need to get rid of this problem." The division head may have meant that the employee should be scheduled for more training or transferred to another division. However, the assistant may interpret the statement differently and fire the problem employee.

The specialized or technical language of a trade, field, profession, or social group is called **jargon**. Jargon may be a hybrid of standard language and the specialized language of a group. For example, experts in the computer field use terms such as "gigs," "megs," "RAM," and "bandwidth" that have no meaning to those unfamiliar with computers. The use of jargon makes communication within a close group of colleagues more efficient and meaningful, but outside the group it has the opposite effect. Sometimes a source person comfortable with jargon uses it unknowingly in an attempt to communicate with receivers who do not understand it, thus causing a communication breakdown. For example, one of the authors of this text was discussing his teaching assignment with a friend, who was a health psychologist. When he informed her that he would be teaching a course in "OB" (based on the short form for organizational behaviour), she looked puzzled and asked, "What do you know about obstetrics?" In the health profession, the term "OB" is used to refer to obstetrics, a medical specialty. In other cases, the source might use jargon intentionally to obscure meaning or to show outsiders that he or she belongs to the group that uses the language.

The use of jargon is acceptable if the receiver is familiar with it. Otherwise, it should be avoided. Repeating a message that contains jargon in clearer terms should help the receiver understand it. In general, the source and the receiver should clarify the set of symbols to be used before they communicate. Also, the receiver can ask questions frequently and, if necessary, ask the source to repeat all or part of the message. The source must send the message through a medium appropriate to the message itself and to the intended receiver. For example, a commercial run on an AM radio station will not have its intended effect if the people in the desired market segment listen only to FM radio.

Receiver Several communication problems originate in the receiver, including problems with selective attention, value judgments, source credibility, and overload. Selective attention exists when the receiver attends to only selected parts of a message—a frequent occurrence with oral communication. For example, in a university class some

> **Semantics** is the study of language forms.

> **Jargon** is the specialized or technical language of a trade, profession, or social group.

> Communication problems that originate in the receiver include problems with selective attention, value judgments, source credibility, and overload.

Reprinted with special permission of King Feature Syndicate.

One of the oldest barriers to effective communication in organizations is simply poor writing. If the sender jots down some instructions or other information, but the receiver cannot accurately read the intended message, any number of problems can arise. Of course, the simplest solution is for the receiver to simply ask the sender to "translate" what she or he has written. As shown here, though, some people are reluctant to take this step, and their reluctance can sometimes spell big trouble!

students may hear only part of the professor's lecture as their minds wander to other topics. To focus receivers' attention on the message, senders often engage in attention-getting behaviours such as varying the volume, repeating the message, and offering rewards.

Value judgments are influenced by the degree to which a message reinforces or challenges the receiver's basic personal beliefs. If a message reinforces the receiver's beliefs, he or she may pay close attention and believe it completely, without examination. On the other hand, if the message challenges those beliefs, the receiver may entirely discount it. Thus, if a firm's sales manager predicts that the demand for new baby-care products will increase substantially over the next two years, she or he may ignore reports that the birthrate is declining.

The receiver may also judge the credibility of the source of the message. If the source is perceived to be an expert in the field, the listener may pay close attention to the message and believe it. Conversely, if the receiver has little respect for the source, he or she may disregard the message. The receiver considers both the message and the source in making value judgments and determining credibility. An expert in nuclear physics may be viewed as a credible source if the issue is building a nuclear power plant, yet the same person's evaluation of the birthrate may be disregarded, perhaps correctly. This is one reason that trial lawyers ask expert witnesses about their education and experience at the beginning of testimony: to establish credibility.

A receiver experiencing communication overload is receiving more information than she or he can process. In organizations, this can happen very easily; a receiver can be bombarded with computer-generated reports and messages from superiors, peers, and sources outside the organization. Unable to take in all the messages, decode them, understand them, and act on them, the receiver may use selective attention and value judgments to focus on the messages that seem most important. Although this type of selective attention is necessary for survival in an information-glutted environment, it may mean that vital information is lost or overlooked.

Feedback   The purpose of feedback is **verification**, in which the receiver sends a message to the source indicating receipt of the message and the degree to which it was understood. Lack of feedback can cause at least two problems. First, the source may need to send another message that depends on the response to the first; if the source receives no feedback, the source may not send the second message or may be forced to send the original message again. Second, the receiver may act on the unverified message; if the receiver misunderstood the message, the resulting act may be inappropriate.

Because feedback is so important, the source must actively seek it and the receiver must supply it. Often it is appropriate for the receiver to repeat the original message as an introduction to the response, although the medium or symbols used may be different. Nonverbal cues can provide instantaneous feedback. These include body language and facial expressions, such as anger and disbelief.[36]

The source needs to be concerned with the message, the symbols, the medium, and the feedback from the receiver. Of course, the receiver is concerned with these things too, but from a different point of view. In general the receiver needs to be source-oriented just as the source needs to be receiver-oriented. Table 7.3 gives suggestions for improving the communication process.

> **Verification** is the feedback portion of communication in which the receiver sends a message to the source indicating receipt of the message and the degree to which he or she understood the message.

Improving Organizational Factors in Communication

Organizational factors that can create communication breakdowns or barriers include noise, status differences, time pressures, and overload. As previously stated, disturbances anywhere in the organization can distort or interrupt meaningful communication.

	Source		Receiver	
Focus	**Question**	**Corrective Action**	**Question**	**Corrective Action**
Message	What idea or thought are you trying to get across?	Give more information. Give less information. Give entire message.	What idea or thought does the sender want you to understand?	Listen carefully to the entire message, not just to part of it.
Symbols	Does the receiver use the same symbols, words, jargon?	Say it another way. Employ repetition. Use receiver's language or jargon. Before sending, clarify symbols to be used.	What symbols are being used—for example, foreign language, technical jargon?	Clarify symbols before communication begins. Ask questions. Ask sender to repeat message.
Medium	Is this a channel that the receiver monitors regularly? Sometimes? Never?	Use multiple media. Change medium. Increase volume (loudness)	What medium or media is the sender using?	Monitor several media.
Feedback	What is the receiver's reaction to your message?	Pay attention to the feedback, especially non-verbal cues. Ask questions.	Did you correctly interpret the message?	Repeat message.

TABLE 7.3

Improving the Communication Process

Thus, the noise created by a rumoured takeover can disrupt the orderly flow of task-related information. Status differences between source and receiver can cause some of the communication problems just discussed. For example, a firm's chief executive officer may pay little attention to communications from employees far lower on the organization chart, and employees may pay little attention to communications from the CEO. Both are instances of selective attention prompted by the organization's status system. Time pressures and communication overload are also detrimental to communication. When the receiver is not allowed enough time to understand incoming messages, or when there are too many messages, he or she may misunderstand or ignore some of them. Effective organizational communication provides the right information to the right person at the right time and in the right form.

Reduce Noise   Noise is a primary barrier to effective organizational communication. A common form of noise is the rumour **grapevine**, an informal system of communication that coexists with the formal system.[37] The grapevine usually transmits information faster than official channels do. Because the accuracy of this information often is quite low, however, the grapevine can distort organizational communication. Management can reduce the effects of the distortion by using the grapevine as an additional channel for disseminating information and by constantly monitoring it for accuracy.

The **grapevine** is an informal system of communication that coexists with the formal system.

Foster Informal Communication   Communication in well-run companies was once described as "a vast network of informal, open communications."[38] Informal communication fosters mutual trust, which minimizes the effects of status differences. Open communication can also contribute to better understanding between diverse groups in an organization. WestJet executives often participate in day to day tasks such as helping to clean aircraft and, at least once a year, employees attend small chat sessions where they can voice concerns to management as well as make suggestions.[39]

Open communication also allows information to be communicated when it is needed rather than when the formal information system allows it to emerge. Some experts also describe communication in effective companies as chaotic and intense, supported by the reward structure and the physical arrangement of the facilities. This means that the performance appraisal and reward system, offices, meeting rooms, and work areas are designed to encourage frequent, unscheduled, and unstructured communication throughout the organization.

Develop a Balanced Information Network   Many large organizations have developed elaborate formal information systems to cope with the potential problems of information overload and time pressures. In many cases, however, the systems have created problems rather than solving them. Often they produce more information than managers and decision makers can comprehend and use in their jobs. They also often use only formal communication channels and ignore various informal lines of communication. Furthermore, the systems frequently provide whatever information the computer is set up to provide—information that may not apply to the most pressing problem at hand. The result of all these drawbacks is loss of communication effectiveness.

> Organizations need to balance information load and information-processing capabilities.

Organizations need to balance information load and information-processing capabilities.[40] In other words, they must take care not to generate more information than people can handle. It is useless to produce sophisticated statistical reports that managers have no time to read. Furthermore, the new technologies that are making more information available to managers and decision makers must be unified to produce usable information.[41] Information production, storage, and processing capabilities must be compatible with one another and, equally important, with the needs of the organization.

Some organizations—for example, General Electric, DuPont Canada, Canada Post, and McDonald's—have formalized an upward communication system that uses a corporate "ombudsperson" position.[42] A highly placed executive who is available outside the formal chain of command to hear employees' complaints usually holds this position. The system provides an opportunity for disgruntled employees to complain without fear of losing their jobs and may help some companies achieve a balanced communication system.

Summary of Key Points

- Communication is the process by which two parties exchange information and share meaning. It plays a role in every organizational activity. The purposes of communication in organizations are to achieve coordinated action, share information, and to express feelings and emotions.

- People in organizations communicate through written, oral, and nonverbal means. Written communications include letters, memos, reports, and the like. Oral communication is the type most commonly used. Personal elements, such as facial expressions and body language, and environmental elements, such as office design, are forms of nonverbal communication.

- Communication among individuals, groups, or organizations is a process in which a source sends a message and a receiver responds. The source encodes a message into symbols and transmits it through a medium to the receiver, who decodes the symbols. The receiver then responds with feedback, an attempt to verify the meaning of the original message. Noise—anything that distorts or interrupts communication—can interfere in virtually any stage of the process.

- The fully integrated communication-information office system—the electronic office—links personnel in a communication network through a combination of computers and electronic transmission systems. The full range of effects of such systems has yet to be fully realized.

- Communication networks are systems of information exchange within organizations. Patterns of communication emerge as information flows from person to person in a group. Typical small-group communication networks include the wheel, chain, circle, and all-channel networks.

- The organizational communication network, which constitutes the real communication links in an organization, usually differs from the arrangement on an organization chart. Roles in organizational communication networks include those of gatekeeper, liaison, cosmopolite, and isolate.

- Managing communication in organizations involves understanding the numerous problems that can interfere with effective communication. Problems may arise from the communication process itself and from organizational factors such as status differences.

Discussion Questions

1. How is communication in organizations an individual process as well as an organizational process?

2. Discuss the three primary purposes of organizational communication.

3. Describe a situation in which you tried to carry on a conversation when no one was listening. Were any messages sent during the conversation?

4. A college classroom is a forum for a typical attempt at communication as the professor tries to communicate the subject to the students. Describe classroom communication in terms of the basic communication process outlined in the chapter.

5. Is there a communication network (other than professor-to-student) in the class in which you are using this book? If so, identify the specific roles that people play in the network. If not, why has no network developed? What would be the benefits of having a communication network in this class?

6. Why might educators typically focus most communication training on the written and oral methods and pay little attention to the nonverbal methods? Do you think that more training emphasis should be placed on nonverbal communication? Why or why not?

7. Is the typical classroom means of transferring information from professor to student an effective form of communication? Where does it break down? What are the communication problems in the college or university classroom?

8. Whose responsibility is it to solve classroom communication problems: the students', the professor's, or the administration's?

9. Have you ever worked in an organization in which communication was a problem? If so, what were some causes of the problem?

10. What methods were used, or should have been used, to improve communication in the situation you described in question 9?

11. Would the use of advanced computer information processing or telecommunications have helped solve the communications problem you described in question 9?

12. What types of communication problems will new telecommunications methods probably be able to solve? Why?

Experiencing Organizational Behaviour

Purpose: This exercise demonstrates the importance of feedback in oral communication.

Format: You will be an observer or play the role of either a manager or an assistant manager trying to tell a coworker where a package of important materials is to be picked up. The observer's role is to make sure the other two participants follow the rules and to observe and record any interesting occurrences.

Procedure: The instructor will divide the class into groups of three. (Any extra members can be roving observers.) The three people in each group will take the roles of manager, assistant manager, and observer. In the second trial, the manager and the assistant manager will switch roles.

Trial 1: The manager and the assistant manager should turn their backs to each other so that neither can see the other. Here is the situation. The manager is in another city that he or she is not familiar with but that the assistant manager knows quite well. The manager needs to find the office of a supplier to pick up drawings of a critical component of the company's main product. The supplier will be closing for the day in a few minutes; the drawings must be picked up before closing time. The manager has called the assistant manager to get directions to the office. However, the connection is faulty; the manager can hear the assistant manager but the assistant manager can hear only enough to know the manager is on the line. The manager has redialled once, but there was no improvement in the connection. Now there is no time to lose. The manager has decided to get the directions from the assistant without asking questions.

Just before the exercise begins, the instructor will give the assistant manager a detailed map of the city that shows the locations of the supplier's office and the manager. The map will include a number of turns, stops, stoplights, intersections, and shopping centres between these locations.

The assistant manager can study it for no longer than a minute or two. When the instructor gives the direction to start, the assistant manager describes to the manager how to get from his or her present location to the supplier's office. As the assistant manager gives the directions, the manager draws the map on a piece of paper.

The observer makes sure that no questions are asked, records the beginning and ending times, and notes how the assistant manager tries to communicate particularly difficult points (including points about which the manager obviously wants to ask questions) and any other noteworthy occurrences.

After all pairs have finished, each observer "grades" the quality of the manager's map by comparing it with the original and counting the number of obvious mistakes. The instructor will ask a few managers who believe they have drawn good maps to tell the rest of the class how to get to the supplier's office.

Trial 2: In trial 2, the manager and the assistant manager switch roles, and a second map is passed out to the new assistant managers. The situation is the same as in the first trial, except that the telephones are working properly and the manager can ask questions of the assistant manager. The observer's role is the same as in trial 1—recording the beginning and ending times, the methods of communication, and other noteworthy occurrences.

After all pairs have finished, the observers grade the maps, just as in the first trial. The instructor then selects a few managers to tell the rest of the class how to get to the supplier's office. The subsequent class discussion should centre on the experiences of the class members and the follow-up questions.

Follow-up Questions

1. Which trial resulted in more accurate maps? Why?

2. Which trial took longer? Why?

3. How did you feel when a question needed to be asked but it could not be asked in trial 1? Was your confidence in the final result affected differently in the two trials?

Diagnosing Your Listening Skills

Introduction: Good listening skills are essential for effective communication and are often overlooked when communication is analyzed. This self-assessment questionnaire examines your ability to listen effectively.

Instructions: Go through the following statements, checking "Yes" or "No" next to each one. Mark each question as truthfully as you can in light of your behaviour in the last few meetings or gatherings you attended.

Yes   No

_____ _____ 1. I frequently attempt to listen to several conversations at the same time.

_____ _____ 2. I like people to give me only the facts and then let me make my own interpretation.

_____ _____ 3. I sometimes pretend to pay attention to people.

_____ _____ 4. I consider myself a good judge of nonverbal communications.

_____ _____ 5. I usually know what another person is going to say before he or she says it.

_____ _____ 6. I usually end conversations that don't interest me by diverting my attention from the speaker.

_____ _____ 7. I frequently nod, frown, or in some other way let the speaker know how I feel about what he or she is saying.

_____ _____ 8. I usually respond immediately when someone has finished talking.

_____ _____ 9. I evaluate what is being said while it is being said.

_____ _____ 10. I usually formulate a response while the other person is still talking.

_____ _____ 11. The speaker's delivery style frequently keeps me from listening to content.

_____ _____ 12. I usually ask people to clarify what they have said rather than guess at the meaning.

_____ _____ 13. I make a concerted effort to understand other people's point of view.

_____ _____ 14. I frequently hear what I expect to hear rather than what is said.

_____ _____ 15. Most people feel that I have understood their point of view when we disagree.

Scoring

The correct answers according to communication theory are as follows:

NO for statements 1, 2, 3, 5, 6, 7, 8, 9, 10, 11, 14.

YES for statements 4, 12, 13, 15.

If you missed only one or two responses, you strongly approve of your own listening habits, and you are on the right track to becoming an effective listener in your role as manager. If you missed three or four responses, you have uncovered some doubts about your listening effectiveness, and your knowledge of how to listen has some gaps. If you missed five or more responses, you probably are not satisfied with the way you listen, and your friends and coworkers may not feel you are a good listener either. Work on improving your active listening skills.

Source: Ethel C. Glenn and Elliott A. Pond, "Listening Self-Inventory," from *Supervisory Management*, January 1989, pp. 12–15. Copyright © 1989. Reprinted by permission of American Management Association, Inc. All rights reserved.

Management SkillBuilder

Exercise Overview: Communication skills refer to a manager's ability both to convey ideas and information effectively to others and to receive ideas and information effectively from others. This exercise focuses on communication skills as they involve deciding how to best convey information.

Exercise Background: Assume that you are a middle manager for a large electronics firm. People in your organization generally use one of three means for communicating with one another. The most common way is oral communication, accomplished either face-to-face or by telephone. Electronic mail is also widely used. Finally, a surprisingly large amount of communication is still done on paper, such as through memos, reports, or letters.

During the course of a typical day, you receive and send a variety of messages and other communication. You generally use some combination of all of the communication methods previously noted during the course of any given day. The things that you need to communicate today include the following:

1. You need to schedule a meeting with five subordinates.

2. You need to congratulate a coworker who just had a baby.

3. You need to reprimand a staff assistant who has been coming to work late for the last several days.

4. You need to inform the warehouse staff that several customers have recently complained because their shipments were not properly packed.

5. You need to schedule a meeting with your boss.

6. You need to announce two promotions.

7. You need to fire someone who has been performing poorly for some time.

8. You need to inform several individuals about a set of new government regulations that will soon affect them.

9. You need to inform a supplier that your company will soon be cutting back on its purchases because a competing supplier has lowered its prices, and you plan to shift more of your business to that supplier.

10. You need to resolve a disagreement between two subordinates who both want to take their vacation at the same time.

Exercise Task: Using the information just presented, do the following:

1. Indicate which methods of communication would be appropriate for each situation.

2. Rank-order the methods for each communication situation from best to worst.

3. Compare your rankings with those of a classmate and discuss any differences.

Organizational Behaviour Case for Discussion

Heading off a Permanent Misunderstanding

Mindy Martin was no longer speaking to Al Sharp. She had been wary of him since her first day at Alton Products; he had always seemed distant and aloof. She thought at first that he resented her M.B.A. degree, her fast rise in the company, or her sense of purpose and ambition. But she was determined to get along with everyone in the office, so she had taken him out to lunch, praised his work whenever she could, and even kept track of his son's hockey feats.

But all that ended with the appointment of the new marketing director for Western Canada. Martin had had her sights on the job and thought her chances were good. She was competing with three other managers on her level. Sharp was not in the running because he did not have a graduate degree, but his voice was thought to carry a lot of weight with the top brass. Martin had less seniority than any of her competitors, but her division had become the leader in the company, and upper management had praised her lavishly. She believed that with a good recommendation from Sharp, she would get the job.

But Walt Murdoch received the promotion and moved to Winnipeg. Martin was devastated. It was bad enough that she did not get the promotion, but she could not stand the fact that Murdoch had been chosen. She and Al Sharp had taken to calling Murdoch "Mr. Intolerable" because neither of them could stand his pompous arrogance. She felt that his being chosen was an insult to her; it made her rethink her entire career. When the grapevine confirmed her suspicion that Al Sharp had strongly influenced the decision, she determined to reduce her interaction with Sharp to a bare minimum.

Relations in the office were very chilly for almost a month. Sharp soon gave up trying to get back in Martin's favour, and they began communicating only in short, unsigned memos. Finally, William Attridge, their immediate boss, could tolerate the hostility no longer and called the two in for a meeting. "We're going to sit here until you two become friends again," he said, "or at least until I find out what's bugging you."

Martin resisted for a few minutes, denying that anything had changed in their relationship, but when she saw that Attridge was serious, she finally said, "Al seems more interested in dealing with Walter Murdoch." Sharp's jaw dropped; he sputtered but could not say anything. Attridge came to the rescue.

"Walter's been safely kicked upstairs, thanks in part to Al, and neither of you will have to deal with him in the future. But if you're upset about that promotion, you should know that Al had nothing but praise for you and kept pointing out how this division would suffer if we sent you to Winnipeg. With your bonuses, you're still making as much as Murdoch. If your work here continues to be outstanding, you'll be headed for even better things than the job Murdoch just got."

Embarrassed, Martin looked up at Sharp, who shrugged and said, "You want to go get some coffee?"

Over coffee, Martin told Sharp what she had been thinking for the past month and apologized for treating him unfairly. Sharp explained that what she saw as aloofness was actually respect and something akin to fear: he viewed her as brilliant and efficient. Consequently he was very cautious, trying not to offend her.

The next day, the office was almost back to normal. But a new ritual had been established: Martin and Sharp took a coffee break together every day at 10:00. Soon their teasing and friendly competition loosened up everyone they worked with. Want more test questions? Take the ACE quizzes found on the student website: www.hmco.ca/ob.

Case Questions

1. What might have happened had William Attridge not intervened?

2. Are the sources of misunderstanding between Martin and Sharp common or unusual?

SELF TEST

You have read the chapter and studied the key terms. Think you're ready to ace the exam? Take this sample test to gauge your comprehension of chapter material and check your answers at the back of the book.

T F 1. Communication is a social process.

T F 2. A performance appraisal form is an example of communication.

T F 3. The communication sender must decode his or her message before they transmit it.

T F 4. One downside to telecommuting is the missed social interaction of the office.

T F 5. Communication networks are relatively permanent, even though tasks and organization memberships change.

T F 6. One way a manager can improve communication is to increase filtering.

T F 7. The grapevine usually transmits information faster than official channels do.

8. The primary purpose of communication in organizations is
   a. to inform customers.
   b. to achieve coordinated action.
   c. to understand different cultures.
   d. to share ideas.
   e. to make decisions.

9. The most prevalent form of organizational communication is
   a. written.
   b. visual.
   c. memos and reports.
   d. policy manuals.
   e. oral.

10. Tony wants to transmit a message to his employees, but he wants to be sure they understand how passionately he feels about the issue. He'd be best off to pick which communication media?
    a. letter
    b. e-mail
    c. memo
    d. face-to-face
    e. All of the above have the same carrying capacity, as long as Tony makes his message clear.

11. All of the following are benefits of telecommuting, except
    a. less fatigue for employees.
    b. increased productivity.

c. reduced commuting expenses.
    d. reduced air pollution and overcrowding.
    e. increased control over employees.

12. An organization that has a clear vertical hierarchy likely has which type of communication network?
    a. wheel network
    b. chain network
    c. circle network
    d. all-channel network
    e. virtual network

13. Nichole is a lower-level manager who wants to communicate with the company president. To accomplish this, Nichole will likely have to go through a/an
    a. gatekeeper.
    b. liaison.
    c. cosmopolite.
    d. isolate.
    e. transmitter.

14. Which is the best advice for managers with regard to the use of jargon?
    a. Use jargon to establish expertise in a particular field.
    b. Require the use of jargon by all technical employees.
    c. Use jargon during negotiations to avoid telling the other party too much.
    d. Avoid using jargon if the receiver is unfamiliar with it.
    e. Never use jargon.

15. The recommendation to managers to develop a balanced information network refers to the need to weigh
    a. the capacity of information-processing equipment with the financial cost of this equipment.
    b. the frequency of information usage with the demands on information capacity.
    c. the amount of information people can handle with the amount of information generated.
    d. the technology available to process information with the personal wants and needs of information systems employees.
    e. the information storage capabilities with the needs of the organization.

Foundations of Interpersonal and Group Behaviour

CHAPTER 8

After studying this chapter, you should be able to:

- ▶ **Define the term "group" and discuss why the study of groups is important in managing organizations.**

- ▶ **Explain the differences between formal and informal groups.**

- ▶ **Trace the stages of development of groups from initial introduction to a mature stage of performing.**

- ▶ **Summarize the key factors affecting group performance.**

- ▶ **Describe the important dimensions of inter-group behaviour.**

- ▶ **Explain the difference between normal work groups and teams.**

- ▶ **Discuss the benefits of teams.**

- ▶ **Describe seven types of teams.**

- ▶ **Discuss the factors that managers must consider in managing groups in organizations.**

Building a Successful Team

Few teams have experienced as much success as Canada's National Women's Hockey Team. In fact, the team has never lost a single game to another women's team with the exception of the United States. In the lead up to the 2006 Winter Olympic Games in Turin, Italy, the Canadians were the favourites, but no one was counting out a strong American team. And, despite being the defending champions, having won gold at the 2002 Olympic Games in Salt Lake City, the heartbreaking loss to the American team at the 1998 Olympic Games in Nagano, Japan, was not far from anyone's mind. As a result, Team Canada head coach Melody Davidson was not leaving anything to chance. As a seasoned coach, Davidson understood that the success of the team would depend on cohesiveness and physical preparedness.

Rather than staging open training camps, Davidson had a short list of 27 players, 15 of whom were veterans from the 2002 gold medal team. The players were invited to a three-week mini-camp in June 2005 where they experienced a punishing series of fitness tests and drills, including a triathalon. Goaltender Charline Labonté recalled, "I thought I was going to die in the pool. The camp was hell — I wanted to quit." Two months later, Davidson moved all the invited players to Calgary to live and train full-time. Veteran defenseman, Becky Kellar, moved with her infant son and nanny, leaving her husband behind at their home in Burlington, Ontario.

For the next five months, the team played 43 exhibition games, beating the American squad in eight of ten meetings. The Canadians also went undefeated in 21 games against teams from other nations. Seeking a bigger challenge for the women, Davidson arranged a series of 22 games against boys' midget AAA teams from around Alberta. These teams consisted of big, physical 16- and 17-year-olds. The first games did not go well for the women. They won only one of their first five games and were outscored 20 to 7. At one point, Davidson laid into the players telling them that they had better pick up their level of play or they would not be around to play in the Olympics. It worked! The team won its last three games against the boys' teams. During the final game, Davidson felt that the team was truly beginning to gel. "I saw so much trust," said Davidson, "from the players to each other, from the players to us." They were ready for the Olympics!

As expected, Team Canada breezed through the opening round of Olympic play, outscoring their opponents 36 to 1. After a 12 to 0 pounding of the Russian team, the team was criticized for running up the score. Team U.S. defenceman Angela Ruggiero accused the Canadians of doing a disservice to women's hockey. This comment only served to heighten anticipation of a Canada–U.S.

gold medal matchup. After all, the Americans had never lost a game to anyone other than Canada. But, the unexpected happened in the semi-final game when Sweden defeated the U.S. to advance to the gold medal game against Canada. Despite a game effort from the Swedes, Team Canada won their second straight Olympic gold medal, defeating Sweden 4 to 1.[1]

In this chapter, we discuss groups and teams in organizations. Although the Canadian Women's hockey team is not a business organization, a lot of the factors that lead to success in sports teams are also important in organizational teams. One factor that we alluded to in the opening vignette and discuss in more detail later in the chapter is cohesiveness. Many of the situations engineered by Coach Melody Davidson (and some that came from outside the team) were designed to create a high level of cohesiveness in her team. For example, the process used to select team members, the opportunity for frequent interactions among the team members, the clear objectives, and the success experienced by the team in the period prior to the Olympic tournament all brought the women together and helped lead to their success, as did the criticism directed at the team from external parties.

The notion of groups and teams as a way of organizing work is not new. Neither is it an American or Japanese innovation. One of the earliest uses and analyses of teams was the work of the Tavistock Institute in the late 1940s in the United Kingdom (discussed in more detail in Chapter 15).[2] Major companies such as Hewlett Packard, Xerox, Procter & Gamble, General Motors, and General Mills have been using teams as a primary means of accomplishing tasks for almost 20 years.[3] The popular business press, such as Canadian Business, Fortune, the National Post, Business Week, Forbes, and Wall Street Journal, regularly report on the use of teams in businesses around the world. The use of teams is not a fad of the month or some new way to manipulate workers into producing more at their own expense to enrich owners. Managers and experts agree that teams can be the way to organize and manage successfully in the next century. A Conference Board of Canada survey indicated that 42 percent of Canadian organizations use teams extensively with nearly the same number of organizations reporting moderate use of teams.[4]

This chapter is about work groups and teams in organizations. Large companies around the world are restructuring their organizations around teams to increase productivity and innovation and improve customer service. Here we cover the basics of group dynamics—the reasons for group formation, the types of groups in organizations, and group performance factors. We also consider how organizations are using teams today.

We begin this chapter by defining "group" and summarizing the importance of groups in organizations. Then we describe different types of groups and discuss the stages as they evolve from newly formed groups into mature, high-performing units. Next, we identify four key factors in group performance. Then we move to a discussion of how groups interact with other groups in organizations. Next we define what is meant by "team" and differentiate teams from normal work groups. Then we discuss the rationale for using teams, including both the benefits and the costs. Next, we describe seven types of teams in use in organizations today. Finally, we summarize the important elements in managing groups and teams in organizations.

Figure 8.1 presents a three-phase model of group dynamics. In the first phase, the reasons for forming the group determine what type of group it will be. A process of

---

FIGURE 8.1

A General Model of Group Dynamics

This model serves as the framework for this chapter. In phase one, the reasons for group formation determine what type of group it will be. In the second phase, groups evolve through four stages under the influence of four performance factors. Finally, a mature group emerges that interacts with other groups and can pursue organizational goals; conflicts with other groups sometimes occur.

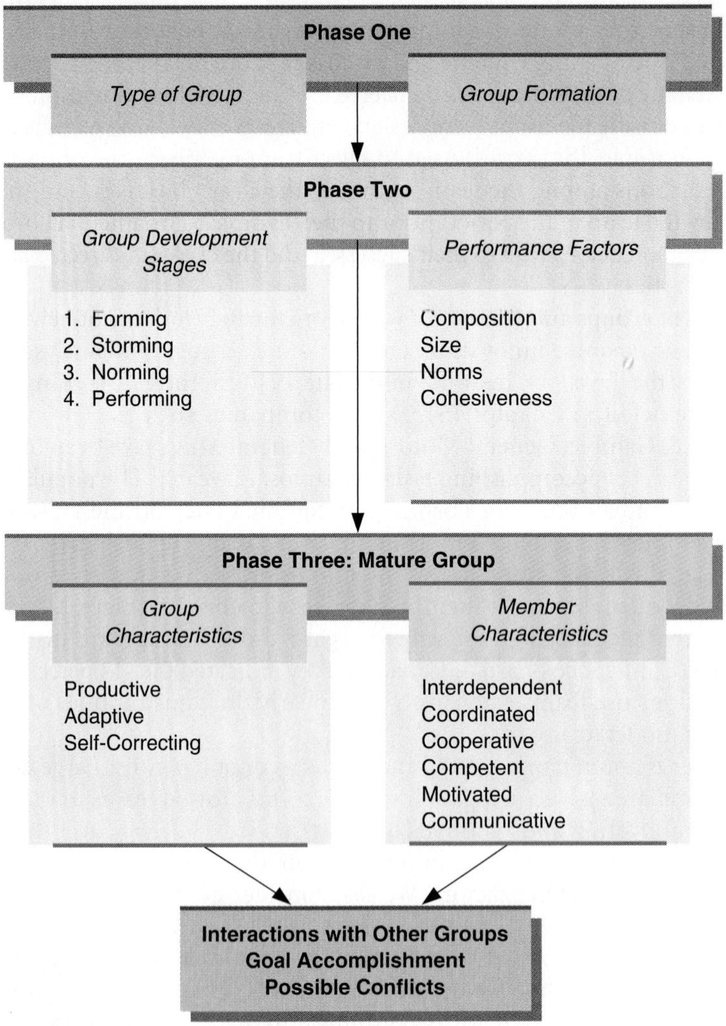

Phase One

| *Type of Group* | *Group Formation* |

Phase Two

| *Group Development Stages* | *Performance Factors* |

1. Forming	Composition
2. Storming	Size
3. Norming	Norms
4. Performing	Cohesiveness

Phase Three: Mature Group

| *Group Characteristics* | *Member Characteristics* |

Productive	Interdependent
Adaptive	Coordinated
Self-Correcting	Cooperative
	Competent
	Motivated
	Communicative

Interactions with Other Groups
Goal Accomplishment
Possible Conflicts

---

group development occurs during the second stage; the precise nature of these steps depends on four primary group performance factors. In the final phase, a mature, productive, adaptive group has evolved. As the model shows, mature groups interact with other groups, meet goals, and sometimes have conflicts with other groups. This model serves as the framework for our discussion of groups in this chapter.

Overview of Groups and Group Dynamics

Work groups consist of people who are trying to make a living for themselves and their families. The work group often is the primary source of social identity for employees, and the nature of the group can affect their performance at work as well as their relationships outside the organization.[5] A group in an organization often takes on a life of its own that transcends the individual members.

Group Defined

Definitions of "group" are as abundant as studies of groups. Groups can be defined in terms of perceptions, motivation, organization, interdependencies, and interactions.[6] A simple and comprehensive definition has been offered by Marvin Shaw: A **group** is two or more persons who interact with one another such that each person influences and is influenced by each other person.[7] The concept of interaction is essential to this definition. Two people who are physically near each other are not a group unless they interact and have some influence on each other. Coworkers may work side by side on related tasks, but if they do not interact they are not a group. The presence of others can influence the performance of a group: an audience can stimulate the performance of actors, or an evaluator can inhibit an employee's behaviour.[8] However, neither the audience nor the evaluator can be considered part of a group unless interaction occurs.

> A **group** is two or more people who interact with one another such that each person influences and is influenced by each other person.

Although groups often have goals, note that our definition does not state that group members must share a goal or motivation. This omission implies that members of a group identify little or not at all with the group's goal. People can be a part of a group and enjoy the benefits of group membership without wanting to pursue any group goal. Members can satisfy needs just by being members, without pursuing anything. Of course, the quality of the interactions and the group's performance can be affected by members' lack of interest in the group goal.

Our definition of group also suggests a limit on group size. A collection of people so large that its members cannot interact with and influence one another does not meet this definition. And in reality, the dynamics of large assemblies of people usually differ significantly from those of small groups. Our focus in this chapter is on small groups in which the members interact with and influence one another.

The Importance of Studying Groups

We cannot study behaviour in organizations without attempting to understand the behaviour of people in group settings. Groups are everywhere in our society. Most people belong to several groups—family, basketball team, church group, fund raising group, or work group at the office.[9] Some groups are formally established in a work or social organization; others are more loosely knit associations of people.

To understand the behaviour of people in organizations, we must understand the forces that affect individuals as well as how individuals affect the organization. The behaviour of individuals both affects and is affected by the group. The accomplishments of groups are strongly influenced by the behaviour of their individual members. For example, adding one key all-star player to a hockey team can make the difference between a bad season and a league championship. At the same time, groups have profound effects on the behaviours of their members.[10] We saw in the Hawthorne Studies described in Chapter 1 that employees will alter their behaviours to fall in line with group norms even when the financial rewards for those employees are decreased as a result. We discuss the development and impact of group norms later in this chapter.

From a managerial perspective, the work group is the primary means by which managers coordinate individuals' behaviour to achieve organizational goals. Managers direct the activities of individuals, but they also direct and coordinate interactions within groups. For example, managers' efforts to boost salespersons' performance has been shown to have both individual and group effects.[11] Therefore, the manager must pay attention to both the individual and the group in trying to improve employee performance. Managers must be aware of individual needs and interpersonal dynamics to manage groups effectively and efficiently, because the behaviour of individuals is key to the group's success or failure.

Group Formation

Groups are formed to satisfy both organizational and individual needs. They form in organizations because managers expect people working together in groups will be better able to complete and coordinate organizational tasks. Organizations of all types are forming teams to improve some aspect of the work, such as productivity or quality.

People join or form groups because they expect to satisfy certain personal needs.

Individuals join groups to satisfy a need. An employee may join a work group to get or keep a job. Individuals may form an informal group or join an existing one for many reasons: attraction to people in the group, to its activities (such as playing bridge, running marathons, or gardening), or to its goals. Some people join groups just for companionship, or to be identified as members of the group. In any case, people join groups for satisfaction of personal needs. In other words, they expect that they will get something in return for their membership in the group.

Understanding why groups form is important in studying individual behaviour in groups. Suppose some people join a bridge group primarily for social contact. If a more competitive player substitutes for a regular player one evening, she or he joins the group (temporarily) with the goal of playing rigorous, competitive bridge. The substitute may be annoyed when the game slows down or stops altogether because the other players are absorbed in a discussion. The regular members, conversely, may be irritated when the substitute interrupts the discussion or criticizes his or her partner for faulty technique. To resolve the resulting conflict, players must understand the reasons why each person joined the group. The inconsistencies in behaviour arise because each member is trying to satisfy a different need. To settle the dispute, the regulars and the substitute may have to be more tolerant of each other's behaviour, at least for the rest of the evening. Even if that occurs, however, the substitute player may not be invited back the next time a regular member cannot attend.

Thus, understanding why people join groups sheds light on apparent inconsistencies in behaviour and the tensions likely to result from them. Managers are better equipped to manage certain kinds of conflict that arise in groups in organizations when they understand why groups form.

Types of Groups

Our first task in understanding group processes is to develop a typology of groups that provides insight into their dynamics. Groups can be loosely categorized according to their degrees of *formalization* (formal or informal) and *permanence* (relatively permanent or relatively temporary). Table 8.1 shows this classification scheme.

	Relatively Permanent	Relatively Temporary	
Formal	**Command Groups**	**Task Groups**	**Affinity Groups**
	Quality-assurance department	Search Committee for a new school superintendent	New product development group
	Cost-accounting group	Task force on new-product quality	
Informal	**Friendship Groups**	**Interest Groups**	
	Friends who do many activities together (attend the theatre, play games, travel)	Basketball group Women's network	

TABLE 8.1

Classification Scheme for Types of Groups

Formal Groups

Formal groups are established by the organization to do its work. Formal groups include command (or functional) groups, task groups, and affinity groups. A **command group** is relatively permanent and is characterized by functional reporting relationships such as having a group manager and those who report to the manager. Command groups are usually included in the organization chart. A **task group** is created to perform a specific task, such as solving a particular quality problem, and is relatively temporary. **Affinity groups** are relatively permanent collections of employees from the same level in the organization who meet on a regular basis to share information, capture emerging opportunities, and solve problems.

In business organizations, most employees work in command groups, as typically specified on an official organization chart. The size, shape, and organization of a company's command groups can vary considerably. Typical command groups in organizations include the quality-assurance department, the industrial engineering department, the cost-accounting department, and the personnel department. Other types of command groups include work teams organized in the Japanese style of management, in which subsections of manufacturing and assembly processes are each assigned to a team of workers. The team members decide among themselves who will do each task.

Teams are becoming widespread in automobile manufacturing. For instance, General Motors has organized its highly automated assembly lines into work teams of between five and twenty workers.[12] Although participative teams are becoming more popular, command groups, whether entire departments or sophisticated work teams, are the dominant type of work group in organizations. Federal Express has organized its clerical workers into teams that manage themselves.[13]

Task, or special-project, groups are usually temporary and are often established to solve a particular problem. The group usually dissolves once it solves the problem or makes recommendations. People typically remain members of their command groups, or functional departments, while simultaneously serving in a task group and continuing to carry out the normal duties of their jobs. The members' command group duties may be temporarily reduced if the task group requires a great deal of time and effort. Task groups exist in all types of organizations around the world. For example, Pope John Paul II established a special task force of cardinals to study the financial condition of the Vatican and develop new ways to raise money.[14]

Affinity groups are a special type of formal group: they are set up by the organization, yet they are not really part of the formal organization structure. They are not really command groups because they are not part of the organizational hierarchy,

A **formal group** is formed by an organization to do its work.

A **command group** is a relatively permanent, formal group with functional reporting relationships and is usually included in the organization chart.

A **task group** is a relatively temporary, formal group established to do a specific task.

Affinity groups are collections of employees from the same level in the organization who meet on a regular basis to share information, capture emerging opportunities, and solve problems.

Friendship and interest groups can be a powerful force in an organization. These medical staffers discovered that a coworker had cancer. In response, the women became an even closer-knit group and worked even harder both to support their friend and to help other cancer patients.

yet they are not task groups because they stay in existence longer than any one task. Affinity groups are groups of employees who share roles, responsibilities, duties, and interests; they represent horizontal slices of the normal organizational hierarchy. Because the members share important characteristics such as roles, duties, and levels, they are said to have an affinity for one another. The members of affinity groups usually have very similar job titles and similar duties but are in different divisions or departments within the organization.

Affinity groups meet regularly, and members have assigned roles, such as recorder, reporter, facilitator, and meeting organizer. Members follow simple rules such as communicating openly and honestly, listening actively, respecting confidentiality, honouring time agreements, being prepared, staying focused, being individually accountable, and being supportive of each other and the group. The greatest benefits of affinity groups are that they cross existing boundaries of the organization and facilitate better communication among diverse departments and divisions across the organization.

Informal Groups

An **informal group** is established by its members.

A **friendship group** is relatively permanent and informal and draws its benefits from the social relationships among its members.

An **interest group** is relatively temporary and informal and is organized around a common activity or interest of its members.

Whereas formal groups are established by an organization, **informal groups** are formed by their members and consist of the friendship group, which is relatively permanent, and the interest group, which may be shorter lived. **Friendship groups** arise out of the cordial relationships among members and the enjoyment they get from being together. **Interest groups** are organized around a common activity or interest, although friendships may develop among members.

Good examples of interest groups are networks of working women. Many of these groups began as informal social gatherings of women who wanted to meet with other women working in male-dominated organizations, but they soon developed into interest groups whose benefits went far beyond their initial social purposes. The networks became information systems for counselling, job placement, and management training. Some networks were eventually established as formal, permanent associations; some remained informal groups based more on social relationships than on any specific interest; others were dissolved. These groups may be partly responsible for the past decade's dramatic increase in the percentage of women in managerial and administrative jobs.[15]

Stages of Group Development

Groups are not static—they typically develop through a four-stage process: (1) forming, (2) storming, (3) norming, and (4) performing. Eventually, teams might reach a fifth stage referred to as adjourning if the team is disbanded.[16] A model of these stages

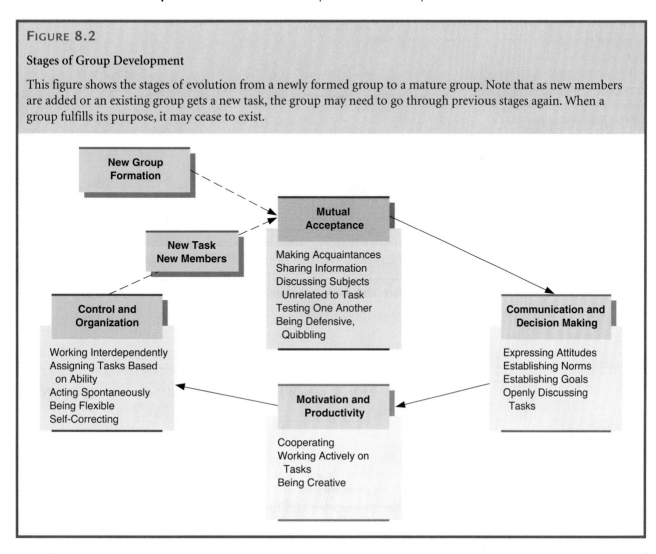

FIGURE 8.2

Stages of Group Development

This figure shows the stages of evolution from a newly formed group to a mature group. Note that as new members are added or an existing group gets a new task, the group may need to go through previous stages again. When a group fulfills its purpose, it may cease to exist.

is shown in Figure 8.2. We treat the stages as separate and distinct. It is difficult to pinpoint exactly when a group moves from one stage to another, however, because the activities in the phases tend to overlap. We also see that, although teams might progress through the stages in an orderly fashion, they may also fall back to a previous stage for various reasons. For example, the addition of a new team member might force the team to reevaluate norms surrounding team member behaviours.

Forming

In the *forming stage* of group development, the group forms and members get to know one another by sharing information about themselves. They often test one another's opinions by discussing subjects that have little to do with the group, such as the weather, sports, or recent events within the organization. Some aspects of the group's task such as its formal objectives, may also be discussed at this stage. However, such discussion probably will not be very productive because the members are unfamiliar with one another and do not know how to evaluate one another's comments. If the members happen to know one another already, this stage may be brief. However, it is unlikely

When groups get to the performing stage of group development, communication and decision making are very effective, but it looks like this team may be stuck in the storming stage. Groups need to openly discuss and agree on their goals, motivations, and individual roles before they can successfully accomplish tasks. It is essential that groups go through all four stages of development in order to become a mature, productive group.

Copyright 2001 by Randy Glasbergen.
www.glasbergen.com

**"My team is having trouble thinking outside the box.
We can't agree on the size of the box, what materials
the box should be constructed from, a reasonable
budget for the box, or our first choice of box vendors."**

to be skipped altogether because this is a new group with a new purpose. Besides, there are likely to be a few members whom the others do not know well or at all.[17]

FORMING → STORMING → NORMING → PERFORMING ---- →ADJOURNING

Storming

The group progresses to the *storming stage* as group members begin to attempt to establish their roles within the group. It is at this stage that interpersonal conflict may emerge as questions arise about leadership and control of group activities. Members may disagree about group goals, individual roles, processes for task achievement, and performance standards. This is a critical stage in group development as the conflict that emerges may result in the collapse of the group.

Norming

In the next stage, *norming,* the emphasis shifts away from personal concerns and viewpoints to activities that will benefit the group. Roles and norms are clarified and group cohesiveness begins to develop. Members perform their assigned tasks, cooperate with each other, and help others accomplish their goals. The members are highly motivated and may carry out their tasks creatively. In this stage, the group is accomplishing its work and moving toward the final stage of development.

Performing

In the final stage, *performing,* the group works effectively toward accomplishing its goals. Tasks are assigned by mutual agreement and according to ability. In a mature group, the members' activities are relatively spontaneous and flexible, rather than subject to rigid structural restraints. Mature groups evaluate their activities and potential outcomes and take corrective actions if necessary. The characteristics of flexibility, spontaneity, and self-correction are very important if the group is to remain productive over an extended period.

Adjourning

Adjourning is the final stage of group development for those groups that have achieved all of their goals and no longer have a purpose for remaining together. This stage often occurs for certain types of organizational groups such as project teams or task forces who are brought together for the express purpose of achieving a particular objective. Groups also end because of restructuring or downsizing. Whatever the reason, members begin to focus on the relationship aspect of the group in recognition of their parting of ways.

Not all groups go through all stages. Some groups disband before reaching the final stage. Others fail to complete a stage before moving on to the next one.[18] Rather than spend the time necessary to get to know one another and build trust, for example, a group may cut short the first stage of development because of pressure from its leader, from deadlines, or from an outside threat (such as the boss). If members are forced into activities typical of a later stage while the work of an earlier stage remains incomplete, they are likely to become frustrated: the group may not develop completely and may be less productive than it could be.[19] Group productivity depends on successful development at each stage. A group that evolves fully through all stages of development usually becomes a mature, effective group.[20] Its members are interdependent, coordinated, cooperative, competent at their jobs, motivated to do them, self-correcting, and in active communication with one another.[21]

Finally, as working conditions and relationships change, either through a change in membership or when a task is completed and a new task is begun, groups may need to re-experience one or more of the stages of development to maintain the cohesiveness and productivity characteristic of a well-developed group. Although these stages are not separate and distinct in all groups, many groups make fairly predictable transitions in activities at about the midpoint of the period available to complete a task.[22] A group may begin with its own distinctive approach to the problem and maintain it until about halfway through the allotted time. The midpoint transition is often accompanied by a burst of concentrated activity, re-examining assumptions, dropping old patterns of activity, adopting new perspectives on the work, and making dramatic progress. Following these midpoint activities, the new patterns of activity may be maintained until close to the end of the period allotted for the activity. Another transition may occur just before the deadline. At this transition, groups often go into the completion stage, launching a final burst of activity to finish the job.

Group Performance Factors

The performance of any group is affected by several factors other than its reasons for forming and the stages of its development. In a high-performing group, a group synergy often develops in which the group's performance is more than the sum of the individual contributions of its members. Several additional factors may account for this accelerated performance.[23] The four basic **group performance factors** are composition, size, norms, and cohesiveness.

> **Group performance factors**—composition, size, norms, and cohesiveness—affect the success of the group in fulfilling its goals.

Composition

The composition of a group plays an important role in determining group productivity.[24] **Group composition** is most often described in terms of the homogeneity or heterogeneity of the members. A group is homogeneous if the members are similar in one or several ways that are critical to the work of the group, such as age, work experience, education, technical specialty, or cultural background. In heterogeneous groups, the

> **Group composition** is the degree of similarity or difference among group members on factors important to the group's work.

Diversity within teams can lead to higher levels of performance, but it appears to depend on a variety of factors. For example, this team is made up of individuals from a variety of ethnic and cultural backgrounds that can increase the creativity and quality of their decisions, but can also lead to more conflict regarding the processes and outcomes of the decision.

members differ in one or more ways that are critical to the work of the group. Homogeneous groups often are created in organizations when people are assigned to command groups based on a similar technical specialty. Although the people who work in such command groups may differ in some ways, such as age or work experience, they are homogeneous in terms of a critical work performance variable: technical specialty.

Much research has explored the relationship between a group's composition and its productivity. The group's heterogeneity in age and tenure within the group has been shown to be related to turnover: groups with members of different ages and experiences with the group tend to experience frequent changes in membership.[25] The Older Workers and . . . Diversity box describes some problems and opportunities that work groups with a population of older workers can face. Table 8.2 summarizes task variables that make a homogeneous or heterogeneous group more effective. A homogeneous group is likely to be more productive in situations where the group task is simple, cooperation is necessary, the group tasks are sequential, or quick action is required. A heterogeneous group is more likely to be productive when the task is complex, requires a collective effort (that is, each member does a different task and the sum of these efforts constitutes the group output), demands creativity, and when speed is less important than thorough deliberations. For example, a group asked to generate ideas for marketing a new product probably needs to be heterogeneous to develop as many different ideas as possible.

TABLE 8.2

Task Variables and Group Composition

A homogeneous group is more useful for:	A heterogeneous group is more useful for:
Simple tasks	Complex tasks
Sequential tasks	Collective tasks
Tasks that require cooperation	Tasks that require creativity
Tasks that must be done quickly	Tasks that need not be done quickly

Source: Based on discussion in Bernard M. Bass and Edward C. Ryterband, *Organizational Psychology* 2nd ed. (Boston: Allyn and Bacon, 1979). Reprinted by permission.

The link between group composition and type of task is explained by the interactions typical of homogeneous and heterogeneous groups. A homogeneous group tends to have less conflict, fewer differences of opinion, smoother communication, and more interaction. When a task requires cooperation and speed, a homogeneous group is therefore more desirable. If, however, the task requires complex analysis of information and creativity to arrive at the best possible solution, a heterogeneous group may be more appropriate because it generates a wide range of viewpoints. More discussion and more conflict are likely, both of which can enhance the group's decision making.

Group composition becomes especially important as organizations become increasingly diverse. Cultures differ in the importance they place on group membership and in

Older Workers and . . . **DIVERSITY**

Work Groups with Older Workers

Age is an important facet of diversity in organizations, and Canada's workforce as a whole is getting older. Between 1991 and 2001, the proportion of working age people between 45 and 64 years of age increased by 35.8 percent, mostly as a result of the baby boomers born between 1946 and 1965. By 2011, this group is projected to make up approximately one-third of Canada's population. Human rights legislation provides protection for employees from discrimination as a result of age and many provinces have banned mandatory retirement. Now, workers can work past the age of 65 should they choose to do so.

Other than the legal issues, the concern for organizations is how to work with older workers who are still around. Canada has one of the fastest aging populations in the industrialized world and it is expected that approximately 35 percent of the population will be over the age of 65 by 2050.

Some young to middle-aged managers have reported certain problems with older workers. A 40-year-old group manager at a major bank reported feeling uncomfortable when older people in his group spoke up; it was as if his parents were telling him what to do. Some managers perceive older workers as rigid, hard to retrain, and too expensive. Numerous studies, however, report just the opposite. In training, studies show older workers may take a little bit longer to train, but once trained they perform just as well as younger workers. In addition, they are usually less likely to be absent or change jobs and have a stronger work ethic than younger workers. Some companies have found that early retirement and other programs that significantly reduced the number of older workers have resulted in major loss of tradition, sense of history, work experience, and maturity in the workforce. At B&Q, a British hardware store, older workers have proved to be more reliable, better at customer service, 39 percent less absent, better at taking care of inventory stock, and good examples for younger workers. B&Q is planning to significantly increase the percentage of older workers in its stores.

Other research has shown that diversity in work groups, in age and other dimensions, has significant positive benefits. A diversity of opinions in the group forces everyone in the group to really pay attention to what is going on. It reduces the comfort level with the status quo, which is becoming a popular trend in industries where top managers are encouraging employees to be creative and develop new solutions to problems. Diverse work groups are better at problem solving and decision making because they challenge the assumptions of the status quo. Homogeneity can make the group too comfortable.

Older workers can provide just the right balance for a group of primarily young white males. Older workers may not be trying to climb the corporate ladder and can help the group analyze problems with an experienced eye and with no political posturing or individualistic personal competition. So rather than move them out when the hair gets a little grey, maybe we should populate our work groups with more older workers and expect productivity to increase and decision quality to rise.

Sources: M. Fougere, M. Merette, and G. Zhu, "Population Aging in Canada and Labour Market Challenges," November 2006, Human Resources and Social Development Canada; Statistics Canada, *2001 Census: Age and Sex;* Sue Shellenbarger and Carol Hymowitz, "As Population Ages, Older Workers Clash with Younger Bosses" *Wall Street Journal*, 13 June 1994, pp. A1, A8; "The Power of Diversity in Work Groups" *Working Age*, September/October 1995, pp. 2–3.

Group composition is an important factor in understanding group dynamics. These women attended a Women in Business seminar for women holding key positions in major corporations. The fact that they are all female gave them a shared frame of reference and common perspectives from which to identify key issues and to help shape the future of their respective businesses.

how they view authority, uncertainty, and other important factors. Increasing attention is being focused on how to deal with groups made up of people from different cultures.[26] Generally, a manager in charge of a culturally diverse group can expect several things. First, members will probably distrust each other. Second, stereotyping also will present a problem, and, third, communication problems will almost certainly arise. Thus, the manager needs to recognize that such groups will seldom function smoothly, at least at first. Therefore, he or she may need to spend more time helping the group through the rough spots as it matures, and they should allow a longer-than-normal time before expecting it to carry out its assigned task.

Many organizations are creating joint ventures and other types of alliances with organizations from other countries. Joint ventures have become common in the automobile and electronics industries, for example, but North American managers tend to exhibit individualistic behaviours in a group setting, whereas managers from the People's Republic of China tend to exhibit more collectivist behaviours.[27] Thus, when these two different types of managers work together in a group, as they might in some type of joint venture, the managers must be trained to be cautious and understanding in their interactions and the types of behaviours that they exhibit. All employees need training in how to work with people from different cultures.

Size

Group size is the number of members of the group; it affects the number of resources available to perform the task.

A group can have as few as two members or as many members as can interact and influence one another. **Group size** can have an important effect on performance. A group with many members has more resources available and may be able to complete a large number of relatively independent tasks. In groups established to generate ideas, those with more members tend to produce more ideas, although the rate of increase in the number of ideas diminishes rapidly as the group grows.[28] Beyond a certain point, the greater complexity of interactions and communication may make it more difficult for a large group to achieve agreement.

Interactions and communication are much more likely to be formalized in larger groups. Large groups tend to set agendas for meetings and to follow a protocol parliamentary procedure to control discussion. As a result, some time that otherwise might be available to work on tasks is taken up in administrative duties such as organizing and structuring the interactions and communications within the group. Also, the large size may inhibit participation of some people[29] and increase absenteeism;[30] some people may stop trying to make a meaningful contribution and may even stop coming to group meetings if repeated attempts to contribute or participate are thwarted by the sheer number of similar efforts by other members. Furthermore, large groups present more opportunities for interpersonal attraction, leading to more social interactions and fewer task interactions. **Social loafing** is the tendency of some members of groups not to put forth as much effort in a group situation as they would working alone.[31] Social loafing often results from the assumption by some members that if they do not work hard other members will pick up the slack. How much of a problem this becomes depends on the nature of the task, the characteristics of the people involved, and the ability of the group leadership to be aware of the potential problem and do something about it.

> **Social loafing** is the tendency of some members of groups not to put forth as much effort in a group situation as they would working alone.

The most effective size of a group, therefore, is determined by the group members' ability to interact and influence each other effectively. The need for interaction is affected by the maturity of the group, the tasks of the group, the maturity of individual members, and the ability of the group leader or manager to manage the communication, potential conflicts, and task activities. In some situations the most effective group size is three or four; other groups can function effectively with fifteen or more members.

Norms

A **norm** is a standard against which the appropriateness of a behaviour is judged.[32] Thus, norms determine the behaviour expected in a certain situation. Group norms usually are established during the second stage of group development (communication and decision making) and carried forward into the maturity stage.[33] By providing a basis for predicting others' behaviours, norms enable people to behave in a manner consistent with and acceptable to the group. Without norms, the activities in a group would be chaotic.

> A **norm** is a standard against which the appropriateness of a behaviour is judged.

Norms result from the combination of members' personality characteristics, the situation, the task, and the historical traditions of the group. Lack of conformity to group norms can result in verbal abuse, physical threats, ostracism, or ejection from the group. Group norms are enforced, however, only for actions that are important to group members.[34] For example, if the office norm is for employees to wear suits to convey a professional image to clients, a staff member who wears blue jeans and a sweatshirt violates the group norm and will hear about it quickly. But if the norm is that dress is unimportant because little contact with clients occurs in the office, the fact that someone wears blue jeans may not even be noticed.

Norms serve four purposes:

1. Norms help the group survive. Groups tend to reject deviant behaviour that does not help meet group goals or contribute to the survival of the group if it is threatened. Accordingly, a successful group that is not under threat may be more tolerant of deviant behaviour.
2. Norms simplify and make more predictable the behaviours expected of group members. Because they are familiar with norms, members do not have to analyze each behaviour and decide on a response. Members can anticipate the actions of others on the basis of group norms, usually resulting in increased productivity and goal attainment.

3. Norms help the group avoid embarrassing situations. Group members often want to avoid damaging other members' self-images and are likely to avoid certain subjects that might hurt a member's feelings.
4. Norms express the central values of the group and identify the group to others. Certain clothes, mannerisms, or behaviours in particular situations may be a rallying point for members and may signify to others the nature of the group.[35]

Cohesiveness

Group cohesiveness is the extent to which a group is committed to staying together.

Group cohesiveness is the extent to which a group is committed to remaining together; it results from "all forces acting on the members to remain in the group."[36] The forces that create cohesiveness are attraction to the group, resistance to leaving the group, and the motivation to remain a member of the group.[37] As shown in Figure 8.3, group cohesiveness is related to many aspects of group dynamics that we already discussed—maturity, homogeneity, manageable size, and frequency of interactions.

Figure 8.3 also shows that group cohesiveness can be increased by competition or by the presence of an external threat.[38] Either factor can focus members' attention on a clearly defined goal and increase their willingness to work together. The threat of management to use replacement workers for those on strike has the immediate effect of unifying the striking employees against management. The employees become more cohesive and vow more strongly than ever to hold out.

Finally, successfully reaching goals often increases the cohesiveness of a group because people are proud to be identified with a winner and to be thought of as competent and successful. This may be one reason behind the popular phrase "success breeds success." A group that is successful may become more cohesive and hence possibly even more successful. One example is the initial success of the design group at Apple Computer as it created the Macintosh personal computer. The members worked and partied together and became quite cohesive. (Of course, other factors can get in the way of continued success, such as personal differences, egos, and the lure of more individual success in other activities.)

Research on group performance factors has focused on the relationship between cohesiveness and group productivity. Highly cohesive groups appear to be more effective at achieving their goals than groups that are low in cohesiveness. However, highly cohesive groups will not necessarily be more productive in an organizational sense than groups with low cohesiveness. As Figure 8.4 illustrates, when a group's goals are compatible with

FIGURE 8.3

Factors That Affect Group Cohesiveness and Consequences of Group Cohesiveness

The factors that increase and decrease cohesiveness and the consequences of high and low cohesiveness indicate that, although it is often preferable to have a highly cohesive group, in some situations the effects of a highly cohesive group can be negative for the organization.

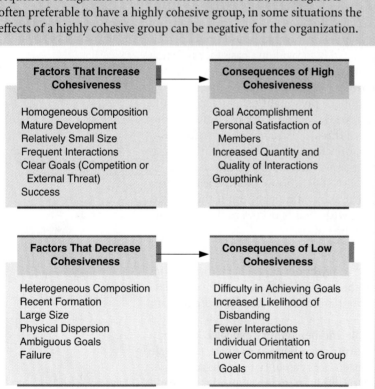

Factors That Increase Cohesiveness

Homogeneous Composition
Mature Development
Relatively Small Size
Frequent Interactions
Clear Goals (Competition or External Threat)
Success

Consequences of High Cohesiveness

Goal Accomplishment
Personal Satisfaction of Members
Increased Quantity and Quality of Interactions
Groupthink

Factors That Decrease Cohesiveness

Heterogeneous Composition
Recent Formation
Large Size
Physical Dispersion
Ambiguous Goals
Failure

Consequences of Low Cohesiveness

Difficulty in Achieving Goals
Increased Likelihood of Disbanding
Fewer Interactions
Individual Orientation
Lower Commitment to Group Goals

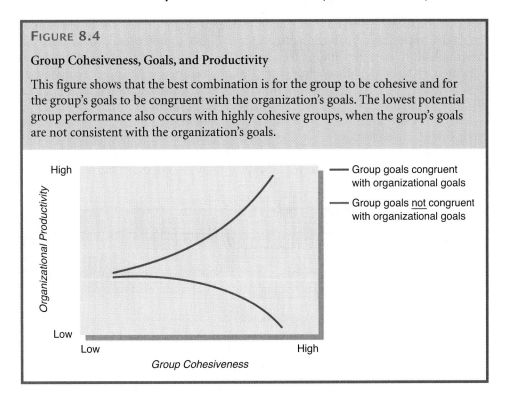

FIGURE 8.4

Group Cohesiveness, Goals, and Productivity

This figure shows that the best combination is for the group to be cohesive and for the group's goals to be congruent with the organization's goals. The lowest potential group performance also occurs with highly cohesive groups, when the group's goals are not consistent with the organization's goals.

the organization's, a cohesive group probably will be more productive than one that is not cohesive. In other words, if a highly cohesive group has the goal of contributing to the good of the organization, it is very likely to be productive in organizational terms. We saw in the opening vignette how focused the players on the Women's Canadian Olympic Hockey team were on achieving their goal of a gold medal, a goal shared by the entire organization. But if such a group decides on a goal that has little to do with the business of the organization, it will probably achieve its own goal even at the expense of any organizational goal. In a study of group characteristics and productivity, group cohesiveness was the only factor that was consistently related to high performance for research and development engineers and technicians.[39]

Cohesiveness may also be an important factor in the development of certain problems for some decision-making groups. An example is *groupthink*, which occurs when a group's overriding concern is a unanimous decision rather than critical analysis of alternatives.[40] (In Chapter 9 we go into more detail in describing groupthink.) These problems, together with the evidence regarding group cohesiveness and productivity, mean that a manager must carefully weigh the pros and cons of fostering highly cohesive groups.

Intergroup Dynamics

A group's contribution to an organization depends on its interactions with other groups as well as on its own productivity. Many organizations are increasing their use of cross-functional teams to address more complex and increasingly important organizational issues. The result has been heightened emphasis on the teams' interactions with other groups. Groups that actively interact with other groups by asking questions, initiating joint programs, and sharing their team's achievements are usually the most productive.

Interactions among groups are based on the characteristics of the interacting groups, the organizational context within which the groups operate, and the task and situational bases of the interactions.

Interactions are the key to understanding intergroup dynamics. The orientation of the groups toward their goals takes place under a highly complex set of conditions that determine the relationship among the groups. The most important of these factors are presented in the model of intergroup dynamics in Figure 8.5. The model emphasizes three primary factors that influence intergroup interactions: group characteristics, organizational factors, and task and situational bases of interaction.

First, we must understand the key characteristics of the interacting groups. Each group brings unique features to the interaction. As individuals become a part of a group, they tend to identify so strongly with the group that their views of other groups become biased, and harmonious relationships can be difficult to achieve.[41] Furthermore, the

FIGURE 8.5

Factors That Influence Intergroup Interactions

The nature of the interactions between groups depends on the characteristics of the groups involved, the organizational setting, and the task and situational setting for the interaction.

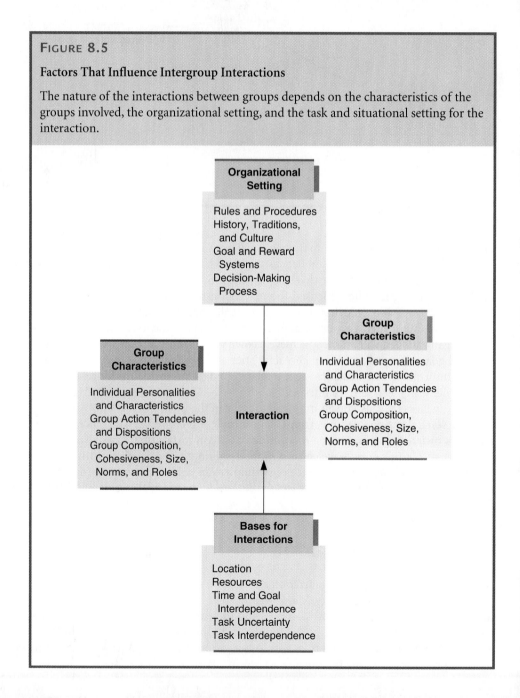

individuals in the group contribute to the group processes, which influences the groups' norms, size, composition, and cohesiveness; all of these factors affect interactions with other groups. Thus, understanding the individuals in the group and the key characteristics of the group can help managers monitor intergroup interactions.

Second, the organizational setting in which the groups interact can have a powerful influence on intergroup interactions. The organization's structure, rules and procedures, decision-making processes, and goals and reward systems all affect interactions. For example, organizations in which frequent interactions occur and strong ties among groups exist usually are characterized as low-conflict organizations.[42]

Third, the task and situational bases of interactions focus attention on the working relationships among the interacting groups and on the reasons for the interactions. As Figure 8.5 shows, five factors affect intergroup interactions: location, resources, time and goal interdependence, task uncertainty, and task interdependence. These factors both create the interactions and determine their characteristics, such as the frequency of interaction, the volume of information exchange among groups, and the type of coordination the groups need to interact and function. For example, if two groups depend heavily on each other to perform a task about which much uncertainty exists, they need a great deal of information from each other to define and perform the task.

Differentiating Teams from Groups

Teams have been used, written about, and studied under many names and organizational programs: self-directed teams, self-managing teams, autonomous work groups, participative management, and many others. Groups and teams are not the same thing, although the two words are often used interchangeably in popular usage. A brief look at a dictionary shows that "group" usually refers to an assemblage of people or objects gathered together, whereas "team" usually refers to people or animals organized to work together.[43] Thus, a "team" places more emphasis on concerted action than a "group."

Specifically in organizations, teams and groups are quite different. As we noted previously, a group is two or more persons who interact with one another such that each person influences and is influenced by each other person. We specifically noted that individuals interacting and influencing each other need not have a common goal. The collection of people who happen to report to the same supervisor or manager in an organization can be called a "work group." Group members may be satisfying their own needs in the group and have little concern for a common objective. This is where a team and a group differ. In a team, all team members are committed to a common goal.

We could therefore say that a team is a group with a common goal. But teams differ from groups in other ways, too, and most experts are a bit more specific in defining teams. A more elaborate definition is this: "A **team** is a small number of people with complementary skills who are committed to a common purpose, performance goals, and approach for which they hold themselves mutually accountable."[44] Several facets of this definition need further explanation. A team includes few people because the interaction and influence processes needed for the team to function can only occur when the number of members is small. When many people are involved, they have difficulty interacting and influencing each other, utilizing their complementary skills, meeting goals, and holding themselves accountable. Regardless of the name, by our definition mature, fully developed teams are self-directing, self-managing, and autonomous. If they are not, then someone from outside the group must be giving directions, so the group cannot be considered a true team.

A **team** is a small number of people with complementary skills who are committed to a common purpose, common performance goals, and an approach for which they hold themselves mutually accountable.

Teams need to have a mix of technical, problem-solving, decision-making, and interpersonal skills.

Teams include people with a mix of skills appropriate to the tasks to be done. Three types of skills are usually required in a team. First, the team needs to have members with the technical or functional skills to do the jobs. Some types of engineering, scientific, technological, legal, or business skills may be necessary. Second, some team members need to have problem-solving and decision-making skills to help the team identify problems, determine priorities, evaluate alternatives, analyze tradeoffs, and make decisions about the direction of the team. Third, members need interpersonal skills to manage communication flow, manage conflict, direct questions and discussion, provide support, and recognize the interests of all members of the team. Not all members will have all of the required skills, especially when the team first convenes; different members will have different skills. However, as the team grows, develops, and matures, team members will come to have more of the necessary skills.

Having a common purpose and common performance goals sets the tone and direction of the team. A team comes together to take action to pursue a goal, unlike a work group, in which members report to the same supervisor or work in the same department. The purpose becomes the focus of the team, which makes all decisions and takes all actions in pursuit of the goal. Teams often spend days or weeks establishing the reason for their existence, which builds strong identification and fosters commitment to it. Usually, the defining purpose comes first, followed by development of specific performance goals. For example, a team of local citizens, teachers, and parents may come together for the purpose of making the local schools the best in the province. Then the team establishes specific performance goals to serve as guides for decision making, to maintain the focus on action, to differentiate this team from other groups who may want to improve schools, and to challenge people to commit themselves to the team. Here is one further note on the importance of purpose and performance goals for teams: Katzenbach and Smith studied more than 30 teams and found that demanding, high-performance goals often challenge members to create a real team, as opposed to a group, because when goals are truly demanding, members must pull together, find resources within themselves, develop and use the appropriate skills, and take a common approach to reach the goals.[45]

Teams differ from groups in their active goal orientation, their job categories, the distribution of authority, and the type of reward systems.

Agreeing on a common approach is especially important for teams, because it is often the approach that differentiates one team from others. The team's approach usually covers how work will be done, social norms regarding dress, attendance at meetings, tardiness, norms of fairness and ethical behaviour, and what will and will not be included in the team activities. One factor that might increase the likelihood that team members agree on a common approach is the homogeneity of personality characteristics of the team members. The Team Performance and . . . Research box highlights recent research linking personality characteristics to team performance.

Finally, the definition states that teams hold themselves mutually accountable for results, rather than merely meeting a manager's demands for results, as in the traditional approach. If the members translate accountability to an external manager into internal, or mutual, accountability, the group moves toward acting like a team. Mutual accountability is essentially a promise that members make to each other to do everything possible to achieve their goals, and it requires the commitment and trust of all members. It is the promise of each member to hold him- or herself accountable for the team's goals that earns each individual the right to express her or his views and the expectation of a fair and constructive hearing. With this promise, members maintain and strengthen the trust necessary for the team to succeed. The clearly stated high-performance goals and the common approach serve as the standards to which the team holds itself. Because teams are mutually accountable for meeting performance goals, three other differences between groups and teams become important: job categories, authority, and reward systems. The differences for traditional work groups and work teams are shown in Table 8.3.

Collective Efficacy and Team Performance

One reason that teams are used so extensively is that they can lead to higher organizational productivity. Pooling the talents of individuals who are working toward a collective goal can be more effective than having those individuals work alone. In Chapter 3, we discussed how self-efficacy can positively affect individual performance. But, how do beliefs about the ability to perform tasks affect performance at the team level? Simon Taggar of Wilfrid Laurier University and his colleagues conducted a series of studies designed to examine the influence of collective efficacy, the team's shared perception of its capability to successfully perform a specific task, on team performance. In addition, these researchers examined the factors that led to collective efficacy.

In one study, Taggar and Gerard Seijts, of the University of Western Ontario, found that collective efficacy resulted in higher levels of performance in teams of four to six business students performing a novel bridge-building task. One of the primary factors that led to higher levels of collective efficacy was staff role efficacy, which the authors defined as their confidence in their ability to engage in a set of behaviours important to effective teamwork. These behaviours included interpersonal skills such as conflict resolution, collaborative problem solving, and communication, as well as self-management skills such as goal setting and performance management, and planning and task coordination behaviours.

In a subsequent study, Kevin Tasa of McMaster University, along with Taggar and Seijts, extended the initial work cited above. As is the case with self-efficacy, these researchers found that collective efficacy was influenced by initial performance feedback. In addition, collective efficacy increased the amount of teamwork behaviours engaged in by team members, which in turn influenced the overall performance of the team. All of this points to the fact that teams that experience success develop even more confidence in their abilities as well as their willingness to pull together as a team. And this tends to breed even more success.

Given the extent to which Canadian organizations are relying on teams to compete effectively, this research is critical. Some organizations already consider applicants' ability to work in teams as important as technical skills.

Sources: Simon Taggar and Gerard H. Seijts, "Leader and Staff Role-Efficacy as Antecedents of Collective-Efficacy and Team Performance," *Human Performance*, 2003, 16(2), pp. 131–156; Kevin Tasa, Simon Taggar, and Gerard H. Seijts, "The Development of Collective Efficacy in Teams: A Multilevel and Longitudinal Perspective," *Journal of Applied Psychology*, January 2007, pp. 17–27.

Issue	Conventional Work Groups	Teams
Job categories	Many narrow categories	One or two broad categories
Authority	Supervisor directly controls daily activities	Team controls daily activities
Reward system	Depends on the type of job, individual performance, and seniority	Based on team performance and individual breadth of skills

TABLE 8.3

Differences Between Teams and Traditional Work Groups

Source: Adapted from Jack D. Orsburn, Linda Moran, and Ed Musselwhite, with Craig Perrin, *Self-Directed Work Teams: The New American Challenge* (Homewood, Illinois: Business One Irwin, 1990), p. 11.

Benefits and Costs of Teams in Organizations

With the popularity of teams increasing so rapidly around the world, it is possible that some organizations are starting to use teams simply because everyone else is doing it, which is obviously the wrong reason. The reason to create teams is because teams make sense for that organization. The best reason to start teams in any organization

> The reason for creating teams in any organization should be because teams make sense for that organization.

is the positive benefits that can result from a team-based environment: enhanced performance, employee benefits, reduced costs, and organizational enhancements. Four categories of benefits and some examples are shown in Table 8.4.

Enhanced Performance

The benefits of working in teams include enhanced productivity and quality, benefits for employees, reduced costs, and increased organizational innovation, creativity, and flexibility.

Enhanced performance can come in many forms, including improved productivity, quality, and customer service. Working in teams enables workers to avoid wasted effort, reduce errors, and react better to customers, resulting in more output for each unit of employee input. Such enhancements result from pooling of individual efforts in new ways and from striving to continuously improve for the benefit of the team. For example, three years after the Honeywell plant in Scarborough, Ontario, made the move to self-directed teams, the plant maintained previous production levels with 40 percent fewer workers.[46]

Employee Benefits

Employees tend to benefit as much as organizations in a team environment. Much attention has focused on the differences between the baby-boom generation and the "post-boomers" in attitudes toward work, its importance to their lives, and what they want from it. In general, younger workers tend to be less satisfied with their work and the organization, to have lower respect for authority and supervision, and to want more than a paycheque every week. Teams can provide the sense of self-control, human dignity, identification with the work, and sense of self-worth and self-fulfilment that current and

---

TABLE.8.4

Benefits of Teams in Organizations

Type of Benefit	Specific Benefit	Organizational Examples
Enhanced performance	• Increased productivity	Ampex: On-time customer delivery rose 98%.
	• Improved quality	K-Shoes: Rejects per million dropped from 5000 to 250.
	• Improved customer service	Tennessee Eastman: Productivity rose 70%.
Employee benefits	• Quality of work life	Milwaukee Mutual: Employee assistance program usage dropped to 40% below industry average.
	• Lower stress	
Reduced costs	• Lower turnover, absenteeism	Kodak: Reduced turnover to one-half the industry average.
	• Fewer injuries	Texas Instruments: Reduced costs more than 50%. Westinghouse: Costs down 60%.
Organizational enhancements	• Increased innovation, flexibility	IDS Mutual Fund Operations: Improved flexibility to handle fluctuations in market activity. Hewlett-Packard: Innovative order-processing system.

Sources: Adapted from Charles C. Manz and Henry P. Sims, Jr., *Business Without Bosses* (New York: Wiley, 1993); Richard S. Wellins, William C. Byham, and George R. Dixon, *Inside Teams* (San Francisco: Jossey-Bass, 1994).

future workers seem to strive for. Rather than relying on the traditional, hierarchical, manager-based system, teams give employees freedom to grow and gain respect and dignity by managing themselves, making decisions about their work, and really making a difference in the world around them.[47] As a result employees have a better work life, face less stress at work, and make less use of employee assistance programs.

Reduced Costs

As empowered teams reduce scrap, make fewer errors, file fewer worker's compensation claims, and reduce absenteeism and turnover, organizations based on teams are showing significant cost reductions. Team members feel that they have a stake in the outcomes, want to make contributions because they are valued, and are committed to their team and do not want to let it down. Wilson Sporting Goods reported saving $10 million per year for five years due to their teams. Colgate Palmolive reported that technician turnover was extremely low—more than 90 percent of technicians were retained after five years[48]—once they moved to a team-based approach.

Organizational Enhancements

Other improvements in organizations that result from moving from a hierarchically based, directive culture to a team-based culture include increased innovation, creativity, and flexibility. Use of teams can eliminate redundant layers of bureaucracy and flatten the hierarchy in large organizations. Employees feel closer to and more in touch with top management. Employees who feel their efforts are important are more likely to make significant contributions. In addition, the team environment constantly challenges teams to innovate and solve problems creatively. If doing something the same old way does not work, empowered teams are free to throw it out and develop a new way. With increasing global competition, organizations must constantly adapt to keep abreast of changes. Teams provide the flexibility to react quickly. One of Motorola's earliest teams challenged a longstanding top-management policy regarding supplier inspections to reduce the cycle times and improve delivery of crucial parts.[49] After several attempts, management finally allowed them to change the system and reaped the expected benefits.

Costs of Teams

The costs of teams are usually expressed in terms of the difficulty of changing to a team-based organization. Managers have expressed frustration and confusion about their new roles as coaches and facilitators, especially if they developed their managerial skills under the old traditional, hierarchical management philosophy. Some managers have felt as if they were working themselves out of a job as they turned over more and more of their old directing duties to the team.[50]

Employees may also feel like losers during the change to a team culture. Some traditional staff groups, such as technical advisory staffs, may feel that their jobs are in jeopardy as teams do more and more of the technical work formerly done by technicians. New roles and pay scales may need to be developed for the technical staff in these situations. Often, technical people have been assigned to a team or a small group of teams and become members who fully participate in team activities.

Another cost associated with teams is the slowness of the process of full team development. As discussed elsewhere in this chapter, it takes a long time for teams to go through the full development cycle and become mature, efficient, and effective. If top management is impatient with the slow progress, teams might be disbanded, returning

Unfortunately, this person probably isn't going to be a very effective team member. That's too bad, because working in teams can result in enhanced performance, a reduction in errors, and an overall enhancement in performance. An organization that promotes a team environment can see positive results in terms of worker creativity, productivity, and job satisfaction.

Copyright 2002 by Randy Glasbergen.   www.glasbergen.com

T.E.A.M.

TOGETHER
EVERYONE
ANNOYS
ME

"Before I begin, I'd just like to make it known that I didn't volunteer to do this presentation."

the organization to its original, hierarchical form with significant losses for employees, managers, and the organization.

Probably the most dangerous cost is premature abandonment of the change to a team-based organization. If top management gets impatient with the team change process and cuts it short, never allowing teams to fully develop and realize benefits and returning to the former directive, hierarchical organization, all of the hard work of employees, middle managers, and supervisors is lost. Employee confidence in management in general and in the decision makers in particular may suffer for a long time. The losses in productivity and efficiency will be very difficult to recoup. Therefore, management must be fully committed before initiating a change to a team-based organization.

Types of Teams

Many types of teams exist in organizations today. Some evolved naturally in organizations that permit various types of participative and empowering management programs. Others have been formally created at the suggestion of enlightened management. One easy way to classify teams is by what they do; for example, some teams make or do things, some teams recommend things, and some teams run things. The most common type of teams are quality circles, work teams, and problem-solving teams; management teams are also quite common.

Quality Circles

Quality circles are small groups of employees from the same work area who regularly meet to discuss and recommend solutions to workplace problems.

Quality circles (QCs) are small groups of employees from the same work area who meet regularly (usually weekly or monthly) to discuss and recommend solutions to workplace problems.[51] QCs were the first type of team created in U.S. organizations, becoming most popular during the 1980s in response to growing Japanese competition. QCs had some success in reducing rework and cutting defects on the shop floors of many manufacturing plants. Some attempts have been made to use QCs in offices and service operations, too. They exist alongside the traditional management structure and are relatively permanent. The role of the QC is to investigate a variety of quality problems that might come up in the workplace. They do not replace the work group or make decisions about how the work is done. Although interest in QCs has dropped somewhat, a large number of organizations still use them. QCs are teams that make recommendations.

Work Teams

Work teams tend to be permanent, like QCs, but they are the teams that do the daily work, rather than auxiliary committees.[52] A team of nurses, orderlies, and various technicians responsible for all patients on a floor or wing in a hospital is a work team. Rather than investigate a specific problem, evaluate alternatives, and recommend a solution or change, a work team does the actual daily work of the unit. The difference between a traditional work group of nurses and the patient care team is that the latter has the authority to decide how the work is done, in what order, and by whom; the entire team is responsible for all patient care. When the team decides how the work is to be organized or done, it becomes a self-managing team, to which accrue all of the benefits described in this chapter. Work teams are teams that make or do things.

> **Work teams** include all the people working in an area, are relatively permanent, and do the daily work, making decisions regarding how the work of the team is done.

Problem-Solving Teams

Problem-solving teams are temporary teams established to attack specific problems in the workplace. Teams can use any number of methods to solve the problem, as discussed in Chapter 12. After solving the problem, the team is usually disbanded, allowing members to return to their normal work. High-performing problem-solving teams are often cross-functional, meaning that team members come from many different functional areas. Crisis teams are problem-solving teams created only for the duration of an organizational crisis and are usually composed of people from many different areas. Problem-solving teams are teams that make recommendations for others to implement.

> **Problem-solving teams** are temporary teams established to attack specific problems in the workplace.

Implementation Teams

Implementation teams are temporary teams designed to incorporate new organizational processes or to assist in the incorporation of major organizational changes. Given the large number of organizations recently undergoing major changes, implementation teams have become rather common. When Transport Canada privatized its Air Navigation System, implementation teams made up of employees from various levels in the organization were created to make the process go as smoothly as possible.

> **Implementation teams** are groups of individuals from various functional groups who are responsible for enacting change in organizations.

Management Teams

Management teams consist of managers from various areas who coordinate work teams. They are relatively permanent because their work does not end with the completion of a particular project or the resolution of a problem. Management teams must concentrate on the teams that have the most impact on overall corporate performance. The primary job of management teams is to coach and counsel other teams to be self-managing by making decisions within the team. The second most important task of management teams is to coordinate work between work teams that are interdependent in some manner. Digital Equipment Corporation abandoned its team matrix structure because the matrix of teams was not well organized and coordinated. Team members at all levels reported spending hours and hours in meetings trying to coordinate among teams, leaving too little time to get the real work done.[53]

> **Management teams** consist of managers from various areas; they coordinate work teams.

Boeing engineers are hard at work designing the next generation of the popular 777 long-haul aircraft. This engineer is part of a team developing new instrumentation systems for the aircraft. The team is using computer simulations to test how various instrument designs can enhance performance of the plane.

Top management teams may have special types of problems. First, the work of the top management team may not be conducive to teamwork. Vice-presidents or heads of divisions may be in charge of different sets of operations that are not related and do not need to be coordinated. Forcing that type of top management group to be a team may be inappropriate. Second, top managers often have reached high levels in the organization because they have certain characteristics or abilities to get things done. For successful managers to alter their style, to pool resources, and to sacrifice their independence and individuality can be very difficult.[54]

Product-Development Teams

Product-development teams design new products or services.

Product-development teams are combinations of work teams and problem-solving teams that create new designs for products or services that will satisfy customer needs. They are similar to problem-solving teams because when the product is fully developed and in production, the team may be disbanded. As global competition and electronic information storage, processing, and retrieving capabilities increase, companies in almost every industry are struggling to cut product-development times. The primary organizational means of accomplishing this important task is the "blue-ribbon" cross-functional team. Boeing's development of the 777 commercial airplane and the platform teams of Chrysler are typical examples.

The rush to market with new designs can lead to numerous problems for product-development teams. The primary problems of poor communication and coordination of typical product-development processes in organizations can be rectified by creating self-managing cross-functional product-development teams.[55]

Virtual Teams

Virtual teams work together by computer and other electronic communication utilities; members move in and out of meetings and the team itself as the situation dictates.

Virtual teams are teams that may never actually meet together in the same room—their activities take place on the computer via teleconferencing and other electronic information systems. Engineers in Canada can connect audibly and visually directly with counterparts all around the globe, sharing files via the Internet, electronic mail, and other communication utilities; all participants can look at the same drawing, print, or specification, so decisions can be made much faster. With electronic communication systems team members can move in or out of a team or a team discussion as the issues warrant.

Managing Group and Intergroup Dynamics in Organizations

Managing groups in organizations is difficult. Managers must know what types of groups—command or task, formal or informal—exist in the organization. If a certain command group is very large, there will probably be several informal subgroups to be managed. A manager might want to take advantage of existing informal groups, formalizing some of them into command or task groups based on a subset of the tasks to be performed. Other informal groups may need to be broken up to make task assignment easier. In assigning tasks to people and subgroups, the manager must also consider individual motivations for joining groups and the composition of groups.

> Managers can change the ways groups interact by altering the physical arrangements, changing the resource distribution, stressing a superordinate goal, training employees to manage group interactions more effectively, and changing the structure of the organization.

Quite often, a manager can help make sure a group develops into a productive unit by nurturing its activities at each stage of development. Helpful steps include encouraging open communication and trust among the members, stimulating discussion of important issues and providing task-relevant information at appropriate times, and helping analyze external factors such as competition and external threats and opportunities. Managers might also encourage the development of norms and roles within the group to help its development.

In managing a group, managers must consider both the goals of individual members and the goals of the group as a whole. Developing a reward structure that lets people reach their own goals by working toward those of the group can result in a very productive group. A manager may also be able to improve group cohesiveness, for example, by trying to stimulate competition, by provoking an external threat to the group, by establishing a goal-setting system, or by employing participative approaches.

Managers must carefully choose strategies for dealing with interactions among groups after thorough examination and analysis of the groups, their goals, their unique characteristics, and the organizational setting in which the interactions occur. Managers can use a variety of strategies to increase the efficiency of intergroup interactions. One common mechanism is to encourage groups to focus on a superordinate goal, as mentioned earlier. In other situations, management might want to use a **linking role**, a position for a person or group that coordinates the activities of two or more organizational groups. This can add a layer of management, but in very important situations it may be worthwhile. Finally, management may need to change reporting relationships, decision–making priorities, and rules and procedures to properly manage group interactions.

> A **linking role** is a position for a person or group that serves to coordinate the activities of two or more organizational groups.

In summary, managers must be aware of the implications—organizational and social—of their attempts to manage people in groups. Groups affect how their members behave, and it is member behaviour that adds up to total group performance. Groups are so prevalent in our society that managers must strive to understand them better.

Chapter Review

Summary of Key Points

- A group is two or more people who interact and influence one another. It is important to study groups because groups are everywhere in our society, because they can profoundly affect individual behaviour, and because the behaviour of individuals in a group is key to the group's success or failure. The work group is the primary means by which managers coordinate individual behaviour to achieve organizational goals. Individuals form or join groups because they expect to satisfy personal needs.

- Groups may be differentiated on the bases of relative permanence and degree of formality. The two types of formal groups are command and task groups. Friendship and interest groups are the two types of informal groups. Command groups are relatively permanent work groups established by the organization and usually are specified on an organization chart. Task groups, although also established by the organization, are relatively temporary and exist only until the specific task is accomplished. In friendship groups, the affiliation among members arises from close social relationships and the enjoyment that comes from being together. The common bond in interest groups is the activity in which the members engage.

- Groups develop in stages: forming, storming, norming, performing, and adjourning. Although the stages are sequential, they may overlap. A group that does not fully develop within each stage will not fully mature as a group, resulting in lower group performance.

- Four additional factors affect group performance: composition, size, norms, and cohesiveness. The homogeneity of the people in the group affects the interactions that occur and the productivity of the group. The effect of increasing the size of the group depends on the nature of the group's tasks and the people in the group. Norms help people function and relate to one another in predictable and efficient ways. Norms serve four purposes: They facilitate group survival, simplify and make more predictable the behaviours of group members, help the group avoid embarrassing situations, and express the central values of the group and identify the group to others.

- To comprehend intergroup dynamics we must understand the key characteristics of groups: that each group is unique, that the specific organizational setting influences the group, and that the group's task and setting have an effect on group behaviour. The five bases of intergroup interactions determine the characteristics of the interactions between groups, including their frequency, how much information is exchanged, and what type of interaction occurs.

- Interactions among work groups involve some of the most complex relationships in organizations. They are based on five factors: location, resources, time and goal interdependence, task uncertainty, and task interdependence. Being physically near one another naturally increases groups' opportunities for interactions. If groups use the same or similar resources, or if one group can affect the availability of the resources needed by another group, the potential for frequent interactions increases. The nature of the tasks groups perform, including time and goal orientation, the uncertainties of group tasks, and group interdependencies, influences how groups interact.

- Managers must be aware of the many factors that affect group performance and understand the individual as well as the group issues.

- Groups and teams are not the same. A team is a small number of people with complementary skills who are committed to a common purpose, common performance goals, and a common approach for which they hold themselves mutually accountable. Teams differ from traditional work groups in their job categories, authority, and reward systems.

- Teams are used because they make sense for a specific organization. Organizational benefits include enhanced performance, employee benefits, and reduced costs, among others.

- Many types of teams exist in organizations. Quality circles are small groups of employees from the same work area who meet regularly to discuss and recommend solutions to workplace problems. Work teams perform the daily operations of the organization and make decisions about how to do the work. Problem-solving teams are temporarily established to solve a particular problem. Implementation teams enact organizational changes. Management teams consist of managers from various areas; these teams are relatively permanent and coach and counsel the new teams. Product development teams are teams assigned the task of developing a new product or service for the organization. Members of virtual teams usually meet via teleconferencing, may never actually sit in the same room together, and often have a fluid membership.

Discussion Questions

1. Why is it useful for a manager to understand group behaviour? Why is it useful for an employee?

2. Our definition of a group is somewhat broad. Would you classify each of the following collections of people as a group? Explain why.
   a. Twenty thousand people at a hockey game
   b. Students taking this course
   c. People in an elevator
   d. People on an escalator
   e. Employees of Scotiabank
   f. Employees of your local college or university bookstore

3. List four groups to which you belong. Identify each as formal or informal.

4. Explain why each group you listed in question 3 formed. Why did you join each group? Why might others have decided to join each group?

5. In which stage of development is each of the four groups listed in question 3? Did any group move too quickly through any of the stages? Explain.

6. Analyze the composition of two of the groups to which you belong. How are they similar in composition? How do they differ?

7. Are any of the groups to which you belong too large or too small to get their work done? If so, what can the leader or the members do to alleviate the problem?

8. List two norms each for two of the groups to which you belong. How are these norms enforced?

9. Discuss the following statement: "Group cohesiveness is the good, warm feeling we get from working in groups and is something that all group leaders should strive to develop in the groups they lead."

10. Consider one of the groups to which you belong and describe the interactions that group has with another group.

11. Why is it important to make a distinction between "group" and "team"? What kinds of behaviours might be different in these assemblages?

12. How are other organizational characteristics different for a team-based organization?

13. Some say that changing to a team-based arrangement "just makes sense" for organizations. What are the four primary reasons why this might be so?

14. If employees are happy working in the traditional boss-hierarchical organization, why should a manager even consider changing to a team-based organization?

15. How are the seven types of teams related to each other?

Self-Assessment Exercise

Group Cohesiveness

Introduction: You are probably a member of many different groups: study groups for school, work groups, friendship groups within a social club such as a fraternity or sorority, and interest groups. You probably have some feel for how tightly knit or cohesive each of those groups is. This exercise will help you diagnose the cohesiveness of one of those groups.

Instructions: First, pick one of the small groups to which you belong for analysis. Be sure that it is a small group, say between three and eight people. Next, rate on the following scale of 1 (poorly) to 5 (very well) how well you feel the group works together.

How well does this group work together?

1. Poorly

2. Not Very Well

3. About Average

4. Pretty Well

5. Very Well

Now answer the following six questions about the group. Put a check in the blank next to the answer that best describes how you feel about each question.

1. How many of the people in your group are friendly toward each other?

_____ (5) All of them

_____ (4) Most of them

_____ (3) Some of them

_____ (2) A few of them

_____ (1) None of them

2. How much trust is there among members of your group?

_____ (1) Distrust

_____ (2) Little trust

_____ (3) Average trust

_____ (4) Considerable trust

_____ (5) A great deal of trust

3. How much loyalty and sense of belonging is there among group members?

_____ (1) No group loyalty or sense of belonging

_____ (2) A little loyalty and sense of belonging

_____ (3) An average sense of belonging

_____ (4) An above-average sense of belonging

_____ (5) A strong sense of belonging

4. Do you feel that you are really a valuable part of your group?

_____ (5) I am really a part of my group

_____ (4) I am included in most ways

_____ (3) I am included in some ways, but not others

_____ (2) I am included in a few ways, but not many

_____ (1) I do not feel I really belong

5. How friendly are your fellow group members toward one another?

_____ (1) Not friendly

_____ (2) Somewhat friendly

_____ (3) Friendly to an average degree

_____ (4) Friendlier than average

_____ (5) Very friendly

6. If you had a chance to work with a different group of people doing the same task, how would you feel about moving to another group?

_____ (1) I would want very much to move

_____ (2) I would rather move than stay where I am

(3) It would make no difference to me

_____ (4) I would rather stay where I am than move

_____ (5) I would want very much to stay where I am

Now add up the numbers you chose for all six questions and divide by 6.

Total from all six questions = _____ / 6 = _____. This is the group cohesiveness score for your group.

Compare this number with the one you checked on the scale at the beginning of this exercise about how well you feel this group works together. Are they about the same, or are they quite different? If they are about the same, then you have a pretty good feel for the group and how it works. If they are quite different, then you probably need to analyze what aspects of the group functioning you misunderstood. (This is only part of a much longer instrument; it has not been scientifically validated in this form and is to be used for class discussion purposes only.)

Source: The six questions were taken from the Groupthink Assessment Inventory by John R. Montanari and Gregory Moorhead, "Development of the Groupthink Assessment Inventory," *Educational and Psychological Measurement*, 1989, vol. 39, pp. 209–219. Reprinted by permission of Gregory Moorhead.

Purpose: This exercise will help you understand some of the benefits of teamwork .

Format: Your instructor will divide the group into teams of four to six people. (These could be previously formed teams or new teams.) Teams should arrange their desks or chairs so that they can interact and communicate well with each other.

Procedure: Your team is an engineering design team assigned to work out this difficult problem, which is the key to getting a major purchase contract from a large influential buyer. The task seems simple, but working out such tasks (at different levels of complexity) can be very important to organizations.

1. It is important for your team to work together to develop your solution.

2. Look at the accompanying figure. Your task is to create a single square by making only two straight-line cuts and then reassembling the pieces so that all material is used in the final product.

The Figure:

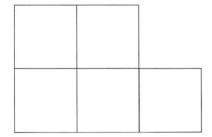

3. It might be easier to trace the design onto stiff paper or cardboard to facilitate working with the pieces.

4. Your instructor has access to the correct answer key from the Instructor's Resource Manual.

Follow-up Questions

1. How did the other members of your team help or hinder your ability to solve the problem?

2. Did your team have a leader throughout the exercise? If so, can you identify why that person emerged as the leader?

3. What type of training would have helped your team solve the problem better or faster?

Source: From John W. Newstrom and Edward E. Scannell, *Games Trainers Play: Experiential Learning Exercises*, p. 259. Copyright © 1980. Reproduced by permission of The McGraw-Hill Companies.

Teams at Evans RV Wholesale Supply and Distribution Company

Evans RV Wholesale Supply and Distribution Company sells parts, equipment, and supplies for recreational vehicles—motor homes, travel trailers, campers, and similar vehicles. In addition, Evans has a service department for the repair and service of RVs. The owner, Alex Evans, bought the company five years ago from its original owner, changed the name of the company, and has finally made it profitable, although it has been rough going. The

organization is set up in three divisions: service, retail parts and supplies, and wholesale parts and supplies. Alex, the owner, CEO, and president, has a vice president for each operating division and a vice president of finance and operations. The organization chart shows these divisions and positions.

In the warehouse there are three groups: receiving (checking orders for completeness, returning defective merchandise, stocking the shelves, filling orders), service parts, and order filling for outgoing shipments. The warehouse group is responsible for all activities related to parts and supplies receiving, storage, and shipping.

The retail sales division includes all functions related to selling of parts and supplies at the two stores and in the mobile sales trailer. Personnel in the retail division include salespeople and cashiers. The retail salespeople also work in the warehouse because the warehouse also serves as the showroom for walk–in customers.

In the service department the service manager supervises the service writers, one scheduler, and lead mechanics and technicians. The service department includes the collision repair group at the main store and the service department at the satellite store. The collision repair group has two service writers who have special expertise in collision repair and insurance regulations. Two drivers who move RVs around the yard also work in the service division.

The accounting and finance groups do everything related to the money side of the business, including accounts payable and receivable, cash management, and payroll. Also in this group is the one person who handles all of the traditional personnel functions.

Alex has run other small businesses and is known as a benevolent owner, always taking care of the loyal employees who work hard and are the backbone of any small business. He is also known as being really tough on anyone who loafs on the job or tries to take unfair advantage of Alex or the company. Most of the employees are either veterans of the RV industry at Evans or elsewhere, or are very young and still learning the business. Alex is working hard to develop a good work ethic among the younger employees and to keep the old-timers fully involved. Since he bought the business, Alex has instituted new, modern, employee-centred human resource policies. However, the company is still a traditional hierarchically structured organization (see chart).

The company is located in a major metropolitan area that has a lot of potential customers for the RV business. The region has many outdoor recreational activities and an active retirement community whose members either live in RVs or use them for recreation. The former owner of the business specifically chose not to be in the RV sales business, figuring that parts and service was the better end of the business. Two stores are strategically located on opposite ends of the metropolitan area, and a mobile sales office is moved around the major camping and recreational areas during the peak months of the year.

When Alex bought the company, the parts and supplies business was only retail, relying on customers to walk in the door to buy something. After buying the business, Alex applied good management, marketing, and cash-management principles to get the company out of the red and into profitability. Although his was not the only such business in town, it was the only one locally owned, and it had a good local following.

About two years ago, Alex recognized that the nature of the business was changing. First, he saw the large nationwide retailers moving into town. These retailers were using discount pricing in large warehouse-type stores. These large retail stores could use volume purchasing to get lower prices from manufacturers, and they had the large stores necessary to store and shelve the large inventory. Alex, with only two stores, was unable to get such low prices from manufacturers. He also noted that retired people were notorious for shopping around for the lowest prices, but they also appreciated good, friendly customer service. People interested in recreational items also seemed to be following the national trend to shop via catalogues.

So for a variety of reasons Alex began to develop a wholesale business by becoming a wholesale distributor to the many RV parts and supply businesses in the small towns located in the recreational areas around the province. At the same time, he created the first catalogue for RV parts and supplies, featuring all the brand-name parts and supplies by category and supplier. The catalogue had a very attractive camping scene on the cover, a combination of attractively displayed items and pages full of all the possible parts and supplies that the RV owner could think of. Of course, he made placing an order very easy, by phone, mail, or fax, and accepted many easy payment methods. He filled both distributor orders and catalogue orders from his warehouse in the main store using standard mail and parcel delivery services, charging the full delivery costs to the customers. He credits the business's survival so far to his diversification into the warehouse and catalogue business through which he can directly compete with the national chains.

Although it is now barely profitable, Alex is concerned about the changes in the industry and the competition and about making the monthly payments on the $5 million loan he got from the bank to buy the business in the first place. In addition, he reads about the latest management techniques and attends various professional conferences around the country. He has been hearing and reading about this team-based organization idea and thinks it might be just the thing to energize his company and take it to the next level of performance and profitability. At the annual strategic planning retreat in August, Alex announced to his top management team that starting on October 1 (the beginning of the next fiscal year,) the company would be changing to a team-based arrangement.

Case Questions

1. What mistakes has Alex already made in developing a team-based organization?

2. If Alex were to call you in as a consultant, what would you tell Alex to do?

SELF TEST

You have read the chapter and studied the key terms. Think you're ready to ace the exam? Take this sample test to gauge your comprehension of chapter material and check your answers at the back of the book.

T   F   1. Interpersonal relations are a vital part of all managerial activities.

T   F   2. A collection of coworkers must share a goal to qualify as a group.

T   F   3. Norming is usually the last stage of group development.

T   F   4. A group must fully complete one stage of development before it can move on to the next stage.

T   F   5. A homogeneous group tends to have less conflict than a heterogeneous group.

T   F   6. The use of teams is a recent innovation in the management process.

T   F   7. The members of teams hold themselves mutually accountable for results.

8. According to the authors of your text, a group has all of the following except
   a. two or more people.
   b. interaction among the group members.
   c. mutual influence among the group members.
   d. motivation to stay together.

9. Hannah is the manager of the large appliance department at a home improvement store. She supervises six appliance salespeople. This is an example of a
   a. task group.
   b. command group.
   c. affinity group.
   d. interest group.
   e. project group.

10. The first stage of group development is
    a. forming.
    b. storming.
    c. norming.
    d. performing.
    e. adjourning.

11. A homogeneous group is likely to be more productive when the group task is
    a. highly challenging and long term.
    b. risky and short term.
    c. new and uncertain.
    d. simple and cooperation is necessary.
    e. complex and requires collective effort.

12. Group norms are usually established during which stage of group development?
    a. forming.
    b. storming.
    c. norming.
    d. performing.
    e. adjourning.

13. One basic difference between a group and a team is
    a. a group is usually larger.
    b. team members are committed to a common goal.
    c. group members have complementary skills.
    d. team members are more concerned with individual performance.
    e. a team is evaluated as a whole.

14. In traditional work groups, the supervisor directly controls the daily activities. In teams, who performs this function?
    a. customers
    b. senior managers
    c. the team itself
    d. unaffiliated supervisors
    e. management trainees

15. Which of the following is not a benefit that may result from the use of teams?
    a. Reduced frustration for managers in their new roles
    b. Enhanced performance, such as increased output
    c. Employee benefits and a sense of self-control
    d. Reduced costs
    e. Organizational enhancements and eliminated bureaucracy

16. Kim is a member of a permanent team that does the daily work of her department. Kim is a member of a
    a. management team.
    b. problem-solving team.
    c. development team.
    d. quality circle.
    e. work team.

Decision Making

CHAPTER 9

After studying this chapter,
you should be able to:

- ▌ Discuss the nature of different types of decisions made in organizations.

- ▌ Describe four different ways of making decisions in organizations.

- ▌ Discuss escalation of commitment and ethics in decision making.

- ▌ Explain group decision making.

- ▌ Discuss creativity and the creative process in organizations.

Innovation at GoodLife Fitness

GoodLife Fitness Clubs was founded in 1979 when David Patchell-Evans opened a 186 square metre facility in London, Ontario. Today, GoodLife is the largest group of fitness clubs in Canada. The company employs

4000 associates and has over 300 000 members at over 120 locations. Patchell-Evans, who prefers to be called Patch, is a former champion rower who built his company by doing things differently. In a business where members come and go, client retention is key. In order to attract and retain customers, Patchell-Evans has introduced numerous client services such as onsite childcare, tanning salons, low cost DVD rentals, and massage therapy. The company also offers a Corporate Wellness program that offers individual and group discounts to its corporate partners, recognizing that fitter employees are more productive and are absent less. The GoodLife Fitness website outlines the specific benefits of the program for both employees and employers.

Patchell-Evans has received numerous awards over the years paying homage to his business acumen, including being named Most Innovative CEO in 2005 by *Canadian Business* magazine. In addition, GoodLife Fitness has been on the list of the 50 Best Managed Companies in Canada several times. And for good reason. In 2004, Patchell-Evans acquired the exclusive Canadian rights to Visual Fitness Planner, a software tool that allows clients to visualize themselves before and after they have achieved their fitness goals. After inputting client information, including genetic and lifestyle factors, the software produces an image of the client along with customized diet and exercise recommendations. For women who feel intimidated by working out in a co-ed environment, Patchell-Evans introduced a series of women-only facilities in locations such as supermarkets. This also enables busy women to have a workout while picking up the groceries. According to its founder, GoodLife Fitness is not finished growing. Patchell-Evan's stated goal is to have 200 clubs across Canada by 2009.[1]

David Patchell-Evan's innovative approach to building GoodLife Fitness Clubs into the largest chain of fitness clubs in Canada exemplifies a fundamental part of the management process in any organization—making decisions. Indeed, some experts believe that decision making is the most basic of all management activities. Some decisions, such as those described above, involve major events that have a dramatic impact on a firm's future growth, profits, and even survival. Others, such as choosing the colours of the firm's new letterhead or deciding when to reorder office supplies, are much less significant. But all decisions are important on some level, so managers need to understand how decisions are made.

This chapter explores decision making in detail. We start by examining the nature of decision making. Next we describe several different approaches to understanding the decision-making process. We then identify and discuss two related behavioural aspects of decision making. Next we consider several important issues in group decision making. We conclude by presenting a powerful approach to negotiation.

The Nature of Decision Making

Decision making is the process of choosing from among several alternatives.

Decision making is choosing one alternative from among several. Consider football, for example. The quarterback can run any of perhaps a hundred plays. With the goal of scoring a touchdown always in mind, he chooses the play that seems to promise the best outcome. His choice is based on his understanding of the game situation, the likelihood of various outcomes, and his preference for each outcome.

Managers' decisions usually are guided by a goal.

Figure 9.1 shows the basic elements of decision making. A decision maker's actions are guided by a goal. Each of several alternative courses of action is linked with various

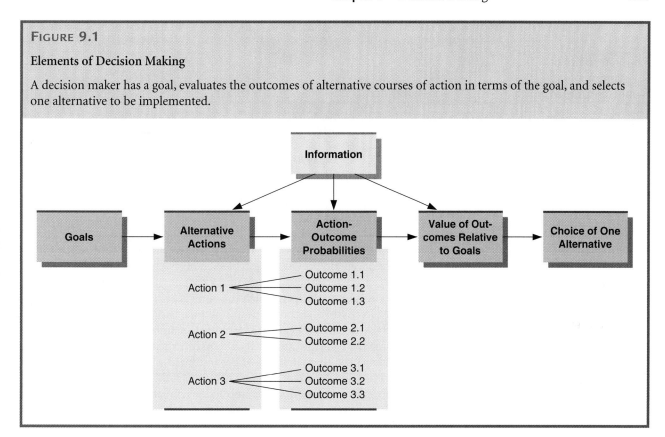

FIGURE 9.1

Elements of Decision Making

A decision maker has a goal, evaluates the outcomes of alternative courses of action in terms of the goal, and selects one alternative to be implemented.

outcomes. Information is available on the alternatives, on the likelihood that each outcome will occur, and on the value of each outcome relative to the goal. The decision maker chooses one alternative on the basis of his or her evaluation of the information.

Decisions made in organizations can be classified according to frequency and to information conditions. In a decision-making context, frequency is how often a particular decision recurs and information conditions describe how much information is available about the likelihood of various outcomes.

Types of Decisions

The frequency of recurrence determines whether a decision is programmed or nonprogrammed. A **programmed decision** recurs often enough for a decision rule to be developed. A **decision rule** tells decision makers which alternative to choose once they have information about the decision situation. The appropriate decision rule is used whenever the same situation is encountered. Programmed decisions usually are highly structured; that is, the goals are clear and well known, the decision-making procedure is already established, and the sources and channels of information are clearly defined.[2]

Airlines use established procedures when a piece of equipment breaks down and cannot be used on a particular flight. Passengers may not view the issue as a programmed decision, because they experience this situation relatively infrequently. But the airlines know that equipment problems that render a plane unfit for service arise regularly. Each airline has its own set of clear procedures to use in the event of equipment problems. A given flight might be delayed, cancelled, or continued on a different plane, depending on the nature of the problem and other circumstances (such as the

A **programmed decision** is a decision that recurs often enough for a decision rule to be developed.

A **decision rule** is a statement that tells a decision maker which alternative to choose based on the characteristics of the decision situation.

TABLE 9.1

Characteristics of Programmed and Nonprogrammed Decisions

Characteristics	Programmed Decisions	Nonprogrammed Decisions
Type of Decision	Well structured	Poorly structured
Frequency	Repetitive and routine	New and unusual
Goals	Clear, specific	Vague
Information	Readily available	Not available, unclear channels
Consequences	Minor	Major
Organizational Level	Lower levels	Upper levels
Time for Solution	Short	Relatively long
Basis for Solution	Decision rules, set procedures	Judgment and creativity

number of passengers booked, the next scheduled flight for the same destination, and so forth).

When a problem or decision situation has not been encountered before, however, a decision maker cannot rely on previously established decision rules. Such a decision is called a **nonprogrammed decision**, and it requires problem solving. **Problem solving** is a special form of decision making in which the issue is unique—it requires developing and evaluating alternatives without the aid of a decision rule. Nonprogrammed decisions are poorly structured; because information is ambiguous, there is no clear procedure for making the decision, and the goals are often vague.[3]

Table 9.1 summarizes the characteristics of programmed and nonprogrammed decisions. Note that programmed decisions are more common at the lower levels of the organization, whereas a primary responsibility of top management is to make the difficult, nonprogrammed decisions that determine the organization's long-term effectiveness. By definition, the strategy decisions for which top management is responsible are poorly structured and nonroutine and have far-reaching consequences.[4] Programmed decisions, then, can be made according to previously tested rules and procedures. Nonprogrammed decisions generally require that the decision maker exercise judgment and creativity.[5] In other words, all problems require a decision, but not all decisions require problem solving.

> A **nonprogrammed decision** is a decision that recurs infrequently and for which there is no previously established decision rule.

> **Problem solving** of decision making in which the issue is unique and alternatives must be developed and evaluated without the aid of a programmed decision rule.

> Problems require a decision, but not all decisions require problem solving.

Information Required for Decision Making

Decisions are made to bring about desired outcomes, but the information available about those outcomes varies. The range of available information can be considered as a continuum whose endpoints represent complete certainty, when all alternative outcomes are known, and complete uncertainty, when alternative outcomes are unknown. At points between the two extremes, risk is involved; the decision maker has some information about the possible outcomes and may be able to estimate the probability of their occurrence.

Different information conditions present different challenges to the decision maker.[6] For example, suppose a marketing manager at Microsoft is trying to determine whether to launch an expensive promotional effort for a new video game developed for the Xbox 360 (see Figure 9.2). For simplicity, assume there are only two alternatives: to promote the game or not to promote it. Under a condition of *certainty*, the manager knows the outcomes of each alternative. If the new game is promoted heavily, the company will realize a $10 million profit. Without promotion, the company will realize only a $2 million profit. Here the decision is simple: Promote the game. (Note: These figures are created for the purposes of this example and are not actual profit figures for any company.)

Under a condition of *risk*, the decision maker cannot know with certainty what the outcome of a given action will be but has enough information to estimate the probabilities of various outcomes. Thus, working from information gathered by the market research department, the marketing manager in our example can estimate the likelihood of each outcome in a risk situation. In this case, the alternatives are defined by

FIGURE 9.2

Alternative Outcomes Under Different Information Conditions

The three decision-making conditions of certainty, risk, and uncertainty for the decision about whether to promote a new video game to the market.

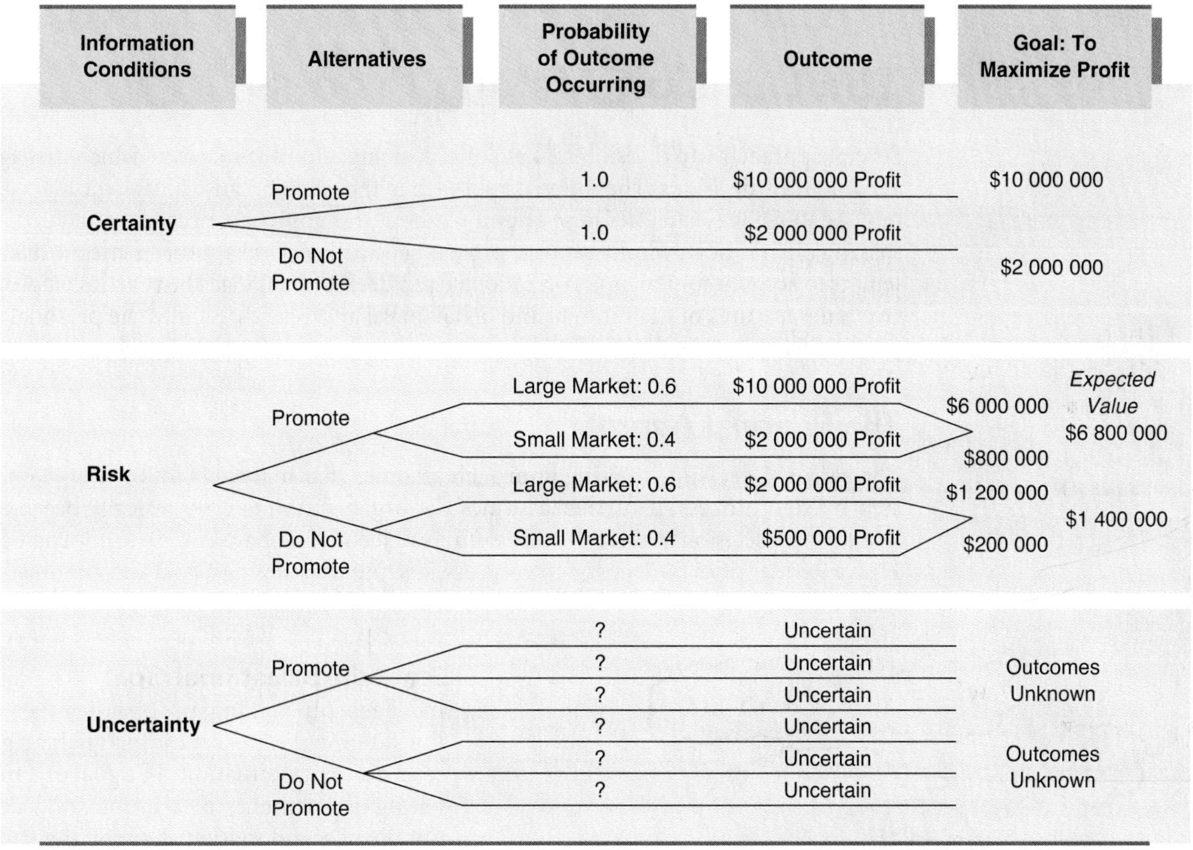

Information Conditions	Alternatives	Probability of Outcome Occurring	Outcome	Goal: To Maximize Profit
Certainty	Promote	1.0	$10 000 000 Profit	$10 000 000
	Do Not Promote	1.0	$2 000 000 Profit	$2 000 000
Risk	Promote	Large Market: 0.6	$10 000 000 Profit	$6 000 000 *Expected Value* $6 800 000
		Small Market: 0.4	$2 000 000 Profit	$800 000
	Do Not Promote	Large Market: 0.6	$2 000 000 Profit	$1 200 000 $1 400 000
		Small Market: 0.4	$500 000 Profit	$200 000
Uncertainty	Promote	?	Uncertain	
		?	Uncertain	Outcomes Unknown
		?	Uncertain	
	Do Not Promote	?	Uncertain	
		?	Uncertain	Outcomes Unknown
		?	Uncertain	

the size of the market. The probability for a large video game market is 0.6, and the probability for a small market is 0.4. The manager can calculate the expected value of the promotional effort based on these probabilities and the expected profits associated with each. To find the expected value of an alternative, the manager multiplies each outcome's value by the probability of its occurrence. The sum of these calculations for all possible outcomes represents that alternative's expected value. In this case, the expected value of alternative 1—to promote the new game—is as follows:

$$0.6 \times \$10\ 000\ 000 = \$6\ 000\ 000$$
$$+0.4 \times \$2\ 000\ 000 = \$800\ 0000$$
$$\overline{\text{Expected value of alternative 1} = \$6\ 800\ 000}$$

The expected value of alternative 2 (shown in Figure 9.2) is $1 400 000. The marketing manager should choose the first alternative, because its expected value is higher. The manager should recognize, however, that although the numbers look convincing, they are based on incomplete information and only estimates of probability.

The decision maker who lacks enough information to estimate the probability of outcomes (or perhaps even to identify the outcomes at all) faces a condition of *uncertainty*.[7] In the Xbox 360 example, this might be the case if sales of video games had recently collapsed and it was not clear whether the precipitous drop was temporary or permanent or when information to clarify the situation would be available. Under such circumstances, the decision maker may wait for more information to reduce uncertainty or rely on judgment, experience, and intuition to make the decision.

The Decision-Making Process

Several approaches to decision making offer insights into the process by which managers arrive at their decisions. The rational approach is appealing because of its logic and economy. Yet these very qualities raise questions about this approach, because actual decision making often is not a wholly rational process. The behavioural approach, meanwhile, attempts to account for the limits on rationality in decision making. The practical approach combines features of the rational and behavioural approaches. Finally, the personal approach focuses on the decision-making processes individuals use in difficult situations.

The Rational Approach

The **rational decision-making approach** is a systematic, step-by-step process for making decisions.

The **rational decision-making approach** assumes that managers follow a systematic, step-by-step process. It further assumes the organization is economically based and managed by decision makers who are entirely objective and have complete information.[8] Figure 9.3 identifies the steps of the process, starting with stating a goal and running logically through the process until the best decision is made, implemented, and controlled.

State the Situational Goal The rational decision-making process begins with the statement of a situational goal, or goal for a particular situation. The goal of a marketing department, for example, may be to obtain a certain market share by the end of the year. (Some models of decision making do not start with a goal. We include it because it is the standard used to determine whether there is a decision to be made.)

Identify the Problem The purpose of problem identification is to gather information that bears on the goal. If there is a discrepancy between the goal and the actual state, action may be needed. In the marketing example, the group may gather information about the company's actual market share and compare it with the desired market share. A difference between the two represents a problem that necessitates a decision. Reliable information is very important in this step. Inaccurate information can lead to an unnecessary decision or no decision when one is required.

Risk propensity refers to the extent that a person is willing to gamble when making a decision. Those with lower risk propensity often struggle to reach a decision because they may worry too much about the risk associated with various options. This executive, for example, is clearly having trouble deciding on an option, perhaps because he has a low propensity for risk.

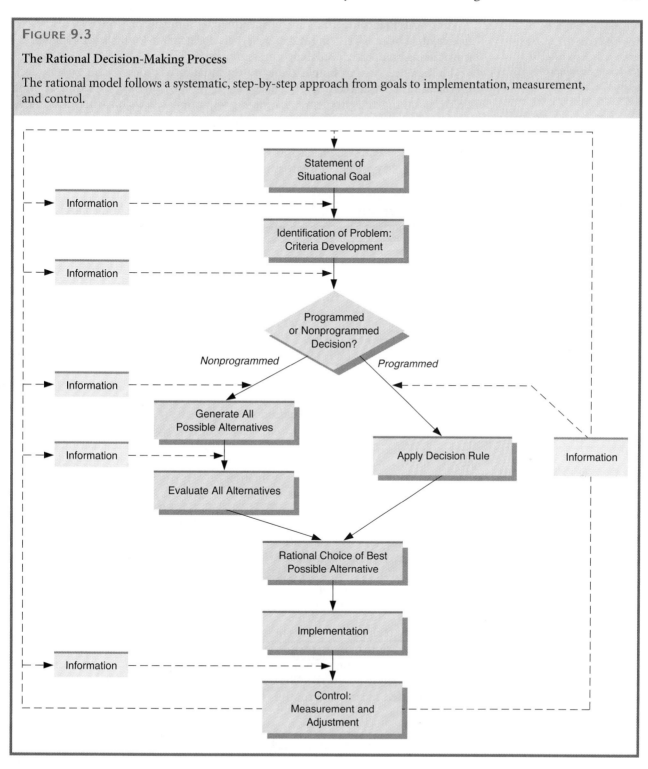

FIGURE 9.3

The Rational Decision-Making Process

The rational model follows a systematic, step-by-step approach from goals to implementation, measurement, and control.

Determining Decision Type   Next, the decision makers must determine if the problem represents a programmed or a nonprogrammed decision. If a programmed decision is needed, the appropriate decision rule is invoked, and the process moves on to the choice among alternatives. A programmed marketing decision may be called for if

Determining the decision type means deciding whether a decision is to be programmed or nonprogrammed.

analysis reveals that competitors are outspending the company on print advertising. Because creating print advertising and buying space for it are well-established functions of the marketing group, it requires only a programmed decision.

Although it may seem simple to diagnose a situation as programmed, apply a decision rule, and arrive at a solution, mistakes can still occur. Choosing the wrong decision rule or assuming the problem calls for a programmed decision when a nonprogrammed decision actually is required can result in poor decisions. The same caution applies to the determination that a nonprogrammed decision is called for. If the situation is wrongly diagnosed, the decision maker wastes time and resources seeking a new solution to an old problem, or reinventing the wheel.

Generate Alternatives   The next step in making a nonprogrammed decision is to generate alternatives. The rational process assumes that decision makers will generate all the possible alternative solutions to the problem. However, this assumption is unrealistic, because even simple business problems can have scores of possible solutions. Decision makers may rely on education and experience as well as knowledge of the situation to generate alternatives. In addition, they may seek information from other people, such as peers, subordinates, and supervisors. Decision makers may analyze the symptoms of the problem for clues or fall back on intuition or judgment to develop alternative solutions.[9] If the marketing department in our example determines that a nonprogrammed decision is required, it will need to generate alternatives for increasing market share.

Evaluate Alternatives   Evaluation involves assessing all possible alternatives in terms of predetermined decision criteria. The ultimate decision criterion is "Will this alternative bring us nearer to the goal?" In each case, the decision maker must examine each alternative for evidence that it will reduce the discrepancy between the desired state and the actual state. The evaluation process usually includes (1) describing the anticipated outcomes (benefits) of each alternative, (2) evaluating the anticipated costs of each alternative, and (3) estimating the uncertainties and risks associated with each alternative.[10] In most decision situations, the decision maker does not have perfect information regarding the outcomes of all alternatives. At one extreme, as shown earlier in Figure 9.2, outcomes may be known with certainty; at the other, the decision maker has no information whatsoever, so the outcomes are entirely uncertain. But risk is the most common situation.

Choose an Alternative   The choice of an alternative is usually the most crucial step in the decision-making process. Choosing consists of selecting the alternative with the highest possible payoff, based on the benefits, costs, risks, and uncertainties of all alternatives. In the Xbox 360 game promotion example, the decision maker evaluated the two alternatives by calculating their expected values. Following the rational approach, the manager would choose the one with the largest expected value.

Even with the rational approach, however, difficulties can arise in choosing an alternative. First, when two or more alternatives have equal payoffs, the decision maker must obtain more information or use some other criterion to make the choice. Second, when no single alternative will accomplish the objective, some combination of two or three alternatives may have to be implemented. Finally, if no alternative or combination of alternatives will solve the problem, the decision maker must obtain more information, generate more alternatives, or change the goals.[11]

An important part of the choice phase is the consideration of **contingency plans**—alternative actions that can be taken if the primary course of action is unexpectedly disrupted or rendered inappropriate.[12] Planning for contingencies is part of the transition between choosing the preferred alternative and implementing it. In developing contingency plans, the decision maker usually asks questions such as: What if something unexpected happens during the implementation of this alternative?" or "If the economy goes into a recession, will the choice of this alternative ruin the company?" or "How can we alter this plan if the economy suddenly rebounds and begins to grow?"

Contingency plans are alternative actions to take if the primary course of action is unexpectedly disrupted or rendered inappropriate.

Implement the Plan   Implementation puts the decision into action. It builds on the commitment and motivation of those who participated in the decision-making process (and may actually bolster individual commitment and motivation). To succeed, implementation requires the proper use of resources and good management skills. Following the decision to promote the new Nintendo game heavily, for example, the marketing manager must implement the decision by assigning the project to a work group or task force. The success of this team depends on the leadership, the reward structure, the communications system, and group dynamics. Sometimes the decision maker begins to doubt a choice already made. This doubt is called post–decision dissonance or more generally, **cognitive dissonance**.[13] To reduce the tension created by the dissonance, the decision maker may seek to rationalize the decision further with new information.

Cognitive dissonance is the anxiety a person experiences when two sets of knowledge or perceptions are contradictory or incongruent.

Control: Measure and Adjust   In the final stage of the rational decision-making process, the outcomes of the decision are measured and compared with the desired goal. If a discrepancy remains, the decision maker may restart the decision-making process by setting a new goal (or reiterating the existing one.) The decision maker, unsatisfied with the previous decision, may modify the subsequent decision-making process to avoid another mistake. Changes can be made in any part of the process, as Figure 9.3 illustrates by the arrows leading from the control step to each of the other steps. Decision making therefore is a dynamic, self-correcting, and ongoing process in organizations.

Suppose a marketing department implements a new print advertising campaign. After implementation, it constantly monitors market research data and compares its new market share to the desired market share. If the advertising has the desired effect, no changes will be made in the promotion campaign. If, however, the data indicate no change in the market share, additional decisions and implementation of a contingency plan may be necessary. For example, when Nissan introduced its luxury car line Infiniti, it relied on a series of Zen-like ads that featured images of rocks, plants, and water—but no images of the car. At the same time, Toyota was featuring pictures of its new luxury car line, Lexus, which quickly established itself in the market. When Infiniti managers realized their mistake, they quickly pulled the old ads and started running new ones centred on images of their car.[14]

Strengths and Weaknesses of the Rational Approach   The rational approach has several strengths. It forces the decision maker to consider a decision in a logical, sequential manner, and the in-depth analysis of alternatives enables the decision maker to choose on the basis of information rather than emotion or social pressure. But the rigid assumptions of this approach often are unrealistic.[15] The amount of information available to managers usually is limited by either time or cost constraints, and most decision makers have limited ability to process information about the alternatives. In addition, not all alternatives lend themselves to quantification in terms that will allow for easy comparison. Finally, because they cannot predict the future, it is unlikely that decision makers will know all possible outcomes of each alternative.[16]

The Behavioural Approach

Whereas the rational approach assumes that managers operate logically and rationally, the behavioural approach acknowledges the role and importance of human behaviour in the decision-making process. In particular, a crucial assumption of the behavioural approach is that decision makers operate with bounded rationality rather than with the perfect rationality assumed by the rational approach.

Bounded rationality is the idea that although individuals seek the best solution to a problem, the demands of processing all the information bearing on the problem, generating all possible solutions, and choosing the single best solution are beyond the capabilities of most decision makers. Thus, they accept less-than-ideal solutions based on a process that is neither exhaustive nor entirely rational. For example, one study found that under time pressure, groups usually eliminate all but the two most favourable alternatives and then process the remaining two in great detail.[17] Thus, decision makers operating with bounded rationality limit the inputs to the decision-making process and base decisions on judgment and personal biases as well as logic.[18]

The **behavioural approach** is characterized by (1) the use of procedures and guidelines, (2) suboptimizing, and (3) satisficing. Uncertainty in decision making can initially be reduced by relying on procedures and rules of thumb. If, for example, increasing print advertising has increased a company's market share in the past, that linkage may be used by company employees as a rule of thumb in decision making. When the previous month's market share drops below a certain level, the company might increase its print advertising expenditures by 25 percent during the following month.

Suboptimizing is knowingly accepting less than the best possible outcome. Frequently it is not feasible to make the ideal decision in a real-world situation given organizational constraints. The decision maker often must suboptimize to avoid unintended negative effects on other departments, product lines, or decisions.[19] An automobile manufacturer, for example, can cut costs dramatically and increase efficiency if it schedules the production of one model at a time. Thus, the production group's optimal decision is single-model scheduling. But the marketing group, seeking to optimize its sales goals by offering a wide variety of models, may demand the opposite production schedule: short runs of entirely different models. The groups in the middle, design and scheduling, may suboptimize the benefits the production and marketing groups seek by planning long runs of slightly different models. This is the practice of the large auto manufacturers, such as General Motors and Ford, which make several body styles in numerous models on the same production line.

The final feature of the behavioural approach is **satisficing**: examining alternatives only until a solution that meets minimal requirements is found and then ceasing to look for a better one.[20] The search for alternatives usually is a sequential process guided by procedures and rules of thumb based on previous experiences with similar problems. The search often ends when the first minimally acceptable choice is encountered. The resulting choice may narrow the discrepancy between the desired and the actual states, but it is not likely to be the optimal solution. As the process is repeated, incremental improvements slowly reduce the discrepancy between the actual and desired states.

The Practical Approach

Because of the unrealistic demands of the rational approach and the limited, short-run orientation of the behavioural approach, neither is entirely satisfactory. However,

Bounded rationality is the idea that decision makers cannot deal with information about all the aspects and alternatives pertaining to a problem and therefore choose to tackle some meaningful subset of it.

The **behavioural approach** uses guidelines, suboptimizing, and satisficing in making decisions.

Suboptimizing is knowingly accepting less than the best possible outcome to avoid unintended negative effects on other aspects of the organization.

Satisficing is examining alternatives only until a solution that meets minimal requirements is found.

Although the rational approach to decision making suggests that we should fully evaluate all alternatives against all decision criteria, the reality is that many important decisions are not made in that manner. One reason for this is that decisions must sometimes be made very quickly and there simply is not time to fully evaluate all the alternatives. Individuals who trade shares on the Toronto Stock Exchange (TSX) must make snap decisions about whether to buy or sell. Many managerial decisions involve short time frames within which they must be made.

the worthwhile features of each can be combined into a practical approach to decision making, shown in Figure 9.4. The steps in this process are the same as in the rational approach; however, the conditions recognized by the behavioural approach are added to provide a more realistic process. For example, **the practical approach** suggests that rather than generating all alternatives, the decision maker should try to go beyond rules of thumb and satisficing limitations and generate as many alternatives as time, money, and other practicalities of the situation allow. In this synthesis of the two approaches, the rational approach provides an analytical framework for making decisions, whereas the behavioural approach provides a moderating influence.

In practice, decision makers use some hybrid of the rational, behavioural, and practical approaches to make the tough day-to-day decisions in running organizations. Some decision makers use a methodical process of gathering all available information, developing and evaluating alternatives, and seeking advice from knowledgable people before making a decision. Others fly from one decision to another, making seemingly hasty decisions and barking out orders to subordinates. The second group would seem to not use much information or a rational approach to making decisions. Recent research, however, has shown that managers who make decisions very quickly probably are using just as much, or more, information and generating and evaluating as many alternatives as slower, more methodical decision makers.[21]

> **The practical approach** to decision making combines the steps of the rational approach with the conditions in the behavioural approach to create a more realistic process for making decisions in organizations.

The Personal Approach

Although the models just described have provided significant insight into decision making, they do not fully explain the processes people engage in when they are nervous, worried, and agitated over making a decision that has major implications for them, their organization, or their families. In short, they still do not reflect the conditions under which many decisions are made. One attempt to provide a more realistic view of individual decision making is the model presented by Irving Janis and Leon Mann.[22] The Janis-Mann process, called the **conflict model**, is based on research in social psychology and individual decision processes and is a very personal approach to

> **The conflict model** is a very personal approach to decision making because it deals with the personal conflicts that people experience in particularly difficult decision situations.

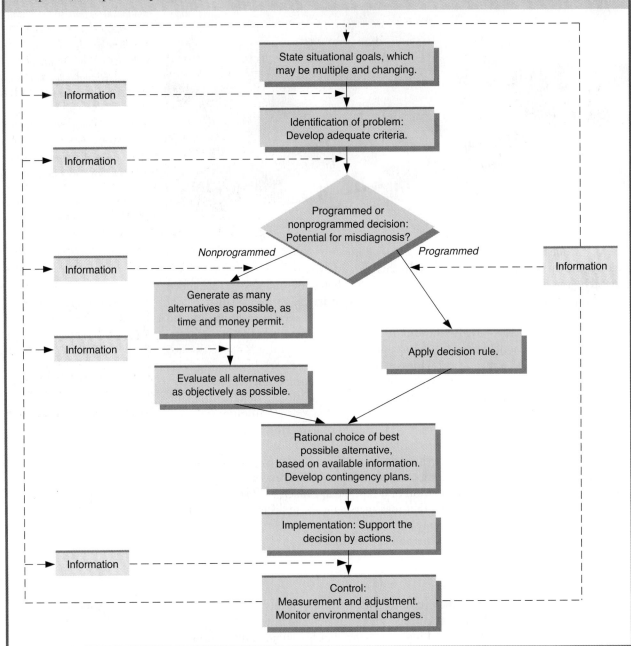

FIGURE 9.4

Practical Approach to Decision Making with Behavioural Guidelines

The practical model applies some of the conditions recognized by the behavioural approach to the rational approach to decision making. Although similar to the rational model, the practical approach recognizes personal limitations at each point (or step) in the process.

decision making. Although the model may appear complex, if you examine it one step at a time and follow the example in this section, you should easily understand how it works. The model has five basic characteristics:

1. It deals only with important life decisions—marriage, schooling, career, major organizational decisions—that commit the individual or the organization to a certain course of action following the decision.
2. It recognizes that procrastination and rationalization are mechanisms by which people avoid making difficult decisions and coping with the associated stress.
3. It explicitly acknowledges that some decisions probably will be wrong and that the fear of making an unsound decision can be a deterrent to making any decision at all.
4. It provides for **self-reactions**—comparisons of alternatives with internalized moral standards. Internalized moral standards guide decision making as much as economic and social outcomes do. A proposed course of action may offer many economic and social rewards, but if it violates the decision maker's moral convictions, it is unlikely to be chosen.
5. It recognizes that at times the decision maker is ambivalent about alternative courses of action; in such circumstances, it is very difficult to make a wholehearted commitment to a single choice. Major life decisions seldom allow compromise, however; usually they are either-or decisions that require commitment to one course of action.

The Janis-Mann conflict model of decision making is shown in Figure 9.5. A concrete example will help explain each step. Our hypothetical individual is Richard, a 30-year-old engineer with a working wife and two young children. Richard has been employed at a large manufacturing company for eight years. He keeps abreast of his career situation through visits with peers at work and in other companies, through feedback from his manager and others regarding his work and future with the firm, through the alumni magazine from his university, and from other sources. At work one morning, Richard learns that he has been passed over for a promotion for the second time in a year. He investigates the information, which can be considered negative feedback, and confirms it. As a result, he seeks out other information regarding his career at the company, the prospect of changing employers, and the possibility of going back to graduate school to get an MBA. At the same time, he asks himself: "Are the risks serious if I do not make a change?" If the answer is no, Richard will continue his present activities. In the model's terms, this option is called **unconflicted adherence**. If the answer is yes or maybe, Richard will move to the next question in the model.

The second step asks: "Are the risks serious if I do change?" If Richard goes on to this step, he will gather information about potential losses from making a change. He may, for example, find out whether he would lose health insurance and pension benefits if he changed jobs or went back to graduate school. If he believes that changing presents no serious risks, Richard will make the change, called an **unconflicted change**. Otherwise, he will move on to the next step.

But suppose Richard has determined that the risks are serious whether or not he makes a change. He believes he must make a change because he will not be promoted further in his present company, yet serious risks are also associated with making a change—perhaps loss of benefits, uncertain promotion opportunities in another company, and lost income from going to graduate school for two years. In the third step, Richard wonders: "Is it realistic to hope to find a better solution?" He continues to look for information that can help him make the decision. If the answer to this third question is no, Richard may give up the hope of finding anything better and opt for what Janis and Mann call **defensive avoidance**; that is, he will make no change and avoid

Self-reactions are comparisons of alternatives with internalized moral standards.

Unconflicted adherence entails continuing with current activities if doing so does not entail serious risks.

Unconflicted change involves making changes in present activities if doing so presents no serious risks.

Defensive avoidance entails making no changes in present activities and avoiding any further contact with associated issues because there appears to be no hope of finding a better solution.

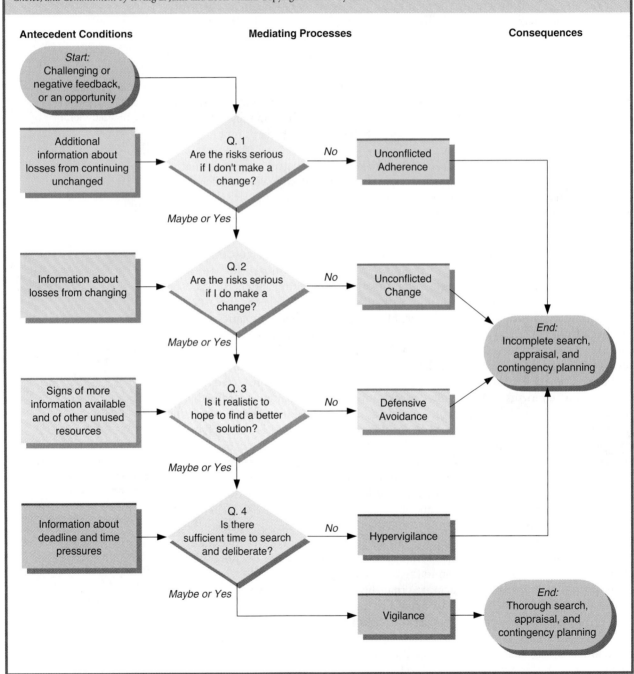

FIGURE 9.5

Janis-Mann Conflict Model of Decision Making

A decision maker answering "Yes" to all four questions will engage in vigilant information processing.

Source: Adapted with the permission of The Free Press, a division of Simon & Schuster from *Decision Making: A Psychological Analysis of Conflict, Choice, and Commitment by* Irving L. Janis and Leon Mann. Copyright © 1977 by The Free Press.

any further contact with the issue. A positive response, however, will move Richard to the next step.

Defensive avoidance entails making no changes in present activities and avoiding any further contact with associated issues because there appears to be no hope of finding a better solution. Here the decision maker, who now recognizes the serious risks involved yet expects to find a solution, asks: "Is there sufficient time to search and deliberate?" Richard now asks himself how quickly he needs to make a change. If he believes he has little time to deliberate, perhaps because of his age, he will experience what Janis and Mann call **hypervigilance**. In this state, he may suffer severe psychological stress and engage in frantic, superficial pursuit of some satisficing strategy. (This might also be called panic!) If, on the other hand, Richard believes he has two to three years to consider various alternatives, he will undertake **vigilant information processing**, in which he will thoroughly investigate all possible alternatives, weigh their costs and benefits before making a choice, and develop contingency plans.

Negative answers to the questions in the conflict model lead to responses of unconflicted adherence, unconflicted change, defensive avoidance, and hypervigilance. All are coping strategies that result in incomplete search, appraisal, and contingency planning. A decision maker who gives the same answer to all the questions will always engage in the same coping strategy. However, if the answers change as the situation changes, the individual's coping strategies may change as well. The decision maker who answers yes to each of the four questions is led to vigilant information processing, a process similar to that outlined in the rational decision-making model. The decision maker objectively analyzes the problem and all alternatives, thoroughly searches for information, carefully evaluates the consequences of all alternatives, and diligently plans for implementation and contingencies.

> **Hypervigilance** is frantic, superficial pursuit of some satisficing strategy.

> **Vigilant information processing** involves thoroughly investigating all possible alternatives, weighing their costs and benefits before making a decision, and developing contingency plans.

Related Behavioural Aspects of Decision Making

The behavioural, practical, and personal approach each has behavioural components, but the manager must be aware of other behavioural aspects of decision making as well. These include political forces, intuition, escalation of commitment, risk propensity, and ethics.

Political Forces in Decision Making

Political forces can play a major role in how decisions are made. We cover political behaviour in Chapter 10, but one major element of politics, coalitions, is especially relevant to decision making. A **coalition** is an informal alliance of individuals or groups formed to achieve a common goal. This common goal is often a preferred decision alternative. For example, coalitions of shareholders frequently band together to force a board of directors to make a certain decision. Indeed, many of the recent power struggles between management and dissident shareholders at Disney Corporation have relied on coalitions as each side tried to gain the upper hand against the other.[23]

> A **coalition** is an informal alliance of individuals or groups formed to achieve a common goal.

The impact of coalitions can be either positive or negative. They can help astute managers get the organization on a path toward effectiveness and profitability, or they can strangle well-conceived strategies and decisions. Managers must recognize when to use coalitions, how to assess whether coalitions are acting in the best interests of the organization, and how to constrain their dysfunctional effects.[24]

Intuition

Intuition is an innate belief about something without conscious consideration. Managers sometimes decide to do something because it "feels right" or they have a hunch. This feeling is usually not arbitrary, however. Rather, it is based on years of experience and practice in making decisions in similar situations. An inner sense may help managers make an occasional decision without going through a full-blown rational sequence of steps. The best-selling book by Malcolm Gladwell entitled *Blink: The Power of Thinking Without Thinking* made strong arguments that intuition is both used more commonly and results in better decisions than had previously been believed.

A few years ago the New York Yankees called three major running shoe manufacturers, Nike, Reebok, and Adidas, and informed them that they wanted to make a sponsorship deal. While Nike and Reebok were carefully and rationally assessing the possibilities, managers at Adidas quickly realized that a partnership with the Yankees made a lot of sense for them. They responded very quickly to the idea, and ended up hammering out a contract while the competitors were still analyzing details.[25] Of course, all managers, but most especially inexperienced ones, should be careful not to rely on intuition too heavily. If rationality and logic are continually flaunted for what "feels right," the odds are that disaster will strike one day.

Escalation of Commitment

Sometimes people continue to try to implement a decision despite clear and convincing evidence that substantial problems exist. **Escalation of commitment** is the tendency to persist in an ineffective course of action when evidence indicates that the project is doomed to failure. A good example is the decision by the government of British Columbia to hold EXPO '86 in Vancouver. Originally, the organizers expected the project to break even financially, so the province would not have to increase taxes to pay for it. As work progressed, it became clear that expenses would be far greater than had been projected. But organizers considered it too late to call off the event, despite the huge losses that obviously would occur. Eventually, the province conducted a $300 million lottery to try to cover the costs.[26] As we point out in the caption accompanying the photograph below, the British Columbia government may be facing a similar dilemma regarding the financing of the 2010 Winter Olympics to be held in Vancouver-Whistler. It is difficult for decision makers to ignore sunk costs in such large, public investments. Similar examples abound in stock market investments, in political and military situations, and in organizations developing any type of new project.

Barry Staw has suggested several possible reasons for escalation of commitment.[27] Some projects require much front-end investment and offer little return until the end, so the investor must stay in all the way to get any payoff. These all-or-nothing projects require unflagging commitment. Furthermore, investors' or project leaders' egos often become so involved with their project that their identities are totally wrapped up in it.[28] Failure or cancellation seems to threaten their reason for existence. Therefore, they continue to push the project as potentially successful despite strong evidence to the contrary. Other times, the social structure, group norms, and group cohesiveness support a project so strongly that cancellation is impossible. Organizational inertia also may force an organization to maintain a failing project. Thus, escalation of commitment is a phenomenon that has a strong foundation.

How can an individual or organization recognize that a project needs to be stopped before it results in throwing good money after bad? Several suggestions have been made; some are easy to put to use, and others are more difficult. Having good information about a project is always a first step in preventing the escalation problem.

freedom   liberté   ste'we gitah'

Find your freedom in sport
Vis ta liberté dans le sport
vancouver2010.com

Because highly public decisions are more prone to escalation of commitment, it is not surprising that some of the most glaring examples are associated with large international events such as the Olympic Games. The city of Montreal only finished paying off its debt for the 1976 Olympic Games in Montreal in December 2006. Interestingly, similar cost overruns are now plaguing the upcoming 2010 Vancouver Winter Olympic Games. Although the true costs are still under dispute, one report indicated that the Games might cost B.C. taxpayers $1 billion more than initially budgeted. However, the Games are still in the future so the end result will not be known for some time.

Usually it is possible to schedule regular sessions to discuss the project, its progress, the assumptions on which it originally was based, the current validity of these assumptions, and any problems with the project. An objective review is necessary to maintain control. The Escalation of Commitment and . . . Research box discusses the avoidance of the escalation of commitment phenomenon.

Some organizations have begun to make separate teams responsible for the development and implementation of a project to reduce ego involvement. Often the people who initiate a project are those who know the most about it, however, and their expertise can be valuable in the implementation process. Staw suggests that a general strategy for avoiding the escalation problem is to try to create an "experimenting organization in which every program and project is reviewed regularly and managers are evaluated on their contribution to the total organization rather than to specific projects.[29]

A recent example of an organization cutting its losses occurred when Canadian brewing giant Molson divested its interests in a Brazilian brewing company in 2006. Of course, this happened only after the organization learned a difficult lesson, which is described in greater detail in the chapter end case.

Risk Propensity and Decision Making

The behavioural element of **risk propensity** is the extent to which a decision maker is willing to gamble when making a decision. (Recall that we introduced risk propensity back in Chapter 3.) Some managers are cautious about every decision they make. They try to adhere to the rational model and are extremely conservative in what they do. Such managers are more likely to avoid mistakes, and they infrequently make decisions that lead to big losses. Other managers are extremely aggressive in making decisions and are willing to take risks.[30] They rely heavily on intuition, reach decisions quickly, and often risk big investments on their decisions. As in gambling, these managers are more likely than their conservative counterparts to achieve big successes with their

Risk propensity is the extent to which a decision maker is willing to gamble in making a decision.

Escalation of Commitment and . . .    RESEARCH

When Do Smart People Make Bad Decisions?

Even highly skilled individuals sometimes make bad decisions. Glen Whyte, a professor at the University of Toronto, has suggested that the way we frame our decisions has an impact on whether we will "throw good money after bad." When individuals frame decisions as a choice between losses, there is a tendency to prefer the riskier decision. Rather than accept a sure loss, decision makers prefer to take the chance that they will overcome the odds and succeed. Consideration of these sunk costs was probably behind a number of government decisions to invest further in money losing ventures.

Research by Whyte, Alan Saks, and Sterling Hook of the University of Toronto suggests that individuals with high self-efficacy are more likely to persist in the face of decision failure. Whyte and his colleagues note that previous success, an important factor in the development of self-efficacy, may make decision makers overconfident in their ability to turn a losing course of action into another success. In related research, Whyte suggests that efficacy at the group level can also account for bad decisions at the team level in groups contaminated by groupthink.

High collective efficacy can contribute to the negative framing of decisions and, when making critical decisions, can lead to a preference for riskier decisions and a greater concurrence seeking. These factors can cause the group to pursue a decision option that has a higher likelihood for failure. Subsequent research by Kevin Tasa of McMaster University and Whyte found that moderate levels of collective efficacy were more conducive to vigilant decision making (i.e., using decision-making procedures that are deliberate and analytic in their approach) than either high or low collective efficacy and that this vigilance led to better decisions.

Sources: Glen Whyte, Alan M. Saks, and Sterling Hook, "When Success Breeds Failure: The Role of Self-Efficacy in Escalating Commitment to a Losing Course of Action," *Journal of Organizational Behavior*, September 1997, pp. 415–432; Glen Whyte, "Recasting Janis's Groupthink Model: The Key Role of Collective Efficacy in Decision Fiascoes," *Organizational Behavior and Human Decision Processes*, February/March 1998, pp. 185–209; Kevin Tasa and Glen Whyte, "Collective Efficacy and Vigilant Problem Solving in Group Decision Making: A Non-Linear Model," *Organizational Behavior and Human Decision Processes*, 2005, pp. 119–129.

decisions; they are also more likely to incur greater losses.[31] The organization's culture is a prime ingredient in fostering different levels of risk propensity.

Ethics and Decision Making

Ethics are an individual's personal beliefs about what is right and wrong or good and bad.

As we noted in Chapter 2, **ethics** are a person's beliefs about what constitutes right and wrong behaviour. Ethical behaviour is that which conforms to generally accepted social norms; unethical behaviour does not conform to generally accepted social norms. Some decisions made by managers may have little or nothing to do with their own personal ethics, but many other decisions are influenced by the manager's ethics. For example, decisions involving such disparate issues as hiring and firing employees, dealing with customers and suppliers, setting wages and assigning tasks, and maintaining one's expense account are all subject to ethical influences.

In general, ethical dilemmas for managers may centre on direct personal gain, indirect personal gain, or simple personal preferences. Consider, for example, a top executive contemplating a decision about a potential takeover. His or her stock option package may result in enormous personal gain if the decision goes one way, even though shareholders may benefit more if the decision goes the other way. An indirect personal gain may result when a decision does not directly add value to a manager's personal worth but does enhance her or his career. Or the manager may face a choice about relocating a company facility where one of the options is closest to his

Downsizing Decisions and . . . **CHANGE**

Dealing with Losses at DaimlerChrysler

As discussed in Chapter 3, the decision by management to downsize the organization by laying off employees is a frequent response to declining profits. And sometimes downsizing has the desired effect of reducing costs and returning the firm to profitability. However, in many cases, the decision to downsize also has a negative impact on the organization's ability to be innovative. Take the automobile sector as an example. In 2006, DaimlerChrysler lost well over $1 billion and responded by laying off 13 000 workers in North America, including 2000 at their Ontario plants in Windsor and Brampton. The other members of the North American "Big Three," Ford and GM, responded in a similar fashion. In the meantime, Japanese auto makers, Toyota and Honda, are expanding their operations in Ontario. Toyota, for example, announced its intention to build a new plant in Woodstock, not far from its existing facilities in Cambridge.

So, what is causing the stark differences in the performance of the Japanese auto makers from that of their North American counterparts? The answer appears to be innovative decision making. For years, GM, Ford, and DaimlerChrysler have been increasing their capacity to build luxury gas-guzzlers such as SUVs. However, recent events such as increasing oil and fuel prices and increased public concern for environmental issues have resulted in a rapid change in the new vehicle market. Consumers became more interested in saving money by driving more fuel efficient vehicles and protecting the environment by driving vehicles that use alternative energy sources. Both Toyota and Honda, sensing this change in the market, focused their development efforts on fuel efficiency and hybrid technology.

And how are downsizing and innovation connected? For one thing, employees who survive downsizing tend not to be invested in the company. Once the layoff notices begin to be issued, their thoughts turn to when they could be the next ones to go. And when employees are not invested in a company, innovation tends to suffer. The siege mentality experienced by survivors changes the culture of the organization from one of innovation to one of self-protection.

Source: Jay Somerset, "Downsize this? Cutbacks 1, Innovation 0," *Canadian Business*, 2 April 2007, www.canadianbusiness.com.

or her residence. Sometimes, managers' decisions involve outright deception for personal gain.

Managers should carefully and deliberately consider the ethical context of every one of their decisions. The goal, of course, is for the manager to make the decision that is in the best interest of the firm, as opposed to the best interest of the manager. This requires personal honesty and integrity. Managers also find it helpful to discuss potential ethical dilemmas with colleagues. Others can often provide an objective view of a situation that may help a manager avoid unintentionally making an unethical decision.

Group Decision Making

People in organizations work in a variety of groups—formal and informal, permanent and temporary. Most of these groups make decisions that affect the welfare of the organization and the people in it. Here we discuss several issues surrounding how groups make decisions: group polarization, groupthink, and group problem solving.

Group Polarization

Members' attitudes and opinions with respect to an issue or a solution may change during group discussion. Some studies of this tendency have showed the change to be a fairly consistent movement toward a more risky solution, called "risky shift."[32] Other studies and analyses have revealed that the group-induced shift is not always toward more risk; the group is just as likely to move toward a more conservative view.[33] Generally, **group polarization** occurs when the average of the group members' post-discussion attitudes tends to be more extreme than average pre-discussion attitudes.[34]

Group polarization is the tendency for a group's average post-discussion attitudes to be more extreme than its average pre-discussion attitudes.

Several features of group discussion contribute to polarization.[35] When individuals discover in group discussion that others share their opinions, they may feel more strongly about their opinions, resulting in a more extreme view. Persuasive arguments also can encourage polarization. If members who strongly support a particular position are able to express themselves cogently in the discussion, less avid supporters of the position may become convinced that it is correct. In addition, members may believe that because the group is deciding, they are not individually responsible for the decision or its outcomes. This diffusion of responsibility may enable them to accept and support a decision more radical than those they would make as individuals.

Polarization can profoundly affect group decision making. If group members are known to lean toward a particular decision before a discussion, it may be expected that their post-decision position will be even more extreme. Understanding this phenomenon may be useful for one who seeks to affect their decision.

Groupthink

As discussed in Chapter 8, highly cohesive groups and teams often are very successful at meeting their goals, although they sometimes have serious difficulties as well. One problem that can occur is groupthink. **Groupthink**, according to Irving L. Janis, is "a mode of thinking that people engage in when they are deeply involved in a cohesive in-group, when the members' strivings for unanimity override their motivation to realistically appraise alternative courses of action."[36] When groupthink occurs, the group unknowingly makes unanimity rather than the best decision its goal. Individual members may perceive that raising objections is not appropriate. Groupthink can occur in many decision-making situations in organizations. The current trend toward increasing use of teams in organizations may increase instances of groupthink due to the susceptibility of self-managing teams to this type of thought.[37]

Groupthink is a mode of thinking that occurs when members of a group are deeply involved in a cohesive in-group and desire for unanimity offsets their motivation to appraise alternative courses of action.

Symptoms of Groupthink   Figure 9.6 outlines the revised groupthink process. The three primary conditions that foster the development of groupthink are cohesiveness, the leader's promotion of his or her preferred solution, and insulation of the group from experts' opinions. Based on analysis of the disaster associated with the explosion of the space shuttle *Challenger* in 1986, the original idea was enhanced to include the effects of increased time pressure and the role of the leader in not stimulating critical thinking in developing the symptoms of groupthink.[38] A group in which groupthink has taken hold exhibits eight well-defined symptoms:

1. *An illusion of invulnerability*, shared by most or all members, that creates excessive optimism and encourages extreme risk taking.
2. *Collective efforts to rationalize or discount warnings* that might lead members to reconsider assumptions before recommitting themselves to past policy decisions.
3. *An unquestioned belief in the group's inherent morality*, inclining members to ignore the ethical and moral consequences of their decisions.
4. *Stereotyped views of "enemy" leaders as too evil* to warrant genuine attempts to negotiate or as too weak or stupid to counter whatever risky attempts are made to defeat their purposes.

FIGURE 9.6

The Groupthink Process

Groupthink can occur when a highly cohesive group with a directive leader is under time pressure; it can result in a defective decision process and low probability of successful outcomes.

Source: Gregory Moorhead, Richard Ference, and Chris P. Neck, "Group Decision Fiascoes Continue: Space Shuttle *Challenger* and a Revised Groupthink Framework, *Human Relations*, 1991, vol. 44, 1991, pp. 539–550. Used by permission of Sage Publications.

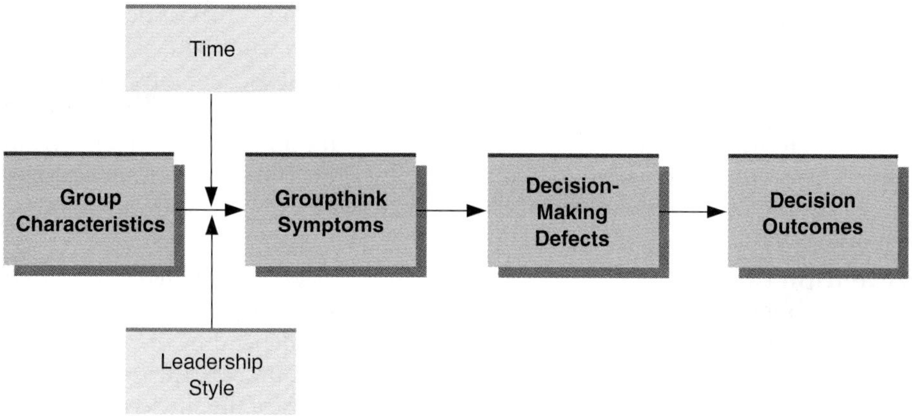

5. *Direct pressure on a member who expresses strong arguments against any of the group's stereotypes, illusions, or commitments*, making clear that such dissent is contrary to what is expected of loyal members.
6. *Self-censorship of deviations* from the apparent group consensus, reflecting each member's inclination to minimize the importance of his or her doubts and counterarguments.
7. *A shared illusion of unanimity*, resulting partly from self-censorship of deviations, augmented by the false assumption that silence means consent.
8. *The emergence of self-appointed "mindguards,"* members who protect the group from adverse information that might shatter their shared complacency about the effectiveness and morality of their decisions.[39]

Janis contends that the group involved in the 1972 Watergate cover-up in the United States—President Richard Nixon, H. R. Haldeman, John Ehrlichman, and John Dean—may have been a victim of groupthink. Evidence of most of the groupthink symptoms can be found in the unedited transcripts of the group's deliberations.[40]

Decision-Making Defects and Decision Quality When groupthink dominates group deliberations, the likelihood that decision-making defects will occur increases. The group is less likely to survey a full range of alternatives and may focus on only a few (often one or two). In discussing a preferred alternative, the group may fail to examine it for nonobvious risks and drawbacks. The group may not reexamine previously rejected alternatives for nonobvious gains or some means of reducing apparent costs even when they receive new information. The group may reject expert opinions that run counter to its own views and may choose to consider only information that supports its preferred solution. A major contributing factor to the groupthink may be the collective efficacy of the team, which can be defined as a group's belief in their ability to successfully pursue a particular course of action. The decision to launch the space shuttle *Challenger* in January 1986 and the explosion of the space shuttle *Columbia* in February 2003 may have been a product of groupthink, because, due to the increased time pressure to make a decision, overconfidence of the group, and the leaders' style, negative information was ignored by the group that made the decision.[41] Finally, the group may not consider any potential setbacks or counter moves by competing groups and therefore may fail to develop contingency plans. It should be noted that Janis contends that these six defects may arise from other common problems as well: fatigue, prejudice, inaccurate information, information overload, and ignorance.[42]

Defects in decision making do not always lead to bad outcomes or defeats. Even if its own decision-making processes are flawed, one side can win a battle because of the poor decisions made by the other side's leaders. Nevertheless, decisions produced by defective processes are less likely to succeed.

Although the arguments for the existence of groupthink are convincing, the hypothesis has not been subjected to rigorous empirical examination. Research supports parts of the model but leaves some questions unanswered.[43]

Prevention of Groupthink   Several suggestions have been offered to help managers reduce the probability of groupthink in group decision making.[44] Summarized in Table 9.2, these prescriptions fall into four categories depending on whether they apply to the leader, the organization, the individual, or the process. All are designed to facilitate the critical evaluation of alternatives and discourage the single-minded pursuit of unanimity.

Participation

A major issue in group decision making is the degree to which employees should participate in the process. Early management theories, such as those of the scientific management

TABLE 9.2

Prescriptions for Preventing Groupthink

A. Leader prescriptions
1. Assign everyone the role of critical evaluator.
2. Be impartial; do not state preferences.
3. Assign the devil's advocate role to at least one group member.
4. Use outside experts to challenge the group.
5. Be open to dissenting points of view.

B. Organizational prescriptions
1. Set up several independent groups to study the same issue.
2. Train managers and group leaders in groupthink prevention techniques.

C. Individual prescriptions
1. Be a critical thinker.
2. Discuss group deliberations with a trusted outsider; report back to the group.

D. Process prescriptions
1. Periodically break the group into subgroups to discuss the issues.
2. Take time to study external factors.
3. Hold second-chance meetings to rethink issues before making a commitment.

school, advocated a clear separation between the duties of managers and workers: Management was to make the decisions, and employees were to implement them.[45] Other approaches have urged that employees be allowed to participate in decisions to increase their ego involvement, motivation, and satisfaction.[46] Numerous research studies have shown that whereas employees who seek responsibility and challenge on the job may find participation in the decision-making process both motivating and enriching, other employees may regard such participation as a waste of time and a management imposition.[47]

Whether employee participation in decision making is appropriate depends on the situation. In tasks that require an estimation, a prediction, or a judgment of accuracy—usually referred to as judgmental tasks—groups typically are superior to individuals, simply because more people contribute to the decision-making process.[48] However, one especially capable individual may make a better judgment than a group.

In problem-solving tasks, groups generally produce more and better solutions than do individuals. But groups take far longer than individuals to develop solutions and make decisions. An individual or very small group may be able to accomplish some things much faster than a large, unwieldy group or organization. In addition, individual decision making avoids the special problems of group decision making, such as groupthink or group polarization. If the problem to be solved is fairly straightforward, it may be more appropriate to have a single capable individual concentrate on solving it. On the other hand, complex problems are more appropriate for groups. Such problems can often be divided into parts and the parts assigned to individuals or small groups, who bring their results back to the group for discussion and decision making.

An additional advantage to group decision making is that it often creates greater interest in the task.[49] Heightened interest can increase the time and effort given to the task, resulting in more ideas, a more thorough search for solutions, better evaluation of alternatives, and improved decision quality.

The Vroom-Yetton-Jago model of leadership (discussed in Chapter 11) is one popular approach to determining the appropriate degree of employee participation.[50] The model includes decision styles that vary from autocratic (the leader alone makes the decision) to democratic (the group makes the decision, with each member having an equal say). The choice of style rests on eight considerations that concern the characteristics of the situation and the subordinates.

Participation in decision making is also related to organizational structure. For example, decentralization involves delegating some decision-making authority throughout the organizational hierarchy. The more decentralized the organization, the more its employees tend to participate in decision making. Whether one views participation in decision making as pertaining to leadership, organization structure, or motivation, it remains an important aspect of organizations that continues to occupy managers and organizational scholars.[51]

Group Problem Solving

A typical interacting group may have difficulty with any of several steps in the decision-making process. One common problem arises in the alternative-generation phase: The search may be arbitrarily ended before all plausible alternatives have been identified. Several types of group interactions can have this effect. If members immediately express their reactions to the alternatives as they are first proposed, potential contributors may begin to censor their ideas to avoid embarrassing criticism from the group. Less confident group members, intimidated by members who have more experience,

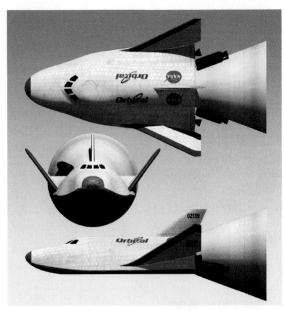

Brainstorming is a common technique for promoting the identification of new alternatives in group decision-making situations. Engineers at Northrop Grumman are helping the next generation of space vehicles to replace the aging shuttle fleet. The firm often uses groups to brainstorm new ideas. One such group, for instance, came up with this possible option—a "Space Taxi" that would take off like an airplane but still be capable of supersonic speeds.

Brainstorming is a technique used in the idea-generation phase of decision making that assists in development of numerous alternative courses of action.

With the **nominal group technique (NGT)**, group members follow a generate-discuss-vote cycle until they reach an appropriate decision.

higher status, or more power, also may censor their ideas for fear of embarrassment or punishment. In addition, the group leader may limit idea generation by enforcing requirements concerning time, appropriateness, cost, feasibility, and the like.

To improve the alternative-generation process, managers can employ any of three techniques—brainstorming, the nominal group technique (NGT), or the Delphi technique—to stimulate the group's problem-solving capabilities.

Brainstorming   **Brainstorming**, a technique made popular in the 1950s, is most often used in the idea-generation phase of decision making and is intended to solve problems that are new to the organization and have major consequences. In brainstorming, the group convenes specifically to generate alternatives. The members present ideas and clarify them with brief explanations. Each idea is recorded in full view of all members, usually on a flip chart. To avoid self-censoring, no attempts to evaluate the ideas are allowed. Group members are encouraged to offer any ideas that occur to them, even those that seem too risky or impossible to implement. (The absence of such ideas, in fact, is evidence that group members are engaging in self-censorship.) In a subsequent session, after the ideas have been recorded and distributed to members for review, the alternatives are evaluated.

The intent of brainstorming is to produce totally new ideas and solutions by stimulating the creativity of group members and encouraging them to build on the contributions of others. Brainstorming does not provide the resolution to the problem, an evaluation scheme, or the decision itself. Instead, it should produce a list of alternatives that is more innovative and comprehensive than one developed by the typical interacting group.

The Nominal Group Technique (NGT)   The **nominal group technique** is another means of improving group decision making. Whereas brainstorming is used primarily to generate alternatives, this technique may be used in other phases of decision making, such as identification of the problem and of appropriate criteria for evaluating alternatives. To use this technique, a group of individuals convenes to address an issue. The issue is described to the group, and each individual writes a list of ideas; no discussion among the members is permitted. Following the five- to ten-minute idea-generation period, individual members take turns reporting their ideas, one at a time, to the group. The ideas are recorded on a flip chart, and members are encouraged to add to the list by building on the ideas of others. After all ideas have been presented, the members may discuss them and continue to build on them or proceed to the next phase. This part of the process can also be carried out without a face-to-face meeting or by mail, telephone, or computer. A meeting, however, helps members develop a group feeling and puts interpersonal pressure on the members to do their best in developing their lists.[52]

After the discussion, members privately vote on or rank the ideas or report their preferences in some other agreed-upon way. Reporting is private to reduce any feelings of intimidation. After voting, the group may discuss the results and continue to generate and discuss ideas. The generation-discussion-vote cycle can continue until an appropriate decision is reached.

The nominal group technique has two principal advantages. It helps overcome the negative effects of power and status differences among group members, and it can be used to explore problems to generate alternatives, or to evaluate them. Its primary disadvantage lies in its structured nature, which may limit creativity.

The Delphi Technique   The **Delphi technique** was originally developed by Rand Corporation as a method to systematically gather the judgments of experts for use in developing forecasts. It is designed for groups that do not meet face to face. For instance, the product-development manager of a major toy manufacturer might use the Delphi technique to probe the views of industry experts to forecast developments in the dynamic toy market.

> The **Delphi technique** is a method of systematically gathering judgments of experts for use in developing forecasts.

The manager who wants the input of a group is the central figure in the process. After recruiting participants, the manager develops a questionnaire for them to complete. The questionnaire is relatively simple in that it contains straightforward questions that deal with the issue, trends in the area, new technological developments, and other factors the manager is interested in. The manager summarizes the responses and reports back to the experts with another questionnaire. This cycle may be repeated as many times as necessary to generate the information the manager needs.

The Delphi technique is useful when experts are physically dispersed, anonymity is desired, or the participants are known to have trouble communicating with one another because of extreme differences of opinion.[53] On the one hand, this method also avoids the intimidation problems that may exist in decision-making groups. On the other hand, the technique eliminates the often fruitful results of direct interaction among group members.

Creativity in Organizations

Creativity is yet another important component of individual behaviour in organizations. The ability of its workers to be creative can sometimes mean the difference between success and failure for organizations in today's fast-paced environment. **Creativity** is the ability to generate new ideas or to conceive of new perspectives on existing ideas. What makes a person creative? How do people become creative? How does the creative process work? Although psychologists have not yet completely answered these questions, examining a few general patterns helps us understand the sources of individual creativity within organizations.[54]

> **Creativity** is a person's ability to generate new ideas or to conceive of new perspectives on existing ideas.

The Creative Individual

Numerous researchers have attempted to describe the common attributes of creative individuals. These attributes generally fall into three categories: *background experiences, personal traits,* and *cognitive abilities.*[55]

Background Experiences and Creativity   Researchers have observed that many creative individuals were raised in environments that nurtured creativity. Mozart was raised in a family of musicians and began composing and performing music at age six. Pierre and Marie Curie, great scientists in their own right, raised a daughter, Irene, who won the Nobel Prize in chemistry. Thomas Edison's creativity was nurtured by his mother.

Personal Traits and Creativity   Certain personal traits have also been linked to creativity in individuals. The traits shared by most creative people are openness, an attraction to complexity, high levels of energy, independence and autonomy, strong self-confidence, and a strong belief that one is, in fact, creative. Individuals who possess these traits are more likely to be creative than are those who do not.

Cognitive Abilities and Creativity   Cognitive abilities are an individual's power to think intelligently and to analyze situations and data effectively. Intelligence may be a precondition for individual creativity—although most creative people are highly intelligent, not all intelligent people are necessarily creative. Creativity is also linked with the ability to think divergently and convergently. *Divergent thinking* allows people to see differences among situations, phenomena, or events. *Convergent thinking* allows people to see similarities among situations, phenomena, or events. Creative people are generally very skilled at both divergent and convergent thinking.

To develop these abilities in their employees, many large Canadian organizations, such as the Royal Bank and Ciba Vision, provide training in creative thinking. Interestingly, Japanese managers have recently questioned their own creative abilities. The concern is that their emphasis on group harmony has perhaps stifled individual initiative and hampered the development of individual creativity. As a result, many Japanese firms, including Omron Corporation, Fuji Photo, and Shimizu Corporation, have launched employee training programs intended to boost the creativity of their employees.[56]

The Creative Process

Although creative people often report that ideas seem to come to them in a flash, individual creative activity actually tends to progress through a series of stages.

While Figure 9.7 summarizes the major stages of the creative process, we use the story of Bruce Roth to illustrate how the creative process can work in an individual. Keep in mind that not all creative activity has to follow these four stages, but much of it does.

Creativity often makes the difference between business success and failure, particularly among those starting new businesses. Albert Lai is no stranger to entrepreneurial ventures. At age 18, he founded MyDesktop, which he sold for seven figures in 1999. By the age of 28, Lai had sold a number of companies worth millions, and he is not finished yet. He is already planning another new venture and expects to start several more in the future. One of the keys to Lai's success is his ability to develop simple, innovative solutions to complex problems.

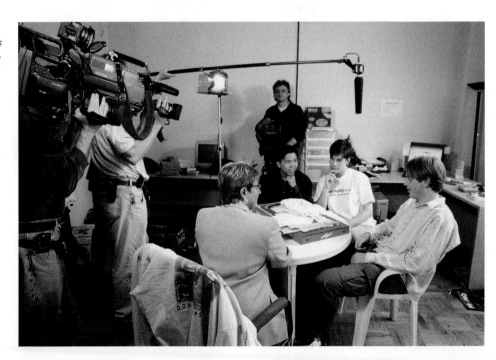

Preparation   The creative process normally begins with a period of **preparation**. Formal education and training are usually the most efficient ways to acquire a strong foundation of knowledge. To make a creative contribution to business management or business services, people must usually receive formal training and education in business. This is one reason for the strong demand for undergraduate and master's-level business education. Formal business education can help a person get up to speed and begin making creative contributions quickly. Managers' experiences on the job after completing formal training can also contribute to the creative process. Bruce Roth earned a Ph.D. in chemistry and then spent years working in the pharmaceutical industry learning more and more about chemical compounds and how they work in human beings. In an important sense, the education and training of creative people never really ends. It continues as long as they remain interested in the world and curious about how things work.

Preparation, usually the first stage in the creative process, includes education and formal training.

Incubation   The second phase of the creative process is **incubation**— a period of less intense conscious concentration during which the knowledge and ideas acquired during preparation mature and develop. A curious aspect of incubation is that it is often helped along by pauses in concentrated rational thought. Some creative people rely on physical activity such as jogging or swimming to provide a break from thinking. Others read or listen to music. Sometimes sleep may even supply the needed pause. Bruce Roth eventually joined Warner-Lambert, an up-and-coming drug company, to help develop medication to lower cholesterol. In his spare time, Roth read mystery novels and hiked in the mountains. He later acknowledged that this was when he did his best thinking.

Insight   Usually occurring after preparation and incubation, insight is a breakthrough in which the creative person achieves a new understanding of some problem or situation. **Insight** represents a coming together of all the scattered thoughts and ideas that were maturing during incubation. It may occur suddenly or develop slowly over time. Insight can be triggered by some external event, such as a new experience or an encounter with new data that forces the individual to think about old issues and problems in new ways, or it can be a completely internal event in which patterns of thought finally coalesce in ways that generate new understanding. One day Bruce Roth was reviewing some data from some earlier studies that had found the new drug under development to be no more effective than other drugs already available. But this time he saw some statistical relationships that had not been identified previously. He knew then that he had a major breakthrough on his hands.

Verification   Once an insight has occurred, **verification** determines the validity or truthfulness of the insight. For many creative ideas, verification includes scientific experiments to determine whether the insight actually leads to the results expected. Verification may also include the development of a product or service prototype. A *prototype* is one product (or very few) built to see if the ideas behind them actually work. Product prototypes are rarely sold to the public, but are very valuable in verifying the insights developed in the creative process. Once the new product or service is

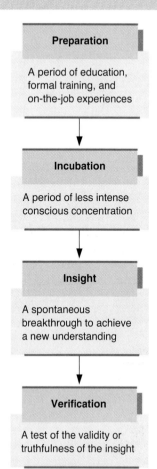

FIGURE 9.7

The Creative Process

The creative process generally follows the four steps illustrated here. Of course, there are exceptions and the process is occasionally different. In most cases, however, these steps capture the essence of the creative process.

Preparation
A period of education, formal training, and on-the-job experiences

Incubation
A period of less intense conscious concentration

Insight
A spontaneous breakthrough to achieve a new understanding

Verification
A test of the validity or truthfulness of the insight

Incubation is the stage of less intense conscious concentration during which a creative person lets the knowledge and ideas acquired during preparation mature and develop.

Insight is the stage in the creative process when all the scattered thoughts and ideas that were maturing during incubation come together to produce a breakthrough.

In **verification,** the final stage of the creative process, the validity or truthfulness of the insight is determined.

developed, verification in the marketplace is the ultimate test of the creative idea behind it. Bruce Roth and his colleagues set to work testing the new drug compound and eventually won approval from the organizations that oversee the licensing of new drugs. The drug, named Lipitor, is already the largest-selling pharmaceutical in history. And Pfizer, the firm that bought Warner-Lambert in a hostile takeover, is expected to soon earn more than $10 billion a year on the drug.[57]

Enhancing Creativity in Organizations

Managers who wish to enhance and promote creativity in their organizations can do so in a variety of ways. One important method is to make it a part of the organization's culture, often through explicit goals. Firms that truly want to stress creativity, such as 3M and Rubbermaid, for example, state as a goal that some percentage of future revenues are to be gained from new products. This clearly communicates that creativity and innovation are valued.

Another important part of enhancing creativity is to reward creative successes, while being careful to not punish creative failures. Many ideas that seem worthwhile on paper fail to work in reality. If the first person to come up with an idea that fails is fired or otherwise punished, others in the organization will become more cautious in their own work, and fewer creative ideas will emerge.

Summary of Key Points

- Decision making is the process of choosing one alternative from several. The basic elements of decision making include choosing a goal, considering alternative courses of action, assessing potential outcomes of the alternatives each with its own value relative to the goal, and choosing one alternative based on evaluation of the outcomes. Information is available regarding the alternatives, outcomes, and values.

- Programmed decisions are well-structured, recurring decisions made according to set decision rules. Non-programmed decisions involve nonroutine, poorly structured situations with unclear sources of information; these decisions cannot be made according to existing decision rules. Decision making may also be classified according to the information available. The classifications—certainty, risk, and uncertainty—reflect the amount of information available regarding the outcomes of alternatives.

- The rational approach views decision making as a completely rational process in which goals are established, a problem is identified, alternatives are generated and evaluated, a choice is made and implemented, and control is exercised. The behavioural model is characterized by the use of procedures and rules of thumb, suboptimizing, and satisficing. The rational and behavioural views can be combined into a practical model. The Janis-Mann conflict model recognizes the personal anxiety individuals face when they must make important decisions.

- Two related behavioural aspects of decision making are escalation of commitment and ethics. Escalation of commitment to an ineffective course of action occurs in many decision situations. It may be caused by psychological, social, ego, and organizational factors. Ethics also play an important role in many managerial decisions.

- Group decision making involves problems as well as benefits. One possible problem is group polarization, the shift of members' attitudes and opinions to a more extreme position following group discussion. Another difficulty is groupthink, a mode of thinking in which the urge toward unanimity overrides the critical appraisal of alternatives. Yet another concern involves employee participation in decision making.

The appropriate degree of participation depends on the characteristics of the situation.

- Creativity is a person's ability to generate new ideas or to conceive of new perspectives on existing ideas. Background experiences, personal traits, and cognitive abilities affect an individual's creativity. The creative process usually involves four steps: preparation, incubation, insight, and verification.

Discussion Questions

1. Some have argued that people, not organizations, make decisions and that the study of "organizational" decision making is therefore pointless. Do you agree with this argument? Why or why not?

2. What information did you use in deciding to enter the school you now attend?

3. When your alarm goes off each morning, you have a decision to make: whether to get up and go to school or work, or to stay in bed and sleep longer. Is this a programmed or nonprogrammed decision? Why?

4. Describe at least three points in the decision-making process at which information plays an important role.

5. How does the role of information in the rational model of decision making differ from the role of information in the behavioural model?

6. Why does it make sense to discuss several different models of decision making?

7. Can you think of a time when you satisficed when making a decision? Have you ever suboptimized?

8. Describe a situation in which you experienced escalation of commitment to an ineffective course of action. What did you do about it? Do you wish you had handled it differently? Why or why not?

9. How are group polarization and groupthink similar? How do they differ?

10. Describe a situation in which you came up with a new idea following the basic steps in the creative process described in the text.

Experiencing Organizational Behaviour

Purpose: This exercise will allow you to take part in making a hypothetical decision and help you understand the difference between programmed and nonprogrammed decisions.

Format: You will be asked to perform a task both individually and as a member of a group.

Procedure: Following is a list of typical organizational decisions. Your task is to determine whether they are programmed or nonprogrammed. Number your paper, and write P for programmed or N for nonprogrammed next to each number.

Your instructor will divide the class into groups of four to seven. All groups should have approximately the same number of members. Your task as a group is to make the determinations outlined above. In arriving at your decisions, do not use techniques such as voting or negotiating ("Okay, I'll give in on this one if you'll give in on that one").

The group should discuss the difference between programmed and nonprogrammed decisions and each decision situation until all members at least partly agree with the decision.

Decision List

1. Hiring a specialist for the research staff in a highly technical field.

2. Assigning workers to daily tasks.

3. Determining the size of dividend to be paid to shareholders in the ninth consecutive year of strong earnings growth.

4. Deciding whether to officially excuse an employee's absence for medical reasons.

5. Selecting the location for another branch of a 150-branch bank in a large city.

6. Approving the appointment of a new law school graduate to the corporate legal staff.

7. Making annual assignments of graduate assistants to faculty.

8. Approving an employee's request to attend a local seminar in his or her special area of expertise.

9. Selecting the appropriate outlets for print advertisements for a new college textbook.

10. Determining the location for a new fast-food restaurant in a small but growing town on the major highway between two very large metropolitan areas.

Follow-up Questions

1. To what extent did group members disagree about which decisions were programmed and which were nonprogrammed?

2. What primary factors did the group discuss in making each decision?

3. Were there any differences between the members' individual lists and the group lists? If so, discuss the reasons for the differences.

Self-Assessment Exercise

Rational Versus Practical Approaches to Decision Making

Managers need to recognize and understand the different models that they use to make decisions. They also need to understand the extent to which they are predisposed to be relatively autocratic or relatively participative in making decisions. To develop your skills in these areas, perform the following activity.

First, assume you are the manager of a firm that is rapidly growing. Recent sales figures strongly suggest the need for a new plant to produce more of your firm's products. Key issues include where the plant might be built and how large it might be (for example, a small, less expensive plant to meet current needs that could be expanded in the future versus a large and more expensive plant that might have excess capacity today but meet long-term needs better).

Using the rational approach diagrammed in Figure 9.3, trace the process the manager might use to make the decision. Note the kinds of information that might be required and the extent to which other people might need to be involved in making the decision at each point.

Next, go back and look at various steps in the process where behavioural processes might intervene and affect the overall process. Will bounded rationality come into play? How about satisficing?

Finally, use the practical approach shown in Figure 9.4 and trace through the process again. Again note where other input may be needed. Try to identify places in the process where the rational and practical approaches are likely to result in the same outcome and places where differences are most likely to occur.

Source: Reprinted with the permission of Pocket Books, a division of Simon & Schuster, from *The Win-Win Negotiator: How to Negotiate Favorable Agreements That Last* by Ross R. Reck, Ph.D., and Brian G. Long, Ph.D. Copyright © 1985, 1987 by Brian G. Long and Ross R. Reck.

Organizational Behaviour
Case for Discussion

Decision Making at Molson's Brewery

Molson Breweries is one of Canada's oldest and largest breweries. It was founded in Montreal in 1786 by John Molson and today has over 3000 employees across Canada. The company name is ubiquitous in Canada. Even their flagship beer is called Canadian! In addition to their brewing business, the company owned the National Hockey League's Montreal Canadiens, one of the most storied franchises in sports.

Yet, despite having such dominance in the Canadian beer market, the company fell on hard times in the 1990s. In the years leading up to that period, management pursued a strategy of diversification and, in addition to the Canadiens, Molson owned varied companies such as Beaver Lumber and Home Depot, among others. However, this lack of focus partially resulted in Molson's market share slipping from 52.2 percent in 1989 to 45.8 percent in 1997. In addition, the beer market in Canada had been going through an extended flat period and there was greater competition from imports and microbreweries.

In 1999, Dan O'Neill joined Molson as President and CEO, after stints in the United States with Campbell Soup Co. and H. J. Heinz. The early years of O'Neill's tenure at the helm of Molson were marked with significant success. His first task was to cut $100 million from Molson's costs over a three-year period, which he referred to as "Project 100." In that period, O'Neill closed underperforming facilities and sold a large portion of

Molson's shares in the Montreal Canadiens. In 2000, Molson launched the now famous "I AM CANADIAN" marketing campaign. O'Neill's cost cutting measures were so successful he raised the target to $150 million. Within three years, operating profit had increased by two thirds and company shares tripled in value.

Despite O'Neill's success at returning Molson to profitability, the company's market share in Canada continued to slide. The world beer market was consolidating and Molson's chief Canadian rival, Labatt, became a division of Belgium's Interbrew, one of the largest breweries in the world. Sensing a need to increase Molson's presence on the international market to compensate for declining domestic sales, O'Neill engineered the 2002 purchase of Brazilian brewer Cervejarias Kaiser SA for U.S. $765 million. At the time, the move was hailed with great fanfare. However, things turned sour for Molson very quickly.

Kaiser was purchased from the Coca-Cola Bottlers of Brazil, who held 76 percent of the company's stock and were responsible for distribution of the product. Upon entering the Brazilian market, Molson was forced to rely on these same bottlers for distribution of their product. This arrangement did not go well for Molson. Kaiser's market share in Brazil plummeted and Molson's profits and share prices fell accordingly. The move into Brazil, once seen as Molson's beginnings as a player on the world beer market, considerably weakened the company's financial position, making Canada's largest independent brewer a takeover target. In 2004, Molson announced that it would merge with Coors, the third-largest brewer in the United States to form Molson Coors Brewing Co. In May, 2005, O'Neill announced that he was leaving the company. In January, 2006, Molson Coors sold its stake in Cervejarias Kaiser for less than one tenth what Molson had paid for it less than four years earlier.

Case Questions

1. Identify the many different decisions that Molson and Dan O'Neill made that eventually led to its problems.

2. What type of decision was each of these?

3. Which of the decision-making problems described in the chapter may have occurred here?

Sources: Andy Holloway, "The Molson Way," *Canadian Business*, April 9, 2007, www.canadianbusiness.com; Martin Braun, "Amid Feuding at Molson, CEO O'Neill Stands Tall," *Globeandmail.com*, July 3, 2004; Steve Maich, "Molson to Merge with Coors," *Maclean's*, August 2, 2004, www.thecanadianencyclopedia.com; "Molson Gulps Down Brazilian Brewery Kaiser," *CBC News*, March 18, 2002, www.cbc.ca; "Molson Sells Stake in Ill-Fated Brazilian Brewery," *CBC News*, January 16, 2006, www.cbc.ca; "The Molson Companies Limited Business Information, Profile, and History," companies.jrank.org, May 10, 2007.

SELF TEST

You have read the chapter and studied the key terms. Think you're ready to ace the exam? Take this sample test to gauge your comprehension of chapter material and check your answers at the back of the book. Want more test questions? Take the ACE quizzes found on the student website: www.hmco.ca/ob.

T F 1. Decision making is finding the correct answer to a question.

T F 2. Predicting the roll of the dice occurs under a decision condition of risk.

T F 3. A contingency plan is the action managers expect their competitors to take.

T F 4. Coalitions can help astute managers get the organization on a path toward effectiveness and profitability.

T F 5. It is important to reward creative successes and punish creative failures.

6. When managers make programmed decisions, they apply
   a. a condition of risk.
   b. a decision rule.
   c. their intuition.
   d. their creativity.
   e. the choice of a coalition.

7. Kevin owns a small business and is considering opening a second store in a different location. He has consulted with several small business experts regarding his decision and now is able to predict the probabilities that the new store will reach certain profit levels. Kevin is operating under which decision condition?
   a. Programmed
   b. Certainty
   c. Risk
   d. Uncertainty
   e. Expertise

8. Decision makers ask the question "What if something happens during the implementation of this alternative?" in order to develop
   a. group consensus.
   b. ethical guidelines.
   c. post-decision dissonance.
   d. contingency plans.
   e. nonprogrammed decisions.

9. The practical decision-making approach suggests managers should
   a. use rules of thumb to make decisions.
   b. generate as many alternatives as time and money allow.
   c. satisfice whenever possible.

d. never satisfice.
   e. train others to make their own decisions.

10. Which of the following questions is not one decision makers ask themselves in the conflict model of decision making proposed by Janis and Mann?
    a. Are the risks serious if I do not make a change?
    b. Are the risks serious if I do make a change?
    c. Is it realistic to hope to find a better solution?
    d. Has this decision been made before in the past?
    e. Is there sufficient time to search and deliberate?

11. Which of the following managers would be best suited to rely on his or her intuition?
    a. An experienced manager with practice in making similar decisions
    b. An inexperienced manager with a degree in advanced decision sciences
    c. A manager who is part of a strong coalition
    d. A manager who is extremely creative
    e. A manager who is extremely ethical

12. Which of the following is an example of group polarization?
    a. Two members of a group have a clash of personalities.
    b. Individually, the members of a group try to take the group in different directions.
    c. As a whole, a group becomes more extreme in its position following a discussion than it was before.
    d. A highly cohesive group avoids seeking outside advice.
    e. A group splits in half after an emotional debate on an important issue.

13. Cameron is considering using a group to solve a problem. He knows groups generally produce better decisions than do individuals. However, which of the following disadvantages should Cameron expect?
    a. Groups usually focus on decisions that benefit themselves.
    b. Groups take far longer than individuals to develop solutions and make decisions.
    c. Groups of experts are unlikely to agree.
    d. Groups tend to reduce the interest individuals have in the task.
    e. Groups that have become polarized can never be repaired.

Conflict, Negotiation, Power, and Politics in Organizations

When Workplace Aggression Becomes Deadly

Conflicts within organizations are not unusual. Managers deal with conflict on a regular basis. However, sometimes conflict at work can escalate to the point where the consequences are deadly. In one such instance, a workplace fight in May 2006, between two employees of Richmond, B.C.-based cabinet-maker, Nickels Custom Cabinets, resulted in the death of Sukhjit Johal. His coworker was charged with second-degree murder.

In another high profile case, nurse Lori Dupont was murdered in the recovery room of the Hotel-Dieu Grace Hospital in Windsor, Ontario by Dr. Marc Daniel, an anesthesiologist at the same hospital. Daniel committed suicide shortly thereafter. This incident represented the culmination of a series of acts of aggression and harassment toward Dupont and several other nurses. Prior to Dupont's murder, two nurses had filed formal harassment grievances against Daniel.

Although the vast majority of instances of workplace aggression do not result in death and include other behaviours than physical assaults, a Statistics Canada study released in February 2007 revealed that there were over 356 000 violent incidents in the Canadian workplace in 2004. Both organizations and governments are beginning to recognize the seriousness of workplace aggression, which can include such behaviours as assault, bullying, intimidation, stalking, and verbal or psychological harassment. Several provinces, such as British Columbia and Quebec have enacted legislation compelling employers to address the issue. And, as we see in the Workplace Aggression and . . . Research box, organizations can reduce the likelihood of aggressive behaviours by employees when employees perceive that such actions will be punished by the organization.[1]

Not all conflicts in organizations are as dramatic as those described above, but conflict does arise frequently. Conflict often occurs when individuals and groups interact in organizations. In its simplest form, **conflict** is disagreement among parties. When people, groups, or organizations disagree over significant issues, conflict is often the result. Often it is generated by political behaviour or battles over limited resources. In particular, it frequently occurs when a person or a group believes its attempts to achieve its goal are being blocked by another person or group. For example, conflict may arise over financial resources, the number of authorized positions in work groups, or the number of computers to be purchased for departments. Conflict can also result from anticipating trouble. For example, a person may behave antagonistically toward another person whom he or she expects to pose obstacles to goal achievement.[2] Conflict can also arise from personal differences. Differences in communication style can create misunderstandings that escalate into conflict. These differences in communication style can stem from any number of causes, such as gender, race, values, or personality. Such conflicts can have far-reaching implications for organizations because they can lead to instances of workplace aggression such as those described previously. In the Workplace Aggression and . . . Research box, we describe recent research that has examined factors predicting workplace aggression.

Although conflict often is considered harmful, and thus something to avoid, it can also have some benefits. A total absence of conflict can lead to apathy and lethargy. A moderate degree of focused conflict, on the other hand, can stimulate new ideas, promote healthy competition, and energize behaviour. In some organizations, especially profit-oriented ones, many managers believe that conflict is dysfunctional. On the other hand, managers in not-for-profit organizations view conflict as beneficial and conducive to higher-quality decision making.[3] In many cases, the impact of conflict on performance can take the form shown in Figure 10.1. Either too little or too much conflict may result in low performance, while a moderate level of conflict may lead to higher performance.

Conflict is disagreement among parties. It has both positive and negative characteristics.

285

Workplace Aggression and . . . **RESEARCH**

Predicting Workplace Aggression

Whether workplace aggression takes extreme forms, such as physical assaults or even homicide, or occurs in less severe forms, such as verbal or psychological abuse, its toll on individual well-being and organizational functioning is significant. A stream of research conducted by Julian Barling and his colleagues at Queen's University, as well as his former students now at Memorial University of Newfoundland and Saint Mary's University has examined factors that predict incidents of workplace aggression as well as their consequences.

In one study, Manon LeBlanc and Kevin Kelloway at Saint Mary's University found that coworker aggression had negative effects on both emotional and psychosomatic well-being as well as on affective commitment (see Chapter 3) and turnover intentions. Subsequently, Kathryn Dupré, of Memorial University of Newfoundland, and Barling found that workers were more likely to engage in acts of aggression against their supervisors when they felt that they were unjustly treated. However, the likelihood of aggression was reduced when the organization imposed sanctions on aggressive behaviour.

Finally, a recent meta-analysis that combined the results of 57 separate studies on workplace aggression found that interpersonal aggression in the workplace was influenced by both individual factors, such as trait anger, and situational factors, such as interpersonal conflict. What remains to be determined in future research on this topic concerns what factors predict whether the targets of aggressive behaviours will be coworkers or supervisors. To this point, researchers have not examined this distinction. Given that it is likely that these factors will differ, a greater understanding will provide organizations with more effective intervention options.

Sources: M. M. LeBlanc, and E. K. Kelloway, "Predictors and Outcomes of Workplace Violence and Aggression," *Journal of Applied Psychology*, June 2002, pp. 444–453; K. E. Dupré, and J. Barling, "Predicting and Preventing Supervisory Workplace Aggression," *Journal of Occupational Health Psychology*, January 2006, pp. 13–26; M. S. Herscovis, N. Turner, J. Barling, K. A. Arnold, K. E. Dupré, M. Inness, M. M. LeBlanc, and N. Sivanathan, "Predicting Workplace Aggression: A Meta-Analysis," *Journal of Applied Psychology*, January 2007, pp. 228–238.

FIGURE 10.1

The Nature of Organizational Conflict

Either too much to too little conflict can be dysfunctional for an organization. In either case, performance may be low. However, an optimal level of conflict that sparks motivations, creativity, innovation, and initiative can result in higher levels of performance.

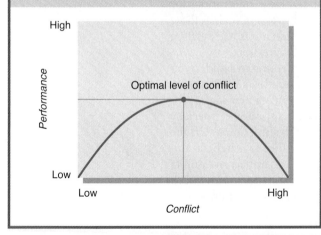

The Nature of Conflict

Conflict may take a number of forms. In addition, it may be caused by a wide array of factors in an organization.

Common Forms of Conflict

In general, there are three basic forms of conflict that exist within an organization. There are additional forms that can relate to conflict between organizations. **Task conflict** refers to conflict regarding the goals and content of the work. For instance, suppose one manager believes that the firm should strive to maximize profits and shareholder value. This individual will feel strongly that the organization should avoid social causes and instead focus its efforts on increasing revenues and/or lowering costs to the exclusion of most other activities. Another manager in the same firm, however, may believe the business should have a pronounced social agenda and be an active participant in relevant social programs. While this manager recognizes the importance of profits, he or she also sees the importance of corporate citizenship. To the extent that their differences lead to disagreements over substantive issues, it represents task conflict.

Process conflict occurs when the parties agree on the goals and content of work, but disagree on how to achieve the goals and actually do the work. For example, suppose the two executives noted above actually both believe in the importance of a social agenda and support the concept of sharing corporate profits with society. Hence, they have no task conflict. However, one thinks the best way to do this is to simply give a portion of the firm's profits to one or more social causes. The other, however, thinks the company should be more active; for instance, she or he wants the firm to sponsor ongoing building projects through Habitat for Humanity. While they share the same goals, they see different processes as the best way to achieve those goals.

Relationship conflict occurs when the parties have interpersonal issues. For instance, suppose one person has very strict conservative religious beliefs. This person is offended by the use of vulgar language, believes strongly in the importance of regular church attendance, and has no qualms about voicing his or her beliefs to others. A coworker, however, may frequently use off-colour words and joke about the need to sleep late on weekends to recover from late nights in bars. While conflict between these two individuals is not certain, there is a reasonable likelihood that they will at least occasionally let the other know that they value different things. As detailed more fully in The Family Business and . . . Change box, relationship conflict can be especially difficult in a family-owned business.

At a somewhat different level, **legal conflict** can arise when there are differences in perceptions between organizations. For instance, if one firm sees a competitor as engaging in predatory pricing practices or a supplier as failing to live up to the terms of a contract, it may bring legal action against the other firm. Given that legal conflict has tightly prescribed procedures and processes in place for resolution, much of our discussion will focus on task, process, and relationship conflict.

Causes of Conflict

Interpersonal Conflict   Conflict between two or more individuals is almost certain to occur in any organization, given the great variety in perceptions, goals, attitudes, and so forth among its members. William Gates, founder and CEO of Microsoft, and Kazuhiko Nishi, a former business associate from Japan, ended a long-term business relationship because of interpersonal conflict. Nishi accused Gates of becoming too political, while Gates charged that Nishi became too unpredictable and erratic in his behaviour.[4]

A frequent source of interpersonal conflict in organizations is what many people call a personality clash—when two people distrust each other's motives, dislike one another, or for some other reason simply can't get along.[5] Conflict also may arise between people who have different beliefs or perceptions about some aspect of their work or their organization. For example, one manager may want the organization to require that all employees use Microsoft Office software to promote standardization. Another manager may believe a variety of software packages should be allowed in order to recognize individuality. Similarly, a male manager may disagree with his female colleague over whether the organization is guilty of discriminating against women in promotion decisions.

Conflict also can result from excess competitiveness among individuals. Two people vying for the same job, for example, may resort to political behaviour in an effort to gain an advantage. If either competitor sees the other's behaviour as inappropriate, accusations are likely to result. Even after the "winner" of the job is determined, such

---

Task conflict refers to conflict regarding the goals and content of the work.

Process conflict occurs when the parties agree on the goals and content of work, but disagree on how to achieve the goals and actually do the work.

Relationship conflict occurs when the parties have interpersonal issues.

Legal conflict may arise when there are differences in perceptions between organizations.

The Family Business and . . .   **CHANGE**

Keeping It in the Family

Family businesses in Canada employ over half of the nation's workers and contribute 45 percent of the gross national product. They also grow into large businesses—some of Canada's wealthiest families, such as the Thomsons, Aspers, Irvings, Sobeys, and Péladeaus became so over several generations by building their family businesses. Family businesses tend to be conservative and traditional. Family name and reputation are keys to their success, making them reluctant to change. Yet family businesses are just as susceptible as larger firms to changes such as increased competition and outsourcing. How can family businesses manage change, without experiencing too much conflict?

Succession is a problem area, as families decide which members of the next generation will assume leadership of the company. The problem is so thorny that many firms do not survive a generational change. Even those that do can experience significant upheaval on both the business and relationship aspects. Perhaps the best known succession conflict in recent memory occurred at New Brunswick food giant McCain. For years, the company was jointly run by brothers Harrison and Wallace McCain. As the brothers approached retirement age, the question of succession arose. The trouble began when Wallace unilaterally appointed his son, Michael, then CEO of the American branch of the McCain empire as

the successor. Harrison was opposed to the appointment and the ensuing lengthy and very public battle resulted in the ousting of Wallace McCain from the company he and his brother had built. Wallace and his sons, Michael and Scott went on to acquire food processing giant, Maple Leaf Foods, a competitor of McCain.

Although conflict over succession is a thorny issue for family businesses, it does not always have to result in high profile strife. Some family business owners recognize that, if the business is to survive and thrive, it is sometimes necessary to seek out talent outside of the family. An example of this is Moosehead Breweries, based in Saint John, New Brunswick. The business has been owned and operated by the Oland family for five generations. However, rather than appoint one of his sons to succeed him as president, Derek Oland opted to hire outside the family. In 1997, Bruce McCubbin became the first non-Oland to run the company. He was succeeded in 2006 by Stephen Poirier, a senior executive at Moosehead since 1997.

Sources: Merle MacIsaac, "Picking Up the Pieces," *Canadian Business,* March 1995, pp. 29–44; Andy Holloway, "Derek Oland: 'Beer People Are Wonderful, Friendly People. They Sell Hospitality, But They Are Hospitable," *Canadian Business,* October 24, 2005, www.canadianbusiness .com on May 9, 2007; www.moosehead.ca/moosehead.com/corporate/ pressroom/on May 9, 2007.

conflict may continue to undermine interpersonal relationships, especially if the reasons given in selecting one candidate are ambiguous or open to alternative explanation.

Intergroup Conflict   Conflict between two or more organizational groups is also quite common. For example, the members of a firm's marketing group may disagree with the production group over product quality and delivery schedules. Two sales groups may disagree over how to meet sales goals, and two groups of managers may have different ideas about how best to allocate organizational resources.

At a J.C. Penney's department store, conflict arose between stockroom employees and sales associates. The sales associates claimed that the stockroom employees were slow in delivering merchandise to the sales floor so that it could be priced and shelved. The stockroom employees, in turn, claimed that the sales associates did not give them enough lead time to get the merchandise delivered or acknowledge that the stockroom employees had additional duties besides carrying merchandise to the sales floor.

Just like people, different departments often have different goals. Further, these goals may often be incompatible. A marketing goal of maximizing sales, achieved partially by offering many products in a wide variety of sizes, shapes, colours, and models, probably conflicts with a production goal of minimizing costs, achieved partially by long production runs of a few items. Reebok recently confronted this very situation. One group of managers wanted to introduce a new sportswear line as quickly as possible, while other managers wanted to expand more deliberately and cautiously. Because the two groups were not able to reconcile their differences effectively, conflict between the two factions led to quality problems and delivery delays that plagued the firm for months.

Competition for scarce resources can also lead to intergroup conflict. Most organizations—especially universities, hospitals, government agencies, and businesses in depressed industries—have limited resources. The Buick, Pontiac, and Chevrolet divisions of General Motors have frequently fought over the rights to manufacture various new products developed by the company.

Conflict Between Organization and Environment   Conflict that arises between one organization and another is called interorganizational conflict. A moderate amount of interorganizational conflict resulting from business competition is, of course, expected, but sometimes conflict becomes more extreme. For example, Air Canada and WestJet were involved in a protracted dispute over allegations that WestJet has spied on Air Canada, accessing information by hacking into an internal website. After two years, WestJet admitted that it was guilty of the accusations, apologized, and paid $15.5 million in penalties and costs.[6] The Xerox and . . . Technology box provides still other examples.

Conflict can also arise between an organization and other elements of its environment. For example, an organization may conflict with a consumer group over claims it makes about its products. McDonald's faced this problem a few years ago when it published nutritional information about its products that omitted details about fat content. Or a firm might conflict with a supplier over the quality of raw materials. The firm may think the supplier is providing inferior materials, while the supplier thinks the materials are adequate. Finally, individual managers may obviously have disagreements with groups of workers. For example, a manager may think her workers are doing poor-quality work and that they are unmotivated. The workers, on the other hand, may believe they are doing a good job and that the manager is doing a poor job of leading them.

Task Interdependence   Task interdependence can also result in conflict across any of the levels noted previously. The greater the interdependence between departments, the greater the likelihood that conflict will occur. There are three major forms of interdependence: pooled, sequential, and reciprocal.[7]

Pooled interdependence represents the lowest level of interdependence and results in the least amount of conflict. Units with pooled interdependence operate with little interaction—the output of the units is pooled at the organizational level. The Gap clothing stores operate with pooled interdependence. Each store is considered a "department" by the parent corporation. Each has its own operating budget, staff, and so forth. The profits or losses from each store are "added together" at the organizational level. The stores are interdependent to the extent that the final success or failure of one store affects the others, but they do not generally interact on a day-to-day basis.

In **sequential interdependence**, the output of one unit becomes the input for another in a sequential fashion. This creates a moderate level of interdependence and a somewhat higher potential for conflict. At Nissan, for example, one plant assembles engines and then ships them to a final assembly site at another plant where the cars are completed. The plants are interdependent in that the final assembly plant must

Pooled interdependence represents the lowest level of interdependence, and hence results in the least amount of conflict.

In sequential interdependence, the output of one unit becomes the input for another in a sequential fashion; this creates a moderate level of interdependence and a somewhat higher potential for conflict.

Xerox and . . . **TECHNOLOGY**

Whose Idea Was This, Anyway?

Xerox is a company long known for innovative technology. Its first copier, for instance, was an instant success, and today many people use "xeroxing" as a synonym for "photocopying." Following its success in the copier business, Xerox diversified into computers and continued to spend substantial amounts on R&D.

In the firm's research laboratory in Palo Alto, California, Xerox built one of the world's first personal computers. The Alto, released in 1981, included many elements that are still used today, such as the mouse, icons, point-and-click, and windows. In spite of the innovations, Xerox was unable to duplicate its previous success and exited the PC industry in 1989.

However, ideas from the Alto were adopted by others, and that was the beginning of Xerox's conflicts and legal troubles with competitors. In December 1989, Xerox sued Apple, alleging copyright infringement. After months in court, the case was dismissed. Apple's lawyers successfully argued that while Apple borrowed ideas from Xerox, ideas are not protected by copyrights. The judge also noted that the case was out of date because technology had already changed so much.

Ironically, at that time, Apple was vigorously defending its own copyrights. Apple was suing Microsoft, IBM, and Hewlett-Packard over their use of a Macintosh-style user interface called "Windows," exactly the same charge Xerox was making about Apple. Like Xerox, Apple lost their lawsuits and the market.

Unfortunately for Xerox, the players change but the problem remains the same. Xerox has bogged down in legal disputes when it develops a concept that is then adopted by a more profitable rival. In the latest example, in 1997 Xerox sued Palm (now known as PalmOne) over the use of a handwriting recognition program. Xerox's claims were denied in May 2004. As before, Palm made money from Xerox's ideas and the legal challenge came far too late.

According to the firm's website, "Xerox . . . explores the unknown, invents next-generation technology . . . and creates new business opportunities." Xerox has mastered exploration and invention; now it needs to focus on selling those new products.

> "*Xerox . . . explores the unknown, invents next-generation technology . . . and creates new business opportunities.*"
>
> XEROX WEBSITE

Sources: "Innovation," "Online Fact Book," "The Story of Xerography," Xerox website, www.xerox.com on June 11, 2005 (quotation); Andrew Pollack, "Most of Xerox's Suit Against Apple Barred," *New York Times*, March 24, 1990, www.nytimes.com on June 11, 2005; Laura Rohde, "Xerox Loses Patent Claim Against PalmOne," *Computer Weekly*, June 21, 2005; www.computerweekly.com on June 11, 2005.

have the engines from engine assembly before it can perform its primary function of producing finished automobiles. But the level of interdependence is generally one-way—the engine plant is not necessarily dependent on the final assembly plant. In this example, though, if the engine assembly plant is constantly late with its deliveries, it will quickly encounter problems with managers at the final assembly plant.

Reactions to Conflict

The most common reactions to conflict are avoidance, accommodation, competition, collaboration, and compromise.[8] Whenever conflict occurs between groups or organizations, it is really the people who are in conflict. In many cases, however, people are acting as representatives of the groups to which they belong. In effect, they work together, representing their group as they strive to do their part in helping the group achieve its goals. Thus, whether the conflict is between people acting as individuals or people acting as representatives of groups, the five types of interactions can be analyzed in terms of relationships among the goals of the people or the groups they represent.

Reactions to conflict can be differentiated along two dimensions: how important each party's goals are to that party, and how compatible the goals are, as shown in Figure 10.2. The importance of reaching a goal may range from very high to very low. The degree of **goal compatibility** is the extent to which the goals can be achieved simultaneously. In other words, the goals are compatible if one party can meet its goals without preventing the other from meeting its goals. The goals are incompatible if one party's meeting its goals prevents the other party from meeting its goals. The goals of different groups may be very compatible, completely incompatible, or somewhere in between.

Avoidance   **Avoidance** occurs when an interaction is relatively unimportant to either party's goals and the goals are incompatible, as in the bottom left corner of Figure 10.2. Because the parties to the conflict are not striving toward compatible goals and the issues in question seem unimportant, the parties simply try to avoid interacting with one another. For example, one government agency may simply ignore another agency's requests for information. The requesting agency can then practise its own form of avoidance by not following up on the requests.

Accommodation   **Accommodation** occurs when the goals are compatible but the interactions are not considered important to overall goal attainment, as in the bottom right corner of Figure 10.2. Interactions of this type may involve discussions of how the parties can accomplish their interdependent tasks with the least expenditure of time and effort. This type of interaction tends to be very friendly. For example, during a college's course scheduling period, potential conflict exists between the marketing and economic departments. Both departments offer morning classes. Which department is allocated the 9 A.M. time slot and which one the 10 A.M. time slot is not that important to either group. Their overall goal is that the classes are scheduled so that students will be able to take courses from both departments.

Competition   **Competition** occurs when the goals are incompatible and the interactions are important to each party's meeting its goals, as in the top left corner of Figure 10.2. If all parties are striving for a goal but only one can reach the goal, the parties will be in competition. As we noted earlier, if a competitive situation gets out of control, as when overt antagonism occurs and there are no rules or procedures to follow, competition can result in conflict. Thus, competition may

> The nature of the interactions between people and groups depends on the importance of the issues and the compatibility of the groups' goals.

> **Goal compatibility** is the extent to which the goals of more than one person or group can be achieved at the same time.

> **Avoidance** occurs when the interacting parties' goals are incompatible and the interaction between groups is relatively unimportant to the attainment of the goals.

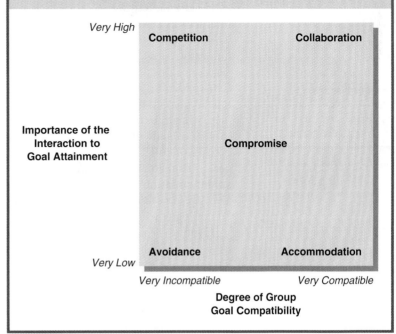

FIGURE 10.2

Five Types of Reactions to Conflict

The five types of reactions to conflict stem from the relative importance of interaction to goal attainment and the degree of goal compatibility.

Accommodation occurs when the parties' goals are compatible but the interaction between groups is relatively unimportant to the goals' attainment.

Competition occurs when the goals are incompatible and the interactions between groups are important to meeting goals.

Collaboration occurs when the interaction between groups is very important to goal attainment and the goals are compatible.

Compromise occurs when the interaction is moderately important to meeting goals and the goals are neither completely compatible nor completely incompatible.

lead to conflict. Sometimes conflict can also change to competition if the parties agree to rules to guide the interaction and conflicting parties agree to not be hostile toward each other.

In one freight warehouse and storage firm, the first, second, and third shifts each sought to win the weekly productivity prize by posting the highest productivity record. Workers on the winning shift received recognition in the company newspaper. Because the issue was important to each group and the interests of the groups were incompatible, the result was competition.

The competition among the shifts encouraged each shift to produce more per week, which increased the company's output and eventually improved its overall welfare (and thus the welfare of each group). Both the company and the groups benefited from the competition because it fostered innovative and creative work methods, which further boosted productivity. After about three months, however, the competition got out of control. The competition among the groups led to poorer overall performance as the groups started to sabotage other shifts and inflate records. The competition became too important, open antagonism resulted, rules were ignored, and the competition changed to open conflict, resulting in actual decreases in work performance.[9]

Collaboration   **Collaboration** occurs when the interaction between groups is very important to goal attainment and the goals are compatible, as in the top right corner of Figure 10.2. In the class scheduling situation mentioned earlier, conflict may arise over which courses to teach in the first semester and which ones in the second. Both departments would like to offer specific courses in the fall. However, by discussing the issue and refocusing their overall goals to match students' needs, the marketing and economics departments can collaborate on developing a proper sequence of courses. At first glance, this may seem to be simple interaction in which the parties participate jointly in activities to accomplish goals after agreeing on the goals and their importance. In many situations, however, it is no easy matter to agree on goals, their importance, and especially the means for achieving them. In a collaborative interaction, goals may differ but be compatible. Parties to a conflict may initially have difficulty working out the ways in which all can achieve their goals. However, because the interactions are important to goal attainment, the parties are willing to continue to work together to achieve the goals. Collaborative relationships can lead to new and innovative ideas and solutions to differences among the parties.[10]

Compromise   **Compromise** occurs when the interactions are moderately important to goal attainment and the goals are neither completely compatible nor completely incompatible. In a compromise situation, parties interact with others striving to achieve goals, but they may not aggressively pursue goal attainment in either a competitive or collaborative manner because the interactions are not that important to goal attainment. On the other hand, the parties may neither avoid one another nor be accommodating because the interactions are somewhat important. Often each party gives up something, but because the interactions are only moderately important, they do not regret what they have given up.

Contract negotiations between union and management are an example of compromise. Each side brings numerous issues of varying importance to the bargaining table. The two sides give and take on the issues through rounds of offers and counteroffers. The complexity of such negotiations is increasing as negotiations spread to multiple plants in different countries. Agreements between management and labour in a plant in the United States may be unacceptable to both parties in Canada.[11] Weeks of negotiations ending in numerous compromises usually result in a contract agreement between the union and management. Sometimes, however, one side is in a much more

Collective bargaining between labour and management is an every day fact of life in many organizations. Typically, each party has some leverage that can push negotiations forward. However, there are times when the power of each party's positions are not equal and this can lead to the less powerful party giving up more in the negotiated outcome than they may like. National Hockey League commissioner, Gary Bettman, on the behalf of NHL team owners, locked out the players and then canceled the 2004–2005 season as a means of extracting greater financial concessions from the NHL Players' Association.

powerful position than the other and can extract greater concessions while giving up very little in the process. An example of this occurred with the 2004–2005 National Hockey League lockout of the players by the owners. This action forced the National Hockey League Players' Association (NHLPA) to agree to a large salary rollback for all players and a far more strict salary cap than they actually wanted in order to strike a collective bargaining agreement with the owners.

In summary, when groups are in conflict they may react in several different ways. If the goals of the parties are very compatible, the parties may engage in mutually supportive interactions, that is, collaboration or accommodation. If the goals are very incompatible, each may attempt to foster its own success at the expense of the others, engaging in competition or avoidance.

Managing Conflict

One must know when to resolve conflict and when to stimulate it if one is to avoid its potentially disruptive effects. When a potentially harmful conflict situation exists, a manager needs to engage in **conflict resolution**. As Figure 10.3 shows, conflict needs to be resolved when it causes major disruptions in the organization and absorbs time and effort that could be used more productively. Conflict should also be resolved when its focus is on the group's internal goals rather than on organizational goals.

We describe the principal conflict-handling strategies later in this section. First, remember that sometimes a manager should be concerned about the absence of conflict. An absence of conflict may indicate that the organization is stagnant and that employees are content with the status quo. It may also suggest that work groups are not motivated to challenge traditional and well-accepted ideas.[12] **Conflict stimulation** is the creation and constructive use of conflict by a manager.[13] Its purpose is to bring about situations where differences of opinion are exposed for examination by all. For example, if competing organizations are making significant changes in products, markets, or technologies, it may be time for a manager to stimulate innovation and creativity

Conflict resolution occurs when a manager resolves a conflict that has become harmful or serious.

Conflict stimulation is the creation and constructive use of conflict by a manager.

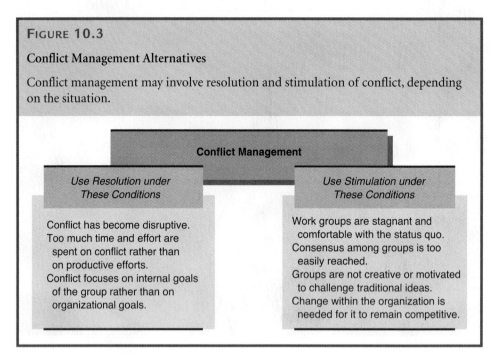

FIGURE 10.3

Conflict Management Alternatives

Conflict management may involve resolution and stimulation of conflict, depending on the situation.

Conflict Management

Use Resolution under These Conditions

Conflict has become disruptive. Too much time and effort are spent on conflict rather than on productive efforts.
Conflict focuses on internal goals of the group rather than on organizational goals.

Use Stimulation under These Conditions

Work groups are stagnant and comfortable with the status quo.
Consensus among groups is too easily reached.
Groups are not creative or motivated to challenge traditional ideas.
Change within the organization is needed for it to remain competitive.

by challenging the status quo. Conflict may give employees the motivation and opportunity to reveal differences of opinion that they previously kept to themselves. When all parties to the conflict are interested enough in an issue to challenge other groups, they often expose their hidden doubts or opinions. This, in turn, allows the parties to get to the heart of the matter and often to develop unique solutions to the problem. Indeed, the interactions may lead the groups to recognize that a problem in fact exists. Conflict, then, can be a catalyst for creativity and change in an organization.

> Depending on the circumstances, a manager may need to either resolve or stimulate conflict.

Several methods can be used to stimulate conflict under controlled conditions.[14] These include altering the physical location of groups to stimulate more interaction, forcing more resource sharing, and implementing other changes in relationships among groups. In addition, training programs can be used to increase employee awareness of potential problems in group decision making and group interactions. Adopting the role of devil's advocate in discussion sessions is another way to stimulate conflict among groups. In this role, a manager challenges the prevailing consensus to ensure that all alternatives have been critically appraised and analyzed. Although this role is often unpopular, it is a good way to stimulate constructive conflict.

Of course, too much conflict is also a concern. If conflict becomes excessive or destructive, the manager needs to adopt a strategy to reduce or resolve it. Managers should first attempt to determine the source of the conflict. If the source of destructive conflict is a particular person or two, it might be appropriate to alter the membership of one or both groups. If it is due to differences in goals, perceptions of the difficulty of goal attainment, or the importance of the goals to the conflicting parties, the manager can attempt to move the conflicting parties into one of the five types of reactions to conflict, depending on the nature of the conflicting parties.

> A **superordinate goal** is an organizational goal that is more important to the well-being of the organization and its members than the more specific goals of interacting parties.

To foster collaboration, it might be appropriate to try to help people see that their goals are really not as different as they seem to be. The manager can help groups view their goals as part of a superordinate goal to which the goals of both conflicting parties can contribute. A **superordinate goal** is a goal of the overall organization and is more important to the well-being of the organization and its members than the more specific goals of the conflicting parties. If the goals are not really that important and are very incompatible, the manager may need to develop ways to help the conflicting parties avoid each other. Similarly, accommodation, competition, or compromise might be appropriate for the conflicting parties.

Third-Party Conflict Management

There are many instances in which individuals in organizations must intervene in a conflict between two other people or groups. For example, a manager may have two departments competing for scarce organizational resources or two employees who work together may have personality differences that lead to conflict. Despite the widespread instances of such conflicts, until recently, there has been scant research attention paid to the need for a framework for third party conflict intervention. Blair Sheppard was one of the first to advocate the need for such a framework. He proposed that this framework should be composed of three parts: (1) a comprehensive set of conflict intervention procedures, (2) a set of criteria or outcomes for evaluating conflict intervention procedures, and (3) a description of situational factors that have an impact on the effectiveness of conflict intervention procedures. More recently, A. R. Elangovan of the University of Victoria developed a prescriptive model of third-party conflict strategy selection based on Sheppard's suggestions as well as the Vroom-Yetton model of decision making discussed in Chapter 11.[15]

Objectives of Third-Party Intervention

When third parties intervene in conflicts (**third-party conflict intervention**), they attempt to address at least four objectives or criteria.[16] Although all four objectives or criteria are considered important, it is often not possible to satisfy all of them. The first, and perhaps primary, objective of third-party intervention is *effectiveness*. A dispute is effectively resolved if the intervention addresses the concerns of the disputing parties as well as those of the organization. An effective intervention addresses the underlying issues and ensures that the same conflict does not arise in the future. A second objective of third party intervention is *efficiency*. The dispute should be resolved in a timely manner and should not unnecessarily tie up important organizational resources. Managers are also concerned with *procedural fairness* and *participant satisfaction*. These last two criteria focus more on the reactions of the disputing parties to how the conflict is handled and are particularly important because it is more likely that the dispute will be resolved when the parties believe they have been fairly treated. In addition, disputants are more likely to be committed to implementing the solution when they are satisfied with both the outcome of the dispute and the process by which the dispute was settled.

As you can imagine, there is no one best way of intervening in a conflict.[17] According to Elangovan's model, there are many situational factors that influence the choice of intervention strategy. The choice of conflict intervention strategies is also determined by the role of a third party. In many contexts, the role of the third party is a formal one. For example, arbitrators or mediators are often appointed to intervene in labour-management disputes with the goal of facilitating a settlement. They are typically neutral third parties with no vested interest in the outcome of the dispute and no history of interaction with the disputing parties. For example, a mediator was appointed to help resolve the dispute between the Saskatchewan government and the Saskatchewan Government and General Employees' Union (SGEU/NUPGE) in early 2007. Managers, however, frequently must intervene in disputes between subordinates

> **Third-party conflict intervention** occurs when a manager attempts to resolve a dispute between individuals or groups of employees.

with whom they have ongoing relationships. Furthermore, these disputes often place the manager in the position of having to balance the interests of the disputants and the organization, as well as any interests that the manager may have in the outcome of the dispute. Thus, the range of strategy options may be different for informal third parties (e.g., a manager) than for formal third parties (e.g., a judge or mediator).

There is a wide variety of strategies available to managers when intervening in a conflict between employees. Most of these strategies vary in the degree to which the manager controls the process or the outcome of the conflict.[18] To determine what types of conflict intervention strategies that managers use most frequently, Sheppard conducted interviews with managers.[19] The three most frequently occurring procedures were what Sheppard called *inquisitorial intervention, adversarial intervention*, and *providing impetus*. Although not as widely used by managers, a fourth option involves *mediation*. We can see in Figure 10.4 how these four conflict intervention strategies differ along the dimensions of process and outcome control.

Inquisitorial intervention involves the manager soliciting evidence from the disputants and then making a decision. Managers using this approach have high outcome control because they retain the right to decide the outcome of the dispute. They also have high process control because they decide what information will be gathered and used in deciding the outcome.

Adversarial intervention occurs with the manager listening to both parties presenting evidence to support their cases, and then making a decision. This approach is similar to arbitration, an intervention strategy sometimes used in labour disputes. In such cases, however, the arbitrator is a neutral third party, unlike managers. The major distinction between adversarial and inquisitorial interventions is that the manager exercises a high degree of control over how information is gathered and used in the inquisitorial approach, but not in the adversarial approach. They are similar in that the manager decides the outcome in both intervention procedures.

Providing impetus involves the manager providing a strong incentive for the disputants to reach an agreement on their own. The incentive may be the threat of dire consequences should the parties be unable to resolve their dispute. Despite the threat, managers exercise little or no control over the outcome or the process by which the dispute is resolved. Their only concern is that the dispute be resolved within a certain period of time. This approach is more likely to be used when the outcome of the dispute does not have an impact on organizational functioning.

Mediation is an intervention strategy that has not been widely used by managers, perhaps because it requires a skilled individual. A manager who uses mediation controls the way in which the disputants interact with one another. Thus, mediation involves a high degree of process control. However, unlike the adversarial and inquisitorial approaches, the manager does not attempt to impose a settlement on the disputing parties. This lack of control over the outcome may be another reason that managers don't use mediation as often as adversarial and inquisitorial approaches. However,

Inquisitorial intervention involves the manager soliciting evidence from the disputants and then making a decision.

Adversarial intervention involves the manager listening to both parties present evidence to support their cases and then making a decision.

Providing impetus involves the manager providing a strong incentive for the disputants to reach an agreement on their own.

FIGURE 10.4

Third-Party Conflict Intervention Strategies

When managers intervene in conflicts between individuals or groups of employees, there are four primary approaches they can follow. These intervention strategies vary along two dimensions: the extent to which the manager controls the manner in which the disputants interact (process control), and the extent to which the manager controls the final dispute resolution (outcome control). According to Elangovan's model of third-party conflict intervention, the best approach depends on a variety of situational factors.

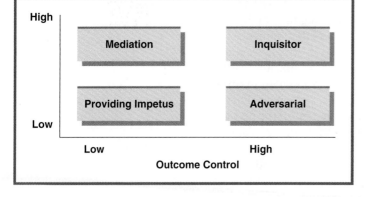

when the disputants themselves determine the outcome, it is more likely that they will be satisfied with that outcome.

Negotiation

One special way that decisions are made in organizations is through negotiation. **Negotiation** is the process in which two or more parties (people or groups) reach agreement even though they have different preferences. In its simplest form the parties involved may be two individuals who are trying to decide who will pay for lunch. A little more complexity is involved when two people, such as an employee and manager, sit down to decide on personal performance goals for the next year against which the employee's performance will be measured. Even more complex are the negotiations that take place between labour unions and management of a company, or between two companies as they negotiate the terms of a joint venture. The key issues are that at least two parties are involved, their preferences are different, and they need to reach agreement.

Four Approaches to Negotiation

The study of negotiation has grown steadily since the 1960s. Four primary approaches to negotiation have dominated this study: individual differences, situational characteristics, game theory, and cognitive approaches. Each of these is briefly described in the following sections.

Individual Differences   The early psychological approaches concentrated on the personality traits of the negotiators.[20] The traits investigated have included demographic characteristics and personality variables. Demographic characteristics have included age, gender, and race, among others. Personality variables have included risk-taking, locus of control, tolerance for ambiguity, self-esteem, authoritarianism, and Machiavellianism. The assumption of this type of research was that the key to successful negotiation was selecting the right person to do the negotiation, one who had the appropriate demographic characteristics or personality. This assumption seemed to make sense because negotiation is such a personal and interactive process. However, the research rarely showed the positive results expected because situational variables negated the effects of the individual differences.[21]

Situational Characteristics   Situational characteristics are the context within which negotiation takes place. They include such things as the types of communication between negotiators, the potential outcomes of the negotiation, the relative power of the parties (both positional and personal), the time frame available for negotiation, the number of people representing each side, and the presence of other parties. Some of this research has contributed to our understanding of the negotiation process. However, the shortcomings of the situational approach are similar to those of the individual characteristics approach. Many situational characteristics are external to the negotiators and beyond their control. Often the negotiators cannot change their relative power positions or the setting within which the negotiation occurs. So, although we have learned a lot from research on the situational issues, we still need to learn much more about the process.

Game Theory   Game theory was developed by economists using mathematical models to predict the outcome of negotiation situations. It requires that every alternative and outcome be analyzed with probabilities and numerical outcomes reflecting

Mediation involves the manager assisting the disputants in the resolution of their conflict by controlling the manner in which they interact, but without enforcing a solution.

Negotiation is the process in which two or more parties (people or groups) reach agreement even though they have different preferences.

the preferences for each outcome. In addition, the order in which different parties can make choices and every possible move are predicted along with associated preferences for outcomes. The outcomes of this approach are exactly what negotiators want: a predictive model of how negotiation should be conducted. One major drawback is that it requires the ability to describe all possible options and outcomes for every possible move in every situation before the negotiation starts. This is often very tedious, if possible at all. Another problem is that it assumes that negotiators are rational at all times. Other research in negotiation has shown that negotiators often do not act rationally. Therefore, this approach, while elegant in its prescriptions, is usually unworkable in a real negotiation situation.

Cognitive Approaches   The fourth approach is the cognitive approach, which recognizes that negotiators often depart from perfect rationality during negotiation; it tries to predict how and when negotiators will make these departures. Howard Raiffa's decision analytic approach focuses on providing advice to negotiators actively involved in negotiation.[22] Bazerman and Neale have added to Raiffa's work by specifying eight ways that negotiators systematically deviate from rationality.[23] The types of deviations they describe include escalation of commitment to a previously selected course of action, overreliance on readily available information, assuming that the negotiations produce fixed-sum outcomes, and anchoring negotiation in irrelevant information. These cognitive approaches have advanced the study of negotiation a long way beyond the early individual and situational approaches. Negotiators can use them to attempt to predict in advance how the negotiation might take place.

Win-Win Negotiation

In addition to the approaches to negotiation described above, a group of approaches proposed by consultants and advisors are meant to give negotiators a specific model to use in carrying out difficult negotiations. One of the best of these is the "win-win negotiator" developed by Ross Reck and his associates.[24] The win-win approach does not treat negotiation as a game in which there are winners and losers. Instead, it approaches negotiation as an opportunity for both sides to be winners, to get what they want out of the agreement. The focus is on both parties reaching agreement in which they are both committed to fulfilling their end of the agreement and to returning for more agreements in the future. In other words, both parties want to have their needs satisfied. In addition, this approach does not advocate either a tough-guy or a nice-guy approach to negotiation, both of which are popular in the literature. It assumes that both parties work together to find ways to satisfy both parties at the same time.

The PRAM model guides the negotiator through the four steps of planning for agreement, building relationships, reaching agreement, and maintaining relationships.

The win-win approach is a four-step approach illustrated in the **PRAM model** shown in Figure 10.5. The PRAM four-step approach proposes that proper planning, building relationships, getting agreement, and maintaining the relationship are the key steps to successful negotiation. *Planning* requires that each negotiator set his or her own goals, anticipate the goals of the other, determine areas of probable agreement, and develop strategies for reconciling areas of probable disagreement.

Developing a win-win *relationship* requires that negotiators plan activities that allow positive personal relationships to develop, cultivate a sense of mutual trust, and allow the relationship to fully develop before discussing business in earnest. The development of trust between the parties is probably the single most important key to success in negotiation.

Forming win-win *agreements* requires that each party confirm the other party's goals, verify areas of agreement, propose and consider positive solutions to reconcile areas of disagreement, and jointly resolve any remaining differences. The key in reaching agreement is to realize that many of the goals are shared by both parties. The number of areas of disagreement is usually small.

Finally, win-win *maintenance* entails providing meaningful feedback based on performance, holding up your end of the agreement, keeping in contact, and reaffirming trust between the parties. The assumption is that both parties want to keep the relationship going so that future mutually beneficial transactions can occur. Both parties must uphold their ends of the agreement and do what they said they would do. Keeping in touch is as easy as a telephone call or lunch visit.

In summary, the PRAM model provides simple advice for conducting negotiations. The four steps are easy to remember and carry out as long as the negotiator does not get distracted by games played by other parties. The focus is on planning, agreeing on goals, trust, and keeping your commitments.

Power in Organizations

Power is one of the most significant forces that exists in organizations; it can be an extremely important ingredient in organizational success—or organizational failure. The Wal-Mart and . . . Ethics box provides an interesting discussion of the potential misuse of power. Although we often think of power as resting in the hands of managers by virtue of their position in the organization, we see that many individuals in an organization can have power over others depending on the context. We discuss leadership more fully in the next chapter, but power is an important aspect of leadership whether that leadership is formal (as in the case of a manager) or informal (as in the case of a highly skilled or respected team member). In this section we first describe the nature of power. Then we examine the types and uses of power.

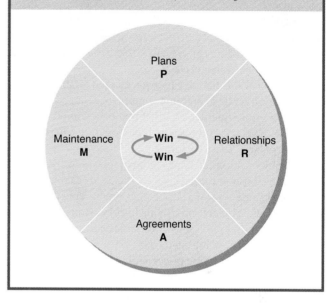

FIGURE 10.5

PRAM Model of Negotiation

The PRAM model shows the fours steps in setting up negotiation so that both parties win.

Source: Reprinted with the permission of Pocket Books, a division of Simon & Schuster, from *The Win-Win Negotiator: How to Negotiate Favorable Agreements That Last* by Ross R. Reck, Ph.D., and Brian G. Long, Ph.D. Copyright © 1985, 1987 by Brian G. Long and Ross R. Reck.

The Nature of Power

Power has been defined in dozens of different ways; no one definition is generally accepted. Drawing from the more common meanings of the term, we define **power** as the potential ability of a person or group to exercise control over another person or group.[25] Power is distinguished from influence due to the element of control; the more powerful control the less powerful. Thus, power might be thought of as an extreme form of influence.[26]

> **Power** is the potential ability of a person or group to exercise control over another person or group.

One obvious aspect of our definition is that it expresses power in terms of potential; that is, we may be able to control others but may choose not to exercise that control. Nevertheless, simply having the potential may be enough to influence others in some settings. We should also note that power can reside in individuals (such as managers and informal leaders), in formal groups (such as departments and committees), and in informal groups (such as a clique of influential people). Finally, we should note the direct link between power and influence. If a person can convince another person to change his or her opinion on some issue, to engage in or refrain from some behaviour,

Wal-Mart and . . .  **ETHICS**

Is Wal-Mart Invading Customer Privacy?

According to the Wal-Mart website, "Years ago, [Wal-Mart founder] Sam Walton challenged all Wal-Mart associates to practice what he called 'aggressive hospitality.' "Today, Wal-Mart is clearly more aggressive in offering low prices than excellent service. Those low prices are the result of dozens of strategic actions, including the use of automated data collection and analysis. Relentless data management reduces prices, but it also introduces concerns about customer privacy.

Wal-Mart, a technology pioneer, has 460 terabytes of information on its mainframe computers, twice as much as on the entire Internet. Much of that data is about stores or products, but some of it is about customers. "We know who every customer is," says Wal-Mart chief information officer Linda M. Dillman. Through credit cards, checks, and drivers' licenses, Wal-Mart can link to customers' home address and e-mail, credit reports, buying patterns, criminal and driving history, bank account balances, marital status, medical conditions, and more.

The information is legal to gather and is used to manage inventory, determine prices, and target advertising. For its part, Wal-Mart claims that it is more interested in aggregate patterns than in the behaviour of any one customer. But the potential for misuse is evident.

Wal-Mart's next wave of technology will be radio-frequency ID tags, or RFIDs. These smart-chips with tiny antennas can hold a significant amount of data and communicate with transmitters. One RFID costs about 25 cents today, but that price is expected to fall to 2 cents within two years, making it an affordable replacement for bar codes. Benetton is considering including RFIDs in its undergarments, where they will transmit information about wear patterns and even bra size! Gillette is already using RFIDs in its expensive razors to control shoplifting.

For now, observers agree that Wal-Mart is not abusing its power, but the data and the technology are available and Wal-Mart's intentions could change at any time. The power lies with the giant retailer. Who is ensuring justice for customers?

> *"We know who every customer is."*
>
> LINDA M. DILLMAN,
> CHIEF INFORMATION OFFICER,
> WAL-MART

Sources: "Exceeding Customer Expectations," Wal-Mart website, www.walmartstores.com on June 11, 2005; Patrick Dixon, "RFIDs: Great New Logistics Business or Brave New World?" Global Change website, www.globalchange.com on June 11, 2005; Constance L. Hays, "What They Know About You," *New York Times*, November 14, 2004, pp. BU1, 9.

or to view circumstances in a certain way, that person has exercised influence—and used power.

Considerable differences of opinion exist about how thoroughly power pervades organizations. Some people argue that virtually all interpersonal relations are influenced by power, whereas others believe that exercise of power is confined only to certain situations. Whatever the case, power is undoubtedly a pervasive part of organizational life. It affects decisions ranging from the choice of strategies to the colour of the new office carpeting. It makes or breaks careers. And it enhances or limits organizational effectiveness.

Types of Power

Within the broad framework of our definition, there obviously are many types of power. These types usually are described in terms of bases of power and position power versus personal power.

Bases of Power   The most widely used and recognized analysis of the bases of power is the framework developed by John R. P. French and Bertram Raven.[27] French

High-profile union leader Buzz Hargrove (left) of the Canadian Auto Workers has led many contract negotiations with the various auto manufacturers in Canada. Auto-sector labour negotiations often occur in "rounds," during which the CAW irons out agreements with automakers.

and Raven identified five general bases of power in organizational settings: legitimate, reward, coercive, expert, and referent power.

Legitimate power, essentially the same thing as authority, is granted by virtue of one's position in an organization. Managers have legitimate power over their subordinates. The organization specifies that it is legitimate for the designated individual to direct the activities of others. The bounds of this legitimacy are defined partly by the formal nature of the position involved and partly by informal norms and traditions. For example, it was once commonplace for managers to expect their secretaries to not only perform work-related activities such as typing and filing but also to run personal errands such as picking up laundry and buying gifts. In highly centralized, mechanistic, and bureaucratic organizations such as the military, the legitimate power inherent in each position is closely specified, widely known, and strictly followed. In more organic organizations, such as research and development labs and software firms, the lines of legitimate power often are blurry. Employees may work for more than one boss at the same time, and managers and followers may be on a nearly equal footing.

> **Legitimate power** is power that is granted by virtue of one's position in the organization.

Reward power is the extent to which a person controls rewards that are valued by another. The most obvious examples of organizational rewards are pay, promotions, and work assignments. If a manager has almost total control over the pay his subordinates receive, can make recommendations about promotions, and has considerable discretion to make job assignments, he or she has a high level of reward power. Reward power can extend beyond material rewards. As we noted in our discussions of motivation theory in Chapters 4 and 5, people work for a variety of reasons in addition to pay. For instance, some people may be motivated primarily by a desire for recognition and acceptance. To the extent that a manager's praise and acknowledgment satisfy those needs, that manager has even more reward power.

> **Reward power** is the extent to which a person controls rewards that another person values.

Coercive power exists when someone has the ability to punish or physically or psychologically harm another person. For example, some managers berate subordinates in front of everyone, belittling their efforts and generally making their lives miserable. Certain forms of coercion may be subtle. In some organizations, a particular division may be notorious as a resting place for people who have no future with the company. Threatening to transfer someone to a dead-end branch or some other undesirable location is thus a form of coercion. Clearly, the more negative the sanctions a person can

> **Coercive power** is the extent to which a person has the ability to punish or physically or psychologically harm someone else.

One's position within the organizational hierarchy influences the amount of power that individual has over others in the organization. Officers within the Canadian military can reasonably expect that the subordinates will follow those orders.

bring to bear on others, the stronger is her or his coercive power. At the same time, the use of coercive power carries a considerable cost in employee resentment and hostility.

Control over expertise or, more precisely, over information is another source of power. For example, to the extent that an inventory manager has information that a sales representative needs, the inventory manager has **expert power** over the sales representative. The more important the information and the fewer the alternative sources for getting it, the greater the power. Expert power can reside in many niches in an organization; it transcends positions and jobs. Although legitimate, reward, and coercive power may not always correspond exactly to formal authority, they often do. Expert power, on the other hand, may be associated much less with formal authority. Upper-level managers usually decide on the organization's strategic agenda, but individuals at lower levels in the organization may have the expertise those managers need to do the tasks. A research scientist may have crucial information about a technical breakthrough of great importance to the organization and its strategic decisions. Or an assistant may take on so many of the boss's routine and mundane activities that the manager loses track of such details and comes to depend on the assistant to keep things running smoothly. In other situations, lower-level participants are given power as a way to take advantage of their expertise.

Referent power is power through identification. If Marie-Josée is highly respected by Adam, Marie-Josée has referent power over Adam. Like expert power, referent power does not always correlate with formal organizational authority. In some ways, referent power is similar to the concept of charisma in that it often involves trust, similarity, acceptance, affection, willingness to follow, and emotional involvement. Referent power usually surfaces as imitation. For example, suppose a new department manager is the youngest person in the organization to have reached that rank. Further, it is widely believed that she is being groomed for the highest levels of the company. Other people in the department may begin to imitate her, thinking that they too may be able to advance. They may begin dressing like her, working the same hours, and trying to pick up as many work-related pointers from her as possible.

Position Versus Personal Power   The French and Raven framework is only one approach to examining the origins of organizational power. Another approach categorizes power in organizations in terms of position or personal power.

Expert power is the extent to which a person controls information that is valuable to someone else.

Referent power is power through identification and imitation.

Position power is power that resides in the position, regardless of who holds it. Thus, legitimate, reward, and some aspects of coercive and expert power can all contribute to position power. Position power is thus similar to authority. In creating a position, the organization simultaneously establishes a sphere of power for the person filling that position. He or she will generally have the power to direct the activities of subordinates in performing their jobs, to control some of their potential rewards, and to have a say in their punishment and discipline. There are, however, limits to a manager's position power. A manager cannot order or control activities that fall outside his or her sphere of power, for instance, directing a subordinate to commit crimes, to perform personal services, or to take on tasks that clearly are not part of the subordinate's job.

Position power resides in the position, regardless of who is filling that position.

Personal power is power that resides with an individual, regardless of his or her position in the organization. Thus, the primary bases of personal power are referent and some traces of expert, coercive, and reward power. Charisma may also contribute to personal power. Someone usually exercises personal power through rational persuasion or by playing on followers' identification with him or her. An individual with personal power often can inspire greater loyalty and dedication in followers than someone who has only position power. The stronger influence stems from the fact that the followers are acting more from choice than from necessity (as dictated, for example, by their organizational responsibilities) and thus will respond more readily to requests and appeals. Of course, the influence of a leader who relies only on personal power is limited, because followers may freely decide not to accept his or her directives or orders.

Personal power resides in the person, regardless of the position being filled.

The distinctions between formal and informal leaders are also related to position and personal power. A formal leader will have, at minimum, position power. And an informal leader will similarly have some degree of personal power. Just as a person may be both a formal and an informal leader, he or she can have both position and personal power simultaneously. Indeed, such a combination usually has the greatest potential influence on the actions of others. Figure 10.6 illustrates how personal and position power may interact to determine how much overall power a person has in a particular situation. An individual with both personal and position power will have the strongest overall power. Likewise, an individual with neither personal nor position power will have the weakest overall power. Finally, when either personal or position power is high but the other is low, the individual will have a moderate level of overall power.

The Uses of Power in Organizations

Power can be used in many ways in an organization. But because of the potential for its misuse and the concerns that it may engender, it is important that managers fully understand the dynamics of using power. People develop strong feelings of distrust if they perceive that their manager is not using his or her power appropriately.

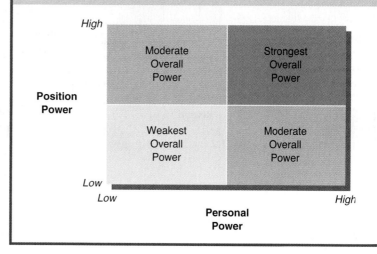

FIGURE 10.6

Position Power and Personal Power

Position power resides in a job, whereas personal power resides in an individual. When these two types of power are broken down into high and low levels and related to one another, the two-by-two matrix shown here is the result. For example, the upper right cell suggests that a leader with high levels of both position and personal power will have the highest overall level of power. Other combinations result in differing levels of overall power.

Gary Yukl has presented a useful perspective for understanding how power can be wielded.[28] His perspective includes two closely related components. The first relates power bases, requests from individuals possessing power, and probable outcomes in the form of prescriptions for the manager. Table 10.1 indicates the three outcomes that can result when a manager tries to exert power.[29] These outcomes depend on the manager's base of power, how that base is operationalized, and the subordinate's individual characteristics (for example, personality traits or past interactions with the manager).

Commitment will probably result from an attempt to exercise power if the subordinate accepts and identifies with the leader. Such an employee will be highly motivated by requests that seem important to the leader. For example, a leader might explain that a new piece of software will greatly benefit the organization if it is developed soon. A committed subordinate will work just as hard as the leader to complete the project, even if that means working overtime. Sam Walton once asked all Wal-Mart employees to start greeting customers with a smile and an offer to help. Because Wal-Mart employees generally were motivated by and loyal to Walton, most of them accepted his request.

Compliance means the subordinate is willing to carry out the leader's wishes as long as doing so will not require extra effort. That is, the person will respond to normal, reasonable requests that are perceived to clearly be within the normal boundaries of the job. But the person will not be inclined to do anything extra or to go beyond the normal expectations for the job. Thus, the subordinate may work at a reasonable pace but refuse to work overtime, insisting that the job will still be there tomorrow. Many ordinary requests from a boss meet with compliant responses from subordinates.

Resistance occurs when the subordinate rejects or fights the leader's wishes. For example, suppose an unpopular leader asks employees to volunteer for a company-sponsored community activity project. The employees may reject this request, largely because of their feelings about the leader. A resistant subordinate may even deliberately

TABLE 10.1

Uses and Outcomes of Power

Source of Leader Influence	Types of Outcome		
	Commitment	Compliance	Resistance
Referent Power	*Likely* If request is believed to be important to leader	*Possible* If request is perceived to be unimportant to leader	*Possible* If request is for something that will bring harm to leader
Expert Power	*Likely* If request is persuasive and subordinates share leader's task goals	*Possible* If request is persuasive but subordinates are apathetic about leader's task goals	*Possible* If leader is arrogant and insulting, or subordinates oppose task goals
Legitimate Power	*Possible* If request is polite and very appropriate	*Likely* If request or order is seen as legitimate	*Possible* If arrogant demands are made or request does not appear proper
Reward Power	*Possible* If used in a subtle, very personal way	*Likely* If used in a mechanical, impersonal way	*Possible* If used in a manipulative arrogant way
Coercive Power	*Very Unlikely*	*Possible* If used in a helpful, nonpunitive way	*Likely* If used in a hostile or manipulative way

Source: Table adapted by Gary A. Yukl from information in John R. P. French, Jr., and Bertram Raven, "The Bases of Social Power," in Dorwin P. Cartwright (ed.), *Studies in Social Power* (Ann Arbor, Mich.: Institute for Social Research, University of Michigan, 1959), pp. 150–167. Data used by permission of the Institute for Social Research.

neglect the project to ensure that it is not done as the leader wants. Mac Cuddy's sons often ignored their superiors and tried to wrest control of Cuddy International on several occasions before they were ousted.

Table 10.2 suggests ways for leaders to use various kinds of power most effectively. By effective use of power we mean using power in the way that is most likely to engender commitment or at the least compliance and that is least likely to engender resistance. For example, to suggest a somewhat mechanistic approach, managers may enhance their referent power by choosing subordinates with backgrounds similar to their own. They might, for instance, build a referent power base by hiring several subordinates who went to the same college they did. A more subtle way to exercise referent power is through role modelling: the leader behaves as she or he wants subordinates to behave. As noted earlier, since subordinates relate to and identify with the leader with referent power, they may subsequently attempt to emulate that person's behaviour.[30]

In using expert power, managers can subtly make others aware of their education, experience, and accomplishments. To maintain credibility, a leader should not pretend to know things that he or she really does not know. A leader whose pretensions are exposed will rapidly lose expert power. A confident and decisive leader demonstrates a

Basis of Power	Guidelines for Use
Referent Power	Treat subordinates fairly
	Defend subordinates' interests
	Be sensitive to subordinates' needs, feelings
	Select subordinates similar to oneself
	Engage in role modelling
Expert Power	Promote image of expertise
	Maintain credibility
	Act confident and decisive
	Keep informed
	Recognize employee concerns
	Avoid threatening subordinates' self-esteem
Legitimate Power	Be cordial and polite
	Be confident
	Be clear and follow up to verify understanding
	Make sure request is appropriate
	Explain reasons for request
	Follow proper channels
	Exercise power regularly
	Enforce compliance
	Be sensitive to subordinates' concerns
Reward Power	Verify compliance
	Make feasible, reasonable requests
	Make only ethical, proper requests
	Offer rewards desired by subordinates
	Offer only credible rewards
Coercive Power	Inform subordinates of rules and penalties
	Warn before punishing
	Administer punishment consistently and uniformly
	Understand the situation before acting
	Fit punishment to the infraction
	Punish in private

TABLE 10.2

Guidelines for Using Power

Source: Reprinted from Gary A. Yukl, *Leadership in Organization*, 6th ed., ©2006, pp. 148–158. Reprinted by permission of Pearson Education, Inc., Upper Saddle River, NJ.

firm grasp of situations and takes charge when circumstances dictate. Managers should also keep themselves informed about developments related to tasks that are valuable to the organization and relevant to their expertise.

A leader who recognizes employee concerns works to understand the underlying nature of these issues and takes appropriate steps to reassure subordinates. For example, if employees feel threatened by rumours that they will lose office space after an impending move, the leader might ask them about this concern and then find out just how much office space there will be and tell the subordinates. Finally, to avoid threatening the self-esteem of subordinates, a leader should be careful not to flaunt expertise or behave like a know-it-all.

Generally, a leader exercises legitimate power by formally requesting that subordinates do something. The leader should be especially careful to make requests diplomatically if the subordinate is sensitive about his or her relationship with the leader. This might be the case, for example, if the subordinate is older or more experienced than the leader. But although the request should be polite, it should be made confidently. The leader is in charge and needs to convey his or her command of the situation. The request should also be clear. Thus, the leader may need to follow up to ascertain that the subordinate has understood it properly. To ensure that a request is seen as appropriate and legitimate to the situation, the leader may need to explain the reasons for it. Often subordinates do not understand the rationale behind a request and consequently are unenthusiastic about it. It is important, too, to follow proper channels when dealing with subordinates.

Suppose a manager has asked a subordinate to spend his day finishing an important report. Later, while the manager is out of the office, the boss comes by and asks the subordinate to drop that project and work on something else. The subordinate will then be in the awkward position of having to choose which of two higher-ranking individuals to obey. Exercising authority regularly will reinforce its presence and legitimacy in the eyes of subordinates. Compliance with legitimate power should be the norm, because if employees resist a request, the leader's power base may diminish. Finally, the leader exerting legitimate power should attempt to be responsive to subordinates' problems and concerns in the same ways we outlined for using expert power.

Reward power is, in some respects, the easiest base of power to use. Verifying compliance simply means that leaders should find out whether subordinates have carried out their requests before giving rewards; otherwise, subordinates may not recognize a performance–reward linkage. The request that is to be rewarded must be both reasonable and feasible, because even the promise of a reward will not motivate a subordinate who thinks a request should not or cannot be carried out.

The same can be said for a request that seems improper or unethical. Among other things, the follower may see a reward linked to an improper or unethical request, such as a bribe or other shady offering. Finally, if the leader promises a reward that subordinates know she or he cannot actually deliver, or if they have little use for a reward the manager can deliver, they will not be motivated to carry out the request. Further, they may grow skeptical of the leader's ability to deliver rewards that are worth something to them.

Coercion is certainly the most difficult form of power to exercise. Because coercive power is likely to cause resentment and to erode referent power, it should be used infrequently, if at all. Compliance is about all one can expect from using coercive power, and that only if the power is used in a helpful, nonpunitive way—that is, if the sanction is mild and fits the situation and if the subordinate learns from it. In most cases, resistance is the most likely outcome, especially if coercive power is used in a hostile or manipulative way.

The first guideline for using coercive power—that subordinates should be fully informed about rules and the penalties for violating them—will prevent accidental violations of a rule, which pose an unpalatable dilemma for a leader. Overlooking an infraction on the grounds that the perpetrator was ignorant can undermine the rule or the leader's legitimate power, but carrying out the punishment probably will create resentment. One approach is to provide reasonable warning before inflicting punishment, responding to the first violation of a rule with a warning about the consequences of another violation. Of course, a serious infraction such as a theft or violence warrants immediate and severe punishment.

The disciplinary action needs to be administered consistently and uniformly, because doing so shows that punishment is both impartial and clearly linked to the infraction. Leaders should obtain complete information about what has happened before they punish, because punishing the wrong person or administering unwarranted punishment can stir great resentment among subordinates. Credibility must be maintained, because a leader who continually makes threats but fails to carry them out loses both respect and power. Similarly, if the leader uses threats that subordinates know are beyond his or her ability to impose, the attempted use of power will be fruitless. Obviously, too, the severity of the punishment generally should match the seriousness of the infraction. Finally, punishing someone in front of others adds humiliation to the penalty, which reflects poorly on the leader and makes those who must watch and listen uncomfortable as well.

Politics and Political Behaviour

A concept closely related to power in organizational settings is politics, or political behaviour. We can define **organizational politics** as activities people perform to acquire, enhance, and use power and other resources to obtain their preferred outcomes in a situation where there is uncertainty or disagreement.[31] Thus, political behaviour is the general means by which people attempt to obtain and use power. Put simply, the goal of such behaviour is to get one's own way about things.[32]

> **Organizational politics** are activities carried out by people to acquire, enhance, and use power and other resources to obtain their desired outcomes.

The Pervasiveness of Political Behaviour

A classic survey conducted by Victor Murray of York University and Jeffrey Gandz of the University of Western Ontario provides some interesting insights into how managers perceive political behaviour in their organizations.[33] Roughly one-third of the 428 managers who responded to this survey believed political behaviour influenced salary decisions in their organizations, whereas 28 percent felt it affected hiring decisions. Moreover, three-quarters of the respondents also believed political behaviour is more prevalent at higher levels of the organization than at lower levels. More than half believed that politics is unfair, unhealthy, and irrational but also acknowledged that successful executives must be good politicians and that it is necessary to behave politically to get ahead. The survey results suggest that managers see political behaviour as an undesirable but unavoidable facet of organizational life.[34]

Politics often are viewed as synonymous with dirty tricks or backstabbing and therefore as something distasteful and best left to others. But the results of the survey just described demonstrate that political behaviour in organizations, like power, is pervasive. Thus, rather than ignoring or trying to eliminate political behaviour, managers might more fruitfully consider when and how organizational politics can be used constructively.

Figure 10.7 presents an interesting model of the ethics of organizational politics.[35] In the model, a political behaviour alternative (PBA) is a given course of action, largely political in character, in a particular situation. The model considers political behaviour ethical and appropriate under two conditions: (1) if it respects the rights of all affected parties and (2) if it adheres to the canons of justice (that is, to a common-sense judgment of what is fair and equitable). Even if the political behaviour does not meet

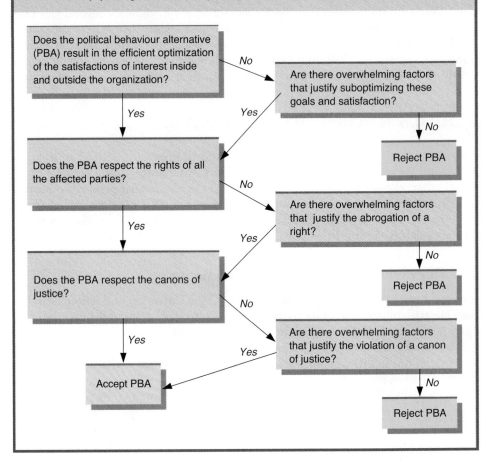

FIGURE 10.7

A Model of Ethical Political Behaviour

Political behaviour can serve both ethical and unethical purposes. This model helps illustrate circumstances in which political behaviour is most and least likely to have ethical consequences. By following the paths through the model, a leader concerned about the ethics of an impending behaviour can gain insights into whether ethical considerations are really a central part of the behaviour.

Source: Gerald F. Cavanaugh, Dennis J. Moberg, and Manuel Velasquez, "The Ethics of Organizational Politics," *Academy of Management Review*, July 1981, p. 368. Used by permission.

these tests, it may be ethical and appropriate under certain circumstances. For example, politics may provide the only possible basis for deciding which employees to let go during a recessionary period of cutbacks. In all cases where nonpolitical alternatives exist, however, the model recommends rejecting political behaviour that abrogates rights or justice.

To illustrate how the model works, consider Susan Jackson and Bill Thompson, two assistant professors of English. University regulations stipulate that only one of the assistant professors can be tenured; the other must be let go. Both Susan and Bill submit their credentials for review. By most objective criteria, such as number of publications and teaching evaluations, the two faculty members' qualifications are roughly the same. Because he fears termination, Bill begins an active political campaign to support a tenure decision favouring him. He continually reminds the tenured faculty of his intangible contributions, such as his friendship with influential campus administrators. Susan decides to say nothing and let her qualifications speak for themselves. The department ultimately votes to give Bill tenure and let Susan go.

Was Bill's behaviour ethical? Assuming that his comments about himself were accurate and that he said nothing to disparage Susan, his behaviour did not affect her rights; that is, she had an equal opportunity to advance her own cause but chose not to do so. Bill's efforts did not directly hurt Susan but only helped himself. On the other hand, it might be argued that Bill's actions violated the canons of justice because clearly defined data on which to base the decision were available. Thus, one could argue that Bill's calculated introduction of additional information into the decision was unjust.

This model has not been tested empirically. Indeed, its very nature may make it impossible to test. Further, as the preceding demonstrates, it often is difficult to give an unequivocal yes or no answer to the questions, even under the simplest circumstances. Thus, the model serves as a general framework for understanding the ethical implications of various courses of action managers might take.

How, then, should managers approach the phenomenon of political behaviour? Trying to eliminate political behaviour will seldom, if ever, work. In fact, such action may well increase political behaviour because of the uncertainty and ambiguity it creates. At the other extreme, universal and freewheeling use of political behaviour probably will lead to conflict, feuds, and turmoil.[36] In most cases, a position somewhere in between is best: the manager does not attempt to eliminate political activity, recognizing its inevitability, and might try to use it effectively, perhaps following the ethical model just described. At the same time, the manager can take certain steps to minimize the potential dysfunctional consequences of abusive political behaviour.

Managing Political Behaviour

Managing organizational politics is not easy. The very nature of political behaviour makes it tricky to approach in a rational and systematic way. Success will require a basic understanding of three factors: the reasons for political behaviour, common techniques for using political behaviour, and strategies for limiting the effects of political behaviour.

Reasons for Political Behaviour   Political behaviour occurs in organizations for five basic reasons: ambiguous goals, scarce resources, technology and environment, nonprogrammed decisions, and organizational change (see Figure 10.8).[37]

Most organizational goals are inherently ambiguous. Organizations frequently espouse goals such as "increasing our presence in certain new markets" or "increasing our market share." The ambiguity of such goals provides an opportunity for political behaviour, because people can view a wide range of behaviours as helping meet the goal. In reality, of course, many of these behaviours may actually be designed for the personal gain of the individuals involved. For example, a top manager might argue that the corporation should pursue its goal of entry into a new market by buying out another firm instead of forming a new division. The manager may appear to have the good of the corporation in mind—but what if he owns some of the target firm's stock and stands to make money on a merger or acquisition?

Whenever resources are scarce, some people will not get everything they think they deserve or need. Thus, they are likely to engage in political behaviour as a means of inflating their share of the resources. In this way, a manager seeking a larger budget

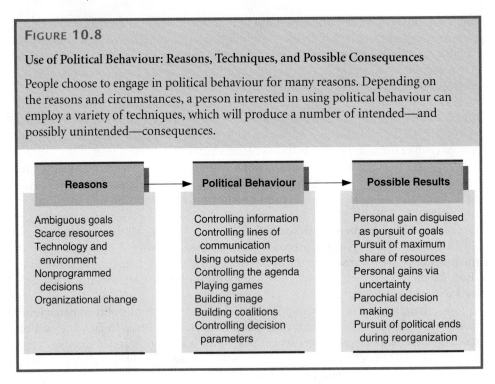

FIGURE **10.8**

Use of Political Behaviour: Reasons, Techniques, and Possible Consequences

People choose to engage in political behaviour for many reasons. Depending on the reasons and circumstances, a person interested in using political behaviour can employ a variety of techniques, which will produce a number of intended—and possibly unintended—consequences.

Reasons	Political Behaviour	Possible Results
Ambiguous goals	Controlling information	Personal gain disguised as pursuit of goals
Scarce resources	Controlling lines of communication	Pursuit of maximum share of resources
Technology and environment	Using outside experts	Personal gains via uncertainty
Nonprogrammed decisions	Controlling the agenda	Parochial decision making
Organizational change	Playing games	Pursuit of political ends during reorganization
	Building image	
	Building coalitions	
	Controlling decision parameters	

might present accurate but misleading or incomplete statistics to inflate the perceived importance of her department. Because no organization has unlimited resources, incentives for this kind of political behaviour are always present.[38]

Technology and environment can influence the overall design of the organization and its activities. The influence stems from the uncertainties associated with nonroutine technologies and dynamic, complex environments. These uncertainties favour the use of political behaviour because, in a dynamic and complex environment, it is imperative that an organization respond to change. An organization's response generally involves a wide range of activities, from purposeful activities to uncertainty to a purely political response. In the last case, a manager might use an environmental shift as an argument for restructuring his or her department to increase his or her own power base.

Political behaviour is also likely to arise whenever many nonprogrammed decisions need to be made. Nonprogrammed-decision situations involve ambiguous circumstances that allow ample opportunity for political manoeuvring. The two faculty members competing for one tenured position is an example. The nature of the decision allowed political behaviour and, in fact, from Bill's point of view, the nonprogrammed decision demanded political action.

As we discuss in Chapter 15, changes in organizations occur regularly and can take many forms. Each such change introduces some uncertainty and ambiguity into the organizational system, at least until it has been completely institutionalized. The period during which this is occurring usually affords much opportunity for political activity. For instance, a manager worried about the consequences of a reorganization might resort to politics to protect the scope of his or her authority.

The Techniques of Political Behaviour   Several techniques are used in practising political behaviour. Unfortunately, because these techniques have not been systematically studied, our understanding of them is based primarily on informal observation and inference.[39] To further complicate this problem, the participants themselves may not even be aware that they are using particular techniques. Figure 10.8 summarizes the most frequently used techniques.[40]

One technique of political behaviour is to control as much information as possible. The more critical the information and the fewer the people who have access to it, the larger the power base and influence of those who do. For example, suppose a top manager has a report compiled as a basis for future strategic plans.

Rather than distributing the complete report to peers and subordinates, he shares only parts of it with the few managers who must have the information. Because no one but the manager has the complete picture, he has power and is engaging in politics to control decisions and activities according to his own ends.

Similarly, some people create or exploit situations to control lines of communication, particularly access to others in the organization. Secretaries frequently control access to their bosses. A secretary might put visitors in contact with the boss, send them away, delay the contact by ensuring that phone calls are not returned promptly, and so forth. People in these positions often find that they can use this type of political behaviour quite effectively.

Using outside experts, such as consultants or advisers, can be an effective political technique. The manager who hires a consultant may select one whose views match her own. Because the consultant realizes that the manager was responsible for selecting him, he feels a certain obligation to the manager. Although the consultant truly attempts to be objective and unbiased, he may unconsciously recommend courses of action favoured by the manager. Given the consultant's presumed expertise and neutrality, others in the organization accept the recommendations without challenge. By using an outside expert, the manager has ultimately received what she wanted.

Controlling the agenda is another common political technique. Suppose a manager wants to prevent a committee from approving a certain proposal. The manager first tries to keep the decision off the agenda entirely, claiming that it is not yet ready for consideration, or attempts to have it placed last on the agenda. As other issues are decided, she or he sides with the same set of managers on each decision, building up a certain assumption that they are a team. When the controversial item comes up, he or she can defeat it through a combination of collective fatigue, the desire to get the meeting over with, and the support of carefully cultivated allies. This technique, then, involves group polarization. A less sophisticated tactic is to prolong discussion of prior agenda items so that the group never reaches the controversial one. Or the manager may raise so many technical issues and new questions about the proposal that the committee decides to table it. In any of these cases, the manager will have used political behaviour for his or her own ends.

Game playing is a complex technique that can take many forms. When playing games, managers simply work within the rules of the organization to increase the probability that their preferred outcomes will come about. Suppose a manager is in a position to cast the deciding vote on an upcoming issue. She or he does not want to alienate either side by voting on it. One game the manager might play is to arrange to be called out of town on a crucial business trip when the vote is to take place. Assuming that no one questions the need for the trip, the manager will successfully maintain her or his position of neutrality and avoid angering either camp.[41]

Another game would involve using any of the techniques of political behaviour in a purely manipulative or deceitful way. For example, a manager who will soon be making recommendations about promotions tells each subordinate, in strictest confidence, that he or she is a leading candidate and needs only to increase his or her performance to have the inside track. Here the manager is using control over information to play games with subordinates. A power struggle at W. R. Grace further illustrates manipulative practices. One senior executive fired the CEO's son and then allegedly attempted to convince the board of directors to oust the CEO and to give him the job. The CEO, in response, fired his rival and then publicly announced that the individual had been forced out because he had sexually harassed Grace employees.[42]

The technique of building coalitions has as its general goal convincing others that everyone should work together to accomplish certain things. A manager who believes she or he does not control enough votes to pass an upcoming agenda item may visit with other managers before the meeting to urge them to side with her. If her or his preferences are in the best interests of the organization, this may be a laudable strategy to follow. But if she or he is the principal beneficiary, the technique is not desirable from the organization's perspective. The technique of controlling decision parameters can be used only in certain situations and requires much subtlety. Instead of trying to control the actual decision, the manager backs up one step and tries to control the criteria and tests on which the decision is based. This allows the manager to take a less active role in the actual decision but still achieve his or her preferred outcome. For example, suppose a district manager wants a proposed new factory to be constructed on a site in his or her region. If the manager tries to influence the decision directly, his or her arguments will be seen as biased and self-serving. Instead, the manager may take a very active role in defining the criteria on which the decision will be based, such as target population, access to rail transportation, tax rates, distance from other facilities, and the like. If he or she is a skillful negotiator, the manager may be able to influence the decision parameters so that his desired location subsequently appears to be the ideal site as determined by the criteria he or she has helped shape. Hence, the manager gets just what he or she wants without playing a prominent role in the actual decision.

Limiting the Effects of Political Behaviour   Although it is virtually impossible to eliminate political activity in organizations, managers can limit its dysfunctional consequences. The techniques for checking political activity target both the reasons it occurs in the first place and the specific techniques that people use for political gain.

Opening communication is one very effective technique for restraining the impact of political behaviour. For instance, with open communication the basis for allocating scarce resources will be known to everyone. This knowledge, in turn, will tend to reduce the propensity to engage in political behaviour to acquire those resources, because people already know how decisions will be made. Open communication also limits the ability of any single person to control information or lines of communication.

A related technique is to reduce uncertainty. Several of the reasons political behaviour occurs—ambiguous goals, nonroutine technology, an unstable environment, and organizational change—and most of the political techniques themselves are associated with high levels of uncertainty. Political behaviour can be limited if the manager can reduce uncertainty. Consider an organization about to transfer a major division from Ontario to Alberta. Many people will resist the idea of moving west and may resort to political behaviour to forestall their own transfer. However, the manager in charge of the move could announce who will stay and who will go at the same time that news of the change spreads throughout the company, thereby curtailing political behaviour related to the move.

The adage "forewarned is forearmed" sums up the final technique for controlling political activity. Simply being aware of the causes and techniques of political behaviour can help a manager check their effects. Suppose a manager anticipates that several impending organizational changes will increase the level of political activity. As a result of this awareness, the manager quickly infers that a particular subordinate is lobbying for the use of a certain consultant only because the subordinate thinks the consultant's recommendations will be in line with his or her own. Attempts to control the agenda, engage in game playing, build a certain image, and control decision parameters often are transparently obvious to the knowledgable observer. Recognizing such behaviours for what they are, an astute manager may be able to take appropriate steps to limit their impact.

Impression Management in Organizations

Impression management is a subtle form of political behaviour that deserves special mention. **Impression management** is a direct, intentional effort by someone to enhance his or her image in the eyes of others. People engage in impression management for a variety of reasons. For one thing, they may do so to further their own careers. By making themselves look good, they think they are more likely to receive rewards, attractive job assignments, and promotions. They may also engage in impression management to boost their own self-esteem. When people have a solid image in an organization, others make them aware of it through their compliments, respect, and so forth. Another reason people use impression management is to acquire more power and hence more control.

People attempt to manage how others perceive them through a variety of mechanisms. Appearance is one of the first things people think of. Hence, a person motivated by impression management will pay close attention to choice of attire, selection of language, and the use of manners and body posture. People interested in impression management are also likely to jockey to be associated only with successful projects. By being assigned to high-profile projects led by highly successful managers, a person can begin to link his or her own name with such projects in the minds of others.

Sometimes people too strongly motivated by impression management become obsessed by it and resort to dishonest or unethical means. For example, some people have been known to take credit for others' work in an effort to make themselves look better. People have also been known to exaggerate or even falsify their personal accomplishments in an effort to enhance their image.[43]

> **Impression management** is a direct and intentional effort by someone to enhance his or her own image in the eyes of others.

Chapter Review

Summary of Key Points

- Conflict is a disagreement between parties; it is a common cause of stress in organizations. Five types of reactions to conflict are avoidance, accommodation, competition, collaboration, and compromise. The types of interactions are determined by the compatibility of goals and the importance of the interaction to group goal attainment. Managers should recognize that conflict can be beneficial as well as harmful.

- Third party intervention is often required of managers when conflict erupts between individual or groups of employees. Four intervention strategies that managers can use include inquisitorial intervention, adversarial intervention, providing impetus, and mediation. The best approach to intervention depends on situational factors surrounding the conflict.

- Negotiation is the process through which two or more parties (people or groups) reach agreement even though they have different preferences. Research on negotiation has examined individual differences, situational characteristics, game theory, and cognitive approaches. The win-win approach provides a simple four-step model to successful negotiation: planning, relationships, agreement, and maintenance.

- Power is the potential ability of a person or group to exercise control over another person or group. The five bases of power are legitimate power (granted by virtue of one's position in the organization), reward power (control of rewards valued by others), coercive power (the ability to punish or harm), expert power (control over information that is valuable to the organization), and referent power (power through personal identification). Position power is tied to a position regardless of the individual who holds it. Personal power is power that resides in a person regardless of position. Attempts to use power can result in commitment, compliance, or resistance.

- Organizational politics is activities people perform to acquire, enhance, and use power and other resources to obtain their preferred outcomes in a situation where uncertainty or disagreement exists. Research indicates that most managers do not advocate use of political behaviour but acknowledge that it is a necessity of organizational life. Because managers cannot eliminate political activity in the organization, they must learn to cope with it. Understanding how to manage political behaviour requires understanding why it occurs, what techniques it employs, and strategies for limiting its effects.

- Impression management is a direct, intentional effort by someone to enhance his or her image in the eyes of others. People engage in impression management for a variety of reasons and use a variety of methods to influence how others see them.

Discussion Questions

1. Do you agree or disagree with the assertion that conflict can be both good and bad? Cite examples of both cases.

2. Mediation is the most effective means of resolving a conflict between disputing parties. Argue both for and against this statement.

3. Describe a situation in which you negotiated an agreement, maybe buying a car or a house. How did the negotiation process compare to the PRAM approach? How did it differ? Were you satisfied with the result of the negotiation?

4. What might happen if two people, each with significant, equal power, attempt to influence each other?

5. Cite examples based on a professor–student relationship to illustrate each of the five bases of organizational power.

6. Is there a logical sequence in the use of power bases that a manager might follow? For instance, should the use of legitimate power usually precede the use of reward power, or vice versa?

7. Cite examples in which you have been committed, compliant, and resistant as a result of efforts to influence you. Think of times when your attempts to influence others led to commitment, compliance, and resistance.

8. Do you agree or disagree with the assertion that political behaviour is inevitable in organizational settings?

9. The term "politics" is generally associated with governmental bodies. Why do you think it has also come

Wal-Mart Plays Hardball

With 1.7 million workers worldwide, Wal-Mart is the planet's largest employer. The company's leaders pride themselves on creating jobs, providing decent working conditions and pay, and treating individuals with respect. Wal-Mart proclaims, "Our people make the difference." However, many Wal-Mart workers tell a very different story. In Canada, Wal-Mart has bitterly fought attempts of workers to unionize. Meanwhile, in the U.S., the company stands accused of gender discrimination.

Wal-Mart entered the Canadian market in 1994 by buying 122 discount department stores from the Canadian subsidiary of Woolco. Interestingly, Wal-Mart passed on 22 other Woolco outlets, including all 10 unionized stores.

The battle with Canadian unions began in British Columbia in 2004 when the United Food and Commercial Workers (UFCW) Union won labour board approval to allow employees at seven Wal-Mart stores to vote on a proposal to unionize. The proposal was voted down by employees at that time, but the following year, the union got approval from the labour board to allow workers at the Cranbrook, B.C., store to hold a similar vote. This time, the employees voted in favour of unionization. Wal-Mart appealed the ruling and, at a second hearing, the company lost its bid to block unionization. However, that decision was overturned by a reconsideration panel consisting of only one member of the Labour Board.

Attempts to unionize at outlets in other parts of Canada were met with resistance from Wal-Mart. In April 2004, the UFCW applied for certification in Weyburn, Saskatchewan. Wal-Mart filed an application to the Supreme Court of Canada stating that the Saskatchewan Labour Relations Act was a violation of its Charter rights. Despite the refusal of the Supreme Court to hear the case, employees of the Weyburn store continue to wait to see if they can bargain collectively.

Wal-Mart also lost a battle to prevent union certification at its store in Jonquière, Quebec. Unlike other jurisdictions in Canada, Quebec labour law allows unions to certify without elections. Instead, if the majority of employees sign union cards, the union is automatically certified by the province and management is required by law to negotiate a collective bargaining agreement. If no

agreement is reached, the government can appoint an arbitrator who has the power to impose a contract.

After initially failing to acquire the required number of signatures, the UFCW petitioned for a secret vote. Employees narrowly voted against certification. Afterward, a group of managers gathered outside the door and taunted union supporters as they left. This enraged a number of individuals who had voted against unionization. Sensing an opportunity, the union began a second campaign to acquire signed union cards. This time, the UFCW was successful, gaining certification before the company even realized what was happening. The union was automatically certified in August 2004. The negotiations that followed were bitter and failed to produce a contract. In early 2005, Wal-Mart announced that it was closing the Jonquière store.

Meanwhile, in the United States, women employed or formerly employed by Wal-Mart accuse the giant firm of gender-based discrimination. In a document requesting that the U.S. District Court in California allow a class-action lawsuit, the plaintiffs introduce their case. "Since at least 1997, female employees of Wal-Mart Stores have been paid less than comparable male employees . . . despite having, on average, higher performance ratings and more seniority . . . Female employees at Wal-Mart Stores also receive far fewer promotions to management than do male employees, and those who are promoted must wait longer." The document goes on to note that women account for two-thirds of employees at Wal-Mart but just one-third of managers. The plaintiffs also allege that the discrimination is on-going, is worsening, and is not representative of the retail industry, where women typically hold over 50 percent of management jobs.

Wal-Mart is vigorously fighting the lawsuit and some of the actions the company has taken appear very suspect. As with the union in Saskatchewan, delay has been Wal-Mart's first tactic. They have spent more than two years disputing the plaintiffs' rights to file as a class, instead suggesting that every woman must file a separate claim. This would increase legal costs and discourage claimants. Next, Wal-Mart has argued that pay and promotion are two separate issues that must be tried separately, again increasing costs for the female workers. Finally, Wal-Mart has claimed that the firm is composed of four different business units and thousands of stores, each of which acts autonomously. Thus, even if a pattern of discrimination is found, the company claims the blame should rest with individual store managers and not with the corporation. Wal-Mart seems unlikely to succeed in any of these tactics, but they do delay the trial and increase expenses, which can be very difficult for working families.

> **❝** *[F]emale employees of Wal-Mart Stores have been paid less than comparable male employees . . . despite having, on average, higher performance ratings and more seniority.* **❞**
>
> JOCELYN LARKIN AND CHRISTINE E. WEBER,
> ATTORNEYS FOR PLAINTIFFS

3. Choose one of Wal-Mart's actions mentioned in the case. In your opinion, who is hurt most by this action? Who benefits most? Use the answer to those two questions to determine whether the action is ethical or not. Explain your reasons.

Case Questions

1. How would you characterize Wal-Mart's approach to handling conflict? Why?

2. If you were asked to intervene in one of these conflicts, what approach would you take?

Sources: "No Union Please, We're Wal-Mart," *BusinessWeek*, February 13, 2006, www.businessweek.com; "Wal-Mart Closing Unionized Store," CNNMoney.com, February 9, 2005; Roy Adams, "Organizing Wal-Mart: The Canadian Campaign," *Just Labour*, Autumn 2005, pp. 1–11; Joe Schneider, "Wal-Mart Win Keeps Union from British Columbia Store," Bloomberg.com, May 2, 2007; "Betty Dukes et. al. v. Wal-Mart Stores Inc.— Plaintiffs' Reply in Support of Class Certification," Cohen, Milstein, Hausfield & Toll website, www.cmht.com on June 11, 2005; Jonathan D. Glazer, "Attention Wal-Mart Plaintiffs: Hurdles Ahead," *New York Times*, June 27, 2004, p. BU5; Joe Hansen, "Hold Wal-Mart Accountable," UFCW website, www.ufcw.org on June 11, 2005; Joe Hansen, "More Villain than Victim," *USA Today*, April 17, 2005, www.usatoday.com on June 11, 2005.

SELF TEST

You have read the chapter and studied the key terms. Think you're ready to ace the exam? Take this sample test to gauge your comprehension of chapter material and check your answers at the back of the book.

T   F   1. Conflict usually refers to a specific event.

T   F   2. Process conflict occurs when the parties disagree on how to achieve the goals and actually do the work.

T   F   3. Competition for scarce resources is unlikely to lead to intergroup conflict.

T   F   4. If interaction is unimportant to two parties, and their goals are incompatible, the two parties are likely to avoid interacting with each other.

T   F   5. The identification of a superordinate goal may help two parties resolve their conflict.

T   F   6. A person with coercive power has the ability to physically or psychologically punish another person.

T   F   7. Subtly making others aware of your education, experience, and accomplishments is a good way to use legitimate power.

T   F   8. Managers should do their best to eliminate all political activity in their organizations.

9. Which of the following is not a potential benefit of conflict?
   a. stimulates new ideas
   b. facilitates downsizing
   c. energizes behaviour
   d. conducive to higher-quality decisions
   e. promotes healthy competition

10. Conflict regarding the goals and content of the work is called
    a. task conflict.
    b. process conflict.
    c. relationship conflict.
    d. labour conflict.
    e. legal conflict.

11. Which form of interdependence results in the greatest potential for conflict?
    a. relationship interdependence
    b. process interdependence
    c. reciprocal interdependence
    d. sequential interdependence
    e. pooled interdependence

12. Greg and Gina have incompatible goals, but in order for them each to meet their individual goals, they have to interact. Which of the following is the likely reaction to this situation?
    a. avoidance
    b. accommodation
    c. competition
    d. compromise
    e. collaboration

13. People engage in impression management for all of the following reasons, except
    a. to further their own careers.
    b. to improve the image of their company.
    c. to receive rewards and promotions.
    d. to acquire more power.
    e. to boost their own self-esteem.

14. Lawrence is a manager over fifteen employees in his organization. At a minimum, Lawrence has which base of power?
    a. managerial
    b. expert
    c. legitimate
    d. coercive
    e. referent

15. To prevent accidental violations of a rule, a manager who wants to use coercive power should first
    a. make reasonable and feasible requests.
    b. fully inform subordinates about the rules and the penalties for violating them.
    c. be polite and confident.
    d. make subordinates aware of the manager's education, expertise, and accomplishments.
    e. be responsive to subordinates' problems and concerns.

16. What advice would you give managers with regard to handling political behaviours within an organization?
    a. Eliminate all political behaviour.
    b. Allow political behaviour at the top of the organization, but not at the bottom.
    c. Allow political behaviour at the bottom of the organization, but not at the top.
    d. Minimize the potential dysfunctional consequences of abusive political behaviour.
    e. Let the political "market" of the organization govern itself.

CHAPTER 11

Leadership Models and Concepts

▶ **Explain the meaning of leadership and differentiate it from management.**

▶ **Summarize the trait and behavioural approaches to leadership.**

▶ **Describe the LPC theory of leadership.**

▶ **Explain the path-goal theory of leadership.**

▶ **Describe the Vroom-Yetton-Jago model of leadership.**

▶ **Summarize the leader-member exchange theory.**

▶ **Summarize the transformational and charismatic approaches to leadership.**

Chapter Outline

Transforming Manulife Financial

D ominc D'Alessandro has helped to transform Manulife in a number of ways ever since he became its CEO in 1994. One major change was the "demutualization" of the company, which entailed changing the ownership structure from being owned by policy holders to a publicly traded company. He has led Manulife through a series of acquisitions, the largest of which was the merger with John Hancock in the United States. At the time, that was the largest cross-border acquisition, valued at over $15 billion. He has also been instrumental in entering other international markets. Manulife currently operates in 19 countries, has over 20,000 employees, and is one of the largest Canadian corporations in terms of its market capitalization.

He encapsulates his vision on how the company and its employees should work in the acronym "PRIDE." PRIDE stands for Professionalism, Real Value to Customers, Integrity, Demonstrated Financial Strength, and Employer of Choice. The philosophy has permeated the organization. Manulife has been recognized as being one of the best employers in Canada, possessing one of the best corporate cultures, being one of the "greenest" financial services companies in Canada, one of the most respected companies, for its excellence in corporate governance practices, service quality, and was even recognized for its community involvement in Hong Kong.

D'Alessandro believes strongly in community service. He is an active participant in a number of volunteer causes, including the United Way, the Corporate Fund for Breast Cancer Research, the Salvation Army, and helping immigrants adjust to Canada. Here again, the company he leads reflects his personal values. Manulife has a very active corporate philanthropy program, focusing on health and education. It also has a program that matches charitable donations made by its employees. Additionally, it has an employee volunteerism program—in 2005, Manulife employees logged over 44 000 hours of volunteer time.

At the same time, the bottom line has not suffered: Manulife posted 12 consecutive years of growing profits. D'Alessandro has received numerous awards and recognition for his visionary leadership in financial services and his commitment to the community. He was selected as Canada's Top CEO in 2002; named to the Order of Canada in 2003; named most respected CEO in 2004 among other achievements.[1]

Dominic D'Alessandro is a manager. But more than that, he is also a leader. By using a wide array of skills and by effectively playing both roles, D'Alessandro is leading Manulife toward new ways of doing business to remain competitive and grow in a globalizing business environment. Like D'Alessandro, many of today's executives are expected to be both able managers and strong leaders, including having strong values and ethics. Most experts believe they understand the basic ideas underlying effective management, but leadership is a much more elusive phenomenon. Indeed, the mystique of leadership is one of the most widely debated, studied, and sought-after commodities of organizational life.[2] Managers talk about the characteristics that make an effective leader, and organizational scientists have extensively researched the issue. Unfortunately, neither group can answer some basic questions about leadership.[3]

Leaders have no significant effect on organizations in some situations. But in others, leaders make the difference between enormous success and overwhelming failure. Although some leaders are effective in one organization but not in others, some succeed no matter where they are.[4] Yet despite hundreds of studies on leadership, researchers have found no simple way to account for these inconsistencies. Why, then, should we study leadership? First, leadership is of great practical importance to organizations. Second, researchers have isolated and verified some key variables that influence leadership effectiveness.[5]

We begin this chapter with a discussion of the meaning of leadership, including its definition and further distinctions between leadership and management. Then we turn to historical views of leadership, focusing on the trait and behavioural approaches, as well as an early contingency theory—the LPC theory developed by Fiedler. Next, we examine two leadership theories that have formed the basis for much leadership research, the path-goal theory, and the Vroom-Yetton-Jago model. We conclude by describing two contemporary models of leadership that are attracting a significant amount of attention among researchers and practitioners, the leader-member exchange (LMX) theory and charismatic and transformational leadership.

The Nature of Leadership

Because leadership is a term that is often used in everyday conversation, you might assume that it has a common meaning. Just the opposite is true—like other key organizational behaviour terms, such as personality and motivation, leadership is used in a variety of ways. Thus, we first clarify its meaning as used in this book.

The Meaning of Leadership

Leadership is both a process and a property. As a process, leadership involves the use of noncoercive influence. As a property, leadership is the set of characteristics attributed to someone who is perceived to use influence successfully.

We will define **leadership** in terms of both process and property.[6] As a process, leadership is the use of noncoercive influence to direct and coordinate the activities of group members to meet a goal. As a property, leadership is the set of characteristics attributed to those who are perceived to use such influence successfully.[7] From an organizational viewpoint, leadership is vital because it has such a powerful influence on individual and group behaviour. Moreover, because the goal toward which the group directs its efforts is often the desired goal of the leader, it may or may not mesh with organizational goals.[8]

Leadership involves neither force nor coercion. A manager who relies solely on force and formal authority to direct the behaviour of subordinates is not exercising leadership.[9] Thus, as described more fully below, a manager or supervisor may or may not also be a leader. It is also important to note that a leader may possess the characteristics attributed to him or her or the leader may merely be perceived as possessing them.

Leadership Versus Management

From these definitions, it should be clear that leadership and management are related, but they are not the same. A person can be a manager, a leader, both, or neither.[10] Some of the basic distinctions between the two are summarized in Table 11.1. On the left side of the table are four elements that differentiate leadership from management. The two columns show how each element differs when considered from a management and a leadership point of view. For example, when executing plans, managers focus on monitoring results, comparing them with goals, and correcting deviations. In contrast, the leader focuses on energizing people to overcome bureaucratic hurdles to help reach goals.

To further underscore the differences, consider the various roles that might typify managers and leaders in a hospital setting. The chief of staff of a large hospital is clearly a manager by virtue of the position itself. At the same time, this individual may not be respected or trusted by others and may have to rely solely on the authority vested in the position to get people to do things. But an emergency-room nurse with no formal authority may be quite effective at taking charge of a chaotic situation and directing others in how to deal with specific patient problems. Others in the emergency room may respond because they trust the nurse's judgment and have confidence in the nurse's decision-making skills.

Activity	Management	Leadership	
Creating an agenda	**Planning and budgeting.** Establishing detailed steps and timetables for achieving needed results; allocating the resources necessary to make those needed results happen	**Establishing direction.** Developing a vision of the future, often the distant future, and strategies for producing the changes needed to achieve that vision	**TABLE 11.1** **Distinctions Between Management and Leadership**
Developing a human network for achieving the agenda	**Organizing and staffing.** Establishing some structure for accomplishing plan requirements, staffing that structure with individuals, delegating responsibility and authority for carrying out the plan, providing policies and procedures to help guide people, and creating methods or systems to monitor implementation	**Aligning people.** Communicating the direction by words and deeds to all those whose cooperation may be needed to influence the creation of teams and coalitions that understand the vision and strategies and accept their validity	
Executing plans	**Controlling and problem solving.** Monitoring results vs. plan in some detail, identifying deviations, and planning and organizing to solve these problems	**Motivating and inspiring.** Energizing people to overcome major political, bureaucratic, and resource barriers to change by satisfying very basic, but often unfulfilled, human needs	
Outcomes	Produces a degree of predictability and order and has the potential to consistently produce major results expected by various stakeholders (e.g., for customers, always being on time; for stockholders, being on budget)	Produces change, often to a dramatic degree, and has the potential to produce extremely useful change (e.g., new products that customers want, new approaches to labour relations that help make a firm more competitive)	

Source: Adapted with permission of The Free Press, a Division of Simon & Schuster Inc. from *A Force for Change: How Leadership Differs from Management,* by John P. Kotter. Copyright ©1990 by John P. Kotter, Inc.

The head of pediatrics, supervising a staff of 20 other doctors, nurses, and attendants, may also enjoy their complete respect, confidence, and trust. They readily take advice and follow directives without question, and often go far beyond what is necessary to help carry out the unit's mission. Thus, being a manager does not ensure that a person is also a leader—any given manager may or may not also be a leader. Similarly, a leadership position can also be formal, as when someone appointed to head a group has leadership qualities, or informal, as when a leader emerges from the ranks of the group according to a consensus of the members. The chief of staff described above is a manager but not a leader. The emergency-room nurse is a leader but not a manager. And the head of pediatrics is both.

Organizations need both management and leadership if they are to be effective. For example, leadership is necessary to create and direct change and to help the organization get through tough times. And management is necessary to achieve coordination and systematic results and to handle administrative activities during times of stability and predictability. Management in conjunction with leadership can help achieve planned orderly change, and leadership in conjunction with management can keep the organization properly aligned with its environment. In addition, managers and leaders also play a major role in setting the moral climate of the organization and in determining the role of ethics in its culture.

Many successful businesses are led by people who understand how to be effective leaders as well as effective managers. Meg Whitman is president and CEO of eBay, the popular online auction business. Ms. Whitman used her managerial acumen to assemble a strong top management team, shown with her here. By aligning people effectively and motivating and inspiring them to succeed, she is laying the foundation for the continued success of eBay.

Early Approaches to Leadership

Although leaders and leadership have profoundly influenced the course of human events, careful scientific study began only about a century ago. Early study focused on the traits, or personal characteristics, of leaders.[11] Later research shifted to examine actual leader behaviours.

Trait Approaches to Leadership

Lincoln, Napoleon, Joan of Arc, Hitler, and Gandhi are names that most of us know quite well. Early researchers believed that notable leaders such as these had some unique set of qualities or traits that distinguished them from their peers. Moreover, these traits were presumed to be relatively stable and enduring. Following this **trait approach**, these researchers focused on identifying leadership traits, developing methods for measuring them, and using the methods to select leaders.[12]

The **trait approach** to leadership attempted to identify stable and enduring character traits that differentiated effective leaders from nonleaders.

Hundreds of studies guided by this research agenda were conducted during the first several decades of the 1900s. The earliest writers believed that important leadership traits included intelligence, dominance, self-confidence, energy, activity, and task-relevant knowledge. The results of subsequent studies gave rise to a long list of additional traits. Unfortunately, the list quickly became so long as to lose any semblance of practical value. In addition, the results of many studies were inconsistent.

For example, one early argument was that effective leaders such as Lincoln tended to be taller than ineffective leaders. But critics were quick to point out that Hitler and Napoleon, both effective leaders in their own way, were not tall. Some writers have even tried to relate leadership to such traits as body shape, astrological sign, or handwriting patterns. The trait approach also had a significant theoretical problem in that it could neither specify nor prove how presumed leadership traits are connected to leadership per se.[13] For these and other reasons, the trait approach was all but abandoned several decades ago.

In recent years, however, the trait approach has received renewed interest. For example, Robert Lord and his colleagues re-examined some of the early trait research evidence.[14] They reported that some traits do seem to be important for leader emergence. Note that this argument differs from the assumption of earlier researchers who thought that leader traits were related to performance. Lord and his colleagues on the other hand suggest that people hold stereotypical views about the characteristics that leaders should possess. Individuals who possess traits that fit with the stereotype are perceived to have leadership potential, and are more likely to attain leadership positions. Other researchers have sought to reintroduce a limited set of traits back into the leadership literature. These traits include drive, motivation, honesty and integrity, self-confidence, cognitive ability, knowledge of the business, and charisma.[15] Some people also believe that biological factors may play a role in leadership as well. Although it is too early to know whether these traits have validity from a leadership perspective, it does appear that a serious and scientific assessment of appropriate traits may further our understanding of the leadership phenomenon.

Michaëlle Jean, the governor-general of Canada, possesses many traits thought to be common among leaders. She is passionate about human rights, and delivers her messages effectively and with great poise.

Similarly, other work has also started examining the role of gender and other diversity factors in leadership. For example, do women and men tend to lead differently? Some early research suggests that there are indeed fundamental differences in leadership as practised by women and men. However, more recent research suggests that gender role, that is whether someone is more masculine, feminine, or androgynous in their behaviour, is more important than biological sex.[16] Still other research demonstrates that male and female leaders are perceived very differently, which is the subject of the Psychology and . . . Research box.

The role of national culture may also be important. There may be important leadership differences in different cultures.[17] Business leaders in the U.S and Canada often talk today about growth, profits, strategy, and competition. But Japanese leaders are more prone to stress group cohesiveness and identity. And, Kun-Hee Lee chair of South Korea's Samsung group, emphasises the importance of competition, like his western counterparts, but also the importance of harmony and community interdependence.[18] Thus, as with gender, ethnicity, and age, researchers need to place attention on cultural differences in leadership traits, roles, and behaviours.

Behavioural Approaches to Leadership

In the late 1940s, most researchers began to shift away from the trait approach and to look at leadership as an observable process or activity. The goal of the so-called **behavioural approach** was to determine what behaviours are associated with effective

The **behavioural approach** to leadership tried to identify behaviours that differentiated effective leaders from nonleaders.

Psychology and . . .   **RESEARCH**

Understanding the Psychological Processes That May Explain the Glass Ceiling

The "Glass Ceiling" is a term used to describe the invisible barrier that continues to keep females from top leadership roles in organizations. Despite many years of recognition of the glass ceiling, the introduction of employment equity practices, and ever increasing female participation in the workforce, the barrier continues to exist.

Kristen Scott of the University of Toronto at Scarborough and Douglas Brown of the University of Waterloo did a series of experiments to understand the psychological processes that may lead to many people—both males and females—to conclude that females do not fit our shared image of a leader and therefore be reluctant to put females into positions of power. In their study, published in 2006, they first noted that the glass ceiling continues to persist into the twenty-first century. Citing data from the U.S. Bureau of Labor Statistics gathered in 2005, they note that while females hold slightly more that 35% of all management positions, they hold only about 8% of top management positions. European data show a similar trend.

Why is this so? Scott and Brown reviewed previous studies and suggested that a clash of stereotypes may cause females not to be perceived as leaders. That is, the stereotypic traits and behaviours of females are more "communal": women are expected to be kind, nurturing, and concerned about building relationships. Stereotypical male behaviour, on the other hand, is assumed to be "agentic," more goal oriented, individualistic, and competitive. What can cause the problem for females not to be seen as leaders is that the "leader stereotype" is also agentic. Consequently, stereotypic "female" behaviours do not fit the expectations for stereotypic "leader" behaviours.

In their first study, Scott and Brown tested response times of subjects to a visual display task. Subjects were flashed a series of sentences that described a person displaying a behaviour, then flashed either a real word or nonsense series of jumbled letters. The subjects' task was to as quickly as possible determine whether a real word or nonsense syllable had been presented. The real test of the clash of stereotypes was to see how long it took for subjects to respond to a pairing of a sentence such as "Jane works late to finish important assignments" followed by the word "determined." Following from above,

Scott and Brown hypothesized that it would take subjects longer to recognize a word representing a stereotypically male trait (determined) when exhibited by a female target (Jane), than if the same trait had been exhibited by a male. They also expected the opposite that it would also take longer to process when a male exhibited a stereotypical female trait. The results of the first study showed that it did take subjects longer to process when a female target exhibited an "agentic" (typically male) trait. However, there were no differences across target genders when processing "communal" traits.

In their second study, Scott and Brown further explored the difference in how people process agentic behaviours when displayed by either male or female managers. This time, they looked at how "trait activation," or the degree to which a particular trait is raised in people's consciousness affects what traits people see in themselves. In this study, subjects were asked to read descriptions of male or female managers displaying either agentic or communal behaviours. Scott and Brown hypothesized that subjects were more likely to see themselves as possessing agentic traits when they read a description of a scene where stereotypes were confirmed, that is, when male managers displayed agentic behaviours. They made this hypothesis on the basis that agentic traits would be activated when the subjects read a story that confirmed their stereotypes. However, agentic traits would not be activated as strongly when the entire scene was ambiguous due to the clash of stereotypes when a female demonstrated agentic behaviours. The results of their study confirmed the hypothesis.

Although the studies examined very particular and precise psychological processes, the results have some important implications. One implication is somewhat disheartening: gender stereotypes run deep, down to the level of basic understanding of whether female behaviour "fits" our perceptions of leaders. Female leaders continue to have a hard time to be accepted as leaders. Still, there is hope for a better future. One action that Scott and Brown suggests is for organizations to actively try to change their organizational cultures, to recognize that both stereotypically male and female traits and behaviours are important attributes for leaders. Other

(Continued)

> (*Continued*)
>
> research has also suggested that there is growing awareness that "androgynous" styles that combine both typically male and female behaviours are successful in modern organizations that rely more on teamwork than a traditional top-down style. Finally, Scott and Brown suggest that females might try to be seen as "leaders first" and "female second" in an attempt to break the
>
> normal information processing cycle. That said, they also recognize that the results of their studies suggest that this may be difficult to execute.
>
> *Source:* Kristyn A. Scott and Douglas J. Brown, "Female First and Leader Second? Gender Bias in the Encoding of Leadership Behavior", *Organizational Behavior and Human Decision Processes*, 2006, vol. 101, pp. 230–242.

leadership.[19] The researchers assumed that the behaviours of effective leaders differed somehow from the behaviours of less effective leaders and that the behaviours of effective leaders would be the same across all situations. The behavioural approach to the study of leadership has been largely influenced by early work referred to as the Michigan studies and the Ohio State studies.[20]

The Michigan Studies   The **Michigan leadership studies** were a program of research conducted at the University of Michigan.[21] The goal of this work was to determine the pattern of leadership behaviours that results in effective group performance. From interviews with supervisors and subordinates of high- and low-productivity groups in several organizations, the researchers collected and analyzed descriptions of supervisory behaviour to determine how effective supervisors differed from ineffective ones. Two basic forms of leader behaviour were identified—job-centred and employee-centred—as shown in the top portion of Figure 11.1.

The leader who exhibits **job-centred leader behaviour** pays close attention to the work of subordinates, explains work procedures, and is mainly interested in performance. The leader's primary concern is efficient completion of the task. The leader who engages in **employee-centred leader behaviour** attempts to build effective work groups with high performance goals. The leader's main concern is with high performance, but that is to be accomplished by paying attention to the human aspects of the group. These two styles of leader behaviour were presumed to be at opposite ends of a single dimension. Thus, Likert and his associates suggested that any given leader could exhibit either job-centred or employee-centred leader behaviour, but not both at the same time. Moreover, they suggested that employee-centred leader behaviour was more likely to result in effective group performance than was job-centred leader behaviour.

The Ohio State Studies   The **Ohio State leadership studies** were conducted about the same time as the Michigan studies (in the late 1940s and early 1950s).[22] During this program of research, behavioural scientists at the Ohio State University developed a questionnaire that they administered in both military and industrial settings, to assess subordinates' perceptions of their leaders' behaviour. The Ohio State studies identified several forms of leader behaviour but tended to focus on the two most significant ones: consideration and initiating-structure.

When engaging in **consideration behaviour**, the leader is concerned with the subordinates' feelings and respects subordinates' ideas. The leader-subordinate relationship is characterized by mutual trust, respect, and two-way communication. When using **initiating-structure behaviour**, the leader clearly defines the leader-subordinate roles so that subordinates know what is expected of them. The leader also establishes channels of communication and determines the methods for accomplishing the group's task.

The **Michigan leadership studies** defined job-centred and employee-centred leadership as opposite ends of a single leadership dimension.

Job-centred leader behaviour involves paying close attention to the work of subordinates, explaining work procedures, and demonstrating a strong interest in performance.

Employee-centred leader behaviour involves attempting to build effective work groups with high performance goals.

The **Ohio State leadership studies** defined leader consideration and initiating-structure behaviours as independent dimensions of leadership.

Consideration behaviour involves being concerned with subordinates' feelings and respecting subordinates' ideas.

Initiating-structure behaviour involves clearly defining the leader-subordinate roles so that subordinates know what is expected of them.

Unlike the employee-centred and job-centred leader behaviours, consideration and initiating structure were not thought to be on the same continuum. Instead, as shown in the bottom portion of Figure 11.1, they were seen as independent dimensions of the leader's behavioural repertoire. As a result, a leader could exhibit high initiating-structure and low consideration or low-initiating structure and high consideration. A leader could also exhibit high or low levels of each behaviour simultaneously. For example, a leader may clearly define subordinates' roles and expectations but exhibit little concern for their feelings. Alternatively, she or he may be concerned about subordinates' feelings but fail to define roles and expectations clearly. But the leader might also demonstrate concern for performance expectations and employee welfare simultaneously.

The Ohio State researchers also investigated the stability of leader behaviours over time. They found that a given individual's leadership pattern appeared to change little as long as the situation remained fairly constant.[23] Another topic they looked at was the combinations of leader behaviours that were related to effectiveness. At first, they believed that leaders who exhibit high levels of both behaviours would be most effective. An early study at International Harvester (now Navistar Corporation), however, found that employees of supervisors who ranked high on initiating-structure were higher performers but also expressed lower levels of satisfaction. Conversely, employees of supervisors who ranked high on consideration had lower performance ratings but also had fewer absences from work.[24] Later research showed that these conclusions were misleading because the studies did not consider all the important variables. In other words, the situational context limits the extent to which consistent and uniform relationships exist between leader behaviours and subordinate responses. As a result, there are no simple explanations of what constitutes effective leader behaviour because leader effectiveness varies from one situation to another.

The Michigan and Ohio State behavioural models attracted considerable attention from managers and behavioural scientists. Unfortunately, later research on each model revealed significant weaknesses. For example, they were not always supported by research and were even found to be ineffective in some settings.[25] The behavioural approaches were valuable in that they identified several fundamental leader behaviours that are still used in most leadership theories today. Moreover, they moved leadership research away from the narrow trait theory. The Michigan and Ohio State studies were exploratory in nature, and they have given researchers several fundamental insights into basic leadership processes. However, in trying to precisely specify a set of leader behaviours effective in all situations the studies overlooked the enormous complexities of individual behaviour in organizational settings.

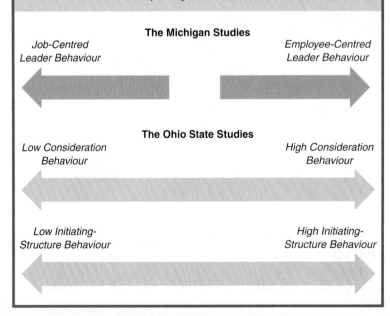

FIGURE 11.1

Early Behavioural Approaches to Leadership

Two of the first behavioural approaches to leadership were the Michigan and Ohio State studies. The results of the Michigan studies suggested that there are two fundamental types of leader behaviour, job-centred and employee-centred, which were presumed to be at opposite ends of a single continuum. The Ohio State studies also found two similar kinds of leadership behaviour, consideration and initiating-structure, but this research suggested that these two types of behaviour were actually independent dimensions.

The Michigan Studies

Job-Centred Leader Behaviour   *Employee-Centred Leader Behaviour*

The Ohio State Studies

Low Consideration Behaviour   *High Consideration Behaviour*

Low Initiating-Structure Behaviour   *High Initiating-Structure Behaviour*

In the end, their most basic shortcoming was that they failed to meet their primary goal—to identify universal leader-behaviour and follower-response patterns and relationships. Managers and behavioural scientists thus realized that still different approaches were needed to accommodate the complexities of leadership. Consequently, they began to focus on contingency theories to better explain leadership and its consequences. These theories assume that appropriate leader behaviour will vary across settings. Their focus is on better understanding how different situations call for different forms of leadership. One of the earliest contingency approaches that was subsequently widely criticized is the LPC theory.

The LPC Theory of Leadership

Fred Fiedler developed the **LPC theory of leadership**. The LPC theory attempts to explain and reconcile both the leader's personality and the complexities of the situation.[26] (This theory was originally called the contingency theory of leadership. However, because this label has come to have generic connotations, new labels are being used to avoid confusion. LPC stands for least-preferred coworker, a concept we explain later in this section). The LPC theory contends that a leader's effectiveness depends on the situation and, as a result, some leaders may be effective in one situation or organization but not in another. The theory also attempts to explain why this discrepancy may occur and identifies leader-situation matches that should result in effective performance.

> The **LPC theory of leadership** suggests that a leader's effectiveness depends on the situation.

Task Versus Relationship Motivation Fiedler and his associates maintain that leadership effectiveness depends on the match between the leader's personality and the situation. Fiedler devised special terms to describe a leader's basic personality traits vis-à-vis leadership: *task motivation* versus *relationship motivation*. He also conceptualized the situational context in terms of its favourableness for the leader, ranging from highly favourable to highly unfavourable.

In some respects, the ideas of task and relationship motivation resemble the basic concepts identified in the behavioural approaches. Task motivation closely parallels job-centred and initiating-structure leader behaviour, and relationship motivation is similar to employee-centred and consideration leader behaviour. A major difference, however, is that Fiedler viewed task versus relationship motivation as being grounded in personality in a way that is basically constant for any given leader.

The degree of task or relationship motivation in a given leader is measured by the **least-preferred coworker scale (LPC)**.[27] The LPC instructions ask respondents (i.e., leaders) to think of all the persons with whom they have worked and to then select their least-preferred coworker. Respondents who describe their least-preferred coworker in relatively positive terms receive a high LPC score, whereas those who use relatively negative terms receive a low LPC score.

> The **least-preferred coworker scale (LPC)** presumes to measure a leader's motivation.

Fiedler assumed that these descriptions actually say more about the leader than about the least-preferred coworker. He believed, for example, that everyone's least preferred coworker is likely to be equally unpleasant and that differences in descriptions actually reflect differences in personality traits among the leaders responding to the LPC scale. Fiedler contended that high-LPC leaders are more concerned with interpersonal relations, whereas low-LPC leaders are more concerned with task-relevant problems. Not surprisingly, controversy has always surrounded the LPC scale. Researchers have offered several interpretations of the LPC score, arguing that it may be an index of behaviour, personality, or some other unknown factor.[28] Indeed, the LPC measure—and its interpretation—have long been among the most debated aspects of this theory.

Situational Favourableness   Fiedler also identified three factors that determine the favourableness of the situation. In order of importance (from most to least important), these factors are leader-member relations, task structure, and leader position power.

Leader-member relations refers to the personal relationship that exists between subordinates and their leader. It is based on the extent to which subordinates trust, respect, and have confidence in their leader, and vice versa. A high degree of mutual trust, respect, and confidence obviously indicates good leader-member relations, and a low degree indicates poor leader-member relations.

Task structure is the second most important determinant of situational favourableness. A structured task is routine, simple, easily understood, and unambiguous. The LPC theory presumes that structured tasks are more favourable because the leader need not be closely involved in defining activities and can devote time to other matters. On the other hand, an unstructured task is one that is nonroutine, ambiguous, and complex. Fiedler argues that this is more unfavourable, because the leader must play a major role in guiding and directing the activities of subordinates.

Finally, *leader position power* is the power inherent in the leader's role itself. If the leader has considerable power to assign work, reward and punish employees, and recommend them for promotion, position power is high and favourable. If, however, the leader must have job assignments approved by someone else, does not control rewards and punishment, and has no voice in promotions, position power is low and unfavourable; that is, many decisions are beyond the leader's control.

Leader Motivation and Situational Favourableness   Fiedler and his associates conducted numerous studies examining the relationships among leader motivation, situational favourableness, and group performance. They contend that a task-oriented leader is appropriate for very favourable as well as very unfavourable situations. For example, the LPC theory predicts that if leader-member relations are poor, the task is unstructured, and leader position power is low, a task-oriented leader will be effective. It also predicts that a task-oriented leader will be effective if leader-member relations are good, the task is structured, and leader position power is high. Finally, for situations of intermediate favourability, the theory suggests that a person-oriented leader will be most likely to get high group performance.

Leader-Situation Match   What happens if a person-oriented leader faces a very favourable or very unfavourable situation or a task-oriented leader faces a situation of intermediate favourability? Fiedler refers to these leader-situation combinations as mismatches. Recall that a basic premise of his theory is that leadership behaviour is a personality trait. Thus, the mismatched leader cannot adapt to the situation and achieve effectiveness. Fiedler contends that when a leader's style and the situation do not match, the only available course of action is to change the situation through job engineering.[29]

For example, Fiedler suggests that if a person-oriented leader ends up in a situation that is very unfavourable, the manager should attempt to improve matters by spending more time with subordinates to improve leader-member relations and by laying down rules and procedures to provide more task structure. Fiedler and his associates have also developed a widely used training program for supervisors on how to assess situational favourability and change the situation to achieve a better match.[30] Weyerhauser and Boeing are among the firms that have experimented with Fiedler's training program.

Evaluation and Implications   The validity of Fiedler's LPC theory has been heatedly debated due to the inconsistency of the research results. Apparent shortcomings of the theory are that the LPC measure lacks validity, the theory is not always supported by research, and Fiedler's assumptions about the inflexibility of leader be-haviour are unrealistic.[31] The theory itself, however, does represent an important con-tribution because it returned the field to a study of the situation and explicitly considered not only the behaviours of the leaders, but also the organizational context and its role in effective leadership.

We now turn our attention to more modern and well accepted approaches, and begin with a discussion of two more recent contingency theories, the path-goal theory, and the Vroom-Yetton-Jago model of leadership.

The Path-Goal Theory of Leadership

Developed jointly by Martin Evans of the University of Toronto and Robert House (formerly at the University of Toronto), the path-goal theory focuses on the situation and leader behaviours rather than on fixed traits of the leader.[32] The path-goal theory thus allows for the possibility of adapting leadership to the situation.

> The **path-goal theory of leadership** suggests that effective leaders clarify the paths (behaviours) that will lead to desired rewards (goals).

Basic Premises

The path-goal theory has its roots in the expectancy theory of motivation discussed in Chapter 4. Recall that expectancy theory says that a person's attitudes and behaviours can be predicted from the degree to which the person believes job performance will lead to various outcomes (expectancy) and the value of those outcomes (valences) to the individual. The **path-goal theory of leadership** argues that subordinates are mo-tivated by their leader to the extent that the behaviours of that leader influence their ex-pectancies. In other words, the leader affects subordinates' performance by clarifying the behaviours (paths) that will lead to desired rewards (goals). Ideally, of course, getting a reward in an organization depends on effec-tive performance. Path-goal theory also sug-gests that a leader may behave in different ways in different situations.

Leader Behaviours As Figure 11.2 shows, path-goal theory identifies four kinds of leader behaviour: directive, supportive, par-ticipative, and achievement-oriented. With *directive leadership*, the leader lets subordi-nates know what is expected of them, gives specific guidance as to how to accomplish tasks, schedules work to be done, and main-tains definitive standards of performance for subordinates. A leader exhibiting *supportive leadership* is friendly and shows concern for subordinates' status, well-being, and needs. With participative leadership, the leader consults with subordinates about issues and

The path-goal theory of leadership encompasses four kinds of leader behaviour. Andrea Jung, chair and CEO of Avon, uses each of these behaviours on a regular basis. For example, she occasionally uses directive behavior to set performance expectations and provide guidance. Jung also demonstrates supportive behaviour through her care and interest in those she works with. Finally, she also uses achievement-oriented leadership in that she sets challenging goals and provides constant encouragement for everyone to work toward those goals.

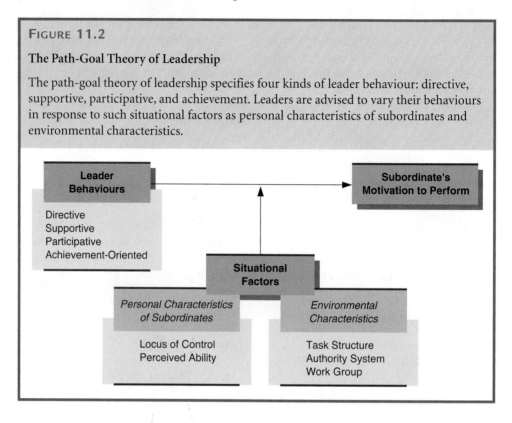

FIGURE 11.2

The Path-Goal Theory of Leadership

The path-goal theory of leadership specifies four kinds of leader behaviour: directive, supportive, participative, and achievement. Leaders are advised to vary their behaviours in response to such situational factors as personal characteristics of subordinates and environmental characteristics.

takes their suggestions into account before making a decision. Finally, *achievement-oriented leadership* involves setting challenging goals, expecting subordinates to perform at their highest level, and showing strong confidence that subordinates will put forth effort and accomplish the goals.[33] Unlike Fiedler's contingency theory, path-goal theory assumes that leaders can change their behaviour and exhibit any or all of these leadership styles. The theory also predicts that the appropriate combination of leadership styles depends on situational factors.

Situational Factors   The path-goal theory proposes two types of situational factors that influence how leader behaviour relates to subordinate satisfaction: the personal characteristics of the subordinates and the characteristics of the environment (see Figure 11.2).

Two important personal characteristics of subordinates are locus of control and perceived ability. Locus of control, discussed in Chapter 3, refers to the extent to which individuals believe that what happens to them results from their own behaviour or from external causes. Research indicates that individuals who attribute outcomes to their own behaviour may be more satisfied with a participative leader (because they feel their own efforts can make a difference), whereas individuals who attribute outcomes to external causes may respond more favourably to a directive leader (because they think their own actions are of little consequence).[34] Perceived ability pertains to how people view their ability with respect to the task. Employees who rate their own ability relatively high are less likely to feel a need for directive leadership (because they think they know how to do the job), whereas those who perceive their own ability to be relatively low may prefer directive leadership (because they think they need someone to show them how to do the job).

Canadian Tire and . . . **CHANGE**

Maintaining a Canadian Retail Icon

Canadian Tire was founded in 1922, incorporated in 1927, and launched its first catalogue in 1928. Since then, the retailer has largely grown and prospered. However, the retail industry is extremely competitive and the last 10 to 15 years witnessed a number of changes that might have severely challenged Canadian Tire's business had its leaders not been flexible. These changes include the emergence of e-business, the growing popularity of "big box" retailers, the entry of Wal-Mart into Canada, and the growth of specialty retailers such as Home Depot.

Wayne Sales, the CEO of Canadian Tire from 2000 to 2006 was respected for his low-key, team oriented approach to leadership. While in the top job at Canadian Tire, the company made a number of significant changes to counter the competitive threats in the Canadian retail environment.

One major change was the overhaul of its website in 2002. Initially introduced well after the online boom of the late 1990s, Canadian Tire first introduced its retail website in 2000. In 2002, it spent over $28 million to improve its website, which is now considered one of the best retail websites in Canada.

In an effort to diversify its business, Canadian Tire acquired Mark's Work Warehouse in 2002. It later introduced branded credit cards and other banking services to add new revenue streams.

It has also undertaken a significant upgrading of its stores, following what it calls its Concept 20/20 design. Concept 20/20 is a plan to add more floor space and product selection. Canadian Tire is also working to make its stores more attractive to female customers.

The results of the innovative approaches have been very good. Canadian Tire's revenues have grown. Its stock price more than tripled during Sales' tenure as CEO, and Sales himself was named Canada's Top CEO by *Canadian Business* magazine in 2005.

Sources: Zena Olijnyk, "TOP CEO 2005: Wayne Sales, Canadian Tire Corp. Ltd." *Canadian Business*, April 25 2005, pp. 42–44; Andy Holloway, "Give like Santa..." *Canadian Business*, December 9, 2002, p. 109; Mike Duff, "Canadian Tire focuses on 20/20 format—marketing concept—Company Profile" *DSN Retailing Today*, January 26, 2004 ; Canadian Tire website: http://www2.canadiantire.ca/CTenglish/h_ourstory.html.

Important environmental characteristics are task structure, the formal authority system, and the primary work group. The path-goal theory proposes that leader behaviour will motivate subordinates if it helps them cope with environmental uncertainty created by those characteristics. In some cases, however, certain forms of leadership will be redundant, decreasing subordinate satisfaction. For example, when task structure is high, directive leadership is less necessary and therefore less effective; similarly, if the work group gives the individual plenty of social support, a supportive leader will not be especially attractive. Thus, the extent to which leader behaviour matches the people and environment in the situation is presumed to influence subordinates' motivation to perform. The Canadian Tire and . . . Change box describes how the CEO at Canadian Tire has worked to match his leadership behaviour with various situational elements to lead the firm to renewed success.

For another example, consider the success of Margaret (Peggy) Kent, the CEO of Century Mines, which operates gold mines in Quebec and is developing interests in South America. To get her idea from the drawing board into the business world, Kent had to use directive leadership to organize her employees. When she met with investors, she had to demonstrate achievement-oriented leadership to convey her goals, strategies, and belief that the projects will be successful.[35]

Evaluation and Implications

The path-goal theory was designed to provide a general framework for understanding how leader behaviour and situational factors influence subordinate attitudes and behaviours. But the intention of the path-goal theorists was to stimulate research on the theory's major propositions, not to offer definitive answers. Researchers hoped that a more fully developed, formal theory of leadership would emerge from continued study. Further work actually has supported the theory's major predictions, but it has not validated the entire model.[36] Moreover, many of the theory's predictions remain overly general and have not been fully refined and tested.

The Vroom-Yetton-Jago Model of Leadership

The **Vroom-Yetton-Jago model** of leadership attempts to prescribe how much participation subordinates should be allowed in making decisions.

The second major theory of leadership is the **Vroom-Yetton-Jago model**, first proposed by Victor Vroom and Philip Yetton and later revised and expanded by Vroom and Arthur Jago.[37] Like the path-goal theory, the model attempts to prescribe a leadership style appropriate to a given situation. It also assumes that the same leader can display several leadership styles. But the Vroom-Yetton-Jago model concerns itself with only a single aspect of leader behaviour: subordinate participation in decision making. The goals of the model are to protect the quality of the decision while ensuring acceptance of the decision by subordinates.

Basic Premises

The Vroom-Yetton-Jago model assumes that the degree to which subordinates should be encouraged to participate in decision making depends on the characteristics of the situation. In other words, no one decision-making process is best for all situations. After evaluating each of the problem attributes (characteristics of the problem or decision), the leader determines an appropriate decision style that specifies the amount of subordinate participation.

Vroom and Jago's expansion of the original model requires the use of decision trees.[38] To use one of the trees, the manager assesses the situation in terms of several factors. This assessment involves providing "yes" or "no" answers to a series of questions. The answers guide the manager through the paths of the decision tree to a recommended course of action. There are actually four trees: two for group-level decisions and two for individual-level decisions. One of each is for use when time is of the utmost importance and the other for when time is less important and the manager wants instead to develop the subordinate's decision-making abilities.

The decision tree for time-driven group problems is shown in Figure 11.3. The problem attributes (situational factors) are arranged along the top of the decision tree and, as noted above, are expressed as questions. To use the model, the decision maker starts at the left side of the diagram and asks the first question. For instance, the manager first decides whether the problem at hand involves a quality requirement; that is, are there quality differences in the alternatives, and do they matter? For example, choosing between blue and green uniforms for the company bowling team from the same supplier has no quality requirement if the uniforms differ only in colour. The answer determines the path to the second node on the decision tree, where the question pertaining to that attribute is asked. This process continues until a terminal node is reached. In this way, the manager identifies an effective decision-making style for the situation.

The various decision styles reflected at the ends of the tree branches represent different levels of subordinate participation that the manager should attempt to adopt in a given situation. The five styles are defined as follows:

FIGURE **11.3**

The Vroom-Yetton-Jago Model (Time-Driven Group Problems)

The Vroom-Yetton-Jago model of leadership depends on the use of decision trees such as the one illustrated here. The model itself helps leaders to determine the optimal level of employee participation to allow in a given situation. To use the tree, the leader first asks the QR (Quality Requirement) question. Depending on the answer (yes or no), the leader continues on through the tree until a recommended level of participation is reached.

Source: Adaptations from Table 2.1, Decision Methods for Group and Individual Problems (p. 13) and Figure 9.3, Decision-Process Flow Chart for Both Individual and Group Problems (p. 194) from Leadership and Decision-Making, by Victor H. Vroom and Philip W. Yetton, © 1973. Reprinted by permission of the University of Pittsburgh Press.

QR	*Quality Requirement:*	How important is the technical quality of the decision?
CR	*Commitment Requirement:*	How important is subordinate commitment to the decision?
LI	*Leader's Information:*	Do you have sufficient information to make a high-quality decision?
ST	*Problem Structure:*	Is the problem well structured?
CP	*Commitment Probability:*	If you were to make the decision by yourself, is it reasonably certain that your subordinate(s) would be committed to the decision?
GC	*Goal Congruence:*	Do subordinates share the organizational goals to be attained in solving this problem?
CO	*Subordinate Conflict:*	Is conflict among subordinates over preferred solutions likely?
SI	*Subordinate Information:*	Do subordinates have sufficient information to make a high-quality decision?

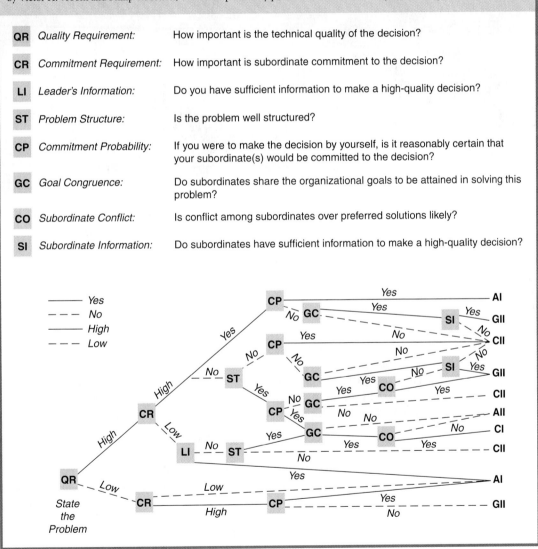

AI: The manager makes the decision alone.

AII: The manager asks for information from subordinates but makes the decision alone. Subordinates may or may not be informed about the situation.

CI: The manager shares the situation with individual subordinates and asks for information and evaluation. Subordinates do not meet as a group, and the manager alone makes the decision.

Vroom's decision tree approach to leadership suggests that leaders should vary the degree of participation they provide to subordinates in making decisions. In the wake of financial scandal after financial scandal, some top managers have begun to systematically increase communication and participation throughout the ranks of their organization. For instance, Steve Odland (standing) is the CEO of AutoZone. He now insists that all top managers fully participate in discussions and decisions regarding the firm's finances. Indeed, he requires that each top manager certify the accuracy of his or her unit's financial performance before the results are submitted to him.

CII: The manager and subordinates meet as a group to discuss the situation, but the manager makes the decision.

GII: The manager and subordinates meet as a group to discuss the situation, and the group makes the decision. (The original model included a GI style, but it was dropped because research found it to be indistinguishable from this GII style.)[39]

The complete Vroom-Yetton-Jago model today is even more complex than Vroom and Yetton's earlier version. The other three trees, for example, include still different situational attributes and decision styles. Moreover, several of the questions now allow more than a simple yes or no answer. To compensate for this difficulty, Vroom and Jago have developed computer software to help managers assess a situation accurately and quickly and then make an appropriate decision regarding employee participation.[40] Many firms, including Halliburton Company, Litton Industries, and Borland International, have provided their managers with training in how to use the Vroom-Yetton-Jago model.

Evaluation and Implications

The expanded Vroom-Yetton-Jago model is relatively new and has not been fully scientifically tested, perhaps because of its complexity. However, the original Vroom-Yetton model attracted a great deal of attention and generally was supported by research.[41] Richard Field of the University of Alberta has done several studies on the Vroom-Yetton model. He found some support for the idea that individuals who make decisions consistent with the predictions of the model are more effective than those who make decisions inconsistent with it. The basic model therefore appears to be a tool that managers can apply with some confidence in deciding how much subordinates should participate in the decision-making process.

The Leader-Member Exchange Model

The **leader-member exchange model (LMX)** of leadership, conceived by Fred Dansereau and George Graen, stresses the importance of variable relationships between supervisors and each of their subordinates.[42] Each superior-subordinate pair is referred to as a *vertical dyad*. The model differs from earlier approaches in that it focuses on the differential relationship leaders often establish with different subordinates.

LMX is based on social exchange theory, similar to the equity theory of motivation discussed in Chapter 4. The differential relationships that form between the leader and each subordinate are a function of the intensity of the exchange within each leader-subordinate dyad. But what is exchanged? The leader provides some subordinates with additional attention, consideration, and time. In return, those subordinates are expected to give the leader enhanced loyalty, commitment, and performance. Figure 11.4 shows the basic concepts of the leader-member exchange theory.

> The **leader-member exchange (LMX) model** of leadership stresses the fact that leaders develop unique working relationships with each of their subordinates.

Basic Premises

The model suggests that supervisors establish a special relationship with some trusted subordinates referred to as the in-group. The in-group usually receives special duties requiring responsibility and autonomy; they may also receive special privileges. Subordinates who are not a part of this group are called the out-group, and they receive less of the supervisor's time and attention. Note in the figure that the leader has a dyadic, or one-to-one, relationship with each of the five subordinates.

FIGURE 11.4

The Leader-Member Exchange (LMX) Model

The LMX model suggests that leaders form unique independent relationships with each of their subordinates. As illustrated here, a key factor in the nature of this relationship is whether the individual subordinate is in the leader's out-group or in-group.

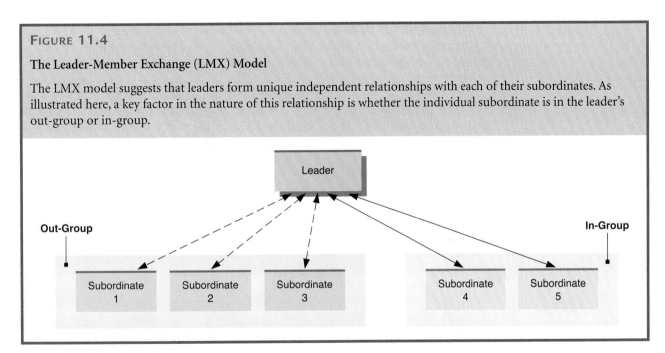

Early in his or her interaction with a given subordinate, the supervisor initiates either an in-group or out-group relationship. It is not completely clear how a leader selects members of the in-group, but the decision may be based more on personal compatibility than subordinates' competence.[43] Research has confirmed the existence of in-groups and out-groups. In addition, studies generally have found that in-group members as compared to out-group members have higher levels of satisfaction, and commitment and demonstrate more organizational citizenship behaviours.[44]

Evaluation and Implications

Exchange quality, a measure of how close a leader is to a subordinate, has been found to be related to satisfaction with supervision, overall satisfaction, organizational commitment, and supervisors' subjective performance appraisal of subordinates' performance.[45] However, exchange quality is very weakly related to objective performance measures, but it should be noted that this result is the outcome of very few studies.[46] There are some criticisms of LMX research. These primarily revolve around methodological issues. In particular it has been noted that while the exchange quality results might be accurate, most LMX studies are based solely on perceptions of subordinates, so it is largely unknown if the actual behaviours of supervisors cause the results.[47]

Notwithstanding these methodological issues, there are a number of important implications from the LMX theory. One of the more important implications that the research clearly shows is that managers can easily fall into a trap of establishing in-group relationships with subordinates on the grounds of interpersonal compatibility, which is frequently based on attitudinal similarity. While this may not be a universally bad practice on its own ground, it can result in less than optimal results. One unfavourable outcome is that individuals who are objectively poorer performers might retain in-group status because of similarities with the leader. This can cause conflict among subordinates. Another equally damaging outcome of this process is that subordinates who could perform at a higher level never get the chance because they are undeservedly put into an out-group because of dissimilarity with the leader. One way of overcoming this is for leaders to receive training on how in- and out-groups form, including sensitivity toward diversity of attitudes and styles. It is hoped that managers who receive such training make more informed decisions on in- and out-group status.[48]

Another set of researchers now suggest that it may be better to try to avoid in-group and out-group differences altogether. They suggest that managers should attempt to be more inclusive by offering in-group status to all of their subordinates.[49] There is some research evidence from a field study that shows that this can work. Supervisors were trained to have meetings with out-group members to establish better working relationships. The results showed that compared to the preintervention period those previous out-group members had higher levels of exchange quality, satisfaction and performance.[50]

More recent research has applied the basic notions of LMX beyond leader-subordinate dyads to groups and larger networks with the premise that better exchange relationships among group and organizational members will result in better psychological and performance outcomes.[51] Kathleen Boies of Concordia University and Jane Howell of the University of Western Ontario demonstrated how this can work. In a study of teams in the Canadian military forces, they found that teams with higher average levels of LMX had higher levels of effectiveness and lower levels of conflict.[52]

The organization of W.L. Gore and Associates—the company that makes Gore-Tex along with hundreds of other products—serves as an example of how this can work. The founder, Bill Gore, believed that innovation, creativity and loyalty is best developed when people get to know each other well. Consequently, W.L. Gore and Associates makes sure that each facility has only between 150 and 200 "associates" at each location so that close relationships can be formed, despite the fact that the company now employs over 6000 people![53] Although LMX is a relatively new theory of leadership, it is gaining more interest from researchers and practising managers.

Transformational and Charismatic Approaches to Leadership

As the pace of globalization, international competition, and rapid advances in technology continue to increase, recent interest has focused on the role that leaders must play in changing their organizations. The new focus differs from the leadership models discussed in previous sections of this chapter. Part of the difference is the notion that leadership is not about maintaining the status quo within organizations. The other major difference is that the focus has shifted away from models that could be used for any level of leaders from first-line supervisor to CEO, toward models that describe leadership from the big picture. Key questions, therefore, are: how can leaders influence change in their organizations and how can people lead from afar? These approaches are transformational leadership and charismatic leadership, and have been labelled by some researchers as being the currently dominant theories of leadership.[54] Moreover, these approaches are now not only of interest to academic researchers, but also to practising managers, as evidenced by the fact that *The Globe and Mail* ran a special section of its paper dedicated to these issues.[55]

Transformational Leadership

Transformational leadership focuses on the basic distinction between leading for change and leading for stability.[56] According to this viewpoint, much of what a leader does occurs in the course of normal, routine work-related transactions—assigning work, evaluating performance, making decisions, and so forth. Occasionally, however, the leader has to initiate and manage major change, such as managing a merger, creating a work group, or defining the organization's culture. The first set of issues involves transactional leadership, whereas the second entails transformational leadership.[57]

Recall from the beginning of this chapter the difference between management and leadership. Transactional leadership is essentially the same as management, in that it involves routine, regimented activities. Closer to the general notion of leadership, however, is **transformational leadership**, the set of abilities that allow the leader to recognize the need for change, to create a vision to guide that change, and to execute the change effectively. Only a leader with tremendous influence can hope to perform these functions successfully. Some experts believe that change is such a vital organizational function that even successful firms need to change regularly to avoid complacency and stagnation[58]; accordingly, leadership for change is also important.

Moreover, some leaders can adopt either transformational or transactional perspectives, depending on their circumstances. Others are able to do one or the other, but not both. For instance, when Gordon Bethune assumed the leadership role at Continental Airlines in the early 1990s, the firm was in desperate straits, heading for its third bankruptcy in a decade. The airline's equipment was aging, it was heavily in debt, and employee morale was at an all-time low. Using dramatic transformational leadership Bethune managed to completely overhaul the firm, revitalizing it along every major dimension, and transforming the airline to become one of the most successful and admired in the world. And after the transformation was complete, Bethune was then able to transition to become a highly effective transactional role and led the firm through several more years of success before retiring in 2005.

> **Transformational leadership** is the set of abilities that allow the leader to recognize the need for change, to create a vision to guide that change, and to execute that change effectively.

Charismatic leadership is a type of influence based on an individual's personal charisma. Nelson Mandela is a clear example of this type of leader. During the struggles of black South Africans to end that nation's oppressive policies of apartheid, Mandela came to reflect both their triumphs and their tragedies. Not surprisingly, when the country abolished apartheid, the newly empowered black majority elected Mandela as the country's first black president. Mandela then extended the hand of reconciliation to members of the former ruling party and quickly united the divided country. And today he is seen as a national hero.

Charisma is a form of interpersonal attraction that inspires support and acceptance from others.

Charismatic leadership is a type of influence based on the leader's personal charisma

At Walt Disney, however, the story has been different. When Michael Eisner took over the firm in 1984 it had become stagnant and was heading into decline. Relying on transformational skills, he turned things around in dramatic fashion. Among many other things, he quickly expanded the company's theme parks, built new hotels, improved Disney's movie business, created a successful Disney cruise line, launched several other major new initiatives, and changed the company into a global media powerhouse. But when the firm began to plateau and needed some time to let the changes all settle in, Eisner was unsuccessful at changing his own approach from transformational leadership to transactional leadership and was recently pressured into announcing his retirement plans.

Charismatic Leadership

Perspectives based on charismatic leadership, like the trait theories discussed earlier, assume that charisma is an individual characteristic of the leader. **Charisma** is a form of interpersonal attraction that inspires support and acceptance. **Charismatic leadership** is accordingly a type of influence based on the leader's personal charisma. All else being equal, then, someone with charisma is more likely to be able to influence others than someone without charisma. For example, a highly charismatic supervisor will be more successful in influencing subordinate behaviour than a supervisor who lacks charisma. Thus, influence is again a fundamental element of this perspective.[59]

Robert House (formerly of the University of Toronto) first proposed a theory of charismatic leadership based on research findings from a variety of social science disciplines.[60] His theory suggests that charismatic leaders are likely to have a lot of self-confidence, firm confidence in their beliefs and ideals, and a strong need to influence people. They also tend to communicate high expectations about follower performance and express confidence in followers. Herb Kelleher, CEO of Southwest Airlines, is an excellent example of a charismatic leader. Kelleher, or "Uncle Herbie" as he is known inside the company, possesses a unique combination of executive skill, honesty, and playfulness. These qualities have attracted a group of followers at Southwest who are willing to follow his lead without question and to dedicate themselves to carrying out his decisions and policies with unceasing passion.[61]

Figure 11.5 portrays the three elements of charismatic leadership in organizations that most experts acknowledge today.[62] First, the leader needs to be able to envision the future, to set high expectations, and to model behaviours consistent with meeting those expectations. Next, the charismatic leader must be able to energize others by demonstrating personal excitement, personal confidence, and patterns of success. Finally, the charismatic leader enables others by supporting them, empathizing with them, and expressing confidence in them.

Charismatic leadership ideas are quite popular among managers today and are the subject of numerous books and articles.[63] Few studies have specifically attempted to

---

FIGURE **11.5**

The Charismatic Leader

The charismatic leader is characterized by three fundamental attributes. As illustrated here, these are behaviours resulting in envisioning, energizing, and enabling. Charismatic leaders can be a powerful force in any organizational setting.

Source: David A. Nadler and Michael L. Tushman, "Beyond the Charismatic Leader: Leadership and Organizational Change," *California Management Review*, Winter 1990, pp. 70–97. Copyright © 1990, by the Regents of The University of California. Reprinted by permission.

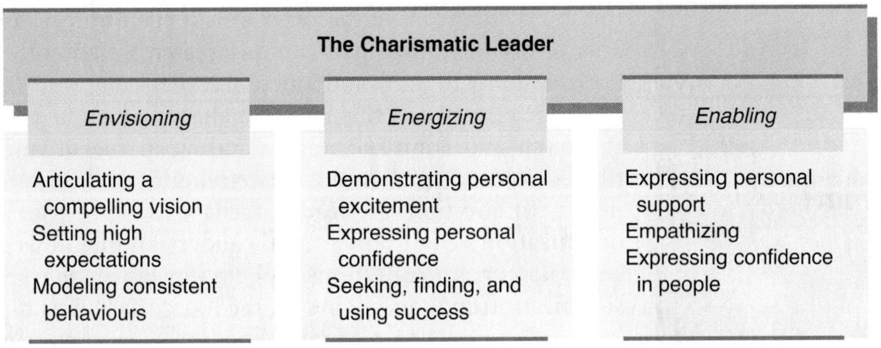

The Charismatic Leader

Envisioning	Energizing	Enabling
Articulating a compelling vision Setting high expectations Modeling consistent behaviours	Demonstrating personal excitement Expressing personal confidence Seeking, finding, and using success	Expressing personal support Empathizing Expressing confidence in people

---

test the meaning and impact of charismatic leadership. However, some researchers suggest that the charismatic behaviours such as expressing a positive vision of the future and expressing confidence in followers motivates followers by appealing to their sense of self-esteem, self-worth, and self-efficacy (discussed in Chapter 5).[64]

Lingering ethical concerns about charismatic leadership also trouble some people. They stem from the fact that some charismatic leaders inspire such blind faith in their followers that they may engage in inappropriate, unethical, or even illegal behaviours, just because the leader instructed them to do so.[65] For example, David Koresh, the infamous leader of the Branch Davidians in Waco, Texas, relied heavily on his personal charisma to influence his followers.

Emerging Issues in Leadership

There are four emerging issues in leadership that warrant discussion. These issues are authentic leadership, strategic leadership, ethical leadership, and virtual leadership.

Interest in *authentic leadership* grew from the concern discussed in the preceding paragraph, that charismatic (and transformational) leaders can use the same tools and techniques towards positive or negative outcomes for their followers. Authentic leaders are thought to be sincere, self-aware, motivated by their own values, and seek to better the lives of their followers.[66] Or conversely, they are not "fake," trying to reflect others' expectations, or try to influence others to attain personal outcomes. Authentic leadership is very early in development, with little research done to confirm the validity of its assumptions, or its effect on individual or organizational outcomes.

Strategic Leadership   Strategic leadership is a new concept that explicitly relates leadership to the role of top management. We will define **strategic leadership** as the

Strategic leadership is the capability to understand the complexities of both the organization and its environment and to lead change in the organization so as to achieve and maintain a superior alignment between the organization and its environment.

Strategic leadership has become a major force in many organizations today. When A. G. Lafley took over the reins at Proctor & Gamble, he systematically revamped the firm's staid culture in order to make the company more responsive to changing consumer tastes and emerging competitive challenges.

capability to understand the complexities of both the organization and its environment and to lead change in the organization so as to achieve and maintain a superior alignment between the organization and its environment. In some ways, then, strategic leadership may be seen as an extension of the transformational leadership role discussed earlier. However, this recent focus has more explicitly acknowledged and incorporated the importance of strategy and strategic decision making. That is, while both transformational and strategic leadership include the concept of change, transformational leadership implicitly emphasizes the ability to lead change as the central focus. Strategic leadership, on the other hand, puts greater weight on the leader's ability to think and function strategically.

To be effective in this role, a manager needs to have a thorough and complete understanding of the organization—its history, its culture, its strengths, and its weaknesses. In addition, the leader needs a firm grasp of the organization's environment. This understanding must encompass current conditions and circumstances as well as significant trends and issues on the horizon. The strategic leader also needs to recognize how the firm is currently aligned with its environment—where it relates effectively, and where it relates less effectively with that environment. Finally, looking at environmental trends and issues the strategic leader works to both improve the current alignment and improve the future alignment.

Dominic D'Allesandro (CEO of Manulife), Michael Dell (founder and CEO of Dell Computer), and A.G. Lafley (CEO of Procter & Gamble) have all been recognized as strong strategic leaders. Reflecting on his dramatic turnaround at Procter & Gamble, for instance, Lafley commented, "I have made a lot of symbolic, very physical changes so people understand we are in the business of leading change." On the other hand, Jurgen Schrempp (CEO of DaimlerChrysler), Raymond Gilmartin (CEO of Merck), and Scott Livengood (CEO of Krispy Kreme) have been singled out by *Business Week* for their poor strategic leadership.[67]

Ethical Leadership   Most people have long assumed that top managers are ethical people. But in the wake of recent corporate scandals at firms like Enron, Boeing, and WorldCom, faith in top managers has been shaken. Hence, perhaps now more than ever high standards of ethical conduct are being held up as a prerequisite for effective leadership. More specifically, top managers are being called upon to maintain high ethical standards for their own conduct, to unfailingly exhibit ethical behaviour, and to hold others in their organizations to the same standards.

The behaviours of top leaders are being scrutinized more than ever, and those responsible for hiring new leaders for a business are looking more and more closely at the backgrounds of those being considered. And the emerging pressures for stronger corporate governance models are likely to further increase commitment to select only those individuals with high ethical standards for leadership positions in business and to hold them more accountable than in the past for both their actions and the consequences of those actions.[68]

Virtual Leadership   Finally, virtual leadership is also emerging as an important issue for organizations. In earlier times, leaders and their employees worked together in the same physical location and engaged in personal (i.e., face-to-face) interactions on a regular basis. But in today's world both leaders and their employees may work in locations that are far from one another. Such arrangements might include people telecommuting from a home office one or two days a week to people actually living and working far from company headquarters and seeing one another in person only very infrequently.

How, then, do managers carry out leadership when they do not have regular personal contact with their followers? And how do they help mentor and develop others? Communication between leaders and their subordinates will still occur, of course, but it may be largely by telephone and e-mail. Hence, one implication may be that leaders in these situations simply need to work harder at creating and maintaining relationships with their employees that go beyond words on a computer screen. While nonverbal communication such as smiles and handshakes may not be possible online, managers can instead make a point of adding a few personal words in an e-mail (whenever appropriate) to convey appreciation, reinforcement, or constructive feedback. Building on this, managers should then also take advantage of every single opportunity whenever they are in face-to-face situations to go further than they might have done under different circumstances to develop a strong relationship.

But beyond these simple prescriptions, there is no theory or research to guide managers functioning in a virtual world. Hence, as electronic communications continues to pervade the workplace, researchers and managers alike need to work together to first help frame the appropriate issues and questions regarding virtual leadership and then to help address those issues and answer those questions.

Chapter Review

Summary of Key Points

- Leadership is both a process and a property. Leadership as a process is the use of noncoercive influence to direct and coordinate the activities of group members to meet goals. As a property, leadership is the set of characteristics attributed to those who are perceived to use such influence successfully. Leadership and management are related but distinct phenomena.

- Early leadership research attempted primarily to identify important traits and behaviours of leaders. The Michigan and Ohio State studies each identified two kinds of leader behaviour, one focusing on job factors, the other on people factors. The Michigan studies viewed these behaviours as points on a single continuum, whereas the Ohio State studies suggested that they were separate dimensions.

- Contingency theories of leadership attempt to identify appropriate leadership styles on the basis of the situation. Fiedler's LPC theory stated that leadership effectiveness depends on a match between the leader's style (viewed as a trait of the leader) and the favourableness of the situation. Situation favourableness, in turn, is determined by task structure, leader-member relations, and leader position power. Leader behaviour is presumed to reflect a constant personality trait and therefore cannot easily be changed.

- The path-goal theory focuses on appropriate leader behaviour for various situations. The path-goal theory suggests that directive, supportive, participative, or achievement-oriented leader behaviour may be appropriate, depending on the personal characteristics of subordinates and the characteristics of the environment. Unlike the LPC theory, this view presumes that leaders can alter their behaviour to best fit the situation.

- The Vroom-Yetton-Jago model suggests appropriate decision-making styles based on situation characteristics. The Vroom-Yetton-Jago theory essentially is a model for deciding how much subordinates should participate in the decision-making process. The model is designed to protect the quality of the decision and ensure decision acceptance by subordinates. Managers ask questions about their situation and follow a series of paths through a decision tree that subsequently prescribes for them how they should make a particular decision.

- The leader-member exchange model focuses on specific relationships between a leader and individual subordinates.

- In recent years, new leadership approaches have attempted to more directly consider the use of influence. Transformational leadership, one such approach, is the set of abilities that allow a leader to recognize the need for change, to create a vision to guide that change, and to execute the change effectively. Another influence-based approach to leadership considers charismatic leadership. Charisma, the basis of this approach, is a form of interpersonal attraction that inspires support and acceptance.

Discussion Questions

1. How would you define leadership? Compare and contrast your definition with the one given in this chapter.

2. Cite examples of managers who are not leaders and leaders who are not managers. What makes them one and not the other? Also, cite examples of both formal and informal leaders.

3. What traits do you think characterize successful leaders? Do you think the trait approach has validity?

4. What other forms of leader behaviour besides those cited in the chapter can you identify?

5. Critique Fiedler's LPC theory. Are other elements of the situation important? Do you think Fiedler's assertion about the inflexibility of leader behaviour makes sense? Why or why not?

6. Do you agree or disagree with Fiedler's assertion that leadership motivation is basically a personality trait? Why?

7. Compare and contrast the LPC and path-goal theories of leadership. What are the strengths and weaknesses of each?

8. Of the three major leadership theories—the LPC theory, the path-goal theory, and the Vroom-Yetton-Jago model—which is the most comprehensive? Which

is the narrowest? Which has the most practical value?

9. How realistic do you think it is for managers to attempt to use the Vroom-Yetton-Jago model as prescribed? Explain.

10. Is it possible for all subordinates to have an in-group relationship with their leader? Why or why not?

11. What limitations are there for first-level supervisors to use transformational or charismatic behaviours?

Purpose: This exercise will help you better understand the behaviours of successful and unsuccessful leaders.

Format: You will be asked to identify contemporary examples of successful and unsuccessful leaders and then to describe how these leaders differ.

Procedure

1. Working alone, each student should list the names of 10 people he or she thinks of as leaders in public life. Note that the names should not necessarily be confined to good leaders, but instead should identify strong leaders.

2. Next, students should form small groups and compare their lists. This comparison should focus on common and unique names, as well as the kinds of individuals listed (i.e., male or female, contemporary or historical, business or nonbusiness, etc.).

3. From all the lists, choose two leaders whom most people would consider very successful and two who would be deemed unsuccessful.

4. Identify similarities and differences between the two successful leaders and between the two unsuccessful leaders.

5. Relate the successes and failures to at least one theory or perspective discussed in the chapter.

6. Select one group member to report your findings to the rest of the class.

Follow-up Questions

1. What role does luck play in leadership?

2. Are there factors about the leaders you researched that might have predicted their success or failure before they achieved leadership roles?

3. What are some criteria of successful leadership?

Applying the Vroom-Yetton-Jago Model

This skillbuilder will help you better understand your own leadership style regarding employee participation in decision making. Mentally play the role described in the following scenario, then make the comparisons suggested at the end of the exercise.

You are the Canadian branch manager of an international manufacturing and sales organization. The firm's management team is looking for ways to increase efficiency. As one part of this effort, the company recently installed an integrated computer network linking sales representatives, customer service employees, and other sales support staff. Sales were supposed to increase and sales expenses to drop as a result.

However, exactly the opposite has occurred: Sales have dropped a bit, and expenses are up. You have personally inspected the new system and believe the hardware is fine. However, you believe the software linking the various computers is less than ideal.

The subordinates you have quizzed about the system think the entire system is fine. They attribute the problems to a number of factors, including inadequate training in how to use the system, a lack of incentive for using it, and generally poor morale. Whatever the reasons given, each worker queried had strong feelings about the issue.

Your boss has just called you and expressed concern about the problems. He has indicated that he has confidence in your ability to solve the problem and will leave it in your hands. However, he wants a report on how you plan to proceed within one week.

First, think of how much participation you would normally be inclined to allow your subordinates in making this decision. Next, apply the Vroom-Yetton-Jago model to the problem and see what it suggests regarding the optimal level of participation. Compare your normal approach to the recommended solution.

Organizational Behaviour
Case for Discussion

The "Reality-Distortion Field" of Steve Jobs

Steve Jobs, a co-founder of Apple Computer, was the visionary behind the first mass-market personal computer, while his co-founder, Steve Wozniak, was the technical wizard. The quirky, creative, and unique culture of Apple was greatly influenced by Jobs, the nonconformist CEO. Apple's unprecedented success paved the way for the PC boom of the 1980s. However, under pressure of competition from mainstream computer makers such as IBM and Compaq, Apple's performance declined. As the PC maker lost its strategic direction, Jobs reluctantly left Apple in 1985. One biography of Jobs sums up the turnover, saying, "While Jobs was a persuasive and charismatic evangelist for Apple, critics also claimed he was an erratic and tempestuous manager." In 1986, Jobs purchased Pixar from George Lucas and became CEO. The computer animation studio produced its first film, *Toy Story*, in 1995. And after a decade of mediocre results at Apple, Jobs again assumed the top spot in 1997.

As Apple's CEO, Jobs developed a reputation for brilliance, originality, and charm. At the same time, he could be arrogant and hypercritical. He expected others to meet his very high standards and was insulting when disappointed. One industry observer portrayed Jobs as intimidating and power hungry, while others said he commanded "a cult-like following from employees and consumers."

> ❝ *The major advantage of having Jobs on the job during uncertain and anxious times is his capacity to dispel feelings of ambiguity.* ❞
> STEVEN BERGLAS, WRITER

widely reputed to be one of the most aggressive egotists in Silicon Valley, has an unrivaled track record when it comes to pulling development teams through start-ups." Referring to the bitter battles waged in the PC industry during the period of rapid growth, Berglas believes that Jobs is an empire builder who "held up IBM as the enemy he needed to destroy." Writing about the history of the PC industry, author Robert X. Cringely states that Jobs had a "reality-distortion field" surrounding him, so that his vision became the one adopted by many in the industry. "The major advantage of having Jobs on the job during uncertain and anxious times is his capacity to dispel feelings of ambiguity," writes Berglas.

But would Jobs's charisma, confidence, and vision allow him to be a successful leader during times of prosperity and success? Berglas and some other industry observers predicted that Jobs would not be able to switch his leadership behaviour to effectively manage the company during good times. However, as Apple's shares reached an all-time high of $80 and the company had the highest revenues and profits in its history in January 2005, Jobs has proved them wrong.

Yet, in spite of occasional criticism, Jobs is clearly a leader who can deliver success in businesses that are evolving, highly technical, and demanding. Writer Steven Berglas says, "Jobs, the enfant terrible

He is more unbeatable than ever. In a 2004 interview, Jobs discussed how his passion and focus enable the company to succeed in any type of situation or environment. "Lots of companies have tons of great engineers and smart people," said Jobs. "But ultimately, there needs to be some gravitational force that pulls it all together . . . That's what was missing at Apple for a while. There were bits and pieces of interesting things floating around, but not that gravitational pull."

Today, Pixar, Apple, and Jobs are riding high. Pixar has released a series of wildly successful movies, such as *Monsters, Inc.*, *Finding Nemo*, and *The Incredibles*. Each film has grossed more than the previous one. *The Incredibles* had sales of $143 million in its opening weekend; the DVD sold five million on the first day of release, setting a daily record of $100 million. Apple has released several versions of the hugely popular iPod, supported by the company's online music store, iTunes. The recent iMac and Mac mini have also been bestsellers, and the new iPhone had millions of potential buyers even before it was released. Jobs's confidence is justified by the company's tremendous success and his confidence is growing. Jobs says, "Apple is doing the best work in its history . . . And there's a lot more coming."

Case Questions

1. Using the Michigan studies framework, describe the leader behaviour of Steve Jobs. Is he likely to be an effective leader? Why or why not?

2. A manager who has very high expectations can be most effective in what types of situations? Use path-goal theory to explain your answer.

3. Based on your answer to the previous question, do you expect Steve Jobs to be an effective manager at Pixar and Apple? Explain.

4. What behaviours does Jobs exhibit that would classify him as a transformational or charismatic leader?

Sources: Steven Berglas, "What You Can Learn from Steve Jobs," *Inc. Magazine*, October 1999, www.inc.com on May 5, 2005 (quotation); Peter Burrows, "Apple's Bold Swim Downstream," *Business Week*, January 24, 2005, pp. 32–35; Peter Burrows, "The Seed of Apple's Innovation," *Business Week*, October 12, 2004, www.businessweek.com on May 16, 2005; Robert X. Cringely, *Accidental Empires*, Addison-Wesley, 1992; Alan Deutschman, *The Second Coming of Steve Jobs*, Broadway Publishing, September 2001; Brent Schlender, "How Big Can Apple Get?" *Fortune*, February 21, 2005, www.fortune.com on May 15, 2005; Mike Snider, "The New Theatrical Event: DVD," *USA Today*, March 21, 2005, www.usatoday.com on May 15, 2005. Jeremy Caplan, "The iPhone Kick-Starts the Competition", *Time*, July 2, 2007, pp. 22–23.

Organizational Behaviour Case for Discussion

Too Much of a Good Thing?

Alexandra (Alex) McIntyre finally got to bed at about 2:00 in the morning. She had just finished the report that was due to her boss the next day. This was the third night this week that Alex had been up very late just finishing her own work. Things at the office were really getting out of hand.

Lately, she had been spending almost all of her time with her 10 subordinates. Everyone wanted her advice and coaching on the projects they were executing. Alex had no time for herself, because of the constant stream of questions coming at her.

Things started to get bad about four weeks ago. McIntyre had recently taken a leadership development seminar. At one lecture, the instructor said that a study done by Leader-Member Exchange theory showed that workers who previously had bad relationships with their boss could be "won over" if the boss offered to build a better working relationship. The previous bad workers became good

workers (or something like that). Alex can't really recall what the instructor said after that, since he was talking on and on and on (again), and Alex dozed off (after all, it was a weekend class, and Alex worked all week long . . .)

So, Alex took the instructor's advice to work the very next day. She called a team meeting and said:

"Look, I know that all of us have not gotten along very well since I joined the company and became the head of this department four months ago. Actually, to be fully honest, I know that I have not really gotten along with any of you. I really want us to get along better. I know that a good portion of our problems have been my fault. Again, to be honest, I've spent the last few months just learning how to do my job. I know it now, so now I have more time for all of you. I know that you want to do your job the best you can, and that you all want to get promoted some day. So, here's the deal: I'll be your friend, and your coach whenever you need help. Need a question answered? Ask me anytime. Need someone just to listen. I'm here anytime for you. . ."

Alex went on like this for about 10 more minutes. By the time she finished, everyone was upbeat and to some extent relieved. It was quite an emotional breakthrough for the group.

The very next day, things got a lot better for the employees, and a lot worse for Alex. There was a flood of questions, opinions sought, and problems shared with Alex. She spent the entire working day, and just about every working day since then being everyone's "friend."

But her own work suffered. Her open door policy was killing her. Alex's boss noticed it also, and commented that Alex was starting to miss deadlines, and had to get her performance up to where it was before she started to be a mentor to everyone. Otherwise, he might consider looking for a new position elsewhere. . .

Case Questions

Answer the following questions using either Leader-member Exchange or Transformational (or Charismatic Leadership).

1. What did Alex do wrong?

2. What should Alex do now? Give specific advice on what should be done, and discuss potential difficulties in implementing your suggestions.

SELF TEST

You have read the chapter and studied the key terms. Think you're ready to ace the exam? Take this sample test to gauge your comprehension of chapter material and check your answers at the back of the book. Want more test questions? Take the ACE quizzes found on the student website: www.hmco.ca/ob.

T F 1. Leadership can be a property or a process, but not both.

T F 2. Leaders use initiating-structure behaviours to show respect for subordinates' feelings and ideas.

T F 3. According to the path-goal theory of leadership, leaders motivate their subordinates by clarifying the behaviours that will be rewarded.

T F 4. Vroom's decision tree approach helps leaders determine how much subordinate participation to include in decision making.

T F 5. The leader-member exchange model suggests that all subordinates should be treated the same way.

T F 6. Transactional leadership is essentially the same as management.

T F 7. Research has shown that charismatic leaders are usually less effective than non-charismatic leaders.

8. Compared to managers, leaders do which of the following?
   a. create and direct change
   b. achieve coordination
   c. handle administrative activities
   d. achieve systematic results
   e. compare results with goals

9. The behavioural theories of leadership focused on which two basic dimensions of leadership?
   a. profit-generating behaviours and cost-reducing behaviours
   b. work-centred behaviours and employee-centred behaviours
   c. personal goal-directed behaviours and organizational goal-directed behaviours
   d. management behaviours and leadership behaviours
   e. public behaviours and private behaviours

10. Situational models of leadership assume
    a. good leaders are made rather than born.
    b. leadership is based on personal characteristics rather than on behaviours.
    c. leaders are most effective when they focus on situations, not on people.
    d. leaders should learn as much as possible about the situation before acting.

e. appropriate leader behaviour varies from one situation to another.

11. According to path-goal theory, when would a directive leadership style be most appropriate?
    a. when subordinates have high motivation
    b. when subordinates have an external locus of control
    c. when subordinates have high ability
    d. when leaders have an internal locus of control
    e. when leaders have low ability

12. According to research on the leader-member exchange model, employees in the out-group are characterized by all of the following except they
    a. receive less attention from the supervisor.
    b. are assigned more mundane work.
    c. experience lower job satisfaction.
    d. receive more responsibility and autonomy.
    e. are given fewer special privileges.

13. Which of the following elements did Fiedler add as another major element of situational favorableness in his LPC theory of leadership?
    a. stress
    b. decision-making style
    c. participation
    d. charisma
    e. rewards

14. Which of the following leadership styles would be most appropriate for a leader who needs to initiate and manage major change?
    a. exchange
    b. telling
    c. selling
    d. transformational
    e. transactional

15. Charismatic leaders possess all of the following except the ability to
    a. set high expectations for themselves and for others.
    b. display personal excitement and confidence.
    c. envision likely future trends and patterns.
    d. build a tight-knit in-group of followers.
    e. support and empathize with followers.

The Success of Groups at Starbucks

The interpersonal interactions of individuals in groups contribute greatly to the success of Starbucks. Baristas and other workers at each Starbucks location make up a group, a collection of individuals who interact with and influence each other. The Starbucks group is a command group, because the individuals are brought together by their official positions and the group includes a store manager to oversee the work of the others.

Each store's group of workers can also be a team, because they work toward a common goal. Starbucks's mission statement serves as the ultimate goal for employees and the statement is prominently displayed at every location. Baristas often hear about the company's commitment to the mission statement's values, such as caring for the environment, fostering innovation, satisfying customers, treating others with dignity and respect, making a profit, and embracing diversity. Starbucks's executives communicate details about company performance and goals with employees, to help employees contribute to the firm. Employees share short-range goals for sales, quality, efficiency, and so on. Starbucks pays bonuses based on company-wide performance, further strengthening the team concept.

However, Starbucks teams do not operate autonomously, so they are not fully mature. The store managers have discretion in hiring, rewarding, and scheduling. Workers may choose tasks and manage their own work to some extent, but store managers oversee the store's operations and direct the baristas, just as the regional and corporate officers oversee and direct the work of store managers.

Starbucks teams are fairly well developed, as members have worked together for some time. Of course, with an annual turnover of 80 percent, team membership changes frequently and there is a constant need to teach new workers about the group's norms. Starbucks provides twenty-four hours of formal training that introduces each new hire to the company's values and culture. The first training also includes an introduction to coffee. Baristas learn about different coffees and methods of coffee brewing. Later training focuses on communication, leadership, and management skills. Another way that Starbucks employees learn about group norms is through direct observation and interaction with peers. Starbucks has a "promote from within" policy, so the store managers know the company's culture and can serve as role models.

Training also helps the company to enforce group norms. At Starbucks, norms include everything from how to dress to how to manage difficult customers. The norms at Starbucks promote friendliness, efficiency, and consistency, which aid the company in accomplishing its goals. However, some feel that the strong norms at Starbucks result in too much consistency and stifle creativity and individual expression. In Canada, two female baristas of Indian ancestry were fired because they wore nose studs. Facial jewelry is prohibited by Starbucks's dress code, but the women argued that the result is unfair bias. "Starbucks' dress code accepts ear piercing . . . [but] rejects other forms of body piercing," claims a leaflet circulated in support of a lawsuit filed by the women. "In prohibiting nose studs, it degrades an important part of South Asian tradition . . . This is cultural racism, an unjustified act of discrimination." Group performance is improved by Starbucks's diversity, where over 60 percent of the workforce is made up of minorities and women. "Embracing diversity is not only the right thing to do socially or ethically, it's good for business," according to former CEO Orin Smith. "As the world becomes more and more complex, having a diverse work team helps us be more adaptive as a company. This is especially critical because we are expanding internationally. Diversity helps us make better decisions." Diversity improves decision quality by increasing the number of different values and viewpoints brought to bear in making a decision. For instance, Starbucks employees make thousands of suggestions each year, based on their unique backgrounds. Each suggestion is investigated and hundreds are adopted, leading to increased innovation and efficiency.

In addition, workforce diversity makes it easier to attract and serve diverse customers. And seeking out diverse applicants increases the applicant pool, making it easier to find personnel when the labour supply is tight. It has been predicted that, by 2008, the majority of workforce entrants will be women and minorities. Thus, Starbucks must recruit from a diverse population in order to find enough workers. To recruit more diverse applicants, Starbucks visits colleges and universities with high minority enrollment, builds relationships with advocacy organizations, and places advertisements in publications with minority readers.

Starbucks explains its stance on diversity with the phrase, "*Honouring* our origins, enriched by our blends." The word "origins" is equated to a single-origin coffee, "with its own unique *flavour,* aroma, and growing conditions." Starbucks emphasizes the importance of the individual worker, who has unique experiences, values, and skills. The word "blends" is compared to blended coffees, which "are woven together, forming a tapestry of taste and texture." This phrase emphasizes the combination of several different individuals to create a group that can do more than each of its individual parts.

Group cohesiveness is an important performance factor at Starbucks. The company works to increase cohesiveness by careful recruiting procedures that identify individuals with outgoing, energetic, and pleasant personalities. Also, store managers are trained in team building, where they learn to create a supportive and upbeat atmosphere. And Starbucks' policy of internal promotions increases cohesiveness, because store employees see managers as being similar to themselves.

Effective interpersonal processes aid the organization in leadership, decision making, and conflict management. Leadership has been an important element of Starbucks' success since 1985, when Howard Schultz bought the small chain. Schultz had two visions, inspired by an experience with Italian coffee houses, which he used to transform the lacklustre company into the retailing giant it is today. First, Schultz saw that Starbucks had the potential for tremendous growth. Second, he realized the appeal of socializing, which is important to the success of European coffee houses. "Great companies must have the courage to examine strategic opportunities that are transformational—as long as they are not inconsistent with the guiding principles and values of the core business," Schultz says.

> **"** *. . . A diverse work team helps us be more adaptive as a company . . . Diversity helps us make better decisions.* **"**
>
> ORIN SMITH, FORMER CEO, STARBUCKS

Starbucks uses a rational decision-making model for many decisions, such as product pricing and store location. However, behavioural factors play a large part in the most important decisions, including the initial concept of the firm. Schultz's decision to purchase Starbucks and change its competitive strategy was based on his intuition. His management training and experiences helped him to quickly realize the company's potential. Schultz also has a high propensity for risk, as shown by his willingness to give up his executive job and invest his own money in an uncertain undertaking. In addition, he drastically changed the focus and strategy of Starbucks, to move into a more competitive industry. Schultz says, "Seek to renew yourself even when you are hitting home runs." With this statement, the Starbucks founder shows that he will not be satisfied with excellent performance. He believes that even excellent performance can be improved, if one is willing to change and take risks.

Schultz has also demonstrated very effective transactional leadership in the years since he acquired Starbucks. He has managed a great deal of growth, international expansion, the transition to a publicly traded firm, and more. Schultz has demonstrated his transactional management abilities by his successful efforts at product development, brand management, and operational efficiencies.

Founder Schultz and other top managers are clearly excellent leaders, as demonstrated by Starbucks' long-term performance. Yet leadership at Starbucks occurs at many levels, not just at the top of the giant firm. Schultz claims as one of his guiding principles, "Don't be threatened by people smarter than you." Therefore, there is an emphasis at the company on developing the team leadership skills of every leader, down to the level of store managers. Starbucks offered a leadership training program called "Servant Leaders Workshop" to over 6000 employees in 2004. The program emphasized "trust, collaboration, people development and ethics."

Servant leadership is an emerging view of leadership, in which the leader sees him- or herself as helping followers, rather than as guiding or directing them. Servant leadership is similar to the idea of leaders as coaches, but takes the concept a step further. Leader-coaches help employees develop the skills they need to function without a lot of oversight and direction from above. Leader-servants lead out of a genuine desire to be of service to employees and the organization, helping them to develop and be more effective. Richard Smith of Creative Leaps International developed the program used at Starbucks. Smith says that his program is designed to help leaders answer the question, "Do those served grow as persons?" Smith explains that servant leadership means that the worker, as a result of what the leader does, should grow and become a better person. Smith's course emphasizes ways that managers, through increased trust and collaboration, give to workers.

Starbucks works hard to create positive personal interactions among its employees, but in a company of this size, conflicts are inevitable. Workers need predictable schedules; managers need flexibility. Workers demand freedom to speak and dress as they please; managers demand that company policies and dress codes be upheld. Until recently, worker-management conflicts were resolved at the store level. However, in early 2004, store 7356, on Madison Avenue in Manhattan, got permission from the National Labor Relations Board (NLRB) to hold a union election. Pro-union sentiment had begun to build, with workers unhappy about pay, hours, and safety. Barista Anthony Polanco says, "Starbucks pays peanuts, and they treat the workers like elephants." Most New York City workers agree that Starbucks's $7.75 hourly rate is a poverty wage for the area. Another barista, Daniel Gross, cites a work environment that causes burns and repetitive stress injuries.

Starbucks prefers that workers are not unionized. Founder Howard Schultz takes the threat of unionization personally. "If workers had faith in me and my motives, they wouldn't need a union," he says. After the call for a union election, Starbucks executives began to visit store 7536, engaging in anti-union discussions with baristas and handing out free pizza and concert tickets. By July 2004, union activists canceled the election, perhaps fearing a loss. Most of the pro-union employees moved on to other stores or other employers.

The NLRB investigated the possibility that Starbucks engaged in unfair labour practices and in 2007 charged Starbucks with 30 violations of the law in their alleged attempt to ward off union activity at the Manhattan outlets. Meanwhile, seven unionized Starbucks outlets in Vancouver were recently decertified, leaving a Regina outlet as the only unionized Starbucks in the world. With a reputation for social responsibility, Starbucks is vulnerable to charges of being anti-labour or anti-worker. In the meantime, the company continues its practices: training, communicating, fostering diversity, and developing leaders. So far, these have been more than sufficient in generating growth and success for Starbucks.

Sources: "Corporate Social Responsibility Report 2004," "Diversity," "Starbucks Mission Statement," Starbucks website, www.starbucks.com on June 30, 2005; "Biography: Howard Schultz, Starbucks," Great Entrepreneurs website, 2000, www.myprimetime.com on June 30, 2005 (quotation); Sharmistha Choudhury, "Brewing Racism in Canada," *The New Nation*, October 1, 2004, nation.ittefaq.com on June 30, 2005; Anya Kamenetz, "Baristas of the World, Unite!" *New York Magazine*, May 30, 2005, www.newyorkmetro.com on June 30, 2005; A.V. Krebs, "Union in NYC Wins Battle to Vote on Union at Starbucks," *The Agribusiness Examiner*, July 14, 2004, www.organic-consumers.org on February 2, 2005; Alison Overholt, "Listening to Starbucks," *Fast Company*, July 2004, pp. 50–56; "Starbucks Workers Union on Canada's National Public Radio CBC The Current," www.iww.org on August 21, 2007.

Integrative Case Questions

1. In what ways does workforce diversity help or benefit Starbucks? In what ways does diversity present challenges or potential problems? Based on your answer, do you think Starbucks should try to increase or decrease the diversity of its workforce? Explain.

2. Starbucks carefully selects team members and offers them training about the company. What else could the company do to improve team effectiveness? What outcomes does Starbucks experience as a result of good teamwork at its stores?

3. Based on what you read about attempts to unionize Starbucks, what is the company's reaction to conflict? In your opinion, is this the optimal response in this situation? If so, explain why. If not, choose a different response and explain why that response might be preferable.

Dimensions of Organization Structure

Chapter Outline

The Nature of Organization Structure

Organization Defined
Organization Structure

Structural Configuration

Division of Labour
Coordinating the Divided Tasks

Structure and Operations

Centralization
Formalization

Responsibility and Authority

Responsibility
Authority
An Alternative View of Authority

Classic Views of Structure

Ideal Bureaucracy
The Classic Principles of Organizing
Human Organization

▌ **Define organization structure and discuss its purpose.**

▌ **Describe structural configuration and summarize its four basic dimensions.**

▌ **Discuss two structural policies that affect operations.**

▌ **Explain the dual concepts of authority and responsibility.**

▌ **Explain the classic views of organization structure.**

Maple Leaf Foods' Intelligent Organization Structure

Maple Leaf Foods is one of Canada's largest food processing companies. Headquartered in Toronto, It produces many meat products under the Maple Leaf brand. It also owns Schneider's Foods, acquired in 2003. As well, Maple Leaf owns a number of product lines such as Dempster's Breads and Olivieri Pastas and sauces, among others.

Maple Leaf achieved its size through a number of methods, including growth from within as well as external acquisitions. Over time, part of its operations became unwieldy and uneconomical. For example, its meat processing was spread over six different units, and it had many suppliers under contracts and in joint ventures.

In late October of 2006, Maple Leaf announced a restructuring of its operations to streamline production. It moved all of its meat processing into a single division, and is moving toward 100 percent ownership of the barns that supply their inputs. It will move all of its primary processing to one location, where six locations had been used in the past.

Additionally, it is redirecting its focus from fresh meats, which were becoming increasingly uncompetitive due largely to the appreciation of the value of the Canadian dollar, and moving more emphasis into value added products. It plans to reduce its inputs by nearly one half, and to use approximately 70 percent of its meat in value-added products while it currently uses only about 20 percent for that purpose.

The change is estimated to cost between $80 and $120 million dollars, will require the sale of many assets, and may result in a number of jobs being lost. However, Maple Leaf and its major shareholder—the Ontario Teachers Pension Plan—expect the plan to succeed. Maple Leaf predicts that its after-tax profits will improve by $100 million annually once the centralization is complete.[1]

When organizations such as Maple Leaf Foods make major structural changes, they do so for some compelling reason. Maple Leaf Foods had become an industry leader in food processing. However, its managers believed that centralizing a major part of its production, and refocusing on value-added products will help improve the company's profitability and meet the demands of foreign competition. This is the first in a two-chapter sequence in which we explore how the structure of an organization can be a major factor in how successfully the organization achieves its goals. In this chapter, we present the basics of organization structure, its building blocks, and the classical ways of designing organization structures. Chapter 13 integrates the basic elements of structure, taking into consideration other factors such as the environment and technology, and presents several perspectives on organization design.

In this chapter, we begin with an overview of organizations and organization structure, defining both terms and placing organization structure in the context of organizational goals and strategy. Second, we discuss the two major perspectives of organizing, the structural configuration view and the operational view. Third we discuss the often confusing concepts of responsibility and authority and present an alternative view of authority. Fourth, we explain several of the classic views of how organizations should be structured.

The Nature of Organization Structure

In other chapters we discuss key elements of the individual and the factors that tie the individual and the organization together. In a given organization, these factors must fit together within a common framework: the organization's structure.

Organization Defined

An **organization** is a group of people working together to achieve common goals.[2] Top management determines the direction of the organization by defining its purpose, establishing the goals to meet that purpose, and formulating strategies to achieve the goals.[3] The definition of purpose gives the organization reason to exist; in effect, it answers the question: "What business are we in?"

Establishing goals converts the defined purpose into specific, measurable performance targets. **Organizational goals** are objectives that management seeks to achieve in pursuing the purpose of the firm. Goals motivate people to work together. Although each individual's goals are important to the organization, it is the organization's overall goals that are most important. Goals keep the organization on track by focusing the attention and actions of the members. They also give the organization a forward-looking orientation. They do not address past success or failure; rather, they force members to think about and plan for the future.

Finally, strategies are specific action plans that enable the organization to achieve its goals and thus its purpose. Pursuing a strategy involves developing an organization structure and the processes to do the organization's work.

> An **organization** is a group of people working together to attain common goals.

> **Organizational goals** are objectives that management seeks to achieve in pursuing the firm's purpose.

> Organizational goals keep the organization on track by focusing the attention and actions of its members.

Organization Structure

Organization structure is the system of task, reporting, and authority relationships within which the work of the organization is done. Thus, structure defines the form and function of the organization's activities. Structure also defines how the parts of an organization fit together, as is evident from an organization chart.

The purpose of an organization's structure is to order and coordinate the actions of employees to achieve organizational goals. The premise of organized effort is that people can accomplish more by working together than they can separately. The work must be coordinated properly, however, if the potential gains of collective effort are to be realized. Consider what might happen if the thousands of employees at a computer manufacturer worked without any kind of structure. Each person might try to build a computer that he or she thought would sell. No two computers would be alike, and each would take months or years to build. The costs of making the computers would be so high that no one would be able to afford them. To produce computers that are both competitive in the marketplace and profitable for the company, there must be a structure in which its employees and managers work together in a coordinated manner.

Kenyan scientist Florence Wambugu has genetically modified foods, such as bananas and sweet potatoes, to help the starving people of her homeland. However, some governments in Africa object to genetically altered food, and people are starving despite the availability of the controversial crops. Wambugu has created a new organization, A Harvest Biotech Foundation International, to serve as a pan-African voice on the issue. With the organizational goal of increasing the availability of genetically modified crops in Africa, the organization will be better able to stay on track and continue its forward momentum.

Strategies are specific action plans that enable the organization to achieve its goals and thus its purpose.

Organization structure is the system of task, reporting, and authority relationships within which the organization does its work.

The task of coordinating the activities of thousands of workers to produce computers that do the work expected of them but are guaranteed and easy to maintain may seem monumental. Yet whether the goal is to mass produce computers or to make soap, the requirements of organization structure are similar. First, the structure must identify the various tasks or processes necessary for the organization to reach its goals. This dividing of tasks into smaller parts is often called division of labour. Even small organizations (those with fewer than 100 employees) use division of labour.[4] Second, the structure must combine and coordinate the divided tasks to achieve a desired level of output. The more interdependent the divided tasks, the more coordination is required.[5] Every organization structure addresses these two fundamental requirements.[6] The various ways they do so are what make one organization structure different from another.

Organization structure can be analyzed in three ways. First, we can examine its configuration, or its size and shape as depicted on an organization chart. Second, we can analyze its operational aspects or characteristics, such as separation of specialized tasks, rules and procedures, and decision making. Finally, we can examine responsibility and authority within the organization. In this chapter, we describe organization structure from all three points of view.

Structural Configuration

An **organization chart** is a diagram showing all people, positions, reporting relationships, and lines of formal communication in the organization.

The **configuration** of an organization is its shape, which reflects the division of labour and the means of coordinating the divided tasks.

The structure of an organization is most often described in terms of its organization chart. A complete **organization chart** shows all people, positions, reporting relationships, and lines of formal communication in the organization. (However, as we discussed in Chapter 7, communication is not limited to these formal channels.) For large organizations, several charts may be necessary to show all positions. For example, one chart may show top management, including the board of directors, the chief executive officer, the president, all vice presidents, and important headquarters, staff units. Subsequent charts may show the structure of each department and staff unit. Figure 12.1 depicts two organization charts for a large firm; top management is shown in the upper portion of the figure and the manufacturing department in the lower portion. Notice that the structures of the different manufacturing groups are given in separate charts.

An organization chart depicts reporting relationships and work group memberships and shows how positions and small work groups are combined into departments, which together make up the **configuration**, or shape, of the organization. The configuration of organizations can be analyzed in terms of how the two basic requirements of structure—division of labour and coordination of the divided tasks—are fulfilled.

Division of Labour

The **division of labour** is the way the organization's work is divided into different jobs to be done by different people.

Division of labour is the extent to which the organization's work is separated into different jobs to be done by different people. Division of labour is one of the seven primary characteristics of structuring described by Max Weber,[7] but the concept can be traced back to the eighteenth-century economist Adam Smith. As we noted in Chapter 5, Smith used a study of pin-making to promote the idea of dividing production work to increase productivity.[8] Division of labour grew more popular as large organizations became more prevalent in a manufacturing society. This has continued, and most research indicates that large organizations usually have more divisions than smaller ones.[9]

Division of labour has been found to have both advantages and disadvantages (see Table 12.1). Modern managers and organization theorists are still struggling with the primary disadvantage: division of labour often results in repetitive, boring jobs that undercut worker satisfaction, involvement, and commitment.[10] In addition, extreme

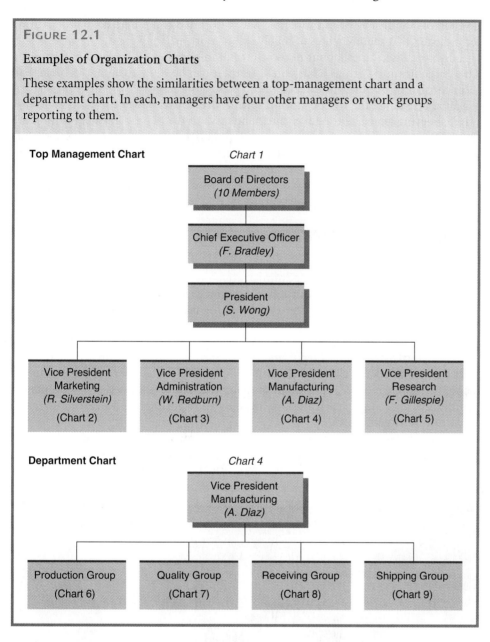

FIGURE 12.1

Examples of Organization Charts

These examples show the similarities between a top-management chart and a department chart. In each, managers have four other managers or work groups reporting to them.

Advantages	Disadvantages
Efficient use of labour	Routine, repetitive jobs
Reduced training costs	Reduced job satisfaction
Increased standardization and uniformity of output	Decreased worker involvement and commitment
Increased expertise from repetition of tasks	Increased worker alienation
	Possible incompatibility with computerized manufacturing technologies

TABLE 12.1

Advantages and Disadvantages of Division of Labour

division of labour may be incompatible with integrated computerized manufacturing technologies that require teams of highly skilled workers.[11]

However, division of labour need not result in boredom. Visualized in terms of a small organization such as a basketball team, it can be quite dynamic. A basketball team consists of five players, each of whom plays a different role on the team. In professional basketball the five positions typically are centre, power forward, small forward, shooting guard, and point guard. The tasks of the players in each position are quite different, so players of different sizes and skills are on the floor at the same time. The teams that win championships, such as the San Antonio Spurs and the Los Angeles Lakers, use division of labour by having players specialize in doing specified tasks, and doing them impeccably. Similarly, organizations must have specialists who are highly trained and know their specific jobs very well.

Coordinating the Divided Tasks

Divided tasks can be combined into departments by function, process, product, customer, and geography.

Three basic mechanisms are used to help coordinate the divided tasks: departmentalization, span of control, and administrative hierarchy. These mechanisms focus on grouping tasks in some meaningful manner, creating work groups of manageable size, and establishing a system of reporting relationships among supervisors and managers.

Departmentalization is the manner in which divided tasks are combined and allocated to work groups.

Departmentalization   **Departmentalization** is the manner in which divided tasks are combined and allocated to work groups. It is a consequence of the division of labour. Because employees engaged in specialized activities can lose sight of overall organizational goals, their work must be coordinated to ensure that it contributes to the welfare of the organization.

There are many possible ways to group, or departmentalize, tasks. The five methods most often used are by business function, by process, by product or service, by customer, and by geography. The first two, function and process, derive from the

This meeting shows Kari Barbar, vice president of sales and marketing operations for IBM's Personal Computing, chairing a meeting discussing IBM's "Think" strategy. Creating divisions, such as the Personal Computing Division, allows employees with different areas of expertise to work more closely together and focus their attention on one product or set of products, in this case personal computers.

internal operations of the organization; the others are based on external factors. Most organizations tend to use a combination of methods, and departmentalization often changes as organizations evolve.[12]

Departmentalization by business function is based on traditional business functions such as marketing, manufacturing, and human resource administration (Figure 12.2). In this configuration employees most frequently associate with those engaged in the same function, which helps in communication and cooperation. In a functional group, employees who do similar work can learn from one another by sharing ideas about opportunities and problems they encounter on the job. The top management structure at Highliner Foods, an international seafood company headquartered in Lunenberg, Nova Scotia, for example, has vice presidents or directors for finance, procurement, and human resources, among others.

Unfortunately, functional groups lack an automatic mechanism for coordinating the flow of work through the organization.[13] In other words, employees in a functional structure tend to associate little with those in other parts of the organization. The result can be a narrow focus that limits the coordination of work among functional groups, as when the engineering department fails to provide marketing with product information because it is too busy testing materials to think about sales. Departmentalization by process is similar to functional departmentalization, except that the focus is much more on specific jobs grouped according to the activity. Thus, as Figure 12.2 illustrates, the firm's manufacturing jobs are divided into certain well-defined manufacturing processes: drilling, milling, heat treating, painting, and assembly. Hospitals often use process departmentalization, grouping the professional employees, such as therapists, according to the types of treatment they provide.

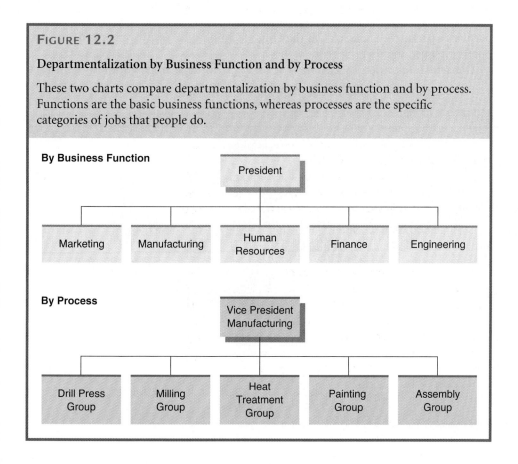

FIGURE 12.2

Departmentalization by Business Function and by Process

These two charts compare departmentalization by business function and by process. Functions are the basic business functions, whereas processes are the specific categories of jobs that people do.

By Business Function

President

- Marketing
- Manufacturing
- Human Resources
- Finance
- Engineering

By Process

Vice President Manufacturing

- Drill Press Group
- Milling Group
- Heat Treatment Group
- Painting Group
- Assembly Group

Process groupings encourage specialization and expertise among employees, who tend to concentrate on a single operation and share information with departmental colleagues. A process orientation may develop into an internal career path and managerial hierarchy within the department. For example, a specialist might become the lead person for that speciality (i.e., lead welder or lead press operator). As in functional grouping, however, narrowness of focus can be a problem. Employees in a process group may become so absorbed in the requirements and execution of their operations that they disregard broader considerations such as overall product flow.[14]

Departmentalization by product or service occurs when employees who work on a particular product or service are members of the same department regardless of their business function or the process in which they are engaged. Petro-Canada uses this sort of structure, with international and offshore, natural gas, and oil sands as some of its major operating divisions.

Colgate-Palmolive changed its organization structure by eliminating the typical functional divisions, such as basic research, processing, and packaging. Instead, employees were organized into teams based on products such as pet food, household products, and oral hygiene products. This configuration is shown in Figure 12.3. Since the reorganization, new-product development has increased significantly and cost savings are estimated to be about $40 million.[15]

Departmentalization according to product or service obviously enhances interaction and communication among employees who produce the same product or service and may reduce coordination problems. In this type of configuration, there may be less process specialization but more specialization in the peculiarities of the specific product or service. Bombardier expects this would allow all employees, from designers to manufacturing workers to marketing experts, to become specialists in a particular product group. The disadvantage is that employees may become so interested in their particular product or service that they miss technological improvements or innovations developed in other departments.

Departmentalization by customer is often called departmentalization by market. Many Canadian banks, for example, have separate departments for personal, commercial,

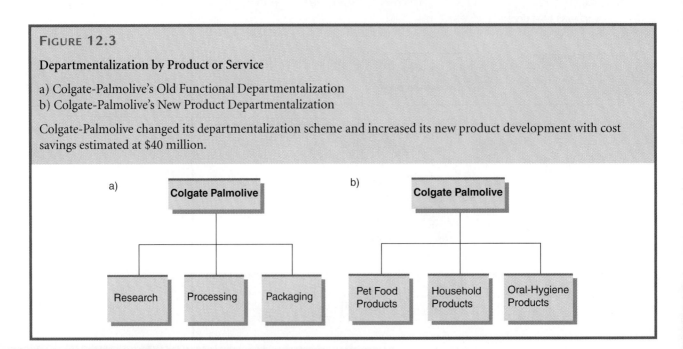

FIGURE 12.3

Departmentalization by Product or Service

a) Colgate-Palmolive's Old Functional Departmentalization
b) Colgate-Palmolive's New Product Departmentalization

Colgate-Palmolive changed its departmentalization scheme and increased its new product development with cost savings estimated at $40 million.

Intel and . . . **CHANGE**

The "Dellification" of Intel

Intel's reorganization gives more attention to customers and makes it resemble Dell Computers, arguably the most customer-focused firm on the planet. Technology editor Ephraim Schwartz makes the connection when he says, "The dot-com boom saw the promise of build-to-order PCs, perfected by Dell. [With Intel's reorganization] we may be seeing the beginning of a design-components-to-order era."

Dell tries to encourage imitation, particularly in its supplier firms, but with scant success. Writer James Surowiecki says, "In theory, any of Dell's competitors could do what Dell does . . . None does, though, in large part because all of them are stuck with out-of-date business models and business structures." Founder Michael Dell says, "These things just don't happen as fast as a lot of people predict. We've seen [potential imitators] come time and time again, and you could see them struggling with the change."

Innovation expert Michael Schrage writes that "[Dell has had] unprecedented success in matching product offerings to customer demand . . . Michael Dell is too smart to think he's smart enough to predict the future . . . Dell is content to ask consumers what they want and then sell it to them." Dell's organization structure supports this sharp departure from a traditional model, where consumers are taught to want what the company can provide.

Surowiecki claims that large groups of ordinary individuals are better at innovation and problem solving than a few experts. Surowiecki applies his model to politics,

> **"Dell's competitors ... are stuck with out-of-date business models and business structures."**
>
> JAMES SUROWIECKI, WRITER

popular culture, and business. Dell has turned Surowiecki's insight into bankable profits. If Surowiecki is correct, and if Dell's evident success continues, Intel may be just one of hundreds of companies that say and truly mean, "The customers are always right."

Sources: Darrell Dunn, "Dell's Manifest Destiny," *Tech Builder*, February 7, 2005, www.techbuilder.org on March 6, 2005; Ephraim Schwartz, "The Age of the Industry-Specific PC," *InfoWorld*, January 28, 2005, www.infoworld.com on February 8, 2005; Michael Schrage, "The Dell Curve," *Wired*, July 2002, www.wired.com on March 6, 2005; James Surowiecki, "The New Economy Was a Myth, Right?" *Wired*, July 2002, www.wired.com on March 6, 2005.

and student loans, as shown in Figure 12.4. When significant groups of customers differ substantially from one another, organizing along customer lines may be the most effective way to provide the best product or service possible. This is why hospital nurses often are grouped by the type of illness they handle; the various maladies demand different treatment and specialized knowledge.[16]

With customer departmentalization there usually is less process specialization, because employees must remain flexible to do whatever is necessary to enhance the relationship with customers. This configuration offers the best coordination of the work flow to the customer; however, it may isolate employees from others in their special areas of expertise. For example, if each of a company's three metallurgical specialists is assigned to a different market-based group, these individuals are unlikely to have many opportunities to discuss the latest technological advances in metallurgy.

Departmentalization by geography means that groups are organized according to a region of the country or world. Sales or marketing groups often are arranged by geographic region. As Figure 12.4 illustrates, the marketing effort of a large multinational corporation can be divided according to major geographical divisions. Using a geographically based configuration may result in significant cost savings and better market coverage. On the other hand, it may isolate work groups from activities in the organization's home office or

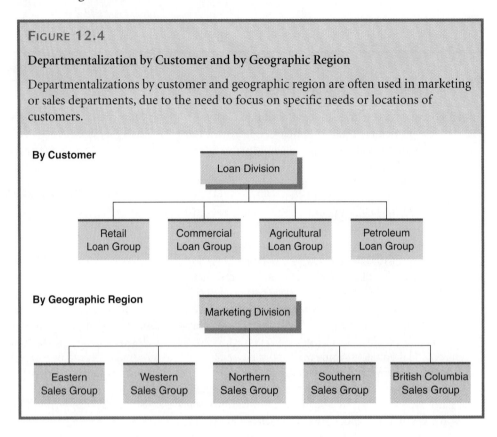

FIGURE 12.4

Departmentalization by Customer and by Geographic Region

Departmentalizations by customer and geographic region are often used in marketing or sales departments, due to the need to focus on specific needs or locations of customers.

By Customer

Loan Division

Retail Loan Group | Commercial Loan Group | Agricultural Loan Group | Petroleum Loan Group

By Geographic Region

Marketing Division

Eastern Sales Group | Western Sales Group | Northern Sales Group | Southern Sales Group | British Columbia Sales Group

in the technological community, because the focus of the work group is solely on affairs within the region. This may foster loyalty to the work group that exceeds commitment to the larger organization. In addition, work-related communication and coordination among groups may be somewhat inefficient.

Many large organizations use a mixed departmentalization scheme. Such organizations may have separate operating divisions based on products, but within each division departments may be based on business function, process, customers, or geographic region (see Figure 12.5). Which methods work best depends on the organization's activities, communication needs, and coordination requirements. Another type of mixed structure that often occurs in large organizations is called a hybrid structure. These structures have a mix of both functional and product units. Maple Leaf Foods, a portion of which was discussed at the beginning of this chapter has a hybrid structure. It has vice presidents for several functions, such as human resources, communications and consumer affairs, purchasing and supply chain, and corporate engineering. It also has vice presidents responsible for various product lines, such as Maple Leaf Bakery, Canada Fresh Bakery, Consumer Foods, and Animal Nutrition. Joint ventures, which are becoming increasingly popular, are another type of mixed structures. The Nissan and . . . Globalization box gives an example of an international joint venture between Nissan and the Dongfeng Automobile Company in China. It is a good illustration of a typical partnership and the opportunities and challenges that come with such partnerships.

The **span of control** is the number of people who report to a manager.

Span of Control   The second dimension of organizational configuration, **span of control**, is the number of people reporting to a manager; thus, it defines the size of the organization's work groups. Span of control is also called span of management.

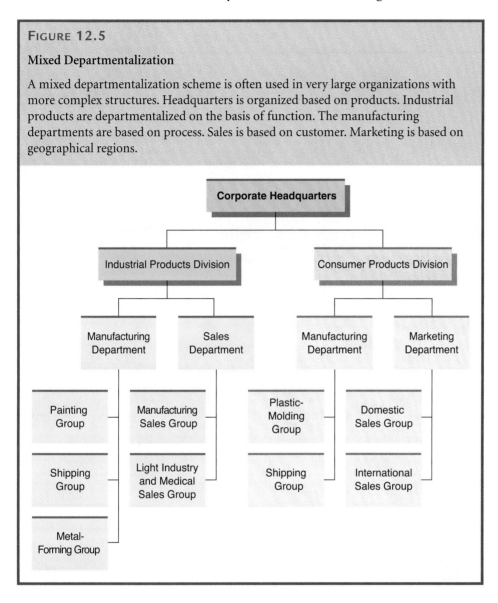

FIGURE 12.5

Mixed Departmentalization

A mixed departmentalization scheme is often used in very large organizations with more complex structures. Headquarters is organized based on products. Industrial products are departmentalized on the basis of function. The manufacturing departments are based on process. Sales is based on customer. Marketing is based on geographical regions.

A manager who has a small span of control can maintain close control over the workers and stay in contact with daily operations. If the span of control is large, close control is not possible. Figure 12.6 shows examples of small and large spans of control. Supervisors in the upper portion of the figure have a span of control of sixteen, whereas in the lower portion their span of control is eight.

A number of formulas and rules have been offered for determining the optimal span of control in an organization,[17] but research on the topic has not conclusively identified a foolproof method.[18] Henry Mintzberg, of McGill University in Montreal, concluded that the optimal unit size, or span of control, depends on five conditions:

1. The coordination requirements within the unit, including factors such as the degree of job specialization
2. The similarity of the tasks in the unit
3. The type of information available or needed by unit members

Nissan and . . . GLOBALIZATION

Nissan's Chinese Venture

As part of sweeping changes and a major reorganization effort, Nissan Motors is increasing its investment in a joint venture with its Chinese partner, Dongfeng Automobile Company. Nissan's first investment in China came in 2000, when the automaker began its partnership with Dongfeng to produce just one sedan model. In 2003, the joint venture was at capacity with a volume of 39 000. Yet Nissan cannot afford to ignore a market that is predicted to be the third-largest purchaser of automobiles by 2012, with annual sales of two million vehicles. Imports from Japan just will not cover demand.

Dongfeng gains valuable expertise and access to resources through its partnership, while Nissan takes advantage of lower production costs and Dongfeng's knowledge of the local market. On the downside, Nissan must consider the impact on their brand if quality slips, as well as the risk of competitors gaining access to confidential information. This fear is especially acute in its relationship with Dongfeng, which also has a joint venture with Honda, one of Nissan's rivals.

Another concern is perhaps even more important, because so many are affected. What happens to global competitors if China is able to produce high-quality goods much more cheaply? One American manufacturer, seeing low-cost components similar to those made by his firm, says, "I can only assume this is 'the China price' . . . It is about half the price." Ohio State University professor and author Oded Shenkar warns firms, "If you still make anything labor intensive, get out now rather than bleed to death . . . You need an entirely new business model to compete."

Nissan is cooperating in China, for now. At the same time, the company *is* adopting an entirely new business model. To read more, see the chapter closing case, "Nissan's New Organization Structure."

Sources: "Dongfeng Automobile Co. Ltd.," China Cars website, www .chinacars.com on March 7, 2005; "Nissan's Revival Plan Bets on New Models in China," Xinhua News Agency, August 21, 2002, www .china.org.cn on March 7, 2005; Brian Bremner, "Nissan's Boss," *Business Week*, October 4, 2004, www.businessweek.com on March 7, 2005; Pete Engardio and Dexter Roberts, "'The China Price,'" *Business Week*, December 6, 2004, www.businessweek.com on March 7, 2005; Yuri Kageyama, "Nissan Beefing Up China Plants with New Company," *The Detroit News*, June 12, 2003, www.detnews.com on March 7, 2005.

4. Differences in the members' need for autonomy
5. The extent to which members need direct access to the supervisor[19]

For example, a span of control of 16 (as shown in Figure 12.6) might be appropriate for a supervisor in a typical manufacturing plant where experienced workers do repetitive production tasks. On the other hand, a span of control of eight or fewer (as shown in Figure 12.6) might be appropriate in a job shop or custom-manufacturing facility in which workers do many different things and the tasks and problems that arise are new and unusual. Research on span of control continues, especially in light of newer forms of organizations, which are generally flatter with many relying more on team-based structures.[20]

> The **administrative hierarchy** is the system of reporting relationships in the organization, from the lowest to the highest managerial levels.

Administrative Hierarchy   The **administrative hierarchy** is the system of reporting relationships in the organization, from the first level up through the president or CEO. It results from the need for supervisors and managers to coordinate the activities of employees. The size of the administrative hierarchy is inversely related to the span of control: organizations with a small span of control have many managers in the hierarchy; those with a large span of control have a smaller administrative hierarchy.

Using Figure 12.6 again, we can examine the effects of small and large spans of control on the number of hierarchical levels. The smaller span of control for the supervisors in the lower portion of the figure requires that there be four supervisors rather than two.

Correspondingly, another management layer is needed to keep the department head's span of control at two. Thus, the span of control is small, the workers are under tighter supervision, and there are more administrative levels. In the upper portion of the figure, production workers are not closely supervised, and there are fewer administrative levels. Because it measures the number of management personnel, or administrators, in the organization, the administrative hierarchy sometimes is called the administrative component, administrative intensity, or administrative ratio.

The size of the administrative hierarchy also relates to the overall size of the organization. As an organization's size increases, so do its complexity and the requirements for coordination, necessitating proportionately more people to manage the business. However, this conclusion defines the administrative component as including the entire administrative hierarchy, that is, all of the support staff groups, such as personnel and financial services, legal staff, and others. Defined in this way, the administrative component in a large company may seem huge compared to the number of production workers. Research that separates the support staff and clerical functions from the management hierarchy has found that the ratio of managers to total employees actually decreases with increases in the organization's size. Other more recent research has shown that the size of the administrative hierarchy and the overall size of the organization are not related in a straightforward manner, especially during periods of growth and decline.[21]

The popular movement toward downsizing has partially been a reaction to the complexity that comes with increasing organization size. Much of the literature on organizational downsizing has proposed that it results in lower overhead costs, less bureaucracy, faster decision making, smoother communications, and increases in productivity.[22] This expectation is due to the effort to reduce the administrative hierarchy by cutting layers of middle managers from the middle of the hierarchy. Unfortunately, many downsizing efforts have resulted in poorer communication, reduced productivity, and lower employee morale because the downsizing is done indiscriminately, without regard for the jobs that people actually do, the coordination needs of the organization, and the additional training that may be necessary for the survivors.[23] Organizational restructuring is sometimes possible, but cannot be done in a mindless copycat fashion that regards people only as costs that can be cut, and not as assets that could be developed through appropriate investments in training and development.[24]

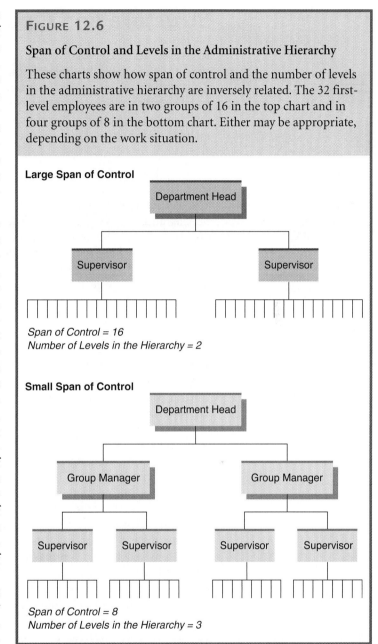

FIGURE 12.6

Span of Control and Levels in the Administrative Hierarchy

These charts show how span of control and the number of levels in the administrative hierarchy are inversely related. The 32 first-level employees are in two groups of 16 in the top chart and in four groups of 8 in the bottom chart. Either may be appropriate, depending on the work situation.

Large Span of Control

Department Head

Supervisor   Supervisor

Span of Control = 16
Number of Levels in the Hierarchy = 2

Small Span of Control

Department Head

Group Manager   Group Manager

Supervisor   Supervisor   Supervisor   Supervisor

Span of Control = 8
Number of Levels in the Hierarchy = 3

Structure and Operations

Some important aspects of organization structure do not appear on the organization chart and thus are quite different from the configurational aspects discussed in the previous section. In this section, we examine the structural policies that affect operations and prescribe or restrict how employees behave in their organizational activities.[25] The two primary aspects of these policies are centralization of decision making and formalization of rules and procedures.

Centralization

Centralization is a structural policy in which decision-making authority is concentrated at the top of the organizational hierarchy.

The first structural policy that affects operations is **centralization**, wherein decision-making authority is concentrated at the top of the organizational hierarchy. At the opposite end of the continuum is decentralization, in which decisions are made throughout the hierarchy.[26] One centralization/decentralization question, about the location and control of research and development is the subject of the R&D and . . . Research box on page 367. Increasingly, centralization is being discussed in terms of participation in decision making.[27] In decentralized organizations, lower-level employees participate in making decisions.

Decision making in organizations is more complex than the simple centralized-decentralized classification indicates. In Chapter 9, we discussed organizational decision making in more depth. One of the major distinctions we made there was that some decisions are relatively routine and require only the application of a decision rule. These decisions are programmed decisions, whereas those that are not routine are nonprogrammed. The decision rules for programmed decisions are formalized for the organization. This difference between programmed and nonprogrammed decisions tends to cloud the distinction between centralization and decentralization. For, even if decision making is decentralized, the decisions themselves may be programmed and tightly circumscribed.

If there is little employee participation in decision making, decision making is centralized, regardless of the nature of the decisions being made. At the other extreme, if individuals or groups participate extensively in making nonprogrammed decisions, the structure can be described as truly decentralized. If individuals or groups participate extensively in decision making but mainly in programmed decisions, the structure is called formalized decentralization. Formalized decentralization is a common way to provide decision-making involvement for employees at many different levels in the organization while maintaining control and predictability.

Participative management has been described as a total management system in which people are involved in the daily decision making and management of the organization.

Participative management has been described as a total management system in which people are involved in the daily decision making and management of the organization. As part of an organization's culture, it can contribute significantly to the long-term success of an organization.[28] It has been described as effective and, in fact, morally necessary in organizations. Thus, for many people, participation in decision making has become more than a simple aspect of organization structure. Caution is required, however, because if middle managers are to make effective decisions, as participative management requires, they must have sufficient information.[29]

Formalization

Formalization is the degree to which rules and procedures shape the jobs and activities of employees.

Formalization is the degree to which rules and procedures shape employees' jobs and activities. The purpose of formalization is to predict and control how employees behave on the job.[30] Rules and procedures can be both explicit and implicit. Explicit

R&D and . . . RESEARCH

Centralizing Research and Development

The question of whether to use centralized or decentralized organization of certain functions may seem a bit dry. However, it can be a key organizational design decision managers must correctly make if the company is to thrive in the long run.

In many modern organizations, the placement of the research and development (R&D) function is one such important decision. Nicholas Argyres of Boston University and Brian Silverman of the University of Toronto examined the effect that centralized versus decentralized R&D structures have the on the impact of the resulting innovations from R&D efforts.

They examined the R&D structures of 71 large, diversified companies that engaged in a significant amount of R&D. They found three types of R&D structures. The first was a "centralized" structure, wherein R&D labs, activities, and budget control were located at the corporate level. The second structure was "decentralized," wherein labs and budget control were found mostly at the subunit or divisional level. The third type was the "hybrid," wherein there were both centralized (corporate) and decentralized (divisional) based R&D activities and where budget control may or may not be centralized.

Argyres and Silverman expected, and found, that the innovations resulting from centralized R&D operations had:

- greater overall impact as measured by regard by other scientists and inventors;
- greater breadth of impact—that a particular discovery would be useful across a number of somewhat unrelated product developments;
- greater breadth of search, that the research done would use research and innovations from other organizations and not just previous findings from within the organization, and;
- broader technological research, that the research done would be more likely to cut across research disciplines.

They also found that the reverse was true for decentralized structures. Hybrid structures on the other hand, demonstrated a variety of results.

Argyres and Silverman argued that these results were due to the roles managers and researchers had depending on whether they worked in centralized or decentralized research units. In centralized R&D units, managers and researchers would work on more abstract and general issues that could be of use to many subunits in the organization. Researchers and managers in decentralized units, on the other hand, would be interested in more specific and market-relevant projects of importance to their own subunits.

The authors caution that their findings do not mean that centralized R&D is necessarily better or more profitable. It is likely that in many cases decentralized R&D may actually be more profitable, at least in the short run. That is because the more decentralized R&D is more market specific, and is likely to produce innovations that are more easily converted into revenue-generating products.

On the other hand, the innovations produced by centralized R&D units may actually be less profitable in the short term, or at least less easily measured for profitability as they are more abstract and general. Still, these innovations are more likely to yield a number of applications and new spin-off technologies, more so than those produced by decentralized R&D efforts.

Consquently, Argyres and Silverman also caution that industries and societies as a whole should be concerned about the organization of R&D efforts. Too much decentralization can lead in the long run to less overall innovation.

Source: Nicholas S. Argyres and Brian S. Silverman, "R&D, Organization Structure, and the Development of Corporate Technical Knowledge," *Strategic Management Journal*, 2004, vol. 25, pp. 929–958.

rules are set down in job descriptions, policy and procedures manuals, or office memos. (In one large company that continually issues directives attempting to limit employee activities, workers refer to them as "Gestapo" memos because they require employees to follow harsh rules.) Implicit rules may develop as employees become accustomed to doing things in a certain way over a period of time.[31] Though unwritten, these established ways of getting things done become standard operating procedures with the same effect on employee behaviour as written rules.

We can assess formalization in organizations by looking at the proportion of jobs that are governed by rules and procedures and the extent to which those rules permit variation. More formalized organizations have a higher proportion of rule-bound jobs and less tolerance for rule violations.[32] Increasing formalization may affect the design of jobs throughout the organization[33] as well as employee motivation[34] and work group interactions.[35] The specific effects of formalization on employees are still unclear, however.[36]

Organizations tend to add more rules and procedures as the need for control of operations increases. The recent passage of the Sarbannes-Oxley act in the United States has forced many businesses both in the US and Canada to signicanlty increase levels of formalization.[37] Some organizations have become so formalized that they have rules for how to make new rules! One large university created such rules in the form of a three-page document entitled *Procedures for Rule Adoption* that was added to the four-inch-thick policy and procedures manual. The new policy first defines terms such as university, board, and rule and lists 10 exceptions that describe when this policy on rule adoptions does not apply. It then presents a nine-step process for adopting a new rule within the university.

Other organizations are trying to become less formalized by reducing the number of rules and procedures employees must follow. Magna International, an automotive parts supplier with billions of dollars of annual revenue, tries to maintain a balance between too many and too few rules. Magna consists of dozens of independently operated factories, whose local management was allowed almost complete autonomy. However, in the late 1980s and early 1990s, Magna lost money. Upper management realized that it needed to set some limits, since budgets were out of control. It introduced new decision-making guidelines, which required factory managers to check with top management to make sure that local plans fit with the company's overall

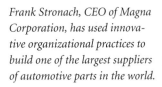

Frank Stronach, CEO of Magna Corporation, has used innovative organizational practices to build one of the largest suppliers of automotive parts in the world.

strategy. Within these broad guidelines, however, local managers still have considerable discretion about how to run their factories.[38]

A relatively new approach to organizational formalization attempts to describe how, when, and why good managers should bend or break a rule.[39] Although rules exist in some form in almost every organization, how strictly they are enforced varies significantly from one organization to another and even within a single organization. Some managers argue that a rule is a rule and all rules must be enforced to control employee behaviour and prevent chaos in the organization. Other managers act as if all rules are made to be broken and see rules as stumbling blocks on the way to effective action. Neither point of view is better for the organization; rather, a more balanced approach is recommended.

The test of a good manager in a formalized organization may be to use appropriate judgment in making exceptions to rules. A balanced approach to making exceptions to rules should do two things. First, it should recognize that individuals are unique and that the organization can benefit from making exceptions that capitalize on exceptional capabilities. For example, suppose an engineering design department with a rule mandating equal access to tools and equipment acquires a limited amount of specialized equipment, such as personal computers. The department manager decides to make an exception to the equal-access rule by assigning the computers to the designers the manager believes will use them most and with the best results instead of making them available for use by all. Second, a balanced approach should recognize the commonalties among employees. Managers should make exceptions to rules only when there is a true and meaningful difference between individuals rather than base exceptions on features such as race, sex, appearance, or social factors.

Responsibility and Authority

Responsibility and authority are related to both configurational and operational aspects of organization structure. For example, the organization chart shows who reports to whom at all levels in the organization. From the operational perspective, the degree of centralization defines the locus of decision-making authority in the organization. However, often there is some confusion about what responsibility and authority really mean for managers and how the two terms relate to each other.

Responsibility

Responsibility is an obligation to do something with the expectation that some act or output will result. For example, a manager might expect an employee to write and present a proposal for a new program by a certain date; thus, the employee is responsible for preparing the proposal.

Responsibility ultimately derives from the ownership of the organization. The owners hire or appoint a group, often a board of directors, to be responsible for managing the organization, making the decisions, and reaching the goals set by the owners. A downward chain of responsibility is then established. The board hires a president to be responsible for running the organization. The president hires more people and holds them responsible for accomplishing designated tasks that enable the president to produce the results expected by the board and the owners. The chain extends throughout the organization, because each manager has an obligation to fulfill: to appropriately employ organizational resources (people, money, and equipment) to meet the owners' expectations. Although managers seemingly pass responsibility on to others to achieve results, each manager is still held responsible for the outputs of those to whom he or she delegates tasks.

Responsibility is an obligation to do something with the expectation of achieving some act or output.

A manager responsible for a work group assigns tasks to members of the group. Each group member is then responsible for doing his or her task. Yet the manager remains responsible for each task and for the work of the group as a whole. This means that managers can take on the responsibility of others but cannot shed their own responsibility onto those below them in the hierarchy.

Authority

Authority is power that has been legitimized within a particular social context.

Authority is power that has been legitimized within a specific social context.[40] (Power is discussed in Chapter 10.) Only when power is part of an official organizational role does it become authority. Authority includes the legitimate right to use resources to accomplish expected outcomes. As we discussed in the previous section, the authority to make decisions can be restricted to the top levels of the organization or dispersed throughout the organization.

Like responsibility, authority originates in the ownership of the organization. The owners establish a group of directors who are responsible for managing the organization's affairs. The directors, in turn, authorize people in the organization to make decisions and to use organizational resources. Thus, they delegate authority, or power in a social context, to others. Authority is linked to responsibility, because a manager responsible for accomplishing certain results must have the authority to use resources to achieve those results.[41] The relationship between responsibility and authority must be one of parity; that is, the authority over resources must be sufficient to enable the manager to meet the output expectations of others.

Authority and responsibility are closely related in that managers must have the authority to carry out their responsibilities.

But authority and responsibility differ in significant ways. Responsibility cannot be delegated down to others (as discussed in the previous section), but authority can. One complaint often heard from employees is that they have too much responsibility but not enough authority to get the job done. This indicates a lack of parity between responsibility and authority. Managers usually are quite willing to hold individuals responsible for specific tasks but are reluctant to delegate enough authority to do the job. In effect, managers try to rid themselves of responsibility for results (which they cannot do), yet they rarely like to give away their cherished authority over resources.

Delegation is the transfer to others of authority to make decisions and use organizational resources.

Delegation is the transfer of authority to make decisions and use organizational resources to others. Delegation of authority to make decisions to lower-level managers is common in organizations today. The important thing is to give lower-level managers authority to carry out the decisions they make. Managers typically have difficulty in delegating successfully. In the Management Skillbuilder exercise at the end of this chapter you will have a chance to practise delegation.

The difficulties that Nortel Networks experienced when its stock price collapsed and the resulting legal wrangling are good examples of the importance of authority and responsibility. The Nortel Networks and . . . Ethics box reports on this case of how quickly a highly respected company can morph into a untrusted organization.

An Alternative View of Authority

So far we have described authority as a top-down function in organizations; that is, authority originates at the top and is delegated downward as the managers at the top consider appropriate. In Chester Barnard's alternative perspective, authority is seen as originating in the individual, who can choose whether or not to follow a directive from above. The choice of whether to comply with a directive is based on the degree to which the individual understands it, feels able to carry it out, and believes it to be in the best interests of the organization and consistent with personal values.[42] This

Nortel Networks and . . . **ETHICS**

Fried Networks and Cooked Books

The 1990s were very good to Nortel Networks, a telecommunications equipment company based in Toronto, Ontario. The company grew throughout that decade as it rode the "dotcom" wave as a provider of computer networking equipment. At one point, it was estimated that Nortel had 47 percent of the market share in optical networking equipment, its share price reached almost $130 in the summer of 2000, and its share price and trading volume made it a dominant stock on the Toronto Stock Exchange. Most remarkably, however, is that at first it apparently survived the "dot-com meltdown" of the late 1990s and early 2000s.

"Apparently" is a very important word in that last sentence. The first rumblings that all was not well came when Nortel's third quarter results for 2000 were not as good as expected. Immediately after that, Nortel made several statements in late 2000 that its sales were robust, its revenue projections were on target, and that it would continue to perform well in 2001. Then, in February of 2001, the company announced that its revenue projections were way off—they would be less than half that was previously stated, to the point that Nortel would lose money in the first quarter of 2001. The market responded immediately, initially driving the stock down to around $30 per share, resulting in a overall loss of over $50 billion of market value.

At first, Nortel management blamed the dot-com meltdown for its troubles: sales were off everywhere and for all equipment providers. However, after a change in management, it was revealed that there had been a number of accounting irregularities. These mostly occurred through the recording of revenues before they were actually realized. Critics of Nortel argued that those accounting practices made the company appear to be more profitable that it actually was. It was later revealed that at least one senior executive left Nortel days before the February

2001 announcement, other executives had exercised stock options shortly before the stock plunged, and at least one acquisition was halted that was going to be based on a stock swap of Nortel shares.

That was just the beginning of Nortel's problems. Throughout the 2000s the company has repeatedly had to restate its financial earnings—the over-aggressive reporting of revenues apparently continued with the new management team. The company has shed more than two-thirds of its workforce. The stock bottomed out at $0.67 in 2002 (but has recovered to trade between $20 and 30). Shareholders have filed class-action suits, alleging that the company knew about its true financial state but deluded its own investors. Several executives were fired "for cause" in 2004, and have now been charged with fraud by the United States Security and Exchange Commission and investigated by Ontario Securities Commission.

What caused all of this? Some people speculate that top managers abused their authority to influence the preparers of financial statements to overstate profits. This increased the value of managers' stock options and bonuses. Other critics blame the board of directors, at least in part, because they did not hold managers accountable for their decisions and performance.

Regardless of the reason, many people have lost trust in Nortel. And perhaps worst of all, many Canadians saw a good portion of their retirement savings evaporate when the Nortel stock collapsed.

Sources: "The crash of Nortel," *Maclean's*, February 26, 2001, p. 5; Katherine Macklem, "Plunge From Grace," *Maclean's*, March 5, 2001, p. 42; Olga Kharif, "Nortel's New CEO Has His Work Cut Out," *Business Week Online*, October 4, 2001; Robert Sheppard, "Nortel Trips Again," *Maclean's*, March 29, 2004, p. 23; Steve Maich, "Nortel's Final Victim," Maclean's, August 2, 2004, p. 23; Andrew Wahl, "Double Trouble," *Canadian Business*, March 26, 2007, pp. 11–12.

---

perspective has been called the **acceptance theory of authority** because it means that the manager's authority depends on the subordinate's acceptance of the manager's right to give the directive and expect compliance.

For example, assume that you are a marketing analyst, and your company has a painting crew in the maintenance department. For some reason your manager has told you to repaint your own office over the weekend. You probably would question your manager's authority to make you do this work. In fact, you would probably refuse to

> The **acceptance theory of authority** says that the authority of a manager depends on the subordinate's acceptance of the manager's right to give directives and expect compliance with them.

do it. If you received a similar request to work over the weekend to finish a report, you would be more likely to accept it and carry it out. Thus, workers can either accept or reject the directives of a supervisor and thus limit supervisory authority.[43] In most organizational situations, employees accept a manager's right to expect compliance on normal, reasonable directives because of the manager's legitimate position in the organizational hierarchy or in the social context of the organization. They may choose to disobey the directive and must accept the consequences if they do not accept the manager's right.

Classic Views of Structure

The earliest views of organization structure combined the elements of organization configuration and operation into recommendations on how organizations should be structured. These views have often been called classical organization theory and include Max Weber's idea of the ideal bureaucracy, the classic organizing principles of Henri Fayol, and the human organization view of Rensis Likert. Although all three are universal approaches, their concerns and structural prescriptions differ significantly.

Ideal Bureaucracy

Weber's **ideal bureaucracy** is characterized by a hierarchy of authority and a system of rules and procedures designed to create an optimally effective system for large organizations.

Weber's **ideal bureaucracy**, presented in Chapter 1, was an organizational system characterized by a hierarchy of authority and a system of rules and procedures that, if followed, would create a maximally effective system for large organizations. Weber, writing at a time when organizations were inherently inefficient, claimed that the bureaucratic form of administration is superior to other forms of management with respect to stability, control, and predictability of outcomes.[44]

Weber's ideal bureaucracy had seven essential characteristics and utilized several of the building blocks discussed in this chapter, including the division of labour, hierarchy of authority, and rules and procedures. Weber intended these characteristics to ensure order and predictability in relationships among people and jobs in the bureaucracy. But it is easy to see how the same features can lead to sluggishness, inefficiency, and red tape. The administrative system can easily break down if any of the characteristics are carried to an extreme or are violated. For example, if endless arrays of rules and procedures bog down employees who must find the precise rule to follow every time they do something, responses to routine client or customer requests may slow to a crawl. Moreover, subsequent writers have said that Weber's view of authority is too rigid and have suggested that the bureaucratic organization would impede creativity and innovation and result in a lack of compassion for the individual in the organization.[45] In other words, the impersonality that is supposed to foster objectivity in a bureaucracy may result in serious difficulties for both employees and the organization. However, some organizations retain some characteristics of a bureaucratic structure while remaining innovative and productive.

The Classic Principles of Organizing

A second classic view was presented at the turn of the century by Henri Fayol, a French engineer and chief executive officer of a mining company. Drawing on his experience as a manager, Fayol was the first to classify the essential elements of management—now usually called management functions—as planning, organizing, command, coordination, and control.[46] In addition, he presented 14 principles of organizing that he considered an indispensable code for managers. These principles are shown in Table 12.2.

Fayol's principles have proved extraordinarily influential; they have served as the basis for the development of generally accepted means of organizing. For example, Fayol's unity of command principle means that employees should receive directions from only one person, and unity of direction means that tasks with the same objective should have a common supervisor. Combining these two principles with division of labour, authority, and responsibility results in a system of tasks and reporting and authority relationships that is the very essence of organizing. Fayol's principles thus provide the framework for the organization chart and the coordination of work.

The classic principles have been criticized on several counts. First, they ignore factors such as individual motivation, leadership, and informal groups—the human element in organizations. This line of criticism asserts that the classic principles result in a mechanical organization into which people must fit, regardless of their interests, abilities, or motivations. The principles have also been criticized for their lack of operational specificity in that Fayol described the principles as universal truths but did not specify the means of applying many of them. Finally, Fayol's principles have been discounted because they were not supported by scientific evidence; Fayol presented them as universal principles, backed by no evidence other than his experience.[47]

Human Organization

Rensis Likert called his approach to organization structure the **human organization**.[48] Because Likert, like others, had criticized Fayol's classic principles for overlooking

> The management functions set forth by Henri Fayol include planning, organizing, command, coordination, and control.

> Rensis Likert's **human organization** approach is based on supportive relationships, participation, and overlapping work groups.

Principle	Fayol's Comments
1. Division of work	Individuals and managers work on the same part.
2. Authority and responsibility	Authority—right to give orders; power to exact obedience; goes with responsibility for reward and punishment.
3. Discipline	Obedience, application, energy, behaviour. Agreement between firm and individual.
4. Unity of command	Employee receives orders from one superior.
5. Unity of direction	One head and one plan for activities with the same objective.
6. Subordination of individual interest to general interest	Objectives of the organization come before objectives of the individual.
7. Remuneration of personnel	Pay should be fair to the organization and the individual; discussed various forms.
8. Centralization	Proportion of discretion held by the manager compared to that allowed to subordinates.
9. Scalar chain	Line of authority from lowest to top.
10. Order	A place for everyone and everyone in his or her place.
11. Equity	Combination of kindness and justice; equality of treatment.
12. Stability of tenure of personnel	Stability of managerial personnel; time to get used to work.
13. Initiative	Power of thinking out and executing a plan.
14. Esprit de corps	Harmony and union among personnel is strength.

TABLE 12.2

Fayol's Classic Principles of Organizing

Source: From *General and Industrial Management* by Henri Fayol. Copyright © Lake Publishing 1984, Belmont, CA 94002. Used by permission.

human factors, it is not surprising that his approach centred on the principles of supportive relationships, employee participation, and overlapping work groups.

The term *supportive relationships* suggests that in all organizational activities, individuals should be treated in such a way that they experience feelings of support, self-worth, and importance. By *employee participation* Likert meant that the work group needs to be involved in decisions that affect it, thereby enhancing the employee's sense of supportiveness and self-worth. The principle of *overlapping work groups* means that work groups are linked, with managers serving as the linking pins. Each manager (except the highest ranking) is a member of two groups: a work group that he or she supervises and a management group composed of the manager's peers and their supervisor. Coordination and communication grow stronger

TABLE 12.3

Characteristics of Likert's Four Management Systems

Characteristic	System 1: Exploitive Authoritative	System 2: Benevolent Authoritative	System 3: Consultative	System 4: Participative Group
Leadership				
• Trust in subordinates	None	None	Substantial	Complete
• Subordinates' ideas	Seldom used	Sometimes used	Usually used	Always used
Motivational Forces				
• Motives tapped	Security, status	Economic, ego	Substantial	Complete
• Level of satisfaction	Overall dissatisfaction	Some moderate satisfaction	Moderate satisfaction	High satisfaction
Communication				
• Amount	Very little	Little	Moderate	Much
• Direction	Downward	Mostly downward	Down, up	Down, up, lateral
Interaction-Influence				
• Amount	None	None	Substantial	Complete
• Cooperative teamwork	None	Virtually none	Moderate	Substantial
Decision Making				
• Locus	Top	Policy decided at top	Broad policy decided at top	All levels
• Subordinates involved	Not at all	Sometimes consulted	Usually consulted	Fully involved
Goal Setting				
• Manner	Orders	Orders with comments	Set after discussion	Group participation
• Acceptance	Covertly resisted	Frequently resisted	Sometimes resisted	Fully accepted
Control Processes				
• Level	Top	None	Some below top	All levels
• Information	Incomplete, inaccurate	Often incomplete, inaccurate	Moderately complete, accurate	Complete, accurate
Performance	Mediocre	Fair to good	Good	Excellent

Sources: Adapted from Rensis Likert, *New Patterns of Management* (New York: McGraw-Hill, 1961), pp. 223–233, and Rensis Likert, *The Human Organization* (New York: McGraw-Hill, 1967), pp. 197, 198, 201, 203, 210, and 211. Reprinted by permission of McGraw-Hill, Inc.

when the managers perform the linking function by sharing problems, decisions, and information both upward and downward in the groups to which they belong. The human organization concept rests on the assumption that people work best in highly cohesive groups oriented toward organizational goals. Management's function is to make sure the work groups are linked for effective coordination and communication.

Likert described four systems of organizing, whose characteristics are summarized in Table 12.3. System 1, the exploitive authoritative system, can be characterized as the classic bureaucracy. System 4, the participative group, is the organization design Likert favoured. System 2, the benevolent authoritative system, and system 3, the consultative system, are less extreme than either system 1 or system 4. Likert described all four systems in terms of eight organizational variables: leadership processes, motivational forces, communication processes, interaction-influence processes, decision-making processes, goal-setting processes, control processes, and performance goals and training. Likert believed that work groups should be able to overlap horizontally as well as vertically where necessary to accomplish tasks. This feature is directly contrary to the classic principle that advocates unity of command. In addition, rather than the hierarchical chain of command, Likert favoured the linking-pin concept of overlapping work groups for making decisions and resolving conflicts.

Research support for Likert's human organization emanates primarily from Likert and his associates' work at the Institute for Social Research at the University of Michigan. Although their research has upheld the basic propositions of the approach, it is not entirely convincing. One review of the evidence suggested that although research has shown characteristics of system 4 to be associated with positive worker attitudes and, in some cases, increased productivity, it is not clear that the characteristics of the human organization caused the positive results.[49] It may have been that positive attitudes and high productivity allowed the organization structure to be participative and provided the atmosphere for the development of supportive relationships. Likert's design has also been criticized for focusing almost exclusively on individuals and groups and not dealing extensively with structural issues. Overall, the most compelling support for this approach is at the individual and work-group levels. In some ways, Likert's system is much like the team-based organization popular today.

Thus, the classic views of organization embody the key elements of organization structure. Each view, however, combined these key elements in different ways and with other management elements. These three classic views are typical of how the early writers attempted to prescribe a universal approach to organization structure that would be best in all situations. In the next chapter we describe other views of organization structure that may be effective, depending on the organizational situation.

Chapter Review

Summary of Key Points

- The structure of an organization is the system of task, reporting, and authority relationships within which the organization does its work. The purpose of organization structure is to order and coordinate the actions of employees to achieve organizational goals. Every organization structure addresses two fundamental issues: dividing available labour according to the tasks to be performed and combining and coordinating divided tasks to ensure that tasks are accomplished.

- An organization chart shows reporting relationships, work-group memberships, departments, and formal lines of communication. In a broader sense, an organization chart shows the configuration, or shape, of the organization. Configuration has four dimensions: division of labour, departmentalization, span of control, and administrative hierarchy. Division of labour is the separation of work into different jobs to be done by different people. Departmentalization is the manner in which the divided tasks are combined and allocated to work groups for coordination. Tasks can be combined into departments on the basis of business function, process, product, customer, and geographic region. Span of control is the number of people reporting to a manager; it also defines the size of work groups and is inversely related to the number of hierarchical levels in the organization. The administrative hierarchy is the system of reporting relationships in the organization.

- Structural policies prescribe how employees should behave in their organizational activities. Such policies include formalization of rules and procedures and centralization of decision making. Formalization is the degree to which rules and procedures shape employees' jobs and activities. The purpose of formalization is to predict and control how employees behave on the job. Explicit rules are set down in job descriptions, policy and procedures manuals, and office memos. Implicit rules develop over time as employees become accustomed to doing things in certain ways.

- Centralization concentrates decision-making authority at the top of the organizational hierarchy; under decentralization, decisions are made throughout the hierarchy.

- Responsibility is an obligation to do something with the expectation of achieving some output. Authority is power that has been legitimized within a specific social context. Authority includes the legitimate right to use resources to accomplish expected outcomes. The relationship between responsibility and authority needs to be one of parity; that is, employees must have enough authority over resources to meet the expectations of others.

- Weber's ideal bureaucracy, Fayol's classic principles of organizing, and Likert's human organization cover many of the key features of organization structure. Weber's bureaucratic form of administration was intended to ensure stability, control, and predictable outcomes. The ideal bureaucracy is characterized by rules and procedures, division of labour, a hierarchy of authority, technical competence, separation of ownership, rights and property differentiation, and documentation.

- Fayol's classic principles included departmentalization, unity of command, and unity of direction; they came to be generally accepted as means of organizing. Taken together, the 14 principles provided the basis for the modern organization chart and for coordinating work.

- Likert's human organization was based on the principles of supportive relationships, employee participation, and overlapping work groups. Likert described the human organization in terms of eight variables based on the assumption that people work best in highly supportive and cohesive work groups oriented toward organization goals.

Discussion Questions

1. Define organization structure and explain its role in the process of managing the organization.

2. What is the purpose of organization structure? What would an organization be like without a structure?

3. In what ways are aspects of the organization structure analogous to the structural parts of the human body?

4. How is labour divided in your college or university? In what other ways could your college or university be departmentalized?

5. What types of organizations could benefit from a small span of control? What types might benefit from a large span of control?

6. Discuss how increasing formalization might affect the role conflict and role ambiguity of employees. How might the impact of formalization differ for research scientists, machine operators, and bank tellers?

7. How might centralization or decentralization affect the job characteristics specified in job design?

8. When a group makes a decision, how is responsibility for the decision apportioned among the members?

9. Why do employees typically want more authority and less responsibility?

10. Consider the job you now hold or one that you held in the past. Did your boss have the authority to direct your work? Why did he or she have this authority?

11. Describe at least four features of organization structure that were important parts of the classic view of organizing.

Experiencing Organizational Behaviour

Purpose: This exercise will help you understand the configurational and operational aspects of organization structure.

Format: You will interview at least five employees in different parts of either the college or university you attend or a small- to medium-sized organization and analyze its structure. (You may want to coordinate this exercise with the exercise in Chapter 13.)

Procedure: If you use a local organization, your first task is to find one with 50 to 500 employees. The organization should have more than two hierarchical levels, but it should not be too complex to understand in a short period of study. You may want to check with your professor before contacting the company. Your initial contact should be with the highest-ranking manager, if possible. Be sure that top management is aware of your project and gives approval.

If you use your college or university, you could talk to professors, secretaries, and other administrative staff in the admissions office, student services department, athletic department, library, or other areas. Be sure to represent a variety of jobs and levels in your interviews.

Using the material in this chapter, interview employees to obtain the following information on the structure of the organization:

1. The type of departmentalization (business function, process, product, customer, geographic region)

2. The typical span of control at each level of the organization

3. The number of levels in the hierarchy

4. The administrative ratio (ratio of managers to total employees and ratio of managers to production employees)

5. The degree of formalization (to what extent are rules and procedures written down in job descriptions, policy and procedures manuals, and memos?)

6. The degree of decentralization (to what extent are employees at all levels involved in making decisions?)

Interview three to five employees of the organization at different levels and in different departments. One should hold a top-level position. Be sure to ask the questions in a way that is clear to the respondents; they may not be familiar with the terminology used in this chapter.

Students should produce a report with a paragraph on each configurational and operational aspect of structure listed in this exercise as well as an organization chart of the company, a discussion of differences in responses from the employees interviewed, and any unusual structural features (for example, a situation in which employees report to more than one person or to no one). You may want to send a copy of your report to the company's top management.

Follow-up Questions

1. Which aspects of structure were the hardest to obtain information about? Why?

2. If there were differences in the responses of the employees you interviewed, how do you account for them?

3. If you were president of the organization you analyzed, would you structure it in the same way? Why or why not? If not, how would you structure it differently?

Management Skillbuilder

Exercise Overview: Managers typically inherit an existing organization structure when they are promoted or hired into a position as manager. Often, however, after working with the existing structure for a while, they feel the need to rearrange the structure to increase the productivity or performance of the organization. This exercise provides you with the opportunity to restructure an existing organization.

Exercise Background: Recall the analysis you did in the "Experiencing Organizational Behaviour" exercise on page 377 in which you analyzed the structure of an existing organization. In that exercise you described the configurational and operational aspects of the structure of a local organization or department at your college or university.

Exercise Task: Develop a different organization structure for that organization. You may utilize any or all of the factors described in this chapter. For example, you could alter the span of control, the administrative hierarchy, and the method of departmentalization as well as the formalization and centralization of the organization. Remember, the key to structure is to develop a way to coordinate the divided tasks. You should draw a new organization chart and develop a rationale for your new design.

Conclude by addressing the following questions:

1. How difficult was it to come up with a different way of structuring the organization?

2. What would it take to convince the current head of that organization to go along with your suggested changes?

Organizational Behaviour Case for Discussion

Molson Coors

The origins of the Molson Brewery Company can be traced back to 1786, when John Molson first started producing beer in Montreal. The company prospered for many years, as an independent operation, reaching iconic status as a Canadian company (and beer!).

As with many companies, it grew and diversified over the years. It introduced new brands, adding to its flagship Molson's Canadian and Molson's Export Ale with newer products such as Molson's Dry and Molson's Ultra—the latter a "low-carb" brew. Over the last 20 years or so, it has also signed a number of distribution partnerships with foreign producers of beer, such as Corona (Mexican), Heineken (Dutch), and Foster's Lager (Australian) among others. Molson's even attempted diversification into unrelated businesses such as home improvement retailers Beaver Lumber and Home Depot, although these ventures were later jettisoned.

Through the 1990s and 2000s the beer industry was globalizing rapidly, with mega-companies such as Anheiser-Busch, ABMiller, and InterBrew growing rapidly and gaining large international market share. All of those companies had made many acquisitions over the previous decade, and were using economies of scale, purchasing power, and integrated distribution networks to penetrate many markets efficiently and effectively.

In the early 2000s Molson's decided to enter a "merger of equals" with the Coors Brewing Company of Golden, Colorado. Executives from both companies stated that the merger was a necessary response to industry concentration and globalization. Some critics, however, allege that Molson's was forced to "sell out" to the American company due to an ill-fated acquisition of a Brazilian brewery that was losing money. In any event, the merger was approved, and the Molson Coors Brewery was formally formed on February 9, 2005.

The combined company now sells the labels listed above as well as Coors Light, and other brands that Coors owned prior to the merger, such as Carling and Carling Black Label. The company hopes to add value by cutting costs—indeed, one Coors brewery in the United States has already closed—and gaining efficiencies in areas such as sales, marketing, and distribution. Some critics are skeptical however, noting that many mergers, particularly between family dominated firms can fail.

Other beer and business critics suggested that the merger fails to resolve the core problem that both Molson's and Coors had prior to their joining: their lead products were losing market share, mostly because they just don't taste very good.

Case Questions

1. What are the organizational advantages and disadvantages for Molson Coors to operate as a merged company?

2. How centralized should be the decision making within the new company? Should some decisions be decentralized on a geographic basis, given the differences across brand preferences and loyalties, and between Canada and the United States?

Sources: Adrienne Carter, "Will This Merger Go Down Smoothly?" *Business Week*, Feb. 21, 2005, pp. 70–71; Steve Maich, "The Story of Kiely & Carly," *Maclean's*, Feb. 28, 2005, p. 29; Robert Barker, "Brews at Bargain Prices," *Business Week*, Aug. 8, 2005, p. 23; Andy Holloway, "Tale of Brews," *Canadian Business*, June 5, 2006, pp. 63–66; Andy Holloway, "The Molson Way," *Canadian Business*, April 9, 2007, pp. 36–40.

Organizational Behaviour Case for Discussion

Changing the Rules at Cosmo Plastics

When Alice Thornton took over as chief executive officer at Cosmo Plastics, the company was in trouble. Cosmo had started out as an innovative company, known for creating a new product just as the popularity of one of the industry's old standbys was fading (i.e., replacing yo-yo's with water guns). In two decades, it had become an established maker of plastics for the toy industry. Cosmo had grown from a dozen employees to four hundred, and its rules had grown haphazardly with it. Thornton's predecessor, Willard P. Blatz, had found the company's procedures chaotic and had instituted a uniform set of rules for all employees. Since then, both research output and manufacturing productivity had steadily declined. When the company's board of directors hired Thornton, they emphasized the need to evaluate and revise the company's formal procedures in an attempt to reverse the trends.

First, Thornton studied the rules Blatz had implemented. She was impressed to find that the entire procedures manual was only 20 pages long. It began with the reasonable sentence "All employees of Cosmo Plastics shall be governed by the following . . ." Thornton had expected to find evidence that Blatz had been a tyrant who ran the company with an iron fist. But as she read through the manual, she found nothing to indicate this. In fact, some of the rules were rather flexible. Employees could punch in anytime between 8 and 10 A.M. and leave nine hours later, between 5 and 7 P.M. Managers were expected to keep monthly notes on the people working for them and make yearly recommendations to the human resources committee about raises, bonuses, promotions, and firings. Except for their one-hour lunch break, which they could take at any time, employees were expected to be in the building at all times.

Puzzled, Thornton went down to the lounge where the research and development people gathered. She was surprised to find a time clock on the wall. Curious, she fed a time card into it and was even more flabbergasted when the machine chattered noisily, then spit it out without registering the time. Apparently R&D was none too pleased with the time clock and had found a way to rig it. When Thornton looked up in astonishment, only two of the twelve employees who had been in the room were still there. They said the others had punched back in when they saw the boss coming.

Thornton asked the remaining pair to tell her what was wrong with company rules, and she got an earful. The researchers, mostly chemists and engineers with advanced graduate degrees, resented punching a time clock and having their work evaluated once a month, when they could not reasonably be expected to come up with something new and worth writing about more than twice a year. Before the implementation of the new rules, they had often received inspiration from going down to the local dime store and picking up five dollars worth of cheap toys, but now they felt they could make such trips only on their own time. And when a researcher came up with an innovative idea, it often took months for the proposal to work its way up the company hierarchy to the attention of someone who could put it into production. In short, all these sharp minds felt shackled.

Concluding that maybe she had overlooked the rigidity of the rules, Thornton walked over to the manufacturing building to talk to the production supervisors. They responded to her questions with one word: anarchy. With employees drifting in between 8:00 and 10:00 and then starting to drift out again by 11:00 for lunch, the supervisors never knew if they had enough people to run a particular operation. Employee turnover was high, but not high enough in some cases; supervisors believed the rules prevented them from firing all but the most incompetent workers before the end of the yearly evaluation period. The rules were so humane that discipline was impossible to enforce.

By the time Alice Thornton got back to her office, she had a plan. The following week, she called in all the department managers and asked them to draft formal rules and procedures for their individual areas. She told them she did not intend to lose control of the company, but she wanted to see if they could improve productivity and morale by creating formal procedures for their individual departments.

Case Questions

1. Do you think Alice Thornton's proposal to decentralize the rules and procedures of Cosmo Plastics will work?

2. What kinds of rules and procedures do you think the department managers will come up with? Which departments will be more formalized? Why?

3. What risks will the company face if it establishes different procedures for different areas?

SELF TEST

You have read the chapter and studied the key terms. Think you're ready to ace the exam? Take this sample test to gauge your comprehension of chapter material and check your answers at the back of the book. Want more test questions? Take the ACE quizzes found on the student website: www.hmco.ca/ob.

T F 1. An organization is a group of jobs tied together with money.

T F 2. The system of authority relationships are part of an organization's structure.

T F 3. A primary disadvantage of division of labour is low worker satisfaction.

T F 4. Nearly all large organizations pick one form of departmentalization for all levels of the company.

T F 5. Formalized decentralization is a common way to allow participation in decision making while maintaining control and predictability.

T F 6. Authority can be delegated down to others, but responsibility cannot.

T F 7. Fayol's classic principles of organizing were criticized because they ignore the human element in organization.

8. The purpose of an organization's structure is to
   a. avoid formal task and reporting relationships.
   b. order and coordinate the actions of employees to achieve organizational goals.
   c. focus on customer needs, not on products or geographic locations.
   d. eliminate differences in authority and responsibility.
   e. make the organization more attractive to customers.

9. Which of the following is not a common basis for departmentalization?
   a. business function
   b. profit levels
   c. process
   d. product
   e. geography

10. With customer departmentalization there is usually less process specialization because
    a. specialists prefer to develop products rather than work with people.
    b. process specialization results in a span of control that is too large.
    c. employees must remain flexible to do whatever is necessary for customers.

    d. market coverage is better with lower process specialization.
    e. process specialization results in lower productivity and higher costs, regardless of the form of departmentalization.

11. Robert wants to work at a company that allows lower-level employees to participate in making decisions. Robert should look for a company
    a. that is departmentalized by geography.
    b. with a narrow span of control.
    c. that refuses to downsize.
    d. that is decentralized.
    e. that is departmentalized by product.

12. You can tell whether an organization is very formalized by
    a. counting the number of levels in its hierarchy.
    b. determining the last time the company downsized.
    c. looking at how many rules it has.
    d. observing whether the departmentalization is based on customers or products.
    e. verifying that responsibility is delegated.

13. The classic management theorist Rensis Likert described several systems of organizing. Which system did Likert favour?
    a. the classic bureaucracy
    b. the participative group
    c. the benevolent authoritative system
    d. the consultative system
    e. the dual-structure system

14. Rensis Likert, a renown management theorist, believed work groups should be able to overlap horizontally as well as vertically where necessary to accomplish tasks. This feature is directly contrary to which classical principle of organizing?
    a. supportive relationships
    b. linking pins
    c. employee participation
    d. unity of command
    e. customer departmentalization

Organization Design

▶ **Describe the basic premise of contingency organization design.**

▶ **Discuss how strategy and the three structural imperatives affect organization structure.**

▶ **Describe five different approaches to organizational design.**

▶ **Discuss contemporary approaches to organization design.**

Chapter Outline

Contingency Approaches to Organization Design

Strategy, Structural Imperatives, and Strategic Choice

> Strategy
> Structural Imperatives
> Strategic Choice

Organizational Designs

> Mechanistic and Organic Designs
> Sociotechnical Systems Designs
> Mintzberg's Designs
> Matrix Organization Design
> Virtual Organizations

Contemporary Organization Design

> Reengineering the Organization
> Rethinking the Organization
> Global Organization Structure and Design Issues
> Dominant Themes of Contemporary Designs

From Radios to Publishing Empire

Selling radios in North Bay, Ontario, during the Depression of the 1930s seems like an unlikely way to start a successful business. It seems even more unlikely that the business would become one of Canada's largest, and make the founder's family one of the wealthiest in Canada. But that is how the Thomson Corporation started.

After failing in farming in Saskatchewan and at running an automobile parts distributorship in Ontario, Roy Thomson's next business adventure was to sell radios in North Bay in 1930. It was a bit of a hard go, in part because radio reception was poor. Thomson's solution: he started his own radio station in 1932. Soon after that, he acquired more radio stations in Ontario, then moved into newspapers, a somewhat related business line in the sense that it was another media outlet.

That early example reflects Thomson's strategy throughout the years—it started or acquired complementary businesses, and sometimes more loosely affiliated business to meets its general goals of growth and profitability. What is now the Thomson Corporation has changed considerably over the years, acquiring and divesting business as it continuously adjusts its strategy to fit with changing times and business environments.

Throughout the 1950s and 1960s Thomson grew largely in print and electronic media. It owned dozens of newspapers and magazines, radio and television stations in several countries. In the late 1960s it moved into unrelated ventures in travel and oil.

When Ken Thomson succeeded his father in the mid-1970s the company was worth an estimated $750 million. Shortly thereafter, more Canadian newspapers were acquired, including *The Globe and Mail*. Educational publishers were acquired. At its peak, Thomson owned over 200 newspapers in Canada and the US, and the second largest academic publishing business in the US.

In the late 1980s and early 1990s, the company began to refocus. First, it divested its oil interests. It also started to acquire Internet-based information service providers to a number of professions in investment, healthcare, and legal services. This decision was driven in part by the decline in newspaper revenues.

Then, in a major shift, in 2000 Thomson sold its newspapers while continuing to acquire more information service providers. In 2007, it sold Thomson Learning, its academic publishing division for nearly $8 billion.

Its main focus is now on providing electronic information services, and its latest move was to acquire the Reuters Group information and news systems—for $17 billion—in an effort to compete directly with Bloomberg financial information services. If the Reuters acquisition is approved by regulators, Thomson will become the largest financial information provider in the world.

The company started by Roy Thomson's efforts in radio sales is now worth over $30 billion, with over $6 billion in annual revenues. It employs over 30 000 people in 37 countries. When he passed away in 2006, Ken Thomson's personal wealth was estimated at $19 billion.[1]

The Thomson Corporation has been in business for almost 80 years. Its many moves in acquisitions and divestments were in response to shifts in the environment. Thomson continuously changed to remain competitive and dominant in the operating environments in which it chose to compete. Why is it that, when some companies' technologies change or competitors emerge, some companies die but other firms adjust and become stronger than ever, like Thomson? One key reason is organization design. Within the organization, design coordinates the efforts of the people, work groups, and departments. Designing a system of task, reporting, and authority relationships that leads to the efficient accomplishment of organizational goals is a challenge managers must be prepared to face. In Chapter 12, we discussed the tools with which managers design a system that enables the organization to be effective. In this chapter, we integrate these basic elements of structure, take into consideration other factors such as the environment and technology, and present several perspectives on organization design. We begin this chapter by discussing organization designs based on the contingency approach. In this discussion we describe how an organization's size, environment, and technology combine with its strategy to determine various aspects of organization design. Next, we examine several organization designs: mechanistic and organic designs, the sociotechnical systems perspective, the Mintzberg framework for classifying organization structures, matrix designs, and virtual organizations. We conclude with an examination of contemporary organization design issues.

Contingency Approaches to Organization Design

In the **universal approach** to organization design, prescriptions or propositions are designed to work in any circumstances.

Under the **contingency approach** to organization design, the desired outcomes for the organization can be achieved in several ways.

Organization designs vary from rigid bureaucracies to flexible matrix systems. Most theories of organization design take either a universal or a contingency approach. A **universal approach** is one whose prescriptions or propositions are designed to work in any situation. Thus, a universal design prescribes the "one best way" to structure the jobs, authority, and reporting relationships of the organization, regardless of factors such as the organization's external environment, the industry, and the type of work to be done. The classical approaches discussed in Chapter 12 are all universal approaches.

A **contingency approach**, on the other hand, suggests that organizational efficiency can be achieved in several ways. In a contingency design, specific conditions such as the environment, technology, and the organization's workforce determine the structure. Figure 13.1 shows the distinction between the universal and contingency approaches. This distinction is similar to the one between universal and contingency approaches to motivation (Chapters 4), job design (Chapter 5), and leadership (Chapter 11). Although no one particular form of organization is generally accepted, the contingency approach most closely represents current thinking.

FIGURE 13.1

Universal and Contingency Approaches to Organization Design

The universal approach looks for the single best way to design an organization regardless of situational issues. The contingency approach designs the organization to fit the situation.

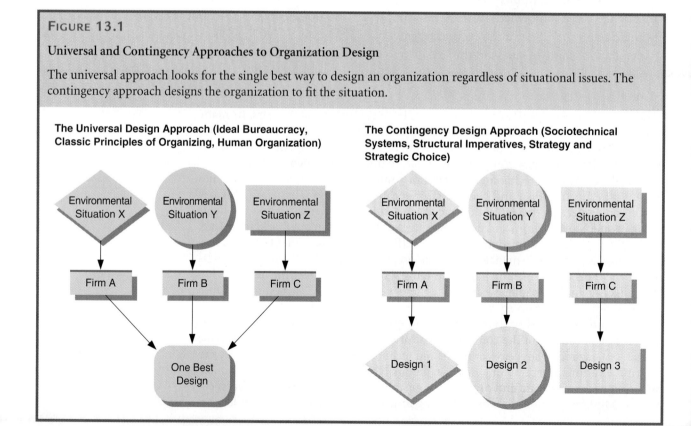

Weber, Fayol, and Likert (see Chapter 12) each proposed an organization design that is independent of the nature of the organization and its environment. Although each of these approaches contributed to our understanding of the organizing process and the practice of management, none has proved to be universally applicable. In this chapter we turn to several contingency designs that attempt to specify the conditions, or contingency factors, under which they are likely to be most effective. The contingency factors include such things as the strategy of the organization, technology, the environment, the organization's size, and the social system within which the organization operates.

The contingency approach has been criticized as unrealistic, in that managers are expected to observe a change in one of the contingency factors and to make a rational structural alteration. On the other hand, Donaldson has argued that it is reasonable to expect organizations to respond to lower organizational performance, which may result from a lack of response to some significant change in one or several contingency factors.[2]

Strategy, Structural Imperatives, and Strategic Choice

> **Strategy** is the plans and actions necessary to achieve organizational goals.

The decision about how to design the organization structure is based on numerous factors. In this section, we present several views of the determinants of organization structure and integrate them to a single approach. We begin with the strategic view.

Strategy

A **strategy** is the plans and actions necessary to achieve organizational goals.[3] Bombardier, for example, has attempted to become the leader in the transportation industry by pursuing a strategy that combines product differentiation and market segmentation. Over the years Bombardier has successfully introduced new products and entered new transportation markets in a diverse array of products ranging from rail cars and jet airplanes, while selling off the personal recreation vehicle division upon which the company was founded.[4]

After studying the history of 70 companies, Alfred Chandler drew certain conclusions about the relationship between an organization's structure and its business strategy.[5] Chandler observed that a growth strategy to expand into a new product line is usually matched with some type of decentralization, a decentralized structure being necessary to deal with the problems of the new product line.

Chandler's structure-follows-strategy concept seems to appeal to common sense. Management must decide what the organization is to do and what its goals are before deciding how to design the organization structure, which is how the organization will meet those goals. This perspective assumes a purposeful approach to designing the structure of the organization.

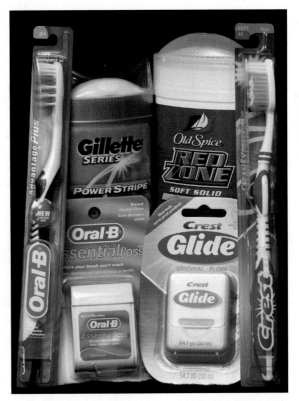

This picture shows just a few of the multiple overlapping products from Procter & Gamble and Gillette following the acquisition of Gillette by Procter & Gamble. The strategy related to personal care products will probably require Procter & Gamble to sell, spin off, license, or combine in some manner some of these overlapping products. The result will be a very different organization design for the new Procter & Gamble.

Structural Imperatives

The structural-imperatives approach to organization design probably has been the most discussed and researched contingency perspective of the last 30 years. This perspective was not formulated by a single theorist or researcher and it has not evolved from a systematic and cohesive research effort; rather, it gradually emerged from a vast number of studies that sought to address the question "What are the compelling factors that determine how the organization must be structured to be effective?" As Figure 13.2 shows, the three factors that have been identified as **structural imperatives** are size, technology, and environment.

> **Structural imperatives**—environment, technology, and size—are the three primary determinants of organization structure.

Size   The size of an organization can be gauged in many ways. Usually it is measured in terms of total number of employees, value of the organization's assets, total sales in the previous year (or number of clients served), or physical capacity. The method of measurement is very important, although the different measures usually are correlated.[6]

Generally, larger organizations have more complex structures than smaller ones. Peter Blau and his associates found that large size is associated with greater specialization of labour, a larger span of control, more hierarchical levels, and greater formalization.[7] These multiple effects are shown in Figure 13.3. Increasing size leads to more specialization of labour within a work unit, which increases the amount of differentiation among work units and the number of levels in the hierarchy, resulting in a need for more intergroup formalization. With greater specialization within the unit, there is less need for coordination within groups; thus, the span of control can be larger. Larger spans of control mean fewer first-line managers, but the need for more intergroup coordination may require more second and third-line managers and staff personnel to coordinate them. Large organizations may therefore be more efficient because of their large spans of control and reduced administrative overhead; however, the greater differentiation among units makes the system more complex. Studies by researchers associated with the University of Aston in Birmingham, England, and others, have shown similar results.[8]

> Larger organizations tend to have more complex organization structures than smaller organizations.

Economies of scale are another advantage of large organizations. In a large operation, fixed costs—for example, plant and equipment—can be spread over more units of output, thereby reducing the cost per unit. In addition, some administrative activities, such as purchasing, clerical work, and marketing, can be accomplished for a large number of units at the same cost as for a small number. Their cost can then be spread over the larger number of units, again reducing unit cost.

Companies such as AT&T Technologies, General Electric's Aircraft Engine Products Group, and S. C. Johnson & Son have gone against the conventional wisdom that larger is always better in manufacturing plants. They cite as their main reasons the smaller investment required for smaller plants, the reduced need to produce a variety of products, and the desire to decrease organizational complexity (that is, reduce the number of hierarchical levels and shorten lines of communication). In a number of instances, smaller plants have resulted in increased team spirit, improved productivity, and higher profits.[9]

Other studies have found that the relationship between size and structural complexity is less clear than the Blau results indicated. These studies suggest that size must be examined in relation to the technology of the organization.[10]

Traditionally, as organizations have grown, several layers of advisory staff

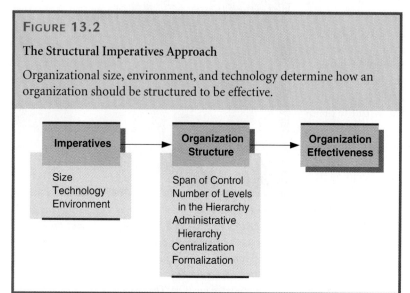

FIGURE 13.2

The Structural Imperatives Approach

Organizational size, environment, and technology determine how an organization should be structured to be effective.

Imperatives	Organization Structure	Organization Effectiveness
Size	Span of Control	
Technology	Number of Levels	
Environment	in the Hierarchy	
	Administrative	
	Hierarchy	
	Centralization	
	Formalization	

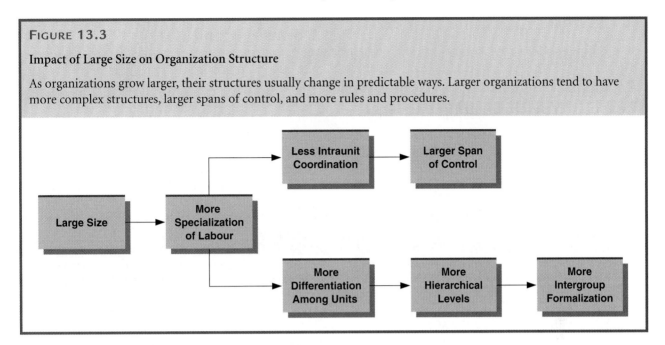

FIGURE **13.3**

Impact of Large Size on Organization Structure

As organizations grow larger, their structures usually change in predictable ways. Larger organizations tend to have more complex structures, larger spans of control, and more rules and procedures.

have been added to help coordinate the complexities inherent in any large organization. In contrast, a current trend is to cut staff throughout the organization. Known as **organizational downsizing**, this popular trend is aimed primarily at reducing the size of corporate staff and middle management to reduce costs. Companies such as Telus and Cisco Systems cut back corporate staff significantly in the early 2000s.[11] The results have been mixed, with some observers noting that indiscriminate across-the-board cuts can leave the organization weak in certain key areas. The Downsizing and . . . Research box describes several studies that examine the consequences and causes of downsizing.

There can be positive results from downsizing, including quicker decision making because fewer layers of management must approve every decision. One review of research on organizational downsizing found that it had both psychological and sociological impacts. This study suggested that in a downsizing environment, size affects organization design in very complex ways.[12]

Technology **Technology** consists of the mechanical and intellectual processes that transform raw materials into products and services for customers. For example, the primary technology employed by McCain Foods transforms raw materials such as potatoes (input) into French fries (outputs). Prudential Insurance uses actuarial tables and information-processing technologies to produce its insurance services. CTV gathers news, then collates, edits, and broadcasts information. Of course, most organizations use multiple technologies. For example, McCain uses marketing research to assist product development and owns a transportation company to help get its product to market.

Although there is general agreement that technology is important, the means by which this technology has been evaluated and measured have varied widely. Five approaches to examining the technology of the organization are shown in Table 13.1. For convenience, we have classified these approaches according to the names of their proponents.

In an early study of the relationship between technology and organization structure, Joan Woodward categorized manufacturing technologies by their complexity: unit or small-batch, large-batch or mass production, and continuous processes.[13] Tom Burns and

Organizational downsizing is a popular trend aimed at reducing the size of corporate staff and middle management to reduce costs.

Technology refers to the mechanical and intellectual processes that transform inputs into outputs.

Downsizing and . . .   **RESEARCH**

Results of Downsizing and Some Possible Reasons Why Downsizing Persists

Many Canadian organizations, in both the private and public sectors have downsized over the past two decades. This has drawn the interest of quite a few Canadian scholars. Indeed, the interest was so great that a special issue of the *Canadian Journal of Administrative Studies* was dedicated to the topic of downsizing and restructuring in 1998.

Terry Wagar of Saint Mary's University in Halifax, Nova Scotia, was one of the contributors to the special issue. His study examined the impact of downsizing in Canadian organizations. 1907 organizations completed a questionnaire, representing a number of private sector industries as well as government, health care and education. Wagar then compared those organizations that had downsized with those that had not. Over 55 percent of the participating organizations had downsized in the two years prior to the survey. As with previous studies of downsizing, he found that those organizations that had downsized experienced a number of negative results including lower employer efficiency, employee satisfaction, and worse employer-employee relationships.

Wagar did a similar analysis in another study several years later, but this time also asked union representatives about their perceptions of downsizing. Not surprisingly, those unions whose organizations had experienced downsizing also reported lower employee satisfaction and poorer management–labour relations.

Given the number of studies that show that downsizing is risky and frequently does not yield the desired or even desirable results, why do organizations persist in attempting the strategy? Marc Mentzer of the University of Saskatchewan has suggested several possible answers, some based on the personality characteristics of executives, and others based on national cultures. He first noted that downsizing has become a wildly popular strategy despite its mixed results: between 19% to a whopping 57% of organizations downsized within a given year in the years between 1988 and 2001. Mentzer observed that downsizing had obviously become a management fad, a strategy that was probably copied by some executives simply because many other companies were doing it. Therefore, he suggests that executives who have personalities that are more risk averse are likely to downsize their organizations, since downsizing might appear to be a relatively more certain strategy given its popularity.

Mentzer also speculated that there may be some national cultural predictors of downsizing. He notes that national cultures are thought to differ from one another on several characteristics. Two of these are "uncertainty avoidance" and "power distance." Like the personality characteristic of risk aversion, Mentzer suggests that countries that are higher in uncertainty avoidance are more likely to have higher rates of downsizing. Power distance, on the other hand is the degree of social separation between the most and least powerful people in a society. Mentzer speculates that countries that have more power distance are likely to have more downsizing, because executives would have less empathy for lower level employees.

Sources: Terry H. Wagar, "Exploring the Consequences of Workforce Reduction," *Canadian Journal of Administrative Studies*, 1998, vol. 15, pp. 300–309; Terry H. Wagar, "Consequences of Work Force Reduction: Some Employer and Union Evidence," *Journal of Labor Research*, 2001, vol. 22, pp. 851–862; Marc S. Mentzer, "Toward a Psychological and Cultural Model of Downsizing," *Journal of Organizational Behavior*, 2005, vol. 26, pp. 993–997.

George Stalker proposed that the rate of change in technology determines the best method of structuring the organization.[14] Charles Perrow developed a technological continuum, with routine technologies at one end and nonroutine technologies at the other, and claimed that all organizations could be classified on his routine-to-nonroutine continuum.[15] James Thompson claimed that all organizations could be classified into one of three technological categories: long-linked, mediating, and intensive.[16] Finally, a group of English researchers at the University of Aston developed three categories of technology based on the type of work flow involved: operations, material, and knowledge.[17] These perspectives on technology are somewhat similar in that all (except the Aston

Approach	Classification of Technology	Example
Woodward (1958 and 1965) (cit. no.13)	Unit or small-batch	Customized parts made one at a time
	Large-batch or mass production	Automobile assembly line
	Continuous process	Chemical plant, petroleum refinery
Burns and Stalker (1961) (cit. no. 14)	Rate of technological change	Slow: large manufacturing; rapid: computer industry
Perrow (1967) (cit. 15)	Routine	Standardized products (Procter & Gamble, General Foods
	Nonroutine	New technology products or processes (computers, telecommunications)
Thompson (1967) (cit. no. 16)	Long-linked	Assembly line
	Mediating	Bank
	Intensive	General hospital
Aston studies: Hickson, Pugh, and Pheysey (1969) (cit. no. 17)	Work flow integration; operations, materials, and knowledge technologies	Technology differs in various parts of the organization

TABLE 13.1

Summary of Approaches to Technology

typology) address the adaptability of the technological system to change. Large-batch or mass production, routine, and long-linked technologies are not very adaptable to change. At the opposite end of the continuum, continuous-process, nonroutine, and intensive technologies are readily adaptable to change.

One major contribution of the study of organizational technology is the recognition that organizations have more than one important technology that enables them to accomplish their tasks. Instead of examining technology in isolation, the Aston group recognized that size and technology are related in determining organization structure.[18] They found that in smaller organizations, technology had more direct effects on the structure. In large organizations, however, they found, like Blau, that structure depended less on the operations technology and more on size considerations such as the number of employees. In large organizations each department or division may have a different technology that determines how that department or division should be structured. In short, in small organizations the structure depended primarily on the technology, whereas in large organizations the need to coordinate complicated activities was the most important factor. Thus, both organizational size and technology are important considerations in organization design.

Global technology variations come in two forms: variations in available technology and variations in attitudes toward technology. The technology available affects how organizations can do business. Many underdeveloped countries, for example, lack electric power sources, telephones, and trucking equipment, not to mention computers and robots. A manager working in such a country must be prepared to deal with many frustrations. A few years ago, some Brazilian officials convinced a U.S. company to build a high-tech plant in their country. Midway through construction, however, the government of Brazil decided it would not allow the company to import some accurate measuring instruments it needed to produce its products. The new plant was abandoned before it opened.[19]

In small organizations the structure depends primarily on the technology, whereas in large organizations the need to coordinate complicated activities may be more important.

Build-A-Bear and . . . **TECHNOLOGY**

The High-Tech Approach to High Touch

When you walk into a Build-A-Bear Workshop (BBW) location, you immediately notice the personal touch and numerous opportunities for interaction and activity. Children select animals, then stuff and dress them. Kids place the stuffing in the clear blower tubes as a game. Staff members groom the bears and sew them up with a needle and thread. It all seems very low technology and high touch. Build-A-Bear CEO Maxine Clark says, "[The store is] the balance to high technology." Yet BBW has found a way to combine high touch with high tech.

One use of high technology is the Name Me computer, which provides games that let children customize their bear's "birth certificate." While the children think they are playing, they are in fact helping to create their own product. Another high-tech application is the insertion of sound chips into the bear during stuffing. Customers can choose from pre-recorded messages or can create their own custom sounds. Best of all, a barcode is also inserted into the bear before final stitching, allowing the toy to be reunited with its owner if it is ever lost.

The company's website has won design awards for its ease in navigation and for the imaginative children's games it provides. The website even allows customers to create a custom birthday party experience, with personalized favours and products.

Build-A-Bear has been very smart about mixing high and low tech and using technology to increase customer appeal. Chris Bryne, editor of a toy industry magazine, states, "Kids live in a technological world now, so technology alone does not impress them . . . It has to be a play experience they really love." Or as Amazon.com CEO Jeffrey P. Bezos, an advocate for online retailing, says, "The physical world is still the best medium ever invented."

Sources: "Awards, Press, Print," "Fact Sheet," "Welcome to Build-A-Bear Workshops!" Build-A-Bear website, www.buildabear.com on March 13, 2005; "Build-A-Bear Creates Value Through Organization Design," video case; Janet Ginsburg, "Xtreme Retailing," *Business Week*, December 20, 1999, www.businessweek.com on March 12, 2005 (quotation).

Attitudes toward technology also vary across cultures. Surprisingly, Japan has only recently begun to support basic research. For many years, the Japanese government encouraged its companies to take basic research findings discovered elsewhere (often in the United States) and figure out how to apply them to consumer products (applied research). In the mid-1980s, however, the government changed its stance and started to encourage basic research as well.[20] Most western nations have a generally favourable attitude toward technology, whereas China and other Asian countries (with the exception of Japan) do not.

Despite all of the emphasis on technology's role as a primary determinant of structure, there is some support for viewing it from the perspective that the strategy and structure of the organization determine what types of technology are appropriate. For example, Wal-Mart and Dell Computers are careful to use only new information technology in ways that support their strategy and structure. Wal-Mart's information systems keep track of its inventory from receipt to shelf placement to purchase, and Dell uses technology to optimize its manufacturing processes. Because both companies started with low-tech processes and then adopted new technologies over time, the technology clearly was a result of each firm's structure and strategy, and not the other way around. The Build-a-Bear and . . . Technology box describes how Build-a-Bear is using technology to bring the customer directly into the manufacturing process.

The **organizational environment** is everything outside an organization and includes all elements—people, other organizations, economic factors, objects, and events—that lie outside the boundaries of the organization.

Environment   The **organizational environment** includes all of these elements— people, other organizations, economic factors, objects, and events—that lie outside the boundaries of the organization. The environment is composed of two layers: the general environment and the task environment. The **general environment** includes all of a broad set of dimensions and factors within which the organization operates, including the political-legal, sociocultural, technological, economic, and international factors. The **task environment** includes specific organizations, groups, and individuals that influence the organization. People in the task environment include customers, donors, regulators, inspectors, and shareholders. Among the organizations in the task environment are competitors, legislatures, and regulatory agencies. Economic factors in the task environment might include interest rates, international trade factors, and the unemployment rate in a particular area. Objects in the task environment include such things as buildings, vehicles, and trees. Events that may affect organizations include weather, elections, or war.

It is necessary to determine the boundaries of the organization to understand where the environment begins. These boundaries may be somewhat elusive, or at least changeable, and thus difficult to define. But for the most part we can say that certain people, groups, or buildings are either in the organization or in the environment. For example, a college student shopping for a personal computer is part of the environment of Dell, IBM, Apple, and other computer manufacturers. However, if the student works for one of these computer manufacturers, he or she is not part of that company's environment but is within the boundaries of the organization.

This definition of organizational environment emphasizes the expanse of the environment within which the organization operates. It may give managers the false impression that the environment is outside their control and interest. But because the environment completely encloses the organization, managers must be constantly concerned about it.

The manager, then, faces an enormous, only vaguely specified environment that somehow affects the organization. Managing the organization within such an environment may seem an overwhelming task. The alternatives for the manager are to (1) ignore the environment because of its complexity and focus on managing the internal operations of the company, (2) exert maximum energy in gathering information on every part of the environment and trying to react to every environmental factor, and (3) pay attention to specific aspects of the task environment, responding only to those that most clearly affect the organization.

To ignore environmental factors entirely and focus on internal operations leaves the company in danger of missing major environmental shifts, such as changes in customer preferences, technological breakthroughs, and new regulations. To expend large amounts of energy, time, and money exploring every facet of the environment may take more out of the organization than it returns.

The third alternative—to carefully analyze segments of the environment that most affect the organization and to respond accordingly—is the most prudent course. The issue, then, is to determine which parts of the environment should receive the manager's attention. In the remainder of this section, we examine two perspectives on the organizational environment: the analysis of environmental components and environmental uncertainty.

Forces in the environment have different effects on different companies. Air Canada for example, is very much influenced by government regulations and scientific developments. McDonald's, on the other hand, is affected by quite different environmental forces: consumer demand, cultural shifts in attitudes about fast food, disposable income,

In a complex and dynamic environment such as the toy industry, the development of new products and redesign of existing products are very risky propositions. In addition to the influence of movies and television programs, even Barbie has a new image and has dumped poor Ken. Mattel hopes the newly designed Barbie may be interested enough in Australian boogie boarder Blaine to spur sales of both dolls. Mattel's organization structure must be able to react quickly to changes in children's preferences for toys.

The **general environment** includes the broad set of dimensions and factors within which the organization operates, including political-legal, sociocultural, technological, economic, and international factors.

The **task environment** includes specific organizations, groups, and individuals that influence the organization.

cost of meat and bread, and gasoline prices. Thus, the task environment, the specific set of environmental forces that influence the operations of an organization, varies among organizations.

The environmental characteristic that brings together all of these different environmental influences and appears to have the most effect on the structure of the organization is uncertainty. **Environmental uncertainty** exists when managers have little information about environmental events and their impact on the organization.[21] Uncertainty has been described as resulting from complexity and dynamism in the environment. *Environmental complexity* is the number of environmental components that impinge on organizational decision making. *Environmental dynamism* is the degree to which these components change.[22] With these two dimensions, we can determine the degree of environmental uncertainty, as illustrated in Figure 13.4.

In cell 1, a low-uncertainty environment, there are few important components, and they change infrequently. A company in the cardboard-container industry might have a highly certain environment when demand is steady, manufacturing processes are stable, and government regulations have remained largely unchanged.

Environmental uncertainty exists when managers have little information about environmental events and their impact on the organization.

FIGURE 13.4

Classification of Environmental Uncertainty

This four-cell matrix describes all four levels of environmental dynamism and complexity and shows how they combine to create low or high environmental uncertainty.

Source: Reprinted from Robert B. Duncan, "Characteristics of Organizational Environments and Perceived Uncertainty," in *Administrative Science Quarterly*, September 1972, vol. 17, no. 3, p. 320, by permission of *Administrative Science Quarterly*. Copyright © 1972 Cornell University. All rights reserved.

	Simple	**Complex**
Static	**Cell 1:** **Low Perceived Uncertainty** 1. Small number of factors and components in the environment. 2. Factors and components are somewhat similar to one another. 3. Factors and components remain basically the same. *Example: cardboard container industry*	**Cell 2:** **Moderately Low Perceived Uncertainty** 1. Large number of factors and components in the environment. 2. Factors and components are not similar to one another. 3. Factors and components remain basically the same. *Example: provincial universities*
Dynamic	**Cell 3:** **Moderately High Perceived Uncertainty** 1. Small number of factors and components in the environment. 2. Factors and components are somewhat similar to one another. 3. Factors and components of the environment continually change. *Example: fashion industry*	**Cell 4:** **High Perceived Uncertainty** 1. Large number of factors and components in the environment. 2. Factors and components are not similar to one another. 3. Factors and components of environment continually change. *Example: banking industry*

Rate of Environmental Change (vertical axis: Static / Dynamic)

Environmental Complexity (horizontal axis: Simple / Complex)

In cell 4, in contrast, many important components are involved in decision making, and they change often. Thus, cell 4 represents a high-uncertainty environment. The banking environment is now highly uncertain. With deregulation and the advent of growing international competition, banks today would like to compete with insurance companies, brokerage firms, and real estate firms. The toy industry also is in a highly uncertain environment. As they develop new toys, toy companies must stay in tune with movies, television shows, cartoons, and with public sentiment.

Environmental characteristics and uncertainty have been important factors in explaining organization structure, strategy, and performance. For example, the characteristics of the environment affect how managers perceive the environment, which in turn affects how they adapt the structure of the organization to meet environmental demands.[23] The environment has also been shown to affect the degree to which a firm's strategy enhances its performance.[24] That is, a certain strategy will enhance organizational performance to the extent that it is appropriate for the environment in which the organization operates. Finally, the environment is directly related to organizational performance.[25] The environment and the organization's response to it are crucial to success.

An organization attempts to continue as a viable entity in a dynamic environment. The environment completely encloses the organization, and managers must be concerned about it constantly. The organization as a whole, as well as departments and divisions within it, is created to deal with challenges, problems, and uncertainties. James Thompson suggested that organizations design a structure to protect the dominant technology of the organization, smooth out any problems, and keep down coordination costs.[26] Thus, organization structures are designed to coordinate relevant technologies and protect them from outside disturbances. Structural components such as inventory, warehousing, and shipping help buffer the technology used to transform inputs into outputs. For instance, the emergence of online shopping, or e-commerce has influenced organizations quite differently. Some companies, such as Amazon, rely completely on online sales, which affects its warehousing and distribution systems. Other companies, such as Canadian Tire, which were traditionally "bricks and mortar" retailers have moved into online sales resulting in "bricks and clicks" operations. These forms require quite different systems of marketing and promotion, warehousing and distribution.[27]

Organizations with international operations must contend with additional levels of complexity and dynamism, both within and across cultures. Many cultures have relatively stable environments. For example, the economies of the United States and Canada are fairly stable. Although competitive forces within them vary, they generally remain strong, free-market economies. In contrast, the environments of other countries are more dynamic. For example, in France each election affects whether the country will favour socialism or private enterprise. At present, rapid changes in the economic and management philosophies in many Asian countries make their environments far more dynamic.

Environments also vary widely in terms of their complexity. The Japanese culture, which is fairly stable, is also quite complex. Japanese managers are subject to an array of cultural norms and values that are far more encompassing and resistant to change than those Canadian managers face. India and China also have extremely complex environments due in part to a number of sub-cultures and rapidly changing approaches to business and education.

Strategic Choice

The previous two sections describe how structure is affected by the strategy of the organization and by the structural imperatives of size, technology, and environment. These approaches may seem to contradict each other considering that both approaches

> When the organizational environment is complex and dynamic, the manager may have little information about future events and have great difficulty predicting them.

> Strategy and the imperatives of size, technology, and environment are the primary determinants of organization design.

attempt to specify the determinants of structure. This apparent clash has been resolved by refining the strategy concept to include the role of the top management decision makers in determining the organization's structure.[28] In effect, this view inserts the manager as the decision maker who evaluates the imperatives and the organization strategy and then designs the organization structure. This distinction can be understood by comparing Figure 13.5 with Figure 13.2.

Figure 13.5 shows structural imperatives as contextual factors within which the organization must operate and that affect the purposes and goals of the organization. The manager's choices for organization structure are affected by the organization's strategy (purposes and goals), the imperatives, and the manager's personal value system and experience.[29] Organizational effectiveness depends on the fit among the size, the technology, the environment, the strategies, and the structure. For example, due to changes in consumer preferences and the regulatory environment in Canada, RBC has expanded its services over the years and expanded its operations into the United States.[30]

Another perspective on the link between strategy and structure is that the relationship may be reciprocal; that is, the structure may be set up to implement the strategy, but the structure may then affect the process of decision making, influencing such matters as the centralization or decentralization of decision making and the formalization of rules and procedures.[31] Thus, strategy determines structure, which in turn affects strategic decision making. A more complex view, suggested by Herman Boschken, is that strategy is a determinant of structure and long-term performance but only when the subunits doing the planning have the ability to do the planning well.[32]

The relationship between strategic choice and structure is actually more complicated than the concept that structure follows strategy conveys. However, this relationship has

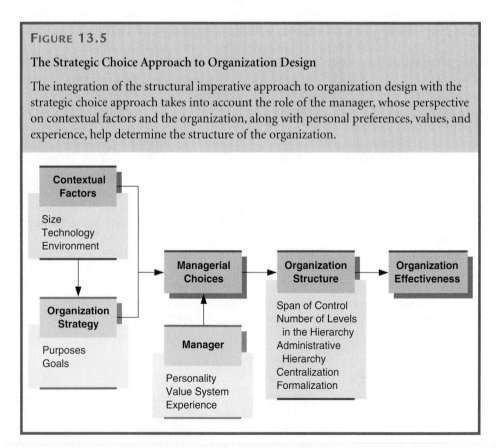

FIGURE 13.5

The Strategic Choice Approach to Organization Design

The integration of the structural imperative approach to organization design with the strategic choice approach takes into account the role of the manager, whose perspective on contextual factors and the organization, along with personal preferences, values, and experience, help determine the structure of the organization.

Contextual Factors

Size
Technology
Environment

Organization Strategy

Purposes
Goals

Manager

Personality
Value System
Experience

Managerial Choices

Organization Structure

Span of Control
Number of Levels
   in the Hierarchy
Administrative
   Hierarchy
Centralization
Formalization

Organization Effectiveness

received less research attention than the idea of structural imperatives. And of course, some might view strategy simply as another imperative, along with size, technology, and environment. But the strategic-choice view goes beyond the imperative perspective because it is a product of both the analysis of the imperatives and the organization's strategy.

Organizational Designs

The previous section described several factors that determine how organizations are structured. In this section we present several organizational designs that have been created to adapt organizations to the many contingency factors they face. We discuss mechanistic and organic structures, the sociotechnical system perspective, Mintzberg's designs, and matrix designs.

Mechanistic and Organic Designs

As we discussed in the previous section, most theorists believe that organizations need to be able to adapt to changes in the technology. For example, if the rate of change in technology is slow, the most effective design is bureaucratic or, to use Burns and Stalker's term, mechanistic. As summarized in Table 13.2, a **mechanistic structure** is primarily hierarchical in nature, interactions and communications are mostly vertical, instructions come from the boss, knowledge is concentrated at the top, and continued membership requires loyalty and obedience. But if the technology is changing rapidly, the organization needs a structure that allows more flexibility and faster decision making so that it can react quickly to change. This design is called organic. An **organic structure** resembles a network—interactions and communications are more lateral, knowledge resides wherever it is most useful to the organization, and membership requires a commitment to the tasks of the organization.

> A **mechanistic structure** is primarily hierarchical; interactions and communications typically are vertical, instructions come from the boss, knowledge is concentrated at the top, and loyalty and obedience are required to sustain membership.

> An **organic structure** is set up like a network; interactions and communications are horizontal, knowledge resides wherever it is most useful to the organization, and membership requires a commitment to the organization's tasks.

Sociotechnical Systems Designs

The foundation of the **sociotechnical systems** approach to organizing is systems theory, discussed in Chapter 1. There we defined a *system* as an interrelated set of elements that function as a whole. A system can have numerous subsystems, each of which, like the overall system, includes inputs, transformation processes, outputs, and feedback. We also defined an *open system* as one that interacts with its environment. A complex system is made up of numerous subsystems in which the outputs of some are the inputs to others. The **sociotechnical systems approach** views the organization as an open system structured to integrate the two important subsystems: the technical (task) subsystem and the social subsystem.

> The **sociotechnical systems approach** to organization design views the organization as an open system structured to integrate the technical and social subsystems into a single management system.

Characteristic	Mechanistic	Organic
Structure	Hierarchical	Network based on interests
Interactions, communication	Primarily vertical	Lateral throughout
Work directions, instructions	From supervisor	Through advice, information
Knowledge, information	Concentrated at top	Throughout
Membership, relationship with organization	Requires loyalty, obedience	Commitment to task, progress, expansion

TABLE 13.2

Mechanism and Organic Organization Design

The *technical (task) subsystem* is the means by which inputs are transformed into outputs. The transformation processes can take many forms. In a steel foundry, it would entail the way steel is formed, cut, drilled, chemically treated, and painted. In an insurance company or financial institution it would be the way information is processed. Often, significant scientific and engineering expertise is applied to these transformation processes to get the highest productivity at the lowest cost. For example, Garrison Guitar of St. John's, Newfoundland—which was purchased by Gibson Guitars in 2007—uses advanced injection moulding processes and just-in-time maufacturing and inventory systems to improve the productivity of its plant. Under this system, component parts arrive just in time to be used in the manufacturing process, reducing the cost of storing them in a warehouse until they are needed.[33] The transformation process usually is regarded as technologically and economically driven; that is, whatever process is most productive and costs the least is generally the most desirable.

The *social subsystem* includes the interpersonal relationships that develop among people in organizations. Employees learn one another's work habits, strengths, weaknesses, and preferences while developing a sense of mutual trust. Social relationships can be manifested in personal friendships and interest groups. Communication, about both work and employees' common interests, may be enhanced by friendship or hampered by antagonistic relationships. The Hawthorne studies (discussed in Chapter 1) were the first serious studies of social subsystems in organizations.[34]

The sociotechnical systems approach was developed by members of the Tavistock Institute of England as an outgrowth of a study of coal mining. The study concerned new mining techniques that were introduced to increase productivity but failed because they entailed splitting up well-established work groups.[35] The Tavistock researchers concluded that the social subsystem had been sacrificed to the technical subsystem. Thus, improvements in the technical subsystem were not realized because of problems in the social subsystem.

The Tavistock group proposed that an organization's technical and social subsystems could be integrated through autonomous work groups. The aim of *autonomous work groups* is to make technical and social subsystems work together for the benefit of the larger system. These groups are developed using concepts of task design, particularly job enrichment, and ideas about group interaction, supervision, and other characteristics of organization design. To structure the task, authority, and reporting relationships around work groups, organizations should delegate to the groups themselves decisions regarding job assignments, training, inspection, rewards, and punishments. Management is responsible for coordinating the groups according to the demands of the work and task environment. Autonomous work groups often evolve into self-managing teams, as was discussed in Chapter 8.

Organizations in turbulent environments tend to rely less on hierarchy and more on the coordination of work among autonomous work groups. Sociotechnical systems theory asserts that the role of management is twofold: to monitor the environmental factors that impinge on the internal operations of the organization and to coordinate social and technical subsystems. Although the sociotechnical systems approach has not been thoroughly tested, it has been tried with some success in the General Foods plant in Topeka, Kansas, the Saab-Scania project in Sweden, the Volvo plant in Kalmar, Sweden,[36] and at Aliant in Canada. The development of the sociotechnical systems approach is significant in its departure from the universal approaches to organization design and its emphasis on jointly harnessing the technical and human subsystems. Popular movements in management today include many of the principles of the sociotechnical systems design approach. The development of cross-functional teams to generate and design new products and services is a good example (see Chapter 8).

Mintzberg's Designs

In this section we describe the concrete organization designs proposed by Henry Mintzberg, a renowned management scholar who has received many awards and honours for his work, including the Order of Canada. The universe of possible designs is large, but fortunately we can divide designs into a few basic forms. Mintzberg proposed that the purpose of organizational design was to coordinate activities and suggested a range of coordinating mechanisms that are found in operating organizations.[37] In his view, organization structure reflects how tasks are divided and then coordinated. Mintzberg described five major ways in which tasks are coordinated: by mutual adjustment, by direct supervision, and by standardization of worker (or input) skills, work processes, or outputs (see Figure 13.6). These five methods can exist side by side within an organization.

Coordination by mutual adjustment (1 in Figure 13.6) simply means that workers use informal communication to coordinate with one another, whereas coordination by direct supervision (2 in Figure 13.6) means that a manager or supervisor coordinates the actions of workers. As noted, standardization can be used as a coordination mechanism in three different ways: we can standardize the worker skills (3 in Figure 13.6) that are inputs to the work process; we can standardize the processes themselves (4 in Figure 13.6), that is, the methods workers use to transform inputs into outputs; or we can standardize the outputs (5 in Figure 13.6), the products or services or the performance levels expected of workers.

Standardization usually is developed by staff analysts and enforced by management so that skills, processes, and output meet predetermined standards.

Mintzberg further suggested that the five coordinating mechanisms roughly correspond to stages of organizational development and complexity. In the very small organization, individuals working together communicate informally, achieving coordination by mutual adjustment. As more people join the organization, coordination needs become more complex, and direct supervision is added. For example, two or three people working in a small fast-food business can coordinate the work simply by talking to each other about incoming orders for hamburgers, fries, and drinks. However, direct supervision becomes necessary in a larger restaurant with more complex cooking and warming equipment and several shifts of workers.

In large organizations, standardization is added to mutual adjustment and direct supervision to coordinate the work. The type of standardization depends on the nature of the work situation—that is, the organization's technology and environment. Standardization of work processes may achieve the necessary coordination when the organization's tasks are fairly routine. Thus, the larger fast-food outlet may standardize the making of hamburger patties: the meat is weighed, put into a hamburger press, and compressed into a patty. McDonald's is well known for this type of standardized process.

In other complex situations, standardization of the output may allow employees to do the work in any appropriate manner as long as the output meets specifications. Thus, the cook may not care how the hamburger is pressed, only that the right amount of meat is used and that the patty is the correct diameter and thickness. In other words, the worker can use any process as long as the output is a standard burger.

Rather than focus on structural imperatives, people, or rules, Mintzberg's description of structure emphasizes the ways activities are coordinated.

Henry Mintzberg of McGill University in Montreal is an internationally respected expert on management strategy, and organizational design.

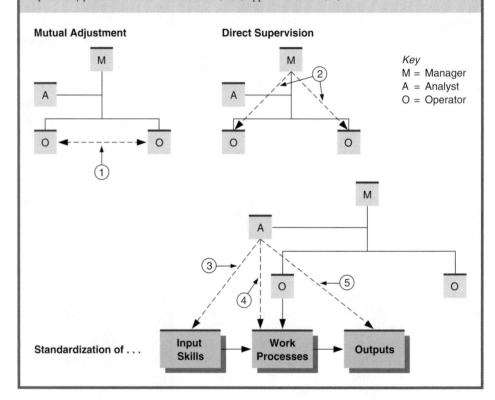

FIGURE 13.6

Mintzberg's Five Coordinating Mechanisms

Mintzberg described five methods of coordinating the actions of organizational participants. The dashed lines in each diagram show the five means of coordination: (1) mutual adjustment, (2) direct supervision, and standardization of (3) input skills, (4) work processes, and (5) outputs.

Source: Henry Mintzberg, *The Structuring of Organizations: A Synthesis of the Research.* © 1979, p. 4. Reprinted by permission of Pearson Education, Inc., Upper Saddle River, NJ.

A third possibility is to coordinate work by standardizing worker skills. This approach is most often adopted in situations where processes and outputs are difficult to standardize. In a hospital, for example, each patient must be treated as a special situation; the hospital process and output therefore cannot be standardized. Similar diagnostic and treatment procedures may be used with more than one patient, but the hospital relies on the skills of the physicians and nurses, which are standardized through their professional training, to coordinate the work. Organizations may have to depend on workers' mutual adjustment to coordinate their own actions in the most complex work situations or where the most important elements of coordination are the workers' professional training and communication skills. In effect, mutual adjustment can be an appropriate coordinating mechanism in both the simplest and the most complex situations.

Mintzberg pointed out that the five methods of coordination can be combined with the basic components of structure to develop five structural forms: the simple structure, the machine bureaucracy, the professional bureaucracy, the divisionalized form, and the adhocracy. Mintzberg called these structures pure or ideal types of designs.

Simple Structure The **simple structure** characterizes relatively small, usually young organizations in a simple, dynamic environment. The organization has little specialization and formalization, and its overall structure is organic. Power and decision making are concentrated in the chief executive, often the owner-manager, and the flow of authority is from the top down. The primary coordinating mechanism is direct supervision. The organization must adapt quickly to survive because of its dynamic and often hostile environment. Most small businesses—a car dealership, a locally owned retail clothing store, or a candy manufacturer with only regional distribution—have a simple structure.

The **simple structure**, typical of relatively small or new organizations, has little specialization or formalization; power and decision making are concentrated in the chief executive.

Machine Bureaucracy The **machine bureaucracy** is typical of large, well-established companies in simple, stable environments. Work is highly specialized and formalized, and decision making is usually concentrated at the top. Standardization of work processes is the primary coordinating mechanism. This highly bureaucratic structure does not have to adapt quickly to changes because the environment is both simple and stable. Examples include large mass-production firms, such as some automobile companies, and providers of services to mass markets, such as insurance companies.

In a **machine bureaucracy**, which typifies large, well-established organizations, work is highly specialized and formalized and decision making is usually concentrated at the top.

Professional Bureaucracy Usually found in a complex and stable environment, the **professional bureaucracy** relies on standardization of skills as the primary means of coordination. There is much horizontal specialization by professional areas of expertise but little formalization. Decision making is decentralized and takes place where the expertise is. The only means of coordination available to the organization is standardization of skills—the professionally trained employees. Although it lacks centralization, the professional bureaucracy stabilizes and controls its tasks with rules and procedures developed in the relevant profession. Hospitals, universities, and consulting firms are examples.

A **professional bureaucracy** is characterized by horizontal specialization by professional area of expertise, little formalization, and decentralized decision making.

Divisionalized Form The **divisionalized form** is characteristic of old, very large firms operating in a relatively simple, stable environment with several diverse markets. It resembles the machine bureaucracy except that it is divided according to the various markets it serves. There is some horizontal and vertical specialization between the divisions (each defined by a market) and headquarters. Decision making is clearly split between headquarters and the divisions, and the primary means of coordination is standardization of outputs. The mechanism of control required by headquarters encourages the development of machine bureaucracies in the divisions.

The **divisionalized form**, typical of old, very large organizations, is divided according to the different markets served; horizontal and vertical specialization exists between divisions and headquarters, decision making is divided between headquarters and divisions, and outputs are standardized.

The classic example of the divisionalized form is General Motors, which, in a reorganization in the 1920s, adopted a design that created divisions for each major car model.[38] Although the divisions have been reorganized and the cars changed several times, the concept of the divisionalized organization is still very evident at GM.[39] Bombardier uses a two-tiered divisionalized structure, dividing its numerous businesses into strategic business units (for example, aerospace, rail products) that are further divided into sectors (aerospace has divisions for regional aircraft, business aircraft, and amphibious aircraft).[40]

Adhocracy The **adhocracy** is typically found in young organizations engaged in highly technical fields where the environment is complex and dynamic. Decision making is spread throughout the organization, and power is in the hands of experts. There is horizontal and vertical specialization but little formalization, resulting in a very organic structure. Coordination is by mutual adjustment through frequent personal communication and liaison. Specialists are not grouped together in functional units but are deployed into specialized market oriented project teams.

In an **adhocracy**, typically found in young organizations in highly technical fields, decision making is spread throughout the organization, power resides with the experts, horizontal and vertical specialization exist, and there is little formalization.

The typical adhocracy is usually established to foster innovation, something to which the other four types of structures are not particularly well suited. Numerous

North American organizations—Johnson & Johnson, Procter & Gamble, Monsanto, and 3M, for example—are known for their innovation and constant stream of new products.[41] These organizations are either structured totally as adhocracies or have large divisions set up as adhocracies. Johnson & Johnson operates more than 200 subsidiary companies that are allowed to operate as independent businesses to encourage continued innovation, creativity, and risk taking.

Mintzberg believed that fit among parts is the most important consideration in designing an organization. Not only must there be a fit among the structure, the structural imperatives (technology, size, and environment), and organizational strategy, but also the components of structure (rules and procedures, decision making, specialization) must fit together and be appropriate for the situation. Mintzberg suggested that an organization will not function effectively when these characteristics are not put together properly.[42]

Matrix Organization Design

One other organizational form deserves attention here: the matrix organization design. Matrix design is consistent with the contingency approach, because it is useful only in certain situations. One of the earliest implementations of the matrix design was at TRW Systems Group in 1959.[43] Following TRW's lead, other firms in aerospace and high-technology fields created similar matrix structures.

The **matrix design** attempts to combine two different designs to gain the benefits of each. The most common matrix form superimposes product or project departmentalization on a functional structure (see Figure 13.7). Each department and project has a manager; each employee, however, is a member of both a functional department and a project team. The dual role means that the employee has two supervisors, the department manager and the project leader.

A matrix structure is appropriate when three conditions exist:

1. There is external pressure for a dual focus, meaning that factors in the environment require the organization to focus its efforts equally on responding to multiple external factors and on internal operations.
2. There is pressure for a high information-processing capacity.
3. There is pressure for shared resources.[44]

In the aerospace industry in the early 1960s, all these conditions were present. Private companies had a dual focus: their customers, primarily the federal government, and the complex engineering and technical fields in which they were engaged. Moreover, the environments of these companies were changing very rapidly. Technological sophistication and competition were increasing, resulting in growing environmental uncertainty and an added need for information processing. The final condition stemmed from the pressure on the companies to excel in a very competitive environment despite limited resources. The companies concluded that it was inefficient to assign their highly professional—and highly compensated—scientific and engineering personnel to just one project at a time.

Built into the matrix structure is the capacity for flexible and coordinated responses to internal and external pressures. Members can be reassigned from one project to another as demands for their skills change. They may work for a month on one project, be assigned to the functional home department for two weeks, and then be reassigned to another project for the next six months. The matrix form improves project coordination by assigning project responsibility to a single leader rather than dividing it among several functional department heads. Furthermore, it improves communication because employees can talk about the project with members of both the project team and the functional unit to which they belong. In this way, solutions to project problems can

The **matrix design** combines two different designs to gain the benefits of each; typically combined are a product or project departmentalization scheme and a functional structure.

The matrix structure attempts to build into the organization structure the ability to be flexible and provide coordinated responses to both internal and external pressures.

FIGURE **13.7**

A Matrix Organization Design

A matrix organization design superimposes two types of departmentalization onto each other—for example,
a functional structure and a project structure.

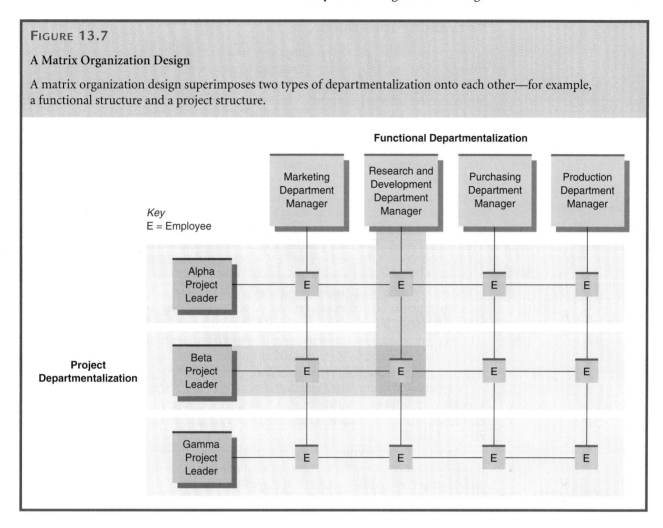

emerge from either group. Many different types of organizations have used the matrix
form of organization, notably large-project manufacturing firms, banks, and hospitals.[45]
AdFarm is a marketing communications firm specializing in agriculture based in Calgary, with offices in Guelph, Ontario; Fargo, North Dakota; and Kansas City, Missouri. It
uses a matrix organization, pulling together experts from all of its locations to work on
particular client accounts through the use of tele- and video-conferencing.[46]

The matrix organizational form thus provides several benefits for the organization.
It is not, however, trouble free. Typical problems include the following:

1. The dual reporting system can cause role conflict among employees.
2. Power struggles can occur over who has authority on which issues.
3. Matrix organization often is misinterpreted to mean that all decisions must be
   made by a group; as a result, group decision-making techniques might be used
   when they are not appropriate.
4. If the design involves several matrices, each laid on top of another, there might be
   no way to trace accountability and authority.[47]

Only under the three conditions listed earlier is the matrix design likely to work. In
any case, it is a complex organizational system that must be carefully coordinated and
managed to be effective.

Virtual Organizations

Some companies do one or two things very well, such as sell to government clients, but struggle with most others, such as manufacturing products with very tight precision. Other companies might be great at close-tolerance manufacturing, but lousy at reaching out to certain types of clients. Wouldn't it be nice if those two organizations could get together to utilize each other's strengths but still retain their independence? They can, and many are doing so in what are called virtual organizations.

A **virtual organization** is a temporary alliance between two or more organizations that band together to accomplish a specific venture. Each partner contributes to the partnership what it does best. The opportunity is usually something that needs a quick response to maximize the market opportunity. A slow response will probably result in losses. Therefore, a virtual organization allows each organization to bring its best capabilities together with others without worrying about learning how to do something that it has never done before. Thus, the reaction time is faster, mistakes are fewer, and profits are quicker. Sharing of information among partners is usually facilitated by electronic technology such as computers, faxes, and electronic mail systems, thereby avoiding the expense of renting new office space for the venture or costly travel time between companies.

Some types of virtual organizations involve *outsourcing*, where a company moves part of its operations or processes that it historically performed to another firm. Outsourcing has become increasingly popular especially in software design and technical support. For example, it is estimated that software development in India costs only 40 percent what it does in North America.

A number of companies, such as General Electric, Dupont Chemicals, and Bell Laboratories, engage in outsourcing activity. Other companies relocate part of their businesses offshore as well. It is estimated that over 25 percent of Dell employees now work in India.[48]

The virtual organization may be just another management fad. On the other hand, it may be the wave of the future for organizations to capitalize on certain types of projects. Management scholars have mixed opinions on the effectiveness of such arrangements. Although it may seem odd, this approach can produce substantial benefits in some situations.

> A **virtual organization** is a temporary alliance between two or more organizations that band together to undertake a specific venture.

Contemporary Organization Design

The current proliferation of design theories and alternative forms of organization gives practising managers a dizzying array of choices. The task of the manager or organization designer is to examine the firm and its situation and to design a form of organization that meets its needs. A partial list of contemporary alternatives includes as downsizing, rightsizing, reengineering the organization, team-based organizations, and the virtual organization. These approaches often make use of total quality management, employee empowerment, employee involvement and participation, reduction in force, process innovation, and networks of alliances. Practising managers must deal with new terminology, the temptation to treat such new approaches as fads, and their own organizational situation before making major organization design shifts. In this section we describe currently popular approaches.

Reengineering the Organization

Reengineering is the radical redesign of organizational processes to achieve major gains in cost, time, and provision of services. It forces the organization to start from scratch to

> **Reengineering** is the radical redesign of organizational processes to achieve major gains in cost, time, and provision of services.

redesign itself around its most important processes rather than beginning with its current form and making incremental changes. It assumes that if a company had no existing structure, departments, jobs, rules, or established ways of doing things, reengineering would design the organization as it should be for future success. The process starts with determining what the customers actually want from the organization and then developing a strategy to provide it. Once the strategy is in place, strong leadership from top management can create and motivate a team of people to design an organizational system to achieve the strategy.[49] Reengineering is a process of redesigning the organization that does not necessarily result in any particular organizational form.

Rethinking the Organization

Also currently popular is the concept of rethinking the organization. Rethinking the organization is also a process for restructuring that throws out traditional assumptions that organizations should be structured with boxes and horizontal and vertical lines. Robert Tomasko makes some suggestions for organizational forms for the future.[50] Tomasko suggests that the traditional pyramid shape of organizations may be inappropriate for current business practices. Traditional structures, he contends, may have too many levels of management arranged in a hierarchy to be efficient and respond to dynamic changes in the environment. Rethinking organizations might entail thinking of the organization structure as a dome rather than a pyramid, the dome being top management, which acts as an umbrella, covering and protecting those underneath but leaving them alone to do their work. Internal units underneath the dome would have the flexibility to interact with each other and with environmental forces. Companies such as Microsoft Corporation and Royal Dutch Petroleum have some of the characteristics of this dome approach to organization design.

> Rethinking the organization means looking at organization design in totally different ways, perhaps even abandoning the classic view of organization as a pyramid.

Global Organization Structure and Design Issues

Managers working in an international environment must consider not only similarities and differences among firms in different cultures but the structural features of multinational organizations.

Between-Culture Issues Between-culture issues are variations in the structure and design of companies operating in different cultures. As might be expected, such companies have both differences and similarities. For example, one study compared the structures of 55 U.S. and 51 Japanese manufacturing plants. Results suggested that the Japanese plants had less specialization, more formal centralization (but less real centralization), and taller hierarchies than their U.S. counterparts. The Japanese structures were also less affected by their technology than the U.S. plants.[51]

Many cultures still take a traditional view of organization structure not unlike the approaches used in North America during the days of classical organization theory. For example, Tom Peters, a leading management consultant and coauthor of *In Search of Excellence*, spent some time lecturing to managers in China. They were not interested in his ideas about decentralization and worker participation, however. Instead, the question most often asked involved how a manager determined the optimal span of control.[52]

In contrast, many European companies are increasingly patterning themselves after successful North American firms. This stems in part from corporate raiders in Europe emulating their North American counterparts and partly from the managerial workforce becoming better educated. Together, these two factors have caused many European firms to become less centralized and to adopt divisional structures by moving from functional to product departmentalization.[53]

Multinational Organization   More and more firms have entered the international arena and have found it necessary to adapt their designs to better cope with different cultures.[54] For example, after a company has achieved a moderate level of international activity, it often establishes an international division or divisions, usually at the same organizational level as other major functional divisions. McCain Foods Ltd. uses this organization design. It has several divisions responsible for the company's business activities in the U.S., Europe, and Canada.

For an organization that has become more deeply involved in international activities, a logical form of organization design is the international matrix. This type of matrix arrays product managers across the top. Project teams headed by foreign market managers cut across the product departments. A company with three basic product lines, for example, might establish three product departments (of course, it would include domestic advertising, finance, and operations departments as well). Foreign market managers can be designated for, say, Japan, Europe, Latin America, and Australia. Each foreign market manager is then responsible for all three of the company's products in his or her market.[55]

Finally, at the most advanced level of multinational activity, a firm might become an international conglomerate. Nestlé and Unilever N.V. fit this type. Each has an international headquarters (Nestlé in Vevey, Switzerland, and Unilever in Rotterdam, Netherlands) that coordinates the activities of businesses scattered around the globe. Nestlé has factories in 50 countries and markets its products in virtually every country in the world. More than 96 percent of its business is done outside of Switzerland, and only about 7 000 of its 160 000 employees reside in its home country.

Dominant Themes of Contemporary Designs

The four dominant themes of current design strategies are the effects of technological and environmental change, the importance of people, the necessity of staying in touch with the customer, and the global organization. Technology and the environment are changing so fast and in so many unpredictable ways that no organization structure will be appropriate for a long time. The changes in electronic information processing, transmission, and retrieval alone are so vast that employee relationships, information distribution, and task coordination need to be reviewed almost daily.[56] The emphasis on productivity through people that was energized by Thomas Peters and Robert Waterman, Jr., in the 1980s continues in almost every aspect of contemporary organization design.[57] In addition, Peters and Austin further emphasized the importance of staying in touch with customers at the initial stage in organization design.[58]

> There is no one best way to design an organization.

These popular contemporary approaches and the four dominant factors argue for a contingency design perspective. Unfortunately, there is no one best way. Managers must consider the impact of multiple factors—sociotechnical systems, strategy, the structural imperatives, changing information technology, people, global considerations, and a concern for end users—on their particular organization and design the organization structure accordingly.

Summary of Key Points

■ Universal approaches to organization design attempt to specify the one best way to structure organizations for effectiveness. Contingency approaches, on the other hand, propose that the best way to design organization structure depends on a variety of factors. Important contingency approaches to organization design centre on the organizational strategy, the determinants of structure, and strategic choice.

■ Initially, strategy was seen as the determinant of structure: The structure of the organization was designed to implement its purpose, goals, and strategies. Taking managerial choice into account in determining organization structure is a modification of this view. The manager designs the structure to accomplish organizational goals, guided by an analysis of the contextual factors, the strategies of the organization, and personal preferences.

■ The structural imperatives are size, technology, and environment. In general, large organizations have more complex structures and usually more than one technology. The structures of small organizations, on the other hand, may be dominated by one core operations technology. The structure of the organization is also established to fit with the environmental demands and buffer the core operating technology from environmental changes and uncertainties.

■ Organization designs can take many forms. A mechanistic structure relies on the administrative hierarchy for communication and directing activities. An organic design is structured like a network; communications and interactions are horizontal and diagonal across groups and teams throughout the organization.

■ In the sociotechnical systems view, the organization is an open system structured to integrate two important subsystems: the technical (task) subsystem and the social subsystem. According to this approach, organizations should structure the task, authority, and reporting relationships around the workgroup, delegating to the group decisions on job assignments, training, inspection, rewards, and punishments. The task of management is to monitor the environment and coordinate the structures, rules, and procedures.

■ Mintzberg's ideal types of organization design were derived from a framework of coordinating mechanisms. The five types are simple structure, machine bureaucracy, professional bureaucracy, divisionalized form, and adhocracy. Most organizations have some characteristics of each type, but one is likely to predominate. Mintzberg believed that the most important consideration in designing an organization is the fit among parts of the organization.

■ The matrix design combines two types of structure (usually functional and project departmentalization) to gain the benefits of each. It usually results in a multiple command and authority system. Benefits of the matrix form include increased flexibility, cooperation, and communication and better use of skilled personnel. Typical problems are associated with the dual reporting system and the complex management system needed to coordinate work.

■ Virtual organizations are temporary alliances between organizations that agree to work together on a specific venture. Reaction time to business opportunities can be very fast with these types of alliances. In effect, organizations create a network of other organizations to enable them to respond to changes in the environment.

■ Contemporary organization design is contingency oriented. Currently popular design strategies are reengineering the organization and rethinking the organization. Four factors influencing design decisions are the changing technological environment, concern for people as valued resources, the need to keep in touch with customers, and global impacts on organizations.

Discussion Questions

1. What are the differences between universal approaches and contingency approaches to organization design?

2. Define organizational environment and organizational technology. In what ways do these concepts overlap?

3. Identify and describe some of the environmental and technological factors that affect your college or university. Give specific examples of how they affect you as a student.

4. How does organization design usually differ for large and small organizations?

5. What might be the advantages and disadvantages of structuring the faculty members at your college or university as an autonomous work group?

6. What do you think are the purposes, goals, and strategies of your college or university? How are they reflected in its structure?

7. Which of Mintzberg's pure forms is best illustrated by a major national political party (Liberal or Reform)? A religious organization? A hockey team? The Canadian Olympic Committee?

8. In a matrix organization, would you rather be a project leader, a functional department head, or a highly trained technical specialist? Why?

9. Discuss what you think the important design considerations will be for organization designers in the year 2010.

10. How would your college or university be different if you rethought or reengineered how it is designed?

Experiencing Organizational Behaviour

Purpose: This exercise will help you understand the factors that determine the design of organizations. These will help you understand the configurational and operational aspects of organization structure.

Format: You will interview at least five employees in different parts of the college or university that you attend or employees of a small- to medium-sized organization and analyze the reasons for its design. (You may want to coordinate this exercise with that in Chapter 12.)

Procedure: If you use a local organization, your first task is to find one with between 50 and 500 employees. (It should not be part of your college or university.) If you did the exercise for Chapter 12, you can use the same company for this exercise. The organization should have more than two hierarchical levels, but it should not be too complex to understand with a short period of study. You may want to check with your professor before contacting the company. Your initial contact should be with the highest-ranking manager you can reach. Make sure that top management is aware of your project and approves.

If you use your local college or university, you could talk to professors, secretaries, and other administrative staff in the admissions office, student services department, athletic department, library, and many others. Be sure to include employees from a variety of jobs and levels in your interviews.

Using the material in this chapter, you will interview employees to obtain the following information on the structure of the organization:

1. What is the organization in business to do? What are its goals and its strategies for achieving them?

2. How large is the company? What is the total number of employees? How many work full time? How many work part time?

3. What are the most important components of the organization's environment?

4. Is the number of important environmental components large or small?

5. How quickly or slowly do these components change?

6. Would you characterize the organization's environment as certain, uncertain, or somewhere in between? If in between, describe approximately how certain or uncertain.

7. What is the organization's dominant technology; that is, how does it transform inputs into outputs?

8. How rigid is the company in its application of rules and procedures? Is it flexible enough to respond to environmental changes?

9. How involved are employees in the daily decision making related to their jobs?

10. What methods are used to ensure control over the actions of employees?

Interview at least five employees of the college or company at different levels and in different departments. One should hold a top-level position. Be sure to ask the questions in a way the employees will understand; they may not be familiar with some of the terminology used in this chapter.

The result of the exercise should be a report describing the technology, environment, and structure of the company. You should discuss the extent to which the structure is appropriate for the organization's strategy, size, technology, and environment. If it does not seem appropriate, you should explain the reasons. If you also used this company for the exercise in Chapter 12, you can comment further on the organization chart and its appropriateness for the company. You may want to send a copy of your report to the cooperating company.

Follow-up Questions

1. Which aspects of strategy, size, environment, and technology were the most difficult to obtain information about? Why?

2. If there were differences in the responses of the employees you interviewed, how do you account for them?

3. If you were the president of the organization you analyzed, would you structure it in the same way? Why or why not? If not, how would you structure it differently?

4. How did your answers to questions 2 and 3 differ from those in the exercise in Chapter 12?

Management Skillbuilder

Diagnosing Organization Structure

Introduction: You are probably involved with many different organizations—the place you work, a social or service club, a church, the college or university you attend. This assessment will help you diagnose the structure of one of those organizations. You could use this assessment on the organization that you analyzed in the previous Experiential Exercise.

Instructions: First, pick one of the organizations you belong to or know a lot about. Then read each statement below and determine the degree to which you agree or disagree with that statement about your organization using the following scale.

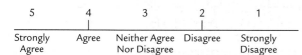

5	4	3	2	1
Strongly Agree	Agree	Neither Agree Nor Disagree	Disagree	Strongly Disagree

Then place the number of the response that best represents your organization in the space before each statement.

_____ 1. If people believe that they have the right approach to carrying out their job, they can usually go ahead without checking with their superior.

_____ 2. People in this organization don't always have to wait for orders from their superiors on important matters.

_____ 3. People in this organization share ideas with their superior.

_____ 4. Different individuals play important roles in making decisions.

_____ 5. People in this organization are likely to express their feelings openly on important matters.

_____ 6. People in this organization are encouraged to speak their minds on important matters, even if it means disagreeing with their superior.

_____ 7. Talking to other people about the problems someone might have in making decisions is an important part of the decision-making process.

_____ 8. Developing employees' talents and abilities is a major concern of this organization.

_____ 9. People are encouraged to make suggestions before decisions are made.

_____ 10. In this organization, most people can have their point of view heard.

_____ 11. Superiors often seek advice from subordinates before making decisions.

_____ 12. Subordinates play an active role in running this organization.

_____ 13. For many decisions, the rules and regulations are developed as we go along.

_____ 14. It is not always necessary to go through channels in dealing with important matters.

_____ 15. Employees do not consistently follow the same rules and regulations.

_____ 16. There are few rules and regulations for handling any kind of problem that may arise in making most decisions.

_____ 17. People from different departments are often put together in task forces to solve important problems.

_____ 18. For special problems, we usually set up a temporary task force until we meet our objectives.

_____ 19. Jobs in this organization are not clearly defined.

_____ 20. In this organization, adapting to changes in the environment is important.

= _____

Total Score

When you finish, add up the numbers to get a total score. Your instructor can help you interpret your scores by referring to the Instructor's Resource Manual.

Source: From Ricky W. Griffin, *Management*, 5th ed., which is adapted from Robert T. Keller, *Type of Management System*. Griffin copyright © 1996 by Houghton Mifflin Company. Keller copyright © 1988. Used by permission of Houghton Mifflin Company and Robert T. Keller.

Organizational Behaviour Case for Discussion

The Right Structure for Build-A-Bear Workshop

In 1995, Maxine Clark resigned from the presidency of Payless ShoeSource. She left the chain of 4 500 stores to start up a new kind of retail firm, Build-A-Bear Workshop. "My ability to connect with people wasn't being tapped," Clark says. "I wanted to . . . make retailing fun again." She has certainly succeeded. Today, Build-A-Bear Workshop (BBW) operates 170 stores in the U.S. and Canada, is franchising in Japan and Korea, and opens 30 new stores each year.

BBW is based on a unique retailing concept. Clark claims, "We don't think of ourselves as a toy company. We sell an experience." Kids of all ages choose a presewn animal body, have it stuffed, and complete it with sounds, grooming, clothes, and accessories. The entire store is designed to create maximum opportunities for interaction between customers and staff. Store visitors are given lavish personal attention. Children enjoy the atmosphere of wacky, kid-friendly fun, and customers appreciate the opportunity to customize the product.

Build-A-Bear is at the forefront of a trend toward customization, interaction, and entertainment in retailing. For example, popular "skater" shoe company Vans has added a skate park to a Los Angeles store. Gibson Guitar allows clients to watch their custom instruments being built. Bass Pro Shops has trout ponds and aquariums at some locations. Lands' End online clothing retailer allows customers to order pants and shirts tailored to their exact body measurements. "Build-A-Bear is a new type of toy store where there's interactivity. Kids love differentiation. They like to have something that's their own," says Jim Silver, toy industry expert.

In the retailing industry, personal service and customization are necessary to counteract "the Wal-Mart" problem, according to Clark. Wal-Mart's low prices have allowed the firm to dominate retailing for more than a decade, yet many customers are now yearning for a different type of retail experience and are willing to pay more to get it. "We're so opposite from [Wal-Mart]," says Clark. "We're not about price."

Build-A-Bear Workshop is a mid-sized retail chain and is rapidly growing, both in the United States and abroad. Therefore, the organization structure needs to be flexible, to accommodate change. At the same time, the organization needs to emphasize standardization, to gain the efficiencies that can come with larger size.

BBW uses small-batch technology—virtually every product is one of a kind. This too, has an effect on organization structure, causing the firm to adopt a flexible structure with a need for close coordination between units and individuals. Finally, BBW faces a fairly high level of environmental uncertainty, with constantly changing customer tastes being the most dynamic element. Many "hot" toy concepts, for example, have suffered dramatic drops in sales after the fad cools off. High uncertainty also mandates an organization structure that has lots of flexibility and need for coordination.

It comes as no surprise, then, that Build-A-Bear Workshop uses an organization structure that is relatively organic. Sales associates, due to their constant interaction with the customers, are a valuable source of information and expertise for the firm. Relationships are relatively informal and information sharing occurs laterally as well as vertically. Everyone in the firm is encouraged and expected to be creative, to suggest improvements, to independently resolve problems within their units, and to participate in making important decisions. In addition, the work environment is fun and relaxed.

Build-A-Bear Workshop uses a simple structure, which is appropriate for a young, small, and growing company, headed by a powerful and effective owner-manager. Again, the simple structure maximizes flexibility, open communication, informality, interaction with customers, and creativity.

Build-A-Bear is continuing to creatively expand the business, licensing BBW-brand clothing, books, and home décor. The firm is also experimenting with non-traditional locations, for example, at the Philadelphia Phillies' baseball park, where customers purchase Major League Baseball merchandise for their bears. Some experts fear that BBW, like any specialty retailer, may be a passing fad or limited in growth beyond their specialty niche. Clark, however, has an answer. "Stuffed animals . . . are one of the most difficult to merchandise . . . They usually get thrown on the shelves," she says. "But I think each shopper is looking for something that appeals to them personally and connects with them, and Build-A-Bear is about connection."

Case Questions

1. Which type of standardization (work processes, output, or worker skills, as described by Mintzberg) should Build-A-Bear Workshop use, and why?

2. There are a number of possible factors that influence the choice of an organization structure. Consider BBW's situation. Do the various factors lead BBW to choose compatible strategies, or do the various influences lead the firm in several different directions as they choose a structure? What effect does this level of agreement or disagreement have on the firm?

3. In your opinion, what will BBW's structure look like after more growth, say, in five to ten years? What factors will lead to the changes you expect?

Sources: David Barry, "Exit Strategies," *Fast Company*, April 2000, www .fastcompany.com on March 12, 2005; Janet Ginsburg, "Xtreme Retailing," *Business Week*, December 20, 1999, www.businessweek.com on March 12, 2005; Olga Kharif, "Of Mice, Men, and Baby Bears," *Business Week*, December 17, 2004, www.businessweek.com on March 12, 2005; Lawrence Meyers, "Build-A-Bear Gets Stuffed," *Motley Fool*, March 8, 2005, biz.yahoo.com on March 12, 2005; Angela Moore, "Build-A-Bear Builds on the Basics," *Reuters*, March 5, 2005, news.yahoo.com on March 12, 2005 (quotation); Ian Ritter, "Build-A-Bear's Maxine Clark," *Globe Street Retailing*, March 7, 2005, www.globest.com on March 12, 2005; Amey Stone,"In Toytown, a New Set of Rules," *Business Week*, December 20, 2004, www.businessweek.com on March 12, 2005.

SELF TEST

You have read the chapter and studied the key terms. Think you're ready to ace the exam? Take this sample test to gauge your comprehension of chapter material and check your answers at the back of the book. Want more test questions? Take the ACE quizzes found on the student website: www.hmco.ca/ob

T F 1. A universal approach considers all the different ways a manager might approach a particular situation.

T F 2. Organizational downsizing usually reduces the size of corporate staff and middle management.

T F 3. Uncertainty in the environment results from the complexity of the environment and the degree to which environmental components change.

T F 4. The technical subsystem in a university is the means by which new freshmen students are turned into graduating seniors.

T F 5. Professional bureaucracies are usually found in simple but rapidly changing environments.

T F 6. The virtual organization appears to be another management fad—its popularity will likely wane in the coming years.

T F 7. Nestlé is an example of a firm that has successfully maintained exclusively domestic operations—in this case, in Switzerland.

8. The contingency factors that affect organizational design include all of the following except
   a. the environment.
   b. the organization's technology.
   c. the organization's structure.
   d. the social system within which the organization operates.
   e. the organization's size.

9. Amanda works in a larger firm than Bruce. Based on what you know about organizational size, which of the following is true?
   a. Bruce's firm will be larger than Amanda's.
   b. Bruce's firm will be more specialized than Amanda's.
   c. Amanda's firm will be less formalized than Bruce's.
   d. Span of control will be larger in Amanda's firm.
   e. Differentiation will be greater in Bruce's firm.

10. In large organizations the need to coordinate complicated activities is the most important factor in determining the firm's structure. In small organizations, the most important factor is
   a. strategy.
   b. technology.

c. culture.
d. environment.
e. size.

11. Structural components such as inventory, warehousing, and shipping help buffer an organization's technology from
   a. the effects of organizational size.
   b. environmental disturbances.
   c. the effects of organizational strategy.
   d. interpersonal conflicts among managers.
   e. interpersonal conflict between managers and subordinates.

12. Thomas is a manager in a very small organization. Which of the following mechanisms would Thomas most likely use to coordinate employees' efforts?
   a. standardized input skills
   b. standardized work processes
   c. mutual adjustment
   d. direct supervision
   e. contingency design

13. The best design that is best suited to foster innovation is the
   a. simple structure.
   b. professional bureaucracy.
   c. divisionalized form.
   d. machine bureaucracy.
   e. adhocracy.

14. For years, Steven's company has lagged behind the competition. Steven has decided to adopt the reengineering approach and completely redesign organizational processes. His first step should be to
   a. start a parallel subsidiary company that offers the same product, but employs completely different workers.
   b. adopt a matrix design and eliminate traditional lines of hierarchy.
   c. eliminate excess staff and as many layers of middle management as possible.
   d. determine what customers actually want from the organization and then provide a strategy to provide it.
   e. "x-engineer" the old processes into new, innovative processes that motivate employees.

Organization Culture

After studying this chapter, you should be able to:

▶ **Define organization culture and explain how it affects employee behaviour.**

▶ **Summarize the historical development of organization culture.**

▶ **Describe two different approaches to culture in organizations.**

▶ **Identify three emerging issues in organization culture.**

▶ **Describe the relationships among organization culture and creativity and innovation.**

▶ **Discuss the key elements of managing the organization culture.**

Ganong and Community Commitment

G anong Brothers Chocolates continues to thrive as a company and as a major contributor to its community. Founded in 1873 in St. Stephen, New Brunswick, by James and Gilbert Ganong, the company has become a "piece of Canadiana,", despite the fact that it was labelled "an anachronism" by a competing candy manufacturer 30 years ago. The label was applied because the competitor said that Ganong's time had passed. There was no way that a small, privately owned candy maker located on the far edge of

Canada could compete in the international arena against such giants as Hershey and Nestlé.

The comment was made to the current president, David Ganong, shortly after he assumed his role in 1977. David refused to believe it. Ganong Brothers has a tradition and culture of strong belief in its mission—which is to be a world-class operation, while staying in and helping St. Stephen to grow, and he was not prepared to give up on the Ganong beliefs.

Ganong employees are like an extended family. Many workers are members of families that have been with Ganong's for generations. One reporter noted the closeness of the workers when he accompanied the President on a tour of Ganong's: just about everyone greeted him with a "Hello David" regardless of whether it was a top executive or a maintenance worker. David Ganong said that the most important lessons he learned from his uncle R. Whidden Ganong, his predecessor as president, was to be fair to the employees, never compromise on quality, and be committed to the local community.

Ganong's has shown its commitment to the community of St. Stephen in a variety of ways. It participates in charitable causes, has contributed to the construction of the local arena and middle school, supports local sports teams, and has even bought a large tract of ecologically sensitive land near St. Stephen, which is now the Ganong Nature Park. It was also instrumental in starting the annual Chocolate Festival, now over twenty years old, and built a chocolate museum in St. Stephen. These projects were contributions to the tourism industry of St. Stephen.

But its most important demonstration of its commitment to the community is its basic business decision to stay in St. Stephen. Operational costs would probably be lower in a larger centre, closer to transportation hubs and with easier access to raw materials. Nonetheless, Ganong's is committed to stay in St. Stephen. When its old factory was in need of replacement, Ganong's decided to build a new plant in St. Stephen, rather than relocate. David Ganong summarized his view: "We don't want to do it in Toronto, we don't want to do it in Chicago, we'll do it first in St. Stephen . . . that's the underlying philosophy I continue to work with."[1]

Many organizations attribute their success to a strong and firmly entrenched culture. The culture at Ganong's has evidently worked quite well for many years. However, they now are trying to change the culture to succeed in the twenty-first century. Other companies may want to create a culture similar to Ganong's, or at least one that works as well, but it is not so easy to create this kind of successful culture for every organization.

We begin this chapter by exploring the nature and historical foundations of organization culture. Next, we describe the process of creating the culture. Then we examine two basic approaches to describing the characteristics of organization culture. We discuss three important issues in organization culture. Finally, we show how organization culture can be managed to enhance the organization's effectiveness.

The Nature of Organization Culture

In the early 1980s, organization culture became a central concern in the study of organizational behaviour. Hundreds of researchers began to work in this area. Numerous books were published, important academic journals dedicated entire issues to the discussion of culture, and almost overnight, organizational behaviour textbooks that omitted culture as a topic of study became obsolete.

Interest in organization culture was not limited to academic researchers. Businesses expressed a far more intense interest in culture than in other aspects of organizational behaviour. *The Globe and Mail*, *Profit*, *Business Week*, *Fortune*, and other business periodicals published articles that touted culture as the key to an organization's success and suggested that managers who could manage through their organization's culture almost certainly would rise to the top.[2] *Canadian Business* regularly publishes articles on the importance of organization culture.

Although the enthusiasm of the early 1980s has waned somewhat, the study of organization culture remains important. The assumption is that organizations with a strong culture perform at higher levels than those without a strong culture.[3] For example, studies have shown that organizations with strong cultures that are strategically appropriate and have norms that permit the organization to change actually do perform well.[4] Other studies have shown that different functional units may require different types of cultures.[5] The research on the impact of culture on organizational performance is mixed, however, depending on how the research is done and what variables are measured.

Many researchers have begun to weave the important aspects of organization culture into their research on more traditional topics. Now there are fewer headline stories in the popular business press about culture and culture management, but organization culture has become a common topic for managers interested in improving organizational performance, as the opening incident about Ganong Brothers illustrates. The enormous amount of research on culture completed in the last 20 years has fundamentally shifted the way both academics and managers look at organizations. Some of the concepts developed in the analysis of organization culture have become basic parts of the business vocabulary, and the analysis of organization culture is one of the most important specialties in the field of organizational behaviour.

CIBC employees show their support for their company's culture by taking part in the CIBC supported Run for the Cure in Toronto.

What Is Organization Culture?

Most definitions of organization culture consider the use of values, symbols, and other factors that communicate the culture to employees.

A surprising aspect of the recent rise in interest in organization culture is that the concept, unlike virtually every other concept in the field, has no single widely accepted definition. Indeed, it often appears that authors feel compelled to develop their own definitions, which range from very broad to highly specific. For example, Deal and Kennedy define a firm's culture as "the way we do things around here."[6] This very broad definition presumably could include the way a firm manufactures its products, pays its bills, treats its employees, and performs any other organizational operation. More specific definitions include those of Schein ("the pattern of basic assumptions that a given group has invented, discovered, or developed in learning to cope with its problems of external adaptation and internal integration"[7]) and Peters and Waterman ("a dominant and coherent set of shared values conveyed by such symbolic means as stories, myths, legends, slogans, anecdotes, and fairy tales."[8]) Table 14.1 lists these and other important definitions of organization culture.

TABLE 14.1

Definitions of Organization Culture

Definition	Source
"A belief system shared by an organization's members"	J. C. Spender, "Myths, Recipes and Knowledge-Bases in Organizational Analysis" (Unpublished manuscript, Graduate School of Management, University of California at Los Angeles, 1983), p. 2.
"Strong, widely shared core values"	C. O'Reilly, "Corporations, Cults, and Organizational Culture: Lessons from Silicon Valley Firms" (Paper presented at the Annual Meeting of the Academy of Management, Dallas, Texas, 1983), p. 1.
"The way we do things around here"	T. E. Deal and A. A. Kennedy, *Corporate Cultures: The Rites and Rituals of Corporate Life* (Reading, Mass.: Addison-Wesley, 1982), p. 4.
"The collective programming of the mind"	G. Hofstede, *Culture's Consequences: International Differences in Work-related Values* (Beverly Hills, Calif.: Sage, 1980), p. 25.
"Collective understandings"	J. Van Maanen and S. R. Barley, "Cultural Organization: Fragments of a Theory" (Paper presented at the Annual Meeting of the Academy of Management, Dallas, Texas, 1983), p. 7.
"A set of shared, enduring beliefs communicated through a variety of symbolic media, creating meaning in people's work lives"	J. M. Kouzes, D. F. Caldwell, and B. Z. Posner, "Organizational Culture: How It Is Created, Maintained, and Changed" (Presentation at OD Network National Conference, Los Angeles, October 9, 1983).
"A set of symbols, ceremonies, and myths that communicates the underlying values and beliefs of that organization to its employees"	W. G. Ouchi, *Theory Z: How American Business Can Meet the Japanese Challenge* (Reading, Mass.: Addison-Wesley, 1981), p. 41.
"A dominant and coherent set of shared values conveyed by such symbolic means as stories, myths, legends, slogans, anecdotes, and fairy tales"	T. J. Peters and R. H. Waterman, Jr., *In Search of Excellence: Lessons from America's Best-Run Companies* (New York: Harper & Row, 1982), p. 103.
"The pattern of basic assumptions that a given group has invented, discovered, or developed in learning to cope with its problems of external adaptation and internal integration"	E. H. Schein, "The Role of the Founder in Creating Organizational Culture," *Organizational Dynamics*, Summer 1985, p. 14.

Despite the apparent diversity of these definitions, a few common attributes emerge. First, all the definitions refer to some set of values held by individuals in a firm. These values define what is good or acceptable behaviour and what is bad or unacceptable behaviour. In some organizations, for example, it is unacceptable to blame customers when problems arise. Here the value "the customer is always right" tells managers what actions are acceptable (not blaming the customer) and what actions are not acceptable (blaming the customer). In other organizations, the dominant values might support blaming customers for problems, penalizing employees who make mistakes, or treating employees as the firm's most valuable assets. In each case, values help members of an organization understand how they should act.

A second attribute common to many of the definitions in Table 14.1 is that the values that make up an organization's culture are often taken for granted; that is, they are basic assumptions made by the firm's employees, rather than being written in a book or made explicit in a training program. It may be as difficult for an organization to articulate these basic assumptions as it is for people to express their personal beliefs and values. Several authors have argued that organization culture is a powerful influence on individuals in firms precisely because it is not explicit but becomes an implicit part of employees' values and beliefs.[9]

Some organizations have been able to articulate the key values in their cultures. Many companies throughout North America and Europe now have written codes of ethics.[10] Mountain Equipment Co-op, a retailer of outdoor adventure equipment states its vision, mission, and values on its website (Figure 14.1). At Hewlett-Packard, a brief summary of The HP Way is given to all new employees. This pamphlet describes the basic values of the culture at Hewlett-Packard.[11] RBC has had a code of ethics for over 20 years.[12]

Even when firms can articulate and describe the basic values that make up their cultures, however, the values most strongly affect actions when people in the organization take them for granted. An organization's culture is not likely to powerfully influence behaviour when employees must constantly refer to a handbook to remember what the culture is. When the culture becomes part of them—when they can ignore what is written in

---

FIGURE 14.1

Statement of Values of Mountain Equipment Co-op

Our Vision
Mountain Equipment Co-op is an innovative, thriving co-operative that inspires excellence in products and services, passion for wilderness experiences, leadership for a just world, and action for a healthy planet.

Our Mission
Mountain Equipment Co-op provides quality products and services for self-propelled wilderness-oriented recreation, such as hiking and mountaineering, at the lowest reasonable price in an informative, respectful manner. We are a member-owned co-operative striving for social and environmental leadership.

Our Values
We conduct ourselves ethically and with integrity. We show respect for others in our words and actions. We act in the spirit of community and co-operation. We respect and protect our natural environment. We strive for personal growth, continual learning, and adventure.

Source: Mountain Equipment Co-operative Website www.mec.ca. Reprinted by permission of Mountain Equipment Co-op, Vancouver.

the book because they already have embraced the values it describes—the culture can have an important impact on their actions.

The final attribute shared by many of the definitions in Table 14.1 is an emphasis on the symbolic means through which the values in an organization's culture are communicated. Although, as we noted, companies sometimes can directly describe these values, their meaning is perhaps best communicated to employees through the use of stories, examples, and even what some authors call myths or fairy tales. Stories typically reflect the important implications of values in a firm's culture. Often they develop a life of their own. As they are told and retold, shaped and reshaped, their relationship to what actually occurred becomes less important than the powerful impact the stories have on the way that people behave every day.

Some organization stories have become famous. Two examples from Hewlett-Packard demonstrate how stories help communicate and reinforce important organizational values. One of the key values listed in The HP Way is that Hewlett-Packard avoids bank debt. A story is told of a senior manager in the finance area who was given free rein to develop a financing plan for a new investment. As she applied the best finance theory, it became clear to her that part of the financial package should include bank debt. When her proposal reached Mr. Hewlett and Mr. Packard, however, it was rejected—not because the financial reasoning was unsound but because at Hewlett-Packard "we avoid bank debt."[13] This story shows that avoiding bank debt is more than a slogan at Hewlett-Packard; it is a fact.

Another value at Hewlett-Packard is that "employees are our most important asset." A story that helps communicate the reality of this value tells what happened when the company was struggling through some difficult financial times. While virtually all other firms in the industry were laying people off, HP asked all its employees to take one day of unpaid vacation every two weeks. By having employees work nine days and then take one day off, the firm was able to avoid layoffs. All employees were hurt because all received less pay, but none had to bear the full cost of the firm's reduced performance.[14] The message communicated by this story is that Hewlett-Packard will go to great lengths to avoid layoffs to keep its employment team intact.

We can use the three common attributes of definitions of culture just discussed to develop a definition with which most authors probably could agree: **Organization culture** is the set of shared values, often taken for granted, that help people in an organization understand which actions are considered acceptable and which are considered unacceptable. Often these values are communicated through stories and other symbolic means.

Organization culture is the set of values that helps the organization's employees understand which actions are considered acceptable and which unacceptable.

Our fundamental understanding of organization culture derives from research in anthropology, sociology, social psychology, and economics.

Historical Foundations

Although research on organization culture exploded onto the scene in the early 1980s, the antecedents of this research can be traced to the origins of social science. Understanding the contributions of other social science disciplines is particularly important in the case of organization culture, for many of the dilemmas and debates that continue in this area reflect differences in historical research traditions.

Anthropological Contributions   Anthropology is the study of human cultures.[15] Of all the social science disciplines, anthropology is most closely related to the study of culture and cultural phenomena. Anthropologists seek to understand how the values and beliefs that make up a society's culture affect the structure and functioning of that society. Many anthropologists believe that to understand the relationship between culture and society, it is necessary to look at a culture from the viewpoint of the people who practise it—from the "native's point of view."[16] To reach this level of understanding, anthropologists immerse themselves in the values, symbols, and stories that people in a society use to bring order and meaning to their lives. Anthropologists usually produce book-length descriptions of the values, attitudes, and beliefs that underlie the behaviours of people in one or two cultures.[17]

Whether the culture is that of a large, modern corporation or a primitive tribe in New Guinea or the Philippines, the questions asked are the same: How do people in this culture know what kinds of behaviour are acceptable and what kinds are unacceptable? How is this knowledge understood? How is this knowledge communicated to new members? Through intense efforts at accurate description, the values and beliefs that underlie actions in an organization become clear. However, these values can be fully understood only in the context of the organization in which they developed. In other words, a description of the values and beliefs of one organization is not transferable to those of other organizations; each culture is unique.

Sociological Contributions   Sociology is the study of people in social systems, such as organizations and societies. Sociologists have long been interested in the causes and consequences of culture. In studying culture, sociologists have most often focused on informal social structure. Émile Durkheim, an important early sociologist, argued that the study of myth and ritual is an essential complement to the study of structure and rational behaviour in societies.[18] By studying rituals, Durkheim argued, we can understand the most basic values and beliefs of a group of people.

Many sociological methods and theories have been used in the analysis of organization cultures. Sociologists use systematic interviews, questionnaires, and other quantitative research methods rather than the intensive study and analysis of anthropologists. Practitioners using the sociological approach generally produce a fairly simple typology of cultural attributes and then show how the cultures of a relatively large number of firms can be analyzed with this typology.[19] The major pieces of research on organization culture that later spawned widespread business interest—including Ouchi's Theory Z, Deal and Kennedy's Corporate Cultures, and Peters and Waterman's *In Search of Excellence*[20]—used sociological methods. Later in this chapter, we review some of this work in more detail.

Social Psychology Contributions   Social psychology is a branch of psychology that includes the study of groups and the influence of social factors on individuals. Although most research on organization culture has used anthropological or sociological methods and approaches, some has borrowed heavily from social psychology. Social psychological theory, with its emphasis on the creation and manipulation of symbols, lends itself naturally to the analysis of organization culture.

For example, research in social psychology suggests that people tend to use stories or information about a single event more than they use multiple observations to make judgments.[21] Thus, if your neighbour had trouble with a certain brand of automobile, you will probably conclude that the brand is bad even though the car company can generate reams of statistical data to prove that the situation with your neighbour's car was a rarity.

The impact of stories on decision making suggests an important reason why organization culture has such a powerful influence on the people in an organization. Unlike other organizational phenomena, culture is best communicated through stories and examples, and these become the basis that individuals in the organization use to make judgments. If a story says that blaming customers is a bad thing to do, then blaming customers is a bad thing to do. This value is communicated much more effectively through the cultural story than through some statistical analysis of customer satisfaction.[22]

Economics Contributions   The influence of economics on the study of organization culture is substantial enough to warrant attention, although it has been less

Talisman Energy and . . .   **ETHICS**

Bad Timing, Bad Judgment, or Bad Ethics?

Sudan, located in Northern Africa adjacent to the southern border of Egypt, has rarely had a peaceful moment since it became independent in 1956. Almost immediately after ceasing to be an English-Egyptian colony, a civil war broke out between the Muslim-dominated North and the Christian-animist South. There have been periods of less violence over the years, but they have been brief. After a military coup in 1989, the fighting flared again. It settled down a bit in the middle to late 1990s.

Sudan is one of the 50 poorest countries in the world. This is somewhat ironic, because major offshore gas reserves were found in the 1960s, followed by the discovery of major onshore oil deposits in the early 1970s. Chevron, an oil company based in the United States made the oil discoveries. It attempted to develop production for more than a decade, but production was disrupted when antigovernment militias attacked its operations and killed several employees in 1984. Chevron eventually sold its Sudanese oil rights in 1992, shortly after the military coup and the escalation of violence. The rights were purchased by ConCorp, a private Sudanese company. ConCorp was unable to develop the fields, so it sold the rights to State

Petroleum, a small company based in Vancouver. It too was unable to finance production and a consortium of international companies bought the rights—25 percent of which was acquired by Arakis, a "junior" Canadian petroleum company.

Enter Talisman Energy, one of Canada's largest oil companies, which acquired Arakis and the Sudanese oil concessions in 1998. Talisman, unlike the previous owners after Chevron pulled out, had both the expertise and access to capital to finally bring the oilfields into production.

And produce it did, earning hundreds of millions of dollars in revenue from its Sudanese holdings. It also paid the Sudanese government millions of dollars in royalties.

Almost immediately after Talisman entered Sudan, two things happened. First, the civil war flared yet again and, second, human rights advocates started to criticize Talisman for doing business in Sudan. Horrific stories emerged from Sudan, alleging that the government was engaged in genocide of the Christians and animists, engaging in rampant murders, rapes, mutilations, and slavery of innocent civilians. Human rights advocates

significant than the influence of anthropology and sociology. Economic analysis treats organization culture as one of a variety of tools that managers can use to create some economic advantage to the organization.

The economics approach attempts to link the cultural attributes of firms with their performance, rather than simply describing the cultures of companies as the sociological and anthropological perspectives do. In Theory Z, for example, Ouchi does not just say that Type Z companies differ from other kinds of companies—he asserts that Type Z firms outperform other firms.[23] When Peters and Waterman say they are in search of excellence, they define excellence, in part, as consistently high financial performance.[24] These authors are using cultural explanations of financial success.

Researchers disagree about the extent to which culture affects organization performance. The conditions under which organization culture is linked with superior financial performance have been investigated by several authors.[25] This research suggests that under some relatively narrow conditions, a link between culture and performance may exist. However, the fact that a firm has a culture does not mean it will perform well; indeed, a variety of cultural traits can actually hurt performance. For example, a firm could have a culture that includes values like "customers are too ignorant to be of much help," "employees cannot be trusted," "innovation is not important," and "quality is too expensive." The firm would have a strong culture, but the culture might impair its performance. On the other hand, a company that seems to value performance over other values also demonstrates a particular type of culture. The Talisman Energy and . . . Ethics box discusses one such example: Talisman Energy's investment in Sudan.

argued that the royalties that Talisman paid to the Sudanese government were helping to finance the atrocities.

It was alleged that one of the reasons for the argued ethical lapse was the prevailing culture at both Talisman and the Government of Canada. One critic noted that although the US government actively discussed punishing businesses with investments in Sudan, the Canadian government seemed more interested in seeing Canadian oil companies grow their international operations. Talisman gave a number of explanations—some would call them rationalizations—for its presence. Talisman claimed that it did not know of the extent of the violence. It also said that it asked the government not to target civilians. Further, it justified its presence by stating that it was building much needed infrastructure in Sudan, through the construction of roads, schools, and water systems. Finally, and much to the outrage of some critics, it stated that if it did not develop the oil, somebody else would. Critics of Talisman said the company was obviously unethical, and more concerned about its profits than human suffering.

Talisman eventually sold its share of the oil fields to an Indian company, completely withdrawing by 2003. At the time of the sale, the company still maintained the position that it had done nothing wrong. Critics said this response demonstrates Talisman never "got it" and think that Talisman sold its interests in Sudan mostly because of pressure from the United States and a looming revolt among investors to divest Talisman shares. Talisman's ethics, or lack thereof, they say, had nothing to do with the sale of the Sudanese assets.

What was probably the last official word on the episode came in September of 2006, when a human-rights violations law suit filed against Talisman was dismissed. The suit was filed in the United States by non-Muslim African and Christian groups in 2001. Although the case was dismissed, the judge noted that the dismissal did not address the fundamental issues on the wisdom or propriety of Talisman's Sudanese operations. Clearly, although no illegalities had been proven, Talisman suffered considerable damage to its reputation.

And what of Sudan? Unfortunately, the conflict continues. The bloodshed in Sudan, most recently in the Darfur region, has been called one of the worst humanitarian catastrophes in history. More than two million people have been killed and another four million refugees have been displaced.

Sources: Luke A. Pater, "State Rules: Oil Companies and Armed Conflict in Sudan," *Third World Quarterly*, 2007, vol. 28, pp. 997–1016; Matthew McClearn, "The End of the Affair," *Canadian Business*, September 25, 2006, pp. 11–12; Mark Brown, "Out of Africa," *Canadian Business*, December 9, 2002, p. 21; "Goodbye Sudan, Hello Takeover? Talisman Finally Caves," *Maclean's*, November 11, 2002, p. 12; Ted Byfield and Virginia Byfield, "Give Jim Buckee a Message—If He's Coming Down the Street, Cross to the Other Side," *Alberta Report*, July 9, 2001, p. 46; "Slaves for Sale," *Maclean's*, May 7, 2001, p. 40; Andrew Nikiforuk, "Company Loves Misery," *Canadian Business*, March 20, 2000, p. 16.

Creating the Organization Culture

To the entrepreneur who starts a business, creating the culture of the company may seem secondary to the basic processes of creating a product or service and selling it to customers or clients. However, as the company grows and becomes successful, it usually develops a culture that distinguishes it from other companies and that is one of the reasons for its success. In other words, a company succeeds as a result of what the company does, its strategy, and how it does it, its culture. The culture is linked to the strategic values, whether one is starting up a new company or trying to change the culture of an existing company.[26] The process of creating an organization culture is really a process of linking its strategic values with its cultural values, much as the structure of the organization is linked to its strategy, as we described in Chapter 13. The process is shown in Table 14.2.

Creating Organizational Culture
Step 1—Formulate Strategic Values
Step 2—Develop Cultural Values
Step 3—Create Vision
Step 4—Initiate Implementation Strategies
Step 5—Reinforce Cultural Behaviours

TABLE 14.2

Creating Organizational Culture

Establish Values

Strategic values are the basic beliefs about an organization's environment that shape its strategy.

The first two steps in the process involve establishing values. First, management must determine the strategic values of the organization. **Strategic values** are the basic beliefs about an organization's environment that shape its strategy. They are developed following an environmental scanning process and strategic analysis that evaluates economic, demographic, public policy, technological, and social trends to identify needs in the marketplace that the organization can meet. Strategic values, in effect, link the organization with its environment. BMO, the Bank of Montreal, has introduced a statement of its core values, focused on valuing relationships with all stakeholders from customers to shareholders to employees, diversity, respect, keeping promises, and sharing innovation to deliver superior customer service.[27]

Cultural values are the values that employees need to have and act on for the organization to act on the strategic values.

The second set of values required are the cultural values of the organization. **Cultural values** are the values employees need to act on for the organization to carry out its strategic values. They should be grounded in the organization's beliefs about how and why the organization can succeed. Organizations that attempt to develop cultural values that are not linked to their strategic values may end up with an empty set of values that have little relationship to its business. In other words, employees need to value work behaviours that are consistent with and support the organization's strategic values: low-cost production, customer service, or technological innovation.

Create Vision

After developing its strategic and cultural values, the organization must establish a vision of the organization's direction. This vision is a picture of what the organization will be like at some point in the future. It portrays how the strategic and cultural values will combine to create the future. For example, an insurance company might establish a vision of "protecting the lifestyles of 2 million families by the year 2010." In effect, it synthesizes both the strategic and cultural values as it communicates a performance target to employees. The conventional wisdom has been that the vision statement is written first, but experience suggests that the strategic and cultural values must be established first for the vision to be meaningful.

Initiate Implementation Strategies

The next step, initiating implementation strategies, builds on the values and initiates the action to accomplish the vision. The strategies cover many factors, from developing the organization design to recruiting and training employees who share the values and will carry them out. Consider a bank that has the traditional orientation of handling customer loans, deposits, and savings. If the bank changes, placing more emphasis on customer service, it may have to recruit a different type of employee, one who is capable of building relationships. The bank will also have to commit to serious, long-term training of its current employees to teach them the new service-oriented culture. The strategic and cultural values are the stimulus for the implementation practices.

Reinforce Cultural Behaviours

The final step is to reinforce the behaviours of employees as they act out the cultural values and implement the organization's strategies. Reinforcement can take many forms. First, the formal reward system in the organization must reward desired behaviours in ways that employees value. Second, stories must be told throughout the organization about employees who engaged in behaviours that epitomize the cultural values. Third, the organization must engage in ceremonies and rituals that emphasize employees doing the things that are critical to carrying out the organization's vision. In effect, the organization must "make a big deal out of employees doing the right things." For example, it pays quarterly bonuses to employees when objectives are met. Reinforcement practices are the final link between the strategic and cultural values and the creation of the organizational culture. An example of how organizations can use performance measurement systems to reinforce their cultures is described in detail in the Culture and . . . Research box.

Approaches to Describing Organization Culture

The models discussed in this section provide valuable insights into the dimensions along which organization cultures vary. No single framework for describing the values in organization cultures has emerged; however, several frameworks have been suggested. Although these frameworks were developed in the 1980s, their ideas about organizational culture are still influential today. Some of the excellent companies that they described are less excellent now, but the concepts are in use in companies all over the world. Managers should evaluate the various parts of the frameworks described and use the parts that fit the strategic and cultural values for their own organization.

The Ouchi Framework

One of the first researchers to focus explicitly on analyzing the cultures of a limited group of firms was William G. Ouchi. Ouchi analyzed the organization cultures of three groups of firms, which he characterized as (1) typical U.S. firms, (2) typical Japanese firms, and (3) **Type Z**.[28]

Through his analysis, Ouchi developed a list of seven points on which these three types of firms can be compared. He argued that the cultures of typical Japanese firms and U.S. Type Z firms are very different from those of typical U.S. firms and that these differences explain the success of many Japanese firms and U.S. Type Z firms and the difficulties faced by typical U.S. firms. The seven points of comparison developed by Ouchi are presented in Table 14.3.

Commitment to Employees According to Ouchi, typical Japanese and Type Z U.S. firms share the cultural value of trying to keep employees. Thus, both types of firms lay off employees only as a last resort. In Japan, the value of "keeping employees

The **Type Z firm** is committed to retaining employees, evaluates workers' performance based on both qualitative and quantitative information, emphasizes broad career paths, exercises control through informal, implicit mechanisms, requires that decision making occur in groups and be based on full information sharing and consensus, expects individuals to take responsibility for decisions, and emphasizes concern for people.

Cultural Value	Expression in Japanese Companies	Expression in Type Z U.S. Companies	Expression in Typical U.S. Companies
Commitment to Employees	Lifetime employment	Long-term employment	Short-term employment
Evaluation	Slow and qualitative	Slow and qualitative	Fast and quantitative
Careers	Very broad	Moderately broad	Narrow
Control	Implicit and informal	Implicit and informal	Explicit and formal
Decision Making	Group and consensus	Group and consensus	Individual
Responsibility	Group	Individual	Individual
Concern for People	Holistic	Holistic	Narrow

TABLE 14.3

The Ouchi Framework

Culture and . . .  **RESEARCH**

Organizational Culture and Performance Measurement Systems

One of the strongest ways that a company can reinforce its cultural values is to measure and reinforce performance that supports the culture. Jean-François Henri, of Université Laval in Quebec, examined the types of performance measurement systems (PMS) used by companies with different organizational cultures.

Previous studies found that organizational cultures can be classified according to where they fall in the range of competing values of control versus flexibility. Cultures more concerned with control have core values centred on planning, production, formalization and standardization (as discussed in Chapter 12). At the other end of the spectrum are cultures with "flexibility" values with emphases on adaptability, innovation, personal development, harmony, and teamwork.

The first key question in designing a performance measurement system is what to measure. Henri specifically looked at the diversity of measurement in his study, which is the range of performance indicators used in the PMS. Organizations can use very few performance measures, such as only financial or only non-financial data. Alternatively, at the other extreme, organizations can use many indicators, both financial and non-financial. Henri suggested that the most diverse PMS types use the "balanced scorecard" approach, which collects information on financial performance, customer trends, internal processes, and employee growth and development indicators.

The gathered information can then be put to a number of uses. Information can be used (a) to "monitor" the organization's performance to provide feedback to managers, (b) to help with "strategic decision making," (c) to "justify" decisions or actions after they are made, and/or (d) as symbolic "attention focusing" symbols to demonstrate to people throughout the organization those aspects of performance that are deemed to be important.

A survey was completed by 383 executives in Canadian manufacturing firms who had annual sales of at least $20 million and at least 150 employees. The executives were asked to assess their firms' culture, whether it valued flexibility or control more highly. They were also asked to rate the diversity of measures used in their PMS, and finally the purposes for which the data from the PMS were used.

The survey results were used to cluster the organizations into having either flexibility or control oriented cultures. The two cultural groupings were compared on their diversity of PMS measures and the use of the PMS data. Henri found that organizations with flexibility oriented cultures generally had greater diversity of measures. That is, they gathered more information than firms with control oriented cultures. He also found that organizations that valued flexibility more highly used the PMS information for strategic planning, legitimization, and attention focusing when compared to companies with control-oriented cultures.

The reasons for these differences appear to be that organizations that value flexibility need to gather more information because of the complexity caused by constantly seeking innovation, growth, and change. Additionally, firms with flexibility oriented cultures need to use information differently, particularly for strategic planning and its symbolic values. In other words, when employees in a company face uncertainty, they can get cues about what is important to top management by understanding what aspects of their performance is measured.

These results suggest that performance management systems and organizational culture can have reciprocal and reinforcing effects. The values of the organization can and should be used to decide what aspects of performance are measured, and how that information can be used. The actual use of the PMS then helps to focus the attention of the organizational members, which should stimulate behaviours that uphold the values of the firm, thereby reinforcing the culture.

Source: Jean-François Henri, "Organizational Culture and Performance Measurement Systems," *Accounting, Organizations, and Society*, 2006, vol. 31, pp. 77–103.

on" often takes the form of lifetime employment. A person who begins working at some Japanese firms has a virtual guarantee that he or she will never be fired. In U.S. Type Z companies, this cultural value is manifested in a commitment to what Ouchi called long-term employment. Under the Japanese system of lifetime employment, employees usually cannot be fired. Under the U.S. system, workers and managers can be fired, but only if they are not performing acceptably.

Ouchi suggested that typical U.S. firms do not have the same cultural commitment to employees as Japanese firms and U.S. Type Z firms. In reality, U.S. workers and managers often spend their entire careers in a relatively small number of companies. Still, there is a cultural expectation that if there is a serious downturn in a firm's fortunes, change of ownership, or a merger, workers and managers will be let go. For example, when Wells Fargo Bank bought First Interstate Bank in Arizona, they expected to lay off about 400 employees in Arizona and 5000 in the corporation as a whole. However, eight months after the purchase it had eliminated over 1000 in Arizona and a total of 10 800. Wells Fargo has a reputation as a vicious cutter following a takeover and seems to be living up to that reputation.[29]

Evaluation   Ouchi observed that in Japanese and Type Z U.S. companies, appropriate evaluation of workers and managers is thought to take a very long time—up to ten years—and requires the use of qualitative as well as quantitative information about performance. For this reason, promotion in these firms is relatively slow, and promotion decisions are made only after interviews with many people who have had contact with the person being evaluated.

In typical U.S. firms, on the other hand, the cultural value suggests that evaluation can and should be done rapidly and should emphasize quantitative measures of performance. This value tends to encourage short-term thinking among workers and managers.

Careers   Ouchi next observed that the careers most valued in Japanese and Type Z U.S. firms span multiple functions. In Japan this value has led to very broad career paths, which may lead to employees gaining experience in six or seven distinct business functions. The career paths in Type Z U.S. firms are somewhat narrower.

However, the career path valued in typical U.S. firms is considerably narrower. Ouchi's research indicated that most U.S. managers perform only one or two different business functions in their careers. This narrow career path reflects, according to Ouchi, the value of specialization that is part of so many U.S. firms.

Control   All organizations must exert some level of control to achieve coordinated action. Thus, it is not surprising that firms in the United States and Japan have developed cultural values related to organizational control and how to manage it. Most Japanese and Type Z U.S. firms assume that control is exercised through informal, implicit mechanisms. One of the most powerful of these mechanisms is the organization's culture.

In contrast, typical U.S. firms expect guidance to come through explicit directions in the form of job descriptions, delineation of authority, and various rules and procedures, rather than from informal and implicit cultural values.

From a functional perspective, organization culture could be viewed as primarily a means of social control based on shared norms and values.[30] Control comes from knowing that someone who matters is paying close attention to what we do and will tell us if our actions are appropriate or not. In organizations, control can come from formal sources, such as the organization structure or your supervisor, or from social sources, such as the organization's culture. In Ouchi's view, control is based on formal organizational mechanisms in typical U.S. firms, whereas control is more social in nature, derived from the organization culture's shared norms and values, in Japanese and Type Z U.S. firms.

Decision Making   Japanese and Type Z U.S. firms have a strong cultural expectation that decision making occurs in groups and is based on principles of full information sharing and consensus. In most typical U.S. firms, individual decision making is considered appropriate.

Responsibility   Closely linked to the issue of group versus individual decision making are ideas about responsibility. Here, however, the parallels between Japanese firms and Type Z U.S. firms break down. Ouchi showed that in Japan, strong cultural norms support collective responsibility; that is, the group as a whole, rather than a single person, is held responsible for decisions made by the group. In both Type Z U.S. firms and typical U.S. firms, individuals expect to take responsibility for decisions.

Linking individual responsibility with individual decision making, as typical U.S. firms do, is logically consistent. Similarly, group decision making and group responsibility, the situation in Japanese firms, seem to go together. But how do Type Z U.S. firms combine the cultural values of group decision making and individual responsibility?

Ouchi suggested that the answer to this question depends on a cultural view we already discussed: slow, qualitative evaluation. The first time a manager uses a group to make a decision, it is not possible to tell whether the outcomes associated with that decision resulted from the manager's influence or the quality of the group. However, if a manager works with many groups over time, and if these groups consistently do well for the organization, it is likely that the manager is skilled at getting the most out of the groups. This manager can be held responsible for the outcomes of group decision-making processes. Similarly, managers who consistently fail to work effectively with the groups assigned to them can be held responsible for the lack of results from the group decision-making process.

Concern for People   The last cultural value examined by Ouchi deals with a concern for people. Not surprisingly, in Japanese firms and Type Z firms, the cultural value that dominates is a holistic concern for workers and managers. Holistic concern extends beyond concern for a person simply as a worker or manager to concern about that person's home life, hobbies, personal beliefs, hopes, fears, and aspirations. In typical U.S. firms, the concern for people is a narrow one that focuses on the workplace. A culture that emphasizes a strong concern for people, rather than one that emphasizes a work or task orientation, can decrease worker turnover.[31]

Theory Z and Performance   Ouchi argued that the cultures of Japanese and Type Z firms help them outperform typical U.S. firms. Toyota imported the management style and culture that succeeded in Japan into its manufacturing facilities in North America. Toyota's success has often been attributed to the ability of Japanese and Type Z firms to systematically invest in their employees and operations over long periods, resulting in steady and significant improvements in long-term performance.

The Peters and Waterman Approach

Tom Peters and Robert Waterman, in their now classic bestseller *In Search of Excellence*, focused even more explicitly than Ouchi on the relationship between organization culture and performance. Peters and Waterman chose a sample of highly successful firms and sought to describe the management practices that led to their success.[32] Their analysis rapidly turned to the cultural values that led to successful management practices. These excellent values are listed in Table 14.4.

Bias for Action   According to Peters and Waterman, successful firms have a bias for action. Managers in these firms are expected to make decisions even if all the facts are not in. Peters and Waterman argued that, for many important decisions, all the facts will never be in. Delaying decision making in these situations is the same as never making a decision. Meanwhile, other firms probably will have captured whatever business initiative existed. On average, according to these authors, organizations with cultural values that include a bias for action outperform firms without such values.

Stay Close to the Customer   Peters and Waterman believe that firms whose organization cultures value customers over everything else outperform firms without this value. The customer is a source of information about current products, a source of ideas about future products, and the ultimate source of a firm's current and future financial performance. Focusing on the customer, meeting the customer's needs, and pampering the customer when necessary all lead to superior performance. Tell Us About Us is a Winnepeg-based company that provides clients with feedback on how well they are performing on customer service. The company has grown rapidly over the last decade as more companies are becoming aware of the importance of quality customer service.[33]

Autonomy and Entrepreneurship   Peters and Waterman maintained that successful firms fight the lack of innovation and the bureaucracy usually associated with large size. They do this by breaking the company into smaller, more manageable pieces and then encouraging independent, innovative activities within smaller business segments. Stories often exist in these organizations about the junior engineer who takes a risk and influences major product decisions, or of the junior manager, dissatisfied with the slow pace of a product's development, who implements a new and highly successful marketing plan.

Productivity Through People   Like Ouchi, Peters and Waterman believe successful firms recognize that their most important assets are their people—both workers and managers—and that the organization's purpose is to let its people flourish. It is a basic value of the organization culture—a belief that treating people with respect and dignity is not only appropriate but essential to success.

Hands-on Management   Peters and Waterman noted that the firms they studied insisted that senior managers stay in touch with the firms' essential business. It is an expectation, reflecting a deeply embedded cultural norm that managers should

Attributes of an Excellent Firm	
1. Bias for action	5. Hands-on management
2. Stay close to the customer	6. Stick to the knitting
3. Autonomy and entrepreneurship	7. Simple form, lean staff
4. Productivity through people	8. Simultaneously loosely and tightly organized

TABLE 14.4

The Peters and Waterman Framework

This shows children aged five and older participating in activities at one of IBM's sixty-seven worldwide childcare centres. IBM is attempting to meet the needs of an increasingly diverse workforce by providing childcare for employees with families. Employees can remain employed and on a career track without worrying about the quality of childcare for their little ones, while still being close enough to be involved in some of the children's activities in the centre. This is just one way that companies are showing concern for their employees and developing a people-oriented culture.

"Sticking to the knitting" is the popular practice in which management chooses not to diversify into many unrelated businesses.

manage not from behind the closed doors of their offices but by wandering around the plant, the design facility, the research and development department, and so on.

Stick to the Knitting   Another cultural value characteristic of excellent firms is their reluctance to engage in business outside their areas of expertise. These firms reject the concept of diversification, the practice of buying and operating businesses in unrelated industries. This notion is currently referred to as relying on the core competencies, or what the company does best.

Simple Form, Lean Staff   According to Peters and Waterman, successful firms tend to have few administrative layers and relatively small corporate staff groups. In excellently managed companies, importance is measured not only by the number of people who report to a manager but by the manager's impact on the organization's performance. The cultural values in these firms tell managers that their staffs' performance rather than their size is important.

Simultaneously Loose and Tight Organization
The final attribute of organization culture identified by Peters and Waterman appears contradictory. How can a firm be simultaneously loosely and tightly organized? The resolution of this apparent paradox is found in the firms' values. The firms are tightly organized because all their members understand and believe in the firms' values. This common cultural bond is a strong glue that holds the firms together. At the same time, however, the firms are loosely organized because they tend to have less administrative overhead, fewer staff members, and fewer rules and regulations. The result is increased innovation and risk taking and faster response times.

The loose structure is possible only because of the common values held by people in the firm. When employees must make decisions, they can evaluate their options in terms of the organization's underlying values—whether the options are consistent with a bias for action, service to the customer, and so on. By referring to commonly held values, employees can make their own decisions about what actions to take. In this sense, the tight structure of common cultural values makes possible the loose structure of fewer administrative controls.

Emerging Issues in Organization Culture

As discussion of the importance of organization culture matures it inevitably changes and develops new perspectives. Many new ideas about productive environments build on earlier views such as those of Ouchi, Peters and Waterman, and others. Typical of these approaches are the total quality management movement, worker participation, and team-based management, which were discussed in earlier chapters. Two other movements are briefly discussed in this section: innovation and empowerment.

Innovation

Innovation is the process of creating and doing new things that are introduced into the marketplace as products, processes, or services. Innovation involves every aspect of the organization, from research through development, manufacturing, into the marketplace and marketing. One of the organization's biggest challenges is to bring innovative products, processes, or technology to the needs of the marketplace in the most cost-effective manner possible.[34] Note that innovation not only involves the technology to create new products. True organizational innovation pervades the organization. According to *Canadian Business* magazine, organizations with strong cultures are more likely to be confident to introduce innovative strategies.[35] Those companies are innovative in every way—staffing, strategy, research, and business processes.

Many risks are associated with being an innovative company. The most basic is the risk that decisions about new technology or innovation will backfire. As research proceeds and engineers and scientists continue to develop new ideas or solutions to problems, there is always the possibility that the innovation will fail to perform as expected. For this reason, organizations commit considerable resources to testing innovations.[36] A second risk is the possibility that a competitor will make decisions enabling them to get an innovation to the market first. The marketplace has become a breeding ground for continuous innovation. Research in Motion, the Waterloo, Ontario based maker of the Blackberry (profiled in Chapter 1) is constantly innovating its products as it goes head to head in competition with companies such as Apple.[37]

Types of Innovation   Innovation can be either radical, systems, or incremental. A radical innovation is a major breakthrough that changes or creates whole industries. Examples include xerography (which was invented by Chester Carlson in 1935 and became the hallmark of Xerox Corporation), steam engines, and the internal combustion engine (which paved the way for today's automobile industry). Systems innovation creates a new functionality by assembling parts in new ways. For example, the gasoline engine began as a radical innovation and became a systems innovation when it was combined with bicycle and carriage technology to create automobiles. Incremental innovation continues the technical improvement and extends the applications of radical and systems innovations. There are many more incremental innovations than there are radical and systems innovations. In fact, several incremental innovations are often necessary to make radical and systems innovations work properly. Incremental innovations force organizations to continuously improve their products and keep abreast or ahead of the competition.

New Ventures   New ventures based on innovations require entrepreneurship and good management to work. The profile of the entrepreneur typically includes a need for achievement, a desire to assume responsibility, a willingness to take risks, and a focus on concrete results. Entrepreneurship can occur inside or outside large organizations. Outside entrepreneurship requires all of the complex aspects of the innovation process. Inside entrepreneurship occurs within a system that usually discourages chaotic activity.

Large organizations typically do not accept entrepreneurial types of activities. Thus, for a large organization to be innovative and develop new ventures, it must actively encourage entrepreneurial activity within the organization. This form of activity, often called **intrapreneurship**, usually is most effective when it is a part of everyday life in the organization and occurs throughout the organization rather than in the research and development department alone.

Corporate Research   The most common means of developing innovation in the traditional organization is through corporate research, or research and development.

> **Innovation** is the process of creating and doing new things that are introduced into the marketplace as products, processes, or services.

> **Intrapreneurship** is entrepreneurial activity that takes place within the context of a large corporation.

Ed Sabol and his son, Steve, developed NFL Films into a $50 million business by doing what they love: watching and filming professional football. Based on Ed's passions for football and videotaping his son's football games, the company has become an innovator in the industry.

Corporate research is usually set up to support existing businesses, provide incremental innovations in the organization's businesses, and explore potential new technology bases. It often takes place in a laboratory, either on the site of the main corporate facility or some distance away from normal operations.

Corporate researchers are responsible for keeping the company's products and processes technologically advanced. Product life cycles vary a great deal, depending on how fast products become obsolete and whether substitutes for the product are developed. Obviously, if a product becomes obsolete or some other product can be substituted for it, the profits from its sales will decrease. The job of corporate research is to prevent this from happening by keeping the company's products current. The corporate culture can be instrumental in fostering an environment in which creativity and innovation occur.

Empowerment

One of the most popular buzz words in management today is empowerment. Almost every new approach to quality, meeting the competition, getting more out of employees, productivity enhancement, and corporate turnarounds deal with employee empowerment. As we discussed in Chapter 5 **empowerment** is the process of enabling workers to set their own goals, make decisions, and solve problems within their

Empowerment is the process of enabling workers to set their own work goals, make decisions, and solve problems within their sphere of responsibility and authority.

spheres of responsibility and authority. Fads are often dismissed as meaningless and without substance because they are misused and overused, and the concept of empowerment, too, can be taken too lightly.

Empowerment is simple and complex at the same time. It is simple in that it tells managers to quit bossing people around so much and to let them do their jobs. It is complex in that managers and employees typically are not trained to do that. A significant amount of time, training, and practice may be needed to truly empower employees. In Chapter 5, we discussed some techniques for utilizing empowerment and conditions in which empowerment can be effective in organizations.

Empowerment can be much more than a motivational technique, however. In some organizations it is the cornerstone of organizational culture. At Nissan, for example, middle-level managers and staff do not only participate in making some decisions, they are also responsible for the decisions. Plant managers have substantial control over budgets, personnel, and training. Cross-functional development teams that include people from design, manufacturing, and marketing have complete responsibility for new cars.[38]

Empowerment can be viewed as liberating employees, but sometimes empowerment entails little more than delegating a task to an employee and then watching over the employee too closely. Employees may feel that this type of participation is superficial and that they are not really making meaningful decisions. The concept of liberating employees suggests that they should be free to do what they think is best without fear that the boss is standing by to veto or change the work done by the employee.[39]

Managing Organization Culture

The work of Ouchi, Peters and Waterman, and many others demonstrates two important facts. First, organizational cultures differ among firms; second, these organizational cultures can affect a firm's performance. Based on these observations, managers have become more concerned about how to best manage the cultures of their organizations. The three elements of managing organizational culture are (1) taking advantage of existing culture, (2) teaching organizational culture, and (3) changing organizational culture.

Taking Advantage of the Existing Culture

Most managers are not in a position to create an organizational culture; rather, they work in organizations that already have cultural values. For these managers, the central issue in managing culture is how best to use the cultural system that already exists. It may be easier and faster to alter employee behaviours within the existing culture than it is to change the history, traditions, and values that already exist.[40]

To take advantage of an existing cultural system, managers must first be fully aware of the culture's values and what behaviours or actions those values support. Becoming fully aware of an organization's values usually is not easy, however; it involves more than reading a pamphlet about what the company believes in. Managers must develop a deep understanding of how organizational values operate in the firm—an understanding that usually comes only through experience.

This understanding, once achieved, can be used to evaluate the performances of others in the firm. Articulating organizational values can be useful in managing others' behaviours. For example, suppose a subordinate in a firm with a strong cultural value of "sticking to its knitting" develops a business strategy that involves moving into a new industry. Rather than attempting to argue that this business strategy is economically flawed or conceptually weak, the manager who understands the corporate culture can point to this organizational value: "In this firm, we believe in sticking to our knitting."

Senior managers who understand their organization's culture can communicate that understanding to lower-level individuals. Over time, as these lower-level managers begin to understand and accept the firm's culture, they require less direct supervision. Their understanding of corporate values guides their decision making.

> It may be easier and faster to alter employee behaviours within the existing culture than it is to change the history, traditions, and values that already exist within the organization.

Teaching the Organization Culture: Socialization

Socialization is the process through which individuals become social beings.[41] As studied by psychologists, it is the process through which children learn to be adults in a society—how they learn what is acceptable and polite behaviour and what is not, how they learn to communicate, how they learn to interact with others, and so on. In complex societies, the socialization process takes many years.

Organizational socialization is the process through which employees learn about their firm's culture and pass their knowledge and understanding on to others. Employees are socialized into organizations, just as people are socialized into societies; that is, they

> **Socialization** is the process through which individuals become social beings.

> **Organizational socialization** is the process through which employees learn about the firm's culture and pass their knowledge and understanding on to others.

come to know over time what is acceptable in the organization and what is not, how to communicate their feelings, and how to interact with others. They learn both through observation and through efforts by managers to communicate this information to them. Research into the process of socialization indicates that for many employees, socialization programs do not necessarily change their values but make them more aware of the differences between personal and organization values and help them develop ways to cope with the differences.[42]

A variety of organizational mechanisms can affect the socialization of workers in organizations. Probably the most important are the examples that new employees see in the behaviour of experienced people. Through observing examples, new employees develop a repertoire of stories they can use to guide their actions. When a decision needs to be made, new employees can ask, "What would my boss do in this situation?" This is not to suggest that formal training, corporate pamphlets, and corporate statements about organization culture are unimportant in the socialization process. However, these factors tend to support the socialization process based on people's close observations of the actions of others.

In some organizations, the culture described in pamphlets and presented in formal training sessions conflicts with the values of the organization as they are expressed in the actions of its people. For example, a firm may say that employees are its most important asset but treat employees badly. In this setting, new employees quickly learn that the rhetoric of the pamphlets and formal training sessions has little to do with the real organization culture. Employees who are socialized into this system usually come to accept the actual cultural values rather than those formally espoused.

Changing the Organization Culture

Much of our discussion to this point has assumed that an organization's culture enhances its performance. When this is the case, learning what an organization's cultural values are and using those values to help socialize new workers and managers is very important, for such actions help the organization succeed. However, as Ouchi's and Peters and Waterman's research indicates, not all firms have cultural values that are consistent with high performance. Ouchi found that Japanese firms and U.S. Type Z firms have performance-enhancing values. Peters and Waterman identified performance-enhancing values associated with successful companies. By implication, some firms not included in Peters and Waterman's study must have had performance-reducing values. What should a manager who works in a company with performance-reducing values do?

The answer to this question is, of course, that top managers in such firms should try to change their organization's cultures. However, this is a difficult thing to do.[43] Culture resists change for all the reasons it is a powerful influence on behaviour—it embodies the basic values in the firm, it is often taken for granted, and it is typically communicated most effectively through stories or other symbols. When managers attempt to change a culture, they are attempting to change people's basic assumptions about what is and is not appropriate behaviour in the organization. Changing from a traditional organization to a team-based organization (discussed in Chapter 8) is an example of changing the culture of an organization. An example of a successful change in organization culture appears in The Yellow Pages and . . . Change box.

Despite these difficulties, some organizations have changed their cultures from performance-reducing to performance-enhancing.[44] This change process will be described in more detail in Chapter 15. The earlier section on creating organizational culture describes the importance of linking the strategic values and the cultural values in creating a new organizational culture. We briefly discuss other important elements of the cultural change process in the following sections.

The Yellow Pages and . . .   CHANGE

The Yellow Pages Finds a New Direction

The Yellow Pages of Canada grew from "a moribund regional phone directories unit buried in Bell Canada" into "a dominant national player with double-digit growth" in four years. How did this happen?

One of the major reasons is that the Yellow Pages were spun out of Bell Canada in 2002, when the parent company determined that producing directories was not part of its core business. As an independent unit, the Yellow Pages had to make it on its own.

Marc Tellier, who was the CEO of the unit while it was still a part of Bell Canada kept the top job after it was bought by independent investors. Shortly after the spin-off, Tellier and a team of senior executives decided to define some new guiding principles, so all of the employees would know the company's values. They decided that open and timely communications were necessary, and that the company wanted to embrace excellence. They next defined six ground rules or values for the company: customer focus, teamwork, passion, respect, open communications, and competing to win.

In order to communicate these values, they were printed on employees' security passes. The company also started to evaluate the employees not only on how well they performed, but also how well they followed company values.

Once that was in place, the Yellow Pages went on a major growth through acquisition strategy. In just a few years, it acquired Advertising Directory Solutions Holdings Inc., which gave it directories in Alberta, British Columbia, and parts of Quebec; Trader Media and Classified Media, which bolstered its online presence and publications in Ontario; and MTS Media and Aliant Directory Services, the companies that owned the directories in Manitoba and Atlantic Canada. These acquisitions gave it coast to coast reach.

Throughout the remarkable expansion, the culture has persisted. The Yellow Pages is recognized as being one of the best places to work and one of the most well respected organizational cultures in Canada. And the bottom line has not suffered either: the Yellow Pages were purchased from Bell Canada for $3 billion in 2002, and was valued at $7.5 billion in 2006. Clearly, a strong culture can lead to success.

Sources: Calvin Leung, "Book Values," *Canadian Business*, October 10, 2005, p. 127; Marty Parker, "Defining Your Corporate Culture," *Canadian Business Online*, March 21, 2007; Marlene Rego, "Marc Tellier," *Canadian Business*, May 21, 2007, p. 47; Andrew Willis, "BCE Plan Could Spark Corporate Culture Change," *The Globe and Mail*, Feb. 2, 2006, p. B18; Grant Robertson, "Yellow Pages Purchase Atlantic Phone Books," *The Globe and Mail*, Feb. 20, 2007, p. B3; Yellow Pages website, www.ypg.com.

Managing Symbols   Research suggests that organization culture is understood and communicated through the use of stories and other symbolic media. If this is correct, managers interested in changing cultures should attempt to substitute stories and myths that support new cultural values for those that support old ones. They can do so by creating situations that give rise to new stories. Suppose an organization traditionally has held the value "employee opinions are not important." When management meets in this company, the ideas and opinions of lower-level people—when discussed at all—are normally rejected as foolish and irrelevant. The stories that support this cultural value tell about managers who tried to make a constructive point only to have that point lost in personal attacks from superiors. An upper-level manager interested in creating a new story, one that shows lower-level managers that their ideas are valuable, might ask a subordinate to prepare to lead a discussion in a meeting and follow through by asking the subordinate to take the lead when the topic arises. The subordinate's success in the meeting will become a new story, one that may displace some of the many stories suggesting that the opinions of lower-level managers do not matter.

The Difficulty of Change   Changing a firm's culture is a long and difficult process. A primary problem is that upper-level managers, no matter how dedicated they are to implementing some new cultural value, may sometimes inadvertently revert to old patterns of behaviour. This happens, for example, when a manager dedicated to implementing the value that lower-level employees' ideas are important vehemently attacks a subordinate's ideas.

This mistake generates a story that supports old values and beliefs. After such an incident, lower-level managers may believe that the boss says he wants their input and ideas, but nothing could be further from the truth. No matter what the boss says or how consistent his behaviour is, some credibility has been lost, and cultural change has been made more difficult.

The Stability of Change   The process of changing a firm's culture starts with a need for change and moves through a transition period in which efforts are made to adopt new values and beliefs. In the long run, a firm that successfully changes its culture will find that the new values and beliefs are just as stable and influential as the old ones. Value systems tend to be self-reinforcing. Once they are in place, changing them requires an enormous effort. Thus, if a firm can change its culture from performance-reducing to performance-enhancing, the new values are likely to remain in place for a long time.

Summary of Key Points

- Organizational culture has become one of the most discussed subjects in the field of organizational behaviour. It burst on the scene in the 1980s with books by Ouchi, Peters and Waterman, and others. Interest has not been restricted to academics, however. Practising managers are also interested in organizational culture, especially as it relates to performance.

- There is little agreement about how to define organizational culture. A comparison of several important definitions suggests that most have three things in common: They define culture in terms of the values that individuals in organizations use to prescribe appropriate behaviour; they assume that these values are usually taken for granted; and they emphasize the stories and other symbolic means through which the values are typically communicated.

- Current research on organizational culture reflects various research traditions. The most important contributions have come from anthropology and sociology. Anthropologists have tended to focus on the organizational cultures of one or two firms and have used detailed description to help outsiders understand organizational culture from the "natives'" point of view." Sociologists typically have used survey methods to study the organizational cultures of larger numbers of firms. Two other influences on current work in organizational culture are social psychology, which emphasizes the manipulation of symbols in organizations, and economics. The economics approach sees culture both as a tool used to manage and as a determinant of performance.

- Creating organizational culture is a five-step process. It starts with formulating strategic and cultural values for the organization. Next, a vision for the organization is created, followed by institution of implementation strategies. The final step is reinforcing the cultural behaviours of employees.

- Although no single framework for describing organization culture has emerged, several have been suggested. The most popular efforts in this area have been Ouchi's comparison of U.S. and Japanese firms and Peters and Waterman's description of successful firms in the United States. Ouchi and Peters and Waterman suggested several important dimensions along which organizational values vary, including treatment of employees, definitions of appropriate means for

decision making, and assignment of responsibility for the results of decision making.

- Emerging issues in the area of organizational culture include innovation and employee empowerment. Innovation is the process of creating and doing new things that are introduced into the marketplace as products, processes, or services. The organizational culture can either help or hinder innovation. Employee empowerment, in addition to being similar to employee participation as a motivation technique, is now viewed by some as a type of organizational culture. Empowerment occurs when employees make decisions, set their own work goals, and solve problems in their own area of responsibility.

- Managing the organizational culture requires attention to three factors. First, managers can take advantage of cultural values that already exist and use their knowledge to help subordinates understand them. Second, employees need to be properly socialized, or trained, in the cultural values of the organization, either through formal training or by experiencing and observing the actions of higher-level managers. Third, managers can change the culture of the organization through managing the symbols, addressing the extreme difficulties of such a change, and relying on the durability of the new organization culture once the change has been implemented.

Discussion Questions

1. A sociologist or anthropologist might suggest that the culture in North American firms simply reflects the dominant culture of the society as a whole. Therefore, to change the organization culture of a company, one must first deal with the inherent values and beliefs of the society. How would you respond to this claim?

2. Psychology has been defined as the study of individual behaviour. Organizational psychology is the study of individual behaviour in organizations. Many of the theories described in the early chapters of this book are based in organizational psychology. Why was this field not identified as a contributor to the study of organization culture along with anthropology, sociology, social psychology, and economics?

3. Describe the culture of an organization with which you are familiar. It might be one in which you currently work, one in which you have worked, or one in which a friend or family member works. What values, beliefs, stories, and symbols are significant to employees of the organization?

4. Discuss the similarities and differences between the organizational culture approaches of Ouchi and Peters and Waterman.

5. Describe how organizations use symbols and stories to communicate values and beliefs. Give some examples of how symbols and stories have been used in organizations with which you are familiar.

6. What is the role of leadership (discussed in Chapter 13) in developing, maintaining, and changing organizational culture?

7. Review the characteristics of organization structure described in earlier chapters and compare them with the elements of culture described by Ouchi and Peters and Waterman. Describe the similarities and differences, and explain how some characteristics of one may be related to characteristics of the other.

8. Discuss the role of organization rewards in developing, maintaining, and changing the organization culture.

9. How are empowerment and procedural justice similar to each other? How do they differ?

10. Describe how the culture of an organization can affect innovation.

Experiencing Organizational Behaviour

Purpose: This exercise will help you appreciate the fascination as well as the difficulty of examining culture in organizations.

Format: The class will divide into groups of four to six. Each group will analyze the organization culture of a university class. Students in most classes that use this book will have taken many courses at the university they attend and therefore should have several classes in common.

Procedure: The class is divided into groups of four to six on the basis of classes the students have had in common.

1. Each group should first decide which class it will analyze. Each person in the group must have attended the class.

2. Each group should list the cultural factors to be discussed. Items to be covered should include:
   a. Stories about the professor
   b. Stories about the exams
   c. Stories about the grading
   d. Stories about other students
   e. The use of symbols that indicate the students' values
   f. The use of symbols that indicate the instructors' values
   g. Other characteristics of the class as suggested by the frameworks of Ouchi and Peters and Waterman.

3. Students should carefully analyze the stories and symbols to discover their underlying meanings. They should seek stories from other members of the group to ensure that all aspects of the class culture are covered. Students should take notes as these items are discussed.

4. After 20 to 30 minutes of work in groups, the instructor will reconvene the entire class and ask each group to share its analysis with the rest of the class.

Follow-up Questions

1. What was the most difficult part of this exercise? Did other groups experience the same difficulty?

2. How did your group overcome this difficulty? How did other groups overcome it?

3. Do you believe your group's analysis accurately describes the culture of the class you selected? Could other students who analyzed the culture of the same class come up with a very different result? How could that happen?

4. If the instructor wanted to try to change the culture in the class you analyzed, what steps would you recommend that he or she take?

An Empowering Culture: What It Is and What It Is Not

Exercise Overview: Typically, managers are promoted or selected to fill jobs in an organization with a given organization culture. As they begin to work, they must recognize the culture and either learn how to work within it or figure out how to change it. If the culture is a performance-reducing one, managers must figure out how to change the culture to a performance-enhancing one. This exercise will give you a chance to develop your own ideas about changing organization culture.

Exercise Background: Assume that you have just been appointed to head the legislative affairs committee of your local student government. As someone with a double major in business and government, you are eager to take on this assignment and really make a difference. This committee has existed at your university for several years, but it has done little because the members use the committee as a social group and regularly throw great parties. In all the years of its existence, the committee has done nothing to have had an impact on the provincial legislature in relation to the issues important to university

students, such as tuition. Since you know that the issue of university tuition will come before the provincial legislature during the current legislative session, and you know that many students could not afford a substantial raise in tuition, you are determined to use this committee to ensure that any tuition increase is as small as possible. However, you are worried that the party culture of the existing committee may make it difficult for you to use it to work for your issues. You also know that you cannot "fire" any of the volunteers on the committee and can add only two people to the committee.

Exercise Task: Using this information as context, do the following:

1. Design a strategy for utilizing the existing culture of the committee to help you influence the legislature regarding tuition.

2. Assuming that the existing culture is a performance-reducing culture, design a strategy for changing it to a performance-enhancing culture.

Surviving Plant World's Hard Times

In ten years, Plant World had grown from a one-person venture into the largest nursery and landscaping business in its area. Its founder, Myta Ong, combined a lifelong interest in plants with a botany degree to provide a unique customer service. Ong had managed the company's growth so that even with 20 full-time employees working in six to eight crews, the organization culture was still as open, friendly, and personal as it had been when her only employees were friends who would volunteer to help her move a heavy tree.

To maintain that atmosphere, Ong involved herself increasingly with people and less with plants as the company grew. With hundreds of customers and scores of jobs at any one time, she could no longer say without hesitation whether she had a dozen arborvitae bushes in stock or when Mrs. Carnack's estate would need a new load of bark mulch. But she knew when Rose had been up all night

with her baby, when Gary was likely to be late because he had driven to see his sick father over the weekend, and how to deal with Ellen when she was depressed because of her boyfriend's behaviour. She kept track of the birthdays of every employee and even those of their children. She was up every morning by 5:30 arranging schedules so that John could get his son out of daycare at 4 P.M. and Martina could be back in town for her afternoon high school equivalency classes.

Paying all this attention to employees may have led Ong to make a single bad business decision that almost destroyed the company. She provided extensive landscaping to a new mall on credit, and when the mall never opened and its owners went bankrupt, Plant World found itself in deep trouble. The company had virtually no cash and had to pay off the bills for the mall plants, most of which were not even salvageable.

One Friday, Ong called a meeting with her employees and levelled with them: either they would not get paid for a month or Plant World would fold. The news hit the employees hard. Many counted on the Friday paycheque to buy groceries for the week. The local unemployment rate was low, however, and they knew they could find other jobs.

But as they looked around, they wondered whether they could ever find this kind of job. Sure, the pay was not the greatest, but the tears in the eyes of some workers were not over pay or personal hardship; they were for Ong, her dream, and her difficulties. They never thought of her as the boss or called her anything but "Myta." And leaving the group would not be just a matter of saying goodbye to fellow employees. If Bernice left, the company baseball team would lose its best pitcher, and the Sunday game was the height of everyone's week. Where else would they find people who spent much of the weekend working on the best puns with which to assail one another on Monday morning? At how many offices would everyone show up 20 minutes before starting time just to catch up with friends on other crews? What other boss would really understand when you simply said, "I don't have a doctor's appointment, I just need the afternoon off"?

Ong gave her employees the weekend to think over their decision: whether to take their pay and look for another job or to dig into their savings and go on working. Knowing it would be hard for them to quit, she told them they did not have to face her on Monday; if they did not show up, she would send them their cheques. But when she arrived at 7:40 Monday morning, she found the entire group already there, ready to work even harder to pull the company through. They were even trying to top one another with puns about being "mall-contents."

Case Questions

1. How would you describe the organization culture at Plant World?

2. How large can such a company get before it needs to change its culture and structure?

You have read the chapter and studied the key terms. Think you're ready to ace the exam? Take this sample test to gauge your comprehension of chapter material and check your answers at the back of the book. Want more test questions? Take the ACE quizzes found on the student website: www.hmco.ca/ob.

T   F   1. The research on the impact of culture has come to the firm conclusion that strong cultures enhance performance.

T   F   2. Culture is often communicated through stories.

T   F   3. Possession of values and vision are essential to creating an organization culture.

T   F   4. According to William Ouchi, a Type Z firm is a typical Japanese firm that tries to develop an American firm culture.

T   F   5. Managers with a bias for action make decisions even if all the facts are not in.

T   F   6. Entrepreneurial activity within an organization is called intrapreneurship.

T   F   7. Organizations that use formal socialization programs to teach employees their culture are usually successful at changing employees' values.

8. A variety of definitions of culture exist. All of the following are common attributes that emerge among these definitions, except
   a. culture refers to some set of values held by individuals.
   b. the values that make up an organization's culture are often taken for granted.
   c. cultural elements create positive situations in the organization.
   d. an organization's culture is communicated through symbolic means.
   e. All of the above are common attributes among the definitions of culture.

9. Paul is interested in studying organizational culture. Which of the following areas would likely be the least helpful to Paul in his research?
   a. sociology
   b. engineering
   c. anthropology
   d. social psychology
   e. economics

10. Lauren is an entrepreneur and is about to open a new business. She wants to start things off correctly by creating a healthy organizational culture. Which of the following would you recommend be Lauren's first step?
   a. become a Type Z organization.
   b. tell as many stories as possible.

   c. let the culture rapidly develop a "taken for granted" nature.
   d. determine the strategic values of the organization.
   e. reinforce cultural behaviours.

11. According to the research performed by William Ouchi, Type Z U.S. and typical Japanese firms share certain cultural values that may explain their success. Which of the following is not one of these values?
   a. trying to keep employees
   b. rapid employee evaluation and promotion
   c. control through informal, implicit mechanisms
   d. group decision making
   e. holistic concern for workers and managers

12. One suggestion in Peters and Waterman's *In Search of Excellence* is to "stick to the knitting." This means
   a. staying close to the customer.
   b. achieving productivity through people.
   c. reluctance to engage in business outside their areas of expertise.
   d. managers should manage by "wandering around" the organization.
   e. breaking the company into smaller pieces and then re-attaching each piece in sequence.

13. Peters and Waterman identified simultaneously loose and tight organization as a valuable cultural characteristic. How is it possible to be simultaneously loosely and tightly organized?
   a. All members understand the firm's values, but there are formal fewer rules and regulations.
   b. Prices are strictly based on market values, but prices are allowed to fluctuate with the market.
   c. Managers have formal authority, but they allow a wide degree of participation by subordinates.
   d. Employees have specific assignments, but they are allowed to schedule their work as they please.
   e. The organization has few administrative layers, and each layer is staffed with only the necessary number of employees.

CHAPTER 15

Organization Change and Development

▶ **Summarize four dominant forces for change in organizations.**

▶ **Describe the process of planned organization change as a continuous process.**

▶ **Discuss several approaches to organization development.**

▶ **Explain organizational and individual sources of resistance to change.**

▶ **Identify six keys to managing successful organization change and development.**

Chapter Outline

Privatizing CN

The privatization of CN Rail was announced in the budget speech by then federal minister of finance Paul Martin on February 27, 1995. The government decided that it no longer wanted to own the railway, which frequently lost hundreds of millions of dollars itself and, with additional indirect subsidies, cost the government billions of dollars to support each year. The actual sale occurred in November of that year.

The move was not a great surprise. Business reporters had been observing that CN appeared to be preparing for privatization for several years. The Crown corporation had been closing or selling unprofitable rail lines, reducing the size of its workforce, and selling off non-rail subsidiaries such as an oil and gas interest, and real estate holdings, including the CN Tower in Toronto.

CN went through a very painful transition. Prior to privatization, it was widely seen as bloated and inefficient. Nonetheless, the magnitude of the early changes was startling: 14 000 of 36 000 jobs were cut during the period from 1992 to 1997. Hundreds of kilometres of rail lines were sold or closed.

But perhaps the most important change was the introduction of a new culture for the organization and the mindset of its managers. CN had to move away from what was called an overly comfortable approach to operations, where performance and financial results were unimportant. After all, as a Crown corporation, the federal government was always in the background, and had a history of bailing out CN when it ran into problems. As a private company, the new culture had to embrace efficiency, competitiveness, and become aggressive if it was to survive. Paul Tellier, the CEO of CN from 1992 to 2003, stated in 1997 that his biggest job at CN was to change its culture.

In actions that helped to prepare CN for privatization, it took on structures and practices that mirrored the private sector. The market apparently recognized that CN could be successful: the initial public offering of its shares on November 17, 1995, was one of the most successful ever in Canada at that point. The initial share price set at $16.25 closed at $20.25 on the first day of trading, and $2.2 billion were eventually raised.

Although gut-wrenching, the initial turnaround occurred remarkably fast. After losing over $180 million in 1992, CN posted a profit of over $450 million in 1996, its first full year as a private company. Since then, CN has grown and prospered, acquiring new rail lines in Canada and the United States. In 2006, it posted a profit of $2.1 billion on revenues of $7.72 billion, its stock was trading at around $51.00 per share.[1]

Companies such as CN Rail constantly face pressures to change. Forecasts of changing economic conditions, consumer purchasing patterns, technological and scientific factors, and competition, both foreign and domestic, force top management to evaluate their organization and consider significant changes.

This chapter presents a view of change in organizations. First we examine the forces for change and discuss several approaches to planned organization change. Then we consider organization development processes and the resistance to change that usually occurs. The chapter briefly covers several international and cross-cultural factors that affect organization change processes. Finally, we discuss how to manage organization change and development efforts in organizations.

Forces for Change

An organization is subject to pressures for change from far too many sources to discuss them all here. Moreover, it is difficult to predict what type of pressure for change will be most significant in the next decade because the complexity of events and the rapidity of change are increasing. However, it is possible—and important—to discuss the broad categories of pressures that probably will have major effects on organizations. The four areas in which the pressures for change appear most powerful involve people,

The complexity of events and the rapidity of change make it difficult to predict future sources of pressure for change.

Category	Examples	Type of Pressure for Change
People	Generation X, Baby boomers, Senior citizens, Workforce diversity	Demands for different training, benefits, workplace arrangements, and compensation systems
Technology	Manufacturing in space Internet Artificial intelligence	More education and training for workers at all levels, more new products, products move faster to market
Information Processing and Communication	Computer, satellite communications Videoconferencing	Faster reaction times, immediate responses to questions, new products, different office arrangements, telecommuting
Competition	Worldwide markets International trade agreements Emerging nations	Global competition, more competing products with more features and options, lower costs, higher quality

technology, information processing and communication, and competition. Table 15.1 gives examples of each of these categories.

People

As of 2006, approximately one-third of the nearly 33 million Canadians were "baby boomers" born between 1945 and 1965.[2] These baby boomers differ significantly from previous generations with respect to education, expectations, and value systems.[3] The special characteristics of baby boomers show up in distinct purchasing patterns that affect product and service innovation, technological change, and marketing and promotional activities.[4] Boomers are now approaching retirement, and being replaced by other generational groups, sometimes labelled "Gen-X" and, following them, the "millennial" generation. Each successive generation has different expectations and attitudes about careers and employment. Consequently, employment practices, compensation systems, promotion and managerial succession systems, and the entire concept of human resource management are also affected.

The increasing diversity of the workforce in the coming years will mean significant changes for organizations. In addition, employees will be faced with a different work environment in this century. The most descriptive word for this new work environment is *change*. Employees must be prepared for constant change. Change is occurring in organizations' cultures, structures, work relationships, customer relationships, and in the actual jobs that people do. People will have to be completely adaptable to new situations while maintaining productivity under the existing system.[5]

Technology

Not only is technology changing, the rate of technological change is increasing. In 1970, for example, all engineering students owned slide rules and used them in almost every class. By 1976, slide rules had given way to portable electronic calculators. In the mid-1980s, some universities began issuing microcomputers to entering students or assuming that students already owned them. Now students cannot make it through university without owning or at least having ready access to a personal computer. The dormitory rooms at many universities are wired for direct computer access for e-mail, class assignments, and access to the Internet. Older university buildings are being retro-fitted for the wireless access for faculty, students, staff, and campus guests that new buildings have. Technological development is increasing so rapidly in almost every field that it is quite difficult to predict which products will dominate ten years from now.

Interestingly, organization change is self-perpetuating. With the advances in information technology, organizations generate more information and it circulates more quickly. Consequently, employees can respond more quickly to problems, so the organization can respond more quickly to demands from other organizations, customers, and competitors.[6] Toyota is a leader in developing and using new technologies in its plants, as described in the Toyota and . . . Technology box.

New technology will affect organizations in ways we cannot yet predict. Artificial intelligence—computers and software programs that think and learn in much the same way as humans do—is already assisting in geological exploration.[7] Several companies are developing systems to manufacture chemicals and exotic electronic components in space. The Internet and the World Wide Web are changing the way companies and individuals communicate, market, buy, and distribute faster than organizations can respond. Thus, as organizations respond more quickly to changes, change occurs more rapidly, which in turn necessitates more rapid responses.

Information Processing and Communication

Advances in information processing and communication have paralleled each other. A new generation of computers, which will mark another major increase in processing power, is being designed. Satellite systems for data transmission are already in use. Today people can carry telephones in their pockets that double as their portable computers, pocket-size televisions, music players, and pagers, all in one device.

In the future, people may not need offices as they work with computers and communicate through new data transmission devices. Workstations, both in and outside of offices, will be more electronic than paper and pencil. For years the capability existed to generate, manipulate, store, and transmit more data than managers could use, but the benefits were not fully realized. Now the time has come to utilize all of that information-processing potential, and companies are making the most of it. Typically, companies received orders by mail in the 1970s, by 800 number in the 1980s, by the fax machine in the late 1980s and early 1990s, and by electronic data exchange in the mid-1990s. Orders used to take a week to process; now they are processed instantaneously. Due to innovations such as linked databases, wireless monitoring, and radio frequency identification systems, companies must be able to respond immediately, all because of changes in information processing and communication.[8]

Cell phone giants such as Nokia, Motorola, and Ericsson have had a stranglehold on the worldwide cellular phone market. However, as new Chinese companies are pairing with software producers Microsoft and Apple, that is changing. Competition within the cell phone market will continue to grow.

Toyota and . . . **TECHNOLOGY**

The Robot-Worker Interface at Toyota

Toyota is pushing the technology envelope with the development of a *kokino robotto,* "advanced robot," that can perform several complex tasks simultaneously. Personal assistant robots are designed to carry heavy packages and help the elderly and the ill out of bed. Another robot is an exoskeleton, shaped like a chair on wheels. A disabled person rides the robot, opening doors with its arms and climbing stairs, tasks impossible for traditional wheelchairs.

The robots will also be used in factory production. While traditional robots perform large-scale operations in welding, painting, and gross assembly, the *kokino robotto* are super robots capable of performing a task as delicate as tightening a screw. Toyota's super robots can manage final assembly and trim operations.

The machines are quick and consistent. Unlike humans, robots never tire, get hurt, or retire, reducing Toyota's short- and long-term expenses. "The two-armed [super robot] is as labor efficient as a human, if not more efficient," says industry observer Burritt Sabin. A Toyota official states, "[With robots], we aim to reduce production costs to the levels in China."

Robots replace factory workers, in short supply in Japan, and keep costs low in a high-wage country. The company plans to add 1000 super robots to its 3000 to 4000 standard robots. "Even this super robot will not result in the total replacement of man by machine; rather, it will reinforce the strengths of the production line," says Sabin.

Competitors are awed by Toyota's high-tech equipment. However, Toyota managers claim their success is founded on training, responsibility, shared values, and respect. Consultant Dennis Pawley sees the performance gap between American and Japanese automakers. Referring to the Detroit Big Three, he says, "They don't understand that they don't understand."

See "Toyota Reinvented," this chapter's closing case, to learn more about changes at Toyota.

Sources: "Toyota to Employ Robots," News24.com website, January 6, 2005, www.news24.com on May 4, 2005; "Toyota's Global New Body Line," Toyota Motor Manufacturing website, www.toyotageorgetown.com on May 4, 2005; Burritt Sabin, "Robots for Babies—Toyota at the Leading Edge," Japan.com website, www.japan.com on May 5, 2005; Christine Tierney, "Big Three Play Catch-Up to Toyota Plant Prowess," *The Detroit News,* February 22, 2004, www.detnews.com on May 4, 2005.

Competition

Although competition is not a new force for change, competition today has some significant new twists. First, most markets are international because of decreasing transportation and communication costs and the increasing export orientation of business. The adoption of trade agreements such as the North American Free Trade Agreement and the General Agreement on Trade and Tariffs has changed the way business operates. Competition from industrialized countries such as Japan and Germany is starting to take a back seat to competition from the booming industries of developing nations such as China and India. Developing nations may soon offer different, newer, cheaper, or higher-quality products while enjoying the benefits of low labour costs, abundant supplies of raw materials, expertise in certain areas of production, and financial protection from their governments that may not be available in the older industrialized states. North American automobile manufacturers General Motors, Ford, and Chrysler are trying to change their organizations to meet the competition of companies such as Toyota.[9]

Processes for Planned Organization Change

External forces may impose change on an organization. Ideally, however, the organization will not only respond to change but also anticipate it, prepare for it through planning, and incorporate it in the organization strategy. Organization change can be viewed from a static point of view, such as that of Lewin, or from a dynamic perspective.

Lewin's Process Model

Planned organization change requires a systematic process of movement from one condition to another. Kurt Lewin suggested that efforts to bring about planned change in organizations should approach change as a multistage process.[10] His model of planned change is made up of three steps—unfreezing, change, and refreezing—as shown in Figure 15.1.

Unfreezing is the process by which people become aware of the need for change. If people are satisfied with current practices and procedures, they may have little or no interest in making changes. The key factor in unfreezing is making employees understand the importance of a change and how their jobs will be affected by it. The employees who will be most affected by the change must be made aware of why it is needed, which in effect makes them dissatisfied enough with current operations to be motivated to change.

Change itself is the movement from the old way of doing things to a new way. Change may entail installing new equipment, restructuring the organization, implementing a new performance appraisal system—anything that alters existing relationships or activities.

Refreezing makes new behaviours relatively permanent and resistant to further change. Examples of refreezing techniques include repeating newly learned skills in a training session and role playing to teach how the new skill can be used in a real-life work situation. Refreezing is necessary because without it, the old ways of doing things might soon reassert themselves while the new ways are forgotten. For example, many employees who attend special training sessions apply themselves diligently and resolve to change things in their organizations. But when they return to the workplace, they find it easier to conform to the old ways than to make waves. There usually are few, if any, rewards for trying to change the organizational status quo. In fact, the personal sanctions against doing so may be difficult to tolerate. Learning theory and reinforcement theory (Chapter 4) can play important roles in the refreezing phase.

> Lewin's three-stage model of planned organization change suggests that change is a systematic process of moving from one stage to another.

> **Unfreezing** is the process by which people become aware of the need for change.

> **Refreezing** is the process of making new behaviours relatively permanent and resistant to further change.

FIGURE 15.1

Lewin's Process of Organization Change

In Lewin's three-step model, change is a systematic process of transition from an old way of doing things to a new way. Inclusion of an unfreezing stage indicates the importance of preparing for the change. The refreezing stage reflects the importance of following up the change to make it permanent.

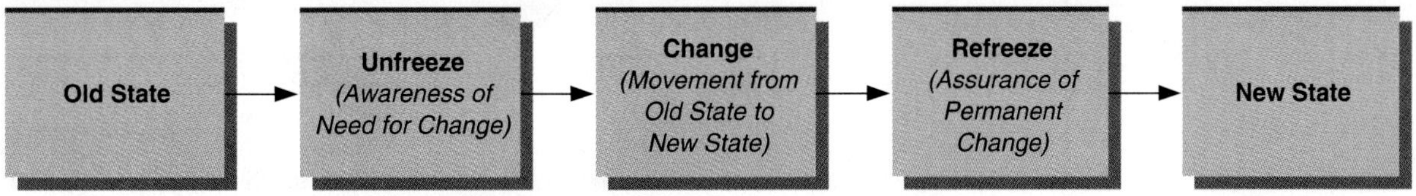

| Old State | → | Unfreeze (Awareness of Need for Change) | → | Change (Movement from Old State to New State) | → | Refreeze (Assurance of Permanent Change) | → | New State |

The Continuous Change Process Model

Perhaps because Lewin's model is very simple and straightforward, virtually all models of organization change use his approach. However, it does not deal with several important issues. A more complex, and more helpful, approach is illustrated in Figure 15.2. This approach treats planned change from the perspective of top management and indicates that change is continuous. Although we discuss each step as if it were separate and distinct from others, it is important to note that as change becomes continuous in organizations, different steps are probably occurring simultaneously throughout the organization. The model incorporates Lewin's concept into the implementation phase.

In this approach, top management perceives that certain forces or trends call for change, and the issue is subjected to the organization's usual problem-solving and decision-making processes (see Chapter 9). Usually, top management defines its goals in terms of what the organization or certain processes or outputs will be like after the change. Alternatives for change are generated and evaluated, and an acceptable one is selected.

Early in the process, the organization may seek the assistance of a **change agent**—a person who will be responsible for managing the change effort. The change agent may also help management recognize and define the problem or the need for the change and may be involved in generating and evaluating potential plans of action. The change agent can be a member of the organization, an outsider such as a consultant, or even someone from headquarters whom employees view as an outsider. An internal change agent is likely to know the organization's people, tasks, and political situations, which may be helpful in interpreting data and understanding the system; but an insider may also be too close to the situation to view it objectively. (In addition, a regular employee would have to be removed from his or her regular duties to concentrate on the transition.) An outsider, then, is often received better by all parties because of his or her assumed impartiality. Under the direction and management of the change

A **change agent** is a person responsible for managing a change effort.

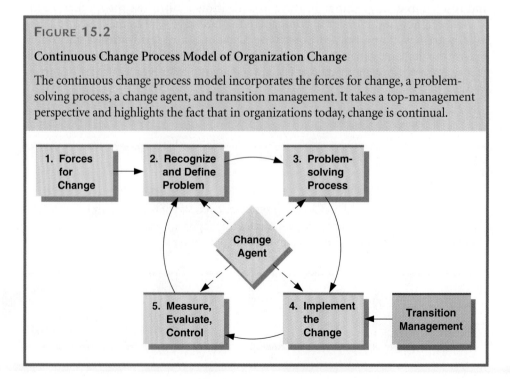

FIGURE 15.2

Continuous Change Process Model of Organization Change

The continuous change process model incorporates the forces for change, a problem-solving process, a change agent, and transition management. It takes a top-management perspective and highlights the fact that in organizations today, change is continual.

agent, the organization implements the change through Lewin's unfreeze, change, and refreeze process.

The final step is measurement, evaluation, and control. The change agent and the top management group assess the degree to which the change is having the desired effect; that is, they measure progress toward the goals of the change and make appropriate changes if necessary. The more closely the change agent is involved in the change process, the less distinct the steps become. The change agent becomes a collaborator or helper to the organization as she or he is immersed in defining and solving the problem with members of the organization. When this happens, the change agent may be working with many individuals, groups, and departments within the organization on different phases of the change process. When the change process is moving along from one stage to another it may not be readily observable because of the total involvement of the change agent in every phase of the project. Throughout the process, however, the change agent brings in new ideas and viewpoints that help members look at old problems in new ways. Change often arises from the conflict that results when the change agent challenges the organization's assumptions and generally accepted patterns of operation.

Through the measurement, evaluation, and control phase, top management determines the effectiveness of the change process by evaluating various indicators of organizational productivity and effectiveness or employee morale. It is hoped that the organization will be better after the change than before. However, the uncertainties and rapid change in all sectors of the environment make constant organization change a certainty for most organizations.

Transition management is the process of systematically planning, organizing, and implementing change, from the disassembly of the current state to the realization of a fully functional future state within an organization.[11] Once change begins, the organization is in neither the old state nor the new state, yet business must go on. Transition management ensures that business continues while the change is occurring, and thus it must begin before the change occurs. The members of the regular management team must take on the role of transition managers and coordinate organizational activities with the change agent. An interim management structure or interim positions may be created to ensure continuity and control of the business during the transition. Communication about the changes to all involved, from employees to customers and suppliers, plays a key role in transition management.[12]

When Micheal Eisner became CEO of Disney in 1984, the company was in the midst of a troubled period. Eisner became the change agent who spurred growth through new activities and projects. While once an agent for change, because it had become clear that he had become the one who needed to be changed, he was ousted in 2004.

Transition management is the process of systematically planning, organizing, and implementing change.

Organization Development

On one level, organization development is simply the way organizations change and evolve. Organization change can involve personnel, technology, competition, and other areas. Employee learning and formal training, transfers, promotions, terminations, and retirements are all examples of personnel-related changes. Thus, in the broadest sense, organization development means organization change.[13] However, the term as used here means something more specific. Over the past 30 years, organization development has emerged as a distinct field of study and practice. Experts now substantially agree as to what constitutes organizational development in general, although arguments about details continue.[14] Our definition of organization development is an attempt to describe a very complex process in a simple manner. It is also an attempt to capture the best points of several definitions offered by writers in the field.

Organization Development Defined

Organization development is the process of planned change and improvement of organizations through the application of knowledge of the behavioural sciences. Three points in this definition make it simple to remember and use. First, organization development involves attempts to plan organization changes, which excludes spontaneous, haphazard initiatives. Second, the specific intention of organization development is to improve organizations. This point excludes changes that merely imitate those of another organization, are forced on the organization by external pressures, or are undertaken merely for the sake of changing. Third, the planned improvement must be based on knowledge of the behavioural sciences, such as organizational behaviour, psychology, sociology, cultural anthropology, and related fields of study, rather than on financial or technological considerations. Under our definition, the replacement of manual personnel records with a computerized system would not be considered an instance of organization development. Although such a change has behavioural effects, it is a technology-driven reform rather than a behavioural one. Likewise, alterations in record keeping necessary to support new government-mandated reporting requirements are not a part of organization development, because the change is obligatory and the result of an external force. The three most basic types of techniques are systemwide, task and technological, and group and individual.

Systemwide Organization Development

The most comprehensive type of organization change involves a major reorganization, usually referred to as a **structural change**—a systemwide rearrangement of task division and authority and reporting relationships. A structural change affects performance appraisal and rewards, decision making, and communication and information-processing systems. As we discussed in Chapter 13, re-engineering and rethinking the organizations are two contemporary approaches to systemwide structural change.

An organization may change the way it divides tasks into jobs, groups jobs into departments and divisions, and arranges authority and reporting relationships among positions. It may move from functional departmentalization to a system based on products or geography, for example, or from a conventional linear design to a matrix or a team-based design. Other changes include dividing large groups into smaller ones or merging small groups into larger ones. In addition, the degree to which rules and procedures are written down and enforced, as well as the locus of decision-making authority, may be altered. Supervisors may become coaches or facilitators in a team-based organization. The organization will have transformed both the configurational and the operational aspects of its structure if all these changes are made.

No systemwide structural change is simple.[15] A company president cannot just issue a memo notifying company personnel that on a certain date they will report to a different supervisor and be responsible for new tasks and expect everything to change overnight. Employees have months, years, and sometimes decades of experience in dealing with people and tasks in certain ways. When these patterns are disrupted, employees need time to learn the new tasks and to settle into the new relationships. Moreover, they may resist the change for a number of reasons; we discuss resistance to change later in this chapter. Therefore, organizations must manage the change process.

> **Organization development** is the process of planned change and improvement of the organization through application of knowledge of the behavioural sciences.

> **Structural change**—a systemwide organization development involving a major restructuring of the organization or instituting programs such as quality of worklife.

Another systemwide change is the introduction of quality-of-worklife programs. J. Lloyd Suttle defined **quality of worklife** as the "degree to which members of a work organization are able to satisfy important personal needs through their experiences in the organization."[16] Quality-of-worklife programs focus strongly on providing a work environment conducive to satisfying individual needs. The emphasis on improving life at work developed during the 1970s, a period of increasing inflation and deepening recession. The development was rather surprising, because an expanding economy and substantially increased resources are the conditions that usually induce top management to begin people-oriented programs. Improving life at work was viewed by top management as a means of improving productivity.

> **Quality of worklife** is the extent to which workers can satisfy important personal needs through their experiences in the organization.

Any movement with broad and ambiguous goals tends to spawn diverse programs, each claiming to be based on the movement's goals, and quality of worklife is no exception. These programs vary substantially, although most espouse a goal of humanizing the workplace. Richard Walton divided them into the eight categories shown in Figure 15.3.[17] Obviously, many types of programs can be accommodated by the categories, from changing the pay system to establishing an employee bill of rights that guarantees workers the rights to privacy, free speech, due process, and fair and equitable treatment.

Total quality management, which was discussed in several earlier chapters, can also be viewed as a systemwide organization development program. In fact, some might consider total quality management as a broad program that includes structural change as well as quality of worklife. It differs from quality of worklife in that it emphasizes satisfying customer needs by making quality-oriented changes rather than focusing on satisfying employee needs at work. Often, however, the employee programs are very similar.

The benefits gained from quality of worklife programs differ substantially, but generally they are of three types. A more positive attitude toward the work and the organization, or increased job satisfaction, is perhaps the most direct benefit.[18] Another is increased productivity, although it is often difficult to measure and separate the effects of the quality-of-worklife program from the effects of other organizational factors. A third benefit is increased effectiveness of the organization as measured by its profitability, goal accomplishment, shareholder wealth, or resource exchange. The third gain follows directly from the first two: if employees have more positive attitudes about the organization and their productivity increases, everything else being equal, the organization should be more effective.

Task and Technological Change

Another way to bring about systemwide organization development is through changes in the tasks involved in doing the work, the technology, or both. The direct alteration of jobs usually is

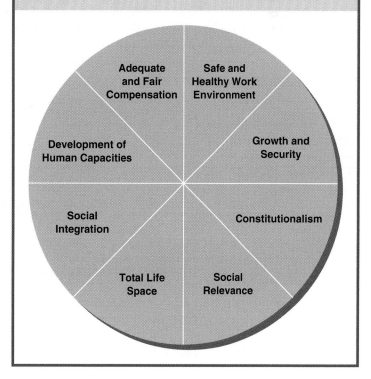

FIGURE 15.3

Walton's Categorization of Quality-of-Worklife Programs

Quality-of-worklife programs can be categorized into eight types. The expected benefits of these programs are increased employee morale, productivity, and organizational effectiveness.

Source: Adapted from Richard E. Walton, "Quality of Worklife: What Is It?" *Sloan Management Review,* Fall 1973, pp. 11–21, by permission of the publisher. Copyright © 1973 by the Sloan Management Review Association. All rights reserved.

- Adequate and Fair Compensation
- Safe and Healthy Work Environment
- Development of Human Capacities
- Growth and Security
- Social Integration
- Constitutionalism
- Total Life Space
- Social Relevance

called task redesign. Changing how inputs are transformed into outputs is called technological change and also usually results in task changes. Strictly speaking, changing the technology is typically not part of organization development, whereas task redesign usually is.

The structural changes discussed in the preceding section are explicitly systemwide in scope. Those we examine in this section are more narrowly focused and may not seem to have the same far-reaching consequences. It is important to remember, however, that their impact is felt throughout the organization. The discussion of task design in Chapter 5 focused on job definition and motivation and gave little attention to implementing changes in jobs. Here we discuss task redesign as a mode of organization change.

Several approaches to introducing job changes in organizations have been proposed. One is by a coauthor of this book, Ricky W. Griffin. Griffin's approach is an integrative framework of nine steps that reflect the complexities of the interfaces between individual jobs and the total organization.[19] The process, shown in Table 15.2, includes the steps usually associated with change, such as recognizing the need for a change, selecting the appropriate intervention, and evaluating the change. But Griffin's approach inserts four additional steps into the standard sequence: diagnosis of the overall work system and context, including examination of the jobs, technology, organization design, leadership, and group dynamics; evaluating the costs and benefits of the change; formulating a redesign strategy; and implementing supplemental changes.

Diagnosis includes analysis of the total work environment within which the jobs exist. It is important to evaluate the organization structure, especially the work rules and decision-making authority within a department, when job changes are being considered.[20] For example, if jobs are to be redesigned to give employees more freedom in choosing work methods or scheduling work activities, diagnosis of the present system must determine whether the rules will allow that to happen. Diagnosis must also include evaluation of the work group and teams and intragroup dynamics (discussed in Chapter 8). Furthermore, it must determine whether workers have or can easily obtain the new skills to perform the redesigned task.

It is extremely important to recognize the full range of potential costs and benefits associated with a job redesign effort. Some are direct and quantifiable; others are indirect and not quantifiable. Redesign may involve unexpected costs or benefits; although

TABLE 15.2
 	
Integrated Framework for Implementation of Task Redesign in Organizations
	Step 1: Recognition of a need for a change
	Step 2: Selection of task redesign as a potential intervention
	Step 3: Diagnosis of the work system and context
	    a. Diagnosis of existing jobs
	    b. Diagnosis of existing work force
	    c. Diagnosis of technology
	    d. Diagnosis of organization design
	    e. Diagnosis of leader behaviour
	    f. Diagnosis of group and social processes
	Step 4: Cost-benefit analysis of proposed changes
	Step 5: Go/no-go decision
	Step 6: Formulation of the strategy for redesign
	Step 7: Implementation of the task changes
	Step 8: Implementation of any supplemental changes
	Step 9: Evaluation of the task redesign effort
	
	Source: Ricky W. Griffin, *Task Design: An Integrative Framework* (Glenview, Ill.: Scott, Foresman, 1982), p. 208. Used by permission.

these cannot be predicted with certainty, they can be weighed as possibilities. Factors such as short-term role ambiguity, role conflict, and role overload can be major stumbling blocks to a job redesign effort.

Implementing a redesign scheme takes careful planning, and developing a strategy for the intervention is the final planning step. Strategy formulation is a four-part process. First, the organization must decide who will design the changes. Depending on the circumstances, the planning team may consist of only upper-level management or may include line workers and supervisors. Next, the team undertakes the actual design of the changes based on job design theory and the needs, goals, and circumstances of the organization. Third, the team decides the timing of the implementation, which may require a formal transition period during which equipment is purchased and installed, job training takes place, new physical layouts are arranged, and the bugs in the new system are worked out. Fourth, strategy planners must consider whether the job changes require adjustments and supplemental changes in other organizational components, such as reporting relationships and the compensation system.

Group and Individual Change

Groups and individuals can be involved in organization change in a vast number of ways. Retraining a single employee can be considered an organization change if the training affects the way the employee does his or her job. Familiarizing managers with the Vroom-Yetton-Jago decision tree (Chapter 11) is an attempt at change. In the first case, the goal is to balance management concerns for production and people; in the second, the goal is to increase the participation of rank-and-file employees in the organization's decision making. In this section, we present an overview of four popular types of people-oriented change techniques: training, management development programs, team building, and survey feedback.

Training   Training generally is designed to improve employees' job skills. Employees may be trained to run certain machines, taught new mathematical skills, or acquainted with personal growth and development methods. Stress management programs are becoming popular for helping employees, particularly executives, understand organizational stress and develop ways to cope with it.[21] Training can

David Hunt, assistant director of the Language Training Centre, teaches Spanish during a class for workers at Delta faucet in Indianapolis. This will allow employees to better interact, and relate to, Hispanic coworkers.

also be used in conjunction with other, more comprehensive organization changes. For instance, if an organization is implementing a management-by-objectives program, training in establishing goals and reviewing goal-oriented performance is probably needed. One important type of training that is becoming increasingly common is training people to work in other countries. Companies such as Motorola give extensive training programs to employees at all levels before they start an international assignment. Training includes intensive language courses, cultural courses, and courses for the family.

Among the many training methods, the most common are lecture, discussion, a lecture-discussion combination, experiential methods, case studies, and films or videotapes. Training can take place in a standard classroom, either on company property or in a hotel, at a resort, or at a conference centre. On-the-job training provides a different type of experience in which the trainee learns from an experienced worker. Most training programs use a combination of methods determined by the topic, the trainees, the trainer, and the organization.

A major problem of training programs is transferring employee learning to the workplace. Often an employee learns a new skill or a manager learns a new management technique but upon returning to the normal work situation finds it easier to go back to the old way of doing things. As we discussed earlier, the process of refreezing is a vital part of the change process, and some way must be found to make the accomplishments of the training program permanent.

Management Development Programs   Management development programs, like employee training programs, attempt to foster certain skills, abilities, and perspectives. Often, when a highly qualified technical person is promoted to manager of a work group, he or she lacks training in how to manage or deal with people. In such cases, management development programs can be important to organizations, both for the new manager and for his or her subordinates.

> **Management development programs** attempt to develop managers' skills, abilities, and perspectives.

Typically, management development programs use the lecture-discussion method to some extent but rely most heavily on participative methods, such as case studies and role playing. Participative and experiential methods allow the manager to experience the problems of being a manager as well as the feelings of frustration, doubt, and success that are part of the job. The subject matter of this type of training program is problematic, however, in that management skills, including communication, problem diagnosis, problem solving, and performance appraisal, are not as easy to identify or to transfer from a classroom to the workplace as the skills required to run a machine. In addition, rapid changes in the external environment can make certain managerial skills obsolete in a very short time. As a result, some companies are approaching the development of their management team as an ongoing, career-long process and require their managers to attend refresher courses periodically.

One training approach involves managers in an intense exercise that simulates the daily operation of a real company. Such simulations emphasize problem-solving behaviour rather than competitive tactics and usually involve extensive debriefing, in which a manager's style is openly discussed and criticized by trained observers as the first step to improvement. IBM and AT&T have commissioned experts to create a simulation specifically for their managers. Although the cost of custom simulations is high, it is reportedly repaid in benefits from individual development.[22]

As corporate North America invests hundreds of millions of dollars in management development, certain guiding principles are evolving: (1) management development is a multifaceted, complex, and long-term process to which there is no quick or simple approach; (2) organizations should carefully and systematically identify their unique developmental needs and evaluate their programs accordingly; (3) management development objectives must be compatible with organizational objectives; and

(4) the utility and value of management development remain more an article of faith than a proven fact.[23]

Team Building   When interaction among group members is critical to group success and effectiveness, team development, or team building, may be useful. *Team building* emphasizes members' working together in a spirit of cooperation and generally has one or more of the following goals:

1. To set team goals and priorities
2. To analyze or allocate the way work is performed
3. To examine how a group is working—that is, to examine processes such as norms, decision making, and communications
4. To examine relationships among the people doing the work[24]

Total quality management efforts usually focus on teams, and the principles of team building must be applied to make them work. Team participation is especially important in the data-gathering and evaluation phases of team development. In data gathering, the members share information on the functioning of the group.

The opinions of the group thus form the foundation of the development process. In the evaluation phase, members are the source of information about the effectiveness of the development effort.[25]

Like total quality management and many other management techniques, team building should not be thought of as a one-time experience, perhaps something undertaken on a retreat from the workplace; rather, it is a continuing process. It may take weeks, months, or years for a group to learn to pull together and function as a team. Team development can be a way to train the group to solve its own problems in the future. Research on the effectiveness of team building as an organization development tool so far is mixed and inconclusive. For more details on developing teams in organizations, please refer to Chapter 8.

In this photo, managers of Motorola are working on their presentation skills with members of Second City Communications. This training combines improvisational skills—those most often associated with comedy—to help workers communicate more effectively.

Survey Feedback   Survey feedback techniques can form the basis for a change process. In this process, data are gathered, analyzed, summarized, and returned to those who generated them to identify, discuss, and solve problems. A survey feedback process is often set in motion by either the organization's top management or by a consultant to management. By providing information about employees' beliefs and attitudes, a survey can help management diagnose and solve an organization's problems. A consultant or change agent usually coordinates the process and is responsible for data gathering, analysis, and summary. The three-stage process is shown in Figure 15.4.[26]

The use of survey feedback techniques in an organization development process differs from their use in traditional attitude surveys. In an organization development process, data are (1) returned to employee groups at all levels in the organization and (2) used by all employees working together in their normal work groups to identify and solve problems. In traditional attitude surveys, top management reviews the data and may or may not initiate a new program to solve problems the survey has identified.

In the data-gathering stage, the change agent interviews selected personnel from appropriate levels to determine the key issues to be examined. Information from these interviews is used to develop a survey questionnaire that is distributed to a large sample of employees. The questionnaire may be a standardized instrument, an instrument developed specifically for the organization, or a combination of the two. The questionnaire data are analyzed and aggregated by group or department to ensure that respondents remain anonymous.[27] Then the change agent prepares a summary of the results for the group feedback sessions. From this point on, the consultant is involved in the process as a resource person and expert.

The feedback meetings generally involve only two or three levels of management. Meetings are usually held serially, first with a meeting of the top management group followed by meetings of employees throughout the organization. Sessions typically are led by the group manager rather than the change agent, to transfer ownership of the data from the change agent to the work group. The feedback consists primarily of profiles of the group's attitudes toward the organization, the work, the leadership, and other topics on the questionnaire. During the feedback sessions, participants discuss reasons for the scores and the problems that the data reveal.

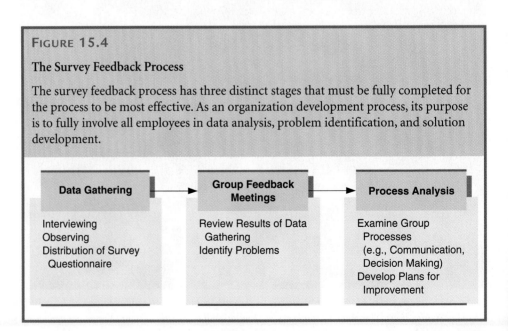

FIGURE 15.4

The Survey Feedback Process

The survey feedback process has three distinct stages that must be fully completed for the process to be most effective. As an organization development process, its purpose is to fully involve all employees in data analysis, problem identification, and solution development.

Data Gathering	Group Feedback Meetings	Process Analysis
Interviewing Observing Distribution of Survey Questionnaire	Review Results of Data Gathering Identify Problems	Examine Group Processes (e.g., Communication, Decision Making) Develop Plans for Improvement

In the process analysis stage, the group examines the process of making decisions, communicating, and accomplishing work, usually with the help of the consultant. Unfortunately, groups often overlook this stage as they become absorbed in the survey data and the problems revealed during the feedback sessions. Occasionally, group managers simply fail to hold feedback and process analysis sessions. Change agents should ensure that managers hold these sessions and that they are rewarded for doing so. The process analysis stage is important because its purpose is to develop action plans to make improvements. Several sessions may be required to discuss the process issues fully and settle on a strategy for improvements. Groups often find it useful to document the plans as they are discussed and to appoint a member to follow up on implementation. Generally, the follow-up assesses whether communication and communication processes have actually been improved. A follow-up survey can be administered several months to a year later to assess how much these processes have changed since they were first reported.

The survey feedback method is probably one of the most widely used organization change and development interventions. If any of its stages are compromised or omitted, however, the technique becomes less useful. A primary responsibility of the consultant or change agent, then, is to ensure that the method is fully and faithfully carried through.

Resistance to Change

Change is inevitable; so is resistance to change. Paradoxically, organizations both promote and resist change. As an agent for change, the organization asks prospective customers or clients to change their current purchasing habits by switching to the company's product or service and asks current customers to change by increasing their purchases. The organization resists change in that its structure and control systems protect the daily tasks of producing a product or service from uncertainties in the environment. The organization must have some elements of permanence to avoid mirroring the instability of the environment. Yet it must also react to external shifts with internal change to maintain currency and relevance in the marketplace.

> Resistance to change within the organization can come from sources that are either external or internal to the organization.

A commonly held view is that all resistance to change needs to be overcome, but that is not always the case. Resistance to change can be used for the benefit of the organization and need not be eliminated entirely. By revealing a legitimate concern that a proposed change may harm the organization or that other alternatives might be better, resistance may alert the organization to re-examine the change.[28] For example, an organization may be considering acquiring a company in a completely different industry. Resistance to such a proposal may cause the organization to examine the advantages and disadvantages of the move more carefully. Without resistance, the decision might be made before the pros and cons have been sufficiently explored.

> Managing resistance to change means working with the sources of resistance rather than trying to overpower or overcome resistance.

Resistance may come from the organization, the individual, or both. Determining the ultimate source is often difficult, however, because organizations are composed of individuals. Table 15.3 summarizes various types of organizational and individual sources of resistance.

Organizational Sources of Resistance

Daniel Katz and Robert Kahn have identified six major organizational sources of resistance: overdetermination, narrow focus of change, group inertia, threatened expertise, threatened power, and changes in resource allocation.[29] Of course, not every organization or every change situation displays all six sources.

TABLE 15.3

Organizational and Individual Sources of Resistance

Organizational Sources	Examples
Overdetermination	Employment system, job descriptions, evaluation and reward system
Narrow Focus of Change	Structure changed with no concern given to other issues, e.g., jobs, people
Group Inertia	Group norms
Threatened Expertise	People move out of area of expertise
Threatened Power	Decentralized decision making
Resource Allocation	Increased use of part-time help

Individual Sources	Examples
Habit	Altered tasks
Security	Altered tasks or reporting relationships
Economic Factors	Changed pay and benefits
Fear of the Unknown	New job, new boss
Lack of Awareness	Isolated groups not heeding notices
Social Factors	Group norms

Overdetermination   Organizations have several systems designed to maintain stability. For example, consider how organizations control employees' performance. Job candidates must have certain specific skills so that they can do the job the organization needs them to do. New employees are given a job description, and the supervisor trains, coaches, and counsels the employee in job tasks. The new employee usually serves some type of probationary period that culminates in a performance review; thereafter, the employee's performance is regularly evaluated. Finally, rewards, punishment, and discipline are administered depending on the level of performance. Such a system is said to be characterized by **overdetermination**, or *structural inertia*,[30] in that employee performance could probably be evaluated with fewer procedures and safeguards. In other words, the structure of the organization produces resistance to change because it was designed to maintain stability.

Overdetermination occurs because numerous organizational systems are in place to ensure that employees and systems behave as expected to maintain stability.

Narrow Focus of Change   Many efforts to create change in organizations adopt too narrow a focus. Any effort to force change in the tasks of individuals or groups must take into account the interdependencies among organizational elements such as people, structure, tasks, and the information system. For example, some attempts at redesigning jobs fail because the organization structure within which jobs must function is inappropriate for the redesigned jobs.[31]

Group Inertia   When an employee attempts to change his or her work behaviour, the group may resist by refusing to change other behaviours that are necessary complements to the individual's changed behaviour. In other words, group norms may act as a brake on individual attempts at behaviour change.

Threatened Expertise   A change in the organization may threaten the specialized expertise that individuals and groups have developed over the years. A job redesign or a structural change may transfer responsibility for a specialized task from the current expert to someone else, threatening the specialist's expertise and building his or her resistance to the change.

Threatened Power   Any redistribution of decision-making authority, such as with re-engineering or team-based management, may threaten an individual's power relationships with others. If an organization is decentralizing its decision making, managers who wielded their decision-making powers in return for special favours from others may resist the change because they do not want to lose their power base.

Resource Allocation   Groups that are satisfied with current resource allocation methods may resist any change they believe will threaten future allocations. Resources in this context can mean anything from monetary rewards and equipment to additional seasonal help to more computer time.

These six sources explain most types of organization-based resistance to change. All are based on people and social relationships. Many of these sources of resistance can be traced to groups or individuals being afraid of losing something—resources, power, or comfort in a routine.

Individual Sources of Resistance

Individual sources of resistance to change are rooted in basic human characteristics such as needs and perceptions. Researchers have identified six reasons for individual resistance to change: habit, security, economic factors, fear of the unknown, lack of awareness, and social factors (see Table 15.3).[32]

Habit   It is easier to do a job the same way every day if the steps in the job are repeated over and over. Learning an entirely new set of steps makes the job more difficult. For the same amount of return (pay), most people prefer to do easier rather than harder work.

Security   Some employees like the comfort and security of doing things the same old way. They gain a feeling of constancy and safety from knowing that some things stay the same despite all the change going on around them. People who believe their security is threatened by a change are likely to resist the change.

Economic Factors   Change may threaten employees' steady paycheques. Workers may fear that change will make their jobs obsolete or reduce their opportunities for future pay increases.

Fear of the Unknown   Some people fear anything unfamiliar. Changes in reporting relationships and job duties create anxiety for such employees. Employees become familiar with their bosses and their jobs and develop relationships with others within the organization, such as contact people for various situations. These relationships and contacts help facilitate their work. Any disruption of familiar patterns may create fear because it can cause delays and foster the belief that nothing is getting accomplished.

Lack of Awareness   Because of perceptual limitations, such as lack of attention or selective attention, a person may not recognize a change in a rule or procedure and thus may not alter his or her behaviour. People may pay attention only to things that support their point of view. As an example, employees in an isolated regional sales office may not notice—or may ignore—directives from headquarters regarding a change in reporting procedures for expense accounts. They may therefore continue the current practice as long as possible.

Social Factors   People may resist change for fear of what others will think. As we mentioned before, the group can be a powerful motivator of behaviour. Employees may believe change will hurt their image, result in ostracism from the group, or simply make them different. For example, an employee who agrees to conform to work rules established by management may be ridiculed by others who openly disobey the rules.

On the other hand, some people may not resist change. A study done by researchers at the University of Western Ontario found that some employees are more committed to change than others, but the nature of the commitment to change will affect the success of the change. The findings are explained in the Organizational Change and . . . Research box.

Managing Successful Organization Change and Development

In conclusion, we offer six keys to managing change in organizations. They relate directly to the problems identified earlier and to our view of the organization as a

Organizational Change and . . .   RESEARCH

Employee Commitment

Lynn Herscovitch who was then a PhD student, and John Meyer of the University of Western Ontario noted that employee commitment to change has frequently been argued to be essential for the success of a planned organizational change. However, there has been little research to either measure commitment to change or its importance for successful change.

Building upon previous research into organizational commitment and a more general model of commitment (see chapter 3), they developed a three-component theory and measurement of commitment to change. Affective commitment occurs when individuals desire the change and want to support it. Continuance commitment to change is evident when people feel that not supporting a change can be costly. People have a normative commitment to change when they feel obliged to make the change for some reason. In short, the three forms of commitment can be summarized that ". . . employees can feel bound to support a change because they want to, have to and/or ought to."

Commitment, the authors state, should be able to predict two types of behaviour. Focal behaviours are those that result from people being bound by commitment. In the context of organizational change, the main focal behaviour is compliance with the formal requirements of the change. Resistance, on the other hand, is a failure to comply. Discretionary behaviours are not actually formally required by the change, they are more voluntary in nature. Cooperating with or championing a change attempt are examples of discretionary behaviours.

After performing a simulation study using university students to validate the commitment to change survey

instrument, Herscovitch and Meyer did two additional surveys, both using hospital nurses as subjects. The nurses were asked to describe a recent or current organizational change that affected them, and to complete the surveys that assessed their commitment and their behavioural responses to the change.

The combined results showed that all three components of commitment to change were related to compliance with the formal requirements of the change. They also found, as they predicted, that only affective and normative commitment to change predicted the more discretionary behaviours of cooperation and championing the change.

The implications from their study are first, that although any form of commitment apparently predicts compliance, compliance alone is unlikely to lead to a truly successful change. Real change will require cooperation and champions. As a consequence, the second implication is that affective and normative commitment to change should be fostered in order to make effective changes. This can be done through the mechanisms described in this chapter—by having people participate in the decision making leading up to the change, and reinforcing positive behaviours and attitudes towards the change. Finally, as with many other studies, this research demonstrates that changes cannot simply be dictated. Individuals' emotions and attitudes must be taken into account.

Source: Lynn Herscovitch and John P. Meyer, "Commitment to Organizational Change: Extension of a Three Component Model," *Journal of Applied Psychology*, 2002, vol. 87, pp. 474–487, quotation p. 475.

Key	Impact
Consider international issues.	Global competition is a force for change, and change is accepted differently in different cultures.
Take a holistic view of the organization.	Anticipate effects on social system and culture.
Secure top management support.	Get dominant coalition on the side of change, safeguard structural change, head off problems of power and control.
Encourage participation by those affected by the change.	Minimize transition problems of control, resistance, and task redefinition.
Foster open communication.	Minimize transition problems of resistance and information and control systems.
Reward those who contribute to change.	Minimize transition problems of resistance and control systems.

TABLE 15.4

Managing Successful Organization Change and Development

comprehensive social system. Each can influence the elements of the social system and may help the organization avoid some of the major problems in managing the change. Table 15.4 lists the points and their potential impacts.

International Influences

One factor to consider is how international environments dictate organization change. As we already noted, the environment is a significant factor in bringing about organization change. Given the additional environmental complexities multinational organizations face, it follows that organization change may be even more critical to them than to purely domestic organizations.

A second point to remember is that acceptance of change varies widely around the globe. Change is a normal and accepted part of organization life in some cultures. In other cultures, change causes many more problems. Managers should remember that techniques for managing change that have worked routinely back home may not work at all and may even trigger negative responses if used indiscriminately in other cultures.[33]

Take a Holistic View

Managers must take a holistic view of the organization and the change project. A limited view can endanger the change effort because the subsystems of the organization are interdependent. A holistic view encompasses the culture and dominant coalition as well as the people, tasks, structure, and information subsystems.

Secure Top Management Support

The support of top management is essential to the success of any change effort. As the organization's probable dominant coalition, it is a powerful element of the social system, and its support is necessary to deal with control and power problems. For example, a manager who plans a change in the ways tasks are assigned and responsibility is delegated in his or her department must notify top management and gain its support. Complications can arise if disgruntled employees complain to high-level managers who have not been notified of the change or do not support it. The employees' complaints might jeopardize the manager's plan—and perhaps her or his job.

Successfully managing organization change means taking a holistic view of the organization, obtaining top management support, encouraging participation by all those affected, fostering open communication, and rewarding those who contribute to the change effort.

Encourage Participation

Problems related to resistance, control, and power can be overcome by broad participation in planning the change. Allowing people a voice in designing the change may give them a sense of power and control over their own destinies, which can help to win their support during implementation.

Foster Open Communication

Open communication is an important factor in managing resistance to change and overcoming information and control problems during transitions. Employees typically recognize the uncertainties and ambiguities that arise during a transition and seek information on the change and their place in the new system. In the absence of information, the gap may be filled with inappropriate or false information that can endanger the change process. Rumours tend to spread through the grapevine faster than accurate information can be disseminated through official channels. A manager should always be sensitive to the effects of uncertainty on employees, especially in a period of change; any news, even bad news, seems better than no news.

Reward Contributors

Although this last point is simple, it can easily be neglected. Employees who contribute to the change in any way need to be rewarded. Too often, the only people acknowledged after a change effort are those who tried to stop it. Those who quickly grasp new work assignments, work harder to cover what otherwise might not get done in the transition, or help others adjust to changes deserve special credit—perhaps a mention in a news release or the internal company newspaper, special consideration in a performance appraisal, a merit raise, or a promotion. From a behavioural perspective, individuals need to benefit in some way if they are to willingly help change something that eliminates the old, comfortable way of doing the job.

In the current dynamic environment, managers must anticipate the need for change and satisfy it with more responsive and competitive organization systems. These six keys to managing organization change can also serve as general guidelines for managing organizational behaviour, because organizations must change or face elimination.

Summary of Key Points

■ Change may be forced on an organization, or an organization may change in response to the environment or an internal need. Forces for change are interdependent and influence organizations in many ways. Currently, the areas in which the pressures for change seem most powerful involve people, technology, information and communication, competition, and social trends.

■ Planned organization change involves anticipating change and preparing for it. Lewin described organization change in terms of unfreezing, the change itself, and refreezing. In the continuous change process model, top management recognizes forces encouraging change, engages in a problem-solving process to design the change, and implements and evaluates the change.

■ Organization development is the process of planned change and improvement of organizations through the application of knowledge of the behavioural sciences. It is based on a systematic change process and focuses on managing the culture of the organization. The most comprehensive change involves altering the structure of the organization through a reorganization of departments, reporting relationships, or authority systems.

■ Quality-of-worklife programs focus on providing a work environment in which employees can satisfy individual needs. Task and technological changes alter the way the organization accomplishes its primary tasks. Along with the steps usually associated with change, task redesign entails diagnosis, cost-benefit analysis, formulation of a redesign strategy, and implementation of supplemental changes.

■ Frequently used group and individual approaches to organization change are training and management development programs, team building, and survey feedback techniques. Training programs are usually designed to improve employees' job skills, to help employees adapt to other organization changes (such as a management-by-objectives program), or to develop employees' awareness and understanding of problems such as workplace safety or stress. Management development programs attempt to foster in current or future managers the skills, abilities, and perspectives important to good management. Team-building programs are designed to help a work team or group develop into a mature, functioning team by helping it define its goals or priorities, analyze its tasks and the way they are performed, and examine relationships among the people doing the work. As used in the organization development process, survey feedback techniques involve gathering data, analyzing and summarizing them, and returning them to employees and groups for discussion and to identify and solve problems.

■ Resistance to change can arise from several individual and organizational sources. Resistance may indicate a legitimate concern that the change is not good for the organization and warrant a re-examination of plans.

■ To manage change in organizations, international issues must be considered and managers should take a holistic view of the organization. Top management support is needed, and those most affected must participate. Open communication is important, and those who contribute to the change effort should be rewarded.

Discussion Questions

1. Is most organization change forced on the organization by external factors or fostered from within? Explain.

2. What broad category of pressures for organization change other than the five discussed in the chapter can you think of? Briefly describe it.

3. Which sources of resistance to change present the most problems for an internal change agent? For an external change agent?

4. Which stage of the Lewin model of change do you think is most often overlooked? Why?

5. What are the advantages and disadvantages of having an internal change agent rather than an external change agent?

6. How does organization development differ from organization change?

7. How and why would organization development differ if the elements of the social system were not interdependent?

8. Do quality-of-worklife programs rely more on individual or organizational aspects of organizational behaviour? Why?

9. Describe how the job of your professor could be re-designed. Include a discussion of other subsystems that would need to be changed as a result.

10. Which of the five suggestions for successfully managing an organizational change effort seem to be the most difficult to manage? Why?

Experiencing Organizational Behaviour

Purpose: This exercise will help you understand the complexities of change in organizations.

Format: Your task is to plan the implementation of a major change in an organization.

Procedure:

Part 1

The class will divide into five groups of approximately equal size. Your instructor will assign each group one of the following changes:

1. A change from the semester system to the quarter system (or the opposite, depending on the school's current system).

2. A requirement that all work—homework, examinations, term papers, problem sets—be done on computer.

3. A requirement that all students live on campus.

4. A requirement that all students have reading, writing, and speaking fluency in at least three languages, including English (or French) and Chinese, to graduate.

5. A requirement that all students room with someone in the same major.

First, decide what individuals and groups must be involved in the change process. Then decide how the change will be implemented using Lewin's process of organization change (Figure 15.1) as a framework. Consider how to deal with resistance to change, using Tables 15.3 and 15.4 as guides. Decide whether a change agent (internal or external) should be used. Develop a realistic timetable for full implementation of the change. Is transition management appropriate?

Part 2

Using the same groups as in Part 1, your next task is to describe the techniques you would use to implement the change described in Part 1. You may use structural changes, task and technology methods, group and individual programs, or any combination of these. You may need to go to the library to gather more information on some techniques.

You should also discuss how you will utilize the five keys to successful change management discussed at the end of the chapter.

Your instructor may make this exercise an in-class project, but it is also a good semester-ending project for groups to work on outside class. Either way, the exercise is most beneficial when the groups report their implementation programs to the entire class. Each group should report on which change techniques are to be used, why they were selected, how they will be implemented, and how problems will be avoided.

Follow-up Questions

Part 1

1. How similar were the implementation steps for each change?

2. Were the plans for managing resistance to change realistic?

3. Do you think any of the changes could be successfully implemented at your school? Why or why not?

Part 2

1. Did various groups use the same technique in different ways or to accomplish different goals?

2. If you did outside research on organization development techniques for your project, did you find any techniques that seemed more applicable than those in this chapter? If so, describe one of them.

Support for Change/Introduction

The questions below are designed to help people understand the level of support or opposition to change within an organization. Scores on this scale should be used for classroom discussion only.

Instructions: Think of an organization that you have worked for in the past or an organization to which you currently belong, and consider the situation when a change was imposed at some point in the recent past. Then check the space that best represents your feeling about each statement or question.

1. Values and Vision

    (Do people throughout the organization share values or vision?)

2. History of Change

    (Does the organization have a good track record in handling change?)

    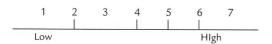

3. Cooperation and Trust

    (Do they seem high throughout the organization?)

    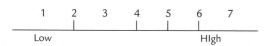

4. Culture

    (Is it one that supports risk taking and change?)

    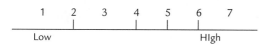

5. Resilience

    (Can people handle more?)

    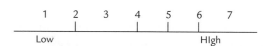

6. Rewards

    (Will this change be seen as beneficial?)

    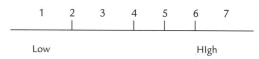

7. Respect and Face

    (Will people be able to maintain dignity and self-respect?)

8. Status Quo

    (Will this change be seen as mild?)

A guide to scoring and explanation is available in the Instructor's Resource Manual.

Source: Beyond the Wall of Resistance: Unconventional Strategies That Build Support for Change. © 1996, by Rick Maurer (Austin: Bard Press, 1996), pp. 104–105. Reprinted by permission. For order information, contact: www.bardpress.com.

Toyota Reinvented

In 2003, Toyota Motors was catching up with the Big Three U.S. automakers—GM, Ford, and Chrysler. It was a risky strategy to overtake the industry's largest competitors, but one that would pay off with a gradual increase in sales and profits. What did Toyota do next? The company immediately set out to reinvent itself.

One of the first changes was the introduction of a host of new designs. Although an early version of the hybrid-fuel Prius came to the American market in 2000, an improved design was unveiled in 2004. Ford licensed Toyota's hybrid technology because, "Toyota is ahead of the game. Ford is playing catch up," claim writers James Mackintosh and Michiyo Nakamoto. Toyota capitalized on the popularity of the hybrid Prius by introducing the world's first hybrid luxury sport-utility vehicle, the RX 400h. Toyota engineers in Europe designed the compact Yaris for sale there. The Yaris is now being imported to Japan for sale to buyers who prefer a European look. Sales of the Scion, designed for hip younger buyers, are double Toyota's initial prediction.

Toyota has a reputation as one of the world's leading cost-cutters, beginning with the company's invention of the *kaizen* (continuous improvement) and *kanban* (just-in-time inventory) systems. Even so, managers have begun to search even more diligently for ways to reduce expenses. Katsuaki Watanabe, executive vice president, targeted 180 key parts and asked for a 30 percent price reduction. No part was too small, or too large. Designers cut the number of parts in a door grip from thirty-four to five, reducing purchasing costs by 40 percent and installation time by 75 percent. From 2000 to 2005, Toyota cut costs by $10 billion, without any layoffs or plant closings, and it plans to cut another $2 billion this year.

Toyota is making a number of low-tech changes to bring cost savings and improve speed and quality. One simple change requires designers, engineers, suppliers, and workers to meet face to face as they hash out the details of a new product design. An over-reliance on teleconferencing and e-mail was inefficient. It took Toyota just nineteen months to develop the new Solara, compared to the industry average of three years. However, the auto giant has not forgotten the high technology for which it is famous. The process technology has been improved with the change to a global production line that allows Toyota to build multiple models on the same production line at the same time. A robotic system assists workers in identifying defects, flashing lights when a mistake is spotted. Toyota's research and development budget has been steadily rising. In 2004, Toyota spent $15 billion on R&D, compared to $7 billion at GM and $7.4 at Ford.

Toyota is not content to make changes only in design, processes, and technology. The firm is also updating its organization structure and replacing many of its top managers. It is further integrating some of its other divisions, such as the business unit that is the biggest seller of single-family homes in Japan. Alliances with Peugeot and even GM are being revitalized and clarified. Katsuaki Watanabe, known for his aggressive cost-cutting and quality control measures, succeeded former CEO Fujio Cho when he retired in 2005. That choice was "part of a wide reshuffle designed to bring new blood to the ranks of upper management," according to business writer Chester Dawson. Watanabe's promotion signals Toyota's continuing commitment to change.

To support these many changes, Toyota leaders are updating the organization's culture. Toyota has often been accused of being too conservative in design, too focused on the Japanese market, and too timid and slow in adopting revolutionary innovations. Maryann Keller, an auto industry consultant, offers faint praise for Toyota, saying, "They find a hole and they plug it. They methodically study problems and they solve them." But that was about to change. Watanabe said, "I feel that being successful may make us arrogant and want to stay in a comfort zone. That is the threat." He plans on pushing for more reform, more openness, more alliances, more speed, and more risk taking. Former CEO Fujio Cho added, "This is a company that does not fear failure."

Toyota is racking up win after win. The Prius was named North American Car of the Year for 2004. That year also showed Toyota producing more than 30 percent of the new cars sold in America, a record high, and in 2006 becoming the world's largest car maker. According to writers David Welch and Dan Beucke, "Toyota Motor Corp., Nissan Motor Corp., and other more nimble competitors ate GM's lunch." Growth has not come at the expense of profits—operating profit margins at Toyota were an impressive 9.4 percent in December 2004. The company also has $30 billion in liquid assets, to fuel further R&D and growth. Reinvention, at Toyota, looks like a winning strategy.

Case Questions

1. What are the forces acting for change in the auto industry?

2. What areas of Toyota are undergoing organization change? Give an example of a change taking place in each area.

3. In your opinion, are Toyota workers likely to resist the changes? Why or why not? How might Toyota help workers overcome their resistance to change?

Sources: "Scoring the World's Carmakers," Standard and Poor's Ratings News, www2.standardandpoors.com on May 4, 2005; "Toyota, Nissan Lift U.S. Auto Sales—SUV Sales Slide," *Agence France Presse*, dailynews.yahoo.com on May 4, 2005; Jeff Bennett, "New Direction for Lexus," *Detroit Free Press*, January 7, 2004, www.freep.com on May 4, 2005; Brian Bremmer and Chester Dawson, "Can Anything Top Toyota?" *Business Week*, November 17, 2003, pp. 114–122 (quotation); Chester Dawson, "The New Boss Driving Toyota," *Business Week*, February 10, 2005, www.businessweek.com on May 4, 2005; Gail Edmondson, "Revved Up For Battle," *Business Week*, January 10, 2005, www.businessweek.com on May 4, 2005; James Mackintosh and Michiyo Nakamoto, "Japanese Carmakers Reach Milestone: 30 Percent of U.S. Auto Sales," *The Financial Times*, January 6, 2005, www.newstarget.com on May 4, 2005; Jathon Sapsford, "Toyota Revs Up Operations to Rival GM as No. 1," *The Wall Street Journal*, November 2, 2004, pp. A1, A12; David Welch and Dan Beucke, "Why GM's Plan Won't Work," *Business Week*, May 9, 2005, pp. 85–93.

**Organizational Behaviour
Case for Discussion**

Spooked by Computers

The Maritimes Arts Project had its headquarters above an Italian restaurant in Halifax, Nova Scotia. The project had five full-time employees and, during busy times of the year, particularly the month before Christmas, it hired as many as six part-time workers to write letters, address envelopes by hand, and send out mailings. Although each of the five full-timers had a title and a formal job description, an observer would have had trouble telling their positions apart. Suzanne McIsaac, for instance, was the executive director, the head of the office, but she could be found keyboarding or licking envelopes just as often as Martin Welk, who had been working for less than a year as office coordinator, the lowest position in the project's hierarchy.

Despite a constant sense of being a month behind, the office ran relatively smoothly. No outsider would have had a prayer of finding a mailing list or a budget in the office, but project employees knew where almost everything was, and after a quiet fall they did not mind having their small space packed with workers in November. But a number of the federal and provincial funding agencies on which the project relied began to grumble about the cost of the part-time workers, the amount of time the project spent handling routine paperwork, and the chaotic condition of its financial records. The pressure to make a radical change was on. Finally Martin Welk said it: "Maybe we should computerize our records—you know, build a database to process mail more quickly and build spreadsheets to do the budget."

To Welk, fresh out of university, where he had written his papers on a word processor, computers were just another tool to make a job easier. But his belief was not shared by the others in the office, the youngest of whom had 15 years more seniority than he. A computer would not speed up the project's mailing processes, and since the mailing list changed so frequently, they would spend more time updating the list than they would simply inputting addresses on individual letters and envelopes. A computerized database could send the wrong things to the wrong people, insulting them and convincing them that the project had become another faceless organization that did not care. They swapped horror stories about incorrect computer-generated mailings that had charged them thousands of dollars for purchases they had never made or had assigned the same airplane seat to five people.

"We'll lose all control," Suzanne McIsaac complained. She knew that the office needed more automation, yet she kept thinking she would probably quit before it came about. She liked hand-addressing mailings to arts patrons whom she had met, and she felt sure that the recipients contributed more because they recognized her neat blue printing. She remembered the agonies of typing class in high school and later struggling just to learn simple word processing software and believed she was too old to take on something new and bound to be much more confusing. Two other employees, with whom she had worked for a decade, called her after work to ask if the prospect of more automated systems in the office meant they should be looking for other jobs. "I have enough trouble with English grammar," one of them wailed. "I'll never be able to learn Access or Excel or whatever these new languages are."

One morning McIsaac called Martin Welk into her office, shut the door, and asked him if he could recommend any computer consultants. She had read an article that explained how a company could waste thousands of dollars by adopting integrated office automation in the wrong way, and she figured the project would have to

hire somebody for at least six months to get new machines working and to teach the staff how to use them. Welk was pleased because McIsaac evidently had accepted the idea of using modern software in the office. But he also realized that as the resident authority on computers, he had a lot of work to do before they went shopping for systems.

Case Questions

1. Is organization development appropriate in this situation? Why or why not?

2. What kinds of resistance to change have the employees of the project displayed?

3. What can Martin Welk do to overcome the resistance?

SELF TEST

You have read the chapter and studied the key terms. Think you're ready to ace the exam? Take this sample test to gauge your comprehension of chapter material and check your answers at the back of the book. Want more test questions? Take the ACE quizzes found on the student website: www.hmco.ca/ob.

T   F   1. Baby boomers differ from previous generations in terms of their education; however, they hold similar value systems.

T   F   2. Advances in information processing and communication have actually slowed business operations because of the extra time needed to enter data.

T   F   3. A change agent may come from inside or outside the organization.

T   F   4. Quality-of-work-life programs are used by medical research firms to extend the average career length of working adults.

T   F   5. A major problem of training programs is transferring employee learning to the workplace.

T   F   6. Managers should learn that all resistance to change needs to be overcome.

T   F   7. Truly successful, systemwide changes in large organizations start off small.

8. Which of the following is not one of the major categories of pressures that influence organizations to change?
a. competition
b. information processing and communication
c. legislation
d. technology
e. people

9. Most markets are now global because of
a. limits on competition.
b. emergent organizational change.
c. planned organizational change.
d. decreasing transportation and communication costs.
e. smaller domestic markets.

10. Brian has been assigned the role of transition manager as part of a change effort in his company. Brian's role will likely involve which of the following?
a. Act as a liaison between the organization and its competitors during the change.
b. Bridge the gap between potential and actual performance.
c. Change the organization back to the way it was initially.
d. Deal with unintended consequences of the change.
e. Eliminate resistance to the change.

11. Quality-of-worklife programs generally result in which of the following benefits?
a. limited resistance to change
b. increased job satisfaction
c. a shorter "refreezing" stage
d. fewer unintended consequences of change
e. innovative technological change

12. Daniel wants to analyze the way work is performed, examine relationships among the people doing the work, and examine how the work groups he supervises are working. Daniel ought to consider which of the following change techniques?
a. training
b. management development programs
c. team building
d. survey feedback
e. total quality management

13. Structural inertia means
a. the culture of the organization has initiated a change effort.
b. the technology of the organization has become obsolete but is still in use.
c. the strategy of the organization is to resist change for as long as possible, but not indefinitely.
d. the people in the organization have adopted a positive attitude toward organizational change efforts.
e. the structure of the organization produces resistance because it was designed to maintain stability.

14. Open communication during a change effort is important because
a. in the absence of accurate information, the gap may be filled with rumours and false information.
b. open communication can replace the need for top management support.
c. it allows an organization to begin its change effort on a small scale.
d. a holistic view requires communication among lower-level employees.
e. employees are used to open communication during periods of stability.

Structure and Success at Starbucks

Founder Howard Schultz purchased Starbucks Coffee Company in 1985 and transformed the little company into one of the most powerful retailing operations in the world. Along with individual and interpersonal forces, organizational factors play a significant role in Starbucks' success.

For the last two decades, the firm's organizational structure has remained the same. At the lowest level, stores are organized into regions. Regional managers report to one of two executive vice presidents, one for the United States and one for international locations. Top managers oversee support functions such as purchasing, marketing, legal, human resources, and information resources. Other groups at the highest level of the company oversee corporate social responsibility and organization culture. Starbucks also has high-level executives in charge of innovation. They focus on emerging businesses and the company's new entertainment ventures.

To attain economies of scale and to ensure consistent quality, most decisions, such as purchasing coffee, developing drinks, store design, and so on, are centralized. Company policies are centrally determined to ensure fairness. However, some decisions are decentralized. Store managers hire and evaluate baristas, and local managers are responsible for ensuring that operational goals are met. Starbucks uses the distinction between centralized and decentralized issues to allow decisions to be made at the most appropriate level—the level where the decision makers are most involved in gathering information and implementing the decision.

The organization design that Starbucks has evolved relies on differentiation strategy; Starbucks presents itself as a distinctive and superior company. The organization design supports the company's differentiation strategy by offering unique and desirable features to customers. These include selling high-quality products, providing excellent customer service, and creating an upscale, entertaining environment. Another important part of Starbucks' strategy is growth. Again, the organization design is simple and consists of multiple small, one-store units. This structure makes it easy to add stores, accommodating growth.

The relative youth of the firm is another important factor affecting organization structure. Starbucks began its current strategic direction just eighteen years ago. Therefore, the organization structure is fairly simple. Although the company has grown tremendously, it does not have many layers of management for a firm of its size. Middle managers and support staff are fewer than in older, more established firms. However, as Starbucks grows and ages, a more complex organization structure will be required. Already the firm is moving away from a simple structure, as defined by Mintzberg, toward a machine bureaucracy. A machine bureaucracy relies more on administrative coordination and standardization of work. At Starbucks, a machine bureaucracy structure is demonstrated when important decisions are made centrally and workers are trained to ensure product consistency.

Finally, the environment has a significant impact on organization structure. The quick-serve food industry, including technology, the economy, and competitors, is changing slowly. Since Starbucks itself is responsible for much of the change that has occurred in coffee houses in recent years (formulating new drinks, selling CDs), this makes the changes very easy for Starbucks to predict. An environment that is low in uncertainty allows Starbucks to concentrate attention internally. This leads to rapid growth, high efficiency, and innovation.

Along with an effective and evolving organization design, Starbucks has a unique organization culture. Schultz and other leaders at Starbucks understand the importance of organization culture in creating a successful firm. "It's extremely valuable to have people proud to work for Starbucks and we make decisions that are consistent with what our employees expect of us," Schultz says.

The culture began with the values held by founder Howard Schultz. He states again and again two important purposes for Starbucks: "to build a company with a soul" and "to pursue the perfect cup of coffee." Company executives, led by then CEO Schultz, wrote the first official statement about the organization culture in 1990.

The vision statement that resulted said, "Put people first and profits last." The mission statement elaborated further, laying out principles such as respect, diversity, and excellence. Many corporations uphold similar values, but Starbucks places a uniquely strong emphasis on ethics and social responsibility, as well as innovation.

The company has a number of policies that demonstrate its ethical treatment of workers. For example, every employee is referred to as a "partner." Workers, even many part-timers, receive generous benefits. The company is committed to a total pay package that provides a decent standard of living for its workers.

Starbucks is more transparent than most organizations. It shares financial and other information with workers, and it also actively solicits input and feedback from workers. It publishes several newsletters and has education programs for workers. A business conduct help line is available for anonymous help with questions about ethics and business conduct. Starbucks conducts a Mission Review program that encourages workers to submit reports and questions about the company's performance on the values stated in the firm's mission. In 2004, workers contacted the company 3500 times, resulting in many changes in operations and policies.

Starbucks is also active in philanthropic giving. Store managers can donate funds and merchandise for local projects. The company supports causes related to education, youth, and poverty, such as Gift of Words, a philanthropic program funded by Starbucks Coffee Canada and developed and managed by ABC CANADA Literacy Foundation. It supports literacy and learning initiatives in communities across the country. Through the distribution of grants to schools, libraries, and literacy organizations, the program helps create or expand permanent book collections and develop or maintain reading circles. Starbucks also spends millions of dollars supporting healthcare, sanitation, and literacy in coffee-producing countries. Starbucks gains positive publicity from its charitable programs, which is especially useful in courting young, affluent customers. Barista Daniel Gross says, "Starbucks is selling an image more than coffee."

Observing Starbucks's growth and development over the last 18 years, the most striking aspect of the firm is its commitment to innovation. No part of the firm is too important or too insignificant to escape change. Starbucks was the first firm to popularize Italian-style specialty coffee beverages in the United States. There are 167 million Americans who drink coffee, about the same number as ten years ago. However, Americans spend $31 per capita on coffee, a sharp increase over the last decade. The increase is due to increased consumption of more expensive specialty drinks. Over 63 percent of Canadians over the age of 18 drink coffee on a daily basis making coffee the number one beverage choice of adult Canadians. Coffee is a more popular beverage in Canada than the United States with just 49 percent of Americans drinking coffee on a daily basis and with Starbucks commanding a small, but growing part of the Canadian market, the opportunities for growth are significant. Starbucks constantly develops new products, including iced coffees, teas, hot chocolate, coffee ice creams, and even seasonal flavours, such as pumpkin spice coffee at Halloween. New food offerings include sandwiches and salads. Lunch food sales are expected to contribute $30 000 in profits per store.

Starbucks has expanded its product offerings beyond food and drink. The firm offers CDs, publishes a children's holiday book, and sells the board game Cranium. The company offers a branded Visa card and most locations offer wireless Internet service. That creates what Schultz refers to as "the Third Place," a space for socializing that is somewhere between home and work. The usual Starbucks visit is just five minutes long, but Internet users stay forty-five minutes on average, creating more sales opportunities. Also, Internet customers visit after peak morning hours, generating revenue during otherwise "light" periods. "If we'd only thought of ourselves as a coffee company, we wouldn't have done this," says Anne Saunders, marketing senior vice president.

Operations provides another area for innovation. One-third of new stores now offer drive-through lanes for speedier service. The company has switched to faster, automated espresso machines. New store designs increase the selling space, provide more effective displays, and optimize inventory and food preparation areas. The company acquired several smaller coffee companies to increase brand depth. Alternate distribution channels include whole-bean, bottled coffee, and ice cream sales through traditional supermarkets, as well as deals with food wholesaler Sysco. Starbucks's brewed coffee is available in Chapters bookstores and the Loblaw's chain of supermarkets. Recently, the company introduced a coffee liqueur available through outlets such as the Liquor Control Board of Ontario.

Starbucks is expanding its demographic base to attract more young, urban, and diverse customers. The firm is trying to move beyond its narrow niche market of white, educated, wealthy consumers. Peter Kafka of *Forbes* writes, "Starbucks may be the only consumer company in the U.S. that boasts that its customer base is becoming less affluent." The company has begun to build stores in small towns and inner cities, allowing them to reach a broader market.

The company continually reinvents itself. "Whenever you reach a plateau, it's time to rethink," Schultz says. "If you're number one . . . maybe it's time to reconsider . . . Create a broader definition of the industry, and develop a new plan to conquer it." Starbucks has certainly heeded that advice. First it switched from coffee bean retailer to coffee house. Then it became the "Third Place" for socializing and working. Its next concept, called Hear Music, is the company's third major transformation in less than twenty years.

With Hear Music customers can purchase CDs or create their own. Hear Music's marketing plan helped *Genius Loves Company*, an album of Ray Charles duets, win a Grammy. The CD sold over 1 million copies in just three months and earned Album of the Year for 2004. More recently, Hear Music released Paul McCartney's 2007 studio album *Memory Almost Full*, which debuted at number 3 on the Billboard Top 200 chart, McCartney's highest chart debut in a decade. The same year, Starbucks became the exclusive retailer to sell the Dave Matthews Band's *Live Trax* CD. Previously, the series of live compilation tracks from DMB concerts were only available at the band's concerts or website. In southern California, Miami, and Austin, stores provide tablet PCs for customers to select and legally burn music CDs from the company's library of more than 150 000 songs. The buyer chooses the music ($8.99 for the first seven songs, $.99 for each additional song) and can create label and cover art. "In the time it takes you to order a latte, you could have any CD burned on demand for you," says vice president Don MacKinnon. The service is likely to appeal to older buyers who are not technology savvy and who feel ignored by traditional music stores and radio stations. "This is training wheels for digital," MacKinnon says. These customers are willing to pay for ease and convenience.

Innovation is ongoing at Starbucks. "Schultz is doing something quite unusual in business. He's already looking ahead, doing the arithmetic and saying, 'Well, our current model is not forever.' There are probably a few more years of growth left in coffee shops, and he's asking, 'How do we manage that inevitable slowdown a couple of years

> **❝ *The hardest thing is to stay small while you get big.* ❞**
> HOWARD SCHULTZ,
> FOUNDER, STARBUCKS

from now?'" says consultant Adrian Slywotzky. Starbucks plans to continue growing. Yet while the company is growing and changing, Starbucks's leaders are working to help the company retain its culture, image, and small-store appeal. "The hardest thing is to stay small while you get big, to figure out how to stay intimate with your customers and your people, even as your reach gets bigger," says Schultz.

Integrative Case Questions

1. What changes in organization structure do you anticipate the firm will make as it grows and ages? What benefits will these structure changes bring? What are some potential problems that these structure changes will bring?

2. Use the Ouchi framework to describe the organization culture at Starbucks. Is the company most like a Japanese firm, a Type Z North American company, or a typical North American company?

3. What types of resistance to change is Starbucks likely to encounter? What can the company do to overcome resistance to change?

Sources: "Corporate Social Responsibility Report 2004," "Mission Statement," "Ray Charles Nominated for 10 Grammy Awards," "Starbucks Recaps 2002–2004 Successes," "Starbucks Lays Out Global Growth Strategy," "Starbucks' Strong Innovation Pipeline," Starbucks website, www.starbucks.com on February 2, 2005; "U.S. Coffee Consumption Shows Impressive Growth," *Food and Drink Weekly,* February 16, 2004, www.foodanddrink.com on June 30, 2005; Robert D. Hof, "Building an Idea Factory," *Business Week,* October 11, 2004, www.businessweek.com on January 31, 2005; Stanley Holmes, "Maybe They'll Call It Starbooks," *Business Week,* October 25, 2004, www.businessweek.com on January 31, 2005; Stanley Holmes, "Starbucks Tunes In to Digital Music," *Business Week,* March 16, 2004, www.businessweek.com on January 31, 2005; Peter Kafka, "Bean Counter," *Forbes,* February 28, 2005, www.forbes.com on June 30, 2005; Anya Kamenetz, "Baristas of the World, Unite!" *New York Metro,* www.newyorkmetro.com on June 30, 2005; Alison Overholt, "Listening to Starbucks," *Fast Company,* July 2004, pp. 50–56 (quotation); Christopher Palmeri, "March of the Toys—Out of the Toy Section," *Business Week,* November 29, 2004, www.businessweek.com on January 31, 2005; Amy Tsao, "Starbucks: A Bit Overheated?" *Business Week,* April 5, 2004, www.businessweek.com on January 31, 2005; Amy Tsao, "Starbucks' Plan to Brew Growth," *Business Week,* April 5, 2004, www.businessweek.com on January 31, 2005; "2003 Canadian Coffee Drinking Survey," www.coffeeassoc.com on August 21, 2007; www.starbucks.ca on August 21, 2007.

Endnotes

Chapter 1

1. For a classic discussion of the meaning of organizational behaviour, see Larry Cummings, "Toward Organizational Behavior," *Academy of Management Review*, January 1978, pp. 90–98. For recent updates, see the annual series *Research in Organizational Behavior* (Greenwich, Connecticut: JAI Press), edited by Larry Cummings and Barry Staw. See also Jerald Greenberg (ed.), *Organizational Behavior—The State of the Science* (Hillsdale, New Jersey: Lawrence Erlbaum Associates, 1994); and Cary L. Cooper and Denise M. Rousseau (eds.), *Trends in Organizational Behavior* (New York: John Wiley & Sons, 1995).

2. See "Work and Family," *Business Week*, 28 June 1993, pp. 80–88, for some insights into the role of work and organizations in our everyday lives.

3. Daniel A. Wren, *The Evolution of Management Thought*, 4th ed. (New York: Wiley, 1994), Chapters 1 and 2. See also Stephen J. Carroll and Dennis A. Gillen, "Are the Classical Management Functions Useful in Describing Managerial Work?" *Academy of Management Review*, January 1987, pp. 38–51; and Daniel A. Wren, "Management History: Issues and Ideas for Teaching and Research," *Journal of Management*, Summer 1987, pp. 339–350.

4. Frederick W. Taylor, *Principles of Scientific Management* (New York: Harper, 1911).

5. Max Weber, *Theory of Social and Economic Organization*, trans. A. M. Henderson and T. Parsons (London: Oxford University Press, 1921).

6. Elton Mayo, *The Human Problems of Industrial Civilization* (New York: Macmillan, 1933); Fritz J. Roethlisberger and William J. Dickson, *Management and the Worker* (Cambridge, Massachusetts: Harvard University Press, 1939).

7. Alex Carey, "The Hawthorne Studies: A Radical Criticism," *American Sociological Review*, June 1967, pp. 403–416; Lyle Yorks and David A. Whitsett, "Hawthorne, Topeka, and the Issue of Science versus Advocacy in Organizational Behavior," *Academy of Management Review*, January 1985, pp. 21–30.

8. Douglas McGregor, *The Human Side of Enterprise* (New York: McGraw-Hill, 1960); Abraham Maslow, "A Theory of Human Motivation," *Psychological Review*, July 1943, pp. 370–396. See also Paul R. Lawrence, "Historical Development of Organizational Behavior," in Jay W. Lorsch (ed.), *Handbook of Organizational Behavior* (Englewood Cliffs, New Jersey: Prentice-Hall, 1987), pp. 1–9.

9. See "Conversation with Lyman W. Porter," *Organizational Dynamics*, Winter 1990, pp. 69–79.

10. See Lorsch, *Handbook of Organizational Behavior*, for an overview of the current state of the field. See also the annual *Research in Organizational Behavior* series edited by Larry Cummings and Barry Staw.

11. Joseph W. McGuire, "Retreat to the Academy," *Business Horizons*, July–August 1982, pp. 31–37; Kenneth Thomas and Walter G. Tymon, "Necessary Properties of Relevant Research: Lessons from Recent Criticisms of the Organizational Sciences," *Academy of Management Review*, July 1982, pp. 345–353. See also Jeffrey Pfeffer, "The Theory-Practice Gap: Myth or Reality?" *Academy of Management Executive*, February 1987, pp. 31–32.

12. Fremont Kast and James Rosenzweig, "General Systems Theory: Applications for Organization and Management," *Academy of Management Journal*, December 1972, pp. 447–465.

13. See Fremont Kast and James Rosenzweig (eds.), *Contingency Views of Organization and Management* (Chicago: SRA, 1973), for a classic overview and introduction.

14. James Terborg, "Interactional Psychology and Research on Human Behavior in Organizations," *Academy of Management Review*, October 1981, pp. 569–576; Benjamin Schneider, "Interactional Psychology and Organizational Behavior," in Larry Cummings and Barry Staw (eds.), *Research in Organizational Behavior* (Greenwich, Connecticut: JAI Press, 1983), V, pp. 1–32; Daniel B. Turban and Thomas L. Keon, "Organizational Attractiveness: An Interactionist Perspective," *Journal of Applied Psychology*, 1993, vol. 78, no. 2, pp. 184–193.

15. Jeffrey Pfeffer, "The Theory–Practice Gap: Myth or Reality?" *Academy of Management Executive*, February 1987, pp. 31–33.

16. Eugene Stone, *Research Methods in Organizational Behavior* (Santa Monica, California: Goodyear, 1978).

17. Fred N. Kerlinger, *Foundations of Behavioral Research*, 3rd ed. (New York: Holt, Rinehart & Winston, 1987).

18. Richard L. Daft, Ricky W. Griffin, and Valerie Yates, "Retrospective Accounts of Research Factors Associated with Significant and Not-So-Significant Research Outcomes," *Academy of Management Journal*, December 1987, pp. 763–785.

19. Richard L. Daft, "Learning the Craft of Organizational Research," *Academy of Management Review*, October 1983, pp. 539–546.

20. Larry L. Cummings and Peter Frost, *Publishing in Organizational Sciences* (Homewood, Illinois: Irwin, 1985).

21. D. T. Campbell and J. C. Stanley, *Experimental and Quasi-Experimental Designs for Research* (Chicago: Rand McNally, 1963).

22. R. Yin and K. Heald, "Using the Case Study Method to Analyze Policy Studies," *Administrative Science Quarterly*, June 1975, pp. 371–381.

23. Kerlinger, *Foundations of Behavioral Research*.

24. Ramon J. Aldag and Timothy M. Stearns, "Issues in Research Methodology," *Journal of Management*, June 1988, pp. 253–276.

25. See C. A. Schriesheim et al., "Improving Construct Measurement in Management," *Journal of Management*, Summer 1993, pp. 385–418.

26. Cynthia D. Fisher, "Laboratory Experiments," in Thomas S. Bateman and Gerald R. Ferris (eds.), *Method and Analysis in Organizational Research* (Reston, Virginia: Reston, 1984); Edwin Locke (ed.), *Generalizing from Laboratory to Field Settings* (Lexington, Massachusetts: Lexington Books, 1986).

27. Stone, *Research Methods in Organizational Behavior.*

28. Phillip M. Podsakoff and Dan R. Dalton, "Research Methodology in Organizational Studies," *Journal of Management,* Summer 1987, pp. 419–441.

29. Stone, *Research Methods in Organizational Behavior.*

30. Kerlinger, *Foundations of Behavioral Research.*

31. Mary Ann Von Glinow, "Ethical Issues in Organizational Behavior," *Academy of Management Newsletter,* March 1985, pp. 1–3.

Chapter 2

1. David Finlayson, "Management Kudos for CCI," *The Edmonton Journal,* 21 March 2006, www.canada.com; Robert Gibbons, "Outstanding in the Field," *The Montreal Gazette,* 26 February 2007, www.canada.com; Gary Lamphier, "Arctic Spas Makes a Splash," *The Edmonton Journal,* 15 April 2006, www.canada.com.

2. Henry Mintzberg, "Rounding Out the Manager's Job," *Sloan Management Review,* Fall 1994, pp. 11–26.

3. Brian Dumaine, "The New Non-Manager Managers," *Fortune,* 22 February 1993, pp. 80–84.

4. Mauro F. Guillen, "The Age of Eclecticism: Current Organizational Trends and the Evolution of Managerial Models," *Sloan Management Review,* Fall 1994, pp. 75–86.

5. David H. Freedman, "Is Management Still a Science?" *Harvard Business Review,* November–December 1992, pp. 26–38.

6. Henry Mintzberg, "The Manager's Job: Folklore and Fact," *Harvard Business Review,* July–August 1975, pp. 49–61.

7. Robert L. Katz, "The Skills of an Effective Administrator," *Harvard Business Review,* September–October 1987, pp. 90–102.

8. Calvin Leung, "Culture Club: Effective Corporate Cultures," *Canadian Business,* October 9-22, 2006 (Online: www .canadianbusiness.com/shared/print.jsp?content=200610>, accessed 11 December 2006).

9. Mary Lamey, "Mall Owners Shop for Deals Abroad," *Financial Post,* 22 June 2006, www.canada.com.

10. Wojtek Dabrowski "Nortel to Slash 2,900 Jobs in Latest Cost-Cutting," Reuters.com, February 7, 2007.

11. Marjorie Armstrong-Stassen, "The Influence of Prior Commitment on the Reactions of Layoff Survivors to Organizational Downsizing," *Journal of Occupational Health Psychology,* 2004, vol. 9, no. 1, pp. 46–60; Marjorie Armstrong-Stassen, "Coping with Downsizing: A Comparison of Executive-Level and Middle Managers," *International Journal of Stress Management,* 2005, vol. 12, no. 2, pp. 117–141; Marjorie Armstrong-Stassen, "Determinants of How Managers Cope with Organisational Downsizing," *Applied Psychology: An International Review,* 2006, vol. 55, no. 1, pp. 1–26.

12. Patricia L. Nemetz and Sandra L. Christensen, "The Challenge of Cultural Diversity: Harnessing a Diversity of Views to Understand Multiculturalism," *Academy of Management Review,* 1996, vol. 21, no. 2, pp. 434–462; Frances J. Milliken and Luis L. Martins, "Searching for Common Threads: Understanding the Multiple Effects of Diversity in Organizational Groups," *Academy of Management Review,* 1996, vol. 21, no. 2, pp. 402–433.

13. Andrew Wahl, Zena Olijnyk, Peter Evans, Andy Holloway, and Erin Pooley, "Best Workplaces of 2006: Lessons from Some of the Best," *Canadian Business,* 10–23 April 2006, www.canadianbusiness.com.

14. Brian Dumaine, "Times Are Good? Create a Crisis," *Fortune,* 28 June 1993, pp. 123–130.

15. Peter F. Drucker, "The Information Executives Truly Need," *Harvard Business Review,* January–February 1995, pp. 54–62.

16. Rahul Jacob, "The Struggle to Create an Organization for the Twenty-first Century," *Fortune,* 3 April 1995, pp. 90–99; Susan Sonnesyn Brooks, "Managing a Horizontal Revolution," *HRMagazine,* June 1995, pp. 52–57.

17. Michael Porter, *Competitive Strategy* (New York: Free Press, 1980).

18. Jeffrey Pfeffer, "Producing Sustainable Competitive Advantage Through the Effective Management of People," *Academy of Management Executives,* 1995, vol. 9, no. 1, pp. 55–69; Carl Long and Mary Vickers-Koch, "Using Core Capabilities to Create Competitive Advantage," *Organizational Dynamics,* Summer 1995, pp. 39–55.

19. Geert Hofstede, *Culture's Consequences: International Differences in Work-Related Values* (Beverly Hills: Sage Publications, 1980).

20. "How to Fix Corporate Governance," *Business Week,* May 6, 2002, pp. 68–78.

21. Max Boisot, *Knowledge Assets* (Oxford: Oxford University Press, 1998).

22. M. L. Tushman and C. A. O'Reilly, *Winning Through Innovation* (Cambridge, MA: Harvard Business School Press, 1996).

23. M. A. Von Glinow, *The New Professionals* (Cambridge, MA: Ballinger, 1988).

24. T. W. Lee and S. D. Maurer, "The Retention of Knowledge Workers with the Unfolding Model of Voluntary Turnover," *Human Resource Management Review,* 1997, vol. 7, pp. 247–276.

25. G. T. Milkovich, "Compensation Systems in High-Technology Companies," in *High Technology Management,* eds. A. Klingartner and C. Anderson (Lexington, MA: Lexington Books, 1987).

26. Ross Johnson and William O. Winchell, *Management and Quality* (Milwaukee, Wisconsin: American Society for Quality Control, 1989).

27. "Quality," *Business Week,* 30 November 1992, pp. 66–75.

28. Joel Dreyfuss, "Victories in the Quality Crusade," *Fortune,* 10 October 1988, pp. 80–88.

29. Patricia Sellers, "Companies That Serve You Best," *Fortune,* 31 May 1993, pp. 74–88.

30. "Service Productivity Is Rising Fast—And So Is the Fear of Lost Jobs," *Wall Street Journal,* 8 June 1995, pp. A1, A10.

31. Graham Lowe, "Here in Body, Absent in Productivity," *Canadian HR Reporter,* 2 December 2002, pp. 5–6.; "Still Go to Work When Sick, Most Employees Admit," *Kitchener-Waterloo Record,* 28 October 2006, p. F6.

Chapter 3

1. Scott Deveau, "It's All in the Genes," *Financial Post,* February 9, 2007, www.canada.com; Jason Kirby and Steve Maich, "The Frank Factor," *Maclean's,* May 28, 2007, www.macleans.ca; Gideon D. Markman and Robert A. Baron, "Person–entrepreneurship Fit:

Why Some People Are More Successful as Entrepreneurs Than Others," *Human Resource Management Review*, 2003, Volume 13, pp. 281–301; Mark A. Ciavarella et al., "The Big Five and Venture Survival: Is There a Linkage?" *Journal of Business Venturing*, 2004, Volume 19, pp. 465–483; www.timhortons.com; www.jimpattison.com.

2. Denise M. Rousseau and Judi McLean Parks, "The Contracts of Individuals and Organizations," in Larry L. Cummings and Barry M. Staw (eds.), *Research in Organizational Behavior* (Greenwich, Connecticut: JAI Press, 1993), XV, pp. 1–43.

3. Denise M. Rousseau, "Changing the Deal While Keeping the People," *Academy of Management Executive*, February 1996, pp. 50–58. See also Erica Gordon Sorohan, "When the Ties That Bind Break," *Training and Development*, February 1994, pp. 28–35.

4. Richard A. Guzzo, Katherine A. Noonan, and Efrat Elron, "Expatriate Managers and the Psychological Contract," *Journal of Applied Psychology*, vol. 79, no. 4, pp. 617–626.

5. Jennifer A. Chatman, "Improving Interactional Organizational Research: A Model of Person–Organization Fit," *Academy of Management Review*, July 1989, pp. 333–349; Charles A. O'Reilly III, Jennifer Chatman, and David F. Calwell, "People and Organizational Culture: A Profile Comparison Approach to Assessing Person–Organization Fit," *Academy of Management Journal*, September 1991, pp. 487–516.

6. Amy L. Kristof, "Person–Organization Fit: An Integrative Review of Its Conceptualizations, Measurement, and Implications," *Personnel Psychology*, Spring 1996, pp. 1–49.

7. Lawrence Pervin, "Personality," in Mark Rosenzweig and Lyman Porter (eds.), *Annual Review of Psychology* (Palo Alto, California: Annual Reviews, 1985), XXXVI, pp. 83–114; S. R. Maddi, *Personality Theories: A Comparative Analysis*, 4th ed. (Homewood, Illinois: Dorsey, 1980).

8. Jennifer George, "The Role of Personality in Organizational Life: Issues and Evidence," *Journal of Management*, 1992, vol. 18, pp. 185–213.

9. Lawrence Pervin, *Current Controversies and Issues in Personality*, 2nd ed. (New York: Wiley, 1984).

10. L. R. Goldberg, "An Alternative 'Description of Personality': The Big Five Factor Structure," *Journal of Personality and Social Psychology*, 1990, vol. 59, pp. 1216–1229; M. R. Barrick and M. K. Mount, "The Big Five Personality Dimensions and Job Performance," *Personnel Psychology*, 1991, vol. 44, pp. 1–26.

11. Barrick and Mount, "The Big Five Personality Dimensions and Job Performance."

12. Michael K. Mount, Murray R. Barrick, and J. Perkins Strauss, "Validity of Observer Ratings of the Big Five Personality Factors," *Journal of Applied Psychology*, 1994, vol. 79, no. 2, pp. 272–280.

13. A. L. Hammer, *Introduction to Types and Careers* (Palo Alto, California: Consulting Psychologists Press, 1993).

14. See Daniel Goleman, *Emotional Intelligence: Why It Can Matter More Than IQ* (New York: Bantam Books, 1995).

15. J. D. Mayer and P. Salovey, "What Is Emotional Intelligence?" In P. Salovey and D. Sluyter (Eds.), *Emotional Development and Emotional Intelligence: Educational Implications* (pp. 3–31), 1997, New York: Basic Books.

16. Stéphane Côté and Christopher T. H. Miners, "Emotional Intelligence, Cognitive Intelligence, and Job Performance," *Administrative Science Quarterly*, 2006, vol. 51, no. 1, pp. 1–28; Arla L. Day and Sarah Carroll, "Using An Ability-Based Measure of Emotional Intelligence to Predict Individual Performance, Group Performance, and Group Citizenship Behaviours," *Personality and Individual Differences*, 2004, vol. 36, pp. 1443–1458.

17. J. B. Rotter, "Generalized Expectancies for Internal vs. External Control of Reinforcement," *Psychological Monographs*, 1966, vol. 80, pp. 1–28; Bert De Brabander and Christopher Boone, "Sex Differences in Perceived Locus of Control," *Journal of Social Psychology*, 1990, vol. 130, pp. 271–276.

18. Angelo J. Kinicki and Robert P. Vecchio, "Influences on the Quality of Supervisor–Subordinate Relations: The Role of Time-pressure, Organizational Commitment, and Locus of Control," *Journal of Organizational Behavior*, 1994, vol. 15, pp. 75–82; Daniel F. Coleman, P. Gregory Irving, and Christine L. Cooper, "Another Look at the Locus of Control-Organizational Commitment Relationship: It Depends on the Form of Commitment," *Journal of Organizational Behavior*. In Press.

19. Marilyn E. Gist and Terence R. Mitchell, "Self-Efficacy: A Theoretical Analysis of Its Determinants and Malleability," *Academy of Management Review*, April 1992, pp. 183–211.

20. Peg Thoms, Keirsten S. Moore, and Kimberly S. Scott, "The Relationship Between Self-Efficacy for Participating in Self-Managed Work Groups and the Big Five Personality Dimensions," *Journal of Organizational Behavior*, 1996, vol. 17, pp. 349–362; Cynthia Lee and Phillip Bobko, "Self-Efficacy Beliefs: Comparison of Five Measures," *Journal of Applied Psychology*, 1994, vol. 79, no. 3, pp. 364–369.

21. T. W. Adorno, E. Frenkel-Brunswick, D. J. Levinson, and R. N. Sanford, *The Authoritarian Personality* (New York: Harper & Row, 1950).

22. "Who Becomes an Authoritarian?" *Psychology Today*, March 1989, pp. 66–70.

23. Jon L. Pierce, Donald G. Gardner, and Larry L. Cummings, "Organization-Based Self-Esteem: Construct Definition, Measurement, and Validation," *Academy of Management Journal*, 1989, vol. 32, pp. 622–648.

24. Roy J. Blitzer, Colleen Petersen, and Linda Rogers, "How to Build Self-Esteem," *Training and Development*, February 1993, pp. 58–65.

25. Michael Harris Bond and Peter B. Smith, "Cross-Cultural Social and Organizational Psychology," in Janet Spence (ed.), *Annual Review of Psychology*, vol. 47 (Palo Alto, California: Annual Reviews, 1996), pp. 205–235.

26. "One Man's Accident Is Shedding New Light on Human Perception," *Wall Street Journal*, 30 September 1993, pp. A1, A13.

27. William H. Starbuck and John M. Mezias, "Opening Pandora's Box: Studying the Accuracy of Managers' Perceptions," *Journal of Organizational Behavior*, 1996, vol. 17, pp. 99–117.

28. Frank E. Saal and S. Craig Moore, "Perceptions of Promotion Fairness and Promotion Candidates' Qualifications," *Journal of Applied Psychology*, 1993, vol. 78, pp. 105–110.

29. Mark J. Martinko and William L. Gardner, "The Leader/Member Attribution Process," *Academy of Management Review*, April 1987, pp. 235–249; Jeffrey D. Ford, "The Effects of Causal Attributions on Decision Makers' Responses to Performance

Downturns," *Academy of Management Review*, October 1985, pp. 770–786.

30. Lee D. Ross, "The Intuitive Psychologist and His Shortcomings: Distortions in the Attribution Process," in L. Berkowitz (ed.), *Advances in Experimental Social Psychology*, vol. 10 (New York: Academic Press, 1977).

31. Charles E. Kimble, *Social Psychology: Studying Human Interaction* (Dubuque, Iowa: William C. Brown, 1990); Frank E. Saal and Patrick A. Knight, *Industrial/Organizational Psychology* (Belmont, California: Brooks/Cole, 1988).

32 Amy S. Wharton and Rebecca J. Erickson, "Managing Emotions on the Job and at Home: Understanding the Consequences of Multiple Emotional Roles," *Academy of Management Journal*, September 1993, pp. 457–486.

33. Bobby J. Calder and Paul H. Schurr, "Attitudinal Processes in Organizations," in Larry L. Cummings and Barry M. Staw (eds.), *Research in Organizational Behavior* (Greenwich, Connecticut: JAI Press, 1981), III, pp. 283–302.

34. Leon Festinger, *A Theory of Cognitive Dissonance* (Palo Alto, California: Stanford University Press, 1957).

35. Cliff Hakim, "Boost Morale to Gain Productivity," *HRMagazine*, February 1993, pp. 46–53.

36. Timothy. A. Judge, Daniel Heller, and Michael K. Mount, "Five-Factor Model of Personality and Job Satisfaction: A Meta-Analysis," *Journal of Applied Psychology*, 2002, vol. 87, no. 3, 530–541.

37. Chris Lackner, "Money Isn't Everything, Job Satisfaction Poll Shows," *The Ottawa Citizen*, March 30, 2007, www.canada.com; www.jobquality.ca/indicator_e/rew002.stm.

38. Frederick F. Reichheld, "Loyalty-Based Management," *Harvard Business Review*, March–April 1993, pp. 64–73.

39. John P. Meyer and Natalie J. Allen, *Commitment in the Workplace: Theory, Research, and Application* (Thousand Oaks, California: Sage, 1997).

40. John P. Meyer, Natalie J. Allen, and Catherine A. Smith, "Commitment to Organizations and Occupations: Extension and Test of a Three-Component Conceptualization," *Journal of Applied Psychology*, 1993, vol. 78, no. 4, pp. 538–551.

41. See Rick D. Hackett, Peter Bycio, and Peter A. Hausdorf, "Further Assessments of Meyer and Allen's (1991) Three-Component Model of Organizational Commitment," *Journal of Applied Psychology*, 1994, vol. 79, no. 1, pp. 15–23; John P. Meyer, David J. Stanley, Lynne Herscovitch, Laryssa Topolnytsky, "Affective, continuance, and normative commitment to the organization: A meta-analysis of antecedents, correlates, and consequences," Journal of Vocational Behavior, 2002, vol. 61, no. 1, pp. 20–52.

42. Meyer, Allen, and Smith, "Commitment to Organizations and Occupations: Extension and Test of a Three-Component Conceptualization"; P. Gregory Irving, Daniel F. Coleman, and Christine L. Cooper, "Further Assessments of a Three-Component Model of Occupational Commitment: Generalizability and Differences Across Occupations," *Journal of Applied Psychology*, 1997, vol. 82, no. 3, pp. 444–452.

43. Leslie E. Palich, Peter W. Hom, and Roger W. Griffeth, "Managing in the International Context: Testing Cultural Generality of Sources of Commitment to Multinational Enterprises," *Journal of Management*, 1995, vol. 21, no. 4, pp. 671–690.

44. For research work in this area, see Jennifer M. George and Gareth R. Jones, "The Experience of Mood and Turnover Intentions: Interactive Effects of Value Attainment, Job Satisfaction, and Positive Mood," *Journal of Applied Psychology*, 1996, vol. 81, no. 3, pp. 318–325; Larry J. Williams, Mark B. Gavin, and Margaret Williams, "Measurement and Nonmeasurement Processes with Negative Affectivity and Employee Attitudes," *Journal of Applied Psychology*, vol. 81, no. 1, pp. 88–101.

45. See Jerald Greenberg and Jason Colquitt, *Handbook of Organizational Justice* (Mahwah, NJ: Lawrence Erlbaum Associates, 2004) for a comprehensive discussion and review of the literature on justice in organization.

46. Lori Francis and Julian Barling, "Organizational Injustice and Psychological Strain," *Canadian Journal of Behavioural Science*, 2005, vol. 37, no. 4, pp. 250–261.

47. Sandra L. Robinson and Rebecca Bennett, "A Typology of Deviant Workplace Behaviors: A Multidimensional Scaling Study," *Academy of Management Journal*, 1995, vol. 38, no. 2, pp. 555–572.

48. Daniel P. Skarlicki and Robert Folger, "Retaliation in the Workplace: The Roles of Distributive, Procedural, and Interactional Justice," *Journal of Applied Psychology*, 1997, vol. 82, no. 3, pp. 434–443.

49. See for example Gary Johns, "Absenteeism Estimates by Employees and Managers: Divergent Perspectives and Self-serving Perceptions," *Journal of Applied Psychology*, 1994, vol. 79, no. 2, pp. 229–239; Ian R. Gellatly, "Individual and Group Determinants of Employee Absenteeism: Test of a Causal Model," *Journal of Organizational Behavior*, 1995, vol. 16, pp. 469–485.

50. See Anne O'Leary-Kelly, Ricky W. Griffin, and David J. Glew, "Organization-Motivated Aggression: A Research Framework," *Academy of Management Review*, January 1996, pp. 225–253.

51. See Dennis W. Organ, "Personality and Organizational Citizenship Behavior," *Journal of Management*, 1994, vol. 20, no. 2, pp. 465–478, for a review of findings regarding this behaviour.

52. Brian P. Niehoff and Robert H. Moorman, "Justice as a Mediator of the Relationship Between Methods of Monitoring and Organizational Citizenship Behavior," *Academy of Management Journal*, September 1993, pp. 527–556.

53. Dennis W. Organ, "Organizational Citizenship and the Good Soldier," in Michael G. Rumsey et al. (eds.), *Personnel Selection and Classification* (Hillsdale, New Jersey: Lawrence Erlbaum Associates, 1994).

Chapter 4

1. Katherine Macklem, "No. 1: Vancity confidential," *Maclean's*, October 10, 2004. Andrew Wahl, "Best Workplaces," *Canadian Business*; April 2006. Andrew Wahl, "On the Money," *Canadian Business*, April 2006. Jill Lambert, "The Economics of Happiness," *Canadian Business,* May 2005.

2. Richard M. Steers and Lyman W. Porter, *Motivation and Work Behavior*, 5th ed. (New York: McGraw-Hill, 1991), pp. 5–6. See also Ruth Kanfer, "Motivational Theory and Industrial

and Organizational Psychology," in M. D. Dunnette and L. M. Hough (eds.), *Handbook of Industrial and Organizational Psychology*, 2nd ed. (Palo Alto, California: Consulting Psychologists Press), I, pp. 75–170; Frank J. Landy and Wendy S. Becker, "Motivation Theory Reconsidered," in Larry L. Cummings and Barry M. Staw (eds.), *Research in Organizational Behavior* (Greenwich, Connecticut: JAI Press, 1987), IX, pp. 1–38.

3. Roland E. Kidwell, Jr., and Nathan Bennett, "Employee Propensity to Withhold Effort: A Conceptual Model to Intersect Three Avenues of Research," *Academy of Management Review*, July 1993, pp. 429–456.

4. Victor H. Vroom, *Work and Motivation* (New York: Wiley, 1964).

5. Craig C. Pinder, *Work Motivation in Organizational Behavior* (Upper Saddle River, New Jersey: Prentice Hall, 1998).

6. Frederick W. Taylor, *Principles of Scientific Management* (New York: Harper, 1911).

7. Ibid., pp. 46–47.

8. See Charles D. Wrege and Amedeo G. Perroni, "Taylor's Pig-Tale: A Historical Analysis of Frederick W. Taylor's Pig-Iron Experiment," *Academy of Management Journal*, March 1974, pp. 6–27.

9. Pinder, *Work Motivation in Organizational Behavior*. See also Daniel Wren, *The Evolution of Management Thought*, 4th ed. (New York: Wiley, 1994).

10. Steers and Porter, *Motivation and Work Behavior*.

11. Abraham H. Maslow, "A Theory of Human Motivation," *Psychological Review*, 1943, vol. 50, pp. 370–396; Abraham H. Maslow, *Motivation and Personality* (New York: Harper & Row, 1954).

12. Gerald R. Salancik and Jeffrey Pfeffer, "An Examination of Need-Satisfaction Models of Job Attitudes," *Administrative Science Quarterly*, September 1977, pp. 427–456.

13. Mahmond A. Wahba and Lawrence G. Bridwell, "Maslow Reconsidered: A Review of Research on the Need Hierarchy Theory," *Organizational Behavior and Human Performance*, April 1976, pp. 212–240.

14. Ibid.

15. Clayton P. Alderfer, *Existence, Relatedness, and Growth* (New York: Free Press, 1972).

16. Frederick Herzberg, Bernard Mausner, and Barbara Synderman, *The Motivation to Work* (New York: Wiley, 1959); Frederick Herzberg, "One More Time": How Do You Motivate Employees?" *Harvard Business Review*, January–February 1968, pp. 53–62.

17. Herzberg, Mausner, and Synderman, *The Motivation to Work*.

18. Herzberg, "One More Time—; Ricky W. Griffin, *Task Design: An Integrative Approach* (Glenview, Illinois: Scott, Foresman, 1982).

19. Pinder, *Work Motivation in Organizational Behavior*.

20. Marvin Dunnette, John Campbell, and Milton Hakel, "Factors Contributing to Job Satisfaction and Job Dissatisfaction in Six Occupational Groups," *Organizational Behavior and Human Performance*, May 1967, pp. 143–174; Charles L. Hulin and Patricia Smith, "An Empirical Investigation of Two Implications of the Two-Factor Theory of Job Satisfaction," *Journal of Applied Psychology*, October 1967, pp. 396–402.

21. Nathan King, "A Clarification and Evaluation of the Two-Factor Theory of Job Satisfaction," *Psychological Bulletin*, July 1970, pp. 18–31. See also Dunnette, Campbell, and Hakel, "Factors Contributing to Job Satisfaction," and R. J. House and L. Wigdor, "Herzberg's Dual-Factor Theory of Job Satisfaction and Motivation: A Review of the Evidence and a Criticism," *Personnel Psychology*, Summer 1967, pp. 369–389.

22. Pinder, *Work Motivation in Organizational Behavior*.

23. Ibid.

24. B. F. Skinner, *Science and Human Behavior* (New York: Macmillan, 1953), and *Beyond Freedom and Dignity* (New York: Knopf, 1972).

25. Fred Luthans and Robert Kreitner, *Organizational Behavior Modification and Beyond* (Glenview, Illinois: Scott, Foresman, 1985).

26. Ibid.

27. "Workers: Risks and Rewards," *Time*, 15 April 1991, pp. 42–43.

28. See Richard Arvey and John M. Ivancevich, "Punishment in Organizations: A Review, Propositions, and Research Suggestions," *Academy of Management Review*, April 1980, pp. 123–132 for a review of the literature on punishment.

29. Fred Luthans and Robert Kreitner, *Organizational Behavior Modification* (Glenview, Illinois: Scott, Foresman, 1975); Luthans and Kreitner, *Organizational Behavior Modification and Beyond*.

30. See David A. Harrison, Meghna Virick, and Sonja William, "Working Without a Net: Time, Performance, and Turnover Under Maximally Contingent Rewards," *Journal of Applied Psychology*, 1996, vol. 81, no. 4, pp. 331–345.

31. Pinder, *Work Motivation in Organizational Behavior*.

32. Ibid.

33. Ibid.

34. Gary P. Latham and Craig C. Pinder, "Work Motivation Theory and Research at the Dawn of the Twenty-First Century," *Annual Review of Psychology*, 2005, pp. 485–516.

35. Daniel P. Skarlicki and Robert Folger, "Retaliation in the Workplace: The Roles of Distributive, Procedural and Interactional Justice," *Journal of Applied Pschology*, 1997, vol. 82, pp. 434–443.

36. J. Stacy Adams, "Toward an Understanding of Inequity," *Journal of Abnormal and Social Psychology*, November 1963, pp. 422–436. See also Richard T. Mowday, "Equity Theory Predictions of Behavior in Organizations," in Richard M. Steers and Lyman W. Porter (eds.), *Motivation and Work Behavior*, 4th ed. (New York: McGraw-Hill, 1987), pp. 89–110.

37. Paul S. Goodman, "Social Comparison Processes in Organizations," in Barry M. Staw and Gerald R. Salancik (eds.), *New Directions in Organizational Behavior* (Chicago: St. Clair, 1977), pp. 97–131.

38. J. Stacy Adams, "Inequity in Social Exchange," in L. Berkowitz (ed.), *Advances in Experimental Social Psychology*, II (New York: Academic Press, 1965), pp. 267–299.

39. Oliver Bertin, "Air Canada Grounded as Pilots Walk Out," *The Globe and Mail*, 2 September 1998.

40. Pinder, *Work Motivation in Organizational Behavior*.

41. Richard A. Cosier and Dan R. Dalton, "Equity Theory and Time: A Reformulation," *Academy of Management Review*, April 1983, pp. 311–319. See also Jerald Greenberg, "Cognitive Reevaluation of Outcomes in Response to Underpayment Inequity," *Academy of Management Journal*, March 1989, pp. 174–184.

42. Jerald Greenberg and Suzyn Ornstein, "High Status Job Title as Compensation for Underpayment: A Test of Equity Theory," *Journal of Applied Psychology*, 1983, vol. 68, pp. 285–297; Jerald Greenberg, "Determinants of Perceived Fairness of Performance Evaluations," *Journal of Applied Psychology*, 1986, vol. 71, pp. 340–342.

43. Richard C. Huseman, John D. Hatfield, and Edward W. Miles, "A New Perspective on Equity Theory: The Equity Sensitivity Construct," *Academy of Management Review*, October 1987, pp. 222–234. See also Wesley C. King, Jr., Edward W. Miles, and D. David Day, "A Test and Refinement of the Equity Sensitivity Construct," *Journal of Organizational Behavior*, 1993, vol. 14, pp. 301–317.

44. Randall P. Settoon, Nathan Bennett, and Robert C. Liden, "Social Exchange in Organizations: Perceived Support, Leader-Member Exchange, and Employee Reciprocity," *Journal of Applied Psychology*, June 1996, pp. 219–227.

45. G.S. Leventhal, "What Should Be Done with Equity Theory?" In R.J. Gergen, M.S. Greenberg, and R.H. Willis (Eds.). *Social Exchange: Advances in Theory and Research*. (New York: Plenum Press, 1980).

46. Daniel P. Skarlicki, Robert Folger, and Paul Tesluk, "Personality as a moderator in the Relationship Between Fairness and Retaliation," *Academy of Management Journal*, 1999, vol. 42, pp. 100–108.

47. Stefanie E. Naumann, Nathan Bennett, Robert J. Bies, and Christopher L. Martin, "Laid Off, but Still Loyal: The Influence of Perceived Justice and Organizational Support" *International Journal of Conflict Management*, 1998, Vol. 9, pp. 356–368.

48. Laurie J. Barclay, Daniel P. Skarlicki, and S. Douglas Pugh, "Exploring the role of emotions in injustice perceptions and retaliation", *Journal of Applied Psychology*, 2005, vol. 90, pp. 629–643.

49. Edward C. Tolman, *Purposive Behavior in Animals* (New York: Appleton-Century-Crofts, 1932); Kurt Lewin, *The Conceptual Representation and the Measurement of Psychological Forces* (Durham, North Carolina: Duke University Press, 1938).

50. Victor Vroom, *Work and Motivation* (New York: Wiley, 1964).

51. Lyman W. Porter and Edward E. Lawler, *Managerial Attitudes and Performance* (Homewood, Illinois: Dorsey Press, 1968).

52. See Terence R. Mitchell, "Expectancy Models of Job Satisfaction, Occupational Preference, and Effort: A Theoretical, Methodological, and Empirical Appraisal," *Psychological Bulletin*, 1974, vol. 81, pp. 1096–1112; and John P. Campbell and Robert D. Pritchard, "Motivation Theory in Industrial and Organizational Psychology," in Marvin D. Dunnette (ed.), *Handbook of Industrial and Organizational Psychology* (Chicago: Rand McNally, 1976), pp. 63–130 for reviews.

53. Pinder, *Work Motivation in Organizational Behavior.*

54. Ibid.

55. Campbell and Pritchard, "Motivation Theory in Industrial and Organizational Psychology."

56. Pinder, *Work Motivation in Organizational Behavior.*

57. Ibid.

58. Nancy Adler, *International Dimensions of Organizational Behavior*, 3rd ed. (Boston: PWS-Kent, 1997).

59. David A. Nadler and Edward E. Lawler, "Motivation: A Diagnostic Approach," in J. Richard Hackman, Edward E. Lawler, and Lyman W. Porter (eds.), *Perspectives on Behavior in Organizations*, 2nd ed. (New York: McGraw-Hill, 1983), pp. 67–78.

60. S. H. Hulse, J. Deese, and H. Egeth, *The Psychology of Learning*, 7th ed. (New York: McGraw-Hill, 1992). See also Gib Akins, "Varieties of Organizational Learning," *Organizational Dynamics*, Autumn 1987, pp. 36–48.

61. Hulse, Deese, and Egeth, *The Psychology of Learning*. For recent perspectives, see also Douglas F. Cellar and Gerald V. Barrett, "Script Processing and Intrinsic Motivation: The Cognitive Sets Underlying Cognitive Labels," *Organizational Behavior and Human Decision Processes*, August 1987, pp. 115–135; and Max H. Bazerman and John S. Carroll, "Negotiator Cognition," in L. L. Cummings and Barry M. Staw (eds.), *Research in Organizational Behavior* (Greenwich, Connecticut: JAI Press, 1987), IX, pp. 247–288.

62. See Robert Wood and Albert Bandura, "Social Cognitive Theory of Organizational Management," *Academy of Management Review*, July 1989, pp. 361–384.

63. Albert Bandura, *Self-Efficacy: The Exercise of Control* (New York: W.H. Freeman and Company, 1997).

64. Ibid.

65. Albert Bandura, "Human Agency in Social Cognitive Theory," *American Psychologist*, 1989, vol. 44, 1175–1184.

66. Latham and Pinder, "Work Motivation Theory and Research at the Dawn of the Twenty-First Century."

67. Alexander D. Stajkovic and Fred Luthans, "Self-efficacy and Work-Related Performance: A Meta-analysis", *Psychological Bulletin*, 1998, vol. 124, pp. 240–261. Alan M. Saks, "Longitudinal Field Investigation of the Moderating and Mediating Effects of Self-Efficacy on the Relationship Between Training and Newcomer Adjustment," *Journal of Applied Psychology*, 1995, vol. 80, pp. 211–225.

Chapter 5

1. Michelle Magnan, "People Power", *Canadian Business*, 10/10/2005, Vol. 78, Issue 20; Andrew Wahl, "Culture Shock" *Canadian Business*, October 10, 2005, vol. 78, issue 20; Norma Ramage, "Cummings keeps *WestJet* employees in cockpit" *Marketing Magazine*; January 29, 2007, vol. 112, issue 2, p. 30; *Joe Castaldo*, "Consumer Reports Department" *Canadian Business*; October 9, 2006, vol. 79, issue 20, pp. 140–142; Tamara Gignac, "WestJet lifts off despite shaky start in '06" *Calgary Herald*, December 29, 2006; John Gray "Staying Power: strong brands" *Canadian Business,* November 6, 2006; Jenn Hardy, "All Star Execs: The Class of 2004, Top Exec of 2004. Clive Beddoe." *Canadian Business*, April 25, 2005, vol. 78 (9).

2. A. Bandura, *Self-Efficacy: The Exercise of Control* (New York: W.H. Freeman and Company, 1997).

3. See Edwin A. Locke, "Toward a Theory of Task Performance and Incentives," *Organizational Behavior and Human Performance*, 1968, vol. 3, pp. 157–189.

4. Anthony J. Mento, Robert P. Steel, and Ronald J. Karren, "A Meta-Analytic Study of the Effects of Goal Setting on Task Performance," *Organizational Behavior and Human Decision Processes*, vol. 39, 1987, pp. 52–83.

5. Gary P. Latham and J. J. Baldes, "The Practical Significance of Locke's Theory of Goal Setting," *Journal of Applied Psychology*, 1975, vol. 60, pp. 187–191.

6. Mento, Steel, and Karren, "A Meta-Analytic Study of the Effects of Goal Setting on Task Performance."

7. Mark E. Tubbs, "Commitment as a Moderator of the Goal-Performance Relation: A Case for Clearer Construct Definition," *Journal of Applied Psychology*, 1993, vol. 78, pp. 86–97.

8. Andew Wahl, "Best Workplaces 2006: On the Money—Vancity," *Canadian Business*, April 10, 2006.

9. See Stephen J. Carroll and Henry L. Tosi, *Management by Objectives* (New York: Macmillan, 1973).

10. Robert Rodgers, John E. Hunter, and Deborah L. Rogers, "Influence of Top Management Commitment on Management Program Success," *Journal of Applied Psychology*, 1993, vol. 78, pp. 151–155.

11. Shawn K. Yearta, Sally Maitlis, and Rob B. Briner, "An Exploratory Study of Goal Setting in Theory and Practice: A Motivational Technique That Works?" *Journal of Occupational and Organizational Psychology*, vol. 68, pp. 237–252.

12. Edwin A. Locke and Gary P. Latham, "Building a Practically Useful Theory of Goal Setting and Task Motivation: A 35 Year Odyssey," *American Psychologist*, 2002, vol. 57, pp. 705–715.

13. Craig C. Pinder, *Work Motivation in Organizational Behavior* (Upper Saddle River, New Jersey: Prentice Hall, 1998).

14. Robert Rodgers and John E. Hunter, "Impact of Management by Objectives on Organizational Productivity," *Journal of Applied Psychology*, 1991, vol. 76, pp. 322–336; Rodgers, Hunter, and Rogers, "Influence of Top Management Commitment on Management Program Success."

15. Adam Smith, *An Inquiry into the Nature and Causes of the Wealth of Nations* (New York: Modern Library, 1937). Originally published in 1776.

16. Charles Babbage, *On the Economy of Machinery and Manufactures* (London: Charles Knight, 1832).

17. Frederick W. Taylor, *The Principles of Scientific Management* (New York: Harper & Row, 1911).

18. C. R. Walker and R. Guest, *The Man on the Assembly Line* (Cambridge, Massachusetts: Harvard University Press, 1952).

19. Jia Lin Xie and Gary Johns, "Job Scope and Stress: Can Job Scope Be Too High?" *Academy of Management Journal*, 1995, vol. 38, no. 5, pp. 1288–1309.

20. Ricky W. Griffin, *Task Design: An Integrative Approach* (Glenview, Illinois: Scott, Foresman, 1982).

21. H. Conant and M. Kilbridge, "An Interdisciplinary Analysis of Job Enlargement: Technology, Cost, Behavioral Implications," *Industrial and Labor Relations Review*, 1965, vol. 18, no. 7, pp. 377–395.

22. Frederick Herzberg, "One More Time: How Do You Motivate Employees?" *Harvard Business Review*, January–February 1968, pp. 53–62; Frederick Herzberg, "The Wise Old Turk," *Harvard Business Review*, September–October 1974, pp. 70–80.

23. E. D. Weed, "Job Enrichment 'Cleans Up' at Texas Instruments," in J. R. Maher (ed.), *New Perspectives in Job Enrichment* (New York: Van Nostrand, 1971).

24. Griffin and McMahan, "Motivation Through Job Design," and Griffin, *Task Design*.

25. Robert J. House and L. Wigdor, "Herzberg's Dual-Factor Theory of Job Satisfaction and Motivation: A Review of the Evidence and a Criticism," *Personnel Psychology*, 1967, vol. 20, 1967, pp. 369–389.

26. J. Richard Hackman and Greg Oldham, "Motivation Through the Design of Work: Test of a Theory," *Organizational Behavior and Human Performance*, 1976, vol. 16, pp. 250–279. See also Michael A. Campion and Paul W. Thayer, "Job Design: Approaches, Outcomes, and Trade-Offs," *Organizational Dynamics*, Winter 1987, pp. 66–78.

27. Ibid.

28. J. Richard Hackman, "Work Design," in J. Richard Hackman and J. L. Suttle (eds.), *Improving Life at Work: Behavioral Science Approaches to Organizational Change* (Santa Monica, California: Goodyear, 1977).

29. Griffin, *Task Design*.

30. Griffin, Task Design. See also Karlene H. Roberts and William Glick, "The Job Characteristics Approach to Task Design: A Critical Review," *Journal of Applied Psychology*, 1981, vol. 66, pp. 193–217; and Ricky W. Griffin, "Toward an Integrated Theory of Task Design," in Larry L. Cummings and Barry M. Staw (eds.), *Research in Organizational Behavior* (Greenwich, Connecticut: JAI Press, 1987), IX, pp. 79–120.

31. Yitzhak Fried and Gerald Ferris, "The Validity of the Job Characteristics Model: A Review and Meta-Analysis," *Personnel Psychology*, 1987, vol. 40, pp. 287–322.

32. John L. Cordery and Peter P. Sevastos, "Responses to the Original and Revised Job Diagnostic Survey: Is Education a Factor in Responses to Negatively Worded Items?" *Journal of Applied Psychology*, 1993, vol. 78, pp. 141–143. See also Brian T. Loher, Raymond A. Noe, Nancy L. Moeller, and Michael P. Fitzgerald, "A Meta-Analysis of the Relation of Job Characteristics to Job Satisfaction," *Journal of Applied Psychology*, 1985, vol. 70, pp. 280–289.

33. Roberts and Glick, "The Job Characteristics Approach to Task Design."

34. For examples, see Donald J. Campbell, "Task Complexity: A Review and Analysis," *Academy of Management Review*, January 1988, pp. 40–52; Donald G. Gardner, "Task Complexity Effects on Non-Task-Related Movements: A Test of Activation Theory," *Organizational Behavior and Human Decision Processes*, 1990, vol. 45, pp. 209–231; Barry M. Staw and Richard D. Boettger, "Task Revision: A Neglected Form of Work Performance," *Academy of Management Journal*, September 1990, pp. 534–559.

35. Gerald Salancik and Jeffrey Pfeffer, "An Examination of Need-Satisfaction Models of Job Attitudes," *Administrative Science Quarterly*, 1977, vol. 22, pp. 427–456; Gerald Salancik and Jeffrey Pfeffer, "A Social Information Processing Approach to Job Attitudes and Task Design," *Administrative Science Quarterly*, 1978, vol. 23, pp. 224–253.

36. Salancik and Pfeffer, "A Social Information Processing Approach."

37. Joe Thomas and Ricky W. Griffin, "The Social Information Processing Model of Task Design: A Review of the Literature," *Academy of Management Review*, October 1983, pp. 672–682. See also Griffin, "Toward an Integrated Theory of Task Design."

38. Charles A. O'Reilly and D. F. Caldwell, "Informational Influence as a Determinant of Perceived Task Characteristics and Job Satisfaction," *Journal of Applied Psychology*, 1979, vol. 64, pp. 157–165; Ricky W. Griffin, "Objective and Social Sources of Information in Task Redesign: A Field Experiment," *Administrative Science Quarterly*, June 1983, pp. 184–200. See also Griffin, "Toward an Integrated Theory of Task Design," and Donald J. Campbell, "Task Complexity: A Review and Analysis," *Academy of Management Review*, January 1988, pp. 40–52.

39. David J. Glew, Anne M. O'Leary-Kelly, Ricky W. Griffin, and David D. Van Fleet, "Participation in Organizations: A Preview of the Issues and Proposed Framework for Future Analysis," *Journal of Management*, 1995, vol. 21, no. 3, pp. 395–421.

40. John A. Wagner III, "Participation's Effects of Performance and Satisfaction: A Reconsideration of Research Evidence," *Academy of Management Review*, 1994, vol. 19, no. 2, pp. 312–330.

41. See Putai Jin, "Work Motivation and Productivity in Voluntarily Formed Work Teams: A Field Study in China," *Organizational Behavior and Human Decision Processes*, vol. 54, 1993, pp. 133–155, for an interesting example.

42. Baxter W. Graham, "The Business Argument for Flexibility," *HRMagazine*, May 1996, pp. 104–110.

43. A. R. Cohen and H. Gadon, *Alternative Work Schedules: Integrating Individual and Organizational Needs* (Reading, Massachusetts: Addison-Wesley, 1978).

Chapter 6

1. http://www.ctv.ca/servlet/ArticleNews/story/CTVNews/20060227/nursing_burnout_060227/20060227?hub=Health (accessed on February 19, 2007); http://www.cbc.ca/news/story/2006/10/04/qc-teachersburnout.html on February 19, 2007; http://www.statcan.ca/Daily/English/061211/d061211b.htm on February 19, 2007; Michael P. Leiter, "Perception of risk: An organizational model of occupational risk, burnout, and physical symptoms," *Anxiety, Stress & Coping: An International Journal*, Vol 18(2), June 2005, pp. 131–144.

2. See James C. Quick and Jonathan D. Quick, *Organizational Stress and Preventive Management* (New York: McGraw-Hill, 1984), for a review.

3. Hans Selye, *The Stress of Life* (New York: McGraw-Hill, 1976).

4. Ibid.

5. Meyer Friedman and Ray H. Rosenman, *Type A Behavior and Your Heart* (New York: Knopf, 1974).

6. Ibid.

7. Joshua Fischman, "Type A on Trial," *Psychology Today*, February 1987, pp. 42–50.

8. "Prognosis for the 'Type A' Personality Improves in a New Heart Disease Study," *Wall Street Journal*, 14 January 1988, p. 27.

9. Susan C. Kobasa, "Stressful Life Events, Personality, and Health: An Inquiry Into Hardiness," *Journal of Personality and Social Psychology*, January 1979, pp. 1–11; Susan C. Kobasa, S. R. Maddi, and S. Kahn, "Hardiness and Health: A Prospective Study," *Journal of Personality and Social Psychology*, January 1982, pp. 168–177.

10. Todd D. Jick and Linda F. Mitz, "Sex Differences in Work Stress," *Academy of Management Review*, October 1985, pp. 408–420; Debra L. Nelson and James C. Quick, "Professional Women: Are Distress and Disease Inevitable?" *Academy of Management Review*, April 1985, pp. 206–218.

11. "Complex Characters Handle Stress Better," *Psychology Today*, October 1987, p. 26.

12. Jeffrey R. Edwards, "An Examination of Competing Versions of the Person–Environment Fit Approach to Stress," *Academy of Management Journal*, 1996, vol. 39, no. 2, pp. 292–339.

13. Selye, *Stress of Life*. See also Stephan J. Motowidlo, John S. Packard, and Michael R. Manning, "Occupational Stress: Its Causes and Consequences for Job Performance," *Journal of Applied Psychology*, vol. 71, 1986, pp. 618–629.

14. Peter Kuitenbrouwer, "St. Efficiency's Caring Ways: Toronto's St. Michael's Hospital Is a Lean, Cost-Efficient Machine. But Staff Is Harried and Administrators Are Beginning to Wonder About Quality of Patient Care," *Financial Post*, 7/9 February 1998, pp. 8–9; Jane Auman and Brian Draheim, "The Downside to Downsizing: When a Company Eliminates a Large Number of Its Staff, Disability Costs Should Also Shrink, Right? Wrong, Say Experts," *Benefits Canada*, 1997, vol. 21, no. 5, pp. 31–33.

15. Robert I. Sutton and Anat Rafaeli, "Characteristics of Work Stations as Potential Occupational Stressors," *Academy of Management Journal*, June 1987, pp. 260–276.

16. See Edward R. Kemery, Arthur G. Bedeian, Kevin W. Mossholder, and John Touliatos, "Outcomes of Role Stress: A Multisample Constructive Replication," *Academy of Management Journal*, June 1985, pp. 363–375, for an examination of the effects of role demands.

17. See Karyl E. MacEwan and Julian Barling, "Daily Consequences of Work Interference with Family and Family Interference with Work," *Work and Stress*, 1994, vol. 8, no. 3, pp. 244–254; Karyl E. MacEwan, Julian Barling, and E. Kevin Kelloway, "Effects of Short-Term Role Overload on Marital Interactions," *Work and Stress*, 1992, vol. 6, no. 2, pp. 117–126; and Wendy Stewart and Julian Barling, "Daily Work Stress, Mood, and Interpersonal Job Performance: A Mediational Model," *Work and Stress*, 1996, vol. 10, no. 4, pp. 336–351.

18. For research in this area, see Donna L. Wiley, "The Relationship Between Work/Nonwork Role Conflict and Job-Related Outcomes: Some Unanticipated Findings," *Journal of Management*, Winter 1987, pp. 467–472; and Arthur G. Bedeian, Beverly G. Burke, and Richard G. Moffett, "Outcomes of Work–Family Conflict Among Married Male and Female Professionals," *Journal of Management*, September 1988, pp. 475–485.

19. See Donna M. Randall, "Multiple Roles and Organizational Commitment," *Journal of Organizational Behavior*, vol. 9, 1988, pp. 309–317.

20. See Gary M. Kaufman and Terry A. Beehr, "Interactions Between Job Stressors and Social Support: Some Counterintuitive

Results," *Journal of Applied Psychology*, vol. 71, 1986, pp. 522–526 for an interesting study in this area.

21. David R. Frew and Nealia S. Bruning, "Perceived Organizational Characteristics and Personality Measures as Predictors of Stress/Strain in the Work Place," *Academy of Management Journal*, December 1987, pp. 633–646.

22. Quick and Quick, *Organizational Stress and Preventive Management*.

23. Thomas H. Holmes and Richard H. Rahe, "The Social Readjustment Rating Scale," *Journal of Psychosomatic Research*, vol. 11, 1967, pp. 213–218.

24. Evelyn J. Bromet, Mary A. Dew, David K. Parkinson, and Herbert C. Schulberg, "Predictive Effects of Occupational and Marital Stress on the Mental Health of a Male Workforce," *Journal of Organizational Behavior*, vol. 9, 1988, pp. 1–13.

25. Quick and Quick, *Organizational Stress and Preventive Management*. See also John M. Ivancevich and Michael T. Matteson, *Stress and Work: A Managerial Perspective* (Glenview, Illinois: Scott, Foresman, 1980).

26. Quick and Quick, *Organizational Stress and Preventive Management*.

27. Ibid.

28. Ibid.

29. Quick and Quick, *Organizational Stress and Preventive Management*. See also "Stress: The Test Americans Are Failing," *Business Week*, 18 April 1988, pp. 74–76.

30. "Employers on Guard for Violence," *Wall Street Journal*, 5 April 1995, pp. 3A.

31. Raymond T. Lee and Blake E. Ashforth, "A Meta-Analytic Examination of the Correlates of the Three Dimensions of Job Burnout," *Journal of Applied Psychology*, 1996, vol. 81, no. 2, pp. 123–133.

32. See Susan E. Jackson, Richard L. Schwab, and Randall S. Schuler, "Toward an Understanding of the Burnout Phenomenon," *Journal of Applied Psychology*, 1986, vol. 71, pp. 630–640; and Daniel W. Russell, Elizabeth Altmaier, and Dawn Van Velzen, "Job-Related Stress, Social Support, and Burnout Among Classroom Teachers," *Journal of Applied Psychology*, 1987, vol. 72, pp. 269–274.

33. See Michael P. Leiter, "Burnout as a Developmental Process: Consideration of Models," in W. B. Schaufeli, C. Maslach, and T. Marek (eds.), *Professional Burnout: Recent Developments in Theory and Research* (Washington, D.C.: Taylor and Francis, 1993), pp. 237–250; and Michael P. Leiter and Christina Maslach, "The Impact of Interpersonal Environment on Burnout and Organizational Commitment," *Journal of Organizational Behavior*, 1991, vol. 12, no. 2, pp. 297–308.

34. Lee and Ashforth, *A Meta-Analytic Examination of the Correlates of the Three Dimensions of Burnout*.

35. Quick and Quick, *Organizational Stress and Preventive Management*.

36. C. Folkins, "Effects of Physical Training on Mood," *Journal of Clinical Psychology*, April 1976, pp. 385–390.

37. John W. Lounsbury and Linda L. Hoopes, "A Vacation from Work: Changes in Work and Nonwork Outcomes," *Journal of Applied Psychology*, 1986, vol. 71, pp. 392–401.

38. "Eight Ways to Help You Reduce the Stress in Your Life," *Business Week Careers*, November 1986, p. 78.

39. Daniel C. Ganster, Marcelline R. Fusilier, and Bronston T. Mayes, "Role of Social Support in the Experiences of Stress at Work," *Journal of Applied Psychology*, 1986, vol. 71, pp. 102–110.

40. Randall S. Schuler and Susan E. Jackson, "Managing Stress Through PHRM Practices: An Uncertainty Interpretation," in K. Rowland and G. Ferris (eds.), *Research in Personnel and Human Resources Management* (Greenwich, Connecticut: JAI Press, 1986), IV, pp. 183–224.

41. Quick and Quick, *Organizational Stress and Preventive Management*.

42. Ibid.

43. Richard A. Wolfe, David O. Ulrich, and Donald F. Parker, "Employee Health Management Programs: Review, Critique, and Research Agenda," *Journal of Management*, Winter 1987, pp. 603–615.

44. "A Cure for Stress?" *Newsweek*, 12 October 1987, pp. 64–65.

45. Linda Thiede Thomas and Daniel C. Ganster, "Impact of Family-Supportive Work Variables on Work-Family Conflict and Strain: A Control Perspective," *Journal of Applied Psychology*, 1995, vol. 80, no. 1, pp. 6–15; Victoria J. Doby and Robert D. Caplan, "Organizational Stress as Threat to Reputation: Effects on Anxiety at Work and at Home," *Academy of Management Journal*, 1995, vol. 38, no. 4, pp. 1105–1123.

Chapter 7

1. "Community," "Founders Letter," "The Company," eBay website, www.ebay.com on April 17, 2005 (quotation); Michelle Conlin, "The eBay Way," *Business Week,* November 29, 2004, www.businessweek.com on February 14, 2005; Rob Hof, "Meet eBay's Auctioneer-in-Chief," *Business Week,* May 29, 2003, www.businessweek.com on April 17, 2005; Sarah Lacy, "Getting with the Program on eBay," *Business Week,* November 1, 2004, www.businessweek.com on February 14, 2005; Kate Murphy, "eBay Merchants Trust Their Eyes, and the Bubble Wrap," *New York Times,* October 24, 2004, p. BU 7; Amey Stone, "Well Spent," *Business Week,* February 9, 2005, www.businessweek.com on April 17, 2005.

2. Charles A. O'Reilly, III, and Louis R. Pondy, "Organizational Communication," in Steven Kerr (ed.), *Organizational Behavior* (Columbus, Ohio: Grid, 1979), p. 121.

3. Otis W. Baskin and Craig E. Aronoff, *Interpersonal Communication in Organizations* (Santa Monica, California: Goodyear, 1980), p. 2.

4. Laura Ramsay, "Communication Key to Workplace Happiness," *Financial Post*, 6/8 December 1997, p. 58.

5. "How Merrill Lynch Moves Its Stock Deals All Around the World," *Wall Street Journal*, 9 November 1987, pp. 1, 8.

6. William J. Seiler, E. Scott Baudhuin, and L. David Shuelke, *Communication in Business and Professional Organizations* (Reading, Massachusetts: Addison-Wesley, 1982).

7. Jeanne D. Maes, Teresa G. Weldy, and Marjorie L. Icenogle, "A Managerial Perspective: Oral Communication Competency Is Most Important for Business Students in the Workplace," *Journal of Business Communication,* January 1997, pp. 67–80.

8. Melinda Knight, "Writing and Other Communication Standards in Undergraduate Business Education: A Study of Current Program Requirements, Practices, and Trends," *Business Communication Quarterly,* March 1999, p. 10.

9. Robert Nurden, "Graduates Must Master the Lost Art of Communication," *The European,* March 20, 1997, p. 24.

10. Silvan S. Tompkins and Robert McCarter, "What and Where Are the Primary Affects? Some Evidence for a Theory," *Perceptual and Motor Skills,* February 1964, pp. 119–158.

11. Robert T. Keller and Winfred E. Holland, "Communicators and Innovators in Research and Development Organizations," *Academy of Management Journal,* December 1983, pp. 742–749.

12. See Everett M. Rogers and Rekha Agarwala-Rogers, *Communication in Organizations* (New York: Free Press, 1976), for a brief review of the background and development of the source-message-channel-receiver model of communication.

13. Charles A. O'Reilly, III, "Variations in Decision Makers' Use of Information Sources: The Impact of Quality and Accessibility of Information," *Academy of Management Journal,* December 1982, pp. 756–771.

14. See Richard L. Daft and Robert H. Lengel, "Information Richness: A New Approach to Managerial Behavior and Organization Design," in Barry M. Staw and L. L. Cummings (eds.), *Research in Organizational Behavior* (Greenwich, Connecticut: JAI Press, 1984), VI, pp. 191–233, for further discussion of media and information richness.

15. See Janet Fulk and Brian Boyd, "Emerging Theories of Communication in Organizations," *Journal of Management,* 1991, pp. 407–446, for a good review of the research on choice of medium for message transmission.

16. Anat Rafaeli and Robert I. Sutton, "The Expression of Emotion in Organizational Life," in Larry L. Cummings and Barry M. Staw (eds.), *Research in Organizational Behavior* (Greenwich, Connecticut: JAI Press, 1989), XI, pp. 1–42.

17. See Jerry C. Wofford, Edwin A. Gerloff, and Robert C. Cummins, *Organizational Communication* (New York: McGraw-Hill,1977), for a discussion of channel noise.

18. Donald R. Hollis, "The Shape of Things to Come: The Role of IT," *Management Review,* June 1996, p. 62.

19. Kym France, "Computer Commuting Benefits Companies," *Arizona Republic,* 16 August 1993, pp. E1, E4.

20. Starr R. Hiltz, "User Satisfaction with Computer-Mediated Communication Systems," *Management Science,* June 1990, pp. 739–764; Carol S. Saunders, "Management Information Systems, Communications, and Department Power: An Integrative Model," *Academy of Management Review,* July 1981, pp. 431–442.

21. Oren Harari, "Turn Your Organization into a Hotbed of Ideas," *Management Review,* December 1995, pp. 37–39.

22. Paul S. Goodman and Eric D. Darr, "Exchanging Best Practices Through Computer-Aided Systems," *Academy of Management Executive,* May 1996, pp. 7–18.

23. Richard Bray, "Petro-Canada Builds Home Port for Intranet Users," CIO Canada, 1 November 2006.

24. See Daniel Katz and Robert L. Kahn, "The Social Psychology of Organizations, 2nd ed. (New York: Wiley, 1978), for more about the role of organizational communication networks.

25. Peter R. Monge, Jane A. Edwards, and Kenneth K. Kirste, "Determinants of Communication Network Involvement: Connectedness and Integration," Group & Organization Studies, March 1983, pp. 83–112.

26. Irving S. Shapiro, "Managerial Communication: The View from the Inside," *California Management Review,* Fall 1984, pp. 157–172.

27. "GM Boots Perot," *Newsweek,* 15 December 1986, pp. 56–62.

28. Bruce H. Goodsite, "General Motors Attacks Its Frozen Middle," *IABC Communication World,* October 1987, pp. 20–23.

29. See R. Wayne Pace, *Organizational Communication: Foundations for Human Resource Development* (Englewood Cliffs, New Jersey: Prentice Hall, 1983), for further discussion of the development of communication networks.

30. David Krackhardt and Lyman W. Porter, "The Snowball Effect: Turnover Embedded in Communication Networks," *Journal of Applied Psychology,* February 1986, pp. 50–55.

31. Monge, Edwards, and Kirste, "Determinants of Communication Network Involvement."

32. Karl E. Weick and Larry D. Browning, "Argument and Narration in Organizational Communication," *Journal of Management,* Summer 1986, pp. 243–259.

33. "Small Is Beautiful Now in Manufacturing," *Business Week,* 22 October 1984, pp. 152–156.

34. Pace, *Organizational Communication.*

35. Losana E. Boyd, "Why 'Talking It Out' Almost Never Works Out," *Nation's Business,* November 1984, pp. 53–54.

36. Robert A. Snyder and James H. Morris, "Organizational Communication and Performance," *Journal of Applied Psychology,* August 1984, pp. 461–465.

37. Keith Davis and John W. Newstrom, *Human Behavior at Work: Organizational Behavior,* 7th ed. (New York: McGraw-Hill, 1985), pp. 314–323.

38. Thomas J. Peters and Robert H. Waterman, Jr., *In Search of Excellence: Lessons from America's Best-Run Companies* (New York: Harper & Row, 1982), p. 121.

39. Michelle Magnan, "People Power," *Canadian Business,* October 2005, www.canadianbusiness.com.on May 15, 2007.

40. Charles A. O'Reilly, "Individual and Information Overload in Organizations: Is More Necessarily Better?" *Academy of Management Journal,* December 1980, pp. 684–696.

41. James L. McKenney and F. Warren McFarlan, "The Information Archipelago—Maps and Bridges," *Harvard Business Review,* September–October 1982, pp. 109–119.

42. Michael Brody, "Listen to Your Whistleblower," *Fortune,* 24 November 1986, pp. 77–78.

Chapter 8

1. Jonathon Gatehouse, "The Girls Go Wild," *Maclean's,* March 6, 2006, pp. 39–41.

2. Eric L. Trist and K. W. Bamforth, "Some Social and Psychological Consequences of the Longwall Method of Goal-Getting," *Human Relations,* February 1951, pp. 3–38; Jack D. Orsburn, Linda Moran, and Ed Musselwhite, with John Zenger, *Self-Directed Work Teams: The New American Challenge* (Homewood, Illinois: Business One Irwin, 1990).

3. Charles C. Manz and Henry P. Sims, *Business Without Bosses: How Self-Managing Teams Are Building High-Performance Companies* (New York: Wiley, 1993), pp. 12–14.

4. P. Booth, *Challenge and Change: Embracing the Team Concept* (Report 123-94, Ottawa: The Conference Board of Canada, 1994).

5. Blake E. Ashforth and Fred Mael, "Social Identity Theory and the Organization," *Academy of Management Review*, January 1989, pp. 20–39.

6. Marvin E. Shaw, *Group Dynamics: The Psychology of Small Group Behavior*, 3rd ed.(New York: McGraw-Hill, 1981).

7. Ibid., p. 11.

8. Gerald R. Ferris and Kendrith M. Rowland, "Social Facilitation Effects on Behavioral and Perceptual Task Performance Measures: Implications for Work Behavior," *Group & Organization Studies*, December 1983, pp. 421–438; Jeff Meer, "Loafing Through a Tough Job," *Psychology Today*, January 1985, p. 72.

9. J. Paul Sorrels and Bettye Myers, "Comparison of Group and Family Dynamics," *Human Relations*, May 1983, pp. 477–490.

10. Alfred W. Clark and Robert J. Powell, "Changing Drivers" Attitudes Through Peer Group Decision," *Human Relations*, February 1984, pp. 155–162.

11. Francis J. Yammarino and Alan J. Dubinsky, "Salesperson Performance and Managerially Controllable Factors: An Investigation of Individual and Work Group Effects," *Journal of Management*, 1990, vol. 16, pp. 87–106.

12. "Detroit Versus the UAW: At Odds over Teamwork," *Business Week*, 24 August 1987, pp. 54–55.

13. Brian Dumaine, "Who Needs a Boss?" *Fortune*, 7 May 1990, pp. 52–60.

14. Shawn Tully, "The Vatican's Finances," *Fortune*, 21 December 1987, pp. 28–40.

15. "Women at Work," *Business Week*, 28 January 1985, pp. 80–85.

16. Bernard M. Bass and Edward C. Ryterband, *Organizational Psychology*, 2nd ed. (Boston: Allyn and Bacon, 1979), pp. 252–254.

17. John P. Wanous, Arnon E. Reichers, and S. D. Malik, "Organizational Socialization and Group Development: Toward an Integrative Perspective," *Academy of Management Review*, October 1984, pp. 670–683.

18. Wanous, Reichers, and Malik, "Organizational Socialization and Group Development."

19. Steven L. Obert, "Developmental Patterns of Organizational Task Groups: A Preliminary Study," *Human Relations*, January 1983, pp. 37–52.

20. Bass and Ryterband, *Organizational Psychology*, pp. 252–254.

21. Bernard M. Bass, "The Leaderless Group Discussion," *Psychological Bulletin*, September 1954, pp. 465–492.

22. Connie J. G. Gersick, "Marking Time: Predictable Transitions in Task Groups," *Academy of Management Journal*, vol. 32, 1989, pp. 274–309.

23. James H. Davis, *Group Performance* (Reading, Massachusetts: Addison-Wesley, 1964), pp. 82–86.

24. Shaw, *Group Dynamics*.

25. Charles A. O'Reilly III, David F. Caldwell, and William P. Barnett, "Work Group Demography, Social Integration, and Turnover," *Administrative Science Quarterly*, March 1989, vol. 34, pp. 21–37.

26. Nancy Adler, *International Dimensions of Organizational Behavior*, 3rd ed. (Boston, Massachusetts: PWS–Kent), pp. 132–133.

27. P. Christopher Earley, "Social Loafing and Collectivism: A Comparison of the United States and the People's Republic of China," *Administrative Science Quarterly*, 1989, pp. 565–581.

28. Shaw, *Group Dynamics*, pp. 173–177.

29. Davis, *Group Performance*, p. 73.

30. Steven E. Markham, Fred Dansereau, Jr., and Joseph A. Alutto, "Group Size and Absenteeism Rates: A Longitudinal Analysis," *Academy of Management Journal*, December 1982, pp. 921–927.

31. Nigel Nicholson (ed.), *The Blackwell Encyclopedic Dictionary of Organizational Behavior* (Cambridge, Massachusetts: Blackwell, 1995), p. 522.

32. Davis, *Group Performance*, p. 82.

33. Bass and Ryterband, *Organizational Psychology*, pp. 252–254.

34. Shaw, *Group Dynamics*, pp. 280–293.

35. Daniel C. Feldman, "The Development and Enforcement of Group Norms," *Academy of Management Review*, January 1984, pp. 47–53.

36. L. Festinger, "Informal Social Communication," *Psychological Review*, September 1950, p. 274.

37. William E. Piper, Myriam Marrache, Renee Lacroix, Astrid M. Richardson, and Barry D. Jones, "Cohesion as a Basic Bond in Groups," *Human Relations*, February 1983, pp. 93–108.

38. Davis, *Group Performance*, pp. 78–81.

39. Robert T. Keller, "Predictors of the Performance of Project Groups in R&D Organizations," *Academy of Management Journal*, December 1986, pp. 715–726.

40. Irving L. Janis, *Groupthink*, 2nd ed. (Boston: Houghton Mifflin, 1982), p. 9.

41. Blake E. Ashforth and Fred Mael, "Social Identity Theory and the Organization," *Academy of Management Review*, January 1989, pp. 20–39.

42. Reed E. Nelson, "The Strength of Strong Ties: Social Networks and Intergroup Conflict in Organizations," *Academy of Management Journal*, June 1989, pp. 377–401. Reprinted by permission. "Now That It's Cruising, Can Ford Keep Its Foot to the Gas?" *Business Week*, 11 February 1985, pp. 48–52.

43. *The American Heritage Dictionary of the English Language*, 3rd ed. (Boston: Houghton Mifflin, 1992), pp. 800, 1842.

44. See Katzenbach and Smith, *The Wisdom of Teams*, p. 45.

45. Ibid., p. 3.

46. John Southerest, "Now Everyone Can Be a Boss," *Canadian Business*, May 1994, pp. 48–50.

47. Manz and Sims, *Business Without Bosses*, pp. 10–11.

48. Richard S. Wellins, William C. Byham, and George R. Dixon, *Inside Teams* (San Francisco: Jossey-Bass, 1994), pp. 335–336.

49. Katzenbach and Smith, *The Wisdom of Teams*, pp. 184–189.

50. Manz and Sims, *Business Without Bosses*, pp. 74–76.

51. Nigel Nicholson, *Encyclopedic Dictionary of Organizational Behavior*, p. 463.

52. Brian Dumaine, "The Trouble with Teams," *Fortune*, 5 September 1994.

53. Ibid.

54. Ellen Hart, "Top Teams," *Management Review*, February 1996, pp. 43–47.

55. Dan Dimancescu and Kemp Dwenger, "Smoothing the Product Development Path," *Management Review*, January 1996, pp. 36–41.

Chapter 9

1. Erin Pooley, "Most Innovative CEO 2005: David Patchell-Evans, GoodLife Fitness Clubs," *Canadian Business*, April 25–May 8, 2005, www.canadianbusiness.com; GoodLife Fitness website, www.goodlifefitness.com.

2. Herbert Simon, *The New Science of Management Decision* (New York: Harper & Row, 1960), p. 1.

3. Simon, *The New Science of Management Decision*.

4. Nandini Rajagopalan, Abdul M. A. Rasheed, and Deepak K. Datta, "Strategic Decision Processes: Critical Review and Future Directions," *Journal of Management*, vol. 19, no. 2, pp. 349–384.

5. See Bernard M. Bass, *Organizational Decision Making* (Homewood, Illinois: Irwin, 1983), pp. 13–15, for a discussion of poorly structured and well-structured problems.

6. See George P. Huber, *Managerial Decision Making* (Glenview, Illinois: Scott, Foresman, 1980), pp. 90–115, for a discussion of decision making under conditions of certainty, risk, and uncertainty.

7. See Bass, *Organizational Decision Making*, pp. 83–89, for a discussion of uncertainty.

8. See Bass, *Organizational Decision Making*, pp. 27–31, on the economic theory of the firm.

9. "'90s Style Brainstorming," *Forbes ASAP*, 25 October 1993, pp. 44–61.

10. Milan Zeleny, "Descriptive Decision Making and Its Application," *Applications of Management Science*, 1981, vol. 1, pp. 327–388; Henry Mintzberg, Duru Raisinghani, and André Thoret, "The Structure of 'Unstructured' Decision Processes," *Administrative Science Quarterly*, June 1976, pp. 246–275.

11. See E. Frank Harrison, *The Managerial Decision Making Process*, 2nd ed. (Boston: Houghton Mifflin, 1981), pp. 41–43, for more on choice processes.

12. Donald C. Hambrick and David Lei, "Toward an Empirical Prioritization of Contingency Variables for Business Strategy," *Academy of Management Journal*, December 1985, pp. 763–788; Ari Ginsberg and N. Ventrakaman, "Contingency Perspectives of Organizational Strategy: A Critical Review of the Empirical Research," *Academy of Management Review*, July 1985, pp. 412–434.

13. Leon Festinger, *A Theory of Cognitive Dissonance* (Palo Alto, California: Stanford University Press, 1957).

14. Patricia Sellers, "The Dumbest Marketing Ploys," *Fortune*, 5 October 1992, pp. 88–94.

15. See Harrison, *The Managerial Decision Making Process*, pp. 53–57, for more on the advantages and disadvantages of the rational approach.

16. See Paul C. Nutt, "The Formulation Processes and Tactics Used in Organizational Decision Making," *Organization Science*, 1993, vol. 4, no. 2, pp. 226–236.

17. Craig D. Parks and Rebecca Cowlin, "Group Discussion as Affected by Number of Alternatives and by a Time Limit," *Organizational Behavior and Human Decision Processes*, pp. 267–275, June 1995, vol. 62, no. 3.

18. See James G. March and Herbert A. Simon, *Organizations* (New York: Wiley, 1958), for more on the concept of bounded rationality.

19. Herbert A. Simon, *Administrative Behavior: A Study of Decision-Making Processes in Administrative Organizations*, 3rd ed. (New York: Free Press, 1976).

20. Richard M. Cyert and James G. March, *A Behavioral Theory of the Firm* (Englewood Cliffs, New Jersey: Prentice Hall, 1963), p. 113; Simon, *Administrative Behavior*.

21. Kathleen M. Eisenhardt, "Making Fast Strategic Decisions in High-Velocity Environments," *Academy of Management Journal*, September 1989, pp. 543–576.

22. Irving L. Janis and Leon Mann, *Decision Making: A Psychological Analysis of Conflict, Choice, and Commitment* (New York: Free Press, 1977).

23. "Stage Set for Conflict at Disney Meeting," *USA Today*, February 22, 2005, p. B1.

24. Kimberly D. Elsbach and Greg Elofson, "How the Packaging of Decision Explanations Affects Perceptions of Trustworthiness," *Academy of Management Journal*, 2000, vol. 43, pp. 80–89.

25. Charles P. Wallace, "Adidas—Back in the Game," *Fortune*, August 18, 1997, pp. 176–182.

26. Jerry Ross and Barry M. Staw, "EXPO '86: An Escalation Prototype," *Administrative Science Quarterly*, June 1986, pp. 274–297.

27. Barry M. Staw, "Escalation of Commitment to a Course of Action," *Academy of Management Review*, October 1981, pp. 577–587.

28. Joel Brockner, Robert Houser, Gregg Birnbaum, Kathy Lloyd, Janet Dietcher, Sinaia Nathanson, and Jeffrey Z. Rubin, "Escalation of Commitment to an Ineffective Course of Action: The Effect of Feedback Having Negative Implications for Self-Identity," *Administrative Science Quarterly*, March 1986, 109–126.

29. Barry M. Staw and Jerry Ross, "Good Money After Bad," *Psychology Today*, February 1988, pp. 30–33.

30. Gerry McNamara and Philip Bromiley, "Risk and Return in Organizational Decision Making," *Academy of Management Journal*, 1999, vol. 42, pp. 330–339.

31. See Brian O'Reilly, "What It Takes to Start a Startup," *Fortune*, June 7, 1999, pp. 135–140, for an example.

32. James A. F. Stoner, "Risky and Cautious Shifts in Group Decisions: The Influence of Widely Held Values," *Journal of Experimental Social Psychology*, October 1968, pp. 442–459; M. A. Wallach, N. Kogan, and D. J. Bem, "Group Influence on Individual Risk Taking," *Journal of Abnormal and Social Psychology*, August 1962, pp. 75–86.

33. Dorwin Cartwright, "Risk Taking by Individuals and Groups: An Assessment of Research Employing Choice Dilemmas," *Journal of Personality and Social Psychology*, December 1971, pp. 361–378.

34. S. Moscovici and M. Zavalloni, "The Group as a Polarizer of Attitudes, *Journal of Personality and Social Psychology*, June 1969, pp. 125–135.

35. See Marvin E. Shaw, *Group Dynamics: The Psychology of Small Group Behavior* (New York: McGraw-Hill, 1981), pp. 68–76, for further discussion of group polarization.

36. Irving L. Janis, *Groupthink*, 2nd ed. (Boston: Houghton Mifflin, 1982), p. 9.

37. Mindy West, Gregory Moorhead, and Christopher P. Neck, "The Relevance of Groupthink for the 21st Century: A Self-Managing Team Perspective," paper presented at the Academy of Management Meeting, Cincinnati, Ohio, August 1996.

38. Gregory Moorhead, Richard Ference, and Chris P. Neck, "Group Decision Fiascoes Continue: Space Shuttle Challenger and a Revised Groupthink Framework," *Human Relations*, 1991, vol. 44, pp. 539–550.

39. Irving L. Janis, *Victims of Groupthink* (Boston: Houghton Mifflin, 1972), pp. 197–198.

40. Janis, *Groupthink*.

41. Moorhead, Ference, and Neck, "Group Decision Fiascoes Continue"; Kevin Tasa and Glen Whyte, "Collective Efficacy and Vigilant Problem Solving in Group Decision Making: A Non-Linear Model," Organizational Behavior and Human Decision Processes, 2005, vol. 96, pp. 119–129.

42. Janis, *Groupthink*, pp. 193–197; Gregory Moorhead, "Groupthink: Hypothesis in Need of Testing," *Group and Organization Studies*, December 1982, pp. 429–444.

43. Gregory Moorhead and John R. Montanari, "Empirical Analysis of the Groupthink Phenomenon," *Human Relations*, May 1986, pp. 399–410; John R. Montanari and Gregory Moorhead, "Development of the Groupthink Assessment Inventory," *Educational and Psychological Measurement*, Spring 1989, vol. 49, pp. 209–219.

44. Janis, *Groupthink*.

45. Sean Silicoff, "The Sky's Your Limit," *Canadian Business*, April 1997, pp. 58–66.

46. Rensis Likert, *New Patterns of Management* (New York: McGraw-Hill, 1961); Chris Argyris, *Personality and Organization* (New York: Harper & Row, 1957).

47. N. C. Morse and E. Reimer, "The Experimental Change of a Major Organizational Variable," *Journal of Abnormal and Social Psychology*, January 1956, pp. 120–129; Lester Coch and John R. P. French, "Overcoming Resistance to Change," *Human Relations*, 1948, vol. 1, pp. 512–532.

48. See Marvin E. Shaw, *Group Dynamics*, pp. 57–68.

49. See Huber, *Managerial Decision Making*, pp. 140–148.

50. Victor H. Vroom and Arthur G. Jago, *The New Leadership* (Englewood Cliffs, New Jersey: Prentice Hall, 1988).

51. See Carrie R. Leana, Edwin A. Locke, and David M. Schweiger, "Fact and Fiction in Analyzing Research on Participative Decision Making: A Critique of Cotton, Vollrath, Froggatt, Lengnick-Hall, and Jennings," *Academy of Management Review*, January 1990, pp. 137–146; John L. Cotton, David A. Vollrath, Mark L. Lengnick-Hall, and Mark L. Froggatt, "Fact: The Form of Participation Does Matter—A Rebuttal to Leana, Locke, and Schweiger," *Academy of Management Review*, January 1990, pp. 147–153.

52. See Bass, *Organizational Decision Making*, pp. 162–163, for further discussion of the nominal group technique.

53. George P. Haber, *Managerial Decision Making* (Glenview, Illinois: Scott Foresman, 1980), pp. 205–212, for more details on the Delphi technique.

54. See Richard W. Woodman, John E. Sawyer, and Ricky W. Griffin, "Toward a Theory of Organizational Creativity," *Academy of Management Review*, April 1993, pp. 293–321.

55. See Thomas V. Busse and Richard S. Mansfield, "Theories of the Creative Process: A Review and a Perspective," *Journal of Creative Behavior*, 1980, pp. 91–103.

56. Emily Thornton, "Japan's Struggle to Be Creative," *Fortune*, 19 April 1993, pp. 129–134.

57. John Simons, "The $10 Billion Pill," *Fortune*, January 20, 2003, pp. 58–68.

Chapter 10

1. Canadian Press, "Nova Scotia Tackles Workplace Violence," *The Vancouver Province*, December 17, 2006; Matthew Ramsey, "Workplace Fight Leaves Employee Dead," *The Vancouver Province*, May 14, 2006; Doug Schmidt, "Murder 'Unforeseen,' Hospital Report Says," *The Windsor Star*, August 31, 2006.

2. See Stephen P. Robbins, *Managing Organizational Conflict* (Englewood Cliffs, New Jersey: Prentice Hall, 1974), for a classic review.

3. Charles R. Schwenk, "Conflict in Organizational Decision Making: An Exploratory Study of Its Effects in For-Profit and Not-for-Profit Organizations," *Management Science*, April 1990.

4. "How 2 Computer Nuts Transformed Industry Before Messy Breakup," *Wall Street Journal*, August 27, 1996, pp. A1, A10.

5. Bruce Barry and Greg L. Stewart, "Composition, Process, and Performance in Self-Managed Groups: The Role of Personality," *Journal of Applied Psychology*, 1997, vol. 82, no. 1, pp. 62–78.

6. Jay Bryan, "WestJet Swallows a Bitter Pill," *The Montreal Gazette*, May 30, 2006, www.canada.com on February 21, 2007.

7. James Thompson, *Organizations in Action* (New York: McGraw-Hill, 1967). For another discussion, see Bart Victor and Richard S. Blackburn, "Interdependence: An Alternative Conceptualization," *Academy of Management Review*, July 1987, pp. 486–498.

8. Robert R. Blake, Herbert A. Shepard, and Jane S. Mouton, *Managing Intergroup Conflict in Industry* (Houston: Gulf, 1964).

9. Alfie Kohn, "How to Succeed Without Even Vying," *Psychology Today*, September 1986, pp. 22–28.

10. Andrew S. Grove, "How to Make Confrontation Work for You," *Fortune*, 23 July 1984, pp. 73–75.

11. "Ford of Canada Reaches Tentative Pact with Union Similar to Chrysler Contract," *Wall Street Journal*, 2 October 1987, p. 5; "What's Throwing a Wrench into Britain's Assembly Lines?" *Business Week*, 29 February 1988, p. 41.

12. Janis, *Groupthink*.

13. Robbins, *Managing Organizational Conflict*.

14. Ibid.

15. Blair H. Sheppard, "Third-Party Conflict Intervention: A Procedural Framework," in B. M. Staw and L. L. Cummings (Eds.), *Research in Organizational Behavior*, Volume 6 (Greenwich, Connecticut: JAI Press, 1984), pp. 141–190;

A. R. Elangovan, "Managerial Third-Party Dispute Intervention: A Prescriptive Model of Strategy Selection," *Academy of Management Review*, October 1995, pp. 800–830.

16. Ibid.

17. Kenneth Thomas, "Manager and Mediator: A Comparison of Third-Party Roles Based Upon Conflict-Management Goals," in G. Bomers and R. Peterson (eds.), *Conflict Management and Industrial Relations* (Boston: Kluwer/Nijhoff, 1982), pp. 119–140.

18. John W. Thibaut and Laurens Walker, *Procedural Justice: A Psychological Analysis* (New York: Wiley, 1975).

19. Blair H. Sheppard, "Managers as Inquisitors: Some Lessons From the Law," in M. Bazerman and R. Lewicki (eds.), *Negotiating in Organizations* (Beverly Hills, California: Sage, 1983), pp. 93–213; Rehka Karambayya and Jeanne M. Brett, "Managers Handling Disputes: Third-Party Roles and Perceptions of Fairness," *Academy of Management Journal*, December 1989, pp. 687–704; Roy Lewicki and Blair H. Sheppard, "Choosing How to Intervene: Factors Affecting the Use of Process and Outcome Control in Third-Party Dispute Resolution," *Journal of Occupational Behavior*, January 1985, pp. 49–64.

20. J. Z. Rubin and B. R. Brown, *The Social Psychology of Bargaining and Negotiation* (New York: Academic Press, 1975).

21. R. J. Lewicki and J. A. Litterer, *Negotiation* (Homewood, Illinois: Irwin, 1985).

22. Howard Raiffa, *The Art and Science of Negotiation* (Cambridge, Massachusetts: Belknap, 1982).

23. K. H. Bazerman and M. A. Neale, *Negotiating Rationally* (New York: Free Press, 1992).

24. Ross R. Reck and Brian G. Long, *The Win-Win Negotiator* (Escondido, California: Blanchard Training and Development, 1985).

25. For reviews of the meaning of power, see Henry Mintzberg, *Power in and Around Organizations* (Englewood Cliffs, New Jersey: Prentice Hall, 1983); Jeffrey Pfeffer, *Power in Organizations* (Marshfield, Massachusetts: Pitman Publishing, 1981); John Kenneth Galbraith, *The Anatomy of Power* (Boston: Houghton Mifflin, 1983); Gary A. Yukl, *Leadership in Organizations*, 3rd ed. (Englewood Cliffs, New Jersey: Prentice Hall, 1994).

26. Thomas A. Stewart, "Get with the New Power Game," *Fortune*, 13 January 1997, pp. 58–62.

27. John R. P. French and Bertram Raven, "The Bases of Social Power," in Darwin Cartwright (ed.), *Studies in Social Power* (Ann Arbor, Michigan: University of Michigan Press, 1959), pp. 150–167. See also Philip M. Podsakoff and Chester A. Schriesheim, "Field Studies of French and Raven's Bases of Power: Critique, Reanalysis, and Suggestions for Future Research," *Psychological Bulletin*, 1985, vol. 97, pp. 387–411.

28. Yukl, *Leadership in Organizations*, Chapter X.

29. See also Thomas A. Stewart, "New Ways to Exercise Power," *Fortune*, 6 November 1989, pp. 52–64.

30. French and Raven, "Bases of Social Power."

31. Pfeffer, *Power in Organizations*.

32. Christopher P. Parker, Robert L. Dipboye, and Stacy L. Jackson, "Perceptions of Organizational Politics: An Investigation of Antecedents and Consequences," *Journal of Management*, 1995, vol. 21, no. 5, pp. 891–912.

33. Victor Murray and Jeffrey Gandz, "Games Executives Play: Politics at Work," *Business Horizons*, December 1980, pp. 11–23. See also Jeffrey Gandz and Victor Murray, "The Experience of Workplace Politics," *Academy of Management Journal*, June 1980, pp. 237–251.

34. See Stefanie Ann Lenway and Kathleen Rehbein, "Leaders, Followers, and Free Riders: An Empirical Test of Variation in Corporate Political Involvement," *Academy of Management Journal*, December 1991, pp. 893–905.

35. Gerald F. Cavanaugh, Dennis J. Moberg, and Manuel Valasquez, "The Ethics of Organizational Politics," *Academy of Management Review*, July 1981, pp. 363–374.

36. Pfeffer, *Power in Organizations*.

37. Robert H. Miles, *Macro Organizational Behavior* (Glenview, Illinois: Scott, Foresman, 1980). See also Carrie R. Leana, "Power Relinquishment Versus Power Sharing: Theoretical Clarification and Empirical Comparison of Delegation and Participation," *Journal of Applied Psychology*, 1987, vol. 72, pp. 228–233.

38. Timothy A. Judge and Robert D. Bretz, Jr., "Political Influence Behavior and Career Success," *Journal of Management*, 1994, vol. 20, no. 1, pp. 43–65.

39. Pfeffer, Power *in Organizations*; Mintzberg, *Power in and Around Organizations*.

40. The techniques in Figure 10.8 are based on Pfeffer, *Power in Organizations*; Mintzberg, *Power in and Around Organizations*; and Galbraith, *Anatomy of Power*.

41. Michael Macoby, *The Gamesman* (New York: Simon & Schuster, 1976).

42. "How the Two Top Officials of Grace Wound Up in a Very Dirty War," *Wall Street Journal*, 18 May 1995, pp. Al, A8.

43. See William L. Gardner, "Lessons in Organizational Dramaturgy: The Art of Impression Management," *Organizational Dynamics*, Summer 1992, pp. 51–63; Elizabeth Wolf Morrison and Robert J. Bies, "Impression Management in the Feedback-Seeking Process: A Literature Review and Research Agenda," *Academy of Management Review*, July 1991, pp. 522–541.

Chapter 11

1. Manulife website: http://www.manulife.com/corporate/corporate2.nsf/Public/awards2007.html; Jeff Sanford and John Gray, "Top CFO 2005: Laurence Sellyn, Gildan Activewear Inc," *Canadian Business,* April 25, 2005. Ontario Research and Innovation Council Website: http://www.mri.gov.on.ca/ORIC/english/bios/DominicDAlessandro.asp; Keith Kalawsky, "Manulife in Merger Spotlight: D'Alessandro Named Outstanding CEO", *Financial Post,* November 5, 2005.

2. For a recent review of leadership, see Gary Yukl, *Leadership in Organizations*, 5th ed. (Upper Saddle River, New Jersey: Prentice Hall, 2002).

3. Bernard M. Bass, *Bass and Stogdill's Handbook of Leadership*, 3rd ed. (Riverside, New Jersey: Free Press, 1990). See also James R. Meindl and Sanford B. Ehrlich, "The Romance of Leadership and the Evaluation of Organizational Performance," *Academy of Management Review*, January 1987, pp. 91–109.

4. William G. Pagonis, "The Work of the Leader," *Harvard Business Review*, November–December 1992, pp. 118–126.

5. Ralph M. Stogdill, *Handbook of Leadership* (New York: Free Press, 1974). See also Bass, *Bass and Stogdill's Handbook of Leadership*.

6. See Gary Yukl and David D. Van Fleet, "Theory and Research on Leadership in Organizations," in M. D. Dunnette and L. M. Hough (eds.), *Handbook of Industrial and Organizational Psychology* (Palo Alto, California: Consulting Psychologists Press, 1992), III, pp. 148–197.

7. Arthur G. Jago, "Leadership: Perspectives in Theory and Research," *Management Science*, March 1982, pp. 315–336.

8. John W. Gardner, *On Leadership* (New York: Free Press, 1990).

9. Jay A. Conger, "Leadership: The Art of Empowering Others," *Academy of Management Executive*, August 1989, pp. 17–24.

10. See John P. Kotter, "What Leaders Really Do," *Harvard Business Review*, May–June 1990, pp. 103–111. See also Abraham Zaleznik, "Managers and Leaders: Are They Different?" *Harvard Business Review*, March–April 1992, pp. 126–135.

11. David D. Van Fleet and Gary A. Yukl, "A Century of Leadership Research," in D. A. Wren and J. A. Pearce II (eds.), *Papers Dedicated to the Development of Modern Management* (Chicago: The Academy of Management, 1986), pp. 12–23.

12. Bass, *Bass and Stogdill's Handbook of Leadership*.

13. See Walter Kiechel III, "Beauty and the Managerial Beast," *Fortune*, 10 November 1986, pp. 201–203, for an interesting discussion about leadership traits.

14. Robert G. Lord, Christy DeVader, and George M. Alliger, "A Meta-Analysis of the Relation Between Personality Traits and Leadership Perceptions: An Application of Validity Generalization Procedures," *Journal of Applied Psychology*, 1986, vol. 71, pp. 402–410.

15. Shelly A. Kirkpatrick and Edwin A. Locke, "Leadership: Do Traits Matter?" *Academy of Management Executive*, May 1991, pp. 48–60.

16. Russell L. Kent and Sherry E. Moss, "Effects of Sex and Gender Role of Leader Emergence," *Academy of Management Journal*, 1994, vol. 37, no. 5, pp. 1335–1346.

17. For example, see Sheila Puffer, "Understanding the Bear: A Portrait of Russian Business Leaders," *Academy of Management Executive*, 1994, vol. 8, no. 1, pp. 41–49.

18. www.samsung.com/AboutSAMSUNG/SAMSUNGGROUP/Chairman/CEOMessage/index.htm

19. Philip M. Podsakoff, Scott B. MacKenzie, Mike Ahearne, and William H. Bommer, "Searching for a Needle in a Haystack: Trying to Identify the Illusive Moderators of Leadership Behaviors," *Journal of Management*, 1995, vol. 21, no. 3, pp. 422–470.

20. See Gary A. Yukl, *Leadership in Organizations*.

21. Rensis Likert, *New Patterns of Management* (New York: McGraw-Hill, 1961).

22. Edwin Fleishman, E. F. Harris, and H. E. Burtt, *Leadership and Supervision in Industry* (Columbus, Ohio: Bureau of Educational Research, Ohio State University, 1955).

23. See Edwin A. Fleishman, "Twenty Years of Consideration and Structure," in Edward A. Fleishman and James G. Hunt (eds.), *Current Developments in the Study of Leadership* (Carbondale, Ill.: Southern Illinois University Press, 1973), pp. 1–40.

24. Fleishman, Harris, and Burtt, *Leadership and Supervision in Industry*.

25. See Gary A. Yukl, *Leadership in Organizations*.

26. See Fred E. Fiedler, *A Theory of Leadership Effectiveness* (New York: McGraw-Hill, 1967).

27. Fred E. Fiedler, "The Effects of Leadership Training and Experience: A Contingency Model Interpretation," *Administrative Science Quarterly*, vol. 77, no. 4 (December 1972), p. 455. Used by permission of *Administrative Science Quarterly*. Copyright © 1972 Cornell University. All rights reserved.

28. See Chester A. Schriesheim, B. D. Bannister, and W. H. Money, "Psychometric Properties of the LPC Scale: An Extension of Rice's Review," *Academy of Management Review*, April 1979, pp. 287–294.

29. See Fred E. Fiedler, "Engineering the Job to Fit the Manager," *Harvard Business Review*, September–October 1965, pp. 115–122.

30. See Fred E. Fiedler, Martin M. Chemers, and Linda Mahar, *Improving Leadership Effectiveness: The Leader Match Concept* (New York: Wiley, 1976).

31. Chester A. Schriesheim, Bennett J. Tepper, and Linda A. Tetrault, "Least Preferred Coworkers Score, Situational Control, and Leadership Effectiveness: A Meta-Analysis of Contingency Model Performance Predictions," *Journal of Applied Psychology*, 1994, vol. 79, no. 4, pp. 561–573.

32. See Martin G. Evans, "The Effects of Supervisory Behavior on the Path-Goal Relationship," *Organizational Behavior and Human Performance*, May 1970, pp. 277–298; Robert J. House, "A Path-Goal Theory of Leadership Effectiveness," *Administrative Science Quarterly*, September 1971, pp. 321–339; Robert J. House and Terence R. Mitchell, "Path-Goal Theory of Leadership," *Journal of Contemporary Business*, Autumn 1974, pp. 81–98.

33. See House and Mitchell, "Path-Goal Theory of Leadership."

34. See Terence R. Mitchell, "Motivation and Participation: An Integration," *Academy of Management Journal*, June 1973, pp. 160–179.

35. Drew Hasselback, "Juniors in for a Rocky Ride: Miner," *Financial Post*, Nov. 7, 2006.

36. J. C. Wofford and Laurie Z. Liska, "Path-Goal Theories of Leadership: A Meta-Analysis," *Journal of Management*, 1993, vol. 19, no. 4, pp. 857–876. Chester A. Schreisheim and Linda Neider, "Path-goal Leadership Theory: The Long and Winding Road", *Leadership Quarterly*, 1996, vol. 7, pp. 317–322.

37. See Victor H. Vroom and Philip H. Yetton, *Leadership and Decision Making* (Pittsburgh: University of Pittsburgh Press, 1973); Victor H. Vroom and Arthur G. Jago, *The New Leadership* (Englewood Cliffs, New Jersey: Prentice Hall, 1988).

38. Vroom and Jago, *The New Leadership*.

39. Adaptations from Table 2.1 Decision Methods for Group and Individual Problems (p. 13) and Figure 9.3 Decision-Process Flow Chart for Both Individual and Group Problems (p. 194) from Leadership and Decision-Making, by Victor H. Vroom and Philip W. Yetton, © 1973. Reprinted by permission of the University of Pittsburgh Press.

40. Vroom and Jago, *The New Leadership*.

41. See Madeline E. Heilman, Harvey A. Hornstein, Jack H. Cage, and Judith K. Herschlag, "Reaction to Prescribed Leader Behavior as a Function of Role Perspective: The Case of the Vroom-Yetton Model," *Journal of Applied Psychology*, February 1984, pp. 50–60; R. H. George Field, "A Test of the Vroom-Yetton Normative Model of Leadership," *Journal of Applied Psychology*, February 1982, pp. 523–532. R.H.G. Field and Robert J. House, "A Test of the Vroom-Yetton Model Using Manager and Subordinate Reports," *Journal of Applied Psychology*, 1990, vol. 75, pp. 362–366.

42. Fred Dansereau, George Graen, and W. J. Haga, "A Vertical Dyad Linkage Approach to Leadership Within Formal Organizations: A Longitudinal Investigation of the Role-Making Process," *Organizational Behavior and Human Performance*, 1975, vol. 15, pp. 46–78. George Graen and J. F. Cashman, "A Role-Making Model of Leadership in Formal Organizations: A Developmental Approach," in J. G. Hunt and L. L. Larson (eds.), *Leadership Frontiers* (Kent, Ohio: Kent State University Press, 1975), pp. 143–165.

43. Robert C. Liden, Sandy J. Wayne, and Dean Stilwell, "A Longitudinal Study on the Early Development of Leader-Member Exchanges" *Journal of Applied Psychology*, 1993, vol. 78, pp. 662–674.

44. Antoinette S. Phillips and Arthur G. Bedeian, "Leader-Follower Exchange Quality: The Role of Personal and Interpersonal Attributes," *Academy of Management Journal*, 1994, vol. 37,1 no. 4, pp. 990–1001. Remus Ilies, Jennifer D. Nahrgang and Frederick P. Morgeson, "Leader-Member Exchange and Citizenship Behaviors: A Meta-Analysis", *Journal of Applied Psychology*, 2007, vol. 92, pp. 269–277.

45. Charlotte R. Gerstner and David V. Day, "Meta-Analytic Review of Leader-Member Exchange Theory: Correlates and Construct Issues," *Journal of Applied Psychology*, 1997, vol. 82, pp. 827–844.

46. Ibid.

47. Daniel F. Coleman, "An Alternative 'Limited Domain' View of Leader-Member Exchange," in F. Dansereau and F.J. Yammarino (eds.), *Leadership: The Multiple-Level Approaches* (part B). (Stamford, Connecticut: JAI Press INC, 1998), pp. 137–148.

48. Phillips and Bedeian, "Leader-Follower Exchange Quality: The Role of Personal and Interpersonal Attributes."

49. George B. Graen and Mary Uhl-Bien, "Relationship-Based Approach to Leadership: Development of the Leader-Member Exchange (LMX) Theory of Leadership over 25 Years: Applying a Multi-Domain Approach," *Leadership Quarterly*, 1995, vol. 6, pp. 219–247.

50. Terri A. Scandura and George B. Graen, "Moderating Effects of Initial Leader-Member Exchange Status on the Effects of a Leadership Intervention," *Journal of Applied Psychology*, 1984, vol. 69, pp. 428–436.

51. George B. Graen and Mary Uhl-Bien, "Relationship-based Approach to Leadership: Development of Leader-Member Exchange Theory of Leadership Over 25 Years: Applying a Multi-Level Multi-Domain Perspective," *Leadership Quarterly*, 1995, vol. 6, pp. 219–247.

52. Kathleen Boies and Jane M. Howell, "Leader-Member Exchange in Teams: An Examination of the Interaction Between Relationship Differentiation and Mean LMX in Explaining Team-Level Outcomes," Leadership Quarterly, 2006, vol. 17, pp. 246–257.

53. Alan Deutschman, "The Fabric of Creativity," *Fast Company.com*, December, 2004, p. 54.

54. James G. Hunt, "Transformational/Charismatic Leadership's Transformation of the Field: A Historical Essay," *The Leadership Quarterly*, 1999, vol. 10, pp. 129–144.

55. See *The Globe and Mail*, Friday, 15 May 1998, Section C.

56. See James MacGregor Burns, *Leadership* (New York: Harper & Row, 1978), and Karl W. Kuhnert and Philip Lewis, "Transactional and Transformational Leadership: A Constructive/Developmental Analysis," *Academy of Management Review*, October 1987, pp. 648–657.

57. Francis J. Yammarino and Alan J. Dubinsky, "Transformational Leadership Theory: Using Levels of Analysis to Determine Boundary Conditions," *Personnel Psychology*, 1994, vol. 47, pp. 787–800.

58. See Brian Dumaine, "Times Are Good? Create a Crisis," *Fortune*, 28 June 1993, pp. 123–130.

59. Shelley A. Kirkpatrick and Edwin A. Locke, "Direct and Indirect Effects of Three Core Charismatic Leadership Components on Performance and Attitudes," *Journal of Applied Psychology*, 1996, vol. 81, no. 1, pp. 36–51.

60. See Robert J. House, "A 1976 Theory of Charismatic Leadership," in J. G. Hunt and L. L. Larson (eds.), *Leadership: The Cutting Edge* (Carbondale, Illinois: Southern Illinois University Press, 1977), pp. 189–207. See also Jay A. Conger and Rabindra N. Kanungo, "Toward a Behavioral Theory of Charismatic Leadership in Organizational Settings," *Academy of Management Review*, October 1987, pp. 637–647.

61. Kenneth Labich, "Is Herb Kelleher America's Best CEO?" *Fortune*, 2 May 1994, pp. 44–52.

62. David A. Nadler and Michael L. Tushman, "Beyond the Charismatic Leader: Leadership and Organizational Change," *California Management Review*, Winter 1990, pp. 77–97.

63. See Jay A. Conger and Rabindra N. Kanungo, "Charismatic Leadership in Organizations: Perceived Behavioral Attributes and Their Measurement," *Journal of Organizational Behavior*, 1994, vol. 15, pp. 439–452.

64. Boas Shamir, Robert J. House and Michael B. Arthur, "The Motivational Effects of Charismatic Leadership: A Self-Concept Based Theory," *Organization Science*, 1993, vol. 4, pp. 577–594. See also Boas Shamir, Eliav Zakay, Esther Breinin, and Micha Popper, "Correlates of Charismatic Leader Behavior in Military Units: Subordinates' Attitudes, Unit Characteristics, and Superiors' Appraisals of Leader Performance," *Academy of Management Journal*, 1998, vol. 41, pp. 387–409.

65. Daniel Sankowsky, "The Charismatic Leader as Narcissist: Understanding the Abuse of Power," Organizational Dynamics, Summer 1995, pp. 57–67.

66. Bruce J. Avolio and William L. Gardner, "Authentic Leadership Development: Getting to the Root of Positive Forms of Leadership," *Leadership Quarterly*, 2005, vol. 16, pp. 315–338.

67. "The Best (& Worst) Managers of the Year," *Business Week*, January 10, 2005, p. 55.

68. See Kurt Dirks and Donald Ferrin, "Trust in Leadership," *Journal of Applied Psychology*, 2002, vol. 87, no. 4, pp. 611–628.

Chapter 12

1. "The Foodies," *Canadian Business*, December 28, 2003, p. 35. David Parkinson, "Maple Leaf Foods to restructure operations," *Globe and Mail*, October 12, 2006. David Parkinson and Andy Hoffman, "Maple Leaf takes an axe to pork operations," *Globe and Mail*, October 12, 2006. Maple Leaf Foods website, www.mapleleaf.com.

2. See Richard Daft, *Essentials of Organization Theory and Design* (Cincinnati, Ohio: Southwestern, 1998), p. 9, for further discussion of the definition of organization.

3. John R. Montanari, Cyril P. Morgan, and Jeffrey S. Bracker, *Strategic Management* (Hinsdale, Illinois: Dryden Press, 1990), pp. 1–2.

4. A. Bryman, A. D. Beardworth, E. T. Keil, and J. Ford, "Organizational Size and Specialization," *Organization Studies*, September 1983, pp. 271–278.

5. Joseph L. C. Cheng, "Interdependence and Coordination in Organizations: A Role System Analysis," *Academy of Management Journal*, March 1983, pp. 156–162.

6. See Henry Mintzberg, *The Structuring of Organizations* (Englewood Cliffs, New Jersey: Prentice Hall, 1979), for further discussion of the basic elements of structure.

7. Max Weber, *The Theory of Social and Economic Organization*, trans. A. M. Henderson and Talcott Parsons (New York: Free Press, 1947).

8. Adam Smith, *An Inquiry into the Nature and Causes of the Wealth of Nations* (London: Dent, 1910).

9. Nancy M. Carter and Thomas L. Keon, "The Rise and Fall of the Division of Labor, the Past 25 Years," *Organization Studies*, 1986, pp. 54–57.

10. Glenn R. Carroll, "The Specialist Strategy," *California Management Review*, Spring 1984, pp. 126–137.

11. "Management Discovers the Human Side of Automation," *Business Week*, 29 September 1986, pp. 70–75.

12. See Robert H. Miles, *Macro Organizational Behavior* (Santa Monica, California: Goodyear, 1980), pp. 28–34, for a discussion of departmentalization schemes.

13. Mintzberg, *The Structuring of Organizations*, p. 125.

14. Miles, *Macro Organizational Behavior*, pp. 122–133.

15. Ronald Henkoff, "Cost Cutting: How to Do It Right," *Fortune*, 9 April 1990, pp. 40–50.

16. Peggy Leatt and Rodney Schneck, "Criteria for Grouping Nursing Subunits in Hospitals," *Academy of Management Review*, March 1984, pp. 150–165.

17. Lyndall F. Urwick, "The Manager's Span of Control," *Harvard Business Review*, May–June 1956, pp. 39–47.

18. Dan R. Dalton, William D. Tudor, Michael J. Spendolini, Gordon J. Fielding, and Lyman W. Porter, "Organization Structure and Performance: A Critical Review," *Academy of Management Review*, January 1980, pp. 49–64.

19. Mintzberg, *The Structuring of Organizations*, pp. 133–147.

20. Barbara Davison. "Management Span of Control: How Wide Is Too Wide?" *Journal of Business Strategy,* 2003, vol. 24, pp. 22–29; David Van Fleet, "Span of Management Research and Issues," *Academy of Management Journal*, September 1983, pp. 546–552.

21. John R. Montanari and Philip J. Adelman, "The Administrative Component of Organizations and the Rachet Effect: A Critique of Cross-Sectional Studies," *Journal of Management Studies*, March 1987, pp. 113–123.

22. D. A. Heenan, "The Downside of Downsizing," *Journal of Business Strategy*, November– December 1989, pp. 18–23.

23. Wayne F. Cascio, "Downsizing: What Do We Know? What Have We Learned?" *Academy of Management Executive*, February 1993, pp. 95–104.

24. W. F. Cascio, "Strategies for Responsible Restructuring," *Academy of Management Executive,* Nov. 2005, vol. 19, pp. 39–50.

25. Dalton et al., "Organization Structure and Performance."

26. See John Child, *Organization: A Guide to Problems and Practice*, 2nd ed. (New York: Harper & Row, 1984), pp. 145–153, for a detailed discussion of centralization.

27. Richard H. Hall, *Organization: Structure and Process*, 3rd ed. (Englewood Cliffs, New Jersey: Prentice Hall, 1982), pp. 87–96.

28. Daniel R. Denison, "Bringing Corporate Culture to the Bottom Line," *Organizational Dynamics*, Autumn 1984, pp. 4–22.

29. Leonard W. Johnson and Alan L. Frohman, "Identifying and Closing the Gap in the Middle of Organizations," *Academy of Management Executive*, May 1989, pp. 107–114.

30. Mintzberg, *The Structuring of Organizations*, pp. 83–84.

31. Arthur P. Brief and H. Kirk Downey, "Cognitive and Organizational Structures: A Conceptual Analysis of Implicit Organizing Theories," *Human Relations*, December 1983, pp. 1065–1090.

32. Jerald Hage, "An Axiomatic Theory of Organizations," *Administrative Science Quarterly*, December 1965, pp. 289–320.

33. Gregory Moorhead, "Organizational Analysis: An Integration of the Macro and Micro Approaches," *Journal of Management Studies*, April 1981, pp. 191–218.

34. J. Daniel Sherman and Howard L. Smith, "The Influence of Organizational Structure on Intrinsic Versus Extrinsic Motivation," *Academy of Management Journal*, December 1984, pp. 877–885.

35. John A. Pearce II and Fred R. David, "A Social Network Approach to Organizational Design-Performance," *Academy of Management Review*, July 1983, pp. 436–444.

36. Eileen Fairhurst, "Organizational Rules and the Accomplishment of Nursing Work on Geriatric Wards," *Journal of Management Studies*, July 1983, pp. 315–332.

37. Ellen Forian Katz, "By the Numbers," *Fortune*, January 10, 2005, p. 22.

38. "Frank Stronach's Secret? Call It Empower Steering," *Business Week*, 1 May 1995, pp. 63–65.

39. Neil F. Brady, "Rules for Making Exceptions to Rules," *Academy of Management Review*, July 1987, pp. 436–444.

40. See Jeffrey Pfeffer, *Power in Organizations* (Boston: Pittman, 1981), pp. 4–6, for a discussion of the relationship between power and authority.

41. John B. Miner, *Theories of Organizational Structure and Process* (Hinsdale, Illinois: Dryden Press, 1982), p. 360.

42. Chester Barnard, *The Functions of the Executive* (Cambridge, Massachusetts: Harvard University Press, 1938), pp. 161–184.

43. Pfeffer, *Power in Organizations*, pp. 366–367.

44. Weber, *The Theory of Social and Economic Organization*.

45. For more discussion of these alternative views, see John B. Miner, *Theories of Organizational Structure and Process* (Hinsdale, Illinois: Dryden Press, 1982), p. 386.

46. This summary of the classic principles of organizing is based on Henri Fayol, *General and Industrial Management*, trans. Constance Storrs (London: Pittman, 1949), and the discussions in Bedeian, *Organizations: Theory and Analysis*, 2nd ed. (Chicago: Dryden, 1984), pp. 58–59, and Miner, *Theories of Organizational Structure and Process*, pp. 358–381.

47. Miner, *Theories of Organizational Structure and Process*, pp. 358–381.

48. See Rensis Likert, *New Patterns of Management* (New York: McGraw-Hill, 1961); Rensis Likert, *The Human Organization: Its Management and Value* (New York: McGraw-Hill, 1967), for a complete discussion of the human organization.

49. Miner, *Theories of Organizational Structure and Process*, pp. 17–53.

Chapter 13

1. Mathew Schwartz, "Thomson-Reuters deal would create largest provider of financial data," *B to B*, June 4, 2007, p. 14; Tom Tivnan, "7.75bn for Thomson Learning," *Bookseller*, May 18, 2007, p. 9; Stanley Reed, "The Rise of a Financial Data Powerhouse," *Business Week Online*, May 16, 2007; Zena Olijnik, "Kenneth Thomson 1923-2006," *Canadian Business*, June 19, 2006, pp. 88–91, Thomson Corporation website, www.thomson.com.

2. Lex Donaldson, "Strategy and Structural Adjustment to Regain Fit and Performance: In Defense of Contingency Theory," *Journal of Management Studies*, January 1987, pp. 1–24.

3. John R. Montanari, Cyril P. Morgan, and Jeffrey Bracker, *Strategic Management* (Hinsdale, Illinois: Dryden Press, 1990), p. 114.

4. Thomas Watson and Jason Kirby, "Rec 'N' Roll," *Canadian Business*, September 15, 2003, p. 53; Rasha Mourtada, "Diversify or Die," *Canadian Business*, December 7, 2003, pp. 114ff. For a discussion of strategy, see Arthur A. Thompson, Jr., and A. J. Strickland, III, *Strategic Management: Concepts and Cases*, 13th ed. (Whitby, Ont.: McGraw-Hill, 2002).

5. Alfred D. Chandler, *Strategy and Structure: Chapters in the History of the American Industrial Enterprise* (Cambridge, Massachusetts: MIT Press, 1962).

6. John R. Kimberly, "Organizational Size and the Structuralist Perspective: A Review, Critique, and Proposal," *Administrative Science Quarterly*, December 1976, pp. 571–597.

7. Peter M. Blau and Richard A. Schoenherr, *The Structure of Organizations* (New York: Basic Books, 1971).

8. The results of these studies are thoroughly summarized in Richard H. Hall, *Organizations: Structure and Process*, 3rd ed. (Englewood Cliffs, New Jersey: Prentice Hall, 1982), pp. 89–94. For a recent study in this area, see John H. Cullen and Kenneth S. Anderson, "Blau's Theory of Structural Differentiation Revisited: A Theory of Structural Change or Scale?" *Academy of Management Journal*, June 1986, pp. 203–229.

9. "Small Is Beautiful Now in Manufacturing," *Business Week*, 22 October 1984, pp. 152–156.

10. Richard H. Hall, J. Eugene Haas, and Norman Johnson, "Organizational Size, Complexity, and Formalization," *American Sociological Review*, December 1967, pp. 903–912.

11. "Telus Disconnects 6,000," *Maclean's*, July 22, 2002, p. 14; Chris Talbot, "Cisco Is Streamlining Its Staff," *Computerworld Canada*, May 18, 2001.

12. Robert I. Sutton and Thomas D'Anno, "Decreasing Organizational Size: Untangling the Effects of Money and People," *Academy of Management Review*, May 1989, pp. 194–212.

13. Joan Woodward, *Management and Technology: Problems of Progress in Industry*, no. 3 (London: Her Majesty's Stationery Office, 1958); Joan Woodward, *Industrial Organizations: Theory and Practice* (London: Oxford University Press, 1965).

14. Tom Burns and George M. Stalker, *The Management of Innovation* (London: Tavistock, 1961).

15. Charles B. Perrow, "A Framework for the Comparative Analysis of Organizations," *American Sociological Review*, April 1967, pp. 194–208.

16. James D. Thompson, *Organizations in Action* (New York: McGraw-Hill, 1967).

17. David J. Hickson, Derek S. Pugh, and Diana C. Pheysey, "Operations Technology and Organization Structure: An Empirical Reappraisal," *Administrative Science Quarterly*, September 1969, pp. 378–397.

18. Hickson, Pugh, and Pheysey, "Operations Technology and Organization Structure."

19. Andrew Kupfer, "How to Be a Global Manager," *Fortune*, 14 March 1988, pp. 52–58.

20. "Going Crazy in Japan—In a Break from Tradition, Tokyo Begins Funding a Program for Basic Research," *Wall Street Journal*, 10 November 1986, p. D20.

21. Richard L. Daft, *Organization Theory and Design*, 2nd ed. (St. Paul, Minnesota: West, 1986), p. 55.

22. Robert B. Duncan, "Characteristics of Organizational Environments and Perceived Uncertainty," *Administrative Science Quarterly*, September 1972, pp. 313–327.

23. Masoud Yasai-Ardekani, "Structural Adaptations to Environments," *Academy of Management Review*, January 1986, pp. 9–21.

24. John E. Prescott, "Environments as Moderators of the Relationship Between Strategy and Performance," *Academy of Management Journal*, June 1986, pp. 329–346.

25. Timothy M. Stearns, Alan N. Hoffman, and Jan B. Heide, "Performance of Commercial Television Stations as an Outcome of Interorganizational Linkages and Environmental Conditions," *Academy of Management Journal*, March 1987, pp. 71–90.

26. Thompson, *Organizations in Action*, pp. 51–82.

27. Andy Holloway, "Give Like Santa . . ." *Canadian Business*, December 9, 2002, p. 109; Eliot Bendoly, Doug Blocher, Kurt M. Bretthauer, and M.A. Venkataramanan, "Service and Cost Benefits Through Clicks and Mortar Integration: Implications for the Centralization/Decentralization Debate," *European Journal of Operational Research*, 2007, vol. 180, pp. 426–442.

28. For more information on managerial choice, see John R. Montanari, "Managerial Discretion: An Expanded Model of Organizational Choice," *Academy of Management Review*, April 1978, pp. 231–241; John Child, "Organizational Structure, Environment, and Performance: The Role of Strategic Choice," *Sociology*, January 1972, pp. 1–22.

29. "Determinant of Organizational Structure," *Academy of Management Review*, January 1980, pp. 13–23.

30. Douglas A. Ready, "How to Grow Great Leaders," *Harvard Business Review*, 2004, vol. 82, pp. 92–100.

31. James W. Frederickson, "The Strategic Decision Process and Organization Structure," *Academy of Management Review*, April 1986, pp. 280–297.

32. Herman L. Boschken, "Strategy and Structure: Reconceiving the Relationship," *Journal of Management*, March 1990, pp. 135–150.

33. Andy Holloway, "Between a Rock and a Hard Place," *Canadian Business*, December 27, 2004, pp. 69–71; Tim Shufelt, "Gibson Grooves on Garrison's Guitar," *The Globe and Mail*, July 5, 2007, p. B5.

34. Elton Mayo, *The Human Problems of an Industrial Civilization* (New York: Macmillan, 1933); F. J. Roethlisberger and W. J. Dickson, *Management and the Worker* (Cambridge, Massachusetts: Harvard University Press, 1939).

35. Eric L. Trist and K. W. Bamforth, "Some Social and Psychological Consequences of the Longwall Method of Coal-Getting," *Human Relations*, February 1951, pp. 3–38.

36. Richard E. Walton, "How to Counter Alienation in the Plant," *Harvard Business Review*, November–December 1972, pp. 70–81; Richard E. Walton, "Work Innovations at Topeka: After Six Years," *Journal of Applied Behavioral Science*, July–August–September 1977, pp. 422–433; Pehr G. Gyllenhammar, "How Volvo Adapts Work to People," *Harvard Business Review*, July–August 1977, pp. 102–113.

37. Henry Mintzberg, *The Structuring of Organizations: A Synthesis of the Research* (Englewood Cliffs, New Jersey: Prentice Hall, 1979).

38. See Harold C. Livesay, *American Made: Men Who Shaped the American Economy* (Boston: Little, Brown, 1979), pp. 215–239, for a discussion of Alfred Sloan and the development of the divisionalized structure at General Motors.

39. Anne B. Fisher, "GM Is Tougher Than You Think," *Fortune*, 10 November 1986, pp. 56–64.

40. Thompson and Strickland, *Strategic Management*.

41. Kenneth Labich, "The Innovators," *Fortune*, 6 June 1988, pp. 51–64; Amy Barrett, "J&J: Reinventing How It Invents," *Business Week*, April 17, 2006, pp. 60–61.

42. Henry Mintzberg, "Organization Design: Fashion or Fit," *Harvard Business Review*, January–February 1981, pp. 103–116.

43. Harvey F. Kolodny, "Managing in a Matrix," *Business Horizons*, March–April 1981, pp. 17–24.

44. Stanley M. Davis and Paul R. Lawrence, *Matrix* (Reading, Mass.: Addison-Wesley, 1977), pp. 11–36.

45. Lawton R. Burns, "Matrix Management in Hospitals: Testing Theories of Matrix Structure and Development," *Administrative Science Quarterly*, September 1989, pp. 355–358.

46. Zena Olijnik, "Best Workplaces 2006: The Farm Team-AdFarm", *Canadian Business Online*, April 10, 2006.

47. Ibid., pp. 129–154.

48. Aseem Prakash and Gary Metcalf, "Outsourcing on Steroids," *Canadian Business*, June 20, 2005, p. 21.

49. Michael E. Johnson-Cramer, Robert L. Cross and Aimin Yan, "Sources of Fidelity in Purposive Organizational Change: Lessons from a Re-engineering Case," *Journal of Management Studies*, 2003, vol. 40, pp. 1837–1870.

50. Robert Tomasko, *Rethinking the Corporation* (New York: AMA-COM), 1993.

51. James R. Lincoln, Mitsuyo Hanada, and Kerry McBride, "Organizational Structures in Japanese and U.S. Manufacturing," *Administrative Science Quarterly*, September 1986, pp. 338–364.

52. "The Inscrutable West," *Newsweek*, 18 April 1988, p. 52.

53. Richard I. Kirkland, Jr., "Europe's New Managers," *Fortune*, 29 September 1980, pp. 56–60; Shawn Tully, "Europe's Takeover Kings," *Fortune*, 20 July 1987, pp. 95–98.

54. Henry W. Lane and Joseph J. DiStefano, *International Management Behavior* (Toronto, Ontario: Nelson, 1988).

55. William H. Davison and Philippe Haspeslagh, "Shaping a Global Product Organization," *Harvard Business Review*, July–August 1982, pp. 125–132.

56. John Child, *Organizations: A Guide to Problems and Practice* (New York: Harper & Row, 1984), p. 246.

57. Thomas J. Peters and Robert H. Waterman, Jr., *In Search of Excellence: Lessons from America's Best-Run Companies* (New York: Harper & Row, 1982), pp. 235–278.

58. Thomas J. Peters and Nancy K. Austin, "A Passion for Excellence," *Fortune*, 13 May 1985, pp. 20–32.

Chapter 14

1. David Folster, *Ganong: A Sweet History of Chocolate*, 2006, Goose Lane Editions, Fredericton, New Brunswick (quotation is from page 126); John Demont, "David Ganong, *Maclean's*, July 1, 2002, p. 30; Jason Chesworth, "Growing up Ganong", Sceneandheard.ca July 16, 2007; Ganong Bros. website, www.ganong.com.

2. See Mark MacKinnon, "Firm Designs Culture to Cushion Recession," *The Globe and Mail*, 31 August 1998, p. B9; Tema Frank, "Kinder, Gentler, Smarter," Profit, April–May 1998, pp. 50–52; "Corporate Culture: The Hard-to-Change Values That Spell Success or Failure," *Business Week*, 27 October 1980, pp. 148–160; Charles G. Burck, "Working Smarter," *Fortune*, 15 June 1981, pp. 68–73.

3. Charles A. O'Reilly and Jennifer A. Chatman, "Culture as Social Control: Corporations, Cults, and Commitment," in Barry M. Staw and L. L. Cummings (eds.), *Research in Organizational Behavior*, 1996, vol. 18, pp. 157–200.

4. J. P. Kotter and J. L. Heskett, 1992: *Corporate Culture and Performance* (New York: Free Press, 1992.)

5. Michael Tushman and Charles A. O'Reilly, *Staying on Top: Managing Strategic Innovation and Change for Long-Term Success* (Boston: Harvard Business School Press, 1996).

6. T. E. Deal and A. A. Kennedy, *Corporate Cultures: The Rites and Rituals of Corporate Life* (Reading, Massachusetts: Addison-Wesley, 1982), p. 4.

7. E. H. Schein, "The Role of the Founder in Creating Organizational Culture," *Organizational Dynamics*, Summer 1983, p. 14.

8. Thomas J. Peters and Robert H. Waterman, *In Search of Excellence: Lessons from America's Best-Run Companies* (New York: Harper & Row, 1982), p. 103.

9. See M. Polanyi, *Personal Knowledge* (Chicago: University of Chicago Press, 1958); E. Goffman, *The Presentation of Self in Every Day Life* (New York: Doubleday, 1959); P. L. Berger and T. Luckman, The Social Construction of Reality (Garden City, N.Y.: Anchor, 1967).

10. Jack Mintz, :What's Pork for the Goose," *Canadian Business*, April 25, 2005, p. 19.

11. W. G. Ouchi, *Theory Z: How American Business Can Meet the Japanese Challenge* (Reading, Massachusetts: Addison-Wesley, 1981).

12. Laura Bogomolny, "Good Housekeeping," *Canadian Business*, March 1, 2004, pp. 87–88.

13. A. Wilkins, "Organizational Stories as Symbols Which Control the Organization," in Louis R. Pondy, Peter J. Frost, Gareth Morgan, and Thomas C. Dandridge (eds.), *Organizational Symbolism* (Greenwich, Connecticut: JAI Press, 1983), pp. 81–82.

14. Ibid.

15. A. L. Kroeber and C. Kluckhohn, "Culture: A Critical Review of Concepts and Definitions," in *Papers of the Peabody Museum of American Archaeology and Ethnology*, vol. 47, no. 1 (Cambridge, Massachusetts: Harvard University Press, 1952).

16. C. Geertz, *The Interpretation of Cultures* (New York: Basic Books, 1973).

17. See, for example, B. Clark, *The Distinctive College* (Chicago: Adline, 1970).

18. E. Durkheim, *The Elementary Forms of Religious Life*, trans. J. Swain (New York: Collier, 1961), p. 220.

19. See Ouchi, *Theory Z*, and Peters and Waterman, *In Search of Excellence*.

20. See Ouchi, *Theory Z*; Deal and Kennedy, *Corporate Cultures*; and Peters and Waterman, *In Search of Excellence*.

21. E. Borgida and R. E. Nisbett, "The Differential Impact of Abstract vs. Concrete Information on Decisions," *Journal of Applied Social Psychology*, July–September 1977, pp. 258–271.

22. J. Martin and M. Power, "Truth or Corporate Propaganda: The Value of a Good War Story," in Louis R. Pondy, Peter J. Frost, Gareth Morgan, and Thomas C. Dandridge (eds.), *Organizational Symbolism* (Greenwich, Connecticut: JAI Press, 1983), pp. 93–108.

23. A. Wilkins and W. G. Ouchi, "Efficient Cultures: Exploring the Relationship Between Culture and Organizational Performance," *Administrative Science Quarterly*, September 1983, pp. 468–481; W. G. Ouchi, "Markets, Bureaucracies, and Clans," *Administrative Science Quarterly*, March 1980, pp. 129–141.

24. Peters and Waterman, *In Search of Excellence*.

25. J. B. Barney, "Organizational Culture: Can It Be a Source of Sustained Competitive Advantage?" *Academy of Management Review*, July 1986, pp. 656–665.

26. Richard L. Osborne, "Strategic Values: The Corporate Performance Engine," *Business Horizons*, September-October 1996, pp. 41–47.

27. Rose M. Patten, "From Implicit to Explicit: Putting Corporate Values and Personal Accountability Front and Centre," *Ivey Business Journal*, 2004, vol. 69, pp. 1–4.

28. Ouchi, *Theory Z*.

29. Catherine Reagor, "Wells Fargo Riding Roughshod in State, Some Say," *Arizona Republic*, 8 September 1996, pp. D1, D4; Catherine Reagor, "Wells Fargo to Cut 3000 Additional Jobs," *Arizona Republic*, 20 December 1996, pp. E1, E2.

30. O'Reilly and Chatman, "Culture as Social Control."

31. Lisa A. Mainiero, "Is Your Corporate Culture Costing You?" *Academy of Management Executive*, November 1993, pp. 84–85; John E. Sheridan, "Organizational Culture and Employee Retention," *Academy of Management Journal*, December 1992, pp. 1036–1056.

32. Peters and Waterman, *In Search of Excellence*.

33. "A Tale of Two Brothers," *Canadian Business*, March 26, 2007, pp. 45–47; Tell Us About Us website, www.tellusaboutus.com.

34. Watts S. Humphrey, *Managing for Innovation: Leading Technical People* (Englewood Cliffs, New Jersey, Prentice Hall, 1987).

35. Marty Parker, "Communicating Mission and Values to Internal Stakeholders," *Canadian Business Online*, March 27, 2007.

36. Laurie K. Lewis and David R. Seibold, "Innovation Modification During Intraorganizational Adoption," *Academy of Management Review*, April 1993, vol. 10, no. 2, pp. 322–354.

37. "Research in Motion Tops Street's Estimates for Profit, Sales in the 1st Quarter, Shares Soar," *Canadian Business Online*, June 29, 2007.

38. Matthew J. Kiernan, "The New Strategic Architecture: Learning to Compete in the Twenty-First Century," *Academy of Management Executive*, February 1993, pp. 7–21.

39. Oren Harari, "Stop Empowering Your People," *Management Review*, November 1993, pp. 26–29.

40. See Warren Wilhelm, "Changing Corporate Culture—Or Corporate Behavior? How to Change Your Company," *Academy of Management Executive*, November 1992, pp. 72–77.

41. Socialization has also been defined as "the process by which culture is transmitted from one generation to the next." See J. W. M. Whiting, "Socialization: Anthropological Aspects," in D. Sils (ed.), *International Encyclopedia of the Social Sciences*, XIV (New York: Free Press, 1968), p. 545.

42. J. E. Hebden, "Adopting an Organization's Culture: The Socialization of Graduate Trainees," *Organizational Dynamics*, Summer 1986, pp. 54–72.

43. J. B. Barney, "Organizational Culture: Can It Be a Source of Sustained Competitive Advantage?" *Academy of Management Review*, July 1986, pp. 656–665.

44. James R. Norman, "A New Teledyne," *Forbes*, 27 September 1993, pp. 44–45.

Chapter 15

1. Brent Jang, "CN 'Extremely Optimistic' After Record Profit," *The Globe and Mail*, January 24, 2007, p. B.3; Paul Kaihla, "Back on the Rails," *Maclean's*, January 1, 1997, pp. 36–38. Mathew Ingram, "CN Rail issue burns up the tracks. First instalment jumps $4 on first day in one of the hottest stock debuts on the TSE," *The Globe and Mail*, November 18, 1995, p. B.3; Alan Freeman, "The Budget: Ottawa to sell CN,

Petro-Canada stake, Air navigation system slated to wind up with new non-government agency," *The Globe and Mail,* February 28, 1995, p. B.15; Ann Gibbon, "CN Rail to sell oil and gas business Energy unit lost $4-million last year," *The Globe and Mail,* October 29, 1994, p. B.12; Sandford F. Borins and Barry E. C. Boothman, "Crown Corporations and Economic Efficiency," in D. G. McFetridge, ed., *Canadian Industrial Policy in Action, Research Studies, Royal Commission on the Economic Union and Development Prospects for Canada,* 4, (Toronto: University of Toronto Press, 1986); CN Rail annual reports from CN website, www.cn.ca.

2. Caroline Alphonso and Tenille Bonoguore, "Aging Population set to Alter the Landscape," *The Globe and Mail,* July 18, 2007, p. A. 10; Statistics Canada website, www.StatCan.ca.

3. "Baby Boomers Push for Power," *Business Week,* 2 July 1984, pp. 52–56.

4. Geoffrey Colvin, "What the Baby Boomers Will Buy Next," *Fortune,* 15 October 1984, pp. 28–34.

5. John Huey, "Managing in the Midst of Chaos," *Fortune,* 5 April 1993, pp. 38–48.

6. Peter Nulty, "How Personal Computers Change Managers' Lives," *Fortune,* 3 September 1984, pp. 38–48.

7. "Artificial Language Is Here," *Business Week,* 9 July 1984, pp. 54–62.

8. Cheng Hsu, David M. Livermore, Christopher Carothers, and Gilbert Babin, "Enterprise Collaboration: On-Demand Information Exchange Using Enterprise Databases, Wireless Sensor Networks, and RFID Systems," *IEEE Transactions on Systems, Man, and Cybernetics: Part A,* 2007, vol. 37, pp. 519–532. Thomas A. Stewart, "Welcome to the Revolution," *Fortune,* 13 December 1993, pp. 66–80.

9. Joann Muller, "Relentless" *Forbes,* July 23, 2007, p. 46.

10. Kurt Lewin, *Field Theory in Social Science* (New York: Harper & Row, 1951).

11. Linda S. Ackerman, "Transition Management: An In-Depth Look at Managing Complex Change," *Organizational Dynamics,* Summer 1982, pp. 46–66; David A. Nadler, "Managing Transitions to Uncertain Future States," *Organizational Dynamics,* Summer 1982, pp. 37–45.

12. Noel M. Tichy and David O. Ulrich, "The Leadership Challenge—A Call for the Transformational Leader," *Sloan Management Review,* Fall 1984, pp. 59–68.

13. W. Warner Burke, *Organization Development: Principles and Practices* (Boston: Little, Brown, 1982).

14. Burke, *Organization Development;* Michael Beer, *Organization Change and Development* (Santa Monica, California: Goodyear, 1980).

15. Danny Miller and Peter H. Friesen, "Structural Change and Performance: Quantum Versus Piecemeal-Incremental Approaches," *Academy of Management Journal,* December 1982, pp. 867–892.

16. J. Lloyd Suttle, "Improving Life at Work—Problems and Prospects," in J. Richard Hackman and J. Lloyd Suttle (eds.), *Improving Life at Work: Behavioral Science Approaches to Organizational Change* (Santa Monica, California: Goodyear, 1977), p. 4.

17. Richard E. Walton, "Quality of Worklife: What Is It?" *Sloan Management Review,* Fall 1983, pp. 11–21.

18. Daniel A. Ondrack and Martin G. Evans, "Job Enrichment and Job Satisfaction in Greenfield and Redesign QWL Sites," *Group & Organization Studies,* March 1987, pp. 5–22.

19. Ricky W. Griffin, *Task Design: An Integrative Framework* (Glenview, Illinois: Scott, Foresman, 1982).

20. Gregory Moorhead, "Organizational Analysis: An Integration of the Macro and Micro Approaches," *Journal of Management Studies,* April 1981, pp. 191–218.

21. James C. Quick and Jonathan D. Quick, *Organizational Stress and Preventive Management* (New York: McGraw-Hill, 1984).

22. Peter Petre, "Games That Teach You to Manage," *Fortune,* 29 October 1984, pp. 65–72.

23. Kenneth N. Wexley and Timothy T. Baldwin, "Management Development," *Yearly Review of Management of the Journal of Management,* 1986, pp. 277–294.

24. Richard Beckhard, "Optimizing Team-Building Efforts," *Journal of Contemporary Business,* Summer 1972, pp. 23–27, 30–32.

25. William M. Vicars and Darrel D. Hartke, "Evaluating OD Evaluations: A Status Report," *Group & Organization Studies,* June 1984, pp. 177–188; Bernard M. Bass, "Issues Involved in Relations Between Methodological Rigor and Reported Outcomes in Evaluations of Organizational Development," *Journal of Applied Psychology,* February 1983, pp. 197–201.

26. Beer, *Organization Change and Development.*

27. Jerome L. Franklin, "Improving the Effectiveness of Survey Feedback," *Personnel,* May–June 1978, pp. 11–17.

28. Paul R. Lawrence, "How to Deal with Resistance to Change," *Harvard Business Review,* May–June 1954, reprinted in Gene W. Dalton, Paul R. Lawrence, and Larry E. Greiner (eds.), *Organizational Change and Development* (Homewood, Illinois: Irwin, 1970), pp. 181–197.

29. Daniel Katz and Robert L. Kahn, *The Social Psychology of Organizations,* 2nd ed. (New York: Wiley, 1978), pp. 36–68.

30. See Michael T. Hannah and John Freeman, "Structural Inertia and Organizational Change," *American Sociological Review,* April 1984, pp. 149–164, for an in-depth discussion of structural inertia.

31. Moorhead, "Organizational Analysis: An Integration of the Macro and Micro Approaches."

32. David A. Nadler, "Concepts for the Management of Organizational Change," in J. Richard Hackman, Edward E. Lawler III, and Lyman W. Porter (eds.), *Perspectives on Behavior in Organizations,* 2nd ed. (New York: McGraw-Hill, 1983), pp. 551–561; G. Zaltman and R. Duncan, *Strategies for Planned Change* (New York: Wiley, 1977).

33. Alfred M. Jaeger, "Organization Development and National Culture: Where's the Fit?" *Academy of Management Review,* January 1986, pp. 178–190.

Self Test Answers

Chapter 1

1. F	6. T	11. e
2. F	7. T	12. d
3. T	8. d	13. c
4. F	9. b	14. a
5. F	10. c	

Chapter 2

1. T	6. F	11. a
2. F	7. T	12. c
3. F	8. d	13. b
4. T	9. b	14. c
5. T	10. e	

Chapter 3

1. F	6. T	11. d
2. T	7. F	12. d
3. F	8. c	13. b
4. T	9. e	14. a
5. T	10. b	15. c

Chapter 4

1. F	6. T	11. b
2. T	7. d	12. e
3. T	8. a	13. c
4. F	9. d	14. a
5. F	10. b	

Chapter 5

1. T	6. F	11. a
2. F	7. d	12. b
3. F	8. c	13. e
4. F	9. d	
5. T	10. b	

Chapter 6

1. T	6. F	11. d
2. F	7. T	12. a
3. T	8. d	13. c
4. T	9. b	14. e
5. F	10. e	15. e

Chapter 7

1. T	6. F	11. e
2. T	7. T	12. b
3. F	8. b	13. a
4. T	9. e	14. d
5. F	10. d	15. c

Chapter 8

1. T	7. T	13. c
2. F	8. d	14. b
3. F	9. b	15. a
4. F	10. d	16. e
5. T	11. d	
6. T	12. a	

Chapter 9

1. F	6. b	11. a
2. T	7. c	12. e
3. F	8. d	13. c
4. T	9. b	
5. T	10. d	

Chapter 10

1. F	7. T	13. a
2. T	8. F	14. c
3. F	9. a	15. d
4. T	10. c	16. d
5. T	11. c	
6. F	12. b	

Chapter 11

1. F	6. T	11. b
2. F	7. F	12. d
3. T	8. a	13. b
4. T	9. b	14. d
5. F	10. e	15. d

Chapter 12

1. F	6. F	11. d
2. T	7. T	12. c
3. T	8. b	13. b
4. F	9. b	14. d
5. T	10. c	

Chapter 13

1. F	6. F	11. b
2. T	7. F	12. c
3. T	8. c	13. e
4. T	9. d	14. d
5. T	10. b	

Chapter 14

1. F	6. T	11. b
2. T	7. F	12. c
3. F	8. c	13. a
4. F	9. b	
5. T	10. d	

Chapter 15

1. F	6. F	11. b
2. F	7. T	12. c
3. T	8. c	13. e
4. F	9. d	14. a
5. T	10. d	

Name Index

Subject Index